Corporate Governance and Investment Management

Corporate Governance and Investment Management

The Promises and Limitations of the New Financial Economy

Roger M. Barker

Managing Director, Barker & Associates, UK

Iris H.-Y. Chiu

Professor of Corporate Law and Financial Regulation, University College London, UK

Edward Elgar PUBLISHING

Cheltenham, UK • Northampton, MA, USA

Published by
Edward Elgar Publishing Limited
The Lypiatts
15 Lansdown Road
Cheltenham
Glos GL50 2JA
UK

Edward Elgar Publishing, Inc.
William Pratt House
9 Dewey Court
Northampton
Massachusetts 01060
USA

A catalogue record for this book
is available from the British Library

Library of Congress Control Number: 2017947080

This book is available electronically in the **Elgar**online
Law subject collection
DOI 10.4337/9781784713522

MIX
Paper from responsible sources
FSC® C013056

ISBN 978 1 78471 351 5 (cased)
ISBN 978 1 78471 352 2 (eBook)

Typeset by Columns Design XML Ltd, Reading
Printed and bound in Great Britain by TJ International Ltd, Padstow

Contents

Introduction 1

1. Investment funds in an era of financialisation 10
2. The governance, structures and incentives of investment funds – shaping a model of modern investment management 61
3. Corporate equity ownership and misplaced hope in institutional shareholder stewardship 122
4. Pension funds as corporate governance actors 198
5. Mutual funds as corporate governance actors 257
6. Hedge funds as corporate governance actors 309
7. Private equity funds and their corporate governance actors 351
8. Sovereign wealth funds and their corporate governance roles 380
9. Conclusion: Beyond shareholder stewardship – visions for responsible investment management and a new corporate governance 436

Bibliography 447

Index 505

Introduction

As many universal banks reel from the damage of the global financial crisis 2007-09 and navigate crises such as alleged manipulation of financial benchmarks in the interbank, foreign exchange and precious metals markets, it is an opportune moment to recognise that investment funds and asset managers have become quiet giants in the global financial sector. The fund management sector, which attracts massive global inflows, has become a highly profitable industry in its own right. Fund management is becoming key to liquidity, capital and even credit transformation,[1] on the basis of its role as investment intermediary between savers and users of capital. Many would argue that the fund management sector has also become a key source of systemic risk for the entire global financial system.[2]

In this book, we examine the fund management sector's role in transforming savings into long-term corporate wealth creation. However, we go further than simply examining the sector's role as a bridge between the providers and users of the economy's surplus funds (important as that activity may be). We are particularly interested in an arguably more profound development: the rise of the sector as the main representative of capital in many developed economies (particularly in the United

---

[1] For e.g., pension funds becoming engaged in direct lending such as mortgages, see 'Dutch Pension Funds Turn Mortgage Lenders', *Financial Times* (14 Oct 2015); 'Swiss Pension Funds Push into Mortgages', *Financial Times* (29 Nov 2015) and 'Pension Funds Turn to Mortgage Market in Search for Higher Yield', *Financial Times* (17 Dec 2015).

[2] 'SIFI rules to net more asset managers', *Financial Times* (15 March 2015); Financial Stability Board and the International Organisation of Securities Commissioners, *Assessment Methodologies for Identifying Non-Bank Non-Insurer Global Systemically Important Financial Institutions* (March 2015). Although the FSB and IOSCO, in *Next Steps on the NBNI G-SIFI Assessment Methodologies* (4 July 2015), state that the 'systemic label' for asset managers should give way to individual institutional assessment, the FSB has provided guidance as to the aspects asset managers must pay attention to in terms of systemic risk, such as fund liquidity profiles and possible run pressures. See FSB, 'Proposed Policy Recommendations to Address Structural Vulnerabilities from Asset Management Activities' (22 June 2016).

Kingdom and the United States, but – in an increasingly globalised financial system – in a growing number of other advanced and less developed economies).

In less than three decades, a quiet revolution in corporate ownership has taken place. By becoming major holders of corporate equity, the fund management sector has assumed – almost unnoticed except by specialists and industry participants – a central oversight position astride the corporate governance of a huge range of business enterprises across all sectors and markets. However, in contrast to earlier debates about the merits of public ownership, this is not an ownership revolution that has occurred through conscious policy choices or a public debate about its implications or desirability. Nonetheless, it is a development with subtle but profound implications for the behaviour, competitiveness and performance of underlying economies, and which therefore merits much more careful scrutiny.

Long-term savings funds such as pension funds date back to the post-war period, and as a global phenomenon, the rise of collective savings in pooled vehicles, i.e. investment fund vehicles of various types, is a very marked trend. The rise of the investment management industry is a key aspect of financialisation, i.e. the intermediating of many social needs through the financial economy dominated by the private sector. As key intermediaries of diverse sources of capital, the fund management sector invests in global corporate equity (as well as in other financial assets), carrying out a capital transformation role between savings and long-term corporate wealth creation. This development has been described as 'financier capitalism'[3] by both critical and sympathetic observers of the sector.

Financier capitalism is not only a myriad of private contracts or mandates for investment amongst private individuals. The scale, the time horizons, and the objectives of saving and investment are all matters of social and public interest. Whether such intermediation will become a successful socio-economic mechanism remains uncertain, as policy-makers become aware of the risks that beset the industry – pension deficits, the uncertainties in the vicissitudes of investing in volatile markets, and the unproven capacity of markets alone to resolve social issues such as retirement provision. Furthermore, as we argue in this book, there are significant doubts as to whether the sector can fulfil the

---

[3] Gillian Tett, 'How Savvy Asset Managers can Fend off Regulators', *Financial Times* (14 May 2015).

role of "good corporate owner" in a manner that achieves wider economic and social objectives.

However, this scepticism does not appear to be shared currently by many policy makers. An increasing number are vocal in their demand that funds – as the legitimate owners of corporate equity – should play a more engaged role as corporate governance actors. The UK, for example, has led initiatives aimed at "nudging" shareholder behaviour by encouraging institutions to sign up to and comply with a 'Stewardship Code'[4] that provides a blueprint for constructive engagement with investee companies as part of institutions' corporate governance role.[5] This blueprint is being copied in a number of other major economies.[6] Furthermore, policy initiatives aimed at extending the power of shareholders – over issues ranging from executive pay to approval of significant corporate transactions – are being cut and pasted between jurisdictions as apparent solutions to many of the problems of modern corporate governance. We are sceptical about the likely efficacy of enhancing shareholder power and engagement. Our scepticism is based on the fundamental challenges faced by fund management in reconciling a constructive corporate ownership role with their own business and regulatory objectives.

Indeed, one of the main objectives of this book is to demonstrate that the way in which the investment management industry approaches its corporate governance responsibilities vis-à-vis investee companies is a

[4] See Stewardship Code 2014, https://www.frc.org.uk/Our-Work/Codes-Standards/Corporate-governance/UK-Stewardship-Code.aspx, also see discussion in Iris H-Y Chiu, 'Turning Institutional Investors into "Stewards" – Exploring the Meaning and Objectives in "Stewardship"' (2013) *Current Legal Problems* 1.

[5] The UK has promulgated the first Stewardship Code for institutional investors, geared towards greater engagement in the corporate governance of their investee companies, Stewardship Code 2010, 2012, and discussed in Chapter 3. Many jurisdictions have adapted the UK Code in different ways and for different purposes, and the EU's Shareholder Rights Directive 2017 that will attempt to 'legalise' the concept of shareholder stewardship is at present the most far-reaching measure. See generally, Iris H-Y Chiu, 'Learning from the UK in the Proposed Shareholders' Rights Directive 2014? European Corporate Governance Regulation from a UK Perspective' (2015) 114 *ZVglRWiss* forthcoming.

[6] For example the Stewardship Code introduced by the Japanese securities regulator, see http://www.fsa.go.jp/en/refer/councils/stewardship/20140407/01.pdf. The Italian borsa has also embarked on an initiative to introduce such a code, see http://www.borsaitaliana.it/comitato-corporate-governance/news/20130306.en.pdf, and Denmark is the most recent jurisdiction to adopt such a code, see https://corporategovernance.dk/sites/default/files/media/anbefalinger_for_aktivt_ejerskab.pdf.

direct consequence of its own internal business models, commercial imperatives and regulatory constraints. The narrow interests of the sector are not necessarily aligned with the longer-term flourishing of investee companies or the role of the latter in building broader economic competitiveness. As a result, it is justifiable to question recent trends aimed at 'shareholder empowerment' or 'shareholder activism' as an underpinning of economic reform.

Despite the enthusiasm for shareholder empowerment at the policy level, there has been some recognition of the deficiencies in funds' corporate governance capacities, especially in the wake of the global financial crisis.[7] It is commonly observed that many institutional shareholders seem disengaged from 'monitoring' risky corporate practices and often encourage short-term oriented corporate practices as a means of underpinning near term equity prices.[8] Furthermore, a significant causal connection between corporate performance and institutional shareholder engagement has yet to be demonstrated by rigorous empirical research.[9] As we will observe in this book, investors' corporate governance activities are a relatively unimportant and ineffective instrument in the context of their overall investment management strategy, and give rise to both positive and negative externalities under different circumstances.[10] Hence, we are of the view that extending regulatory governance over certain aspects of investors' corporate governance roles is not an ill-founded suggestion.

This book therefore provides an account of investment management in terms of how it is structured and governed, in order to highlight how its corporate governance role in the wider economy ought to be understood. We call this the 'governance nexus' between the fund management sector

---

[7] See discussion in Iris H-Y Chiu, 'Reviving Shareholder Stewardship: Critically Examining the Impact of Corporate Transparency Reforms in the UK' (2014) 38 *Delaware Journal of Corporate Law* 983.

[8] Lucian Bebchuk and Holger Spamann, 'Regulating Bankers' Pay' (2010) 98 *Georgetown Law Journal* 247; Peter O Mülbert, 'Corporate Governance of Banks after the Financial Crisis: Theory, Evidence, Reforms' (ECGI Working Paper 2010).

[9] E.g. see Sunil Wahal, 'Pension Fund Activism and Firm Performance' (1996) 31 *Journal of Financial and Quantitative Analysis* 1; Jonathan M Karpoff, 'The Impact of Shareholder Activism in Target Companies: A Survey of Empirical Findings' (Sep 2001) at http://papers.ssrn.com/sol3/papers.cfm?abstract_id=885365.

[10] E.g. see Mette Neville, 'The Suspicious Shareholder' in Hanne Birkmose, Mette Neville & Karsten Engsig Sørensen (eds.), *The European Financial Market in Transition* (Alpen aan den Rijn: Kluwer Law International, 2011).

and the corporate sector, and we argue that studying the 'governance nexus' allows us to understand the achievements and limitations of such instrumental assumptions of corporate governance roles by funds. We draw wider implications for the social and policy expectations of what can be achieved by funds' corporate governance role in the wider economy.

Based on the above, it is perhaps unsurprising that we are not as sanguine about the potential role of the fund management sector as an agent of capitalist transformation, as described in earlier literature such as Useem's investor capitalism,[11] or Hawley and Williams' concept of 'fiduciary capitalism'.[12] Both concepts treat the fund management sector as fiduciary intermediaries that bring together the collective power of savers in influencing the governance of the corporate sector. According to this perspective, the connection between savers in the Main Street and corporate giants will pave the way for corporate governance to be shaped in a democratic manner, having a benign and profound impact on the wealth-creating role of the corporate sector for the real economy for the long term. As the UK Kay Review puts it,

> [t]he long term public goal for equity markets is in securing the public purposes of high performing companies and strong returns to savers through an effective asset management industry, and in ensuring that the profits earned by companies are as far as possible translated into returns to beneficiaries by minimising the costs of intermediation.[13]

A realistic assessment of the role of institutional investors to date shows that, by and large, the fund management sector has yet to play this anticipated role in shaping the governance of the corporate sector. Although fund management has been growing relentlessly, with savings pouring in from pension savers in developed countries, current account surpluses in emerging economies and private wealthy individuals, such financialisation[14] of savings into investment has not typically been used to promote corporate governance that favours long-term value creation or economic competitiveness. The financial intermediaries that make up and

---

[11] Michael Useem, *Investor Capitalism: How Money Managers are Rewriting the Rules of Corporate America* (Basic Books, 1999).

[12] James P Hawley and Andrew T Williams, *The Rise of Fiduciary Capitalism: How Institutional Investors Can Make Corporate America More Democratic* (Penn: University of Pennsylvania Press 2000).

[13] BIS, *The Kay Review of UK Equity Markets and Long-Term Decision Making* (Interim Report, Feb 2012), see the Foreword of the Final Report, 23 July 2012.

[14] To be discussed in detail in Chapter 1.

support the fund management sector have focused on value arbitrage through trading and the generation of rents through excessive transactionalisation.[15] From a governance perspective, the sector has been largely behaving as passive rentiers; such behaviour matches the pattern anticipated by Berle and Means[16] in the 1930s, who rightly predicted that such an approach would characterise the investment behaviour of minority shareholders in an economy with a highly dispersed corporate ownership structure. Although these early trends are changing with the arrival of some degree of shareholder activism or engagement,[17] this is also problematic for long-term value creation due to fund management's overriding need to generate short-term financial performance as a means of fulfilling its own business objectives. We do not blithely accept the assumed alignment of funds' shareholder roles with the public interest in securing a well-performing corporate sector in the UK for the long term. Indeed there may be a case for more public-interest oriented regulatory governance over funds' shareholder roles, which are intrinsically bound up in their internal governance, structures and incentives.

We examine the governance, structures and incentives for major investment fund vehicles in this book, and are of the view that these are shaped by market forces and, increasingly, regulatory law. These forces, sometimes contradictory in nature, shape funds' internal governance and incentives. In particular, investment law and regulation endorse certain economic concepts such as modern portfolio management theory, and require regular accountability regarding financial performance and the provision of reasonably certain liquidity in the name of investor protection. These have become crucial to shaping the structures and incentives of investment funds.[18]

---

[15] To be discussed in Chapter 1.

[16] The separation of ownership from control was described by Berle and Means as the 'atomisation of property'. They observed that as shareholding in a corporation became diffuse, fragmentation into smaller holdings occurred as corporations grew. Shareholders became passive, leaving decision-making in the hands of managers. This phenomenon was described as a separation of the spiritual values of ownership from the ownership of stock, see Adolf A Berle and Gardiner C Means, *The Modern Corporation and Private Property* (1932, Transaction Publishers, 1999 edn) at p. 66.

[17] See Iris H-Y Chiu, *The Foundations and Anatomy of Shareholder Activism* (Oxford: Hart 2010); D Katelouzou, 'Worldwide Hedge Fund Activism: Dimensions and Legal Determinants' (2015) 17 *University of Pennsylvania Law Review* 789; 'Shareholder Activism Catches Fire in Japan', *Financial Times* (22 June 2014).

[18] To be discussed in Chapter 2.

Law and regulation are premised on meeting the needs of private accountability in investment mandates, and we are of the view that such an emphasis to an extent contradicts the social and wider economic governance dimensions of the funds phenomenon. As such, we highlight where the structures and incentives of investment funds shaped by market forces, law and regulation create dilemmas in fulfilling ultimate social objectives in saving, and also result in dysfunction in the corporate ownership practices of funds. These dilemmas and dysfunctions, arising through the intersection of private interests, market forces and public policy, give rise to the increasingly unsatisfactory role played by funds at the centre of our corporate governance system.

The requirements of regular accountability and reasonable liquidity are derived from market needs and regulatory law, and they often conflict with the long-term nature of some savings. These will be fleshed out further in Chapter 2. Such requirements on the one hand mitigate the 'agency' problem in investment intermediation, but on the other hand create incentives to compromise long-term investment objectives in favour of the inducement of short-term performance. Such short-termist objectives could in some cases generate more cost in the long term, and at worst could create dysfunctions that cause the long-term objectives to be lost sight of. In the delicate balance of the 'governance nexus' which is shaped by the interaction of various private law and public regulatory regimes, the introduction of the 'Stewardship Code' which narrowly focuses on funds' corporate governance roles may be too myopic and fail to address the incentives arising from funds' underlying business models. Indeed, the call to stewardship may give rise to new forms of financier capitalism known as shareholder activism,[19] stewardship[20] or engagement[21] that could create new issues of concern.

---

[19] A more American term that has evolved from the activism of pension funds such as CalPERS to modern day hedge fund activism, see Chapters 2–4, Iris H-Y Chiu, *The Foundations and Anatomy of Shareholder Activism* (Oxford: Hart 2010).

[20] UK parlance, see the UK Stewardship Code 2010, 2012, https://www.frc.org.uk/Our-Work/Codes-Standards/Corporate-governance/UK-Stewardship-Code.aspx; also Iris H-Y Chiu, 'Turning Institutional Investors into "Stewards" – Exploring the Meaning and Objectives of "Stewardship"' (2013) *Current Legal Problems* 1.

[21] Used in the European Shareholder Rights Directive 2017, Article 3g, Directive (EU) 2017/828 of the European Parliament and of the Council of 17 May 2017 amending Directive 2007/36/EC as regards the encouragement of long-term shareholder engagement.

In sum, this book explores how funds and their asset managers are governed in terms of their investment management business models and regulatory constraints, and explains how their corporate governance roles in the wider economy are essentially derived from that rubric. We highlight wider implications for our understanding of investment funds' intermediating role between the private needs of investment and the social needs of saving. We argue that funds' instrumental assumption of corporate governance roles, which is borne out by our study of the 'governance nexus', is not a panacea for the social concerns of long-term corporate wealth creation in order to deliver savings needs and a competitive corporate economy. Indeed, encouraging the corporate governance role of fund management would only highlight the divergence in the interests of fund management as a business activity and the ideals embodied in shareholder stewardship across the economy as a whole. We are of the view that this divergence needs to be recognised and that if it is to be bridged, much more far-reaching policy and regulatory reforms would need to be introduced.

We will discuss the major fund vehicles in pensions, mutual, alternative investment and sovereign wealth management. We argue that the context of financialisation and the legal and regulatory structures which have developed in response are critical to understanding how modern investment management works for many fund vehicles and their asset managers. For example, why do the funds that seem to be most democratically representative, such as pensions and mutual funds, suffer from chronic short termism in their investment behaviour? We also argue that the character of activism, engagement or stewardship demonstrated by institutional investors and their asset managers may be far from producing beneficial effects for long-term corporate wealth creation. Policy-makers are therefore advised to be more cautious about promoting the beneficial effects of shareholder engagement, activism or stewardship.

SCOPE AND COVERAGE OF THE BOOK

The book comprises two parts. In Part One, there are three chapters featuring general discussions and themes relating to fund structures, incentives and governance and how they affect the corporate governance role of equity-owning fund entities and their delegates. Part Two then provides more detailed treatment of key investment fund entities from Chapters 4 to 8.

Chapter 1 deals with the rise of the investment fund industry to intermediate savings and investment. This phenomenon is often known as financialisation. We discuss the key characteristics of such financialisation as a broad context for understanding the nature of investment management.

Chapter 2 discusses our high-level perspectives on the structures and incentives of the fund management industry. We explore common main themes that pertain to all funds, such as how law and regulation shape short-termist tendencies in the name of investor protection, and how the context of search for yield and liquidity in the financialised environment shapes investment management practices. The investment intermediation business also comprises chains of specialist services, in particular, the services of asset managers and investment consultants. We also explore the inter-relationships within the chains as economic and legal institutions. Chapter 3 then discusses our high level perspectives on the relationship between investment management and the corporate governance roles assumed by equity-owning fund entities and their delegates. In drawing out the 'governance nexus', we will critically appraise the nature of such corporate governance roles and their wider implications for long-term corporate wealth creation. In particular, we argue that caution needs to be exercised in unequivocally endorsing 'stewardship', 'activism' or 'engagement' as the appropriate corporate governance role for funds.

Chapters 4 to 8 provide detailed treatment of key equity owning investment fund entities. We explore how specific aspects of their internal governance, structures and incentives affect their corporate governance roles in different ways. Chapter 4 deals with public and private sector pension funds, Chapter 5 deals with retail collective investment schemes, Chapter 6 deals with hedge funds, Chapter 7 with private equity funds and Chapter 8 deals with sovereign wealth funds. Chapter 9 draws together the analyses in the book and provides brief concluding remarks.

The financialised intermediation of savings for investment is not a panacea for the social dimension of savings needs. Law, regulation and corporate governance practices highlight the broader dilemmas, contests of objectives and interests in the phenomenon of investment management, as it is conceived of in private and public paradigms. This book plays a part in highlighting where such dilemmas and contests lie, by examining the corporate governance roles of equity-owning funds as part of their investment management. We argue that the analysis of the governance nexus provides important insights in the nature of investment management, which, in a financialised era, should be broadly investigated in terms of its promises, sub-optimalities and governance implications.

1. Investment funds in an era of financialisation

A. INTRODUCTION

Investment fund entities are major equity owners in global capital markets. Institutional investors (such as pension funds, mutual funds and insurance companies carrying out collective investment management) are often referred to in corporate governance literature as universal owners,[1] and their ownership roles are discussed in relation to time horizons,[2] passivity[3] and increasingly, stewardship.[4] Alternative investment funds such as hedge and private equity funds are regarded differently[5] and opinions as to their ownership and corporate governance roles are still being developed with the emergence of empirical research.[6] The corporate governance roles of investment fund entities are part and parcel of,

---

[1] J P Hawley and A T Williams, 'Shifting Ground: Emerging Global Corporate-Governance Standards and the Rise of Fiduciary Capitalism' (2005) 37 *Environment and Planning 1995–2013*, *The Rise of Fiduciary Capitalism: How Institutional Investors Can Make Corporate America More Democratic* (University of Pennsylvania Press, 2000) generally; Robert A G Monks, *The New Global Investors* (Capstone, 2001).

[2] Aspen Institute, *Overcoming Short-termism: A Call for a More Responsible Approach to Investment and Business Management* (2009) at http://www.aspeninstitute.org/publications/overcoming-short-termism-call-more-responsible-approach-investment-business-management.

[3] Bernard S Black, "Shareholder Passivity Re-examined" (1990) 89 *Michigan Law Review* 520; John Hendry, Paul Sanderson, Richard Barker and John D Roberts, 'Owners or Traders? Conceptualizations of Institutional Investors and Their Relationship with Corporate Managers' (2006) 59 *Human Relations* 1101.

[4] UK Stewardship Code 2010, 2012, Japanese Stewardship Code 2014, see 'Japan investors face UK-style financial code', *Financial Times* (London, 26 Dec 2013); 'Shareholder activism catches fire in Japan', *Financial Times* (London, 22 June 2014).

[5] See Chapter 4, Iris H-Y Chiu, *The Foundations and Anatomy of Shareholder Activism* (Oxford: Hart, 2010).

[6] Alon A Brav, Wei W Jiang, Randall S R S Thomas and Frank F Partnoy, 'Hedge Fund Activism, Corporate Governance and Firm Performance' (2007) at

or indeed a manifestation of fund investment management strategies and practices, and their growing dominance in global equity markets (and to a lesser extent debt markets).

As we have stated in the Introduction to this book, collective investment fund management is a global phenomenon straddling the private and social paradigms. On the one hand, collective investment fund managements are structures of private mandates and accountability, framed by contract and trust/fiduciary law. On the other hand, the scale of such activities in a financialised era elevates investment management to a dimension of social provision – the management of savings for various real economic needs and the oversight of corporate governance throughout the economy through the acquisition of corporate equity rights.

Regulatory law introduces standards of investor protection and, increasingly, standards on the conduct of such investment management.[7] How investment management is shaped by both private and regulatory law must, in our view, affect funds' corporate governance roles as part of their management of equity portfolios. Hence, we draw out the governance nexus in the book – the connection between the internal governance of funds and their external corporate governance roles – in order to understand how corporate governance of investee companies is carried out as a part of investment management. This is important as we view the current policy fixation[8] on the corporate governance role of funds as a panacea for deficient corporate behaviour and perhaps long-term corporate wealth creation in the wider economy to be rather misguided in light of funds' own internal incentives and motivations.

In examining the corporate governance roles of investment funds as primarily arising as a function of their own business imperatives, we first examine the internal governance, structures and incentives of different

---

http://ssrn.com/abstract=948907; Chris C Clifford, 'Value Creation or Destruction? Hedge Funds as Shareholder Activists' (2007) at http://ssrn.com/abstract=971018; Marco Becht, Julian Franks, Jeremy Grant and Hannes F Wagner, 'The Returns to Hedge Fund Activism: An International Study' (2014) at http://papers.ssrn.com/sol3/papers.cfm?abstract_id=2376271.

[7] For example, the European Shareholder Rights Directive 2015, Arts 3f–h, see discussion in Iris H-Y Chiu, 'European Shareholder Rights Directive Proposals: Convergence or Divergence from the UK Stewardship Code?', ERA Forum, 2016, forthcoming.

[8] E.g. the UK's Stewardship Code, and the EU Shareholder Rights Directive 2017.

types of funds, and explore the key characteristics that drive the corporate governance behaviour of each entity examined in this book.

There is substantial extant literature on how the corporate governance role of shareholders is affected by external contextual factors such as legal institutions and legal traditions. The law and finance thesis[9] may be interpreted as arguing for the importance of minority shareholder protection frameworks in law that shape the corporate governance role of shareholders. The robustness of minority shareholder protection frameworks is important in attracting equity owners, and the corporate governance influence of equity owners may be expressed through securities litigation or corporate governance activism in the US,[10] or through informal shareholder engagement[11] or the market for corporate control in the UK.[12] However we believe that the causal connection between minority shareholder protection frameworks and the corporate governance role of equity-owning funds is an incomplete picture. We observe that internationally active funds play a key part in lobbying for change in the frameworks for minority shareholder protection, such as in Hong Kong.[13] Thus, such funds are driven to shape as well as respond to the corporate governance environment they are in. The study of internal governance factors may be of crucial importance in ultimately understanding how funds conceive of their corporate governance role.

---

[9] R La Porta, F Lopez-de-Silanes, A Shleifer and R Vishny, 'Law and Finance' (1998) 106 *Journal of Political Economy* 1113; R La Porta, F Lopez-de-Silanes and A Shleifer, 'What Works in Securities Laws' (2006) 71 *Journal of Finance* 1.

[10] Steven A Ramirez, 'The Virtues of Private Securities Litigation: An Historic and Macroeconomic Perspective' (2014) 5 *Loyola University of Chicago Law Journal* 669; Martin Gelter, 'The Pension System and the Rise of Shareholder Primacy' (2013) 43 *Seton Hall Law Review* 909.

[11] Iris H-Y Chiu, 'A Confidence Trick: Ex Ante versus Ex Post Frameworks in Minority Investor Protection in the UK' (2014) 11 *European Company Law* 6.

[12] The liberal takeovers regime in the UK is discussed in John Armour and David Skeel Jnr, 'Who Writes the Rules for Hostile Takeovers, and Why – The Peculiar Divergence of US and UK Takeover Regulation' (2006) 95 *Georgetown Law Journal* 1727, who argue that the UK regime is self-regulatory in nature and therefore was susceptible to institutional investor influence from early on.

[13] Roger Barker and Iris H-Y Chiu, 'Protecting Minority Shareholders in Blockholder-Controlled Companies – Evaluating the UK's Enhanced Listing Regime in Comparison with Investor Protection Regimes in New York and Hong Kong' (2015) *Capital Markets Law Journal*, forthcoming.

Funds' corporate governance roles have over the years been discussed and theorised by various commentators in law, economics and business. Below is a brief survey of the key milestones in the literature.

Literature Review of Funds' Corporate Governance Roles

The phenomenon of institutional share-ownership and its implications has already been noted by commentators more than a decade ago. In the early 1990s, Useem[14] discerned that equity ownership of publicly traded corporations in the US was falling into the hands of funds as intermediary owners. He also noted that these intermediary owners had started to adopt a unique corporate governance role which he termed investor capitalism, a movement that sees the rise of investor say and power in how corporations are run. The assumption of investors' corporate governance role as 'owners' is not normatively questioned, largely because of the legal fabrication of shareholders' rights as quasi-proprietary in nature.[15] Hence the legitimacy or credibility of investor capitalism in the form of shareholder activism has not been disputed in principle, but has been examined from the perspective of outcome efficiency – whether activism improves financial performance of companies (albeit mainly from a shareholder perspective).[16]

---

[14] Michael Useem, *Investor Capitalism: How Money Managers are Rewriting the Rules of Corporate America* (Basic Books, 1999).

[15] See Sanford J Grossman and Oliver D. Hart, 'The Costs and Benefits of Ownership: A Theory of Vertical and Lateral Integration' (1986) 94 *Journal of Political Economy* 691–719; Chapter 4, Iris H-Y Chiu, *The Foundations and Anatomy of Shareholder Activism* (Oxford: Hart, 2010); John Armour and Michael Whincop, 'The Proprietary Foundations of Corporate Law' (2007) *Oxford Journal of Legal Studies* 429.

[16] This is a landscape of mixed results, for pension fund activism, see Jonathan MJM Karpoff, 'The Impact of Shareholder Activism in Target Companies: A Survey of Empirical Findings' (Sep 2001) at http://ssrn.com/abstract=885365; Stuart Gillan and Laura T Starks, 'The Evolution of Shareholder Activism in the United States' (2007) at http://papers.ssrn.com/sol3/papers.cfm?abstract_id=959670. The results are mixed in Europe too, see Jean-Michel Sahut, Jean-Sebastien Lantz and Sophie Montandrau, 'Activism of Institutional Investors, Corporate Governance Alerts and Financial Performance' (2010) 15 *International Journal of Business* 221 at http://papers.ssrn.com/sol3/papers.cfm?abstract_id=1735797. Mixed results apply too for hedge funds, see fnt 6 and Lucian A Bebchuk, Alon A Brav and Wei Jiang, 'The Long Term Effects of Hedge Fund Activism' (2013) at http://papers.ssrn.com/sol3/papers.cfm?abstract_id=2291577.

Further, Useem opines that investor capitalism brings about the democratisation of participation in corporate wealth creation, as equity-owning institutional shareholders represent their myriad individual beneficiaries, many of whom are ordinary, saving citizens. Investor capitalism is seen as a form of democratic capitalism, lauded by many commentators as a triumphant form of economic organisation.[17] Hawley and Williams[18] also framed the ownership of corporate equity by institutional funds as ushering in an age of 'fiduciary capitalism' as financial intermediaries act in their corporate governance roles in a representative capacity for myriad savers, democratising the corporate governance process and bringing about the promising prospects of long-term and responsible forms of capitalism under such 'universal ownership'. In many respects, such authors have viewed fund managers as more acceptable representatives of capital than earlier generations of capitalist (e.g. the industrialists or robber barons of the nineteenth century), who were more easily characterised as elitist or exploitative of other stakeholders.

However, more recent commentators have noted that investor or fiduciary capitalism is more correctly described as a form of agency capitalism,[19] intermediary capitalism[20] or money manager

---

[17] J P Hawley and A T Williams, *The Rise of Fiduciary Capitalism: How Institutional Investors Can Make Corporate America More Democratic* (University of Pennsylvania Press, 2000); John C Coffee, Jnr, 'The Future as History: The Prospects for Global Convergence in Corporate Governance and Its Implications' (1999) 93 *Northwestern University Law Review* 641; Henry Hansmann and Reinier Kraakman, 'The End of History for Corporate Law' (2000) 89 *Georgetown Law Journal* 439; which views were defended in a nuanced manner in Henry Hansmann, 'How Close is the End of History' (2005) at http://lesliecaton.com/wordpress/wp-content/uploads/2012/01/7-Hansmann-FINAL.pdf; and in Hansmann and Kraakman, 'Reflections on the End of History for Corporate Law' (2011) at http://papers.ssrn.com/sol3/papers.cfm?abstract_id=2095419.

[18] J P Hawley and A T Williams (2000), above.

[19] Gilson and Gordon describe this phenomenon as a reconcentration of ownership in the hands of intermediaries acting as agents for myriad beneficiaries, Ronald J Gilson and Jeffrey N Gordon, 'Agency Capitalism: Further Implications of Equity Intermediation' (2014) at http://ssrn.com/abstract=2359690.

[20] As a form of intermediary capitalism, it is perhaps arguable that shareholder rights would not necessarily be exercised as it depends on the costs and benefits of the intermediary undertaking this role. The intermediary's business model and incentives affect the undertaking or otherwise of shareholder roles. See Paul H Edelman, Randall S Thomas and Robert B Thompson, 'Shareholder Voting in an Age of Intermediary Capitalism' (2014) at http://ssrn.com/abstract=2401746 arguing that shareholder rights such as voting should only be exercised

capitalism.[21] Beneficial owners are a few steps removed from acting as 'shareholders', as power over investment assets is predominantly exercised by intermediaries.[22] Intermediary institutions choose whether or not to participate in corporate governance roles, giving rise to 'agency aspects' of the intermediary-beneficiary relationship.[23] Beneficiaries can only rely on accountability frameworks that govern their relationships/ mandates with funds in contract, trust or corporate law,[24] and these bodies of law have not articulated precisely in relation to the aspect of fund management that relates to intermediaries' assumption of corporate governance roles in their investee companies.

Agency, intermediary or money manager capitalism is a phenomenon that arises out of the increasing power of the intermediary sector in amassing financial capital and allocating financial flows.[25] Such intermediaries effectively become the primary representatives of capital, and assume all of the powers and privileges inherent in the legal ownership of corporate equity. The growth of the intermediary sector – and the declining influence of the beneficial owners of capital – is part of the larger phenomenon of financialisation.[26] Financialisation can be used as a

---

for reasons of efficiency such as monitoring when their immediate interest tied to residual value is affected or when the Board is conflicted, and when voting is an efficient mechanism for aggregating heterogeneous preferences when the decision differentially affects shareholders and no 'correct' decision is in issue.

[21] Wray quotes Minsky and describes this as a phenomenon of concentrated allocation of investment and savings capital to investment funds that insularly chase ever-higher returns oblivious to the risks, especially systemic risks, they pursue. See L Randall Wray, 'Money Manager Capitalism and the Global Financial Crisis' (2009) at http://ssrn.com/abstract=1478508.

[22] It is argued that beneficial owners are not excluded from the corporate governance process under precepts in trust and fiduciary law. See Ewan McGaughey, 'Does Corporate Governance Exclude the Ultimate Investor?' (2016) 16 *Journal of Corporate Law Studies* 221. However, modern 'agency capitalism' interposes a number of layers in terms of relationship with investee companies and the exercise of corporate governance rights. Hence it would be rather simplistic to treat beneficial owners as 'shareholders'.

[23] Gilson and Gordon, 'Agency Capitalism' (2014), above.

[24] See survey in John K Thompson and Sang-Mok Choi, 'Governance Systems for Collective Investment Schemes in OECD Countries' OECD Occasional Paper (April 2001).

[25] Jonathan Nitzan and Shimshon Bichler, *Capital as Power: A Study of Order and Creorder* (Oxford: Routledge, 2009) argues that capital begets accumulation as an end in itself.

[26] To be explored shortly.

descriptive concept which reflects the growing overall influence of the private financial sector. Alternatively, it can be used to define a normative ideology that views the finance sector as an efficient and desirable means of navigating economic life, and which welcomes its growing role in addressing an ever wider range of economic and social needs.

We adopt the broad term 'financier capitalism' to describe the real world implementation of the ideology of financialisation. Furthermore, we believe that investment fund entities' business models and governance structures have to be understood against the wider backdrop of financialisation. Fund entities' business models and governance structures in turn influence funds' corporate governance roles in the ownership of corporate equity. In Section D below, we argue that fund entities' internal governance is heavily influenced by both market forces and law and regulation, such law and regulation responding to and catering for the needs generated by financialisation. Further, these, in conjunction with recent developments in UK and EU policy framing institutional investors' corporate governance role as 'stewardship',[27] determine the corporate governance roles they assume.

This book intends to go some way in raising questions regarding the legitimacy of funds' corporate governance roles, whether framed as engagement, stewardship or activism.[28] The internal governance, structures and incentives that we discern raise questions regarding the appropriateness of corporate ownership activities undertaken by institutional investors within the quasi-proprietary paradigm of share ownership. The examination of internal governance, structures and incentives could also raise questions as to the continued appropriateness of retaining shareholder primacy over the residual control rights and privileges attached to the ownership of corporate equity, given that increasingly it is funds that are the main actors responsible for exercising such rights.[29]

---

[27] Iris H-Y Chiu, 'Turning Institutional Investors into "Stewards" – Exploring the Meaning and Objectives of "Stewardship"' (2013) *Current Legal Problems* 1.

[28] See Introduction; also Iris H-Y Chiu, *The Foundations and Anatomy of Shareholder Activism* (Oxford: Hart, 2010); the adoption of language of 'stewardship' and 'engagement' in the UK context, as distinguished from 'activism' in the US context. On the meaning of stewardship, see Iris H-Y Chiu (2013), above.

[29] Which was doubted very much by Berle and Means, in pp. 66–69, *The Modern Corporation and Private Property* (NY: Macmillan, 1932).

This chapter proceeds as follows: first, we provide an account of the growth of collective investment management as a phenomenon in financialisation and unpick the characteristics of such financialised investment management. We then point out the role of private and regulatory law in shaping its practices and behaviour. We then turn to the issue of why funds own corporate equity and how their positions as shareholders are treated in the rubric of investment management. This chapter sets the context for examining how corporate governance roles undertaken by funds are an instrumental facet of their own business imperatives and must be understood in that light. This is important as the likely corporate governance role of funds should not be idealised, taken out of context or misunderstood by policy makers.

B. GROWTH OF COLLECTIVE INVESTMENT MANAGEMENT

The OECD reports that growth in collective investment management has been remarkable since the early 1990s.[30] The Price Waterhouse Coopers survey[31] of Asset Management reports that global assets under management stand at about USD$64 trillion at the end of 2013.[32] That relates to assets managed by professional asset managers and does not include those managed in-house. In terms of pensions, as of 2012 total assets under collective management in global pensions (where data has been available) stand at approximately USD$30 trillion, total assets managed by insurance companies at approximately USD$24 trillion and total assets managed by other investment funds at approximately USD$22 trillion.[33] Alternative investment fund assets are estimated to stand at

---

[30] John K Thompson and Sang-Mok Choi, 'Governance Systems for Collective Investment Schemes in OECD Countries' OECD Occasional Paper (April 2001).

[31] PwC, *Asset Management 2020: A Brave New World* (2013) at http://www.pwc.com/gx/en/asset-management/publications/asset-management-2020-a-brave-new-world.jhtml; In Europe, assets under management, including pensions, stood at 13.8 trillion euros at the end of 2011, see EFAMA, *Asset Management in Europe: 6th Annual Review* (2013) at http://www.efama.org/Publications/Statistics/Asset%20Management%20Report/Asset_Management_Report_2013.pdf.

[32] See Andy Haldane's speech estimating global assets managed by institutions to be at USD$87 trillion, at http://www.bankofengland.co.uk/publications/Documents/speeches/2014/speech723.pdf.

[33] http://www.oecd.org/finance/private-pensions/globalpensionstatistics.htm.

more than USD$2 trillion.[34] In 2014, Haldane estimated a figure of total global assets managed by insurance companies, pension funds, mutual funds and others as representing about twice the size of global gross domestic product.[35] Asset managers are estimated in 2017 to have over £4 trillion of UK savings under management in retail and pension funds combined.[36]

The growth of collective investment management is a global phenomenon, although the US and the UK have emerged as the leading geographical locations for the main players in the sector.[37] The key contributing factor to this growth is the rise of pension fund management for retirement savings, making savings work through investment in securities assets.[38] Walter and Sisli[39] refer to the collective investment management of pension funds as a form of partial intermediation as funds flow into managed portfolios of assets instead of being entrusted to banks that perform a full intermediation service (i.e. offering financial claims against themselves in exchange). Pension fund management from both developed countries[40] and emerging economies[41] accounts for the lion's share of global assets under management. In the UK, Congdon documents the institutionalisation of savings starting as early as in the 1960s.[42]

---

[34] Based on Deutsche Bank's *2014 Alternative Investment Survey* at https://www.db.com/medien/en/content/4666_4819.htm.

[35] Andrew Haldane, 'The Age of Asset Management', speech at London Business School (4 April 2014), see fnt 32 above.

[36] FCA, *Asset Management Market Study Final Report* (28 June 2017) at para 1.2, at https://www.fca.org.uk/publication/market-studies/ms15-2-3.pdf.

[37] http://www.theinvestmentassociation.org//assets/files/research/2016/20160929-amsfullreport.pdf p. 15.

[38] Gordon L Clark, 'Institutional Investors and Risk Management' in Gordon L Clark, Adam D Dixon and Ashby HB Monk (eds), *Managing Financial Risks: From Global to Local* (Oxford: OUP 2012) at Chapter 3.

[39] Ingo Walter and Elif Sisli, 'The Asset Management Industry in Asia: Dynamics of Growth, Structure, and Performance' (2007) 16 *Financial Markets, Institutions and Instruments* 1.

[40] Carmen-Pilar Martí-Ballester, 'A Comparative Analysis of the Performance of Collective Investment Institutions' (2012) *Review of Economics and Finance* forthcoming.

[41] Ramón Moreno and Marjorie Santos, 'Pension Systems in EMEs: Implications for Capital Flows and Financial Markets' (2009) at http://ssrn.com/abstract=1992376.

[42] Chapter 2, Tim Congdon, *Money and Asset Prices in Boom and Bust* (London: Institute of Economic Affairs, 2005).

The savings glut from current account surplus countries[43] also contribute to the rise in capital available for investment; these may come from sovereign savings, much of which is managed collectively in sovereign wealth funds, and savings from increasingly wealthy middle classes[44] channelled into retail sector collective investment schemes,[45] or even alternative investment funds.[46] There is also a proportion of the very wealthy private banking clients who channel savings into professionally managed collective investment funds in order to benefit from management brand and expertise in wealth structuring for tax advantages, wealth protection and search for yield.[47] The growth of the high net worth individual sector, especially from emerging economies, is expected to be significant, and Price Waterhouse Coopers predicts that the sector may contribute to as much as two-thirds of investable capital.[48] The increasing popularity of investment as a means to meet a range of financial needs for the sophisticated and the ordinary is supported by (a) policy changes such as shifting the risks of retirement provision to the individual away from the state or employers and (b) macro-economic conditions of cheap money,[49] financial stability and rising asset prices[50] in developed jurisdictions such the US, UK and parts of Europe.

---

[43] Martin Wolf, *Fixing Global Finance* (Conn: Yale University Press, 2008); Chapter 6, Niall Ferguson, *The Ascent of Money* (London: Penguin, 2008).

[44] Tetsuya Kamiyama, 'ASEAN's Investment Trusts Market: Current Conditions and Challenges' (2013) 5 *Nomura Journal of Capital Markets* 1.

[45] Such as unit trusts in the UK, mutual funds in the US and the European UCITs.

[46] Hedge and private equity funds.

[47] Ingo Walter and Elif Sisli, 'The Asset Management Industry in Asia: Dynamics of Growth, Structure, and Performance' (2007) 16 *Financial Markets, Institutions and Instruments* 1.

[48] Price Waterhouse Coopers, *Asset Management 2020: A Brave New World* (2014) at http://www.pwc.com/gx/en/asset-management/publications/asset-management-2020-a-brave-new-world.jhtml.

[49] David Roche and Bob McKee, *New Monetarism* (Independent Strategy, 2007).

[50] See Franklin Allen and Douglas Gale, 'Asset Price Bubbles and Monetary Policy' (2000) at http://finance.wharton.upenn.edu/~allenf/download/Vita/apbm.pdf; Thomas I Palley, *Financialisation: The Economics of Finance Capital Domination* (Basingstoke: Palgrave Macmillan 2013); Robert W Parenteau, 'The Late 1990s US Bubble: Financialization in the Extreme' in Gerald A Epstein (ed.), *Financialization and the World Economy* (Cheltenham: Edward Elgar, 2005) at p. 111.

The collective investment management industry has arisen to meet the need for savings management.[51] Fund houses arise to compete with banks in the intermediation business and provide more choice to savers and investors.[52] Although the partial intermediation offered by fund houses results in greater risk taking by investors and savers, as risk is not absorbed by fully intermediating institutions such as banks, greater choice and chance of higher yields have become attractive to savers and investors. Collective investment management has become a staple form of financial intermediation for the sophisticated as well as the ordinary.[53] Further, fund owners are increasingly delegating portfolio management to the professional asset management industry,[54] creating another link in the chain of intermediation.[55] The Price Waterhouse Coopers survey predicts that by 2020, global assets under management will exceed USD$100 trillion.[56] Financier Capitalism has become a global phenomenon with increasingly developed and mature business models.

The next Section argues that the collective investment management industry has to be understood against the backdrop of financialisation and its practices reflect the normative ideology of financialisation as a positive and efficient development.

C. FINANCIER CAPITALISM AS HALLMARK IN THE AGE OF FINANCIALISATION

As mentioned above, the collective investment management industry has been described as ushering in an age of agency, intermediary or money manager capitalism. Financier Capitalism is a shorthand that captures a broad amalgamation of what has been discussed in academic literature. Intermediary capitalism as Edelman et al[57] describe it, refers to standing inbetween ultimate savers and asset markets. However, the mode of

---

[51] Mary Mellor, *The Future of Money: From Financial Crisis to Public Resource* (New York: Pluto Press 2010).

[52] Arthur E Wilmarth Jnr, 'The Transformation of the Financial Services Industry: 1975-2000, Competition, Consolidation and Increased Risks' (2002) *University of Illinois Law Rev* 215.

[53] Ingo Walter and Elif Sisli (2007), above.

[54] Haldane, 'The Age of Asset Management' (2014), above.

[55] Howard Gospel, Andrew Pendleton and Sigurt Vitols, *Financialization, New Investment Funds and Labour* (Oxford: OUP 2014) at p. 21. This will be discussed in greater detail in Chapter 2.

[56] Price Waterhouse Coopers, *Asset Management 2020* (2014), above.

[57] Edelman et al, 'Shareholder Voting' (2014), above.

standing inbetween creates agency costs, as Gilson and Gordon[58] point out, and the very activity of managing or being in control of someone else's money creates incentives and motivations in terms of how the activity is carried out as a business.[59]

Clark has described the age of financial intermediaries as the 'third stage' of capitalism.[60] The passage towards the age of financial intermediaries was an experience of atomisation of economic activity. From the rise of the entrepreneur and the production of economic activity, economic activity experienced atomisation in the form of separation of ownership from control under the structure of the corporate form,[61] allowing the rise of professional corporate managers. Subsequently, atomisation in the form of separation of capital supply from investment takes place, allowing the rise of investment management intermediaries. Savers and investors relinquish their decisions to such intermediaries, and the role of such intermediaries is framed by client protection standards and/or regulation. The atomisation processes in the passage towards financier capitalism has created an industry devoted to investment. Such specialisation could potentially be economically efficient for mobilising and allocating resources to productive entrepreneurship in the corporate sector.[62] On the other hand, the creation of an industry devoted to amassing investment capital and having the discretionary power to allocate such capital and profit from such activity introduces a unique set of incentives and motivations to the industry, and these could perpetuate self-serving or rent-seeking ends.

Financier capitalism is a manifestation of the financialisation of economic life. Financialisation has been defined as 'the increasing role of financial motives, financial markets, financial actors and financial institutions in the operation of the domestic and international economies',[63] or in a political scientist's view, 'financialisation is the increase in the influence of financial markets, institutions and elites over both the

58 Gilson and Gordon, 'Agency Capitalism' (2014), above.

59 Wray, 'Money Manager Capitalism' (2009), above.

60 Robert C Clark, 'The Four Stages of Capitalism: Reflections on Investment Management Treatises' (1981) 94 *Harvard Law Review* 561.

61 Clark, 'The Four Stages' (1981), above, quoting Berle and Means, *The Modern Corporation* (1932), above.

62 Making equity markets work for savers and corporations is the vision in the Kay Review, BIS, *The Kay Review of UK Equity Markets and Long-Term Decision Making* (Final Report, 23 July 2012).

63 Gerald A Epstein, 'Introduction: Financialization and the World Economy' in Gerald A Epstein ed., *Financialization and the World Economy* (Cheltenham: Edward Elgar, 2005) at p. 3.

economy and other institutions of society, including the government.'[64] The increasing importance of finance may be observed in steady increases in GDP accounted for by the financial sector in the US[65] as well as Europe.[66] In the UK, the Bank of England[67] noted that financial sector output has grown exponentially, although a dip occurred during the period of the global financial crisis 2007–09. In both the US and UK, financial sector output accounts for about just under 10 per cent of GDP. Besides hard figures showing the economic importance of finance, the permeation of finance has occurred in commercial and in everyday life in terms of the use of financial services and products to address a wide range of commercial and social needs.

Van der Zwan[68] argues that financialisation literature mainly deals with three important aspects of the phenomenon: the encouragement of financial accumulation by private individuals, the shareholder value revolution in corporate governance and the permeation of private sector financial solutions into everyday life. The rise of financier capitalism embodies each of these features. First, retail sector savings are encouraged and amassed and professionally managed in order to become the staple mechanism for meeting 'everyday life' needs. Second, such professional management channels savings into investment capital which is used for profit generation through financial instruments and transactions. Financier capitalism then fundamentally affects how corporations, which are at the same time wealth generating productive entities and investible assets on the market, are to be managed and run.

Financier capitalism is supported by the legitimisation of certain 'financialisation norms', which have increasingly embedded themselves into public opinion and social attitudes. The broad context of the norms of financialisation are important for our understanding of supporting law

---

64 Gautam Mukunda, 'The Price of Wall Street's Power' (2014) *Harvard Business Review* 70, on the effects of financialisation upon the American economy.

65 Thomas Philippon, 'Has the U.S. Finance Industry Become Less Efficient? On the Theory and Measurement of Financial Intermediation' (2012) at http://pages.stern.nyu.edu/~tphilipp/papers/Finance_Efficiency.pdf.

66 Guillaume Bazot, 'Financial Consumption and the Cost of Finance: Measuring Financial Efficiency in Europe (1950-2007)' (2014) at http://www.ipp.eu/wp-content/uploads/2014/06/working-paper-2014-17-pse-gbazot.pdf.

67 Stephen Burgess, 'Measuring Financial Sector Output and Its Contribution to UK GDP', *Quarterly Bulletin Q3* (2011) at http://www.bankofengland.co.uk/publications/Documents/quarterlybulletin/qb110304.pdf.

68 Natascha van der Zwan, 'Making Sense of Financialisation' (2014) 12 *Socio-economic Review* 99.

and regulation for this socio-economic model, and these in turn are fundamental to understanding how collective investment fund entities are internally governed. This Section draws out seven such 'financialisation norms' upon which financier capitalism is based.

The seven 'financialisation norms' are: (a) belief in the social importance of investment in financial assets by private individuals; (b) making investment efficient through collective pooling and management; (c) the professionalisation of collective management in portfolio management; (d) making the realisation of investment returns a business and profit-oriented activity; (e) the commoditisation of investible subject matter as asset classes; (f) detachment of investment returns from real productive activity (or the lack of necessary connection between the two); and (g) the widespread acceptance of financial risk-bearing by society. The following elaborates.

(a) Belief in the Social Importance of Investment in Financial Assets by Private Individuals

'Saving' is defined in a mainstream dictionary as the portion of income that is not spent or used immediately.[69] In an era of financialisation, an efficient savings strategy is increasingly seen as implying investment in financial assets,[70] which offers the individual the potential of fulfilling a variety of future needs. Erturk et al[71] describe financialisation as championing a form of democratic participation for households in the investment market, giving opportunities to and empowering households – and no longer just a small number of wealthy individuals – to be engaged in wealth generation through saving in investment. Langley[72] further opines that financialisation underpins the neo-liberal move away from social welfarism to self-care and individual responsibility, promoting the adoption of investing as one of the new liberating technologies that would help the individual realise her power and responsibility in organising her own financial choices and affairs.

---

[69] Merriam Webster online at https://www.merriam-webster.com/.

[70] Gerald F Davis, *Managed by the Markets: How Finance Re-shaped America* (New York: OUP, 2009) at p. 18.

[71] Ismail Erturk, Julie Froud, Sukhdev Johal, Adam Leaver and Karel Williams, 'The Democratization of Finance? Promises, Outcomes and Conditions' (2007) 14 *Review of International Political Economy* 553.

[72] Paul Langley, 'Uncertain Subjects of Anglo-American Financialization' (2007) 65 *Cultural Critique* 67.

The free market for investment promises choice for the deployment of savings into investments that could generate returns to meet an individual's future needs and circumstances. Hence, social needs that need to be met in the future such as ownership of home, consumption of higher education for children and provision in retirement are funnelled into saving through investment. The ramification is that savers would increasingly see investment in financial assets as being the only means to meet the social needs of saving, therefore relying on the investment industry to provide a quasi-necessary good. The investment industry thus moves away from catering for the luxury good of discretionary investment for an elite stratum of society, to providing a quasi-necessary good of investment that realises the social expectations imbued in saving for society as a whole.

However, investment in financial assets generates income and returns not merely by funding real economic productivity but by trading. Returns generated by trading in the markets have been observed in empirical research and in real life often to surpass wealth created by real productive economic activity.[73] Empirical research[74] shows significant income inequalities between finance-generated income and non-finance generated income from real productive economic activity. The potential of realising huge paper gains, therefore, further stimulates the startling ascendancy of investment in financial assets as a potential wealth generating activity for individual savers.

The growing belief in the importance of investment in financial assets by private individuals has the following ramifications: (i) social trust in financier capitalism and the increasing distancing of economic agents

---

[73] Robert Boyer, 'Is a Finance-led Growth Regime a Viable Alternative to Fordism?' (2000) 29 *Economy and Society* 111; Greta Krippner, 'Accumulation and the Profits of Finance' in Ismail Erturk, Julie Froud, Sukhdev Johal, Adam Leaver and Karel Williams (eds), *Financialization At Work: Key Tests and Commentary* (Oxford: Routledge, 2008).

[74] Basak Kus, 'Financialisation and Income Inequality in OECD Nations: 1995–2007' (2012) 43 *The Economic and Social Review* 477; Gerald Epstein and Arjun Jayadev, 'The Rise of Rentier Incomes in OECD Countries: Financialization, Central Bank Policy and Labor Solidarity' in Gerald A Epstein ed., *Financialization and the World Economy* (Cheltenham: Edward Elgar, 2005) at p. 46; Ken-Hou Lin and Donald Tomaskovic-Devey, 'Financialization and U.S. Income Inequality, 1970–2008' (2013) 118 *American Journal of Sociology* 1284; Gerard Dumenil and Dominique Levy, 'Financialization, Neo-liberalism and Income Inequality in the USA' in Ismail Erturk, Julie Froud, Sukhdev Johal, Adam Leaver and Karel Williams (eds), *Financialization At Work: Key Tests and Commentary* (Oxford: Routledge, 2008).

from managing key features of their economic life; (ii) increasing social importance of financier capitalism, with increasing power in the hands of financial intermediaries managing increasing amounts of capital supply; (iii) changes in the balance of economic activity in the corporate sector between real productivity and financial sector activity; and (iv) increasing wealth disparities resulting from the ability to participate in financial market trading and speculation.[75] These are discussed further shortly.

The dominant structure that has arisen for investment intermediation is the organisation of savings into pooled collective investment vehicles managed by collective investment entities.

(b) Making Investment Efficient through Collective Pooling and Management

The organisation of savings into collective pooled investment vehicles is a phenomenon in efficiency as well as in power. Collective pooling of savings into investment funds ensures sufficiently affordable access to investment due to economies of scale. But this gives rise to standardisation in the relational dimension between investment intermediaries and saver-beneficiaries, and therefore (ironically) less prospect for tailor-made financial solutions to specific needs.

Erturk et al[76] critically describes the rise in collective investment management as a form of 'coupon pool' capitalism where the masses become feedstock for finance. Individual beneficiaries meeting their economic and social needs become digitised as units of capital supply. Dembinski[77] argues that financialisation is characterised by the transactionalisation of relationships, tending to be narrowly focused and transient.

The rising tide of capital encourages investment intermediaries to compete for capture of market share, and to engage in marketing and branding in order to attract financial flows. As Bogle[78] opines, the rise in collective pooling and management of investment capital has focused

---

75 See above.

76 Ismail Erturk, Julie Froud, Sukhdev Johal, Adam Leaver and Karel Williams, 'Financialisation, Coupon Pool and Conjuncture' in Ismail Erturk, Julie Froud, Sukhdev Johal, Adam Leaver and Karel Williams (eds), *Financialization At Work: Key Tests and Commentary* (Oxford: Routledge, 2008).

77 Paul H Dembinski, *Finance: Servant or Deceiver* (trans. by Kevin Cook, Basingstoke: Palgrave Macmillan 2009).

78 John C Bogle, *Common Sense on Mutual Funds* (Chichester: John Wiley & Sons, 2011) at pp. 425ff.

investment intermediaries' minds upon capturing as much as possible of the supply of capital, instead of managing such capital as stewards for the needs of the beneficiaries. Despite a lack of supportive empirical evidence, the industry has been highly successful in persuading both private and institutional clients that past fund performance is in some way indicative of future fund performance.[79] In contrast, stewardship activities vis-à-vis investee companies are often treated as relatively insignificant feature of funds' marketing efforts.

Increased accumulation entails a wider breadth of discretionary power over the use and allocation of accumulated capital,[80] in turn sharpening an appetite[81] for further accumulation of capital and power. It also feeds through directly to the profitability of investment management business entities due to the *ad valorem* fee structure of many funds whereby customer revenues are determined by the magnitude of assets under management. Further, accumulation can be further magnified by turning to leverage[82] which provides a multiplier effect on potential gains.

It may be argued that forces of competition and anti-trust regulation are crucial in preventing the rise of substantial disparity of power between the investment intermediaries who are in control of the amassed capital and diffused savers. However research[83] has shown that fund outperformers tend to attract a disproportionate amount of capital flows, and this also gives rise to issues of potential systemic risk due to the

---

[79] Financial Conduct Authority, 'Asset Management Market Study'. Interim Report, November 2016. MS15/2.2, p. 52.

[80] John Scott, *Power: Key Concepts* (Cambridge: Citizenry Press, 2001) at pp. 48, 73.

[81] Jonathan Nitzan and Shimshon Bichler, *Capital as Power: A Study of Order and Creorder* (Oxford: Routledge, 2009) argues that the inherent tendencies of owners or controllers of capital are to accumulate more in order to exercise power. Peter Pelzer, 'Risk as Present Futures: An Elaboration on Risk and Fear' in Susan Long and Burkard Sievers (eds), *Towards a Socioanalysis of Money, Finance and Capitalism* (Oxford: Routledge, 2013) at p. 149 describes the tendencies towards accumulation as an instinct towards the transcendental or god-likeness.

[82] Margaret M Blair, 'Making Money: Leverage and Private Sector Money Creation' (2012) 36 *Seattle University Law Review* 417; Mary Mellor, *The Future of Money: From Financial Crisis to Public Resource* (New York: Pluto Press 2010), but see Tim Congdon, *Money and Asset Prices in Boom and Bust* (London: Institute of Economic Affairs, 2005) who argues that credit does not, strictly speaking, increase the money supply even if the same consequences, such as inflation of asset prices, result.

[83] 'Just 150 will Control UK Funds', *Financial Times* (London, 29 June 2014).

sheer size and economic importance of certain funds in global asset markets.[84] The forces of competition also appear to be limited in finance as financial institutions build up linkages and connections sprawling global geographies in order to trap global financial flows, accumulate capital and power,[85] and entrench the centrality of finance in social and political consciousness.[86] A recent market study of investment management by UK regulators showed that, although there are relatively large numbers of participants in the sector, this does not translate into a high level of price competition that might be of benefit to consumers. Indeed, profit margins in the sector were found to be persistently amongst the highest of any sector in the UK economy.[87]

Gospel et al[88] note that one of the consequences of financialisation is the lengthening of the intermediary chain and an increase in the financial actors who are able to cream off fees and charges to themselves. Such intermediaries may include fund operators, fund managers, custody banks, brokerage and research providers, securities lending providers, investment consultants and online investment platforms, to name but a few. Hence, the division of labour in finance has produced complex chains of linked firms, services and industries that are in a position to influence investment practice in a manner that is not necessarily aligned with principles of sound corporate ownership. The inter-dependencies in finance are now being studied in an attempt to understand the nature of

---

84 Haldane, 'The Age of Asset Management' (2014), above; E Bengtsson, 'Fund Management and Systemic Risk – Lessons from the Global Financial Crisis' (Cityperc Working Paper 2013); Office of Financial Research, *Asset Management and Financial Stability* (Sep 2013) at http://www.treasury.gov/initiatives/ofr/research/Documents/OFR_AMFS_FINAL.pdf; Douglas J Elliott, 'Systemic Risk and the Asset Management Industry' (Brookings Institute, May 2014) at http://www.brookings.edu/~/media/research/files/papers/2014/05/systemic%20risk%20asset%20management%20elliott/systemic_risk_asset_management_elliott.pdf; Massimo Massa, David Schumacher and Yan Wang, 'Who's Afraid of BlackRock?' (2015) at http://papers.ssrn.com/sol3/papers.cfm?abstract_id=2641078.

85 Gordon L Clark and Darius Wójcik, *The Geography of Finance* (Oxford: OUP, 2007) at Chapter 8.

86 Karen Ho, 'Situating Global Capitalisms: A View from Wall Street Investment Banks' (2005) 20 Cultural Anthropology 68.

87 Financial Conduct Authority (2016), above, p. 14.

88 Howard Gospel, Andrew Pendleton and Sigurt Vitols, *Financialization, New Investment Funds and Labour* (Oxford: OUP 2014) at p. 21.

systemic risk which this gives rise to,[89] and in the hope that regulatory efforts to contain systemic risk may be effective.[90]

The structure of collective investment pooling and management, although efficient in saving transaction costs and providing economies of scale, puts investment intermediaries in a powerful position in the management and control of investment capital amassed and accumulated from disparate sources. Given that investment intermediaries are themselves commercial undertakings, with their own business interests, they could easily seek opportunities to exploit their positions of power for self-serving purposes, while regulation in finance and competition are arguably catching up with instead of defining behaviour. One could argue that, on the basis of empirical research showing an aggregate increase in the cost of finance[91] (even in the years of cheap money and liberalised competition), efficiency and transaction-cost savings may have been eroded by the rents extracted by financial intermediaries, evidencing a form of exploitation.

(c) Professionalisation of Collective Management in Portfolio Management

Collective investment management is framed as an activity where intermediaries exercise fiduciary power over entrusted money and assets, and therefore due accountability is owed to beneficiary savers. As will be discussed in Section D, private law and public regulation have to an extent addressed the 'agency' problems of such relationships,[92] but the inequality of power between investment intermediaries and their beneficiaries is an entrenched phenomenon. Such inequality can be reinforced by the perceived professional and epistemic authority of the financial

---

[89] See extensive discussion and literature citations in Chapter 2, Mads Andenas and Iris H-Y Chiu, *The Foundations and Future of Financial Regulation: Governance for Responsibility* (Oxford: Routledge, 2014).

[90] Luigi Zingales, *Capitalism for the People: Recapturing the Lost Genius of American Capitalism* (New York: Basic Books 2012) on structural reforms. He advocates the return of Glass-Steagall in the banking sector, but some jurisdictions, like the UK, are adopting an approach to ring-fence retail from investment banking activities, see Chapter 12, Mads Andenas and Iris H-Y Chiu (2014), above, on UK structural reforms, the Vickers Report 2011 and the ensuing government White Paper and legislation, the Financial Services (Banking Reform) Act 2013.

[91] Bazot, 'Financial Consumption and the Cost of Finance' (2014), above.

[92] However other structural consequences are entailed, as Section D will discuss.

sector and the social trust in such authority. The financial sector holds itself out in epistemic authority, being staffed by extraordinarily talented persons who are remunerated in significant sums,[93] and frames such authority in a technical language of portfolio and risk management which is relatively inaccessible.[94] Further, the financial sector frames its power in a language of knowledge which entrenches it as a key player in shaping global policy and law-making.[95]

Zagzebski[96] expounds on the importance of epistemic authority, as a form of authority that reasonably intelligent and knowledgeable persons would voluntarily succumb to. The expertise of investment intermediaries and asset managers is framed in technical methods in portfolio and risk management and has over the years been supported by the development of quantitative techniques, many of which have received Nobel prize recognition and acclaim.[97] Technical knowledge, systems of administration that are inaccessible to the outside and the perpetuation of

---

[93] Guido Ferranini and Maria Cristina Ungureanu, 'Economics, Politics, and the International Principles for Sound Compensation Practices: An Analysis of Executive Pay at European Banks' (2011) 64 *Vanderbilt Law Review* 432; Gordon L Clark, Nigel Thrift and Adam Tickell, 'Performing Finance: The Industry, the Media and Its Image' (2004) 11 *Review of International Political Economy* 289; Satyajit Das, *Extreme Money: Masters of the Universe and the Cult of Risk* (London: Financial Times, 2011).

[94] Gillian Tett, *Fool's Gold: How Unrestrained Greed Corrupted a Dream, Shattered Global Markets and Unleashed a Catastrophe* (London: Abacus Books, 2010); Frank Partnoy, *Infectious Greed: How Deceit and Risk Corrupted the Financial Markets* (London: Profile Books 2003).

[95] Emanuel Adler and Steven Bernstein, 'Knowledge in Power: The Epistemic Construction of Global Governance' in Michael Barnett and Raymond Duvall (eds), *Power in Global Governance* (Oxford: OUP, 2005) at Chapter 13; Geoffrey RD Underhill, 'Theorizing Governance in a Global Financial System' in Peter Mooschlechner, Helene Schuberth and Beat Weber (eds), *The Political Economy of Financial Market Regulation* (Cheltenham: Edward Elgar 2006), at p. 4; Geoffrey RD Underhill, 'Markets beyond Politics? The State and the Internationalisation of Financial Markets' (1991) 19 *European Journal of Political Research* 197; Geoffrey Underhill and Xiaoke Zhang, 'Norms, Legitimacy, and Global Financial Governance' (2006) WEF Working Paper No 13 http://papers.ssrn.com/sol3/papers.cfm?abstract_id=941389.

[96] Linda Trinkaus Zagzebski, *Epistemic Authority* (Oxford: OUP 2012).

[97] Such as the portfolio theory and the Black-Scholes theory in options pricing.

professionalisation of an industry all reinforce epistemic authority, culminating in the description of financial intermediaries as 'masters of the universe'.[98]

Further, Haugaard[99] argues that the exercise of power can be carried out by dominating the formation of knowledge and the systems for disseminating it. The general financialisation of households, the importance of consumer financial literacy,[100] the rise of shareholder value, the financialisation of the corporate sector,[101] and the financialisation of national economies and in the EU provide the wider backdrop for the acceptance of epistemic authority in professional investment management and the inevitable commitment of social trust. The exercise of power by financial intermediaries has however been framed in the language of efficiency, such that the power of the financial sector seems neutralised in a democratic marketplace where the invisible hand rules.[102] The

---

[98] Richard Wachman, 'Reborn Masters of the Universe', *The Guardian* (London, 19 July 2009); Richard Anderson, 'Masters of the Universe: Meet the World's Best-Paid Men', *BBC News* (London, 2 February 2011).

[99] Mark Haugaard (ed.), *Power: A Reader* (Manchester: Manchester University Press 2002) at Chapter 15; Mark Haugaard, *The Constitution of Power: A Theoretical Analysis of Power, Knowledge and Structure* (Manchester: Manchester University Press 1997) at Chapter 9.

[100] Underlined by the establishment of the Consumer Financial Education Body (Financial Services and Markets Act 2000, sch 6) and www.moneymadeclear.gov.uk, the FCA's website for improving consumer financial awareness, according to its objective (Financial Services and Markets Act 2000, s 3). See also discussion in Toni Williams, 'Empowerment of Whom and for What? Financial Literacy Education and the New Regulation of Consumer Financial Services' (2009) 29 *Law and Policy* 226; Ronen Shamir, 'The Age of Responsibilization: On Market-Embedded Morality' (2008) 37 *Economy and Society* 1.

[101] To be discussed shortly.

[102] Harford rightly describes financial markets as only impressionistic free markets actually dogged by participants with disparities in information and power. Benchmark and currency manipulation scandals further expose the ugly rigged nature of many financial markets. See Tim Harford, 'Why the efficient markets hypothesis merited a Nobel', *Financial Times* (14 Oct 2013). On benchmark manipulation, see 'Barclays hit with £290m Fine over LIBOR Fixing', *The Telegraph* (27 June 2012); 'UBS Latest Bank to be Hit with Multimillion LIBOR Fine', *The Guardian* (13 December 2012); 'RBS Fined £390m for Rigging LIBOR Interest Rate', *The Guardian* (6 February 2013). Martin Wheatley, *The Wheatley Review of LIBOR* (Sep 2012). On foreign exchange manipulation, see 'Citigroup forex trader fired amid global probe', *Financial Times* (10 Jan 2014); 'Deutsche Bank braced for fines in forex probes: sources', *Reuters* (28 May 2014); 'Barclays suspends six foreign exchange traders', *Financial Times* (1 Nov 2013); 'UBS First to Report FX Rigging Shows

financial elites have also been crucially important in shaping international financial law and regulatory standards.[103]

Further, the rise of the wealthy and privileged financial elite[104] has been observed and the typical media representation of the talented and successful banker is an elitist and influential individual, leading a fast-paced and luxurious life.[105] This depiction of a successful financier has however garnered social distaste since the global financial crisis 2007–09 as the extraction of rents and excessive remuneration by financiers continued while social losses were being borne by ordinary taxpayers.

Law and regulation have, since the global financial crisis of 2007–09, taken a more determined stance towards governing such power.[106] Regulatory governance now takes the form of increased direct regulatory intervention into financial activities, markets and even internal structures,[107] as well as the enhancement of client or counterparty accountability. The distrust of finance is a turning point for regulatory reforms post the global financial crisis and the attempt to govern the power of finance has been manifest in many forms of prudential, conduct and

---

EU Immunity Flaws', *Bloomberg* (2 Apr 2014); 'Foreign exchange trading faces SFO criminal investigation', *The Guardian* (21 July 2014).

[103] For example, see Geoffrey R D Underhill, 'Theorizing Governance in a Global Financial System' in Peter Mooschlechner, Helene Schuberth and Beat Weber (eds), *The Political Economy of Financial Market Regulation* (Cheltenham: Edward Elgar 2006), at p. 4; Stefano Pagliari, 'Who Governs Finance? The Shifting Public-Private Divide in the Regulation of Derivatives, Rating Agencies and Hedge Funds' (2012) 18 *European Law Journal* 44. And cites in Chapter 3, Mads Andenas and Iris H-Y Chiu (2014), above.

[104] John Scott, *Power: Key Concepts* (Cambridge: Citizenry Press, 2001) at pp. 78–79. Dembinski, *Finance* (2009), above.

[105] Gordon L Clark, Nigel Thrift and Adam Tickell, 'Performing Finance: The Industry, the Media and Its Image' (2004) 11 *Review of International Political Economy* 289.

[106] See generally the argument made in Mads Andenas and Iris H-Y Chiu, *The Foundations and Future of Financial Regulation* (2014), above regarding how policy-makers anchor new and interventionist regulatory measures on the rhetoric of financial stability and macro-prudential regulation.

[107] Such as the reforms dealing with central clearing of OTC derivatives contracts, transaction transparency and reporting in the Markets in Financial Instruments Regulation II (2014); the European Markets Infrastructure Regulation (2013), the regulatory framework for credit rating agencies in the EU in the Credit Rating Agencies Regulation (2009, amended 2011, 2013), and the direct regulation of bankers' remuneration in the Capital Requirements Directive IV (2013).

structural regulations.[108] The relevant aspects of law and regulation in governing intermediary power will be discussed in greater detail in the chapters dealing with specific investment fund entities in order to assess their impact on changes in behaviour.

(d) Making the Realisation of Investment Returns a Business and Profit-Oriented Activity

Making investment capital productive and yielding a return is essentially an enterprise, a business. Investment intermediation is less a service for social needs than a business susceptible to performance targets. Although good performance would ultimately benefit the beneficiaries who have entrusted investment capital in the first place, it is primarily a business objective to be met by the intermediaries who seek success for the business of investment management as such. Such business success need not be aligned with the expectation of social 'success' in the form of adequate provision for savers' social needs, as investment management is a partially intermediated activity that does not in principle shield investors from the vicissitudes of their investment decisions. This is a relatively disturbing disconnect that the financialised masses have come to accept, largely because of the 'ordinarisation of risk' which will be discussed shortly.

Investment returns are increasingly being generated through trading and making market gains instead of through real productivity.[109] Generating relative or absolute returns (depending on the investment mandate) has become the enterprise objective of collective investment management entities. However, generating a return on financial assets through trading is a fundamentally zero-sum game. In a marketplace, one's decision to buy or sell an asset can only be realised if the counter-party holds a completely contrary view as to the potential returns on the asset. Harford[110] rightly points out that the efficient marketplace is an illusion and financial sector participants engage in arbitrage and zero-sum game

---

[108] Mads Andenas and Iris H-Y Chiu, *The Foundations and Future of Financial Regulation* (Oxford: Routledge, 2014) generally.

[109] Howard Gospel, Andrew Pendleton and Sigurt Vitols, *Financialization, New Investment Funds and Labour* (Oxford: OUP 2014); Kay explains that the rise in trading, i.e. the reliance on marketplaces to generate profit, has replaced relational investments, especially in banking, see John Kay, *Other People's Money* (London: Profile Books 2015) at pp. 16ff.

[110] Tim Harford, 'Why the efficient markets hypothesis merited a Nobel', *Financial Times* (14 Oct 2013).

transactions[111] in order to maximise their respective profits. In which case financialised solutions to meet social needs cannot universally meet all demands and it is inevitable that a portion of social needs will fail to be met.[112] Legal and regulatory frameworks in relation to accountability do not micro-manage or guarantee investment performance. Hence, beneficiaries would have no certainty that their social needs in saving through investment would be met while nevertheless having to pay for the privilege of having accessed the financialised methodologies and processes of investment to meet those needs. The disconnect between the social nature of saving and the enterprise nature of investment is a perennial concern that has yet to be addressed.

In keeping with the enterprise and commercial nature of investment services as a business activity, investment intermediaries engage in profit-seeking. Profit-seeking behaviour underlies a number of practices which may be fundamentally contrary to the social nature of saving needs. For example, the imposition of opaque fee and cost structures by funds is a pervasive phenomenon that may affect the ultimate saving outcomes for beneficiaries.[113]

The enterprise nature of investment management as a business also supports developments in innovative strategies in risk-taking that may obfuscate the nature of risk by employing the language of opportunity.[114] The rise in financial innovation such as derivatives for risk management

---

111 Roger Bootle, *The Trouble with Markets: Saving Capitalism from Itself* (London: Nicholas Brealey Publishing, 2009, 2012).

112 The zero-sum game nature of much of financial activity that is not creative wealth creation but distributive only in nature is noted in Mukunda, 'The Price of Wall Street's Power' (2014), above.

113 Critique in John C Bogle, *Common Sense on Mutual Funds* (Chichester: John Wiley & Sons, 2011). However, it may be argued that whether fees are deserved or otherwise, especially in active management as will be discussed in Chapters 2 and 3, remains highly arguable. See 'We Do Not Need 80% Active Management', *Financial Times* (11 May 2014), quoting a report by the UK's Department for Communities and Local Government. This debate has been played out in CalPERS' decision to drop hedge funds in 2014, which is not supported by many others, including UK pension funds. See 'CalPERS Ditches Hedge Funds', *Financial Times* (16 Sep 2014) and 'UK's £1trn Corporate Pensions Sector Stands by Hedge Funds', *Financial Times* (17 Sep 2014) but the London Pension Funds Authority nevertheless criticised hedge fund fees for being exorbitant, 'UK Pension Fund Criticises Hedge Fund Fees', *Financial Times* (16 Sep 2014).

114 Paddy Ireland, 'The Financialization of Corporate Governance' (2009) at http://ssrn.com/abstract=2068478; Paul H Dembinski, *Finance: Servant or Deceiver* (2009), above.

has given rise to speculative gambling[115] with such instruments in order to generate gains, having the effect of augmenting and multiplying gains and losses in the market using 'other people's money'. The global financial crisis of 2007–09 revealed how the use of derivatives could result in phenomenal losses for institutions on the wrong side of the bet. Zero-sum games in financial markets entail unpredictable distributions of risks and losses, subjecting savers' social needs to the volatility of finance and investment as businesses – as manifested in the need for the public bailout of banks in the global financial crisis.[116] Should finance operate as businesses, a question raised by Arup?[117] It is important to appreciate the impact of profit-seeking and competitive pressures upon the financial sector and how such may distort incentives away from meeting the underlying social needs of savers.

The profit-seeking nature of the investment management enterprise has the following ramifications. The immediate gratification of seeking short-term yield may result in short-termist and sub-optimal investment decisions and behaviour. Short-termist decisions may over-emphasise liquidity and the lack of commitment to investment,[118] chasing fleeting gains deriving from fluctuating market sentiment but disengaged from real productivity, a point that will be taken up again shortly. Sub-optimal decisions may be in the nature of behavioural herding[119] as the perceptions of winning strategies converge[120] upon a few perceived winning practices. Further, sub-optimal decisions may be taken in respect of risk-taking, such as where leverage is employed, raising the question of

---

[115] Emilios Avgouleas, 'Regulating Financial Innovation: A Multifaceted Challenge to Financial Stability, Consumer Protection, and Growth' in *The Oxford Handbook of Financial Regulation* (forthcoming 2014).

[116] Michael Hudson, *Finance Capitalism and its Discontents* (Dresden: Islet Verlag, 2012).

[117] C Arup, 'The Global Financial Crisis: Learning from Regulatory and Governance Studies' (2010) 32 *Law and Policy* 363.

[118] Eckhard Hein, *The Macro-economics of Finance Dominated Capitalism and its Crisis* (Cheltenham: Edward Elgar 2012) at Chapter 3.

[119] Emilios Avgouleas, 'The Global Financial Crisis, Behavioural Finance and Financial Regulation: In Search of a New Orthodoxy' (2009) 9 *Journal of Corporate Law Studies* 23.

[120] Such as closet index hugging, John Authers, 'Active fund managers are closet index huggers', *Financial Times* (London, 12 March 2014); smart beta, see John Authers, 'Is Smart beta smart enough to last?', *Financial Times* (London, 11 June 2014). Even hedge fund strategies that are more flexible and varied may be categorised into a number of dominant themes, see F S L'Habitant, *Hedge Funds: Myths and Limits* (Chichester: Wiley Finance 2002).

whether risks should be so augmented even if profitability may be heightened.[121] Further, as long as short-term yield on investments is achieved, and the business objectives of investment management attained, little attention would be paid to fundamental issues such as whether asset prices may be sustained,[122] whether speculative finance may cause any social damage or harm[123] or whether the disengagement from real productivity increases is a disturbing phenomenon.[124] The spirit of capital formation through pooled collective saving from the masses would be lost in the more myopic business orientation of investment management as an enterprise. It may further be argued that such a business orientation of investment management is supported to an extent by law and regulatory frameworks, leaving the sustainability of investment management practices on the back-burner. The issues of sustainability of business models in investment management and disengagement from the real social needs of beneficiaries are being augmented on a global scale as finance continues to relentlessly expand itself into a global business.[125] Section D will further discuss the part played by law and regulation in reinforcing such short termism.

Turning an activity into a business or enterprise does not need to be an exploitative foray that foists negative externalities onto others. Adam Smith's original vision of enterprise is based on productive wealth creation, fair and efficient trading and regulating against exploitation.[126] It may be argued that it is the rise of contemporary shareholder value-based profit maximisation that has caused business vision to become increasingly tunnelled. The rise in the shareholder value ideology

---

[121] Margaret M Blair, 'Making Money: Leverage and Private Sector Money Creation' (2012) 36 *Seattle University Law Review* 417.

[122] Roche and McKee, *New Monetarism* (2007), above.

[123] Emilios Avgouleas, 'Regulating Financial Innovation: A Multifaceted Challenge to Financial Stability, Consumer Protection, and Growth' in *The Oxford Handbook of Financial Regulation* (forthcoming 2014).

[124] Costas Lapavitsas, 'Financial Capitalism: Crisis and Financial Expropriation' in Costas Lapavitsas ed., Financialization in Crisis (Leiden: Brill Publishers, 2012) at p. 15; James Crotty, 'The Neoliberal Paradox: The Impact of Destructive Product Market Competition and 'Modern' Financial Markets on Nonfinancial Corporation Performance in the Neoliberal Era' in Gerald A Epstein ed., Financialization and the World Economy (Cheltenham: Edward Elgar, 2005) at p. 77.

[125] Karen Ho, 'Situating Global Capitalisms: A View from Wall Street Investment Banks' (2005) 20 *Cultural Anthropology* 68.

[126] Spencer J Pack, *Capitalism as a Moral System* (Cheltenham: Edward Elgar 1991, 2010) at Chapters 2 and 3.

has fundamentally changed business behaviour, causing businesses to focus on short-term calculable value generation at the expense of long-term wealth creation.[127] However the shareholder value ideology is deeply rooted in finance economists' view of the private nature of the corporation[128] and as this book will argue later, is fervently supported by the investment management community in their corporate governance roles. This book will argue that the investment management community's support for the shareholder value ideology is ultimately related to its business objectives in the enterprise of investment management.

The business nature of investment management continues to evolve as investment fund entities and asset managers pick up new opportunities in the post-global financial crisis markets that banks hesitate to tread due to a new raft of regulatory constraints. The growth of shadow banking in the investment management industry,[129] taking on more and expanded maturity transformation functions raises questions as to new risks such activities bring to beneficiaries, society and the global citizenry. Further, socio-analyses of the global financial crisis warn of financial activity becoming an end in itself, and the ethos of service in intermediation becomes lost in the empire-building of an ever-expanding scope of intermediary activities.[130]

---

[127] Paddy Ireland (2009), above; Engelbert Stockhammer, 'Financialization and the Slowdown of Accumulation' in Ismail Erturk, Julie Froud, Sukhdev Johal, Adam Leaver and Karel Williams (eds), *Financialization At Work: Key Tests and Commentary* (Oxford: Routledge, 2008); James Crotty, 'The Neoliberal Paradox: The Impact of Destructive Product Market Competition and 'Modern' Financial Markets on Nonfinancial Corporation Performance in the Neoliberal Era' in Gerald A Epstein ed., *Financialization and the World Economy* (Cheltenham: Edward Elgar, 2005) at p. 77; Chapter 4, Eckhard Hein, *The Macroeconomics of Finance Dominated Capitalism and its Crisis* (Cheltenham: Edward Elgar 2012).

[128] Sanford J Grossman and Oliver D. Hart, 'The Costs and Benefits of Ownership: A Theory of Vertical and Lateral Integration' (1986) 94 *Journal of Political Economy* 691; Frank H Easterbrook and Daniel R Fischel, *The Economic Structure of Corporate Law* (Mass: Harvard University Press, 1991), but see Lynn Stout, *The Shareholder Value Myth: How Putting Shareholders First Harms Investors, Corporations, and the Public* (Berrett-Koehler, 2012).

[129] 'The Lure of Shadow Banking', *The Economist* (10 May 2014) provides an extended discussion of the pros and cons of the rise of shadow banking; Financial Stability Board, *Global Shadow Banking Monitoring Report 2013* and *2012*.

[130] Peter Pelzer, 'Risk as Present Futures: An Elaboration on Risk and Fear' in Susan Long and Burkard Sievers (eds), *Towards a Socioanalysis of Money, Finance and Capitalism* (Oxford: Routledge, 2013) at p. 149; Ian S Miller,

(e) Commoditisation of Investible Subject Matter as Asset Classes and (f) Detachment of Investment Returns from Real Activity

Financialisation has increasingly conditioned our perceptions in terms of what could be marketised, and we have become used to accepting a wide range of subject matter that can be assetised, commodified and traded.[131] As trading becomes a mainstay of generating income from investment, the commodification of various assets into tradeable subject matter is on the rise.[132] Many commentators have opined that investment gains are not generated by putting capital to work in generating real productivity gains – in particular, in support of companies with a distinctive business purpose – but are made in the relatively easier manner of value arbitrage in trading assets.[133] As Walter and Sisli[134] argue, this is not entirely a perspective that is created by the fund industry itself – beneficiaries would also like to enjoy the benefits of yield, liquidity and safety, to have their cake and eat it. Investment intermediaries armed with a glut of supply in capital are in search of tradeable assets that could meet those needs. A key asset class is publicly traded corporate equity, but asset classes[135] include private corporate equity, foreign corporate equity, real

---

'Profit as Organising Meaning' in Susan Long and Burkard Sievers (eds), *Towards a Socioanalysis of Money, Finance and Capitalism* (Oxford: Routledge, 2013) at p. 306; Seth Allcorn and Howard F Stein, 'What, Me Worry? Deregulation and its Discontents: Accurate Reality Testing Reveals Flaws to Deregulation' in Susan Long and Burkard Sievers (eds), *Towards a Socioanalysis of Money, Finance and Capitalism* (Oxford: Routledge, 2013) at p. 120.

131 Ho, 'Situating Global Capitalisms' (2005), above; Jonathan Nitzan and Shimshon Bichler, *Capital as Power: A Study of Order and Creorder* (Oxford: Routledge, 2009).

132 Howard Gospel, Andrew Pendleton and Sigurt Vitols, *Financialization, New Investment Funds and Labour* (Oxford: OUP 2014) at p. 19.

133 Branka Mraović, 'A Free Market Capitalism or a Speculative Market Capitalism?' (2011) 7 *Social Responsibility Journal* 578; Stephan Schulmeister, 'On the Manic-Depressive Fluctuation of Speculative Prices' in Eckhard Hein, Torsten Niechoj, Peter Spahn and Achim Truger (eds), *Finance-led Capitalism: Macro-economic Effects of Changes in the Financial Sector* (Marburg: Metropolis Verlag 2009) at p. 309; Roger Bootle, *The Trouble with Markets: Saving Capitalism from Itself* (London: Nicholas Brealey Publishing, 2009, 2012).

134 Walter and Sisli, 'The Asset Management Industry' (2007), above.

135 The UK Financial Services and Markets Act 2000 section 235 defines property that can be collectively managed as capable of being of any description, this is widely interpreted in case law, see *Financial Services Authority v Fradley* [2005] EWCA Civ 1183 CA.

estate, infrastructure, commodities, precious metals, art, wine, antiques, cars, and synthetic 'assets'.

The focus on market gains gives rise to a few ramifications. First, wealth is generated as rentier income,[136] and such a form of wealth generation results in the gradual under-valuation of labour and the diminished capacity of labour to generate wealth through productivity, causing income inequalities between asset-owning classes and those without.[137] Second, the pursuit of market gains can result in driving up the value of asset prices without any connection to the fundamentals of the wealth generating capacity of the assets in question.[138] Asset price bubbles are not further helped in many decades of loose monetary policy[139] which has allowed cheap money to chase asset prices. The desire to manage such volatility results in financial innovation devised to hedge and manage unexpected downturns in asset prices so as to minimise losses. Financial innovation in derivatives has exploded but managing the unknown or unknowable risks[140] remains a challenging pursuit.[141] The desire to capture market profits has been so great that sub-optimal or not-yet-ready risk management models have been put to

---

136 R H Tawney, 'The Rentier and Financier', John Maynard Keynes, 'Speculation, Cyclicality and the Euthanasia of the Rentier' and Greta Krippner, 'Accumulation and the Profits of Finance' in Ismail Erturk, Julie Froud, Sukhdev Johal, Adam Leaver and Karel Williams (eds), *Financialization At Work: Key Tests and Commentary* (Oxford: Routledge, 2008); Gerald Epstein and Arjun Jayadev, 'The Rise of Rentier Incomes in OECD Countries: Financialization, Central Bank Policy and Labor Solidarity' in Gerald A Epstein ed., *Financialization and the World Economy* (Cheltenham: Edward Elgar, 2005) at p. 46.

137 Ken-Hou Lin and Donald Tomaskovic-Devey, 'Financialization and U.S. Income Inequality, 1970–2008' (2013) 118 *American Journal of Sociology* 1284; Eckhard Hein, 'Finance-dominated Capitalism and Redistribution of Income: A Kaleckian Perspective' (2013) at http://ssrn.com/abstract=2198919; Basak Kus, 'Financialisation and Income Inequality in OECD Nations: 1995–2007' (2012) 43 *The Economic and Social Review* 477; Gerard Dumenil and Dominique Levy, 'Financialization, Neo-liberalism and Income Inequality in the USA' in Ismail Erturk, Julie Froud, Sukhdev Johal, Adam Leaver and Karel Williams (eds), *Financialization At Work: Key Tests and Commentary* (Oxford: Routledge, 2008).

138 Michael Hudson, *Finance Capitalism and its Discontents* (Dresden: Islet Verlag, 2012), at pp. 5, 19, 23.

139 Roche and McKee, *New Monetarism* (2007), above.

140 F X Diebold, N Doherty and R J Herring (eds), *The Known, The Unknown and The Unknowable in Financial Risk Management* (Princeton University Press, 2010).

141 Douglas Hubbard, *The Failure of Risk Management: Why It's Broken and How Do We Fix it?* (Chichester: John Wiley & Sons, 2009).

use and overly-relied upon.[142] The story of the global financial crisis is essentially a story of increased securitisation of exotic assets, sub-optimal risk management and asset price bust.[143]

Further, Hudson[144] argues that the dangerous securitisation of various debts such as sovereign, personal, distressed debt etc are pursuant to the desire of extracting value even when such extraction of value results in damaging expropriation of social wealth. Hence, the business of investment management by trading in exotic and questionable assets could be on the whole socially adverse. The assetisation of subject matter for market gains could also distort their nature such that their long-term wealth creating potential may be jeopardised by market pressures.

Publicly traded corporate equity is a case in point. Markets tend to evaluate asset values based disproportionately on short-term earnings prospects, resulting in the phenomenon that investment in publicly traded corporate equity is less and less related to the fundamental value creation undertaken by companies in producing goods and services,[145] but more related to market demands and sentiment. Economic theories such as the Efficient Capital Markets Hypothesis[146] posit that the value of corporate equity at any given time reflects all the information relating to the corporation and that must include its value creation characteristics and potential. However, many behavioural economists[147] have shown that the trading prices of corporate equity are often based on market sentiment

---

142 Riccardo Rebonato, *Plight of the Fortune Tellers: Why we Need to Manage Financial Risk Differently* (NJ: Princeton University Press, 2007).

143 Richard E Mendales, 'Collateralized Explosive Devices: Why Securities Regulation Failed to Prevent the CDO Meltdown, and How to Fix it' [2009] *University of Illinois Law Review* 1359.

144 Michael Hudson, 'From Marx to Goldman Sachs: The Fictions of Fictitious Capital, and the Financialization of Industry' (2010) 38 *Journal of Socialist Theory* 419.

145 Charles J Whelan, 'Money Manager Capitalism: Still Here but Not Quite as Expected' (2002) 36 *Journal of Economic Issues* 401; John Hendry, Paul Sanderson, Richard Barker and John D Roberts, 'Owners or Traders? Conceptualizations of Institutional Investors and Their Relationship with Corporate Managers' (2006) 59 *Human Relations* 1101.

146 Eugene Fama, 'Efficient Capital Markets: A Review of Theory and Empirical Work'(1970) 25 *Journal of Finance* 383.

147 D Langevoort, 'Taming the Animal Spirits of the Stock Markets: A Behavioral Approach to Securities Regulation' (2002) 97 *Northwestern University Law Rev* 135; Thomas Gilovich, Dale Griffin and Daniel Kahneman (eds), *Heuristics and Biases: The Psychology of Intuitive Judgment* (Cambridge: Cambridge University Press 2002); Daniel Kahneman and Amos Tversky (eds), *Choices, Values and Frames* (Cambridge: Cambridge University Press 2003);

and irrational perceptions and valuations, raising the question of disconnect with the fundamentals of businesses that are publicly traded. The treatment of publicly traded corporate equity as liquid market assets has also resulted in excessive commodification of publicly traded companies – as entities that are easily bought or sold for a profit, and as entities out of which value can be extracted for a profit.

Financialisation has fundamentally changed the role of the corporate sector from long-term creators of wealth in real production to a 'loose collection of assets' that could be manipulated, combined and disassembled for the purposes of commodification and generation of value for investors, managers and financial intermediaries.[148] Little thought is given to the distinctive business purpose of each business entity; each entity is viewed purely in terms of its short-term financial characteristics. Further, the rise in the shareholder value ideology has narrowed down the value of the corporation to the value reflected in the price of tradeable corporate equity. The rise in the shareholder value ideology has fundamentally changed management behaviour, causing management to focus on short-term calculable value generation at the expense of investment in long-term productivity enhancements and wealth creation.[149] Such behaviour is compelled by the nature of short-termist investment that lacks commitment and patience.[150] Corporate decisions made on the basis of

---

Robert H Shiller, 'Bubbles, Human Judgment, and Expert Opinion' (2002) 58 *Financial Analysts Journal* 18; *Irrational Exuberance* (Crown Business, 2006).

[148] Paul H Dembinski, *Finance: Servant or Deceiver* (trans. by Kevin Cook, Basingstoke: Palgrave Macmillan 2009); Ken-Hou Lin and Donald Tomaskovic-Devey, 'Financialization and U.S. Income Inequality, 1970–2008' (2013) 118 *American Journal of Sociology* 1284. Also see John Kay, *Other People's Money* (2015), above at pp. 45ff.

[149] Paddy Ireland, 'The Financialization of Corporate Governance' (2009), above; Engelbert Stockhammer, 'Financialization and the Slowdown of Accumulation' in Ismail Erturk, Julie Froud, Sukhdev Johal, Adam Leaver and Karel Williams (eds), *Financialization At Work: Key Tests and Commentary* (Oxford: Routledge, 2008); James Crotty, 'The Neoliberal Paradox: The Impact of Destructive Product Market Competition and 'Modern' Financial Markets on Nonfinancial Corporation Performance in the Neoliberal Era' in Gerald A Epstein ed., *Financialization and the World Economy* (Cheltenham: Edward Elgar, 2005) at p. 77.

[150] Gordon L Clark and Darius Wójcik, *The Geography of Finance* (Oxford: OUP, 2007) at p. 11 describes the deus ex machine of their book as financial institutions whose commitment to corporate executives is conditional and subject to competing market-based investment opportunities.

short-termist value generation include shrinking the asset base of companies to boost returns on net assets,[151] shrinking the capital base of companies by buying back shares or distributing dividends so that short-term returns on equity could be boosted while compromising longer term research and development expenditure.[152] The release of capital into the marketplace does not result in deployment in real productivity but provides a basis for more rentier income to be earned, such as financing leverage.[153] Financialisation also affects companies in terms of their strategic behaviour – many companies increasingly seek sources of income from investment or developing financial products instead of developing innovations in product or productivity.[154] Such strategic changes in business are further reinforced by remuneration structures for management being aligned with performance defined according to shareholder value.[155] The partnership between business and finance has flourished in the financialisation era and has boosted the power of financial intermediaries who design and execute numerous financialised transactions for corporations. The financialisation of the corporate sector has however resulted in the stagnation of wealth creation in the corporate

---

151 Mukunda, 'The Price of Wall Street's Power' (2014), above; William Lazonick and Mary O'Sullivan, 'Shareholder Value and Corporate Governance' both in Ismail Erturk, Julie Froud, Sukhdev Johal, Adam Leaver and Karel Williams (eds), *Financialization At Work: Key Tests and Commentary* (Oxford: Routledge, 2008).

152 Eckhard Hein, 'Finance-dominated Capitalism and Redistribution of Income: A Kaleckian Perspective' (2013) at http://ssrn.com/abstract=2198919; Julie Froud, Sukhdev Johal, Adam Leaver and Karel Williams, *Financialization and Strategy: Narrative and Numbers* (Oxford: Routledge 2006) at Chapter 4; William Lazonick and Mary O'Sullivan, 'Shareholder Value and Corporate Governance' in Ismail Erturk, Julie Froud, Sukhdev Johal, Adam Leaver and Karel Williams (eds), *Financialization At Work: Key Tests and Commentary* (Oxford: Routledge, 2008).

153 Michael Hudson, *Finance Capitalism and its Discontents* (Dresden: Islet Verlag, 2012) at p. 222.

154 Greta Krippner, 'Accumulation and the Profits of Finance' in Ismail Erturk, Julie Froud, Sukhdev Johal, Adam Leaver and Karel Williams (eds), *Financialization At Work: Key Tests and Commentary* (Oxford: Routledge, 2008); Julie Froud, Sukhdev Johal, Adam Leaver and Karel Williams, 'GE under Jack Welch: Narrative, Performative and the Business Model' in Ismail Erturk, Julie Froud, Sukhdev Johal, Adam Leaver and Karel Williams (eds), *Financialization At Work: Key Tests and Commentary* (Oxford: Routledge, 2008).

155 Andrew Smithers, *The Road to Recovery: How and Why Economic Policy must Change* (Chichester: John Wiley & Sons, 2013).

sector over the long term.[156] Folkman and others argue that financial intermediaries generate a lot of short-termist corporate restructuring and finance work in order to extract rents rather than to help companies achieve long-term growth and value.[157] Santoro and Strauss also argue that the profit generation by financial intermediaries has become a form of 'profit disjunction' as profits could be generated through complex innovations whether or not the transactions generating such profits are of real utility for productive purposes.[158]

Finally, Martin[159] describes financialisation as bringing about an atomised perception of property – which is a value-driven desire that seeks to combine, disperse and calculate how the proprietary nature of assets can be used to generate value. This results in a calculative mindset that encourages selfish exploitation of assets for extraction of value. The changes to financial, corporate and social culture are enduring and disturbing.

The business model of modern investment management overall leads to an over-reliance on market realisation of profits and a general hampering of putting assets to productive good use, including corporations which are both wealth-generating organisations and marketised tradeable assets in themselves. The reliance on fickle asset prices to generate income and making the real economy a less attractive arena for wealth creation are both unsustainable phenomena. Financialisation increasingly correlates with falling rates of real productivity,[160] such as in developed countries where financialisation has become more and more entrenched. Policy and

---

[156] Carlos Morera Camacho and Jose Antonio Rojas Nieto, 'The Globalisation of Finance Capital 1997-2008' in Costas Lapavitsas ed., Financialization in Crisis (Leiden: Brill Publishers, 2012) at 161; Eckhard Hein, 'Rising Shareholder Power: Effects on Distribution, Capacity Utilisation and Capital Accumulation in Kaleckian and Post-Kaleckian Models' in Eckhard Hein, Torsten Niechoj, Peter Spahn and Achim Truger (eds), *Finance-led Capitalism: Macroeconomic Effects of Changes in the Financial Sector* (Marburg: Metropolis Verlag 2009) at 89.

[157] Peter Folkman and others, 'Working for Themselves: Financial Intermediaries and Present Day Capitalism' (2007) 49 *Business History* 552.

[158] Michael A Santoro and Ronald J Strauss, *Wall Street Values: Business Ethics and the Global Financial Crisis* (Cambridge: Cambridge University Press, 2012), Chapter 2.

[159] Randy Martin 'The Twin Towers of Financialization: Entanglements of Political and Cultural Economies' (2009) 3 The Global South 108.

[160] Jacob Assa, 'Financialization and its Consequences: The OECD Experience' (2012) 1 Finance Research 35; Thomas I Palley, *Financialisation: The Economics of Finance Capital Domination* (Basingstoke: Palgrave Macmillan

law have not questioned[161] how investment management generates its returns, although there is cognisance that investment management is increasingly disconnected with its starting social purposes.[162] It is perhaps timely to make a statement regarding the undesirability of excessive reliance on market gains. It is arguable that investment for value arbitrage is not the same as putting capital to work. Market trading should primarily focus on the needs for liquidity so that it is not overly relied upon as an income generator.

(g) The Widespread Acceptance of Financial Risk-bearing by Individual Citizens

The financial sector appeals to many to participate in financial services and markets as the primary means to meet their needs, but the sector nevertheless is able to evade lofty promises by framing financial participation as a form of liberalised decision-making, autonomy, self-care and individual responsibility.[163] Financialisation thus achieves an effect of convincing users of financial services and markets that they bear the ultimate risk of exposure in the markets.

Financial participation for the many is framed as a form of democratised exposure to market risk. The turning of savings into investment results in the perception that exposure to market risk has become a way of life. The market is framed as a neutral arena, spontaneous order,[164] the 'invisible hand' not subject to the control of particular power,[165] further engendering acceptance of its verdict. For example, the shift from

---

2013); Eckhard Hein, *The Macro-economics of Finance Dominated Capitalism and its Crisis* (Cheltenham: Edward Elgar 2012) at Chapter 4.

[161] Law Commission, *Fiduciary Duties of Investment Intermediaries* (July 2014) at http://lawcommission.justice.gov.uk/areas/fiduciary_duties.htm concluding that there is no need to change the law relating to investment intermediaries' relationships with beneficiaries in order to make equity markets work better for meeting saver needs.

[162] BIS, *Kay Review* (2012), above.

[163] Paul Langley, 'Uncertain Subjects of Anglo-American Financialization' (2007) 65 *Cultural Critique* 67.

[164] The Hayekian view, see F A Hayek, *Individualism and Economic Order* (University of Chicago Press, 1944); *The Constitution of Liberty* (University of Chicago Press, 1960).

[165] Which remains an important cornerstone in understanding economic organisation of life, see Peter J Boettke, 'Teaching Economics, Appreciating Spontaneous Order, and Economics as a Public Science' (2010) at http://papers.ssrn.com/sol3/papers.cfm?abstract_id=1661513.

defined benefit to defined contribution pension schemes in many occupational pension funds across OECD countries in the last decade or so would result in increased exposure of households to market risk.[166] Law and regulation have also played a significant role in maintaining the perceived neutrality, objectivity and fairness of the market as an essential infrastructure.[167] However, Broadbent et al, in studying the effect of shifting from defined benefit pension plans to defined contribution ones, report that the acceptance of exposure to market risk does not mean that households understand what the risks mean or how to manage them. It is curious that this disconnect is accepted and hardly questioned.[168] Pike and Pollard[169] report on the extent and pervasiveness of financial risk across geographies, and it seems that the phenomenon of widespread social acceptance of financial risk-bearing has become universal.

It is arguable that households are sold the responsibility of bearing their ultimate financial risks as the language of empowerment and autonomy that surrounds participation in financial markets glibly convinces the retail constituent of such responsibility. Erturk at al[170] argue that retail constituents could be sold financial services or products they do not really understand and yet come away with the impression that the decision to purchase was an act of responsible self-management. O'Horrigan[171] argues that 'New Finance' championing individual choice and responsibility obscures the fact that individual choice is being exploited by intermediaries who seek to serve their own gains and meet

---

[166] John Broadbent, Michael Palumbo and Elizabeth Woodman, 'The Shift from Defined Benefit to Defined Contribution Pension Plans – Implications for Asset Allocation and Risk Management' (*BIS Working Paper* 2006) at http://www.bis.org/publ/wgpapers/cgfs27broadbent3.pdf.

[167] Such as regulation on market conduct and against market abuse, e.g. EU Market Abuse Regulation 2014, the regulation of price discovery and transparency on markets, The MiFID II recast Directive 2014; the Transparency Directive 2004 amended as of 2014.

[168] Simone Polillo, 'Wildcats in Banking Fields: The Politics of Financial Inclusion' (2011) 40 *Theor Soc* 347 argues that the democratisation of exposure to market risk is a façade used to lure the masses into financial participation to generate fees and income for the financial sector and little consideration is given to the needs of participants.

[169] Andy Pike and Jane Pollard, 'Economic Geographies of Financialization' (2010) 86 *Economic Geography* 29.

[170] Ismail Erturk, Julie Froud, Sukhdev Johal, Adam Leaver and Karel Williams, 'The Democratization of Finance? Promises, Outcomes and Conditions' (2007) 14 *Review of International Political Economy* 553.

[171] James O'Horrigan, 'The Ethics of the New Finance' (1987) 6 *Journal of Business Ethics* 97.

their sales volume targets. Financialisation is underpinned by a form of new ethics that encourages an every man for himself attitude, and myopic self-serving behaviour on the part of intermediaries. In this way, a rhetoric of personal responsibility obscures the unfairness in the uneven distribution of risk or risk management between financial intermediaries and ultimate users. Commentators[172] discuss the prevalent uneven distribution of risk between end-users who are persuaded to participate in finance and the opportunistic profit-making carried out by the financial sector.

However, the idea of encouraging individuals into financial assets has been very much supported by law. For example, disclosure-based regulation surrounding investment is premised on giving choice and responsibility to the investor to make an informed decision. The emphasis placed on financial literacy by policy-makers is also in the vein of supporting the risk-bearing by individuals as a way of life. However, consumer financial literacy education may be limited in helping consumers overcome inherent bounded rationality.[173] Williams[174] and Willis[175] argue fervently against regarding consumer financial literacy education as sufficient to make consumers entirely responsible for weak financial decisions, shielding regulators and the industry from liability or responsibility. The post global financial crisis reforms have however recognised the political unpopularity and systemic risk effects of social absorption of financial risk and losses, and so more paternalism has been rolled out in consumer protection in the US, EU and UK.[176]

Although the balance of financial risk-bearing may be slightly shifted in consumers' favour in the wake of the post-global financial crisis law reforms, exposure to market risk remains a mainstay in the context of

---

172 Paul H Dembinski, *Finance: Servant or Deceiver* (2009), above; Thomas I Palley, 'Financialisation: What it is and Why it Matters' in Eckhard Hein, Torsten Niechoj, Peter Spahn and Achim Truger (eds), *Finance-led Capitalism: Macro-economic Effects of Changes in the Financial Sector* (Marburg: Metropolis Verlag 2009) at p. 29.

173 Geraint Howells, 'The Potential and Limits of Consumer Empowerment by Information' (2005) 32 *Journal of Law and Society* 349.

174 Toni Williams, 'Empowerment of Whom and for What? Financial Literacy Education and the New Regulation of Consumer Financial Services' (2007) 29 *Law and Policy* 226.

175 Lauren E Willis, 'Against Financial Literacy Education' (2008-9) 94 *Iowa Law Review* 197.

176 Chapter 8, Mads Andenas and Iris H-Y Chiu, *The Foundations and Future of Financial Regulation: Governance for Responsibility* (Oxford: Routledge, 2014).

financialisation. Ultimately savers may still have to face disappointment in unmet savings needs, and these are attributed to the vicissitudes of the market.[177] In other words, financialisation has revolutionised how needs are met, how resources are to be allocated and used and how economies are run, yet Martin argues that it is essentially a technique, a method that is sold on the ideologies of liberalism and individualism, not promising any particular outcomes to those whose hopes may be entirely placed in it. Kay[178] also opines that investment management is a matter of 'search and stewardship' for the entrusted savings of savers, but very little intermediation activity is associated with search and stewardship, being concentrated on profit generation through transactionalisation and trading, contributing no real value added to the real economy.

Having sketched the seven 'financialisation norms' that underpin modern collective investment management, we suggest that the 'financialisation' norms, whether or not driven by ideology, business and politics, are at least very much reinforced by law and regulation. The next Section argues that the characteristics of commoditisation, transactionalisation and short-termism in investment management can at least be attributed in part to law and regulation, However, the effects of financialisation and supporting law and regulatory frameworks are greatly supported by the investment management industry as they also underpin the industry's profitability.

D. LEGAL AND REGULATORY LEGITIMATION OF FINANCIALISATION

Investment management has always been underpinned by private law in the UK, in contract, trust and fiduciary law. The role of law is essential to such private transactions in terms of determining the terms of transactional bargains and how they will be enforced. However, as the social scale of collective investment management in the financialised era has greatly accelerated, regulation has been introduced to supplement private law. We argue that although regulation has been introduced in the name of investor protection, it achieves an entrenchment of financialisation in the socio-economy, and produces certain unintended consequences in the

177 Pointed out by Luis A Aguilar, US SEC Commissioner, 1 July 2014, reported in http://blogs.law.harvard.edu/corpgov/2014/07/01/evaluating-pension-fund-investments-through-the-lens-of-good-corporate-governance/.

178 John Kay, *Other People's Money* (2015), above at Chapter 7.

nature of investment management. The more detailed aspects of regulatory law and their consequences for the practice of investment management are fleshed out in Chapter 2, and this chapter paints the broad themes of how law and regulation have supported the needs and trends in financialised collective investment management, as a key means of understanding how investment funds are incentivised and governed.

The private law of contract or trusts in the UK generally constitutes the investment management mandate, which could include the objectives of investment management, accountability frequencies and requirements, the terms of maturity, payouts and redemptions (where applicable). Further, the relationship of investment management involves entrustment of assets, and this attracts the application of fiduciary obligations, which proscribe trustees of assets from acting or putting themselves in positions that potentially conflict with the beneficiaries' interests.[179] The operation of private law ensures that beneficiaries can bring private actions in contract or trust for the breach of terms of the investment management mandate, although not for a disappointment in investment outcomes, which are usually not guaranteed in the mandate. Further, beneficiaries can also bring actions for breach of fiduciary obligations where trustees profit from their positions or have in other ways acted in conflict of interest against their beneficiaries.[180]

The *ex post* nature of private law enforcement may on the one hand be regarded as proportionate for monitoring the outworking of investment management mandates as, after all, investment performance can only be ascertained with certainty with the lapse of the stipulated horizons. But on the other hand, such *ex post* mechanisms may be regarded as insufficient for investor protection, as ongoing monitoring is hard to achieve and private litigation at the end of a disappointed mandate may be expensive. These problems are especially acute in collective investment management where individuals may be relatively unsophisticated or unable to afford or access private litigation actions.

The rise of policy-making in investor protection has therefore coincided with the rise of the social scale of investment and collective investment management. The first regulations in investor protection can be traced back to New Deal regulations introduced in the US in the wake

---

[179] Matthew Conaglen, 'The Nature and Function of Fiduciary Loyalty' (2005) 121 *L.Q.R.* 453; Robert Flannigan, 'The Core Nature of Fiduciary Accountability' (2009) *New Zealand Law Review* 375.

[180] See discussion in Timothy Spangler, *The Law of Private Investment Funds* (Oxford: OUP 2010); Lodewjik van Setten, *The Law of Institutional Investment Management* (Oxford: Oxford University Press 2009).

of the Great Depression, in order to provide investor protection in securities investments through harmonised standards of issuer disclosure.[181] In the UK, investor protection regulations have been only slowly adopted in harmonised standards[182] and in conduct of business regulation of investment intermediaries.[183] However, the rise of regulatory capitalism[184] in investment management is marked, perhaps as a response to the now widely accepted socio-economic model of financialised collective investment management.

The rise of regulation over securities and then investment funds arguably legitimises the ethos of financialisation – i.e. that investment as a means of saving can be regarded as a 'proper' channel as public regulatory law provides a framework for it and therefore induces a sense of confidence for social participation. The existence of regulatory regimes, premised upon re-assuring objectives of investor protection, arguably induces citizenry to buy the case of widespread social acceptance of risk-bearing by citizenry in investment markets. Further, regulation introduces standardisation that not only reduces transaction cost to access, but also induces a sense of comfort in being governed by these standardised terms of investor rights and protection. Most recently in the UK, as will be discussed in Chapter 4, regulation has also achieved the ultimate legitimation of a key aspect of financialisation – making private pensions saving mandatory. Regulation may thus even culminate in having a constituting effect upon financialisation, by making a key aspect of it a staple of socio-economic life, i.e. saving for the long-term to retirement through private investment markets.

---

[181] The Securities Act 1933 and Securities Exchange Act 1934.

[182] Largely under the auspices of EU harmonisation of securities regulation since the 1970s such as Admissions and Listing Particulars Directives, 1979 and 1980 respectively.

[183] Largely self-regulatory until the 1990s when the Securities Investment Board produced high level principles, and subsequently taken over by the Financial Services Authority which introduced more regulation, in coincidence with regulatory harmonisation in the EU, see Markets in Financial Instruments Directives 2004, 2014recast.

[184] John Braithwaite, *Regulatory Capitalism* (Cheltenham: Edward Elgar, 2008); David Levi-Faur, 'The Global Diffusion of Regulatory Capitalism' (2005) 598 *ANNALS of the Academy of Political Science* 12. Regulatory capitalism is the view that regulation is a necessary complement to markets, and that '[t]he state is embedded in the economic and social order; any change in the state is expected to be reflected in the economy and the society, and vice versa.', see Levi-Faur above at p. 21.

Nevertheless, the standardisation effects of regulation in certain aspects of investor protection may change the incentives of investment management and result in unintended consequences. In Chapter 2, we will discuss how two key aspects of investor protection, in regular accountability and liquidity provision, impact upon the internal governance of investment funds, contributing to tendencies that may in turn undermine investor expectations. The role of regulation is therefore a difficult one in achieving a balance of objectives and interests.

First, regulation has provided standardisation in the accountability cycles and content that investment funds should adhere to. These regulatory duties in accountability, to a certain extent, mitigated the disparity in bargaining power between beneficiaries and funds. However, regulatory frameworks that conformed to neo-liberal ideologies may not have been optimally useful for investors/savers, as they favoured minimal regulatory intrusion for fear of limiting choice to savers, and individual responsibility on the part of savers.[185] That is until the global financial crisis of 2007–09 ushered in more protective frameworks and standards.[186]

Standardised regular accountability regimes are imposed whether investment funds have a long management horizon, such as in pensions, or shorter horizons, such as in other retail collective investment funds (or mutual funds). Such regular accountability addresses 'agency' problems perceived by regulators, as funds are forced to report on the ongoing performance of their investment management on a regular basis, to be scrutinised by investors, so that early issues may be addressed without waiting for *ex post* private law mechanisms to materialise. However, it remains uncertain how useful such regular accountability is to savers who may not be able to appraise the financial information disclosed. It is uncertain too how they should exercise discipline as savers are too disparate to make their voices heard, and private litigation seems premature and too expensive. Regulatory regimes seem to substitute regulatory enforcement for enforcing savers' interests, but it is queried

[185] See Chapter 11, Mads Andenas and Iris H-Y Chiu, *The Foundations and Future of Financial Regulation: Governance for Responsibility* (Oxford: Routledge 2014).

[186] The US Dodd-Frank Act 2009 and the EU regulatory initiatives in this area such as the MiFID II recast Directive 2014, the Alternative Investment Fund Managers Directive 2010, and the UK FCA's many thematic reviews of the market for various investment products such as the unit-linked fund sector, the life insurance sector, endowment mortgages and trade finance.

whether such compliance only compels unintended consequences contrary to savers' needs.

As regular accountability of investment management performance compels regular valuations whether or not those correspond with the ultimate liabilities of funds in maturity payouts, this could cause funds to be managed for compliance purposes, to meet the needs of the yearly or half-yearly performance accountability report instead of being managed with the ultimate needs of the fund in mind. We are of the view that the needs of 'investor protection', which is defined according to the agency problem, and hence framed around regular monitoring and accountability, could give rise to short-termist myopia on the part of funds. This model of investor protection also seems to cater for the 'hyper-anxious' investor, instead of a more balanced model of the 'trusting' investor[187] whose vision is fixed on the ultimate maturity of the mandate. The pressures of short-term transparency could drive funds towards desperate searches for yield, excessive transactionalisation and investment management practices that try to 'squeeze out' as much as possible from assets rather than participate in a constructive long-term wealth creation process with business. The need for investor protection on an ongoing basis has become standardised by regulation, and has therefore become a matter for compliance. The regulatory framework could be in conflict with the objectives of patient investment fund management that delivers to meet the liabilities over the longer stipulated term, such as in pensions.

However, we observe that such standardisation in frequency and content of investment fund accountability is proliferating across fund structures, from pensions to collective investment funds, to alternative investment funds. This has been led by EU level legal harmonisation[188] which couples fund regulation issues with market access, i.e. allowing market access only on the basis of compliance with EU-wide harmonised regulation. Market access and the building of an integrated EU market has exacerbated standardisation pressures in regulation, but it needs to be queried whether such regulatory frameworks produce unintended effects in the practices of investment management.

Short-termist myopia in investment funds has become an important aspect of investment management, and may be manifest in different ways – from neglect of their corporate governance roles in equity investments,

---

[187] Advocated in Niamh Moloney, *How to Protect Investors; Lessons from the EC and the UK* (Cambridge: Cambridge University Press 2012).

[188] Undertakings in Collective Investments in Transferable Securities Directive 2009 recast as amended in 2014; Alternative Investment Fund Managers Directive 2011.

focusing only on trading, to being actively engaged for 'value extraction' from investee companies,[189] albeit for a relatively fixed term. Hence, the corporate governance roles of funds are not a phenomenon divorced from their internal governance, structures and incentives, and can only be appraised against that backdrop in order to ascertain what value they add – in terms of sustainable and successful investment performance for their term of mandate and in constructive participation in the wealth-creating role of business for the economy and society.

Further, we are also of the view that the needs of investor liquidity also drive, to a large extent, the internal governance of funds, and this area is becoming more and more important in regulatory policy. When investors may be able to redeem their investments may be a matter of private contract, but in retail investments, liquidity for investors is highly prized as liquidity reduces the contracting cost for investors who are less certain of their commitment horizons. Even if an investor's investment horizon is not particularly short, an investor may prefer to be able to cash out of an investment at short notice. The availability of liquidity induces a sense of safety. Further, investors' preference for liquidity may be attributed to the appeal of potential ease in reallocating capital in this age of choice in global investment opportunities.[190] Whether we characterise investors' preference for liquidity as being short-sighted and lacking in loyalty or as

---

[189] 'Value extraction' is a term that offensive activists such as hedge funds often use to describe their investment strategies in shareholder activism. It is based on a belief that the company's share price does not currently reflect what the price ought to be, and that activists may be able to offer suggestions which, if taken by the company, would allow the market to revalue the share price of the company positively. See also remarks made by Eric Knight, Knight Vinke at *Shareholder Activism in the UK*, a conference held in London, 16 Oct 2008.

[190] However, many commentators urge a nuanced understanding of global mobility of capital. For example, Williams argues that geographical limitations to such mobility may still occur due to market preferences such as home bias or political economy contexts. Colin C Williams, 'A Borderless World Of Hyper-mobile and Homeless Money?' (2004) 2 *Industrial Geographer* 144. Further, journalistic evidence seems to bear out preferences for greater mobility during boom times and withdrawal during uncertain times, see 'Emerging Markets in Retreat', edited by the Financial Times (1 Feb 2015); Suxiao Li, Jakob de Haan, Bert Scholtens and Haizhen Yang, 'Are International Fund Flows Pro- or Counter-Cyclical?' (2015) 22 *Applied Economics Letters* 378. Watson also argues that mobility of capital need not mean spatial mobility, but fungible mobility i.e. the transformation of capital into different risk forms due to the possibilities of financial innovation in hedging and chasing returns, see Matthew Watson, *The Political Economy of International Capital Mobility* (Basingstoke: Palgrave Macmillan 2007) at Chapters 2 and 3.

being hyper-mobile, necessarily transient and efficient, the need for liquidity has fed into investment management practices and regulatory frameworks. As such, harmonised European law has reinforced such investor preferences by mandating such redemptions to be offered regularly, at least twice a month in relation to mutual funds, and funds generally offer daily redemptions. Although alternative investment funds, such as hedge funds and private equity, remain free to stipulate their redemption terms, regulation has mandated regular and independent valuations in order to support investor protection. The needs of liquidity support transactionalisation and trading as being key tenets of financialised investment management.

The perceived need for liquidity has however been criticised by Kay[191] who regards this perceived need as being exaggerated by the financial sector, as underlying beneficiaries do not have such frequent and large scale liquidity needs. Further, funds have also engaged in financial innovation to 'liquefy' investment choices even if underlying assets are less liquid, such as in exchange-traded funds, as will be discussed in Chapter 5. Such financial innovation has been motivated on the demand side by investors' search for yield and on the supply side by investment funds keen to attract more inflows. However, there are hidden dangers[192] in assetisation strategies that involve 'liquefying' relatively less liquid assets.

Although, on the one hand, funds may be driven by short-termist and liquidity pressures, on the other hand such pressures also open up opportunities in financial innovation and the marketisation of finance, and increase prospects of appeal and profitability of the financialised investment management model.[193] Hence, the supporting law and regulatory frameworks are likely welcomed by the investment management sector. More recent changes in regulatory thinking, such as systemic importance and long-termist fund management, may indeed introduce anxieties for the sector.

The next Section turns to why investment funds own corporate equity and the enduring importance of equities as an asset class. This Section also looks at how the rubric of shareholder rights and corporate governance roles forms part of the appeal of equity investment.

---

[191] John Kay, *Other People's Money* (2015) above at pp. 87–95.

[192] 'ETFs to play main role in next crisis', *Financial Times* (28 Dec 2015).

[193] Kathryn Judge, Intermediary Influence (2015) 82 *University of Chicago Law Review* 573.

E. IMPORTANCE OF EQUITIES AS AN ASSET CLASS

Equities are a key asset class for all of the collective investment entities discussed in this book.[194] The dedicated portfolio of 60 per cent stocks and 40 per cent bonds[195] has become a standard in many pension fund allocations for example. Equities are favoured for return purposes. Although market prices in stock are subject to a certain degree of unpredictability, historical analyses have consistently shown that returns on equities exceed fixed income holdings. This is known as the 'equity premium'.[196] It may be argued that much research conducted on the equity premium had been carried out in the 1980s and 90s and hence was based on stock price data that spanned a significant bull run period in the 1980s. If so, it could be questioned whether the equity premium would still hold over a much longer time-span, through different market and economic cycles. Malagoli and Young[197] seem to suggest that the equity premium would hold if stocks were purchased in trough times and therefore under-valued, and held through good cycles. Depending on the timing of purchase and the period of holding, the equity premium may not be significantly higher over fixed income returns. However, more recent research[198] suggests that the equity premium is an enduring phenomenon, especially over the long term. Short termist holdings of equities may not outperform fixed income in trough cycles but riding out cycles will yield an overall superior performance to fixed income. Hence, equities are likely to persist as a favoured asset class whether by collective investment entities managing pensions and retail funds or alternative funds.

---

[194] This is borne out by empirical survey, see FCA, *Asset Management Market Study* (Nov 2015) at para 3.16.

[195] Martin L Leibowitz, 'The Dedicated Bond Portfolio in Pension Funds Parts 1 and 2' (1986) 42 Financial Analysts Journal 68–75 and 47–57 respectively.

[196] Roger G Ibbotson, Richard C Carr and Anthony W Robinson, 'International Equity and Bond Returns' (1982) 38 *Financial Analysts Journal* 61; Rajnish Mehra and Edward C Prescott, 'The Equity Premium: a Puzzle' (1985) 15 *Journal of Monetary Economics* 145–162; taken stock of in Pablo Fernandez, 'The Equity Premium in 150 Textbooks' (2013) at http://papers.ssrn.com/sol3/papers.cfm?abstract_id=1473225.

[197] Andrea Malagoli and Chris Young, 'Stocks for the Long Run: Historical Facts and Statistical Fallacies' (2010) at http://ssrn.com/abstract=1904992.

[198] Michael W Crook and Brian Nick, 'Equities (still) for the Long Run: A New Look at the Future Equity Premium' (2012) at http://ssrn.com/abstract=2172796.

Further, the supply of new publicly traded equity is likely to increase as the global market for listed capital is expected to grow.[199] Fund-raising in public equity markets remains an important avenue in corporate finance despite the high costs of listing in the premium markets of the world. Equity finance may be raised to an extent surpassing what debt or retained earnings in firms could contribute for growth and expansion purposes and offers a permanent and stable form of finance.[200] The foray into raising public equity may be regarded by many firms as a stage of maturation in business,[201] and is important for reputational and branding benefits.[202] A couple of commentators[203] opine that the opportunities for growth for firms are unlikely to be pursued in the absence of raising funds from public equity markets, and block-holders in private companies such as family-owned and controlled businesses would rather dilute their equity in order to be able to capture the potential of growth opportunities. Although there has been a trend of private equity investment in firms in order to avoid the costs of public flotation and the constraints imposed on firms due to listing and regulatory rules,[204] private equity funds have certain investment horizons and need to exit their investments at some point in time. Such exit is usually through a sale to another private equity or through public flotation. Even the firms

---

[199] See Price Waterhouse Coopers, *US Global Equity Watch 2012* reporting growth in initial public offers, and the impact of the US JOBS Act; *Europe IPO Watch Q1 2014* also reports increasingly vibrant activity after a slow-down experienced during the global financial crisis.

[200] C Fritz Foley and Robin Greenwood, 'The Evolution of Corporate Ownership after IPO: The Impact of Investor Protection' (2010) 23 *Review of Financial Studies* 1231; Price Waterhouse Coopers and Baker & McKenzie, *Cross-border IPOs: Choice in an Uncertain World* (Nov 2012) at http://www.pwc.com/en_GX/gx/audit-services/ipo-centre/assets/pwc-cross-border-ipo-trends.pdf.

[201] Julian Franks, Colin Mayer, Paolo Volpin and Hannes F Wagner, 'The Life Cycle of Family Ownership: A Comparative Study of France, Germany, Italy and the UK' (2012) 25 *Review of Financial Studies* 1675.

[202] Gaia Marchisio and Davide Ravasi, 'Family Firms and the Decision to Go Public: A Study of Italian IPOs' (2001) at http://ssrn.com/abstract=278237.

[203] Marco Becht and J Bradford Delong, 'Why Has There Been So Little Block Holding in America?', in Randall Morck (ed.), *A History of Corporate Governance around the World* at 613; C Fritz Foley and Robin Greenwood, 'The Evolution of Corporate Ownership after IPO: The Impact of Investor Protection' (2010) 23 *Review of Financial Studies* 1231.

[204] Ronald J Gilson and Charles K Whitehead, 'Deconstructing Equity: Public Ownership, Agency Costs, and Complete Capital Markets' (2008) 108 *Columbia Law Review* 231.

that have been taken private from public by private equity look towards eventual flotation in due course.[205]

Publicly traded equity would remain a key and enduring asset class for investment fund entities as it is also supported by good market infrastructure in many developed economies – established stock exchanges supported by systems of securities regulation.[206] These are important conditions for attracting investors and keeping the markets liquid.[207] In the European Union, the Financial Services Action Plan 1999 (that kickstarted a legislative harmonisation process for prospectus disclosures by firms intending to go public and transparency obligations for firms listed on securities markets) put in place an infrastructure that could be uniformly implemented across the EU,[208] in both the developed and emerging economies. Some asset classes are not as well-supported by developed markets, such as corporate bonds, certain securitised assets as observed in the global financial crisis, exotic asset classes such as art and wine (although international auction houses play an important role) and infrastructure.

Further, many premium stock exchanges have second tier markets[209] that cater for smaller business listings at lower cost and supported by less demanding rules that attempt to strike a balance between an appropriate level of investor protection and providing corporate finance access to firms. Opportunities for cross-listing and foreign listing have also become more and more accessible. For example, cross-listing in the EU

---

[205] E.g. Elizabeth Rigby, 'Inside the Debenhams deal', *Financial Times* (5 Aug 2007).

[206] Bernard S Black, 'The Legal and Industrial Preconditions for Strong Stock Markets' (*Stanford Law School Working Paper* No. 179, 2001); Price Waterhouse Coopers and Baker & McKenzie, *Cross-border IPOs* (2012), above.

[207] Branding thesis, Layna Mosley and David Andrew Singer, 'Taking Stock Seriously: Equity-Market Performance, Government Policy, and Financial Globalization' (2008) 52 *International Studies Quarterly* 405.

[208] The Prospectus Directive 2003 (European Parliament and Council Directive 2003/71/EC of 4 November 2003 on the prospectus to be published when securities are offered to the public or admitted to trading and amending Directive 2001/34/EC [2003] OJ L345/64) amended as of 2010; the Transparency Directive 2004 (European Parliament and Council Directive 2004/109/EC of 15 December 2004 on the harmonisation of transparency requirements in relation to information about issuers whose securities are admitted to trading on a regulated market and amending Directive 2001/34/EC [2004] OJ L390/38) amended as of 2014.

[209] Such as the Alternative Investment Market in London, the Alternext market operated by Euronext.

is facilitated by the EU prospectus passport brought in place by legislative harmonisation.[210] Globalisation and the global competition of capital markets has also made cross-listing possible and attractive since the 1990s.[211] Firms in emerging economies that may not be able to seek sufficient capital on home turf could seek cross-border capital and embark on growth and maturation on a global stage. In this respect, the privatisation of state-owned companies in many emerging economies is often completed through a flotation process of dispersal of equity. Such privatisations have also been reported to be important to improving future performance of state-owned firms,[212] and at a broader level are a key step in the liberation and development of emerging economies.[213] Cross-border equity raising is also becoming more well-accepted as the equity home bias is disappearing[214] in the broader context of global trade liberalisation – increases in cross-border activity and improvements in information technology that help to overcome information asymmetries. Hence, publicly traded equity as an asset class will continue to cater for both an expanding supply and a demand base at a global level.

---

210 The Prospectus Directive 2003 (European Parliament and Council Directive 2003/71/EC of 4 November 2003 on the prospectus to be published when securities are offered to the public or admitted to trading and amending Directive 2001/34/EC [2003] OJ L345/64) amended as of 2010.

211 See Uri Geiger, 'The Case for the Harmonisation of Securities Disclosure Rules in the Global Market' (1997) 1997 *Columbia Business Law Review* 241, Price Waterhouse Coopers and Baker & McKenzie, *Cross-border IPOs* (2012), above.

212 Seung-Doo Choi, Inmoo Lee and William Megginson, 'Do Privatization IPO Firms Outperform in the Long Run?' (2006) at http://ssrn.com/abstract=676181.

213 Franklin Allen, Jun Q J Qian, Susan Chenyu Shan and Mengxin Zhao, 'The IPO of Industrial and Commercial Bank of China and the 'Chinese Model' of Privatizing Large Financial Institutions' (2012) 20 *European Journal of Finance* 599.

214 Amir A Amadi, 'Equity Home Bias: A Disappearing Phenomenon?' (2004) at http://papers.ssrn.com/sol3/papers.cfm?abstract_id=540662. See also Darius Wójcik, 'The Role of Proximity in Secondary Equity Markets' in Gordon L Clark, Adam D Dixon and Ashby H B Monk (eds), *Managing Financial Risks: From Global to Local* (Oxford: OUP 2012) at Chapter 6, arguing that the home bias still makes sense as local information may be more readily available to proximate investors (due to soft information, presence of local financial intermediaries) and investors feel more charitable towards domestic issuers. But foreign equities supported by harmonisation of information reporting standards, visibility marketing campaigns and foreign expert intermediaries who also have a local presence could also become very attractive.

That said, the nature of publicly traded equity is not necessarily dispersed public equity. Much of publicly traded equity, and even a proportion in the US and UK (two countries that have pronounced dispersed ownership patterns in a majority of publicly traded firms), is a minority stake sitting alongside block-held stakes by states or families. It is noted that the corporate governance issues surrounding block-holders have been raised in relation to countries where block-holders are the norm,[215] and also in the UK[216] and US.[217] Institutional investors and listing authorities are however working towards securing acceptable standards of investor protection in a variety of different firm governance structures[218] and the appeal of publicly traded equities as an asset class would likely be undiminished.

Owners of equities enjoy the usual proprietary rights of dealing and creating security, and governance rights such as rights of participation and voting in publicly traded companies. Such governance rights have been reserved for equity holders and do not extend to other stakeholders on the basis of commitment of capital as a residual claim.[219] Although shareholders' rights are expressed as 'reserve' power in the UK,[220] certain powers are the exclusive province of the general meeting such as removal of directors,[221] amendment of constitution,[222] of substantial transactions,[223] ratification of directors' breaches and most recently, a 3-yearly

---

215 E.g. Stijn Claessens, Simeon Djankov, Joseph P H Fan and Larry H P Lang, 'Expropriation of Minority Shareholders: Evidence from East Asia' (2004) at http://elibrary.worldbank.org/doi/book/10.1596/1813-9450-2088; Meijun Qian, Hongbo Pan and Bernard Yin Yeung, 'Expropriation of Minority Shareholders in Politically Connected Firms' (2010) at http://papers.ssrn.com/sol3/papers.cfm?abstract_id=1719335.

216 Financial Conduct Authority, *Enhancing the Effectiveness of the Listing Regime and Further Consultation* (November 2013); *Response to CP13/15 – Enhancing the Effectiveness of the Listing Regime* (May 2014).

217 E.g. 'Activist urges fix for Silicon Valley', *Financial Times* (23 April 2014).

218 Roger Barker and Iris H-Y Chiu, 'Protecting Minority Shareholders in Blockholder-Controlled Companies – Evaluating the UK's Enhanced Listing Regime in Comparison with Investor Protection Regimes in New York and Hong Kong' (2015) *Capital Markets Law Journal*, forthcoming.

219 See discussion and citations in Chapter 4, Iris H-Y Chiu, *The Foundations and Anatomy of Shareholder Activism* (Oxford: Hart, 2010).

220 Article 4, Model Articles of Public and Private Companies Limited by Shares.

221 S168, Companies Act 2006.

222 S21, Companies Act 2006.

223 Ss190-200, Companies Act 2006.

binding vote on director remuneration packages.[224] With increased publicly listed equity and the dispersal of equity observed in large corporations in the 1930s, Berle and Means have already wondered[225] if the proprietary rights that are conferred on public equity owners should remain the same as those conferred on equity owners who are involved in managing privately-held companies. They were of the view that dispersed public equity owners were likely to be passive and uninterested investors who would focus on dealing on the capital markets. The removal of special property rights from them would then allow corporations to be managed as social institutions for wider societal interest. The point was never taken up in public policy, and corporate law moved away from social and communitarian concerns into individualistic and efficiency concerns.[226] This was a natural development given the wider political backdrop of rising unpopularity of socialist-type rhetoric.

Berle and Means' prediction of the behaviour of equity owners held true for a long time. Shareholders in publicly traded companies treated equity assets as investments to be bought or sold for market gains whether in the short term or over longer periods.[227] Dissatisfaction with companies was expressed through exit i.e. selling of shares. In fact, the appeal of equity investment could also lie in being able to exit in the market for corporate control, as takeover premia would generate positive short-term investment performance for shareholders. The governance attributes of equities as part of the bundle of 'ownership' rights were largely ignored by institutional investors.[228] The sidelining of governance rights by institutional investors in publicly traded equity was due to the relative ease of engaging in trading activities which cost less and more easily realised investment gains. However, taking the perspective of equities as commodified assets in the era of financialisation, the attributes of ownership of equity are constantly being evaluated and exploited in

---

[224] S226B, Companies Act 2006 inserted by s80, Enterprise and Regulatory Reform Act 2013.

[225] See Adolf A Berle and Gardiner C Means, *The Modern Corporation and Private Property* (NY: Macmillan, 1932), p. 66.

[226] Dalia Tsuk, 'From Pluralism to Individualism: Berle and Means and 20th-Century American Legal Thought: The Modern Corporation and Private Property by Adolf A. Berle, Gardiner C. Means Review' (2005) 30 *Law and Social Inquiry* 179.

[227] Lynne Dallas, 'Short-Termism, the Financial Crisis, and Corporate Governance' (2012) 37 *Journal of Corporation Law* 265.

[228] Bernard S Black, 'Shareholder Passivity Re-examined' (1990) 89 *Michigan Law Rev* 520; John C Coffee, 'The Folklore of Investor Capitalism' (1997) 95 *Michigan Law Review* 1970.

order to generate investment gains. Hence, hitherto ignored governance rights could become important to investors if they relate to the potential for investment gains. Such an instrumental approach to corporate governance has been observed in contemporary shareholder activism since the 1990s, as shareholder activism began to arise in corporate America led by public sector pension funds such as CalPERS.[229] Shareholders have started to become engaged with their governance rights as the exploitation of these could relate to financial outcomes and improved investment gains. Hedge fund activism, a more recent phenomenon which will be discussed in Chapter 6, is an almost extreme example of the instrumental approach. The publicisation of hedge fund stakes in companies of a significant threshold, such as at 1 per cent and above, would immediately trigger a stock price response upwards.[230] The earning potential of being engaged in governance has in some cases become a self-fulfilling prophecy.

This book argues that the instrumental approach to corporate governance reflects the financialised character of investment management as a form of financier capitalism. Commentators have earlier positively welcomed institutional engagement with their corporate governance rights and roles. Institutional engagement could compel the development and cascading of better governance standards for companies and result in improvement in corporate performance.[231] Hawley and Williams[232] also see the potential for institutional investor capitalism becoming a beacon for the development of global standards for better governed companies, extending to wider social responsibility and sustainability issues. There is some faith in intermediary institutions serving as representatives of the

[229] See Chapter 1, Iris H-Y Chiu, *The Foundations and Anatomy of Shareholder Activism* (Oxford: Hart, 2010).

[230] Alon A Brav, Wei W Jiang, Randall S R S Thomas and Frank F Partnoy, 'Hedge Fund Activism, Corporate Governance and Firm Performance' (2007) at <http://ssrn.com/abstract=948907; Marco Becht, Julian Franks, Jeremy Grant and Hannes F Wagner, 'The Returns to Hedge Fund Activism: An International Study' (2014) at http://papers.ssrn.com/sol3/papers.cfm?abstract_id=2376271.

[231] Alfred F Conard, 'Beyond Managerialism: Investor Capitalism?' (1988–1989) 22 *U. Mich. J.L. Reform* 117.

[232] J P Hawley and A T Williams, 'Shifting Ground: Emerging Global Corporate-Governance Standards and the Rise of Fiduciary Capitalism' (2005) 37 Environment and Planning 1995–2013, *The Rise of Fiduciary Capitalism: How Institutional Investors Can Make Corporate America More Democratic* (University of Pennsylvania Press, 2000) generally.

saving masses in revolutionising corporate governance for the better.[233] On the other hand, shareholder activism could kickstart corporate asset sales, takeovers or mergers and return of capital, decisions that are less unequivocally beneficial for the companies and their relevant stakeholders. The incentives that underlie the instrumental approach to corporate governance often encourage myopic forms of profit seeking, selfish forms of exploitation and little regard for non-value denominated concerns. In this book, we argue that investment funds' corporate governance roles are necessarily an instrumental facet of their investment management, which has a financialised character and is shaped by pressures of global competition and regulatory frameworks. We will draw out the implications for their roles in the intermediation of savings and investment and in long-term wealth creation of the corporate economy.[234] The next chapter now turns to the common themes in the internal governance, structures and incentives for funds.

---

[233] Gordon L Clark, *Pension Fund Capitalism* (Oxford: Oxford University Press, 2000); Gordon L Clark and Tessa Hebb, 'Why Should They Care? The Role of Institutional Investors in the Market for Corporate Global Responsibility' (2005) 37 *Environment and Planning* 2015; Stuart L Gillan and Laura T Starks, 'Corporate Governance, Corporate Ownership, and the Role of Institutional Investors: A Global Perspective' (2003) 13 *Journal of Applied Finance* 4; Tessa Hebb, *No Small Change: Pension Funds and Corporate Engagement* (Ithaca NY: Cornell University Press, 2008).

[234] Riccardo Bellofiore, 'The Ascent and Crisis of Money-Manager Capitalism' (2011) 40 *International Journal of Political Economy* 5.

2. The governance, structures and incentives of investment funds – shaping a model of modern investment management

A. INTRODUCTION

The model of investment management that mediates savers' needs through professionalised collective investment management is a privatised model governed by market forces, private contracts and law, and increasingly regulatory law. In this chapter, we focus on the key aspects of investment fund structures and governance that are essential to understanding the model of modern investment management. Understanding this model provides the essential context for understanding funds' corporate governance roles. Our discussion is at a high level, as being relevant and common to the fund vehicles we discuss in this book, although at a more granular level, there are important differences between fund vehicles. Chapters 4–8 tease out those granular aspects and the more specific lessons in the 'governance nexus' pertaining to those funds.

Isaksson et al,[1] in a research paper for the OECD, first suggested that the business model of different equity-owning funds accounts for differences in the way they behave as shareholders. The paper argues that there are several determinants of funds' shareholder behaviour including the objectives, accountability, maturity horizons, liability structures, market forces, strategic approach, fee structure, portfolio construction and regulatory framework. Although we do not provide systematic treatment of the above list in this chapter, we agree that the fund industry's structures and incentives are shaped by competitive needs and market forces and by legal and regulatory requirements. Increasingly, regulatory requirements have exerted a dominating and pervasive influence upon funds' internal

[1] Serdar Çelik, Mats Isaksson, 'Institutional Investors as Owners' (*OECD Corporate Governance Working Paper* 2013).

structures and governance. Funds' business models have therefore adapted for compliance purposes but continue to innovate to take advantage of new opportunities. In this chapter, we present a balanced account of the interaction of competitive forces and regulatory compulsion in shaping the model of modern investment management.

First, we underpin the importance of regulation in supporting the growth of private investment management as a financialised socio-economic phenomenon. We argue that the modification of the application of fiduciary law in finance and the introduction of regulation of 'conflicts of interest management' have brought about a rather permissive environment crucial to the business model of collective investment management.

Next, we discuss the structures and incentives of the fund management industry that have been shaped by market forces and the role of regulation in relation to them. In particular, we discuss the use of complex and opaque structures in the chain of fund management, albeit in the interests of professionalising investment management services, as an important context for understanding the implications for the 'governance nexus'. In particular, the professional asset management industry's practices have a profound effect upon shaping the nature of modern investment management.

The role of regulation is indispensable to shaping fund structures and governance whether in the form of imposing obligations or giving rise to regulatory arbitrage. We will explore several aspects of regulatory implications. One is that certain regulatory standardisations for the purposes of investor protection are crucial to causing myopic investment management behaviour. These have a marked impact upon funds' corporate governance roles as part of their investment management, in the form of well-documented corporate short-termism. The UK's recent policy initiatives that exhort institutions to act as 'stewards' in their investee companies are purposed towards addressing the imbalances observed, but Chapter 3 will critically discuss what these may achieve.

Finally, we explore whether more recent introductions of conduct of business regulation into fund management may shape the structures, incentives and governance of funds.

In sum, we argue that the fund industry has developed a modern investment management model that is highly disaggregated, entailing an industry of short-termist and myopic investment management punctuated with agency problems. Regulation has to an extent underpinned this model, in order to meet certain investor protection preferences. Although some regulatory reforms and market-driven forces in favour of socially responsible investing may ameliorate the observed sub-optimalities of mainstream investment management, these have had a limited impact to date. We are sceptical that the model of modern investment management accords with the objectives of connecting long-term saving needs to the long-term wealth-creation role of the corporate economy. This is the context in which funds' corporate governance roles are to be further fleshed out in Chapter 3.

B. THE LEGAL BASIS FOR THE GROWTH OF COLLECTIVE INVESTMENT MANAGEMENT

Collective investment management would, in the absence of legal and regulatory intervention, face legal risk due to the application of fiduciary law. In a private transactional context, a fiduciary relationship often arises in the context of custody of assets and in relationships of trust and reliance. An investment management relationship is characterised as fiduciary in character as it involves custody of assets and monies.[2] Fiduciary law ensures that the investment management intermediary acts in loyalty towards the investor and is proscribed from acting against or being in a position of conflict with the investor's interest.[3] The strict application of fiduciary law would make it difficult for collective investment management to be carried out as there may be conflicts of interest between investors. Further, such strict application would also make it impossible for fund managers to manage more than one fund as there may be conflicts of interest between funds, between managers and fund investors, and between investors.[4]

Legal and regulatory inroads have however been made into the strict application of fiduciary law, whether or not consciously, to support the rise of the financialisation of private saving as a staple socio-economic phenomenon. First, fiduciary law is interpreted as a proscriptive duty that

---

[2] See Timothy Spangler, *The Law of Private Investment Funds* (Oxford; OUP 2008) at paras 4.26–4.45; Lodewjik van Setten, *The Law of Institutional Investment Management* (Oxford: OUP 2009) at paras 3.60–3.69. See also *SPL Private Finance (PF1) IC Limited and 17 Others v Arch Financial Products LLP; SPL Private Finance (PF2) IC Limited and 5 others v Robin Farrell* [2014] EWHC 4268 (Comm); certain aspects in *Första AP-Fonden v Bank of New York Mellon SA/NV, The Bank of New York Mellon (Formerly Known as the Bank of New York), BNY Mellon (Formerly Known as Mellon Bank NA)* [2013] EWHC 3127 (Comm).

[3] Van Setten (2009) above at paras 3.60–3.63.

[4] The dimensions of conflicts of interest are discussed in Guido Palazzo and Lena Rethel, 'Conflicts of Interest in Financial Intermediation' (2008) 81 *Journal of Business Ethics* 193.

prevents one from dealing in a disloyal manner, but the application of investment discretion and powers by the intermediary is a matter of 'care, skill and diligence', which is a common law and not equitable concept.[5]

Next, regulators and policy-makers have been convinced by the financial sector to limit the application of general fiduciary law to the sector in terms of how financial firms manage conflicts of interest. By the early 1990s, it had become more and more accepted in the UK that the intermediary nature of certain businesses could give rise to potential conflicts of interests. However, the financial sector was of the view that they were under no prohibition of conflicts of interests, so avoiding such conflicts was not necessary.[6] The uncertainty in the application of the general fiduciary principle to financial transactions nevertheless entailed increased 'legal risk' that was inimical to the interests of the industry. The financial services industry also saw an interest in exclusive jurisdiction for their own regulatory rules and regarded the courts' application of general fiduciary principles as arbitrary and not helpful in creating a well-functioning regulatory regime. As such, the industry lobbied to support limitations in private law remedies for clients in breach of contract, breach of fiduciary or statutory duties, or tort liability.[7] The English Law Commission, in its 1995 report,[8] concluded that the general law on fiduciary duties could be modified by contractual usages, which, in relation to the financial sector, refers to regulatory law.[9] The clarification provided by the Law Commission's final report meant that financial institutions would be held to regulatory rules on conflicts of interest management and a generally wider legal risk of falling foul of

---

[5] As was put in *Seymour v Ockwell & Co and Ors* [2005] EWHC 1137. Although a 'fiduciary' concept of care arose in older case law such as *Woods v Martins Bank* [1959] 1 QB 55, there is no wider positive duty in fiduciary law recognised in UK law except perhaps the specific duty to disclose wrongdoing in *Item Software (UK) Ltd v Fassihi* [2004] EWCA Civ 1244. Specific positive duties such as the 'duty of prudence' imposed on pension trustees, discussed in Chapter 4, are distinct and positive regulatory duties.

[6] For example, see the Privy Council decision in *Kelly v Cooper* [1993] AC 205 (PC).

[7] Jan J Dalhuisen, *Transnational and Comparative Commercial, Financial and Trade Law*, vol III (5th edn, Oxford: Hart Publishing 2012), Chapter 2 ('Financial Risk, Financial Stability and the Role of Financial Regulation').

[8] See Law Commission, *Fiduciary Duties and Regulatory Rules* (Law Com CP No 124, 1995).

[9] But this would remain subject to judicial review, see Law Commission, *Fiduciary Duties and Regulatory Rules* (Law Com CP No 124, 1995).

fiduciary law should not occur. Further, firms could contractually delineate the scope of their fiduciary liability *vis-à-vis* clients, within the scope of the regulatory principles, and this would be accepted in courts as the substance and extent of any duty owed to clients.[10] Hanrahan rightly points out that general fiduciary law is no longer able to provide the 'public good' of client protection with respect to regulating conflicts of interest.[11]

Regulators see the importance of prescribing a regime for conflicts of interest management for financial firms, as a means of clarifying their safe scope of business, and also to provide investor protection to some extent. The approach adopted in the EU and UK is an approach which allows financial firms to identify, manage and disclose conflicts of interest,[12] without being excessively prescriptive. Firms are required to draw up a policy for how conflicts of interest are addressed and how this is to be communicated to investors.

The management of conflicts of interest is treated as part of financial firms' business model. Expanding business and exposure to more clients that may present conflicts of interest situations is an issue that only needs

---

[10] Blanket exclusions are not allowed, see *Brandeis (Brokers) Limited v Herbert Black, American Iron and Metal Company Incorporated, Lito Trade Incorporated*, 2001 WL 513189. But see Gerard McCormack, 'Conflicts of Interest and the Investment Management Function' (1999) 2 *Company Lawyer* 2. In the Australian context, Hanrahan argues that the private law of fiduciary duty is increasingly likely to tolerate contractual modifications, especially in contracts between sophisticated investors. See Pamela F Hanrahan, 'Fiduciary Duty and the Market: Private Law and the Public Good' (2008) *University of Melbourne Legal Studies Research Paper* No 347 http://ssrn.com/abstract=1184443 accessed 25 January 2013, writing in the context of the Australian Securities and Investment Commission's failed action in fiduciary duty against Citigroup. The court held that Citigroup did not owe a fiduciary duty to one of its clients not to undertake proprietary trading in the client's shares.

[11] Pamela F Hanrahan, 'Fiduciary Duty and the Market: Private Law and the Public Good' (2008), above.

[12] Art 23, Directive 2014/65/EU of the European Parliament and of the Council of 15 May 2014 on markets in financial instruments and amending Directive 2002/92/EC and Directive 2011/61/EU (recast), derived from European Parliament and Council Directive 2004/39/EC of 21 April 2004 on markets in financial instruments amending Council Directives 85/611/EEC and 93/6/EEC and Directive 2000/12/EC of the European Parliament and of the Council and repealing Council Directive 93/22/EEC [2004] OJ L145/1 (Markets in Financial Instruments Directive, MiFID), Art. 18. That said, there are specific regulatory rules for inducements, Art 24 of the MiFID 2014 Directive, above, and for investment research.

to be managed, not necessarily avoided. Although the EU legislation, as of 2014, now includes 'prevention' of conflicts of interest as part of the management of such conflicts, there is no positive mandate to prefer 'prevention' or 'avoidance', which would be the natural outcome of a strict standard of fiduciary duty. Declining business or refraining to act is not regarded as a key strategy in the management of conflicts of interest.[13] In sum, the regulatory regime that deals with conflicts of interest management does not present too much of a threat of constraining business freedom.[14] This liberal approach to financial institutions' business interests can to an extent be attributed to regulatory capture by the powerful financial sector lobby, but on the other hand the regulatory regime also serves policy-makers' interests in supporting financialisation of private savings.

Further, the general expansion of financial intermediation activities may be justified by efficiency arguments even if conflicts of interest abound in the provision of financial intermediary services. A number of commentators[15] point out that the expansion of financial intermediation activities undertaken by any one institution necessarily achieves economies of scale. This may in turn bring about social utility through greater efficiency benefits for clients. This argument is certainly pertinent to the fund management industry where collective investment management achieves economies of scale and can lower costs for everyone, making investment much more accessible to the saving public.

The legal clarification in terms of the limited application of general fiduciary law and the relatively undemanding regulatory regime for managing conflicts of interest in general[16] are crucial to the growth of collective investment management as a financialised phenomenon. The third development that has mitigated the legal risk posed by general fiduciary law to the rise of collective investment management is the separation of fund managers from funds, as discussed below.

---

[13] Christoph Kumpan and Patrick C Leyens, 'Conflicts of Interest of Financial Intermediaries' (2008) 5 *European Company and Financial Law Review* 72.

[14] Richard R West, 'Conflicts of Interest: Substance or Subterfuge?' (1971) 27 *Financial Analysts Journal* 31.

[15] Geoffrey Wood and Mike Wright, 'Wayward Agents, Dominant Elite, or Reflection of Internal Diversity? A Critique of Folkman, Froud, Johal and Williams on Financialisation and Financial Intermediaries' (2010) 52 *Business History* 1048.

[16] Certain specific regulatory regimes are much stricter, which will be discussed shortly.

The discussion above highlights the dilemma of investor protection in regulation – there are often trade-offs between policy options that favour access to financial services and those that impose high standards of investor protection. This dilemma is frequently revisited in policy and regulatory choices and shapes a regulatory regime that cannot reconcile both needs in a consistent manner. Hence, there is substantial regulation that is supportive of and facilitates the business models that financial firms adopt, as we shall discuss. Although investor protection regulation has also been in place, we have only observed much more palpable regulatory controls imposed on financial firms, including the conduct of investment management, in the wake of the global financial crisis 2007–09. We will critically evaluate how they change the incentives and governance of fund management entities and whether there are any unintended consequences.

Next, we turn to discuss the key structures, governance and incentives that constitute modern investment management.

C. THE COMMON ORGANISATIONAL PHENOMENON OF 'SEPARATION OF FUNDS FROM MANAGERS'

Separation of Funds from Managers Explained

Most of the fund entities studied in this book are organised in such a way as to effect a 'separation of fund from management'.[17] This phenomenon means that investors' capital is being placed under the ownership of an entity, the fund, which is a separate legal entity from the fund manager, an investment management company (which is often the one that has constituted the fund). The investor's relationship is with the fund, which may be structured as a trust, company or under contract. The fund entity appoints the management company to invest and manage the fund assets, usually by contract. In this way, investors in a fund do not have a direct legal relationship with the fund manager, who is crucial in making strategic and operational decisions in relation to the investment management of the fund's assets. Such a structure of 'separation of funds from

[17] John Morley, 'The Separation of Funds and Managers: A Theory of Investment Fund Structure and Regulation' (2013–14) 123 *Yale Law Journal* 1228.

management' can be observed in pension funds, which outsource investment management to various portfolio managers,[18] retail collective investment funds such as the popular UCITs,[19] hedge and private equity funds.[20] Such a structure may not always be adopted for sovereign wealth funds,[21] as fund ownership and management could be converged, and there may not be compelling efficiency reasons for separation. This point will become significant shortly.

It may be thought that such a structure is legally disadvantageous to investors, as the investor protection they enjoy under duties of care[22] and relevant fiduciary law[23] would only be owed by the fund entity and not the fund manager or other entities that the fund contracts with. Investors would only have recourse in *ex post* remedies to the fund entity for breaches of duties of care and fiduciary duty by the fund entity. As the responsibility for investment management is disaggregated and reposed in a separate entity from the fund, the scope of legal responsibility owed by the fund manager (and other investment entities contracting with the fund) to the ultimate investor is limited. The fund may take action against fund managers for sub-optimal investment management, but investors do not have direct recourse to such an action, having to rely on instructing the fund as such.[24] In the same vein, the investment management strategy and practice adopted by the management company is usually not susceptible to the fund investor's input or influence.[25] By and large, investment

---

[18] Whether in relation to defined benefit or contribution schemes, employers' fund entities often appoint outside investment managers for portfolios, as will be discussed in Chapter 4.

[19] Discussed in Chapter 5.

[20] Discussed in Chapters 6 and 7 respectively.

[21] Discussed in Chapter 8.

[22] Based on the general law of professional negligence, see Timothy Spangler, *The Law of Private Investment Funds* (2008), above at paras 4.18–4.25; Lodewjik van Setten, *The Law of Institutional Investment Management* (2009), above at paras 3.51–3.59.

[23] Timothy Spangler, *The Law of Private Investment Funds* (2008), above at paras 4.26–4.45; Lodewjik van Setten, *The Law of Institutional Investment Management* (2009), above at paras 3.60–3.69.

[24] But enforcement by fund against fund manager may not be a realistic prospect if the fund manager and the fund are related i.e. the fund is constituted by the management company to begin with. If the manager is an outsourcee, there may be more realistic prospects of discipline by the fund, but this depends on the terms of the management mandate.

[25] Although McGaughey (Ewan McGaughey, 'Does Corporate Governance Exclude the Ultimate Investor?' (2016) 16 *Journal of Corporate Law Studies* 221) refers to old case law to support his argument that ultimate investors are

management can be pursued in isolation of fund investors as long as the terms of the management mandate agreed between the fund entity and management company are adhered to.

The insulation of the investment management company and its investment management practice from the ultimate fund investors may be regarded as a form of arbitrage, in order to avoid the implications of fiduciary and common law duties for investment management. However, this may be an acceptable price to pay for ensuring that fund management is both professionally pursued and cost-effective. Morley provides an account of why investors and fund managers converge upon accepting the structure of separation of fund from management, based on efficiency justifications. We further observe that regulation has endorsed the dominance of that arrangement in the markets. The phenomenon of the separation of funds from managers is also key to the development of chains of intermediation in investment fund management.

Morley[26] is of the view that the separation of funds from management is derived from efficiencies desired by both investors and fund managers. If funds are separate from managers, fund investors enjoy the benefits of not being exposed to fund managers' costs and liabilities. Second, investors are better protected by the fund having its own distinct mandate and risk appetite (even if the manager enjoys a wide breadth of discretion within those parameters), and is not exposed to spillages of risk from other management mandates of the fund manager.[27] Third, the separation of fund entities allows fund managers to operate many funds and obtain economies of scale, therefore lowering fees for all investors across funds, and making access to investment management possible for a wider range of savers. Finally, distinct funds are able to provide better investor

owed fiduciary duties and they can instruct funds, and are therefore not excluded from corporate governance, while the lack of a direct relationship with the fund manager makes investors less incentivized or concerned to do so. Moreover, in a collective investment vehicle, it is hard to see how particular investors' preferences can percolate to the fund management level as the fund mediates investors' preferences as a whole.

26 John Morley, 'The Separation of Funds and Managers: A Theory of Investment Fund Structure and Regulation' (2013–14), above.

27 Although it could be argued that 'other management mandates' would be severely limited due to the operation of fiduciary law and hence investors may actually feel more protected from dedicated management attention. However, investors pay for this privilege in the form of much higher management fees.

protection rights for investors, for example, by offering certain exit terms. This may not be possible in the absence of such 'asset partitioning'.[28]

Further, it may be opined that investors prefer such a structure, in spite of less direct relationships with fund managers, due to the implications of financial and tax regulation. For example, the Pensions Act 1995 requires pension trustees to obtain written advice on their investments before establishing a Statement of Principles,[29] as part of their duty of care.[30] Pension trustees therefore seek professional advice as a proxy for discharge of duty,[31] and also seek to delegate to professional investment management in order to discharge their duties relating to suitable selection of investments and to ensure diversification of assets. Thus, the separation of funds from management allows fund management to be delegated to professionals in order to satisfy the regulatory duties of care. In this respect, both regulators and investors may be taking comfort from the employment of professionalism in investment advice and management, even if this means that the structuring of investment management may become more complex,[32] and that investors have less direct relationships with investment management services providers. Further, for collective retail investment funds, hedge and private equity funds, investors may be attracted to the prospect of incorporating the fund entity in a more tax-friendly jurisdiction, separate from the investment management

---

[28] Although it may be argued in which case that investors would bargain for more control and governance rights, and subject investment management to more robust scrutiny and accountability. This could also meet their investment protection needs although it requires more resources and effort on their part.

[29] Section 35.

[30] Sections 1 and 2, Trustees Act 2000.

[31] Andrew Powell and Georgina Rankin, 'Investment Management and Occupational Pension Schemes' in Dick Frase (ed.), *Law and Regulation of Investment Management* (2nd edn, London: Sweet & Maxwell, 2011) at para 9–034. The case of *Martin v City of Edinburgh District Council* [1988] SLT 329 which has held a trustee liable for breach of duty due to the failure to seek professional advice before withdrawing investments that are connected with the South African regime in the 1980s seems also to have placed professional advice at the heart of discharge of duty. However, in *Cowan v Scargill* [1985] 1 Ch 270, the Judge did not accept that having consulted a professional advisor *per se* means that an investment position taken is to be rubberstamped as sound.

[32] We will turn shortly to how 'inefficient' structures may arise in fund management as a response to regulatory requirements that are interpreted in a way that serves fund managers' interests.

company, so that any capital gains may be taxed less onerously in the jurisdiction of capital location.[33]

Nevertheless, it is important to note that the separation structure entails governance deficits over fund management. The discretionary power of investment management is delegated to the management company whose relationship of accountability is with the fund entity as a whole. Although the fund entity can raise matters with the management company and can sue the management company for failures in mandates,[34] this is less likely to be the case if the fund entity is incorporated by the management company, or they are closely related to each other, such as by means of cross-directorships. Investors face obstacles in mounting any litigation against the management company themselves,[35] although law reform in the UK is afoot to address this. Distance is created between investors and

---

33 F S L'Habitant, *Handbook on Hedge Funds* (Chichester: John Wiley & Sons, 2007) at Chapter 4.

34 E.g. Unilever Superannuation Fund's suit against Mercury Asset Management for failing to meet its benchmark, resulting in a settlement for compensation by the asset manager, see 'Mercury Pays out in Unilever Case', *The Standard* (5 Dec 2001) at http://www.standard.co.uk/news/mercury-pays-out-in-unilever-case-6347143.html.

35 For example, case law has stated that investors in a hedge fund structured as limited partners could sue the management company directly, but by doing so they become 'general partners' in the limited partnership and can be liable for the funds' general liabilities. See *Certain Limited Partners In Henderson PFI Secondary Fund LI LLP (A Firm) Claimants v Henderson PFI Secondary Fund LI LP (A Firm), Henderson Equity Partners Limited (sued on its own behalf and on behalf of all creditors of Henderson PFI Secondary Fund II LP from time to time) Henderson Equity Partners (Gp) Limited (sued on its own behalf and on behalf of all creditors of Henderson PFI Secondary Fund II LP from time to time)* [2012] EWHC 3259. Investors in a fund structured as a company would not be able to take litigation action in the name of the company unless it is a derivative claim which requires approval by the court to proceed. See *Breckland Group Holdings Ltd v London & Suffolk Properties Ltd* [1989] BCLC 100, and s260–263, Companies Act 2006. However, the Limited Partnerships Act 1907 in the UK is to be amended in order to allow investment funds to be structured differently from other limited partnerships viz Private Fund Limited Partnerships where investors as limited partners could participate in a range of management-type activities and exercise more governance rights under a non-exhaustive 'white list'. See Business Innovation and Skills, *Proposal on using Legislative Reform Order to Change Partnership Legislation for Private Equity Investments* (March 2016) at https://www.gov.uk/government/uploads/system/uploads/attachment_data/file/509841/PU1924_Final.pdf.

the investment management practices carried out by management companies, hence weakening investors' discipline over the exercise of discretionary powers in investment management. In this context, investment management practices are dominated by the 'agency capitalist's' incentives and agendas, while investors are relatively disempowered in terms of governance capacity. The relative autonomy of investment management brings into question whether it will ultimately serve investors' interests, or play a benign role in supporting the long-term wealth creation of the corporate economy.

However, these implications are not robustly questioned by regulators and policy-makers, who have more or less endorsed the structures developed by the financial intermediation industry. We suggest that the governance deficits caused by the separation structure, which is further reinforced and exacerbated by the investment chain, to be discussed below, should cause us to question the incentives and nature of modern investment management. Its impact upon the long-term expectations of savers and the long-term well-being of the corporate economy should indeed be examined carefully.

Regulatory Support for the Separation Structure and Implications

The separation of funds from management is a structure that is arguably accepted, if not endorsed, in much of financial regulation. In the EU Undertakings in Collective Interests in Transferable Securities Directive (UCITs),[36] the fund entity is referred to as the 'investment company' and is distinct from the 'management company'. The 'investment company' and 'management company' are subject to different authorisation and regulatory regimes. The separation structure allows funds to be incorporated in low tax jurisdictions within the EU, such as Luxembourg and Ireland, and still enjoy rights of passporting to other EU member states for marketing and distribution.[37] Management companies can be located in other EU member states and are separately authorised. In the wake of the UK's Referendum vote on 23 June 2016 to leave the European Union, it remains possible for UK management companies to set up funds in EU jurisdictions (such as Ireland) in order to market them across the EU. However, these management companies would not necessarily enjoy the

[36] Directive 2009/65/EC of the European Parliament and of the Council of 13 July 2009 on the coordination of laws, regulations and administrative provisions relating to undertakings for collective investment in transferable securities (UCITS) (recast).

[37] See Chapter 5.

passporting rights depending on the status of the UK's trade negotiations with the EU, and may have to incorporate EU-based subsidiaries to manage the funds. The Alternative Investment Fund Managers Directive[38] also recognises that fund entities ('Alternative Investment Funds' or AIFs) are separate from the fund manager, which is the subject of the Directive. AIFs are expressly not regulated under the Directive, and this allows AIFs to incorporate in low tax jurisdictions chosen by the relevant funds and their investors.

However, the Directive places some limitations on the marketing rights attached to non-EU AIFs, therefore introducing incentives for the incorporation of AIFs to move back to the EU. After the UK's Referendum vote, UK-based hedge and private equity fund managers may not enjoy such straight-forward passporting rights to market and manage funds across the EU, and may have to incorporate subsidiary management companies to seek authorisation from an EU member state. Although regulation recognises the separation of funds from managers, EU legislation has now introduced certain regulatory duties owed by management companies directly to investors in some fund vehicles, overcoming some of the governance deficits in such a structure. We will shortly examine the impact of such regulatory reforms.

The separation of funds from management is a common structural design for all of the collective investment fund vehicles examined in this book, except some sovereign wealth funds to which the efficiencies of such separation may be irrelevant. This structural design provides efficiencies and financial advantages for investors, although investors have fewer rights of control and accountability vis-à-vis fund managers, who are the ones exercising the discretionary powers in investment management. One important implication of the separation structure is that investors are able to have relatively stronger exit rights from each distinct fund, and investors may see much less need for control or voice.[39] Strong exit rights for investors are underpinned in the EU legislation for UCITs.[40]

---

[38] Directive 2011/61/EU of the European Parliament and of the Council of 8 June 2011 on Alternative Investment Fund Managers and amending Directives 2003/41/EC and 2009/65/EC and Regulations (EC) No 1060/2009 and (EU) No 1095/2010.

[39] John Morley, 'The Separation of Funds and Managers: A Theory of Investment Fund Structure and Regulation' (2013–14), above.

[40] The UCITs Directive makes it mandatory that redemption prices be published at least twice a month and that unit-holders have a right to redeem. In the UK, redemptions of units should be carried out within the business day

The move towards transactionalisation instead of relationalisation in finance reinforces the disempowerment of investors in their governance capacity to monitor the discretionary exercise of investment management powers and may foster investor apathy in the fulfilment of this role. Although regulation mandates much reporting accountability by funds to investors, it remains uncertain how far such disclosure promotes relational forms of market discipline such as voice.[41] Fund investors tend to prefer exit over voice and this preference has been reflected in regulation to meet the objectives of investor protection. Further, this has implications for investors' interest in the corporate governance roles of their equity-owning funds, as well as fund managers' perception of corporate governance roles as being relevant to investment management.[42] That said, regulation has now made inroads into the separation structure, by imposing certain conduct of business duties on fund managers to be owed directly to fund investors, overcoming the governance deficits in the absence of direct relationships in trust, contract or company law. We will shortly discuss what differences these regulatory requirements make. At this juncture, we turn to the point that the separation structure has given rise to the 'chain of intermediation' in investment management. This phenomenon allows funds to disaggregate fund management functions further, by delegating to different service providers aspects of fund operations or management. The growth of the chain of intermediation can create an appearance of being professionalised and specialised, but the chain structure can make it more difficult for investors to scrutinise or

---

although payment can be made in four business days. The Alternative Investment Managers Directive also specifies that funds must provide a redemption policy allowing redemption at reasonable frequency depending on the nature of the fund. The UK mandates that the funds need to be valued at least yearly, but the frequency of redemption is likely a matter for agreement between investors and funds subject to the general requirement of reasonableness given the nature of the fund. These will be discussed again shortly in Section E.

[41] This point is taken up further to discuss how regulatory accountability becomes perceived as part of the metricisation of de-personalised investment management, which in turn feeds into how investment management is carried out.

[42] We will shortly be looking at investment management strategies in an overview, to argue that these rely heavily on marketised and transactionalised mechanisms which can yield regular and short term results, and are not premised on relational forms of investing. Hence, the relational dimension of corporate governance may in fact be subverted to a form of 'instrumentality' even if funds engage in their shareholder role.

hold funds to account.[43] We are of the view that the chain of intermediation reduces legal accountability for all entities in the chain, insulating investment intermediaries while allowing them to extract numerous transactional charges from the ultimate fund investors. The chain is not always an efficient arrangement as such, but has become a structural feature of investment management.[44]

The Development of the Investment Chain and Role of Regulation

The fund management industry has developed layers of service providers for the investment funds market, some of them in different parts of the same financial group and others in separate firms. These layers of services include professional asset management, trading, research, custody, depositary, prime brokerage etc. The web of relationships for investment management is referred to in the Kay Review as investment chains. The Review is critical about the length and complexity of chains, citing their disengagement from the ultimate fund investors as a matter of concern, as such disengagement is observed to entail decline of trust and misalignment of incentives.[45] The growth of chain entities could result in more rent-seeking behaviour as a whole, while chain entities confer benefits upon each other. Investors do not have direct relationships in contract with chain entities and are unable to call them to account.

Further, a survey carried out by the UK's Department of Business, Innovation and Skills[46] also suggests the value added by various layers in the investment chain is uncertain, but the observed effect is the multiplication of complexity and opacity which has resulted in investors' disengagement from the investment process, affecting their ability to call investment intermediaries to account. The investment chain can create perverse incentives for investment management practice in the form of self-seeking behaviour, and funds' assumption of corporate governance roles with investee companies may be shaped by their asset managers'

---

[43] John Kay, *Other People's Money* (London: Profile Books 2015) at pp. 212–13.

[44] Kathryn Judge, 'Intermediary Influence' (2015) 82 *University of Chicago Law Review* 573.

[45] BIS, *The Kay Review of UK Equity Markets and Long-Term Decision Making* (Final Report, 23 July 2012) at paras 3.9, 3.10, 4.10, 4.12.

[46] BIS, *Exploring the Intermediated Shareholding Model* (January 2016) at https://www.gov.uk/government/uploads/system/uploads/attachment_data/file/489357/bis-16-20-intermediated-shareholding-model.pdf.

incentives, or investment consultant's incentives,[47] which are affected by their position in the chain.

Judge[48] rightly argues that the fund management industry is keenly incentivised to create layers and complexity in the investment chain. Each layer generates transaction fees and is an extremely profitable practice for intermediaries. This phenomenon is almost contrary to the efficiency tenets of Coasean organisation which should predict the reduction of transaction costs. Further, the specialisation of each layer can hardly be faulted in terms of increasing professionalisation of the industry. In this respect, regulation has to an extent supported the investment chain. However, we also see regulatory efforts targeted at disincentivising exploitation of the investor by the chain. The net effects of such regulatory efforts remain to be evaluated.

The Kay Review was of the view that regulation has played a contributory part in the growth of the investment chain[49] by requiring checks between investment service provider entities, for example, the appointment of separate depositaries for UCITs[50] and AIFs,[51] and arguably the appointment of independent valuers.[52] One can appreciate that the separation of functions may prevent collusion, minimise fraud and achieve investor protection. However, it is not always easy to establish which additional transaction costs deliver more investor protection and which are merely exploitative. The regulatory duties imposed on pension

---

[47] See for example Eric R W Knight and Adam D Dixon, 'The Role of Investment Consultants in Transforming Pension Fund Decision Making: The Integration of Environmental, Social, and Governance Considerations into Corporate Valuation' in James Hawley, Shyam Kamath, Andrew Williams (eds), *Corporate Governance Failures* (University of Pennsylvania Press 2014) at Chapter 10, 217, arguing that investment consultants wield significant influence over fund clients' investment decision-making, assessment metrics etc.

[48] Kathryn Judge, 'Intermediary Influence' (2015), above.

[49] BIS, *The Kay Review of UK Equity Markets and Long-Term Decision Making* (Final Report, 23 July 2012) at para 5.36.

[50] Articles 22 and 23, UCITs Directive 2009 as amended by Directive 2014/91/EU of the European Parliament and of the Council of 23 July 2014 amending Directive 2009/65/EC on the coordination of laws, regulations and administrative provisions relating to undertakings for collective investment in transferable securities (UCITS) as regards depositary functions, remuneration policies and sanctions.

[51] Articles 18(4), 21, AIFMD.

[52] Article 19, AIFMD.

trustees mentioned earlier also make it mandatory that pension trustees seek external advice, and hence the appointment of pension consultants.[53]

The investment chain has become a structural phenomenon in investment management. The chain may bring about the advantages of specialisation as well as checks and balances, but there are disadvantages in terms of complexity, opacity and disengagement between investors and the chain entities. In a sense, one cannot fault the efficiencies achieved in having dematerialised shares held on record by the share registrar and the efficiencies of having a custodian for pooled assets of investment. However, the share record does not reflect the complexity of the chain of investment intermediation, neither is the custodian able to apportion investor voice to each entity in the pooled assets. In other words, the structures adopted by the fund industry create distance between investors and investment management practice in general, including funds' assumption of corporate governance roles vis-à-vis their investee companies. Investment management practice is becoming less and less disciplined by investors' governance and is susceptible to governance deficits. In this context, funds' assumption of corporate governance roles as part of their investment management activities may not unequivocally be in investors' interests or indeed be serving a collective good. These roles should indeed be examined more carefully in terms of their motivations and effects. Compared with sovereign wealth funds that do not have to be embedded in structural chains of investment intermediation, the relatively shorter and simpler chain of investment management may be important for the closer engagement between ultimate investor and investee companies, which is observed in many sovereign wealth investments.[54] As Chapter 8 will discuss, many sovereign wealth funds have the unity of fund ownership and management, or just a simple separation between fund ownership (the state) and the state's fund manager (usually a state-instituted body which may or may not delegate to external asset managers). This structure profoundly influences how funds are managed and why they assume corporate governance roles of a different kind to other types of fund.

---

[53] S14, Pensions Act 2005.
[54] Discussed in Chapter 8.

Asset Managers

The separation structure has promoted the professionalisation of portfolio management by asset managers.[55] Funds delegate to asset managers the operational decisions in investment management and the exercise of attendant corporate governance rights. Hence, a key characterisation of modern investment management is the practice of professional asset management.

The rise of the asset management industry provides a market for investment management services, and it is arguable that competition and professionalisation in investment services are positive phenomena for the future of fund management. The asset management industry is particularly important to pension funds, which are largely constituted by employers and, in principle, would therefore benefit from being able to access investment expertise provided by external professionals. For other collective investment products such as collective retail schemes, or alternative investment funds such as private equity or hedge funds, the asset management industry plays the major part in product development, therefore financialising the savings of many citizens.

However, the professionalisation of asset management allows investment management to be turned into an industry dominated by certain commercial and regulatory incentives. The industry of asset management is increasingly disengaged from savers' ultimate goals and the long-term wealth-creation role of investee companies in the corporate sector. The structuring discussed above has arguably introduced perverse incentives that threaten to negate the benefits from the specialisation and professionalisation of asset management. We turn to examine these.

D. THE INSULAR WORLD OF ASSET MANAGEMENT – AGENCY PROBLEMS, SHORT TERMISM AND DISENGAGEMENT FROM DELIVERING A COLLECTIVE GOOD

The financialised and heavily marketised model of investment management offers investors a choice of *savings products*, i.e. something to buy in the marketplace. Asset management services are commoditised as asset

---

[55] For example see Ingo Fender, 'Institutional Asset Managers: Industry Trends, Incentives and Implications For Market Efficiency' (2003) *BIS Quarterly Review* 75.

managers compete to manage mandates from funds. In such a competitive world, Wong[56] observes that asset managers are assessed quarterly on the basis of financial performance. Their financial performance is measured usually on a relative basis, benchmarked against a stock market index for example. Although investment products should compete on the basis of 'credence', which refers to maintaining the continuing performance of a product over the long-term, the FCA has found that the competition for savers' fickle capital allocation can be based on short-termist previous performance data or that performance may not even influence investors, making persistently poor performance possible while maintaining relatively high charges for asset management.[57]

The development of such narrow measures of short-term performance is to an extent attributable to the investor protection impetus underlying regulation, but also meets the market's needs for ease of comparison. Much of asset management mandates is active management, which refers to a practice of investment management where managers pick and trade stocks for market returns, in order to outperform a selected stock market index benchmark. This is the dominant mode of investment management[58] although alternative forms of investment management such as passive investing and exchange-traded funds are growing in importance.[59]

Short-termism

Asset managers are regularly reviewed in terms of whether they are beating the benchmark (by an agreed percentage) or otherwise. Although it may be regarded as prudent that pension funds regularly review their asset managers, and it can be argued that trustee duties in law and regulation would compel such regular review,[60] quarterly assessments have become structurally entrenched in terms of asset managers' business model and remuneration. Asset managers' quarterly results become the basis for institutions' selection decisions in the competitive market for

---

[56] Simon C Y Wong, 'Why Stewardship Is Proving Elusive for Institutional Investors' (2010) 7 *JIBFL* 406; 'Is Institutional Investor Stewardship Still Elusive?' (2015) *Butterworths Journal of Banking and Financial Law* 508.

[57] FCA, *Asset Management Market Study Final Report* (2017) at para 4.9 at https://www.fca.org.uk/publication/market-studies/ms15-2-3.pdf.

[58] Lubos Pastor and Robert F Stambaugh, 'On the Size of the Active Management Industry' (2012) at http://papers.ssrn.com/sol3/papers.cfm?abstract_id=1532268.

[59] To be discussed shortly.

[60] Section 4, Trustees Act 2000. In respect of pensions, similar provisions are found in s36 of the Pensions Act 1995.

asset management services, and work into the incentive structures for asset managers. Asset managers focus on delivering short-term quarterly performance, and this has a profound impact upon the nature of investment management. Investment management has inevitably become short-termist in nature, focusing on trading as market gains are more easily generated in the short term than building success in the underlying corporate investment.[61] The focus on trading is also behaviourally driven. Marginson and McAulay[62] show that under conditions of psychological uncertainty, individuals opt for short-termist behaviour as a means of coping. Juniper[63] also argues that it is human nature to over-value immediate realisation of value and undervalue future returns, hence the need to demonstrate short-term performance would only encourage asset managers to trade excessively to make immediate gains or to cut losses. In the latter case, loss aversion may be a dominant heuristic that compels funds or their asset managers to close out of their positions quickly rather than pursue patient value creation.

In a competitive market for collective investment products, other intermediaries such as fund rating agencies arise as market institutions to serve as information intermediaries for investment products. Morningstar ratings,[64] for example, rate funds regularly on a forward-looking basis in terms of bronze, silver or gold, such ratings based on a range of performance information and Morningstar's proprietary methods of weighting.[65] Funds face a pressing need to maintain constant good performance in order to maintain good ratings, as those are crucial to attract inflows or stem outflows by investors.[66] In essence, short termist

---

[61] Paul Frentrop, 'Short Termism of Institutional Investors and the Double Agency Problem' (2012) at http://ssrn.com/abstract=2249872.

[62] David Marginson and Laurie McAulay, 'Exploring the Debate on Short-Termism: A Theoretical and Empirical Analysis' (2008) 29 *Strategic Management* 273.

[63] James Juniper, 'A Genealogy of Short-Termism in Capital Markets' (1998) at http://papers.ssrn.com/sol3/papers.cfm?abstract_id=219990.

[64] http://www.morningstar.co.uk/uk/research/funds/about.aspx.

[65] Predictive properties are critiqued in Christopher R Blake and Matthew R Morey, 'Morningstar Ratings and Mutual Fund Performance' (1999) at http://papers.ssrn.com/sol3/papers.cfm?abstract_id=168668. See also John A Haslem, 'Morningstar Mutual Fund Measures and Selection Model' (2014) *Journal of Wealth Management* 19.

[66] Diane Del Guercio and Paula A Tkac, 'Star Power: The Effect of Morningstar Ratings on Mutual Fund Flow' (2007) at http://papers.ssrn.com/sol3/papers.cfm?abstract_id=286157.

competitive pressures abound in the market that compel funds and asset managers to focus on short term performance.

Short termist investment management behaviour, also known as investor myopia,[67] is argued to be a key driver for corporate short-termism too. The factors driving the trading of corporate securities in secondary markets feed into the behaviour of the underlying companies. Corporations are sensitive to market demands to keep securities prices up, and corporate behaviour and strategy can become conditioned by these pressures through a variety of mechanisms (e.g. executive pay arrangements, takeover pressures, etc). Corporate short termism is defined as behaviour that is dedicated to short term strategies to keep earnings high whether or not such strategies result in value destruction for the company in the long term.[68] Corporate short termism obscures long-term thinking for the company and is ultimately likely to prove destructive for the long-term wealth creation role of the corporate economy.[69] This contradicts savers' long-term need to realise value through investing in the corporate economy. Examples of corporate short termism might include reducing employment expense, outlays on training and investment, product development and innovation, and research and development expenditures in order to boost short term earnings. Such 'financial discipline' is potentially beneficial to investors who need to show short-termist investment performance on the back of high share prices. Managers in corporations whose remuneration is tied to stock price also tend to have their interests aligned with short-termist investors.[70] Further, commentators also find corporate short-termism to be related to greater indifference to stakeholder or corporate responsibility

---

[67] Danyelle Guyatt, 'Meeting Objectives and Resisting Conventions: A Focus on Institutional Investors and Long-Term Responsible Investing' (2005) 5 *Corporate Governance: The International Journal of Business in Society* 139.

[68] Corporate Values Strategy Group, *Overcoming Short-termism: A Call for a More Responsible Approach to Investment and Business Management* (New York: Aspen Institute Business and Society Programs, 2009), http://www.aspeninstitute.org/publications/overcoming-short-termism-call-more-responsible-approach-investment-business-management; Caitlin Helms, Mark Fox and Robert Kenagy, 'Corporate Short-Termism: Causes and Remedies' (2012) 23 *International and Comparative Company Law Review* 45.

[69] Emeka Duruigbo, 'Tackling Shareholder Short-Termism and Managerial Myopia' (2011–12) 100 *Kentucky Law Journal* 531.

[70] Caitlin Helms, Mark Fox and Robert Kenagy, 'Corporate Short-Termism: Causes and Remedies' (2012), above.

issues, and with the lack of motivation to address social and environmental harms that the corporation is perpetuating.[71] However, Roe does not think that investor myopia is the main reason for corporate short-termism, and argues that the 'transmission mechanism' from investor behaviour to corporate short-termism is not definitively proven.[72] Further, Fried[73] is of the view that managers carry out various strategies to maximise their own interests or the interests of select groups of constituents. So short-termism or long-termism can both reflect such game-strategic choices and principal-agent problems. Hence, vilifying corporate short-termism could be a one-sided account.[74] However, Moore and Walker-Arnott argue that investor myopia is ultimately socially harmful as it involves perpetual transfers of future wealth to the present to meet present needs, and such will ultimately undermine long-term investment performance and the long-term prospects and cost of capital of the corporate sector.[75]

Even if the relationship between investor myopia and corporate short termism is not an exact science, at the broader level, the short-termist measurement of investment performance and corporate performance by market price is a reflection of the financialisation age which emphasises excessive marketisation, and is arguably antithetical to relational dimensions in investment such as managing savers' long-term needs, long-termist shareholder engagement and the patient waiting for the realisation of productivity gains.

Investor myopia is a key characteristic of modern investment management practice as professionalised by asset managers. Investments become meaningful in respect largely of their ability to generate short term gains, and investment management is geared towards generating such gains

---

[71] David Millon, 'Shareholder Social Responsibility' (2012–13) 36 *Seattle University Law Review* 911; Emeka Duruigbo, 'Stimulating Long-term Shareholding' (2011–12) 33 *Cardozo Law Review* 1734.

[72] Mark J Roe, 'Corporate Short-Termism – In the Boardroom and in the Courtroom' (2013) 68 *Business Lawyer* 977.

[73] Jesse M Fried, 'The Uneasy Case for Favoring Long-Term Shareholders' (2015) 124 *Yale Law Journal* 1554.

[74] A further consequence of vilifying short-termism may be to encourage long-termism or treat it as more benign than it is. The article points out various principal-agent problems and value-destroying behaviour in the name of long-termism too.

[75] As above.

through many forms of instrumental means.[76] These include trading, commoditising various assets to become investments, use of hedging strategies and financial innovation, or the instrumental use of proprietary rights associated with shareholding. These instrumental means are a form of investment engineering, and not necessarily connected to the long-term social dimension of savers' provision or sustainable wealth creation by the corporate sector. The industry of asset management has turned the practice of investment management into instrumental forms of investment engineering to meet short-termist needs which are dictated by asset managers' business and regulatory imperatives.

Instrumental Forms of 'Investment Engineering'

Asset managers' investment management practices are purposed towards their performance needs, and hence the proprietary attributes of corporate equity can be subject to various forms of 'investment engineering' in order to meet those needs. For example, the general call to asset managers to be more engaged corporate governance actors may generate perverse incentives such as developing business models for charging customers in relation to corporate access,[77] i.e. that asset managers pay in order to meet and chat with investee company directors, and pass on the cost to funds. This area of malpractice, identified by the Financial Conduct Authority, is widespread and shows how 'corporate governance' roles are being used in an instrumental manner by funds to profit themselves.[78] Edelman et al[79] also comment that funds conduct their

---

[76] Including stock lending which generates a significant income for funds. The impact of stock lending on funds' corporate governance roles will be discussed in Chapter 3.

[77] 'Corporate Access Rules Still Flouted', *Financial Times* (26 Oct 2014).

[78] This area was first identified by the FCA which issued a policy to prohibit corporate access charges from being bundled into dealing commissions, see 'FCA Crack-down on Fund Managers' Charges over Broker Commissions', *Financial Times* (25 Nov 2013). Further, the requirement to be imposed by ESMA in forcing all charges to be unbundled in order to comply with the MiFID II Directive's limited permission on inducements would also force corporate access charges to come under scrutiny if not phased out. See ESMA, *MiFID/MiFIR II* (May 2014) at para 4.3, p. 218.

[79] Paul H Edelman, Randall S Thomas and Robert B Thompson, 'Shareholder Voting in an Age of Intermediary Capitalism' (*ECGI Working Paper* 2014) at http://ssrn.com/abstract=2401746.

corporate governance roles, such as in voting, in an entirely self-interested manner and are therefore unreliable as 'stewards' for the corporate governance of investee companies.

As Chapter 3 will discuss in greater detail, shareholder rights attached to corporate equity can be used in an instrumental manner to generate share price spikes that improve short-term fund performance. Dedicated funds that use such rights in an instrumental manner include 'offensive activists', which Armour and Cheffins define as taking an equity stake in order to perform corporate governance interventions.[80] At one end, private equity funds take large concentrated stakes in order to assume management powers,[81] while at the other end, hedge funds[82] and sovereign wealth funds take minority stakes. Activist hedge funds take minority stakes that are significant enough for their voices to be impactful, while in the relevant cases, sovereign wealth funds take minority stakes in (usually) key national champions in order to work behind the scenes for the long-term well-being and prosperity of the investee company,[83] or in some egregious cases, to engage in tunnelling and self-serving interests. Although the assumption of a corporate governance role with investee companies is not a typical marketised model for generating value, the corporate governance roles of some alternative investment funds reflect an instrumental use of such roles and rights towards value extraction, and there are consequences of such an instrumental approach which need to be considered carefully, as Chapter 3 will further flesh out.

Another example of income generation activity that asset managers may carry out, which can be in conflict with their corporate governance roles, is that of securities lending. Securities lending is particularly important for money creation in repo markets. Poszar and Singh[84] explain how, by lending securities, asset managers provide collateral for short term borrowing by financial institutions, supporting the shadow banking system of generating money. The corporate governance implications of stock lending may be that borrowers of stock could have the right to exercise shareholder rights without necessarily being aligned with the

---

[80] John Armour and Brian Cheffins, 'The Rise and Fall (?) of Shareholder Activism by Hedge Funds' (2012) 14 *Journal of Alternative Investments* 17.

[81] See Chapter 7.

[82] See Chapter 6.

[83] As Chapter 8 discusses, such subtle 'activist' influences are much less observed in relation to sovereign wealth funds' foreign investments.

[84] Zoltan Poszar and Manmohan Singh, 'The Non-Bank-Bank Nexus and the Shadow Banking System' (2011) at http://ssrn.com/abstract=1971440.

incentives for the long-term residual claimant. Securities lending is a type of 'investment engineering' that commoditises corporate equity to generate income for asset managers, and asset managers can choose to be quite oblivious to the corporate governance impact of their securities lending activities, as this area is only governed by soft law.[85]

Asset managers' business models include commoditising their proprietary rights and corporate governance rights attached to corporate equity, and such investment management practices are solely geared towards generating value enhancement for their performance. These practices often have very little to do with the funds' long-term maturity horizons or their 'investment capitalist' role in the long-term wealth-creating role of the corporate sector.

Agency Problems

Asset management is also an industry riddled with agency problems that permeate investment management practice. Asset managers are optimally positioned in the investment chain to generate rents for themselves and other participants in the chain. For example, asset managers are reported to practice 'churning', i.e. excessive trading of securities in order to generate transactions fees and charges.[86] Other examples of rent-seeking for the investment chain as a whole include arrangements made with brokers or trading venues for routing orders and receiving commissions or kickbacks and third-party payments such as research payments bundled in dealing commissions to brokers and analysts.[87] The business

[85] The corporate governance implications are only governed by soft law. Securities lenders cannot vote on lent shares, but they can recall their lent shares if they wish to exercise their rights to vote on them. However, there is no compulsion to do so. The conduct of securities lenders in terms of their corporate governance roles and rights is only governed by soft law, see *Securities Lending: An Introductory Guide* at http://www.bankofengland.co.uk/markets/Documents/gilts/sl_intro_green_9_10.pdf produced under the auspices of the Bank of England, which reflects a joint initiative by the Association of Corporate Treasurers, British Bankers Association, London Investment Banking Association, International Securities Lending Association and London Stock Exchange.

[86] See for example, 'How Fund Managers Spend Your Money', *Financial Times* (6 June 2014). The FCA has also found that asset managers do not optimally keep transaction costs under control, see FCA, *Asset Management Market Study Final Report* (2017), above at para 7.2.

[87] Some of these practices are discussed in Graham Busby, 'Conflicts of Interest and Inducements under MiFID' (2008) *Journal of International Banking Law and Regulation* 1.

model of active management lends itself to the support of other complementary business activities in the investment chain.

The agency problems of active management are however coming under attack from different directions, including market competition and regulatory interventions. However, we are of the view that the changing landscape may only substitute one set of agency problems for another.

Active managers have started to experience decreasing returns as the scale of active management has become too large, and similar behaviour in trading amongst asset managers has flatlined returns.[88] Hence, it is becoming more difficult to generate rents within the investment chain that increase cost for investors. Investors are fighting back by choosing alternative modes of investment management such as passive investing, smart beta,[89] which is a variant of passive investing and exchange-traded funds, as they capitalise on lower cost strategies to boost returns.[90] In the alternative fund management sector, investors are becoming more willing to pay for truly alternative strategies such as hedge fund activism and private equity investing that deploy more hands-on efforts with investee companies to generate investment returns.

Further, regulatory scrutiny into fund management fees and charges, especially for pensions and retail collective investment funds, are driving changes to investment management practices and governance as regulators are not only carrying out surveys into fund charges and questioning their structures and legitimacy, but also introducing legislation to make fees and charges more transparent and justifiable.[91] In the current low-yield and competitive environment, Fama and French[92] have found that fund management fees and charges inevitably reduce or nullify the

---

[88] Lubos Pastor, Robert F Stambaugh and Lucian Taylor, 'Scale and Skill in Active Management' (2014) at http://papers.ssrn.com/sol3/papers.cfm?abstract_id=2318788; John Authers, 'The active fund management model is not fit for purpose', *Financial Times* (20 Feb 2015).

[89] 'Market divided over smart-beta success', *Financial Times* (4 May 2014).

[90] Of course, a particularly egregious practice would be closet index-hugging or closet passive strategies under an active management cover, exploiting the active management fees charged to clients, see for example, 'European markets watchdog examines closet trackers', *Financial Times* (23 Nov 2014).

[91] E.g. FCA, *Market Study: Asset Management: Interim Report* (Nov 2016) at https://www.fca.org.uk/publication/market-studies/ms15-2-2-interim-report.pdf; and FCA, *Asset Management Market Study Final Report* (2017) at https://www.fca.org.uk/publication/market-studies/ms15-2-3.pdf.

[92] Eugene F Fama and Kenneth R French, 'Luck Versus Skill in the Cross Section of Mutual Fund Returns' (2009) at http://papers.ssrn.com/sol3/papers.cfm?abstract_id=1356021.

returns for investors, so policy-makers are now making a targeted push towards lower fund management costs. Government initiatives in the UK include the Department of Work and Pensions' continuous scrutiny of defined contribution scheme charges after the mandatory charge cap of 0.75 per cent of fund assets has been introduced;[93] the Department of Business, Innovation and Skills'[94] as well as the Financial Conduct Authority's[95] studies of fees and charges in the investment chain and whether value for money is delivered. The UK and EU have introduced tighter controls over charges fund managers make to investors, such as in the area of bundled dealing commissions subsidising broker research.[96] The UK and EU have introduced legislation to compel fund charges and fees to be more clearly disclosed and broken down, in the area of UCITs and other retail collective investment schemes,[97] as well as in alternative investment funds.[98] The EU is also keen to extend prescriptive rules for bankers' remuneration to fund managers as well in order to align remuneration incentives with prudent risk-taking.[99] These have put pressures on fund managers serving mainstream institutional and retail investments to move from active management into lower cost strategies. Although such moves are targeted at freeing up more returns to investors, they inevitably impact fund management practices and bring about another set of implications.

---

93 See discussion in Chapter 4, and Department of Work and Pensions, *Landscape and Charges Survey 2013: Charges and Quality in Defined Contribution Pension Schemes* (Feb 2014).

94 BIS, *Exploring the Intermediated Shareholding Model* (January 2016), above.

95 FCA, *Asset Management Market Study Final Report* (2017), above.

96 Art 24(8), MiFID 2014 and Commission delegated legislation specifying that bundled dealing commissions cannot continue to be passed on to investors. Research charges need to be specifically costed up front and passed on to investors with their consent.

97 Art 29, Commission Directive 2010/43/EU of 1 July 2010 implementing Directive 2009/65/EC of the European Parliament and of the Council as regards organisational requirements, conflicts of interest, conduct of business, risk management and content of the agreement between a depositary and a management company; FCA Handbook COLL 4.7.2, 4.7.8.

98 Art 23(i), AIFMD.

99 See 'Fund managers fight banker bonus cap extension', *Financial Times* (17 Jan 2016), although the UK does not currently extend the bonus cap to asset managers, see FCA Handbook SYSC 19C.

Going Passive

Investors may pour into passively managed investment products that track an index or replicate an index composition, and charge lower fees.[100] However, there are inconclusive debates[101] as to whether active or passive

[100] Lodewjik van Setten, *The Law of Institutional Investment Management* (2009), above at paras 4.48ff; 4.86ff.

[101] Kevin R James, 'The Price of Retail Investing in the UK' (*FSA Occasional Paper* 2000) arguing that passive investing works out better for investors as cost is low and eats less into yield. Although active management delivers, cost is generally too high and affects yield; Larry E Swedroe, 'Active versus Passive Investing' in John D Haslem (ed.), *Mutual Funds: Portfolio Structures, Analysis, Management, and Stewardship* (Chichester: John Wiley & Sons 2010) at Chapter 6; 'Active share revealed to have feet of clay', *Financial Times* (where Nomura research doubts the benefits of active investing (25 Jan 2015). See also Hymans Robertson, *LGPS Structure Analysis* (Dec 2013); Department for Communities and Local Government, *Local Government Pension Scheme: Opportunities for Collaboration, Cost Savings and Efficiencies* (May 2014) applying to pension funds; 'Vanguard's record inflows prove passive is massive', *Financial Times* (11 Jan 2014) but see more nuanced assessment in Edward D Tower, 'Performance of Actively Managed versus Index Funds: The Vanguard Case' in John D Haslem (ed.), *Mutual Funds: Portfolio Structures, Analysis, Management, and Stewardship* (2010), above at Chapter 12 and also see generally warnings against making active or passive a binary choice as performance determinations are based on certain assumptions, see Michael W Crook, 'A Stochastic Portfolio Perspective on Utilizing Active and Passive Fund Management' (2012) at http://ssrn.com/abstract=2170776. It is explained that the outperformance of passive funds is largely due to efficient markets in many parts of the world, making it difficult for active managers to beat the market, see Burton G Malkiel, 'Efficient Markets and Mutual Fund Investing: The Advantages of Index Funds' in John D Haslem (ed.), *Mutual Funds: Portfolio Structures, Analysis, Management, and Stewardship* (2010), above at Chapter 7.

But there is also research affirming the superior performance of real active managers, see 'Almost 90% of UK active managers beat the stock market', *Financial Times* (3 Aug 2014); Robert C Jones, 'Active Management in Mostly Efficient Markets' (2011) 67 *Financial Analysts Journal* 29; Valery Polkovnichenko, Kelsey Wei and Feng Zhao, 'Cautious Risk-Takers: Investor Preferences and Demand for Active Management' (2012) at http://ssrn.com/abstract=2022416; Lubos Pastor, Robert F Stambaugh and Lucian A Taylor, 'Scale and Skill in Active Management' (Jan 2014), above arguing that small specialist funds can add value although that value may be eroded with fund scale. See also report that boutique fund managers can add significant value through active investing, 'Fund investors find small is beautiful', *Financial Times* (27 Feb 2014).

management outperforms in the long term, and passive management produces another set of agency costs.

Passively-managed products track an established benchmark such as a stock market index, or can be in the form of exchange-traded products (ETFs) that track an index or synthetic ETFs that aim at correlating with an index. Such products are generally low cost as they have a relatively simpler and predictable strategy, and are based on empirical findings on consistent performance of a basket of indexed stocks. They may offer investors the appeal of simplicity and low cost.

However, passive investing creates another type of agency problem, i.e. that of 'neglect' and ultimate disengagement from the real economy. Investors are tied into a mechanistic approach to stock selection, and it is such a constrained approach that makes the investment management cost-effective. Such an arrangement may appear to entail less agency cost than the active management model. But in essence, investors agree to a relative lack of discretion in investment management in return for exposure to the general vicissitudes of market risk and pro-cyclicality, ultimately leaving it to the wisdom of the markets, and not professional skill and endeavour, to achieve the long-term returns that savers need. Further, as passive investing is engaged with a benchmark and not with the underlying corporate assets as such, the sense of disengagement could be augmented between investors and their funds, and with their ultimate investee companies too. On the other hand, passive funds may feel tied to certain companies in the index – in which they are more or less permanently invested – and thus incentivised to revisit their 'ownership' role in investee companies. There seems to be some evidence that passive and large investors such as BlackRock do take shareholder engagement seriously as part of their investment management practice.[102] However, as passive funds are low cost in nature, the demands of shareholder engagement seem contrary to their cost-conscious approach.[103] The

[102] 'Passive investors, active ownership', *Financial Times* (6 April 2014), 'Passive investors are good corporate stewards', *Financial Times* (19 Jan 2016); Ian R Appel, Todd R Gormley and Donald B Keim, 'Passive Investors not Passive Owners' (2014) at http://www.stern.nyu.edu/sites/default/files/assets/documents/1%20Gormley%20Passive%20Investors%20Not%20Passive%20Owners.pdf.

[103] John Plender, 'Pay-offs and perils of passive investing', *Financial Times* (27 Oct 2013).

stewardship demands placed on passive funds are likely to become increasingly onerous as the number of holdings increases[104] and, at some point, it would seem contradictory to their low cost aims to expect meaningful assumption of corporate governance roles in each investee company.

Moreover, passive investing does very little for the long-term wealth creation by the corporate sector as its indexed products inevitably focus on the quarter of the market that is most liquid and historically popular. Such an investing approach would cause a crowding into a certain section of the market. This form of investing seems contrary to the spirit of intermediating capital allocation in the real economy to promote innovation and entrepreneurship, which is what we expect investment intermediaries to do.

The Rise of Exchange-traded Funds

The rise of exchange-traded funds (ETFs) continues the trend towards investment engineering that appeals to the low cost market. An exchange-traded fund is a portfolio of assets that can be traded on an exchange.[105] The portfolio may comprise assets in equity securities, currencies, commodities, fixed income and real estate.[106] The portfolio can be constructed to passively hug an index or be actively managed. Index-hugging portfolios can be actively managed, such as via a basket of assets with correlation to indexed securities or via derivatives. Investors can trade in and out of the entire portfolio and it would be the fund that has to ensure that the underlying assets are maintained in fungibility and in proportion to investors' trades throughout the day.[107] In the UK, listed exchange-traded funds have to comply with the Listing Authority's

---

[104] Above, opining that passive funds, in order to replicate the index, take on too many stocks in their portfolios. Also see 'Messy portfolios and the be busy syndrome', *Financial Times* (9 May 2014).

[105] David J Abner, *The ETF Handbook: How to Value and Trade Exchange-Traded Funds* (Chichester: John Wiley & Sons, 2010); Gary L Gastineau, 'Mutual Funds versus Exchange-Traded Funds' in John D Haslem (ed.), *Mutual Funds: Portfolio Structures, Analysis, Management, and Stewardship* (2010), above at Chapter 14.

[106] David J Abner, *The ETF Handbook: How to Value and Trade Exchange-Traded Funds* (2010), above at Chapter 1.

[107] David J Abner, *The ETF Handbook: How to Value and Trade Exchange-Traded Funds* (Chichester: John Wiley & Sons, 2010) at Chapter 2, 10.

Listing Rules, which require that the funds be UCITs-compliant.[108] This means that the underlying portfolios must comprise securities or derivative assets covered under the UCITs Directives. The Listing Rules allow ETFs to be constructed synthetically i.e. swap-based and not actually holding the assets in the benchmark that the ETF is based on, provided that the underlying assets are still UCITs compliant.[109] Hence it would appear that the London Stock Exchange does not permit actively managed ETFs that may hold exotic and illiquid assets.[110]

ETFs have been developed as a hedging device for institutions, so that an entire portfolio can be hedged.[111] Hence, commentators see them as useful hedging tools for exotic and relatively illiquid assets.[112] However, the exchange-traded fund structure has become appealing to retail investors as the fund is listed and benefits from the transparency requirements imposed on listed entities. Further, the fund can be traded at any time during the trading day, and such intra-day liquidity is highly desired by investors, when compared to UCITs or other collective investment schemes that allow daily redemptions with one published price every day.[113] Where the ETF is based on an index and is passively managed, the liquidity and transparency features seem to be superior to

---

[108] London Stock Exchange, *Exchange-Traded Funds: Introducing and Operating ETFs in the UK* at http://www.londonstockexchange.com/specialist-issuers/etfs/how-to-issue-etfs/listingandadmissionguide.pdf.

[109] See Eddy Wymeersch, 'The Regulatory Regime for Exchange-Traded Funds in the EU' (2011) at http://ssrn.com/abstract=1986852.

[110] This area is subject to huge debate in terms of whether the apparent safety of ETFs is compromised by active management, but active managers in ETFs are rising due to the difficulty of generating superior returns otherwise, see Michael R Rosella and Domenick Pugliese, 'The Evolution of the Exchange-Traded Fund: Is Active Management on the Horizon?' (2006) 7 *Journal of Investment Compliance* 44.

[111] Gary L Gastineau, 'Mutual Funds versus Exchange-Traded Funds' in John D Haslem (ed.), *Mutual Funds: Portfolio Structures, Analysis, Management, and Stewardship* (2010), above at Chapter 14.

[112] Ilan Guedj and Jennifer Huang, 'Are ETFs Replacing Index Mutual Funds?' (2009) at http://ssrn.com/abstract=1108728.

[113] Gary L Gastineau, *The Exchange-Traded Funds Manual* (Chichester: John Wiley & Sons 2010) at Chapter 1. But empirical research has also found that exchange-traded funds do not consistently outperform the mutual fund that is passively managed, see Mohamed Sharifzadeh and Simin Hojat, 'An Analytical Performance Comparison of Exchange-Traded Funds with Index Funds: 2002–2010' (2012) 13 *Journal of Asset Management* 196–209; Adam Turner, 'Exchange-Traded Funds vs. UK Investment Trusts: A Comparison of Performance' (2010) at http://papers.ssrn.com/sol3/papers.cfm?abstract_id=1689534.

mutual funds that are index-hugging and passively managed too. Exchange-traded funds have also been able to charge lower fees than passively managed mutual funds,[114] thus ensuring that yield is not taken up by fees.

Investors have become attracted to exchange-traded funds and the market has grown phenomenally in the UK.[115] This now seems to be a safe investment option[116] although it would be difficult for the fund to be trading above its NAV in the market for highly liquid securities that are the components of an index.

The growth of the retail ETF market reflects investor preferences for low cost and liquid products, but also reflects a backlash against the agency costs of the actively managed and highly discretionary investment management model. However, as pointed out in our discussion on passive investing above, the switch to 'pre-packaged' baskets of securities that involve little investment management discretion facilitates an investment culture that is based on trading and has little connection with underlying companies. The popularity of ETFs has certain implications for the deployment of savings into investment. As ETFs are largely based on indices of UCITs-compliant securities, this quarter of the market relates purely to highly liquid and historically popular securities. Retail savings channelled into this quarter reinforce the imbalance of financing for already mature and liquid markets as opposed to more diverse, long term and illiquid opportunities. This is unless ETFs are allowed to be developed as a saving or hedging structure for illiquid forms of finance in the UK and EU. Trading in ETFs reinforces a commoditised and marketised model of investment, offering investors the freedom to buy and sell investment products on a fleeting basis, disengaged from underlying corporate business purposes and activities. ETFs are one step more removed than collective investment funds as a means of investing in corporate equity, as underlying assets are not just pooled but are

---

114 Forbes.com, 'What's the Difference? Mutual Funds and Exchange-traded Funds Explained' (July 2013) at http://www.forbes.com/sites/feeonlyplanner/2013/07/18/whats-the-difference-mutual-funds-and-exchange-traded-funds-explained/.

115 'Rapid expansion across UK exchange traded funds industry', *Financial Times* (22 Feb 2011); globally see Exchange traded funds make strongest ever start to a year', *Financial Times* (12 April 2015). See FCA, *Market Study: Asset Management: Interim Report* (Nov 2016) at https://www.fca.org.uk/publication/market-studies/ms15-2-2-interim-report.pdf.

116 But underlying securities can be volatile, see episode involving Black-Rock and Vanguard's exposure to HK listed securities in their ETFs, 'ETFs endure Goldin-Hanergy rollercoaster', *Financial Times* (26 May 2015).

packaged into a basket, losing individual identity completely. ETF investing does not encourage an engaged, long-termist investment philosophy amongst investors, but arguably reinforces a trading and short-termist culture.

In sum, the development of professional asset management has produced two rather extreme and perverse effects. One is substantial agency cost in the exercise of significant amounts of discretion in investment management, while the other is completely market-led and marked by a lack of discretionary intervention. In either case it is highly questionable if meaningful investment intermediation through good corporate ownership is achieved – to connect the long-term expectations of savers with the long-term wealth creation by the corporate economy. The age of asset management has arguably come to represent a form of professionalised and commoditised investment management practice whose outlook is insular and bounded up in agency problems, short-termist and disengaged from both savers' long-term goals and long-term wealth creation processes in the corporate economy.

It can be queried whether structural interventions that might hinder the growth of investment chains would mitigate the problems highlighted above. The Kay Review thinks this is desirable, but structural changes are difficult as their institution has been justified by efficiency factors that benefit investors and intermediaries alike. The disruption of such structures would require fundamental market and regulatory changes.[117] Moreover, funds are subject to regulatory requirements that reinforce the short-term focus. Hence, compliance pressure may still force funds to emphasise short-term performance. We next turn to the aspects of regulation in reinforcing the sub-optimal model of investment management discussed above. This discussion shows the trade-offs between objectives that regulation has to achieve.

E. THE IMPACT AND INFLUENCE OF REGULATION ON INVESTMENT MANAGEMENT

Regulation has inevitably shaped investment management structures and practice. The role of regulation is in securing investor protection but many unintended consequences are entailed. This is an area where a

[117] Structural disintermediation changes may be introduced by innovative fintech, but there is a limit to what new technology can do too, see discussion in Iris H-Y Chiu, 'The Disruptive Implications of Fintech – Policy Themes for Financial Regulators' (*UCL Centre of Ethics and Law Working Paper* 2016).

dilemma of interests persists and is particularly challenging for the design of policy and regulation.

Portfolio Diversification

Portfolio diversification, a regulatory obligation for pension funds[118] and retail collective investment schemes,[119] is derived from modern portfolio theory (MPT), an economic theory endorsed in law with arguably many unintended consequences. Diversification is often described by finance practitioners as a 'free lunch' in terms of its ability to reduce the riskiness of an investment portfolio without necessitating any commensurate reduction in expected return.[120] Furthermore, if the business success of an investment manager is dependent on matching or outperforming the returns achieved by a diversified investment benchmark (e.g. a composite index of the performance of numerous individual stocks), it would typically be viewed as imprudent or even reckless to place 'all one's eggs in one basket' in the form of a highly concentrated investment portfolio. However, a highly diversified investment model largely erodes any incentive that an investment manager may have to fulfil a potentially costly and time-consuming corporate governance role with individual investee companies, or to view investee companies as anything other than a collection of securities with quantified expected return characteristics.

The mandatory requirement to have diversified portfolios also reflects the prudential regulatory objective of mitigating concentration risk so that portfolios are not exposed to the risks of particular issuers. Although prudential regulatory objectives may be met, which allows collective investment products to be labelled more safely as meeting the needs of investor protection, portfolio diversification causes funds and their asset managers to focus on the portfolio as a whole and lose interest in the distinctive business purpose of individual investee companies. Investment management based on portfolio diversification emphasises the balance of risks in the portfolio while seeking return, and necessarily results in investee companies being treated as tradeable and replaceable assets, and not as individual entities for the development of deeper and more

[118] Section 4, Trustees Act 2000. In respect of pensions, similar provisions are found in s36 of the Pensions Act 1995.

[119] See UCITs Directive 2009 at Art 52.

[120] Andrew Balls, 'There is no free lunch, but diversification offers a cheap one'. *Financial Times*, 8 February 2015, at https://www.ft.com/content/9656990e-abac-11e4-8070-00144feab7de

meaningful engagement relationships. A number of commentators[121] thus point out that investment management premised upon mandatory applications of MPT is necessarily biased towards trading behaviour in order to generate investment performance. Without a detailed knowledge and commitment to an entity's distinctive business purpose, it is very difficult for an investor to play a meaningful role as a long-term and engaged corporate owner or steward.[122]

Periodic Regulatory Accountability

The regulation of investment management is premised on procedural safeguards for investors to be assured of the proper exercise of investment management discretion. Law and regulation do not extend to guaranteeing the substantive savings outcomes that an investor is hoping for. This is because an investment is ultimately a bet on future prospects and investment performance is thus subject to the vicissitudes of markets and the economy. The private law of contract between investors and their funds can provide monitoring mechanisms for investors, but private law has largely been overtaken by regulatory standards, such that regulation has become the main source of monitoring mechanisms, principally in regular accountability and reporting.

Where pension funds are concerned, it may be argued that their liabilities will only mature over the long term and hence there may not be a need for regular reporting. However, the exercise of long-term investment discretion is perceived to be susceptible to principal-agent problems, and there is a need to monitor investment performance in more immediate terms in order to detect any early problems in meeting eventual liabilities. Hence, defined benefit pension schemes are required to produce actuarial valuations of their assets every financial year[123] and trustees are obliged to account to the regulator regarding how they intend

[121] James Hawley, Shyam Kamath, Andrew Williams, 'Introduction' in James Hawley, Shyam Kamath, Andrew Williams (eds), *Corporate Governance Failures* (University of Pennsylvania Press 2014); Steven Lydenberg, 'Beyond Risk: Notes Towards a Responsible Investment Theory' in James Hawley, Shyam Kamath, Andrew Williams (eds), *Corporate Governance Failures* (University of Pennsylvania Press 2014) at Chapter 2, 26; Jaap Winter, 'Shareholder Engagement and Stewardship: The Realities and Illusions of Institutional Share Ownership' (2011) at http://ssrn.com/abstract=1867564.

[122] Dalia Tsuk Mitchell, 'Institutional shareholders as Proxies: The Contours of Shareholder Democracy' (2006) 65 *Washington and Lee Law Rev* 4.

[123] S224, Pensions Act 2004.

to manage their investments by submitting a yearly statement of investment principles.[124] Where the statutory funding objective is not met after actuarial valuation is carried out, trustees are also obliged to submit a recovery plan in order to show how they intend to achieve the funding objective and by when.[125] Where defined contribution schemes are concerned, although there is no mandatory reporting frequency due to investors, scheme trustees or the internal governance committee of the employer that monitors contract-based providers should regularly assess investment performance and review objectives.[126] Empirical research shows that such review takes place regularly, frequently on a quarterly basis.[127]

For retail collective investment schemes such as UCITs, as well as non-UCITs open-ended (NURS) and close-ended schemes, similar regulatory provisions deal with regular periodic accountability, which is yearly and half yearly reporting. Investors in UCITs schemes are entitled to ongoing disclosure documents in the form of an annual long report and half-yearly short report.[128] The annual report must contain audited financial statements[129] while the half-yearly report is also highly prescribed in terms of financial and technical information.[130] These requirements have been harmonised for non-UCITs schemes in the UK for retail[131] as well as sophisticated investors.[132] For closed-ended investment schemes in the UK, these are generally structured as investment companies listed on the stock exchange and hence would have to comply with annual corporate reporting[133] under the Companies Act as well as periodic reporting required by the listed market, which is on a half-yearly basis.[134]

---

124 S223, Pensions Act 2004.

125 S226, Pensions Act 2004.

126 S244, Pensions Act 2004.

127 Department of Work and Pensions, *Landscape and Charges Survey 2013* (Feb 2014), above at para 10.2.3.

128 Art 68, recast UCITs Directive 2009.

129 Art 69, 73, recast UCITs Directive 2009.

130 Art 69, recast UCITs Directive 2009.

131 See FCA Handbook COLL 4.5.

132 FCA Handbook COLL 8.3.5R.

133 S394, Companies Act 2006.

134 Article 5, Transparency Directive 2004. Directive 2004/109/EC of the European Parliament and of the Council of 15 December 2004 on the harmonisation of transparency requirements in relation to information about issuers whose securities are admitted to trading on a regulated market and amending Directive 2001/34/EC.

Alternative investment fund managers are subject to harmonised reporting obligations, under EU legislation, to investors on a yearly basis.[135] However, in addition to the mandatory annual report, funds and investors could enter into agreements to have additional reporting frequency such as on a quarterly basis.[136]

Nevertheless, it is to be noted that regular accountability and reporting, as a key mechanism to overcome principal-agent problems in investment management relationships, is imposed on funds to investors, and/or between funds and regulators. In light of the realities of the investment chain, such reporting may nevertheless be rather limited, as investors may not gain much insight into the arrangements between funds and the fund manager, and more remotely, between the fund manager and other entities in the investment chain. Hence, the structure of the investment chain could undermine the monitoring mechanism of regular accountability and reporting.

Regular accountability and reporting entail certain consequences. The insistence of regulatory frameworks on regular evaluation and accountability exacerbates the short-termist preferences in investment management because such evaluation and accountability, pursuant to the need of being standardised and objective, is necessarily based on market price, therefore reinforcing a narrow-minded attention to marketised values.[137] Regular reporting also forces funds to regularly evaluate their performance, and funds may be under pressure to boost such performance from one reporting interval to the next. For open-ended investment schemes, past performance may also be crucial to attracting new inflows. As funds' business models and their employee remuneration incentives are structured around assets under management, they are strongly incentivised to show investment performance at every reporting period.

The regulatory regime for regular reporting has played no small part in encouraging funds and their asset managers to pursue short-termist

---

[135] Art 22, AIFMD.

[136] Where investors use online platforms, hedge funds may even in due course aim to provide weekly or daily accounting transparency. See BNY Mellon, *Risk Roadmap: Hedge Funds and Investors' Evolving Approach to Risk* (August 2012), at http://www.thehedgefundjournal.com/sites/default/files/riskroadmap.pdf.

[137] Short-termism and the marketised model of investment management go together in liquid capital markets and dispersed shareholding, see Maria Maher and Thomas Andersson, 'Corporate Governance: Effects on Firm Performance and Economic Growth' (*OECD Working Paper* 1999).

investment performance.[138] Guyatt argues that investor myopia is entrenched as it is seen as a defensible practice in light of regulatory requirements. Funds and asset managers are reluctant to move away from the norm and adopt 'outlier' modes of investment thinking that do not strictly conform to the dominant practice of short-termist evaluation.[139] There may be a need to reconsider Lord Myners' earlier advice that pension scheme funding requirements should be dropped so as not to exacerbate short-termist pressures on pension funds. Instead, funds could be made to disclose regularly how current funding levels may be managed to meet longer term liabilities.[140]

Further, regulation may also play a part in entrenching conventional or dominant modes of investment management practice without questioning their substantive pros and cons. For example, pensions and investment trustees are subject to the 'prudent person' rule in investment making

---

[138] Some empirical research disagrees although much of empirical research shows that investment management is short-termist in nature. See Brian J Bushee, 'Do Institutional Investors Prefer Near-Term Earnings Over Long-Run Value?' (2001) 18 *Contemporary Accounting Research* 207–46; S Graves and S Waddock, 'Institutional Ownership and Control: Implications for Long-Term Corporate Strategy' (1990) 4 *Academy of Management Perspectives* 75–83; A Manconi, M Massa and A Yasuda, 'The Role of Institutional Investors in Propagating The Crisis of 2007–2008' (2012) 104 *Journal of Financial Economics* 491–518; Michael Porter, *Capital Choices: Changing the way America Invests in Industry* (Mass: Harvard Business School 1994); X Yan and Z Zhang, 'Institutional Investors and Equity Returns: Are Short-Term Institutions Better Informed?' (2009) 22 *Review of Financial Studies* 893–924. But on the contrary, see Jeffrey L Callen and Xiaohua Fang, 'Institutional Investor Stability and Crash Risk: Monitoring Versus Short-Termism?' (2013) 37 *Journal of Banking and Finance* 3047 (arguing that companies with institutional investors that are long-termist in nature do not 'hoard' bad news until the very last minute causing share price crashes and volatility and empirical research reveals that most companies are not subject to such share price crashes and short termist pressures from investors); Mark J Roe, 'Corporate Short-Termism—In the Boardroom and in the Courtroom' (2013), above (arguing that short termist traders are only part of the landscape, the most short termist being high frequency traders, and there are plenty of long-termist institutions whose holding periods have not changed much over the years, e.g. Vanguard and Fidelity).

[139] Danyelle Guyatt, 'Meeting Objectives and Resisting Conventions: A Focus on Institutional Investors and Long-Term Responsible Investing' (2005), above. On herding and group conformance, see David Marginson and Laurie McAulay, 'Exploring the Debate on Short-Termism: A Theoretical and Empirical Analysis' (2008), above.

[140] Paul Myners, *Institutional Investment in the UK: A Review* (2001) at paras 63–67.

decisions in the best interests of their beneficiaries.[141] Although this rule appears flexible, Woods[142] argues that courts have narrowly deferred to prevailing investment practices as the standard of 'prudence'. Hence, if the mainstream investment management practice is focused on managing performance for the short term, then conforming investment management practices would likely meet the requirements of 'prudence', making alternative approaches to investment management likelier to incur legal risk. Thus, mainstream institutions such as pension funds and retail collective investment schemes are unlikely to deviate from prevailing conventional investment management practice.

On the contrary, sovereign wealth funds seem to be least affected by short termism,[143] and this may be due to the lack of regulatory accountability regimes for such funds. The unity of state and fund makes such accountability less externalised and provides flexibility for how the state scrutinises the funds and their management. However, the lack of such regulatory accountability regimes is also due to funds having no particular maturing liabilities and this almost seems to suggest that the ability to invest patiently for the long term is a luxury that is not afforded by the financialised model of large scale saving through collective investment. Indeed, it is interesting that SWFs are often viewed by mainstream investors as 'unsophisticated' investors because they do not necessarily have to operate according to the short-term oriented 'rules of the game' that are defined for most other kinds of institutional investor.[144]

The regulatory requirements discussed above meet the needs of investors in short-term monitoring and accountability, but these may give rise to perverse implications for long-term savings outcomes, because short-termist incentives in investment management may actually damage the prospects of the former. Next, we discuss how regulatory frameworks that support investors' needs for liquidity also reinforce the investor myopia problem, highlighting the dilemma between investment management for long-term savings outcomes and near term liquidity.

---

141 *Learoyd v Whiteley* (1887) 12 App Cas 727.

142 Claire Woods, 'Funding Climate Change: How Pension Fund Fiduciary Duty Masks Trustee Inertia and Short-Termism' in James Hawley, Shyam Kamath, Andrew Williams (eds), *Corporate Governance Failures* (University of Pennsylvania Press 2014) at Chapter 11, 242.

143 As will be discussed in Chapter 8.

144 Borzou Daragahi, 'For cash-laden Emirates, no price tag is too large', *Los Angeles Times*, 6 October 2008. http://articles.latimes.com/2008/oct/06/world/fg-emirates6

Investor Liquidity Needs

Talbot argues that '[h]istorically, we can see that capital (and capitalists) in pursuing surplus, seek to resist all restrictions to its fluidity (or liquidity)' and hence all forms of investors, as capital providers, necessarily seek flexibility and mobility in order to chase the most profitable returns or avoid losses'.[145] The prospect of exit, or 'cashing out' of an investment, may be what drives investment in the first place, explaining the necessity of the secondary securities market for primary issuance of securities.[146] Savers have different investment horizons and different objectives may intrude upon their priorities subsequent to making an investment. Hence, the ability to exit by sale or redemption is important so that an investor can resume the proprietary assumption over her capital, and perhaps at the same time provide a signal for market discipline. This is however not the case for pensions, where savers can only switch. But where the investment relates to voluntary saving such as in retail collective investment schemes or alternative funds, investors' redemptions are generally unquestioned rights, albeit governed by terms of the fund and by regulation.[147] Regulation has played a key part in securing investors' rights in redemption as a means of investor protection, and hence liquidity needs for investors have to an extent been protected by regulation.

The UCITs Directive makes it mandatory that redemption prices be published at least twice a month[148] and that unit-holders have a right to redeem.[149] In the UK, redemptions of units should be carried out within the business day although payment can be made in four business days.[150] The implication of this structure for investors is that their relationship with their investment is more that of a product which can be ditched if unhappy, and less that of an ongoing relational paradigm, very much

---

[145] Lorraine E Talbot, 'Why Shareholders Shouldn't Vote: A Marxist-progressive Critique of Shareholder Empowerment' (2013) 76(5) *MLR* 791.

[146] This works the same way for listed close-ended funds which are structured as investment companies. Further, the natural tendency to look for liquidity may be such that it cannot necessarily be overcome by increased transaction costs such as financial transaction taxes, as is proposed by the Aspen report, see above.

[147] Such as the right to request redemption for UCITs investors which must be honoured, Art 84, UCITs Directive; Art 16, 18, AIFMD.

[148] Art 76, UCITs Directive 2009.

[149] Art 84, UCITs Directive 2009.

[150] FCA Handbook COLL 6.2.16.

characteristic of the financialisation of retail savings products as discussed in Chapter 1. The Alternative Investment Managers Directive also specifies that funds must provide a redemption policy allowing redemption at reasonable frequency depending on the nature of the fund.[151] The UK mandates that the funds need to be valued at least yearly,[152] but the frequency of redemption is likely a matter for agreement between investors and funds subject to the general requirement of reasonableness given the nature of the fund. In close-ended funds, there must be a date of maturity, such as seven to ten years in private equity funds.

The provision of liquidity for investors means that a price for exit has to be regularly, if not constantly, available. This reinforces the marketised model of investment management as exit either takes place on the basis of a marketplace, such as for close-ended listed investment companies and listed exchange-traded funds, or on the basis of valuations that rely heavily on market price, such as for retail collective investment schemes and hedge funds. The marketised model of investment management commoditises corporations as narrowly represented in securities assets that are regularly bought and sold, and reinforces the model of investment gains as derived from trading gains instead of real productivity and operational performance. The regulatory protection of investors' liquidity plays no small part in cementing the trading culture as key to investment management culture, which is deleterious to concepts of long-term investment intermediation in the corporate economy and patient capital.

A number of empirical researchers are of the view that a liquid market for securities may be essential for capital formation but adverse to corporate governance, i.e. investors are not encouraged to be actively engaged with their investments over the long term. Under relative conditions of less liquidity, shareholders are more likely to be engaged.[153] Although it may not be conceivable to undermine the proprietary right in selling shares by shareholders, policy-makers in France and Germany are experimenting with rewarding longer-term shareholders with more voting rights or more dividends so that they may be willing to opt into less liquidity for these rewards.[154] Further, there is now policy consideration for the negative aspects of liquidity especially in relation to systemic risk. The Financial Stability Board is concerned that asset managers may

---

151 Articles 16, 18, AIFMD.

152 FCA Handbook FUND 3.9.5.

153 Kerry Back, Tao Li and Alexander Ljungqvist, 'Liquidity and Governance' (2013) at http://ssrn.com/abstract=2350362.

154 See Emeka Duruigbo, 'Stimulating Long-term Shareholding' (2011–12), above.

make promises of liquidity while fund assets are not that easily liquidated, hence triggering investor panic and implications for severe market risk.[155] Hence there may be some push-back on regulatory support for investor liquidity needs.

In sum, investors' needs for liquidity and regulatory frameworks that support those rights as part of investor protection again present a dilemma of balancing interests – between near-term perceptions of adequate investor protection and a long-term investment culture that engages with the corporate economy to meet savings needs. We are unlikely to see changes to these key investor protections. However, regulatory reforms are afoot to mitigate some of the agency problems and governance deficits in the investment chain. We discuss conduct of business reforms in the EU and UK, and point out that although these reforms intend to overcome agency problems to an extent, the sub-optimalities of modern investment management discussed in Section D are not really addressed. Further, it remains an intractable problem to achieve a sound balance between near-term investor protection and the long-term interests of savers in a sustainable and wealth-creating corporate economy.

The Impact of Conduct of Business Reforms in Post-crisis Regulatory Changes

Post-global financial crisis 2007-09, regulation has started to address the exploitative aspects of the investment chain. One of us has explained elsewhere that consumer and investor protection have been ramped up significantly in the UK and EU due to the changed political economy context and the perception that investor protection is important for public interest objectives such as financial stability.[156] The social distrust in the financial sector generally has allowed policy-makers to introduce more paternalistic forms of regulation for investor protection, such as may have been resisted in pre-crisis times. In terms of investment management, the topical aspect of payment for research has come under regulatory control in order to address 'investment chain' charges that are remote from

---

155 FSB, *Policy Recommendations to Address Structural Vulnerabilities of from Asset Management Activities* (12 Jan 2017) at http://www.fsb.org/2017/01/fsb-publishes-policy-recommendations-to-address-structural-vulnerabilities-from-asset-management-activities/.

156 Mads Andenas and Iris H-Y Chiu, *The Foundations and Future of Financial Regulation* (Oxford: Routledge 2014) at Chapter 8 and citations therein.

investors and yet levied upon them.[157] The UK has reformed investment advice in order to mitigate mis-selling due to conflicts of interest.[158] Further, the Financial Conduct Authority also proposed comprehensive reforms to how fees and charges are levied in order to protect investors from uncompetitive pricing practices.[159]

Addressing Potential Exploitation of Investors

Asset managers charge to funds, and ultimately fund investors, transaction charges in connection with investment management. However, amounts payable to subsidise research in brokerage firms are often bundled in transaction charges. These subsidies are known as 'soft dollars' or 'dealing commissions' and are borne by fund investors although they are incurred remotely from investors in the investment chain. The justification for charging dealing commissions to investors would be that the asset manager benefits from such research in carrying out investment management. However, such benefits accrue globally to the asset manager, a separate entity from the fund, and may not be specific to any fund managed by the manager. EU legislation in 2004 placed some limitations on when 'inducements' can generally be paid, and dealing commissions are not excluded as long as the quality of the investment management service may be demonstrated to be enhanced. Although the EU regulatory regime recast in 2014 retains the same qualification, the European Securities and Markets Authority has decided to introduce bolder reforms to weed out the potential of investor exploitation by the investment chain. The European Securities and Markets Authority now proposes that dealing commissions should no longer be paid out of execution charges. Fund managers need to determine a research budget *ab initio* in order to pay for research, and where research charges should be passed on to investors, asset managers should justify how each fund should contribute to the budget depending

---

157 Art 24(8) and (9), MiFID 2014. ESMA, *Final Report: ESMA's Technical Advice to the Commission on MiFID II and MiFIR* (Dec 2014) at pp. 130–43.

158 The Retail Distribution Review, FSA, 'Distribution of Retail Investments: Delivering the RDR – feedback to CP09/18 and final rules' (March 2010) PS10/6 http://www.fsa.gov.uk/pubs/policy/ps10_06.pdf; FSA, 'Distribution of Retail Investments: Delivering the RDR – Professionalism' (January 2011) PS11/01 http://www.fsa.gov.uk/pubs/policy/ps11_01.pdf and FCA Handbook COBS 6.1A. Also Art 27, MiFID 2014 on the provision of independent advice.

159 FCA, *Asset Management Market Study Final Report* (2017), above.

on the benefits achieved for each fund.[160] This novel attack[161] on the privileges hitherto enjoyed by the fund management industry attempts to mitigate a long-running agency problem in asset management. However, this measure does not address the deeper problem of the fund management business model which has produced rent-seeking incentives throughout the investment chain, and can arguably be circumvented by industry structures.

It may be argued that as restrictions for payments to research kick in, research could be reorganised into a separate business model in the investment chain and may indeed become more expensive if it is no longer subsidised by trading charges. The rise in cost or relative diminution of research would impact investment management in such a way that investors would enjoy fewer cost-savings from economies of scale. However, we also see that some asset managers are absorbing research costs as part of their cost of doing business and not passing on to investors,[162] therefore, possibly being able to give investors 'a better deal'. It remains to be seen what precise structures of contractual terms, fees and charges would be developed by the industry. Another adverse consequence in addressing this agency problem could be more migration into passive investing or ETF investing. Although these may initially appeal, based on low-cost features, this chapter has already argued that such modes of investment management may in fact deprive investors of potentially value-added forms of discretionary management (which albeit come at the cost of agency problems) and are likely adverse to the long-term investment intermediation needs of the real economy.

The FCA has also proposed far-reaching reforms to how asset managers should levy their fees and charges. The FCA found that profits in asset management have remained persistently high although performance delivered to investors may be lacklustre. Price competition for actively-managed and partly-active products is weak partly due to sub-optimal communication of fund objectives to investors. Further, asset managers seemed unmotivated to control costs incurred in the investment chain. Hence, the FCA wishes to impose a single all-in-fee for asset management inclusive of estimated costs and charges. This may motivate asset

---

[160] ESMA, *Final Report: ESMA's Technical Advice to the Commission on MiFID II and MiFIR* (Dec 2014), above at pp. 130–43.

[161] It remains uncertain if the UK regulator will adopt this regime, as it supports transparency for research charges but not to the prescriptive extent of ESMA's report.

[162] 'Fund houses plan to pay for research themselves' *Financial Times* (8 May 2016).

managers to be more willing to control cost in the investment chain and deliver value for money. Further, price transparency would be more standardised and subject to regulatory scrutiny.[163]

Kay has argued that the adverse incentives in the investment chain should be mitigated by making all entities in the chain owe fiduciary duties.[164] However, as the Law Commission[165] has pointed out, chain entities do owe duties to the parties they have a direct transactional relationship with, some of them fiduciary in nature. But even fiduciary law cannot construct such duties to be owed between parties not-transactionally connected, i.e. between fund investors and the fund manager and other entities in the investment chain. The legal structuration of investment services relationship in the investment chain has achieved such remoteness of the fund investor from the actual service providers in investment management that it would take direct regulation to intervene in the dynamics. The FCA also agrees that reform to fiduciary duty may be complex and cumbersome,[166] and perhaps unnecessary in the light of regulatory reform that has introduced direct duties to entities in the investment chain vis-à-vis investors.

On this point, regulatory reform has been introduced to make inroads into the remote positioning of fund investors from the rest of the investment chain. Regulation now prescribes certain conduct of business duties to be owed as regulatory duties by fund managers to investors directly, to be enforceable by the regulator if breached. However, as these duties are for the purposes of investor protection, they can be seen as duties 'owed' to the investor. This is helped by the availability of private litigation for investors on the basis of breach of statutory duty.[167] However, such investors in private litigation would need to prove that fund managers' breaches of the relevant duty caused their precise interests to be jeopardised.

---

[163] FCA, *Asset Management Market Study Final Report* (2017) at Chapter 13 at https://www.fca.org.uk/publication/market-studies/ms15-2-3.pdf.

[164] BIS, *The Kay Review of UK Equity Markets and Long-Term Decision Making* (Final Report, 23 July 2012), above at Chapter 6.

[165] Law Commission, *Fiduciary Duties of Investment Intermediaries* (June 2014) at pp. 183–206.

[166] FCA, *Asset Management Market Study Final Report* (2017) at Chapter 11 at https://www.fca.org.uk/publication/market-studies/ms15-2-3.pdf.

[167] S150, Financial Services and Markets Act 2000.

Impact of Direct Regulatory Duties Owed by Fund Manager to Fund Investor

European regulation has achieved the most significant intervention in the remote positioning of the fund investor from fund management service providers.

As will be discussed in Chapter 5, in 2010, the European Commission introduced an initiative to improve investor protection by imposing conduct of business obligations on management companies of UCITS funds.[168] The Directive prescribes certain proscriptive duties on the part of management companies so that the interests of the ultimate unit-holders in the UCITs funds will be secured. Further, certain duties are imposed on management companies in order to secure the best interests of unit-holders in funds, such as the development of fair and transparent pricing models for asset valuation, and to treat all fund unit-holders fairly and equally.[169] Management companies are to ensure that subscriptions and redemptions are dealt with fairly and in an accountable manner.[170] They must undertake all due diligence in monitoring their portfolios and ensure that the portfolios are managed within the investment limits and risk appetite.[171] Further, management companies are also subject to a duty of best execution when dealing with execution decisions on behalf of funds.[172] Finally, as part of regulating the investment management practices of fund managers, the Directive also imposes a duty on management companies to develop policies on how their voting rights in investee companies should be exercised for the benefit of the funds. Chapter 5 provides more discussion. However, the above paints a picture of rather extensive regulatory duties owed by management companies which can potentially be enforced by fund investors.

The Alternative Investment Fund Managers Directive[173] also provides for investor protection duties owed directly by fund managers to fund investors, despite the remote positioning of investors' relationships to

---

168 Commission Directive 2010/43/EU of 1 July 2010 implementing Directive 2009/65/EC of the European Parliament and of the Council as regards organisational requirements, conflicts of interest, conduct of business, risk management and content of the agreement between a depositary and a management company.

169 Art 22, Commission Directive 2010.

170 Art 15, Commission Directive 2010.

171 Art 23, Commission Directive 2010.

172 Art 25, Commission Directive 2010.

173 Art 12, AIFMD 2011.

fund managers. The duties include care, skill and diligence, the employment of resources effectively for the performance of due functions, the management of conflicts of interest, acting in the best interests of investors, compliance with all regulatory requirements including prudential regulation, and treating investors fairly. The FCA in its 2017 study of the asset management market has reiterated the importance of these direct duties to take care of investors' interests and will require senior managers in asset management firms to be personally responsible for ensuring that such a compliant culture is promoted and maintained.[174]

It may be argued that regulation achieves the 'publicisation' of investment management as a matter of public interest, and overcomes the dilution of investor monitoring and enforcement caused by the investment chain structure. The increasing regulation of investment management can reflect the public interest in the scale of collective investment management and its socio-economic dimension. The regulatory regime reflects the introduction of much-needed regulatory capitalism[175] to curb the unchecked forces of perverse incentives and unaccountability in private investment management services. After all, the regulation of food, medicines and product safety are all examples of mature regulatory regimes developed over decades in order to force business to meet the needs of social utility and not merely private profiteering. The same development could be occurring in relation to financial products and services that grow to attain a socially important stature. The regulatory regime has the potential to force changes in investment management behaviour. For example, in order to comply with the duty to act in investors' best interests, it can be argued that churning tendencies may be mitigated as excessive trading may have to be justified to the financial regulator. Investor-focused practices have now become a matter for regulatory compliance. The UK Financial Conduct Authority is able to commission audits into firm-level practices by using 'skilled persons' appointments,[176] and reviews carried out in this way have allowed the

---

174 FCA, *Asset Management Market Study Final Report* (2017) at para 11.10 at https://www.fca.org.uk/publication/market-studies/ms15-2-3.pdf.

175 John Braithwaite, *Regulatory Capitalism* (Cheltenham: Edward Elgar, 2008); David Levi-Faur, 'The Global Diffusion of Regulatory Capitalism' (2005) 598 *ANNALS of the Academy of Political Science* 12. Regulatory capitalism is the view that regulation is a necessary complement to markets, and that '[t]he state is embedded in the economic and social order; any change in the state is expected to be reflected in the economy and the society, and vice versa', see Levi-Faur above at p. 21.

176 S166, Financial Services and Markets Act 2000.

FCA to supervise firms more effectively and bring deterrent enforcement actions where necessary. However, there may be limits to what direct regulatory duties and enforcement can achieve in terms of changing the nature of modern investment management culture.

The imposition of conduct of business duties would be unlikely to change the nature of short-termist investment management behaviour, as such behaviour can be argued to meet the requirements of diligence and best interests of investors. This area is however being scrutinised by the EU which intends to bring about more public scrutiny of how funds and their asset managers meet the long-term interests of savers.[177] The introduction of regulation to compel management companies to subject their investment management practices to mandatory standards and supervisory scrutiny could also result in a box-ticking approach to compliance, or undertaking superficial compliance while increasing the cost of investment management due to such regulatory burdens.

It can also be argued that it is unlikely that regulators would indeed undertake expensive audits and enforcement of asset and fund managers' discharge of their investment management practices, leaving investor private litigation as the main avenue of enforcement. In such a case, the possibility of investor scrutiny and enforcement is unlikely to translate into real discipline as investors face a collective action problem in mounting expensive litigation. Moreover, investors are still likely to prefer to exit, as regulation has already endorsed their strong exit rights. The near-term investor protection goals embraced by regulation, such as in meeting investors' liquidity needs, provide an ambivalent narrative for investors as to what investor protection really means. In the face of these countervailing incentives introduced by regulation, investors may choose the path of least resistance, which is exit rather than the exercise of monitoring or discipline.

Impending Regulatory Developments

We observe early signs of new thinking amongst regulators in relation to introducing a more thorough and comprehensive regime for regulating investment management practices. The FCA has consulted upon whether competitive obstacles exist for investors in the asset management market

---

[177] See Arts 3g–3i, Directive (EU) 2017/828 of the European Parliament and of the Council of 17 May 2017 amending Directive 2007/36/EC as regards the encouragement of long-term shareholder engagement.

and are inquiring comprehensively into market failures.[178] In particular the FCA will introduce reforms into the governance of funds to ensure that investors' interests are ultimately protected, and seek to improve the way funds levy charges and communicate performance in order to stimulate a more competitive market.[179]

There is also general concern regarding governance deficits in the investment chain in the UK and EU, and proposals have been made to regulate various entities in the chain. In the UK, the Law Commission acknowledges that pension funds use pension consultants to advise them on asset allocation and the appointment of suitable asset managers. As there are only a handful of dominant consultancies in the market, such as Mercer and Towers Watson, and pension funds rely heavily on consultants' advice, the Commission suggests that regulatory standards and scrutiny should be extended to them to ensure that principal-agent problems are mitigated and that consistency be maintained with other regulatory regimes for investment.[180] The FCA also proposes to include investment consultants within the regulatory perimeter.[181]

The EU also proposes to make institutions, asset managers and proxy advisory agencies more publicly accountable for the exercise of their corporate governance rights in investee companies.[182] Further, the Financial Stability Board is exploring whether the investment management sector contributes to systemic risk, such as having an impact on asset prices during fund runs or suffering from liquidity squeezes in crises of mass redemptions.[183]

---

[178] FCA, *Asset Management Market Study* (18 Nov 2015) at https://www.fca.org.uk/news/asset-management-market-study; FCA, *Asset Management Market Study: Interim Report* (Nov 2016) at https://www.fca.org.uk/publication/market-studies/ms15-2-2-interim-report.pdf and FCA, *Asset Management Market Study Final Report* (2017) at https://www.fca.org.uk/publication/market-studies/ms15-2-3.pdf.

[179] FCA, *Asset Management Market Study Final Report* (2017) at https://www.fca.org.uk/publication/market-studies/ms15-2-3.pdf.

[180] Law Commission, *Fiduciary Duties of Investment Intermediaries* (June 2014), above at paras 11.51–11.62.

[181] FCA, *Asset Management Market Study Final Report* (2017) at Chapter 10 at https://www.fca.org.uk/publication/market-studies/ms15-2-3.pdf.

[182] See Arts 3g–3i, Directive (EU) 2017/828 of the European Parliament and of the Council of 17 May 2017 amending Directive 2007/36/EC as regards the encouragement of long-term shareholder engagement.

[183] FSB, *Proposed Policy Recommendations to Address Structural Vulnerabilities from Asset Management Activities* (22 June 2016); (12 Jan 2017).

There is an appetite to frame regulatory regimes for investment management and this book argues that this is an encouraging sign, as regulatory intervention is a direct and most effective means to address the sub-optimal development of the character of investment management driven by market forces. Perverse incentives have dominated the investment chain structure and have weakened the application of private law rights and enforcement. However, we acknowledge that regulation is faced with contesting objectives in investor protection, and the maintenance of near-term investor protection aims may compromise regulatory design for longer-term perspectives. For example, the longer-term interests of pooled investments may be met by reducing investors' liquidity rights, such as by the imposition of limited redemptions or redemption gates where the situation warrants.[184] These trade-offs present intractable policy challenges for regulators. Finally, we turn to an alternative ethos in investment management framed by social responsibility concerns, and we ask whether market forces can indeed provide an answer to address the sub-optimalities of mainstream investment management discussed in this Chapter.

F. INVESTING WITH CORPORATE SOCIAL RESPONSIBILITY IN MIND

It may be argued that if investment funds integrate environment, social and governance (ESG) factors into their investment management, investment management may be made more supportive of long-term value creation. There seems to be an increasingly discernible connection between corporate financial performance and social responsibility performance,[185] thus indicating that not only companies but their

---

[184] For example, the FCA acknowledges that certain commercial property funds' erection of redemption gates after runs on funds in the wake of Brexit need to be carefully considered and communicated to investors in order to achieve the purposes of investor protection and treating investors fairly. Other than a widely worded guidance in terms of principles, more prescriptive measures would be difficult. See FCA, *Guidance on Fund Suspensions* (8 July 2016) at http://www.fca.org.uk/news/guidance-fund-suspensions.

[185] Philip L Baird, Pinar Celikkol Geylani and Jeffrey A Roberts, 'Corporate Social and Financial Performance Re-Examined: Industry Effects in a Linear Mixed Model Analysis' (2012) 109 *Journal of Business Ethics* 367 and also literature review within; Henry L Petersen and Harrie Vredenburg, 'Morals or Economics? Institutional Investor Preferences for Corporate Social Responsibility' (2009) 90 *Journal of Business Ethics* 1.

investors would do well by doing good.[186] The development of market-driven forces towards socially responsible investing may be one means by which good ownership principles could be integrated into the practices of modern investment management.

In this Section, we first discuss whether funds *could* take account of ESG factors or indeed structure themselves as ESG-focused, and whether they *should* do so.

A number of commentators argue that, due to policy and social pressure, pension funds in particular have become more conscious of integrating ESG factors into investment management,[187] although shorter-term fund vehicles such as retail collective investment schemes are less engaged.[188] However, pension funds are not entirely convinced that ESG factors can be integrated into investment management, or indeed that investment management should change to become focused on social responsibility. This is partly due to uncertainty regarding the application of trustee duties in law and regulation.

Pension funds are concerned that integrating ESG factors into investment management is inconsistent with fiduciary duties. First, the fiduciary duty of loyalty does not permit fund managers to integrate their own values, morals or preferences into investment management, and hence the objective pursuit of financial returns is key, although not necessarily paramount.[189] Second, the regulatory duty imposed on trustees to act as 'prudent investors' usually means the practice of portfolio diversification. It is uncertain if pursuing ESG integration into conventional investment management would unduly preclude investing in many companies, making the portfolio less diversified and more risky.[190] Woods[191] also suggests that the 'prudent investor' rule for investment trustees has been

---

[186] Samuel B Graves and Sandra A Waddock, 'Institutional Owners and Corporate Social Performance' (1994) 37 *Academy of Management Journal* 1034, showing that institutions do embrace the socially responsible tenet in selecting their portfolio managers.

[187] Riikka Sievanen, Hannu Rita and Bert Scholtens, 'The Drivers of Responsible Investment: The Case of European Pension Funds' (2013) 117 *Journal of Business Ethics* 137. Also, see the influence of social culture in Scandinavia, Elias Bengtsson, 'A History of Scandinavian Socially Responsible Investing' (2008) 82 *Journal of Business Ethics* 969.

[188] Paul Cox, Stephen Brammer and Andrew Millington, 'An Empirical Examination of Institutional Investor Preferences for Corporate Social Performance' (2004) 52 *Journal of Business Ethics* 27.

[189] *Cowan v Scargill* [1985] 1 Ch 270.

[190] Rosy Thornton, 'Ethical Investments: A Case of Disjointed Thinking' (2008) 67 *Cambridge Law Journal* 396. Question also asked in Benjamin

interpreted narrowly by courts to mean the adoption of prevailing conventional investment management practices, and hence investment trustees are slow to take leadership in embracing 'new-fangled' investment criteria that may be more controversial.

The UNEPFI report, otherwise known as the Freshfields Report[192] has produced a definitive analysis on the compatibility of fiduciary duties with ESG considerations. It recommends that pension funds could take into account ESG considerations, where investments already satisfy the 'business case', where similarly competing investments are presented, and the choice of the one with better ESG performance is not incompatible with fiduciary duties. Further, ESG factors may be imperative where the objective of the fund is for such purpose or where the consent of beneficiaries may be found. Richardson[193] argues that the report supports not only the proposition that ESG factors are not incompatible with the legal and regulatory duties imposed on funds, but that they may be indeed important for the fulfilment of those duties. This is because investment management integrated with ESG concerns may take better account of investee company risks and investing in such companies is a more intelligent form of diversification than conventional and undiscriminating approaches. Empirical research also provides support, finding that investment management integrating ESG concerns are better managed in terms of downside volatility.[194]

However, Yeoh and Sandberg are less sanguine that ESG integration would become mainstream or indeed accepted by funds and their asset

---

Richardson, 'Do the Fiduciary Duties of Pension Funds Hinder Socially Responsible Investment?' (2007) 22 *Review of Banking and Financial Law* 145.

[191] Claire Woods, 'Funding Climate Change: How Pension Fund Fiduciary Duty Masks Trustee Inertia and Short-Termism' in James Hawley, Shyam Kamath, Andrew Williams (eds), *Corporate Governance Failures* (University of Pennsylvania Press 2014) at Chapter 11, 242.

[192] UNEPFI, *Fiduciary Responsibility: Legal and Practical Aspects of Integrating Environmental, Social And Governance Issues Into Institutional Investment* (Geneva: UNEPFI, 2009).

[193] Benjamin Richardson, 'Do the Fiduciary Duties of Pension Funds Hinder Socially Responsible Investment?' (2007), above.

[194] Andreas G F Hoepnerab, Michael Rezec, Sebastian Siegl, 'Does Pension Funds' Fiduciary Duty Prohibit the Integration of Environmental Responsibility Criteria in Investment Processes?' (2011) at http://ssrn.com/abstract=1930189.

managers as being consistent with legal and regulatory duties. Sandberg[195] points out that legal obstacles remain in the way the Freshfields report has been framed – the primacy of the business case for conventional funds remains paramount and ESG factors are only admissible if clearly consistent with this. As there is empirical evidence associating 'socially responsible' investment with weak or underperformance,[196] there is unease in some quarters in assuming that ESG factors are consistent with the business case. Yeoh[197] is also of the view that there remains uncertainty among funds as to the validity of becoming 'socially responsible' and they prefer a more conservative investment management practice as being more 'defensible'.

If not clarified by legislation, the existing uncertainties in the interpretation of legal and regulatory duties may remain an obstacle to investment management adopting the integration of ESG factors. That said, the UN Principles of Responsible Investment have published a compelling Statement[198] to encourage all investment funds to adopt ESG factors in their investment management practice, and said that the duty to do so sits alongside the traditional duties of loyalty and care. Nevertheless, the clarification of the legitimacy of ESG factors in investment management can only go so far. It remains uncertain if the integration of ESG factors into mainstream investment management will definitely pay off. As will be discussed shortly, empirical research on the relationship between dedicated 'socially responsible investing' and investment outperformance

---

195 Joakim Sandberg, 'Socially Responsible Investment and Fiduciary Duty: Putting the Freshfields Report into Perspective' (2011) 101 *Journal of Business Ethics* 143.

196 See empirical research ranging from the UK, Canada and Australia all pointing to there being either no statistical difference between the performance of socially responsible funds and conventional funds or indeed negative performance. There are also positive performance stories in the literature review, but in sum the verdict is mixed. See Rob Bauer, Jeroen Derwall and Rogér Otten, 'The Ethical Mutual Fund Performance Debate: New Evidence from Canada' (2007) 70 *Journal of Business Ethics* 111; Maria Ceu Cortez, Florinda Silva and Nelson Areal, 'The Performance of European Socially Responsible Funds' (2009) 87 *Journal of Business Ethics* 573; Stewart Jones, Sandra van der Laan, Geoff Frost and Janice Loftus, 'The Investment Performance of Socially Responsible Investment Funds in Australia' (2008) 80 *Journal of Business Ethics* 181.

197 Peter Yeoh, 'Socially Responsible Investing: Legal and Related Challenges' (2014) 35 *Company Lawyer* 35.

198 Generation Foundation, UNEP and UNPRI, *Fiduciary Duty for the 21st Century: Statement on Investor Obligations and Duties* (June 2016) at https://www.unpri.org/download_report/19422.

has found mixed results,[199] suggesting that focusing on ESG factors does not guarantee investment success. Although there is social and policy support for integrating ESG factors in investment management practice, the landscape of investment management behaviour has not changed dramatically.

Empirical research suggests that conventional funds that sign up to the adoption of ESG factors still tend to focus on the business case, as this approach is seen to be legally defensible and consistent with industry practice. This is why a purported embrace of ESG factors has had little perceived effect on investment management practice, as investment management is still largely carried out in conventional terms and not specially tailored to ESG factors.[200] ESG factors are generally treated as of secondary importance, subservient to mainstream financial concerns. In sum, the integration of ESG factors in this manner has thus far made little practical difference to the marketised and short-termist investment management model that has been shaped by market and regulatory forces discussed so far.[201]

What about funds that are dedicated to be socially responsible, i.e. branded as socially responsible investing (SRI)? This is arguably a niche sector at the moment, although it is growing as a result of diversification by mainstream funds.

---

[199] See note 196, and Gordon L Clark, Andreas Feiner and Michael Viehs, 'From Stockholder to Stakeholder: How Sustainability Can Drive Financial Outperformance' (March 2015) at http://www.arabesque.com/index.php?tt_down=51e2de00a30f88872897824d3e211b11, which is a meta-study arguing that there is overall evidence supporting a link between the adoption of sustainability practices and investment outperformance in investment management.

[200] Alan Lewis and Carmen Juravle, 'Morals, Markets and Sustainable Investments: A Qualitative Study of "Champions"' (2010) 93 *Journal of Business Ethics* 483, discussing their findings from qualitative surveys carried out on 'champions' for ESG investing in the mainstream sector.

[201] See Kyoko Sakuma-Keck and Manuel Hensmans, 'A Motivation Puzzle: Can Investors Change Corporate Behavior by Conforming to ESG Pressures?' in Suzanne Young and Stephen Gates (eds) *Institutional Investors' Power to Change Corporate Behavior: International Perspectives* (Critical Studies on Corporate Responsibility, Governance and Sustainability, Volume 5, Emerald Group Publishing Limited, 2013), arguing that institutions need to make their ESG focus conform to mainstream targets in performance which are financial in nature, and so the distinctness of ESG is lost in that emphasis and has little impact on the investee company as well.

Empirical research on the whole does not find that socially responsible funds show particularly consistent outperformance compared to conventional funds. A number of commentators[202] are of the view that this is because SRI techniques focus on portfolio composition, derived from conventional investment management techniques, and are thus not likely to perform spectacularly differently from conventional funds.

One of the first key methodologies in SRI is negative screening; shunning stocks in the 'sin sector', such as tobacco, gambling and alcohol and companies that do business with decried regimes. Negative screening techniques have their roots in certain values and convictions, so that investments made are consistent with investor conscience.[203] Negative screening methodologies do not make SRI a force for change: they are passive in nature, avoiding certain issuers and sectors, and there is also no evidence of pro-activity or engagement with the investee companies.

SRI funds which focus on negative screening are unlikely to provide catalytic influence in the corporate sector or investment market. This may also explain why empirical evidence has largely found that SRI funds based on negative screening have generally performed no better and no worse than conventional portfolios,[204] as financial motivation is not the underlying basis for such funds. Some empirical evidence has shown that negatively screened portfolios outperform conventional portfolios but the evidence is generally a mixture of some outperformance, some underperformance and generally no difference.[205]

---

[202] Karen L Benson, Timothy J Brailsford and Jacquelyn E Humphrey, 'Do Socially Responsible Fund Managers Really Invest Differently?' (2006) 65 *Journal of Business Ethics* 337; Deutsche Bank Advisors, Sustainable Investing: Establishing Long Term Value and Performance (2012) at http://www.dbcca.com/research; Carlos Joly, 'Why Responsible Investment Falls Short of Its Purpose and What to Do About It' (2010) 10 *Corporate Governance* 18.

[203] Meir Statman, 'Quiet Conversations: The Expressive Nature of Socially Responsible Investors' [2008] *Journal of Financial Planning* 40, surveys individual investors who choose SRI and the conviction dimension that drives SRI without comparing to returns from conventional portfolios.

[204] Anne-Marie Anderson and David H Myers, 'The Cost of Being Good' (2007) 28 *Review of Business* 5.

[205] Hung-Gay Fung, Sheryl A Law and Jot Yau, *Socially Responsible Investment in a Global Environment* (Cheltenham: Edward Elgar 2010), p. 58.

The post-2000 'second-generation'[206] SRI funds are typically managed by positive screening, which involves selecting companies for their superior performance in ESG matters. There is empirical evidence to support the financial outperformance of SRI funds, as Derwall, Koedijk and Horst's research published in 2011 seems to indicate. Comparing SRI portfolios that use different strategies, funds that use positive screening have outperformed others.[207] An earlier piece by Derwall and others[208] also suggests that positive screening for eco-efficiency leads to higher returns than conventional portfolios. These results are supported by Renneboog, Horst and Zhang's later research,[209] which finds that positive environmental screening leads to outperformance. Engelen and Essen[210] argue that responsibility-related announcements (concerning, for example, environmental liability, managerial fraud, product liability and recalls) may negatively affect stock price and hence are of direct concern to investors. However, positive screening entails research and screening costs, and other empirical analyses show that financial performance may only be on a par with conventional portfolios after taking into account such costs.[211]

'Third generation' SRI funds[212] now employ a mixture of positive and negative screening, with positive screening also including a 'best-in class' approach which selects a group of companies according to a

206 Term used in Luc Renneboog, Jenke ter Horst and Chendi Zhang, 'Is Ethical Money Financially Smart?' (February 2006) *ECGI Finance Working Paper* No 117/2006 http://papers.ssrn.com/sol3/papers.cfm?abstract_id=887162.

207 Jeroen Derwall, Kees Koedijk and Jenke ter Horst, 'A Tale of Values-Driven and Profit-Seeking Social Investors' (2011) 35 *Journal of Banking and Finance* 2137.

208 Jeroen Derwall, Nadja Guenster, Rob Bauer and Kees Koedijk, 'The Eco-Efficiency Premium Puzzle' (2005) 61 *Financial Analysts Journal* 51.

209 Luc Renneboog, Jenke ter Horst and Chendi Zhang, 'Socially Responsible Investments: Methodology, Risk Exposure and Performance' (June 2007) *ECGI Finance Working Paper* No 175/2007 http://papers.ssrn.com/sol3/papers.cfm?abstract_id=985267.

210 Peter Jan Engelen and Marc van Essen, 'Reputational Penalties in Financial Markets: An Ethical Mechanism' in Wim Vanderkerckhove, J Leys, K Alm, B Scholtens, S Signori and H Schäfer (eds), *Responsible Investment in Times of Turmoil* (Dordrecht: Springer 2011), pp. 55ff.

211 Hung-Gay Fung, Sheryl A Law and Jot Yau, *Socially Responsible Investment in a Global Environment* (Cheltenham: Edward Elgar 2010), 58.

212 Term used in Luc Renneboog, Jenke ter Horst and Chendi Zhang, 'Is Ethical Money Financially Smart?' (February 2006) ECGI Finance Working Paper No 117/2006 http://papers.ssrn.com/sol3/papers.cfm?abstract_id=887162 accessed 19 March 2013.

category of performance and ranks them in order to inform investment decisions. This approach refines the positive screening approach by providing for a spectrum of companies' ESG performance.[213] Barnett and Salomon find that intensive screening may initially limit the issuers that SRI funds can invest in, causing a decline in returns due to the limitations on diversification, but this decline is generally overcome by subsequent upward performance.[214] They argue that intensive screening generally allows SRI funds to pick from a pool of best performers and that such stock picking is likely to generate outperformance compared to conventional portfolios. Osthoff and Kempf also find that a portfolio of stocks with higher social responsibility ratings (based on KLD ratings) outperforms a portfolio of stocks with the worst KLD ratings.[215] However, Lobe and Walkshäusl find no improved performance from a basket of screened stocks as compared with a basket of 'sin stocks'.[216] Renneboog, Horst and Zhang find that screened stocks exhibit a mixture of outperformance, of no difference and of worse performance compared to conventional portfolios in the long term.[217]

There are arguably a number of factors affecting SRI fund performance. The lack of diversification, the cost of screening and research, and the comparative undervaluing of 'sin stocks'[218] may explain the inconsistent results in the financial performance of SRI funds. Sandberg[219] and Joly[220] argue overall that SRI has not made a fundamental impact on

---

[213] Hung-Gay Fung, Sheryl A Law and Jot Yau, *Socially Responsible Investment in a Global Environment* (2010), above p. 29.

[214] Michael L Barnett and Robert M Salomon, 'Beyond Dichotomy: The Curvilinear Relationship between Social Responsibility and Financial Performance' (2006) 27 *Strategic Management Journal* 1101.

[215] Peer C Osthoff and Alexander Kempf, 'The Effect of Socially Responsible Investing on Portfolio Performance' (2005) 13 *European Financial Management* 908.

[216] Sebastian Lobe and Christian Walkshäusl, 'Vice vs. Virtue Investing Around the World' (May 2011) http://ssrn.com/abstract=1089827.

[217] Luc Renneboog, Jenke ter Horst and Chendi Zhang, 'Is Ethical Money Financially Smart?' (February 2006), above; also Meir Statman, 'Socially Responsible Investments' (2007) 17 *Journal of Investment Consulting* 37.

[218] Harrison Hong and Marcin Kacperczyk, 'The Price of Sin: The Effects of Social Norms on Markets' (2009) 93 *Journal of Financial Economics* 15.

[219] Joakim Sandberg, 'Socially Responsible Investment and Fiduciary Duty: Putting the Freshfields Report into Perspective' (2011), above.

[220] Carlos Joly, 'Why Responsible Investment Falls Short of Its Purpose and What to Do About It' (2010), above.

investment management behaviour as it relies excessively on conventional investment management techniques such as portfolio composition and is thus not really driving the norms for change. It would seem that investment management practices will only change if alternative values and objectives are adopted, thereby shaping a different universe for a different kind of investment management. The marrying of financial and SRI objectives often results in the subsuming of the latter into the former as the former is much more institutionalised in law and the markets.[221]

'Fourth generation' SRI funds however take on more pro-active behaviour in terms of ESG issues. They may engage in shareholder activism, compelling management to engage in dialogue and change their behaviour. However, an Allianz survey seems to suggest that SRI activism is rare and that SRI techniques are still likely to be based on screening rather than activism.[222] The number of shareholder proposals related to corporate social responsibility was relatively limited in the period 2000–05.[223] But Fung, Law and Yau report stealthy increases since then and argue that threatening to bring a proposal may galvanise companies to commit to changes in behaviour aligned with the proposals.[224] Waygood also reports that investor engagement was key to changing the giant UK pharmaceutical company GlaxoSmithKline's

---

221 For example see Ben Jacobsen, 'Institutional Investor Support for Climate Change Resolutions: A New Challenge To Capitalism Or Co-Opted Activism?' in Suzanne Young and Stephen Gates (eds) *Institutional Investors' Power to Change Corporate Behavior: International Perspectives* (Critical Studies on Corporate Responsibility, Governance and Sustainability, Volume 5, Emerald Group Publishing Limited, 2013) at pp. 279–308, where institutions' integration of environmental concerns in their engagement with companies is inevitably bundled up with financial performance concerns in order to be legitimate and defensible.

222 Alexander Boersch, 'Doing Good by Investing Well? Pension Funds and Socially Responsible Investment: Results of an Expert Survey' (January 2010) *Allianz Global Investors International Pension Paper* No 1/2010 http://papers.ssrn.com/sol3/papers.cfm?abstract_id=1607730. However, earlier empirical research suggests that UK pension funds that carry out ESG monitoring do a combination of screening and engagement, see Sirkku Hellsten and Chris Mallin, 'Are "Ethical" or "Socially Responsible" Investments Socially Responsible?' (2006) 66 *Journal of Business Ethics* 393.

223 Robert Monks, Anthony Miller and Jacqueline Cook, 'Shareholder Activism on Environmental Issues: A Study of Proposals at Large US Corporations (2000–2003)' (2004) 28 *Natural Resources Forum* 317; Anastasia O'Rourke, 'A New Politics of Engagement: Shareholder Activism for Corporate Social Responsibility' (2003) 12 *Business Strategy and the Environment* 227.

224 Hung-Gay Fung, Sheryl A Law and Jot Yau, *Socially Responsible Investment in a Global Environment* (2010), above p. 39.

behaviour in addressing the need for accessibility to affordable medicines by sub-Saharan Africa and that this engagement was premised on social good and not on financial returns.[225] Dhir also documents shareholder activism in Canada against Goldcorp Plc in relation to human rights abuses in Guatemala as being a significant driver for corporate behavioural change.[226] However, Bracking[227] argues to the contrary that shareholder activism may not always be for the common good. In relation to private equity funds investing in infrastructure and development in African emerging economies, their hands-on approach has not brought about a revolutionary institution of social responsibility norms in corporate or investment behaviour. This is because the funds have not invested in developing social responsibility yardsticks and merely adopt minimalist procedural approaches to ensure that the business case is not detrimentally affected by ESG issues. Further, SRI may generate outperformance through the use of shareholder activism which produces a market spike in the near term. The market spike may not persist if the market does not see clearly the value-added in the long term brought about by certain changes of corporate behaviour in favour of ESG factors.

The Deutsche Bank Advisers report[228] however finds that dedicated socially responsible funds that engage in activism for SRI show outperformance on a consistent basis relative to conventional fund managers. On the other hand, funds that practice conventional investment management that attempt to integrate ESG factors do not capture such outperformance. This seems to show that unless SRI becomes a key tenet that changes investment management practice around it, the long-termist sustainable financial performance that companies generate may not be captured by investment funds. It seems possible for us to achieve a paradigm of long-term investment culture in sustainable wealth creation

---

225 Steve Waygood, 'Measuring the Effectiveness of Investor Engagement: GSK and Developing Country Access to Essential Medicines' in Rory Sullivan and Craig MacKenzie (eds), *Responsible Investment* (Sheffield: Greenleaf Publishing 2006), p. 206. See also Nick Robins, 'Shaping the Market: Investor Engagement in Public Policy' in Rory Sullivan and Craig MacKenzie (eds), *Responsible Investment* (Sheffield: Greenleaf Publishing 2006), p. 312.

226 Aaron A Dhir, 'Shareholder Engagement in the Embedded Business Corporation: Investment Activism, Human Rights and TWAIL Discourse' (2012) 22 *Business Ethics Quarterly* 99.

227 Sarah Bracking, 'How do Investors Value Environmental Harm/Care? Private Equity Funds, Development Finance Institutions and the Partial Financialization of Nature-based Industries' (2012) 43 *Development and Change* 271.

228 Deutsche Bank Advisors, Sustainable Investing: Establishing Long Term Value and Performance (2012) at http://www.dbcca.com/research.

by the corporate sector, but this requires a committed capital partnership between the company dedicated to such a cause and its similarly committed investors.[229] Hence, a fundamental change from current investment management practice is required for achieving a shift in investment management culture. This also means a change in current regulatory tenets that support marketisation and short-termism. In view of the heavy lifting required, the compromising regulatory stance towards the tenets of financialisation, and the preference in human nature to deal with the near term, SRI is unlikely to become a dominant form of investment management practice.

G. CONCLUSION

In this chapter, we have drawn together broad level discussions on the structures and incentives in investment fund management, as reflecting a model of financialised business. We argue that most investment funds running a business model of pooled investments have structurally separated funds from managers for efficiency and regulatory reasons. This has further resulted in the growth and lengthening of the investment chain which has implications for the nature of investment management practice including the assumption (or lack of assumption) of corporate governance roles for investment funds and their managers. The industry of professionalised asset management is in particular susceptible to investor myopia and short-termism and is riddled with agency problems. Further, regulatory compliance pressures reinforce market preferences for these behaviours. However, these effects are also by-products of legitimate objectives in investor protection such as regular accountability and ensuring liquidity for investors. We query whether the embrace of ESG factors may change investment behaviour. We note that certain niche funds carry out different investment management practices, adopting ESG factors as a different ethos in their management. They come closer to an investment management paradigm that integrates savers' long-term interests and the long-term wealth-creation role of the corporate economy. However, we do not think there are sufficient market-driven or regulatory forces that would compel such change to become mainstream. Hence, the model of investment management that the fund industry has developed raises considerable questions for the long-term objectives of

229 Also described in Colin Mayer, *Firm Commitment* (Oxford: OUP 2013).

meeting savers' needs and supporting a long-term wealth-creating corporate sector. We are sceptical about whether these fundamental questions will be resolved by a greater emphasis from policy-makers on the corporate governance roles of funds and asset managers, as will be discussed in Chapter 3.

3. Corporate equity ownership and misplaced hope in institutional shareholder stewardship

A. INTRODUCTION

Earlier chapters have depicted the anatomy of financier capitalism,[1] and raised questions surrounding the optimality of the modern investment management model. As fund managers mediate the needs of savers through engagement with wealth-creating actors in the corporate economy, their corporate governance shortcomings come into sharp focus. Their distinctive corporate governance role – which stems from intermediaries' own investment management strategy – impacts on corporate strategy and behaviour in the rest of the economy, bringing with it important public interest implications.

When the growth of institutional fund management took off in the early 1990s, commentators initially expressed euphoric optimism for this privatised and financialised model of collective investment, seeing its potential as a universal governance force in the corporate sector so that savers' long-term needs can be achieved through investing in corporate wealth creation. As discussed in Chapter 1, Useem[2] hailed the arrival of investor capitalism which reflected democratic participation in the corporate sector through investment intermediaries' assumption of the role of shareholder on behalf of myriad savers. Hawley and Williams[3] went further to argue that this is an age of fiduciary capitalism where

[1] Paul H Edelman, Randall S Thomas and Robert B Thompson, 'Shareholder Voting in an Age of Intermediary Capitalism' (2014) at http://ssrn.com/abstract=2401746.

[2] Michael Useem, *Investor Capitalism: How Money Managers are Rewriting the Rules of Corporate America* (Basic Books, 1999).

[3] J P Hawley and A T Williams, 'Shifting Ground: Emerging Global Corporate-Governance Standards and the Rise of Fiduciary Capitalism' (2005) 37 *Environment and Planning* 1995–2013, *The Rise of Fiduciary Capitalism: How Institutional Investors Can Make Corporate America More Democratic* (University of Pennsylvania Press, 2000) generally.

investment intermediaries, representing a broad spectrum of savers and investing widely in the corporate sector, will be in a position to assume a meaningful corporate governance role as part of their fiduciary accountability to savers. It would seem that in the depiction of the 'investor capitalist' or the 'fiduciary capitalist', we have integrated the long-term social interest of savers with the long-term public interest in a wealth-creating and sustainable corporate economy. The depiction of the 'investor capitalist' and 'fiduciary capitalist' now seems to be overly idealistic, as Hawley's recent book[4] acknowledges. Hill[5] also points out that there are varying images of the shareholder that institutions have portrayed – the passive, apathetic shareholder, the subjugated shareholder who succumbs to managerial supremacy, and indeed the powerful shareholder who is engaged or activist. The varying and arguably inconsistent images of the institutional shareholder make it difficult for us to either frame institutions' role descriptively or conceptualise their role normatively.

However, UK policy-makers seem in general to believe that institutions' engagement with their corporate governance roles brings about a form of social or public good, especially on the part of pension funds and funds managing retail savings. Institutions are regarded as able to carry out a 'governance role' for corporations in the wider public interest. In the 1990s, the UK was dogged by a number of high profile corporate scandals, from the fall of BCCI and Polly Peck to the collapse of Barings and the Equitable Life scandal.[6] However, it was perceived – especially by the business community – that there was a limit to how far the heavy hand of government regulation could ensure that companies are well-run. Drawing on this perspective, contemporary scholarship in regulation theory has sought to maximise governance potential in diverse private actors in the regulatory space, as the state increasingly faces limitations in capacity, resources and reach in exercising governance and control.[7]

---

[4] James Hawley, Shyam Kamath and Andrew Williams, 'Introduction' in James Hawley, Shyam Kamath and Andrew Williams (eds), *Corporate Governance Failures* (University of Pennsylvania Press 2014).

[5] Jennifer G Hill, 'Images of the Shareholder – Shareholder Power and Shareholder Powerlessness' (2015) at http://ssrn.com/abstract=2664430.

[6] See generally, Iris H-Y Chiu, *The Foundations and Anatomy of Shareholder Activism* (Oxford: Hart 2010) at Chapter 2.

[7] Colin Scott, 'Analysing Regulatory Space: Fragmented Resources and Institutional Design' (2001) *Public Law* 329; Orly Lobel, 'The Renew Deal: The Fall of Regulation and the Rise of Governance in Contemporary Legal Thought' (2004–05) 89 *Minnesota Law Rev* 342. Julia Black, 'Critical Reflections on

As institutional investors have the proximity and resources to monitor investee corporations and do so, there is potential for their monitoring role to work as a force for governance. Regulation theory, in the wake of the decline of the state[8] and central command-and-control type mechanisms in regulatory control, has been advocating theoretical models of de-centralised governance[9] where various actors, public or private, may act in a 'regulatory space'[10] to exert governance and discipline on each other. Although different theories present different levels of optimism as to how the private interests of various actors may coincidentally produce beneficial public interest effects,[11] and how the patchwork of governance forces may work together, the direction that is clear is that we are increasingly looking for governance potential in a range of different actors, private or public. In that light, institutional investors are being looked at to provide a governance role for the optimal behaviour of the

---

Regulation' (2002) 27 *Australian J of Legal Philosophy* 1; Julia Black, 'Enrolling Actors in Regulatory Systems: Examples from UK Financial Services Regulation' (2003) *Public Law* 63–91; 'Mapping the Contours of Contemporary Financial Services Regulation' (2002) 2 *Journal of Corporate Law Studies* 253–87.

[8] E J Hobsbawm and Prem Shankar Jha, 'The Twilight of the Nation State' in Anne Marie Smith and Kate Nash (eds), *Globalisation and Contemporary Studies on the Nation State* (London: Pluto Press 2006); J Rosenau (ed.), *Governance Without Government* (Cambridge: Cambridge University Press 1992, rep 2000).

[9] Scott Burris, Michael Kempa and Clifford Shearing, 'Changes In Governance – A Cross-disciplinary Review of Current Scholarship' (2008) 41 *Akron Law Review* 1; Orly Lobel, 'The Renew Deal: The Fall of Regulation and the Rise of Governance in Contemporary Legal Thought' (2004–05), above. Julia Black, 'Critical Reflections on Regulation' (2002), above; 'Enrolling Actors in Regulatory Systems: Examples from UK Financial Services Regulation' (2003), above; 'Mapping the Contours of Contemporary Financial Services Regulation' (2002), above.

[10] Colin Scott, 'Analysing Regulatory Space: Fragmented Resources and Institutional Design' (2001) *Public Law* 329.

[11] John S F Wright and Brian Head, 'Reconsidering Regulation and Governance Theory: A Learning Approach' (2009) 31 *Law and Policy* 192; Liesbet Hooghe and Gary Marks, 'Unraveling the Central State, but How? Types of Multi-level Governance' (2003) 97 *American Political Science Review* 233; Shann Turnbull, 'Self Regulation' (1997), article presented at International Conference on Socio-Economics, Montreal, arguing that where there are diverse centres of information, expertise and resources, power is fragmented and issues are complex, and hence, governance has to be provided in part by ground-up private sector locations.

corporate sector, as many of them have – at least in theory – a stake in the long-term wealth-creating role of UK corporations.

Institutional investors' corporate governance roles have also become an issue of public interest as fund management has attained a stature of social importance in the context of financialisation. Investment has moved from being a luxury good, or privilege of the class being left with a 'bounty',[12] to an essential staple for managing the livelihood of saving workers and retiring populations. Public scrutiny of investment management practice has increased and there are increasing calls for more governance of the modern investment management phenomena. Ingley et al suggest[13] that investment management should be subject to third party objective monitoring, and the Ownership Commission[14] is of the view that institutions' engagement rights in corporate governance should be delegated to objective third parties.

The attention paid to how institutions engage in the corporate governance of their investee companies is part of overall public interest in their investment management. However there seems to be a preponderant focus on the use of these corporate governance rights – acquired through ownership of corporate equity on an economy-wide scale – as being representative of an optimal form of investment management which can deliver meaningful monitoring of corporate management. We are highly sceptical of the implicit assumption made by policy-makers: that institutions' investment interest is aligned with the public interest in a well-governed corporate sector providing returns for long-term savers. We do not think that the current nature of institutions' participation in corporate governance will necessarily bring about benign effects for either savers' long-term interests or the long-term interests of the wealth-creating corporate economy.

In this book, we make two key arguments. One is that the varying and inconsistent images of the institutional shareholder are a result of equity-owning funds treating their corporate governance roles as an instrument of their investment management practice, i.e. reflecting the commercial imperatives of their own business models. We argue that such an instrumental assumption of corporate governance roles can be understood in the context of how funds are structured and governed, as has been discussed in Chapter 2. The second argument is that funds'

---

[12] Richard L Nobles, 'The Exercise of Trustees' Discretion under a Pension Scheme' (1992) *Journal of Business Law* 261.

[13] C B Ingley and N T van der Walt, 'Corporate Governance, Institutional Investors and Conflicts of Interest' (2004) 12 *Corporate Governance* 534.

[14] *Ownership Commission Report* (March 2012).

instrumentally-driven corporate governance role brings about certain patterns of behaviour and performance in their investee companies, and these do not match the idealistic expectations that are often placed on institutional shareholders.[15] The implication of the second argument is that societal expectations in respect of funds' corporate governance role should either be scaled back to a more realistic level – with investment management being viewed as just another profit-driven business activity rather than quasi-governmental in nature – or indeed, if there is public policy interest in changing its behaviour, significant reforms are needed in order to change the nature and character of investment management. Such discussions would need to be situated in the larger debate regarding the privatised and financialised model of investment management for savers' needs, in terms of whether and to what extent an element of public interest should be (re-)introduced to reshape this model.

B. THE SIGNIFICANCE OF OWNERSHIP OF CORPORATE EQUITY

Before we consider in more detail the governance activities of institutional investors, it is useful for us to describe the behavioural benchmark against which we would seek to evaluate fund managers in their governance role. This brings us to a discussion of the notion of what it means to hold corporate equity – and the rights and powers claimed by fund managers through their investments in corporations' equity securities – and how these could and should be exercised to best achieve social objectives in terms of wealth creation.

The 'ownership' context in which economic activities take place is a crucial but often neglected aspect of economic functioning. In particular, the way in which institutions as shareholders exercise their unique rights and privileges over corporate enterprises is likely to play a fundamental role in defining both the behaviour and performance of the entire economy. Ownership of corporate equity by institutions should hence be a matter of great interest not only to the entities themselves, but also to society as a whole.

As owners of corporate equity, institutions are in a privileged situation as they enjoy legally-defined powers which enable them to exercise a high level of influence or control over the assets and activities of an

---

[15] Sally Wheeler, 'From Responsible Saver to Stewarded Investor? (2013–14) at http://ssrn.com/abstract=2238612.

enterprise, including the fundamental right to either initiate or terminate its existence. According to economic theorists who conceptualise companies as a 'nexus of contracts', 'ownership' resides in the hands of the constituency with residual rights over key decisions that cannot be determined in advance through contractual arrangements between the various stakeholders involved with the company.[16] Economists tend to justify the primacy of shareholders with the assertion that they are the main 'risk takers' amongst the various stakeholders – with no contractually-determined right to any financial return as long as the enterprise remains a going concern – and therefore needful of a privileged position in terms of corporate decision-making (although in practice much of this risk can be eliminated by means of portfolio diversification).[17]

Although company law does not typically refer to shareholders as the explicit 'owners' of a company,[18] it is nonetheless equity investors that are seen as exercising 'quasi-proprietary' powers[19] over a company in practice, in legal, economic and public discourse. Shareholders in most jurisdictions are granted significant legal rights and powers in decision-making in the company, including the crucial power of being able to appoint or dismiss the board of directors (or governing body) by means of shareholder voting at general meetings,[20] to ratify directors' breaches of duty or default,[21] to approve of certain transactions reserved to shareholders such as loans to directors,[22] capital and business restructuring decisions,[23] and to enjoy the reversion of management powers to the general meeting if the Board should be deadlocked.[24] As a result, it is

---

[16] Oliver Hart, 'An Economist's Perspective on the Theory of the Firm' 89 *Columbia Law Review* 1757–1774 (1989).

[17] For example, see Frank H Knight, 'Risk, Uncertainty and Profit' (1921).

[18] For example, in the Companies Act 2006, the term 'member' is used throughout to refer to the shareholder constituency.

[19] *Her Majesty's Commissioners of Inland Revenue v Laird Group plc* [2003] UKHL 54 at para 35 describing share ownership as conferring a form of ownership over certain rights in a company but not over its property.

[20] Section 168, Companies Act 2006.

[21] Section 239, Companies Act 2006.

[22] See sections 190–214, Companies Act 2006.

[23] E.g. sections s644, 693A, 694, Companies Act 2006.

[24] E.g. *Re Opera Photographic* [1989] B.C.L.C. 763; *Union Music Ltd v Watson Arias Ltd v Blacknight Ltd* [2004] B.C.C. 37. These cases concerned whether a shareholder could ask the court to order the convention of a general meeting in order to resolve any deadlock in management, but the court has used such power carefully so that reversion is granted only when it is necessary for the

perhaps not surprising that shareholders are widely referred to as the 'owners' of the company by a wide range of commentators and market participants.

Our implicit although admittedly normative assumption in what follows is that the most desirable form of ownership of a private sector corporate entity is one which supports and encourages long-term value creation. Such companies will, by definition, generate a surplus above and beyond their overall cost of capital on a sustainable basis, and will thereby be able to survive and flourish to the potential benefit of their various constituencies. We believe that it is this kind of company that is most likely to form the core of an internationally-competitive economy. These are also the kind of enterprises that are likely to be concomitant with high levels of corporate productivity and innovation, well-paid employment opportunities, and a stable corporate tax base from which to finance socially-enriching welfare activities and public goods.

What is the role played by corporate equity owners in nurturing and encouraging a broad range of companies focused on long-term value creation? Such a question was recently addressed by the Ownership Commission set up by the UK Government in the wake of the financial crisis of 2007–09.[25] Its conclusion was, *inter alia*, that 'good ownership' was likely to be underpinned by two interrelated characteristics – stewardship and engagement – which we consider in turn.

Firstly, good 'owners', i.e. shareholders, are likely to exercise stewardship duties vis-à-vis their investee companies. Stewardship has been defined as 'the active and responsible management of entrusted resources now and in the longer term, so as to hand them on in better condition'.[26] To act as a steward of an investee company means that the shareholder will be concerned about the long-term interests of the company as a whole, and not only making maximum financial return for themselves (or their clients) in the short term. This is a much broader responsibility than narrowly concerning oneself with the financial performance of specific funds invested in the company's securities, which could easily be disinvested or promoted at the expense of other corporate stakeholders. It

---

general meeting to make a management decision that otherwise would not be made. The court has refrained from aiding the calling of general meeting with an often amended quorum if doing so will override minority and class rights that were sought to be protected, see *Ross v Telford* [1997] B.C.C. 945.

25 *Ownership Commission Report* (2012), see above.

26 Tomorrow's Company, 'Tomorrow's Stewardship: Why Stewardship Matters' (June 2011), p. 2. The notion of stewardship in the context of the UK Stewardship Code is explored in more detail in Section D below.

is a concept which places shareholders on an analogous footing to the directors of the company – who have fiduciary duties to promote the entire company's best interests – rather than pursuing a self-interested strategy of short-term financial gain for their own investor constituency.

Stewardship is likely to involve guiding the company in defining its distinctive business purpose and vision, encouraging the board and management to remain tightly focused on long-term corporate objectives and strategy, and ensuring that they build a good team and motivated relationships with all of the company's stakeholders (particularly employees). A responsible shareholder will also see the long-term value of the company acting as a reasonable corporate citizen, reflecting societal norms with respect to its interaction with wider society. A responsible shareholder is also likely to be supportive of investments in innovation, new products and company-specific training which – despite potentially adverse effects on financial surpluses in the short term – could enhance its long-term competitiveness and performance. Good stewards will utilise all legally available ownership rights (e.g. voting at General Meetings) in the interests of the company as well as having more informal engagement with boards and management, and they will exercise care in ensuring that their stewardship is not compromised due to other conflicting commercial or personal responsibilities. None of these aspects of stewardship will be driven by altruism, but will arise because good 'owners' understand their positive impact on the company's capacity to generate wealth over the longer term.

Second, good 'owners' are likely to eschew a passive or *laissez-faire* approach to share ownership – akin to an absentee landlord – and seek to actively engage with boards and management over issues such as the business purpose of the company, its long-term strategic approach, its governance framework and its corporate values. Such engagement will not necessarily enmesh itself with the detailed management or oversight of the company (which in most corporations are proper matters for the executive team and the board of directors). But it will involve maintaining a dialogue with the company in respect of its adherence to its mission, vision and values, its longer-term performance, and the composition of its board.

A question that is rarely asked by policy makers is whether existing corporate ownership structures are consistent with the nurturing of companies with a focus on long-term value creation. Ownership of corporate equity does not tend to form a central part of modern debates on economic policy except in relation to certain priority sectors of national importance where government accepts – often reluctantly – that there is no viable alternative other than to either directly own key entities or alternatively heavily regulate them (often through a contingent control mechanism known as a 'golden share'). Prominent companies in the defence, media or utility sectors are typically the subject of this kind of governmental *dirigisme*, although the strategic ownership role of the state may sometimes spread more widely (e.g. in France where various strategic sectors are protected from foreign ownership[27]). For such key companies, a purely private ownership structure is seen by policy makers as too risky or inconsistent with wider aspects of the public interest.

Since the Thatcher-Reagan revolution of the 1980s, a broader role for public ownership has been widely rejected in many developed economies in favour of an overwhelmingly *laissez-faire* ownership approach (particularly in the UK, and to varying degrees in other countries). In accordance with free market wisdom, ownership of private sector entities should be a matter for private sector shareholders whose control over companies should be accorded as much discretion as possible. Furthermore, according to this philosophy, the 'best' corporate equity owners for a company are likely to be those that are self-selected through their willingness to pay the highest price in private transactions between market actors. Whoever has legitimately acquired ownership over the equity securities of a private sector corporate entity should then be left alone to exercise ownership rights and privileges in their own self-interest.

Although market fundamentalism in the sphere of corporate ownership remains influential, its impact is far from absolute. The freedom of action of shareholders over corporate entities is constrained to varying degrees by applicable company law, listing rules, the wider regulatory framework in which the company operates and the direct interventions of government in certain circumstances. These constraints partly reflect the need of wider society to protect itself from the externalities that could be incurred by purely self-interested private sector actors. They may also serve to protect some corporate constituencies from each other (e.g. minority shareholders from majority shareholders). Furthermore, as we will see, policy makers have been attempting in recent years to steer the ownership behaviour of shareholders in a direction more consistent with some aspects of long-term value creation and wider societal legitimacy through the introduction of the UK Stewardship Code and similar codes in a variety of countries. Nonetheless, the prevailing wisdom amongst many business people and policy makers in recent decades has been – and

[27] Peggy Hollinger and George Parker 'France lists sectors to be protected from foreign bids', *Financial Times* (1 September 2005).

largely remains – to minimise constraints on corporate ownership as exercised by shareholders. This is justified by the claim that to do otherwise would be deleterious to corporate value creation and threaten the economic freedom of market actors.

As we have described in Chapter 1, one of the profound consequences of this non-interventionist approach has been the quiet transformation of corporate ownership of listed (and to some extent unlisted) companies in favour of institutional investors – and increasingly non-domestic investors – over the last few decades. Due to their large holdings of corporate equity, it is investment funds that are now in a position to exercise the rights and privileges of share ownership, and the broader corporate governance responsibilities that are associated with it. However, as we will argue, this is not a role that they are particularly well placed to fulfil due to the commercial imperatives of their business models.

C. FUNDS' CORPORATE GOVERNANCE ROLES – INSTRUMENTAL ACTIVITY IN PURSUIT OF SECTORALLY-DETERMINED BUSINESS GOALS

As mentioned in Chapter 2, Isaksson et al,[28] in a research paper for the OECD, first suggested that the business model of different equity-owning funds accounts for differences in the way they behave as shareholders. In this Section, we tease out the different paradigms of shareholder behaviour, from passivity (usually with a focus upon exit) to participation in the market for corporate influence.[29] Our discussion in this Section takes place under the assumption that funds are free to choose their shareholder behaviour within the investment management model discussed in Chapter 2, so that we may be able to compare with the impact of policy and regulatory influence directed at shareholder behaviour in the next Section. We discern the incentives for funds in choosing their shareholder behaviour, which will be contrasted with the next Section that discusses how the UK Stewardship Code and the proposed EU Shareholders' Rights Directive purport to govern funds' shareholder behaviour.

---

[28] Serdar Çelik and Mats Isaksson, 'Institutional Investors as Owners' (*OECD Corporate Governance Working Paper* 2013).

[29] The term is coined by Armour and Cheffins in describing how funds decide to buy into a company in order to exert corporate influence as an essential paradigm of hedge fund activism, see John Armour and Brian Cheffins, 'The Rise and Fall (?) of Shareholder Activism by Hedge Funds' (2012) 14 *Journal of Alternative Investments* 17.

Where Assumption of a Corporate Governance Role is Less Relevant to Funds' Business Model

As discussed in Chapter 2, many funds are subject to pressures to show short-term performance. As such, their investment management model tends to focus on trading as a key strategy. This is the case with actively managed funds.[30] Passively managed funds and ETFs generate trading too in response to market movements. For funds that focus on trading, the assumption of a corporate governance role in investee companies which emphasise stewardship or constructive engagement – as described in section B above – is arguably not part of the business model. A number of commentators have found this to be true with many UK institutions.[31] The landscape is changing however in the UK, and this is largely because of 'stewardship' pressures that are being introduced, which will be discussed shortly.

It may be argued that disinterest in assuming a positive ownership role is a *natural* result of the implications of these funds' business models. For example, Taub,[32] in discussing mutual funds in the US, which are similar to retail collective investment funds in the UK and EU, concludes from empirical research that such funds are apathetic due to a number of factors such as short-termism, focus on trading and conflicts of interest. Although they did not expound a normative line of argument about whether such funds, as shareholders, *should* embrace the assumption of their corporate governance roles, Berle and Means had already in the 1930s predicted[33] that dispersed shareholders who own small fractions of corporate equity and are diversified are unlikely to be interested in participating in corporate governance in the sense implied by notions of constructive ownership or stewardship.

---

[30] See Commandment 10 in Massimiliano Caporin and Michael McAleer, 'The Ten Commandments for Managing Investments' (2009) at http://ssrn.com/abstract=1342265 which emphasises market timing.

[31] Marc Goergen and Luc Renneboog, 'Strong Managers and Passive Institutional Investors in the UK' (1998) at http://ssrn.com/abstract=137068; Marc Goergen, Luc Renneboog and Chendi Zhang, 'Do UK Institutional Shareholders Monitor Their Investee Firms?' (2007) at http://ssrn.com/abstract_id=1124406.

[32] Jennifer S Taub, 'Able but Not Willing: The Failure of Mutual Fund Advisers to Advocate for Shareholders' Rights' (2009) 34 *Journal of Corporation Law* 102.

[33] Adolf A Berle and Gardiner C Means, *The Modern Corporation and Private Property* (NY: Macmillan, 1932), p. 66.

Agency theorists would argue that such apathetic shareholders bear large agency risks in leaving corporate management unchecked. However, such shareholders may mitigate their agency risks by embracing a marketised model of corporate governance without engaging in relational forms of participation in the investee company.[34] They may regard participation in the markets through trading as an adequate channel to manage their investments and provide 'feedback' (in the form of changes in stock prices) to investee companies. Some commentators argue that trading shareholders who exit their investments amount to a market phenomenon that exerts feedback pressure on managers.[35] This is particularly the case in the market for corporate control.[36] Hence, it can be argued that shareholders that focus on trading assume a role in corporate governance that is primarily mediated through the securities markets. This business model does not treat participatory or 'voice' roles in corporate governance as imperative nor the lack thereof as a market failure.

Defensive Activism as a Beneficial Corporate Governance Role?

However, other commentators point out that the lack of an engaged corporate governance role by funds should not be thought of as reflecting a lack of good will on their part, but rather arises due to limitations in their business models and in law. Some of the aspects of their business models that disincentivise the assumption of a meaningful corporate governance role include the tendency to take small percentage stakes in a company's equity capital due to excessive diversification, the collective

---

[34] Daniëlle Adriana Maria Melis, 'The Institutional Investor Stewardship Myth' (2014) at http://ssrn.com/abstract=2445997.

[35] Exit can send a market signal and cause share price to decline, thus subjecting managers to scrutiny or the forces of the market for corporate control, but small stakes may not make a difference. See Anat R Admati and Paul Pfleiderer, 'The "Wall Street Walk" and Shareholder Activism: Exit as a Form of Voice' (2009) 22 *Review of Financial Studies* 2645, but exit can also be a 'noisy' signal and hence its effect as market discipline for managers may be muted, see Amil Dasgupta and Giorgia Piacentino, 'The Wall Street Walk when Blockholders Compete for Flows' (2014) at http://ssrn.com/abstract=1848001.

[36] E.g. James D Parrino and Robert S Harris, 'Takeovers, Management Replacement and Post-acquisition Operating Performance: Some Evidence from the 1980s' in Donald S Chew and Stuart Gillan (eds), *Corporate Governance at the Crossroads: A Book of Readings* (NY: McGraw-Hill Irwin 2005) at p. 385; A Cuervo, 'Corporate Governance Mechanisms: A Plea for Less Code and More Market Control' (2002) 10 *Corporate Governance: An International Review* 84.

action problem of coordinating the activities of numerous minority investors and the cost of assuming such roles in a fiercely competitive investment management market. Nevertheless, certain funds may be willing to assume more pronounced corporate governance roles if things are made easier for them to do so. Such funds may have relatively large stakes and long investment horizons and be concerned by the performance of certain key investee companies in which they wish to remain invested. This is characteristic of a form of shareholder behaviour termed 'defensive activism'.

Defensive shareholder activism is defined as 'a defensive safeguarding of invested capital, which is exposed at hazardous moments in the company's existence because of increasing costs of exit.'[37] This type of shareholder behaviour may be activated in the face of performance failures in an investee company and/or management failures observed to threaten the viability of the investment, in particular governance failures. Funds may be motivated to exercise voice pursuant to defensive activism particularly when problems arising from these situations are observed.[38] Hence, their unwillingness to play a meaningful corporate governance role is not absolute, and there is a case for examining existing barriers to assumption of corporate governance roles in more 'normal' situations, and introducing transaction-cost reducing mechanisms.

A key issue is therefore mitigating the cost funds incur when assuming shareholder engagement roles. Birkmose[39] points out that where the law allows more exercise of shareholder voice, the cost of accessing corporate governance roles is reduced and institutional shareholders could

---

[37] Andreas Jansson, 'No Exit!: The Logic of Defensive Shareholder Activism' (2014) 10 *Corporate Board: Roles, Duties and Composition* 16.

[38] This seems to be characteristic of UK pension and mutual funds, see Peter Cziraki, Luc Renneboog and Peter Szilagyi, 'Shareholder Activism through Proxy Proposals: The European Perspective' (2009) at http://ssrn.com/abstract=1413125, Najah Attig, Sadok El Ghoul and Omrane Guedhami, 'Institutional Investment Horizon and Firm Credit Ratings' in Narjess Boubakri, Jean-Claude Cosset and Hyacinthe Y Somé (eds), *Institutional Investors in Global Capital Market* (Emerald Publishing Ltd 2015), also see general discussion in Chapters 1 and 2, Iris H-Y Chiu, *The Foundations and Anatomy of Shareholder Activism* (2010), above.

[39] Hanne Søndergaard Birkmose and Therese Strand 'Institutional Investors: Active Ownership Through Nomination Committees' in Suzanne Young and Stephen Gates (eds), *Institutional Investors' Power to Change Corporate Behavior: International Perspectives* (Critical Studies on Corporate Responsibility, Governance and Sustainability, Volume 5, Emerald Group Publishing Limited, 2013) at pp. 201–24.

indeed be motivated to assume such roles. She highlights the example of Sweden where the nomination committee of the Board is filled mainly by shareholder representatives, and this has encouraged good shareholder participation in a range of governance issues. Perhaps we should not assume that funds are disinterested in all circumstances and it may be worthwhile to actively lower their barriers to entry into the participatory corporate governance space and motivate them to assume corporate governance roles. UK policy-makers' approach to nudge/increasingly pressure institutions to take on a more constructive role in corporate governance via the 'stewardship' rhetoric should be seen in this light. We will raise a key example to discuss how institutions may be incentivised to engage in corporate governance concerns in 'say on pay' where institutions have shown an extent of interested behaviour.

Say on Pay

Executive pay is fundamentally a contractual issue. The company and executive negotiate with each other, settling upon terms that are to a large extent conditioned by the global market for executive talent. In the UK, social dissatisfaction with levels of high executive pay has been brewing for over 20 years but the government has persistently supported shareholder governance as the main means to govern executive pay. Executive pay has been framed as a 'corporate governance' issue, and shareholders are given increasing powers to scrutinise executive remuneration. We will examine the passage of the policies in the UK but argue that looking to governance in this area from shareholders merely produces inconsistent and sporadic behaviour. As private sector actors themselves, institutions are not incentivised to criticise executive pay when the business performance of investee companies does not raise concerns and such criticisms may draw attention to fund managers' own high levels of remuneration. Furthermore, investor campaigns over executive pay have the potential to bring short-term instability to investee companies and their share prices – if senior executives view such demands as de-motivating – which institutions may not see as in their interests. However, after the global financial crisis 2007–09, institutions have been willing to criticise companies where pay and performance seem significantly misaligned. This could be explained as being relevant to their investment performance interests. Policy-makers remain keen to realise institutions' potential to govern companies in executive pay, although we are of the view that the governance activities that institutions undertake in this field are still driven by their instrumental motivations, and are hardly consistent with the social interest in high executive remuneration and the social concerns this entails, such as income disparity and social inequalities.

In the UK, the furore over executive pay arose in the mid 1990s after media reports of skyrocketing executive pay at privatised utilities companies generated extremely negative opinion. The Greenbury Committee which was tasked to look into this issue took a 'corporate governance' approach in recommending more disclosure to shareholders of the relation between executive remuneration and corporate performance, the more robust involvement of the remuneration committee of the Board in designing appropriate executive remuneration and the presentation of the committee report to shareholders in the annual report.[40]

The policy approach of co-opting shareholders to govern the area of excessive executive remuneration is arguably in line with the British tradition of negotiated regulation, which seeks out a proportionate bottom-up approach to address problems without first resorting to regulation. However, after the Greenbury recommendations were introduced, the quality and comparability of corporate disclosure on executive remuneration made to shareholders were unsatisfactory and generally low.[41] The government took further action to improve disclosure and to introduce an advisory shareholder vote on pay ('say on pay') in order to compel shareholders to engage with the issue, via the Directors' Remuneration Report Regulations 2002. The continued framing of the executive pay issue as a corporate governance issue was perhaps important to the government so that the issue would remain de-politicised and there would be no need for the government to impose further top-down intervention in an area that is essentially private in nature. Hence the objective of the Regulations was, paradoxically, to limit the government's need to further intervene in executive pay.

There is mixed evidence in the UK itself regarding the success of the DRRR prior to the financial crisis. Ferris and Maber[42] find that firms with the weakest governance improved remuneration design to be more aligned with performance, and shareholder engagement on pay – such as significant numbers of negative votes against the remuneration report – would result in companies revising remuneration packages and in some cases removing the CEO altogether. Their conclusion is therefore that the

---

[40] Richard Greenbury, *Report: Directors' Remuneration* (17 July 1995).

[41] Lee Roach, 'The Directors' Remuneration Report Regulations 2002 and the Disclosure of Executive Remuneration' (2005) 25 *Company Lawyer* 141.

[42] Fabrizio Ferri and David A Maber, 'Say on Pay Votes and CEO Compensation: Evidence from the UK' (2012) at http://ssrn.com/abstract=1420394.

advisory vote on pay had a marked governance effect. In contrast, Conyon and Sadler have reached different conclusions. They find little shareholder dissent on pay and little change in companies that have previously experienced negative votes during this period.[43]

The global financial crisis 2007–09 again brought executive pay back into scrutiny as high levels of bankers' remuneration and executive remuneration in general were discussed with social distaste.[44] There was appetite to further call executives to account for high levels of pay, as the US embarked on reform to introduce a binding say on pay every three years, followed by the UK, and now the EU.

The Dodd-Frank Act 2010 provides for the right of the Securities Exchange Commission to prescribe rules on shareholder advisory votes on executive remuneration and golden parachutes. The SEC has prescribed rules requiring issuers to put to an advisory vote at least once every three years the executive pay package for the Chief Executive officer and at least four other named executives.[45] In the UK, the Enterprise and Regulatory Reform Act 2013 was introduced to provide a binding shareholder vote on forward-looking pay policy, to take place at least every three years.[46] Further, an annual shareholder advisory vote will be taken in a backward-looking manner to signal shareholder approval or otherwise on the previous year's implementation of pay packages.[47] The EU has now introduced this as an amended Shareholders' Rights Directive that provides a binding say on pay every four years.[48]

Much faith is placed in institutions' ability to assume a role in say on pay and provide the essential monitoring governance expected of 'good corporate equity owners'. Hence law reform supports this policy direction by first providing institutions with information and then empowering

---

[43] Martin Conyon and Graham Sadler, 'Shareholder Voting and Directors' Remuneration Report Legislation: Say on Pay in the UK' (2010) 18 *Corporate Governance* 296.

[44] John Thannasoulis, 'The Case for Intervening in Bankers' Pay' (2012) 67 *The Journal of Finance* 849; Guido Ferranini and Maria Cristina Ungureanu, 'Economics, Politics, and the International Principles for Sound Compensation Practices: An Analysis of Executive Pay at European Banks' (2011) 64 *Vanderbilt Law Review* 432.

[45] Exchange Act Rule 14a–21(a).

[46] Section 439A of the Companies Act, inserted via the Enterprise and Regulatory Reform Act 2013.

[47] BIS, *Frequently Asked Questions* (March 2013).

[48] Agreed text not yet published but see http://www.consilium.europa.eu/en/press/press-releases/2016/12/16-shareholders-rights-eu-companies/.

them with 'say' in the general meeting. Commentators have observed defensive activism at play as institutions agitated for CEO turnover in light of poor corporate performance.[49] In 2012, defensive activism was particularly observed in relation to shareholder discontent over high executive pay[50] where the performance of the company might not warrant such levels of pay. A 'shareholder spring' over executive pay took place in the UK and has continued to make its presence felt to some degree in the years since then.[51] However, it has been commented[52] that institutions' engagement in say on pay is superficial, relying excessively on headline figures. Furthermore, the overall experience of the UK say on pay – during a period when the ratio between the total pay of FTSE 100 CEOs and median company employees increased from around 50 times in the late 1990s to around 150 times in 2016 – is not suggestive of robust shareholder oversight, at least from a public policy perspective.[53] There remains some scepticism as to the quality of institutions' scrutiny of say on pay, as well as their incentives to provide a consistent and engaged form of monitoring in this area that accords with social expectations.

Other commentators[54] are however of the view that shareholder engagement would only be meaningful and constructive if more were

---

[49] M Strivens, S Espenlaub and M Walker, 'The Influence of Institutional Investors over CEO Turnover in the UK' (2008) at http://ssrn.com/abstract=991595.

[50] M Strivens, S Espenlaub and M Walker, 'The Influence of Institutional Investors Over CEO Remuneration in the UK' (2007), above. This is not to say that such shareholder activism is based on sophisticated research or information processing, as some commentators have found that much of shareholder activism against high pay is responsive to top line figures only. This possibly reveals the superficiality of such shareholder engagement, and also the desire on the part of institutions to minimise cost in demonstrating engagement. See Carsten Gerner-Buerle and Tom Kirschmaier, 'Say on Pay: Do Shareholders Care?' (2016) at http://papers.ssrn.com/sol3/papers.cfm?abstract_id=2720481.

[51] 'Boards wake up to a shareholder spring', *Financial Times* (4 May 2012).

[52] Carsten Gerner-Beuerle and Tom Kirschmaier, 'Say on pay: Do Shareholders Care?' (2016), above.

[53] High Pay Centre. 'Submission to the BIS select committee corporate governance enquiry', October 2016. http://highpaycentre.org/pubs/hpc-submission-to-the-bis-select-committee-corporate-governance-enquiry-oct

[54] Paolo Santella, Enrico Baffi, Carlo Drago and Dino Lattuca, 'A Comparative Analysis of the Legal Obstacles to Institutional Investor Activism in the EU and in the US' (2009) 23 European Business Law Review 257, at http://ssrn.com/abstract=1137491; Mette Neville, 'Active Ownership and the Competition for

done to facilitate such engagement. They support legal reforms to dismantle barriers to shareholder engagement, such as in cross-border shareholding. In particular, they advocate that there is a need to overcome difficulties in ascertaining shareholder rights to vote, and procedural barriers in relation to information provision, appointment of proxies and exercise of voting rights in a cross-border context, which are not yet resolved under the 2007 EU Shareholder Rights Directive. Further, in order to overcome the collective action problem and lack of incentives due to excessive diversification, initiatives (voluntary or instituted by policy-makers) can be introduced to pool information together for institutions, facilitate discussion and dialogue among them, and therefore encourage them to assume corporate governance roles. This point has been taken up in the UK Stewardship Code,[55] and we will shortly discuss the initiatives underway and commentators' proposals in this area.

There may be a case for supporting defensive activism as it is widely seen to be beneficial for the governance of the company,[56] even if noticeable share price effects are not always achieved,[57] or indeed share price declines result.[58] However, the primary limitation in defensive activism lies in its sporadic nature. The high cost of mounting such activism and unpredictable effects on share price[59] may mean that funds are not always keen to assume such a corporate governance role. The assumption of sporadic defensive activism is largely determined by funds' perception of the instrumentality of such behaviour to their

---

International Capital – Recent Trends and Some Implications for Company Law' (2002) *European Business Organisation and Law Review* 440.

55 Principle 5 of the UK Stewardship Code 2014, see https://www.frc.org.uk/Our-Work/Codes-Standards/Corporate-governance/UK-Stewardship-Code.aspx.

56 John H Matheson and Brent A Olson, 'Corporate Law and the Long Term Shareholder Model of Corporate Governance' (1991–92) 76 *Minnesota Law Review* 1313; M Strivens, S Espenlaub and M Walker, 'The Influence of Institutional Investors Over CEO Remuneration in the UK' (2007), above; M Strivens, S Espenlaub and M Walker, 'The Influence of Institutional Investors over CEO Turnover in the UK' (2008) at http://ssrn.com/abstract=991595; M Strivens, S Espenlaub and M Walker, 'The Influence of Institutional Investors Over CEO Remuneration in the UK' (2007), above.

57 Andreas Jansson, 'No Exit!: The Logic of Defensive Shareholder Activism' (2014), above.

58 Peter Cziraki, Luc Renneboog and Peter Szilagyi, 'Shareholder Activism through Proxy Proposals: The European Perspective' (2009), above.

59 Impact on share price is important as the investment objectives of most funds are still framed in financial terms, as Chapter 2 has discussed.

investment performance and self-interest. Such shareholder behaviour is thus not a consistent mechanism of governance in the corporate governance fabric.

The Deleterious Effects of Shareholder Primacy

One should also bear in mind the potential flip side of defensive activism. Encouraging institutions to play a greater role in corporate governance could merely push them towards backing the management as a default position of inertia and of least trouble/cost.[60] They might simply decide to reinforce management decisions, providing no monitoring at all. Such a rubber-stamping of management could be sub-optimal where stakeholder issues are ignored or where externalities are unaddressed. Where shareholders have no underlying incentives to consider stakeholder or externality issues, asking them to assume corporate governance roles could only result in doubly marginalising those issues,[61] and justifying the company in neglecting stakeholder issues and third-party externalities.

Institutional shareholders are arguably mainly engaged in corporate governance roles in order to pursue their private and self-serving interests.[62] In particular, institutions are incentivised to influence their investee companies towards their short-term performance objectives. This is the phenomenon of investor myopia influencing companies to become short-termist in their outlook. As discussed earlier in Chapter 2, corporate short-termism is defined as behaviour that is dedicated to short-term strategies to keep earnings high whether or not such strategies result in value destruction for the company in the long term.[63] Corporate short termism obscures long-term thinking for the company and in due course

---

[60] For example, see 'Fund houses back the boss too often', *Financial Times* (17 May 2015); 'BlackRock, TIAA-CREF are big backers of 'overpaid' CEOs', *Financial Times* (10 May 2015); Beyond the rubber stamp: fund managers and the stewardship dilemma', *Financial Times* (2 April 2015).

[61] William W Bratton and Michael L Wachter, 'Shareholders and Social Welfare' (2013) 36 *University of Seattle Law Review* 489.

[62] Iman Anabtawi, 'Some Skepticism about Increasing Shareholder Power' (2006) 53 *UCLA Law Review* 561; Paul Rose, 'Common Agency and the Public Corporation' (2010) 63 *Vanderbilt Law Review* 1355.

[63] Corporate Values Strategy Group, *Overcoming Short-termism: A Call for a More Responsible Approach to Investment and Business Management* (New York: Aspen Institute Business and Society Programs, 2009), http://www.aspeninstitute.org/publications/overcoming-short-termism-call-more-responsible-approach-investment-business-management; Caitlin Helms, Mark Fox and Robert

could prove destructive for the long-term wealth creation role of the corporate economy.[64] In other words, it is the antithesis of the 'good corporate equity ownership' approach described in Section B above. Examples of corporate short termism are reduction in employment expense and research and development investment in order to boost short-term earnings. The buy-back of shares may also boost short-term share price and earnings, although such reduction in capital may not be optimal for companies' long-term investment plans. Further, commentators also find corporate short-termism to be related to greater indifference to stakeholder or corporate responsibility issues.[65] In this way, asking institutions to assume the corporate governance role of a 'good corporate equity owner' would bring about consequences that are far removed from the idealistic expectations articulated earlier. Instead of using their corporate governance role to connect the long-term interest of savers to wealth-creating companies, institutions may jeopardise that objective by influencing companies to focus on short-term profits and maintaining high share prices.

The reinforcing or indeed compelling effect of institutions' investor myopia syndrome has been criticised by a number of commentators. These commentators[66] argue that investor myopia has contributed greatly to risky practices in investee companies, in particular at banks and financial institutions, in the name of shareholder primacy, in the run-up to the global financial crisis 2007–09. Such excessive risk-taking had been crucial to many global banks' business strategies before the global financial crisis, which culminated in their failure or near-failure when market conditions and asset prices rapidly deteriorated.[67] Hence, there is

---

Kenagy, 'Corporate Short-Termism: Causes and Remedies' (2012) 23 *International and Comparative Company Law Review* 45.

[64] Emeka Duruigbo, 'Tackling Shareholder Short-Termism and Managerial Myopia' (2011-12) 100 *Kentucky Law Journal* 531.

[65] David Millon, 'Shareholder Social Responsibility' (2012–13) 36 *Seattle University Law Review* 911; Emeka Duruigbo, 'Stimulating Long-term Shareholding' (2011–12) 33 *Cardozo Law Review* 1734.

[66] Alan Dignam, 'The Future of Shareholder Democracy in the Shadow of the Financial Crisis' (2013) 36 University of *Seattle Law Review* 639; Jill E Fisch, 'The Mess at Morgan: Risk, Incentives and Shareholder Empowerment' (2015) 83 *University of Cincinnati Law Review* 651; Lawrence E Mitchell, 'The Legitimate Rights of Public Shareholders' (2009) 66 *Washington and Lee Law Review* 1635.

[67] Alan Dignam, 'The Future of Shareholder Democracy in the Shadow of the Financial Crisis' (2013), above; Philip Augar, 'Chasing Alpha: An Ideological Explanation of the Catastrophic Failure in the UK Financial Services Industry' in

no obvious case for encouraging shareholder engagement *as such* as there may well be deleterious effects that shareholder pressure can bring to corporate decision-making.[68]

Empirical research carried out by Buchanan et al[69] finds, very interestingly, that shareholders in the UK, who enjoy more rights under the company law framework in comparison with the US, find it less forbidding to pursue occasional episodes of engagement such as making shareholder proposals at General Meetings. However, their research also suggests that the impact of these proposals on company performance is negative, particularly in comparison to results achieved for US companies. That said, contrary research shows that the desire to please short-termist shareholders can sometimes force companies to be innovative and to re-think their growth and profitability strategies. This can in certain circumstances be beneficial for their long-term performance too.[70]

Nonetheless, it should be recognised that institutions' interest in corporate governance is essentially bound up with their investment management objectives and their assumption of corporate governance roles or influence is necessarily instrumental in nature. The UK and EU should be cautious of treating institutional shareholder engagement as an unequivocal good, and regulatory interest may be better directed at reviewing shareholder power under existing legal frameworks. Shareholder powers may indeed be in need of moderation[71] or recalibration, for example, by the imposition of fiduciary duties, so that self-serving and influential shareholders may be constrained from inflicting long-term damage on the company or other stakeholders' interests.[72]

James Hawley, Shyam Kamath and Andrew Williams (eds), *Corporate Governance Failures* (University of Pennsylvania Press 2014) at Chapter 4, 83.

[68] Lawrence E Mitchell, 'The Legitimate Rights of Public Shareholders' (2009), above.

[69] Bonnie G Buchanan, Jeffrey M Netter, Annette B Poulsen and Tina Yang, 'Shareholder Proposal Rules and Practice: Evidence from a Comparison of the United States and United Kingdom' (2012) 49 *American Business Law Journal* 739.

[70] Mariassunta Gianetti and Xiaoyun Yu, 'The Corporate Finance Benefits of Short Horizon Investors' (*ECGI Working Paper* 2016).

[71] E.g. Lynn Stout, *The Shareholder Value Myth: How Putting Shareholders First Harms Investors, Corporations, and the Public* (Berrett-Koehler Publishers 2012).

[72] Iman Anabtawi and Lynn Stout, 'Fiduciary Duties for Activist Shareholders' (2008) 60 *Stanford Law Rev* 1255; Roberta Karmel, 'Should A Duty To The Corporation Be Imposed On Institutional Shareholders?' (2004) 60 *Business Lawyer* 1.

In the next Section, we will discuss funds for whom the assumption of a meaningful corporate governance role appears to accord with their business model, and posit other concerns in relation to their shareholder behaviour.

Where Funds Embrace a Corporate Governance Role – the Case of Offensive Activism

Some funds may view the assumption of corporate governance roles as essential to their business models and as a strategy to drive investment performance. For example, 'offensive activism', which Armour and Cheffins define as taking an equity stake in order to facilitate corporate governance interventions,[73] has become an important investment management strategy for some funds. We are of the view that the assumption of such a corporate governance role may bring about benefits that in some respects may be aligned with wider public interest, but one must not be too idealistic. These corporate governance roles are first and foremost driven by commercial self-interest and certain undesirable consequences, viewed from the perspective of public interest, could also ensue.

Private equity funds take large concentrated stakes in order to assume management or governance powers, while hedge funds and sovereign wealth funds take minority stakes. Activist hedge funds typically take minority stakes that are significant enough to initiate activism, whereas sovereign wealth funds tend in practice to pursue a more low-profile governance approach despite the commonly-aired suspicion that many may be influenced by the strategic political objectives of the governments in their home countries.[74]

Private equity funds have been both praised and criticised for their approach of concentrated ownership stakes in selected companies. Concentrated stakes allow funds to make their voice heard in corporate strategy and governance. Private equity fund strategies are oriented towards growing or transforming companies and generating value over the maturity of the fund, usually between seven to ten years. Hence involvement in corporate strategy and governance is pursuant to that objective. Empirical research has found that hands-on involvement by private equity fund managers is in general strategically valuable to

---

[73] John Armour and Brian Cheffins, 'The Rise and Fall (?) of Shareholder Activism by Hedge Funds' (2012) 14 *Journal of Alternative Investments* 17.

[74] As Chapter 8 discusses, such subtle 'activist' influences are much less observed in relation to sovereign wealth funds' foreign investments.

investee companies, overall producing beneficial effects for the generation of value for the investee company.[75] Private equity funds invest not only capital but also endeavour and expertise to nurture the productivity of a business in the hope of reaping real competitiveness gains in due course.[76] In this sense, private equity funds could be a model for stewardship and long-term investing that mediates between savers' needs and wealth creation in the corporate economy.

However, private equity funds could also be involved in corporate governance in another sense – usually by increasing the company's leverage. This is justified as a means of exerting discipline on management, as free cash flow is seen as susceptible to the agency problem.[77] However, in this monitoring model, private equity funds may exploit leverage to benefit themselves, such as by paying themselves excessive dividends[78] while the company is laden with debt repayments. There is

[75] Ronald W Masulis and Randall S Thomas, 'Does Private Equity Create Wealth?' (2009) *University of Chicago Law Review* 1; Viral V Acharya, Moritz Hahn and Conor Kehoe, 'Corporate Governance and Value Creation: Evidence from Private Equity' (2009) at http://ssrn.com/abstract=1324016; Viral V Acharya, Conor Kehoe and Michael Reyner, 'Private Equity vs PLC Boards in the U.K.: A Comparison of Practices and Effectiveness' (*ECGI Working Paper*, 2008); Stefano Bonini, 'The Effects of Private Equity Investors on the Governance of Companies' (2015) at http://ssrn.com/abstract=2647219; Natee Amornsiripanitch, Paul A Gompers and Yuhai Xuan, 'More than Money: Venture Capitalists on Boards' (2015) at http://ssrn.com/abstract=2586592; James Jianxin Gong and Steve Yuching Wu, 'CEO Turnover in Private Equity Sponsored Leveraged Buyouts' (2011) 19 *Corporate Governance: An International Review* 195; Steven Toms, Nick Wilson and Mike Wright, 'The Evolution of Private Equity: Corporate Restructuring in the UK, c.1945–2010' (2012) at http://ssrn.com/abstract=2145445.

[76] Douglas Cumming, Donald Siegel and Mike Wright, 'Private Equity, Leveraged Buyouts and Governance' (2007) at http://papers.ssrn.com/sol3/papers.cfm?abstract_id==983802; Ann-Kristin Achleitner, Eva Lutz, Kerry Herman and Josh Lerner, 'New Look: Going Private with Private Equity Support' (2009) at http://ssrn.com/abstract=1120230.

[77] Michael Jensen, 'The Economic Case For Private Equity' (2007) at http://ssrn.com/abstract=963530; Ronald W Masulis and Randall S Thomas, 'Does Private Equity Create Wealth?' (2009), above; Ann-Kristin Achleitner, André Betzer and Jasmin Gider, 'Do Corporate Governance Motives Drive Hedge Funds and Private Equity Activities?' (2009) at http://ssrn.com/abstract=1292896.

[78] Richard P Nielsen, 'The Private Equity-Leveraged Buyout Form of Finance Capitalism: Ethical and Social Issues, and Potential Reforms' (2008) 18 *Business Ethics Quarterly* 379.

empirical evidence[79] and case studies[80] that suggest that such an approach has been deleterious to many investee companies, usually struggling with heavy debt long after the private equity fund has cashed out.[81] In the latter case, the assumption of an 'engaged' corporate governance role by the fund may result in 'raiding' instead of growing the investee company, and involve a ruthlessly instrumental use of corporate governance rights and privileges. These practices have also caused deleterious effects for stakeholders such as employees[82] and may profoundly damage the long-term prospects of affected companies.

Where activist hedge funds are concerned, being minority shareholders means that they are not automatically able to assume powerful corporate governance rights and roles in the manner of a private equity fund with a controlling equity stake. However, they are seen as being able to exert pressure by forging alliances with other investors and their proxy advisors, and by running high profile campaigns in the media. Some view their activism as a much-needed form of monitoring for investee companies,[83] so as to ensure that the management of these companies focuses

---

[79] William W Bratton, 'Private Equity's Three Lessons for Agency Theory' (2008) 3 *Brooklyn Journal of Corporate, Financial & Commercial Law* 1; Peter Harbula, 'Operating Performance, Valuation, Leverage and Corporate Governance Of Leveraged Buy- Out Transactions: A Continental European Perspective' (2011) at http://ssrn.com/abstract=1876454.

[80] Jules Domenichini, 'Public to Private Transactions, Private Equity Ownership and IPOs: A Case Study of Debenhams' (2012) at http://ssrn.com/abstract=1516293; Wolter Lemstra and John P M Groenewegen, 'Private Equity Leveraged Buyout and Public Values: The Bankruptcy of Eircom, Ireland' (2012) at http://ssrn.com/abstract=2032222.

[81] Contrary evidence and opinion also exist, see Frederik Vinten, 'The Performance of Private Equity Buyout Fund Owned Firms' (2007) at http://ssrn.com/abstract=1114603 on how financial engineering introduced by private equity funds generate value for investee companies.

[82] Marc Goergen, Noel O'Sullivan and Geoffrey Wood, 'The Employment Consequences of Private Equity Acquisitions: The Case of Institutional Buy Outs' (2014) at http://ssrn.com/abstract=2459890.

[83] Nicole M Boyson and Robert M Mooradian, 'Corporate Governance and Hedge Fund Activism' (2011) 14 *Rev Deriv Res* 169; Thomas W Briggs, 'Corporate Governance and the New Hedge Fund Activism: An Empirical Analysis' (2007) 32 *Journal of Corporation Law* 681; Shane Goodwin, *Corporate Governance and Hedge Fund Activism* (Aug 2015) at http://ssrn.com/abstract=2646293; Paul Rose and Bernard Sharfman, 'Shareholder Activism as a Corrective Mechanism in Corporate Governance' (2014) *Brigham Young University Law Review* 1015. Further, there is empirical research that shows actual governance improvements such as better financial reporting, see C S Agnes

on value creation. A number of commentators[84] call such activists essential 'governance entrepreneurs' who provide a much-needed role in the market to monitor investee companies where mainstream institutional funds have been excessively passive. Moreover, there seems to be a significant body of consistent[85] empirical evidence on positive operating performance for companies subject to activist campaigns five to ten years after the campaign has concluded and the hedge fund has exited.[86]

However, some commentators[87] are of the view that positive empirical findings supporting the legacy of hedge fund activism could be due to favourable market conditions unrelated to their activist efforts, and it has been observed that hedge funds are highly pro-cyclical. They rely on bull markets to maximise the outcomes of their activist strategies, which may explain why Armour and Cheffins[88] observed a sharp decrease in instances of hedge fund activism in the couple of years during the global financial crisis 2007–09.

At a more general level, hedge fund activism, especially that practised by certain American houses which specialise in running highly visible

---

Cheng, Henry He Huang and Yinghua Li, 'Hedge Fund Intervention and Accounting Conservatism' (2013) at http://ssrn.com/abstract=2519286; and reduction in managerial rent-seeking, see Heqing Zhu, 'The Preventive Effect of Hedge Fund Activism' (2013) at http://ssrn.com/abstract=2369533.

[84] Paul Rose and Bernard Sharfman, 'Shareholder Activism as a Corrective Mechanism in Corporate Governance' (2014), above; Bernard Sharfman, 'A Theory of Shareholder Activism and its Place in Corporate Law' (2015) 82 *Tennessee Law Review* 791.

[85] But see evidence to the contrary, John C Coffee and Darius Palia, 'The Impact of Hedge Fund Activism: Evidence and Implications' (2014) at http://ssrn.com/abstract=2496518; Frank Partnoy, 'U.S. Hedge Fund Activism' (2015) at http://ssrn.com/abstract= 2585290.

[86] Lucian Bebchuk, Alon Brav and Wei Jiang, 'The Long-Term Effects of Hedge Fund Activism' (2015) 115 *Columbia Law Review* 2085; Marco Becht, Julian Franks, Jeremy Grant and Hannes Wagner, 'The Returns to Hedge Fund Activism: An International Study' (2014) at http://ssrn.com/abstract=2376271; Alon Brav, Wei Jiang and Hyunseob Kim, 'The Real Effects of Hedge Fund Activism: Productivity, Asset Allocation, and Labor Outcomes' (2015) at http://ssrn.com/abstract=1551953. On medium term value creation, see Nick W A Stokman, 'Influences of Hedge Fund Activism on the Medium Term Target Value' (2007) at http://ssrn.com/abstract=1019968.

[87] 'Activist investors' success owes much to wider bull run', *Financial Times* (2 March 2015); Mike Burkhart and Amil Dasgupta, 'Activist Funds, Leverage and Procyclicality' (2014) at http://ssrn.com/abstract=2169880.

[88] John Armour and Brian Cheffins, 'The Rise and Fall (?) of Shareholder Activism by Hedge Funds' (2012), above.

(sometimes aggressive), persistent and influential campaigns against incumbent boards and management,[89] could produce a wider effect upon corporate culture. Some commentators find qualitative changes in terms of better corporate governance and management accountability after an episode of hedge fund activism.[90] Senior management of companies could become more aware of being scrutinised and may be incentivised to rectify corporate governance sub-optimalities, engage in responsible behaviour and cover all possible tracks in terms of performance and governance in order not to be targeted.[91] In an 'extreme' way, hedge fund activism could provide the 'scare' factor that redresses the market failure of excessive and unchecked managerial power. Such a role would place hedge fund activists in the position of a 'gatekeeper' as described by Sheehan.[92]

However, other commentators[93] are of the view that hedge fund activism only brings disruption to the management role and makes it more likely that Boards will be captured by short-termist shareholder demands, to the detriment of other stakeholders such as employees. Empirical research[94] shows that only the most disruptive forms of shareholder activism, such as agitating for the merger, sale or sale of part of a company, achieve significant share price reactions. Such disruptive behaviour could be deleterious to wider stakeholder interests and the

---

[89] Dionysia Katelouzou, 'Myths and Realities of Hedge Fund Activism: Some Empirical Evidence' (2013) 7 *Virginia Law and Business Review* 459.

[90] Shane Goodwin, Akshay Singh, Walter Slipetz and Ramesh Rao, 'Myopic Investor Myth Debunked: The Long-term Efficacy of Shareholder Advocacy in the Boardroom' (2014) at http://ssrn.com/abstract=2555701.

[91] 'Navigating Today's Shareholder Activism Landscape', *Harvard Law School Forum* (8 July 2014).

[92] Kym Sheehan, 'Great Expectations, Institutional Investors, Executive Remuneration and Say on Pay', in James Hawley, Shyam Kamath and Andrew Williams (eds), *Corporate Governance Failures* (University of Pennsylvania Press 2014) at Chapter 6, 115.

[93] David J Berger and Kenneth M Murray, 'As the Market Turns: Corporate Governance Litigation in an Age of Stockholder Activism' (2009) 5 *NYU Journal of Law & Business* 207; Dan Bernhardt and Ed Nosal, 'Gambling for Dollars: Strategic Hedge Fund Manager Investment' (2013) at http://ssrn.com/abstract=2367475; William W Bratton, 'Hedge Funds and Governance Targets' (2007) 95 *Georgetown Law Journal* 1375. But see Dionysia Katelouzou, 'Myths and Realities of Hedge Fund Activism: Some Empirical Evidence' (2013), above.

[94] 'Activist hedge funds not so good for shareholders', *Financial Times* (20 May 2015); Marco Becht, Julian Franks, Jeremy Grant and Hannes Wagner, 'The Returns to Hedge Fund Activism: An International Study' (2014) at http://ssrn.com/abstract=2376271.

longer-term prospects for the enterprise.[95] Commentators may be rightly cautious and sceptical of the corporate governance role that hedge fund activists assume in many instances.

Hedge fund activism may therefore be based on an instrumental exploitation of shareholder rights in company law, whether the right to vote, influence or participate in decision-making at general meetings or to exercise voice in more informal ways. Partnoy and Thomas[96] refer to hedge fund activism as a form of 'financial innovation' in investment strategy that is mediated through its corporate governance role. Hedge funds have shown special interest in merger arbitrage, capital issues such as buybacks and dividends, and exploitation of short term information asymmetries, all for the purposes of exploiting for financial gain. Such exploitation could be seen as an application of their quasi proprietary rights, such as in asking for share buybacks in order to extract value from return of capital,[97] or in engagement, voting or litigation pursuant to their profit-extraction agenda.[98] Although in the case of share buybacks it could be argued that the reduction of free cash flow may reduce agency

---

[95] Robby Heuben and Gert Straetmans, 'Shareholder Rights and Responsibilities in the Context of Corporate Social Responsibility' (2016) 27 *European Business Law Review* 615 argue that some forms of offensive activism raise the risk profile of the company, having implications for their cost of raising capital and their longer term prospects.

[96] Frank S Partnoy and Randall S Thomas, 'Gap Filling, Hedge Funds, and Financial Innovation' (2006) at http://ssrn.com/abstract=931254.

[97] The self interests of the activist would be predominant as share repurchases bring about increase in share price and a windfall from the capital return, see Balasingham Balachandran, Keryn Chalmers and Janto Haman, 'On-Market Share Buybacks, Exercisable Share Options and Earnings Management' (2008) 48 *Accounting and Finance* 25; Harrison Liu and Edward P Swanson, 'Are Corporate Share Repurchases Used to Support Overvalued Equity?' (2013) at http://papers.ssrn.com/sol3/papers.cfm?abstract_id=2283764; José-Miguel Gaspar, Massimo Massa, Pedro Matos, Rajdeep Patgiri and Zahid Rehman, 'Can Buybacks be a Product of Shorter Shareholder Horizons?' (2005) at http://papers.ssrn.com/sol3/papers.cfm?abstract_id=649482. This idea also aligns with managerial incentives, see Jesse M Fried, 'Open Market Repurchases: Signaling or Managerial Opportunism?' (2001) 2 *Theoretical Inquiries in the Law* 865 and also again in 'Informed Trading and False Signaling with Open Market Repurchases' (2005) 93 *California Law Review* 1323.

[98] Frank S Partnoy and Randall S Thomas, 'Gap Filling, Hedge Funds, and Financial Innovation' (2006), above.

problems,[99] it also reduces companies' precautionary cash reserves[100] and may divert from useful long-term projects.[101] Further extreme forms of exploitation of proprietary rights in relation to shareholding have been observed where hedge funds engage in empty voting, i.e. exercising the right of voting although they have hedged their interest in the shares away.[102] Although empirical studies suggest that empty voting has yet to impose major negative effects on governance, the perverse incentives in empty voting are of concern to policy-makers.[103] Hence, a number of commentators have argued that the substance of hedge fund activism is short-termist[104] and disruptive in nature.

In the US, the high profile Valeant Pharmaceuticals episode in 2015/2016 exerted a particularly negative impact on public perception and confidence in hedge fund activism. Valeant Pharmaceuticals, a Canadian company listed on the New York and Toronto Stock Exchanges, was targeted in 2015 by Bill Ackman, a well-known activist investor. Following the acquisition of a 9 per cent equity stake by Ackman's activist fund, Pershing Square Capital, Valeant carried out a Board shakeup and added Ackman to the Board. However, in late 2015 Valeant's share price collapsed and continued to fall in the wake of public controversy over its

---

[99] Chuan-San Wang, Norman Strong, Samuel Tung and Steve Lin, 'Share Repurchases, the Clustering Problem, and the Free Cash Flow Hypothesis' (2009) 38 *Financial Management* 487.

[100] Lee Pinkowitz, Rene M Stultz and Rohan Williamson, 'Is There a U.S. High Cash Holdings Puzzle after the Financial Crisis?' (2012) at http://papers.ssrn.com/sol3/papers.cfm?abstract_id=2064046; Tom W Bates, Kathryn M Kahle and Rene M Stultz, 'Why Do U.S. Firms Hold So Much More Cash than They Used To?' (2009) 64 *Journal of Finance* 1985.

[101] Lee Pinkowitz, Rene M Stultz and Rohan Williamson, 'Is There a U.S. High Cash Holdings Puzzle after the Financial Crisis?' (2012), above; Marcel Kahan and Edward B Rock, 'Hedge Funds in Corporate Governance and Corporate Control' (2007) 155 *University of Pennsylvania Law Review* 1021. But see Zhongzhi He, Jiaping Qiu and Tingfeng Tang, 'Hedge Fund Activism and Corporate Innovation' (2014) at http://ssrn.com/abstract=2411739.

[102] Henry T C Hu and Bernard B S Black, 'The New Vote Buying: Empty Voting and Hidden (Morphable) Ownership' (2006) 76 *Southern California Law Review* 811.

[103] Wolf-Georg Ringe, 'Hedge Funds and Risk Decoupling: The Empty Voting Problem in the European Union' (2013) 36 *Seattle University Law Review* 1027.

[104] Véronique Bessière, Michael Kaestner and Anne-Laurence Lafont, 'Hedge Fund Activism: Insights from a French Clinical Study' (2011) 21 *Applied Financial Economics* 1225 on governance being used as an excuse to engage for instrumental returns.

pharmaceutical pricing policies, with extremely negative implications for the financial performance of Ackman's fund and the reputation of the hedge fund industry more generally. The role of activist investors who wish to extract short-term value from targeted companies was widely reported as not being constructive for corporate culture.[105] Developments are now afoot in the US to introduce a Bill to limit hedge fund activists' potency in order to compel the disclosure of their stake promptly and to limit their wolf pack behaviour. Hence, the ambivalence towards hedge fund activism is beginning to be manifested at policy-making levels.

Although activist hedge funds and private equity funds may adopt differing investment management practices from mainstream funds – which tend towards marketisation and disengagement from corporate governance roles – the verdict is mixed on their role in constructively engaging in corporate wealth creation over the long term. It could be argued that their instrumental use of corporate governance powers and rights to extract value are essentially self-serving and near-termist in nature. It is noted that Pacces[106] argues that short-termism should not of itself amount to a negative verdict for hedge fund activism, but the efficiencies and benefits achieved for the company should be assessed on a case by case basis. Nevertheless, even if their instrumental use of corporate governance activism generates significant immediate high returns, it is questionable whether such high returns trickle down to investors in a significant measure. This is because activist hedge fund managers charge high fees and grant themselves generous performance-related rewards for deploying the resources necessary for taking on activist roles.[107]

Where sovereign wealth funds adopt governance roles, we observe that it is largely pursuant to strategic interests, usually in domestic companies, such as national champions. A number of commentators observe that such stakes allow the state to grow and nurture key national companies and industries, and the fund may work behind the scenes, using state

---

[105] 'Activist hedge funds found wanting in essential tasks', *Financial Times* (29 March 2016).

[106] Alessio M Pacces, 'Exit, Voice and Loyalty from the Perspective of Hedge Funds Activism in Corporate Governance' (*ECGI Working Paper*, 2 August 2016) at http://papers.ssrn.com/sol3/papers.cfm?abstract_id=2805982.

[107] Although the performance fee model has been argued to be a key incentive for outperformance by these funds, see Robert C Illig, 'The Promise of Hedge Fund Governance: How Incentive Compensation Can Enhance Institutional Investor Monitoring' (2008) 60 *Alabama Law Review* 41.

influence to help these companies.[108] In such cases, other investors may benefit as free riders from the sovereign wealth funds' strategic involvement over the long term. However, it is also observed that the strategic interests of the state reflected in the sovereign wealth fund stake may not be so benign in some cases, where tunnelling and use of corporate assets or opportunities for self-serving purposes may feature.[109] In such a case, other shareholders, in particular independent minority shareholders in such companies, may be prejudiced and may find it difficult or impossible to obtain redress.

Private Litigation as an Instrumental Assumption of Corporate Governance Rights?

Another way in which corporate governance rights deriving from the ownership of corporate equity may be asserted lies in the use of private litigation to enforce shareholder rights and obtain forms of compensation. Derivative and securities litigation is open to institutional investors in an appropriate case, and the threat of litigation could amount to a powerful form of discipline for management. Derivative litigation can be used to challenge directorial behaviour in cases where directors have behaved negligently or in breach of trust or loyalty. Securities litigation can be used to discipline the investee company and directors in terms of ensuring that the reporting they make is accurate and not misleading.

In the UK however, the scene is very quiet where derivative or securities litigation is concerned, and it does not seem that mounting litigation is an attractive option for institutions. Where derivative litigation is concerned, the UK Companies Act 2006 codifies the common law derivative action, and provides a right for a minority shareholder to take an action on behalf of the company against a wrong-doer, which could be a majority shareholder or director of the company, or a third party. The Act provides for a procedure for claimants to seek permission from the

[108] Adam D Dixon and Ashby H B Monk, 'Rethinking the Sovereign in Sovereign Wealth Funds' (2011) 37 *Transactions of the Institute of British Geographers* 104; Jing Li, 'State As An Entrepreneur: A Study of the Investment Contractual Terms and Level of Control of China's Sovereign Wealth Fund in its Portfolio Firms' (2014) at http://ssrn.com/abstract=2617150; Henry Wai-Chung Yeung, 'From National Development to Economic Diplomacy? Governing Singapore's Sovereign Wealth Funds' (2011) 24 *The Pacific Review* 625.

[109] Jonathan G S Koppell, 'Political Control for China's State-Owned Enterprises: Lessons from America's Experience with Hybrid Organizations' (2007) 20 *Governance* 255–78; Peter A Gourevitch and James Shinn, *Political Power and Corporate Control* (Princeton University Press 2005) at pp. 192–200.

court in order to continue a derivative action on behalf of the company.[110] The court determines whether the action is absolutely barred, based on several criteria, or if not absolutely barred, whether it should be permitted, based on a list of criteria.[111]

Although the legal framework for derivative actions accommodates derivative litigation taken by members of all types of companies, derivative actions have really only been pursued by members of privately held companies. Empirical research by Armour, Black, Cheffins and Nolan[112] shows that only very rarely is a case filed against directors of a publicly traded company under corporate law claiming damages, and one has to go back to the early 1980s to find a reported UK case where a director of a public company was a defendant in a derivative suit. The reasons that deter minority investors in publicly traded companies from taking derivative actions relate to the upfront cost of such actions and cumbersome civil procedure before the UK Companies Act 2006.[113] It

---

110 Section 261, UK Companies Act 2006.

111 Section 263, UK Companies Act 2006. See critical reflections by Arad Reisberg, 'Derivative Claims under the Companies Act 2006: Much Ado About Nothing?' in J Armour and J Payne (eds), *Rationality in Company Law: Essays in Honour of DD Prentice* (Oxford: Hart Publishing, 2009) at p. 17.

112 John Armour, Bernard Black, Brian Cheffins and Richard Nolan, 'Private Enforcement of Corporate Law: An Empirical Comparison of the UK and US' (2009) 6 *Journal of Empirical Legal Studies* 687.

113 Above at 692. The court deciding whether to permit a derivative action must refuse to permit such an action if a reasonable person who has in mind the objective of promoting the success of the company would not seek to continue the claim, or where the matter giving rise to the derivative claim has been authorised or ratified by the company, s263, Companies Act 2006. Ratification can only validly occur if a majority of disinterested shareholders vote in favour of ratification, s239, Companies Act 2006. It can be argued that a derivative claimant going against directors, for example, of a publicly traded company, would face a steeper uphill task than a derivative claimant suing on behalf of a privately held company. In derivative actions brought on behalf of privately held companies, the court has examined various factors to determine if a derivative claimant's action is likely to promote the success of the company, in terms of the size of the claim; the strength of the claim; the cost of the proceedings; the company's ability to fund the proceedings; the ability of the potential defendants to satisfy a judgment; the impact on the company if it lost the claim; any disruption to the company's activities while the claim is pursued; whether the prosecution of the claim would damage the company in other ways, see *Iesini v Westrip Holdings Ltd* [2009] EWHC 2526 (Ch); *Stainer v Lee* [2010] EWHC 1539 (Ch). The court is very conscious of the cost-benefit of permitting the continuation of the derivative claim in relation to impact upon the company. Further, permission to continue the derivative claim has been refused in a case

can be surmised that minority investors in a publicly traded company may not find it worthwhile to incur the cost of a derivative claim as the stakes are just not high enough to justify the cost. Minority investors who are part of the widely dispersed ownership landscape in relation to a publicly traded company may also suffer from a collective action problem in terms of taking the initiative to commence derivative actions.

Given that the corporate governance requirements[114] for publicly traded companies include a balanced slate of executive and independent directors, representations of diversity on the Board and the institution of dedicated committees of the Board such as nomination, remuneration, audit and risk to undertake specific key responsibilities, it is much harder for a derivative claimant to impeach a directorial decision made within the context of optimal corporate governance structures and successfully allege that the derivative claim would have the objective of promoting the success of the company. The court may also view the disruptive potential of a derivative action as being far from the objective of promoting the success of the company. Adverse impact on share price and higher cost of corporate finance for the company may follow, and these factors would prevent a derivative claimant's case from proceeding.

Further, the good faith[115] of the derivative claimant is also relevant for the court's consideration in deciding whether to permit the continuation of a derivative claim. The court has interpreted 'good faith' to mean that the derivative claimant's predominant purpose in the proceedings is to vindicate the company's rights.[116] Where a minority investor in a publicly traded company is concerned, it could be difficult to satisfy the good faith requirement if derivative actions are instituted as a strategy in shareholder activism. This is a strategy not unfamiliar to US-based hedge funds and, although relatively successful in the US,[117] it has been resisted and frowned upon in the UK.[118]

---

where there may be issues of breaches of directors' duties but where the decision could make commercial sense and the company has not been financially jeopardised, see *Kleanthous v Paphitis and Ors* [2011] EWHC 2287 (Ch).

114 UK Corporate Governance Code 2012.

115 Section 263(3)(a), UK Companies Act 2006.

116 *Franbar Holdings Ltd v Patel and others* [2008] EWHC 1534 (Ch); [2008] WLR (D) 220.

117 Stephen J Choi, Jill E Fisch and A C Pritchard, 'Do Institutions Matter? The Impact of the Lead Plaintiff Provision of the Private Securities Litigation Reform Act' (2005) 83 *Washington University Law Quarterly* 869.

118 'Polygon Calls in Lawyers to Halt British Energy Restructuring', *The Independent* (1 Aug 2004); Iris H-Y Chiu, *Foundations and Anatomy of Shareholder Activism* (2010), above at Chapter 3.

Where private securities litigation is concerned, investors may bring an action for enforcement against issuers if they suffered losses as a result of any untrue or misleading statement or material omission in any prospectus or any listing particulars,[119] or in any continuing disclosure that issuers are obliged to make.

The general law on negligent misstatements is applicable to the civil enforcement of securities mis-disclosure. Under the *Hedley Byrne*[120] criteria, an actionable negligent misstatement can only be sustained by parties to whom the issuers owe a duty of care. A duty of care is owed to persons who are in a 'proximate' relationship to the issuer and whose reliance on statements made by the issuer stems from the issuer's assumption of responsibility over them. Further causation of loss has to be proved and losses must satisfy the general tortious standard of remoteness. In one case,[121] the court stated clearly that the subscribers to securities offered to the public in an initial public offer are persons to whom the issuer owes a duty of care because these are sufficiently proximate persons whose reliance on the issuer's disclosure forms the main basis for investment. The court also extended the issuer's duty of care to buyers of these securities in the secondary market in the immediate aftermarket trading.

However, investors have to prove causation of loss as being primarily due to the issuer's disclosure breaches. Therefore, if investors would have bought or sold anyway for reasons other than being influenced by the defective disclosures, civil enforcement may not be successful. The court in *Hall* opined that causation must be actual and reasonable and meet both a subjective and an objective standard.[122]

There is a dearth of private securities litigation in relation to prospectuses for publicly issued securities in the UK. There has only been one case of private securities litigation against a publicly traded issuer between 1990 and 2006.[123] The lack of private securities litigation in relation to prospectuses could be due to the potential cost of litigation in this area. The UK does not support a contingency fee-based system for

---

[119] Prospectus Directive 2003, Art. 6; UK Financial Services and Markets Act 2000, s. 90.

[120] *Hedley Byrne & Co Ltd. v Heller & Partners Ltd* [1964] AC 465.

[121] *Possfund Custodian Trustee Ltd v Diamond* [1996] 1 WLR 1351.

[122] *Hall v Cable and Wireless* [2009] EWHC 1793.

[123] *Axa Equity & Law Life Assurance Society plc v National Westminster Bank* [1998] C.L.C. 1177; J Armour, B Black, B Cheffins and R Nolan, 'Private Enforcement of Corporate Law: An Empirical Comparison of the UK and US' (2009), above.

financing private securities litigation, hence any minority investor would be faced with a free rider problem in organising representative litigation and would have to bear the cost of litigation up front. The UK does provide a class litigation mechanism in the form of a representative action that can be taken by a group of seven claimants or more, and hence in terms of civil procedure, access to justice is not fraught with procedural barriers. However, the forbidding cost of mounting litigation without the support of the contingency fee system is perhaps the main impediment to civil enforcement.

Further, shareholders can potentially sue their investee companies and directors for failure to inform secondary markets of timely disclosure required under the continuing mandatory disclosure regime.[124] However, the legal framework for *ex post* investor enforcement against breaches of mandatory continuing disclosure obligations is highly restrictive in the UK. Investors have a right to bring civil actions for breaches of continuing disclosure requirements only if they establish that they have suffered loss as a result of –

(a) a misleading statement or dishonest omission in certain published information relating to the securities, or
(b) a dishonest delay in publishing such information.[125]

The requirement to prove dishonesty in two of the scenarios of mis-disclosures above would likely pose an uphill challenge for most investors. The standard of dishonesty is one of knowingly or deceitfully concealing information.[126] It is akin to the common law tort of deceit,[127] but investors are able to adduce evidence of dishonesty if no reasonable person would have made a similar decision with regard to the impugned disclosure.[128] The nevertheless challenging evidential bar would effectively mean that investor civil litigation as a form of *ex post* enforcement is highly discouraged.

---

[124] Market Abuse Regulation 2014, Art. 12 which was the same as Art 6, Market Abuse Directive 2003 originally enacted; Transparency Directive 2004, Arts 4, 5 and 7, all enacted in the FCA Handbook DTR.

[125] This is now found in Schedule 10A, Financial Services and Markets Act 2010 (U.K.) by virtue of reg. 3(1) of the Financial Services and Markets Act 2000 (Liability of Issuers) Regulations 2010 (S.I. 2010/1192) (U.K.).

[126] Financial Services and Markets Act 2010, Schedule 10A, Art. 5 (U.K.).

[127] *Derry v Peek* [1889] 14 AC 337.

[128] Financial Services and Markets Act 2010, Schedule 10A, Art. 6

There has only been one case of civil enforcement of continuing disclosure breaches in the UK. In *Hall*,[129] Cable and Wireless, in selling its interest in One2One to DeutscheTelekom in 2002, provided a ratings clause guaranteeing that its credit rating would not fall below a certain point and, should that happen, Cable & Wireless's guarantee for certain tax liabilities for One2One would be triggered. The company failed to disclose in their annual financial statements certain information which, when it came to light, led to losses and a ratings downgrading. Cable & Wireless was subsequently sued by a group of investors who claimed to have suffered loss as a result of such omission to disclose. However, the court in that case was dealing with continuing disclosure obligations as part of the listing rules and not as a statutory requirement. It ruled that the investors did not have standing to sue for a breach of statutory duty. The claimants also failed on the issue of whether a common law action for negligent omission would have sustained because they sold shares before the adverse announcement was made and therefore did not rely on the issuer's continuing disclosure.

Given the substantive difficulties in pursuing derivative and securities litigation in the UK, as well as the dis-incentives involved in starting such litigation, private litigation is rarely used in the instrumental assumption of corporate governance roles by funds. Funds that wish to engage in corporate governance roles have resorted to the market for corporate influence as discussed above.

The discussion above shows that the assumption of corporate governance roles by institutions takes on different forms as driven by different instrumental motivations. The outcomes of such shareholder engagement are mixed and not necessarily an unequivocal good. This is simply down to every shareholder, including the state, having self-interests to serve,[130] and not necessarily having the interests of the company as a whole over the long term, or indeed the public interest, in mind.[131] There is certainly not much alignment between the concept of 'good corporate equity

---

[129] *Hall* v *Cable and Wireless* [2009] EWHC 1793.

[130] Iman Anabtawi, 'Some Skepticism about Increasing Shareholder Power' (2006), above; Paul Rose, 'Common Agency and the Public Corporation' (2010), above. We disagree with the more simplistic version of the unified shareholder presented in George W Dent Jnr, 'The Essential Unity of Shareholders and the Myth of Investor Short-Termism' (2010) 35 *Delaware Journal of Corporate Law* 97.

[131] William W Bratton and Michael L Wachter, 'Shareholders and Social Welfare' (2013), above; Dalia Tsuk Mitchell, 'Shareholders As Proxies: The Contours of Shareholder Democracy' (2006) 63 *Washington and Lee Law Rev*

ownership', which we described in Section B, and the real-world behaviour of institutional shareholders. In this context, there should not be an unquestioning endorsement of shareholder engagement or activism, and indeed there may be a case for examining whether the assumption of a shareholder corporate governance role meets public interest objectives and should itself be subject to forms of governance.[132]

It may be argued that the regulatory moderation of shareholder behaviour is warranted in order to mitigate the more undesirable aspects of funds' instrumental implementation of corporate governance roles. This approach could also compel funds to internalise some aspects of the public interest in their corporate governance roles. However, one may be cautious of introducing too much standardisation or homogenous expectations of how funds should behave as shareholders, or indeed introducing unintended incentives that distort the market for shareholder influence. In this light, we now turn to discuss the UK's and EU's approaches to articulating norms for shareholder behaviour. We critically appraise what may be achieved by these approaches and whether they go any length towards changing the modern investment management model.

D. INSTRUMENTAL ASSUMPTION OF CORPORATE GOVERNANCE ROLES – THE MODERATED APPROACHES IN THE UK AND EU

This Section will discuss chiefly the UK's and EU's efforts at governing institutional shareholder behaviour via the introduction of optimal shareholder engagement standards. UK policy makers have termed such norms of engagement as 'stewardship'. Although 'stewardship' standards were only articulated in 2010, UK policy-makers have kept a close eye on

---

1503; Lawrence E Mitchell, 'The Legitimate Rights of Public Shareholders' (2009), above.

[132] Company law has little to say about minority shareholder activism, e.g. see UK cases such as *Northern Counties Securities Ltd v Jackson & Steeples Ltd* [1974] 1 WLR 1133; *Allen v Gold Reefs of W. Africa Ltd* [1900] 1 Ch 656; *Brown v British Abrasive Wheel Co* [1919] 1 Ch 290; *Dafen Tinplate Co Ltd. v Llanelli Steel Co* [1920] 2 Ch 124; *Arbuthnott v Bonnyman & 18 Ors* [2015] EWCA Civ 536. It is argued that the imbalance in favour of shareholder freedom to exercise their rights is unjustifiable, see R Flannigan, 'Shareholder Fiduciary Accountability' (2014) *Journal of Business Law* 1. Although in the US, majority owners can have fiduciary duties imposed on them, see for example J A C Hetherington, 'Defining the Scope of Controlling Shareholders' Fiduciary Responsibilities' (1987) 22 *Wake Forest Law Review* 9.

institutional shareholder engagement since the 1990s as the belief that institutions can play a governing and constructive role in shaping the well-being of the corporate economy is a strong one and remains so.[133] In particular, UK policy-makers have encouraged institutions to vote and exercise their 'voice'[134] in their corporate governance roles.[135] This exhortation has moved from focusing on voting to engagement more broadly since the 2010s.

In the EU, the desire to promote freedom of movement of capital, in particular to promote cross-border listings and raising of capital, underpinned policy-making in many areas including harmonising securities regulation for the supply side[136] and improving shareholder rights for the demand (investor) side.[137] One of the first steps was the enactment of the Shareholder Rights Directive 2007[138] that aims to make it easier for cross-border shareholders to exercise their rights to vote. This is followed by an amendment Directive[139] to enhance institutions' shareholder engagement roles. The proposed Directive however, as we will discuss,

---

133 For example, since the Cadbury Review in 1992 saw institutions as the main constituents that would hold publicly listed companies to account for their governance practices, e.g. para 6.6, Cadbury Committee, *Financial Aspects of Corporate Governance* (1992). UK policy-makers' convictions about institutions' corporate governance roles is extensively discussed in Chapter 2, Iris H-Y Chiu, *The Foundations and Anatomy of Shareholder Activism* (2010), above.

134 Albert O Hirschmann, *Exit, Voice and Loyalty: Responses to Decline in Firms, Organizations, and States* (Cambridge, MA: Harvard University Press 1970).

135 Paul Myners, *Institutional Investment in the UK: A Review* (2001).

136 Financial Services: Building a Framework for Action, COM (1998) 625 1, and Communication on Implementing the Framework For Financial Markets: Action Plan, COM (1999) (232), as well as its endorsement in the *Final Report of the Committee of Wise Men on the Regulation of European Securities Markets* (15 Feb 2001). K Lannoo and M Levin, 'Securities Market Regulation in the EU' (2003) (Research Study Carried out for the Wise Persons' Committee, Centre for European Policy Studies 2003), available at http://216.239.51.104/search?q=cache:MDFLRqTml-QJ:www.wise-averties.ca/reports/WPC_4.pdf+gros+lannoo+euro+capital&hl=en&ct=clnk&cd=15&client=opera.

137 This is somewhat pursuant to the 'law and finance' approach championed in R La Porta, F Lopez-de-Silanes and A Shleifer, 'What Works in Securities Laws' (2006) 71 *Journal of Finance* 1.

138 Directive 2007/36/EC of the European Parliament and of the Council of 11 July 2007 on the exercise of certain rights of shareholders in listed companies.

139 Directive (EU) 2017/828 of the European Parliament and of the Council of 17 May 2017 amending Directive 2007/36/EC as regards the encouragement of long-term shareholder engagement.

creates both empowerment for institutions to engage and obligations to subject such corporate governance roles to governance and scrutiny.[140]

Compelling or Urging Shareholders to Vote

A key area of institutions' engagement with corporate governance rights that policy-makers scrutinise is the exercise of their voting rights at general meetings. At a foundational level, shareholder voting is seen to be a key shareholder right, as shareholder attendance at the general meeting and exercise of voting power is a doctrinal pillar in the legal framework of UK company law. As Lord Millett opined in *Her Majesty's Commissioners of Inland Revenue v Laird Group plc*:

> It is customary to describe [a share] as 'a bundle of rights and liabilities', and this is probably the nearest that one can get to its character, provided that it is appreciated that it is more than a bundle of contractual rights. ... These rights, however, are not purely personal rights. They confer proprietary rights in the company though not in its property.[141]

The key governance right derived from share ownership is the right to vote. Shareholders are entitled to vote on their shares 'as an incident of property',[142] although share ownership is only regarded as 'quasi-proprietary' in nature.[143] The right of shareholders to vote provides the balance of power between the general meeting and the Board of directors, so that each organ of the company can be constituted in an effective and accountable manner under the division of powers in the company law framework. The right to vote is therefore a key form of investor protection in the agency-based framework of corporate governance. In this light, shareholder voting levels could provide an indication of the strength of investor protection in a capital market and an impression of how well companies in that market are governed.

It has been observed that institutions value their voting rights immensely as regards their overseas investments. As institutions diversify their holdings by accessing global capital markets and becoming foreign

---

140 Iris H-Y Chiu, 'European Shareholder Rights Directive Proposals: A Critical Analysis in Mapping with the UK Stewardship Code?' (2016) *ERA Forum* 1, DOI: 10.1007/s12027-016-0415-6.

141 [2003] UKHL 54 at para 35.

142 *Northern Counties v Jackson & Steeple* [1974] 1 WLR 1133, *North-West Transportation Co Ltd v Beatty* (1887) 12 App Cas 589.

143 *Her Majesty's Commissioners of Inland Revenue v Laird Group plc* [2003] UKHL 54 at para 35.

shareholders, voting rights are seen to be important as part of the mosaic of investor protection.[144] This could be because institutions derive comfort from being able to enjoy similar rights in foreign companies as at home, and voting has become a channel for institutions to exert influence over investee companies where concerns arise.[145] The European Commission, in proposing the Shareholder Rights Directive in 2005,[146] argued that cross-border voting rights are important in case shareholders wish to use them, and should not be unnecessarily impeded. Barriers to effective exercise of voting rights in cross-border holdings could in the larger context be an impediment to the integration of EU capital markets. Thus, the Shareholder Rights Directive, enacted in 2007,[147] provides a facilitative framework to receive communications about general meetings, access and participate in general meetings, ask questions and appoint proxies to vote. It seems that whether or not institutions actually exercise their voting rights, the framework for being able to do so is perceived as crucial to investor appeal and is an important foundation for building attractive securities markets. Taking this perspective, it seems not to be imperative that institutions should be *made to vote* as they should consider to what extent the exercise of corporate governance rights is relevant to their business models.

Indeed in 1998, PIRC's survey of proxy voting by institutional investors in the UK shows voting levels to be low, less than 50 per cent of institutional shareholders would turn up or vote at investee companies' general meetings.[148] The low level of interest in voting is basically a

---

[144] Peter Illiev, Karl V Lins, Darius P Miller and Lukas Roth, 'Shareholder Voting and Corporate Governance Around the World' (2015) 28 *Review of Financial Studies* 2167.

[145] 'Hon Hai faces governance challenge at AGM from global investors', *Financial Times* (24 June 2014); Mangesh Tayde and Nageswara Rao, 'Do Foreign Institutional Investors Exhibit Herding and Positive Feedback Trading in Indian Markets?' in Narjess Boubakri, Jean-Claude Cosset, Hyacinthe Y Somé (eds), *Institutional Investors in Global Capital Markets* (Emerald Publishing Ltd 2015).

[146] European Commission, Proposal for a Directive of the European Parliament and of the Council on the exercise of voting rights by shareholders of companies having their registered office in a Member State and whose shares are admitted to trading on a regulated market and amending Directive 2004/109/EC / COM/2005/0685 final – COD 2005/0265.

[147] Directive 2007/36/EC of the European Parliament and of the Council of 11 July 2007 on the exercise of certain rights of shareholders in listed companies.

[148] PIRC, *Survey of Voting Trends* (1998) at http://www.cix.co.uk/~pirc/pubs/pr98.htm. See also discussion in Rebecca Stratling, 'General Meetings: A

manifestation of the early observation that, left to their own motivations, certain funds regard their corporate governance roles as largely irrelevant to their business model, and hence, resources would unlikely be dedicated to voting. A vote allows an expression of preference between given options, but the nature of the vote is such that only the collective aggregation of votes into a majority matters for the outcome,[149] and hence, the allocation of an individual right to vote does not *per se* entail the exercise of strong powers. For widely diversified institutional shareholders, Berle and Means rightly predicted (in the 1930s) that they would behave in a passive manner, and would not be bothered to vote. This could have been largely due to the high cost of voting at so many investee companies in the diversified portfolios of funds. Hence, the prevalent preference is for exit if an investee company underperforms.[150]

Since institutions that are highly diversified and are minority shareholders in a wide range of portfolio companies are not *naturally incentivised* to vote, there may be a case for Edelman et al's[151] bold proposal that shareholder voting should not be regarded as an immutable fundamental tenet, and should be reviewed as shareholder profiles and the needs of companies change. They argue that in an age where most shareholders are institutions that hold assets on behalf of beneficiaries, their voting power should be aligned according to the efficiencies of their business interests, and it is inappropriate to assume that shareholder voting is the main instrument that checks the agency problem of management in power. They propose that shareholders' votes should be limited to issues in relation to long-term residual value, which affect institutions' long-term investment interests, and where the Board is conflicted and hence unable to assume a mediating role between different constituents in the company's fabric. In all other circumstances, the Board should be allowed to play the chief mediating role for all of the company's constituents. In other words, they advocate that the vote should be made less important as a corporate governance mechanism so

---

Dispensable Tool for Corporate Governance of Listed Companies?' (2003) 11 *Corporate Governance* 74.

149 Kenneth J Arrow, *Social Choice and Individual Values* (Conn: Yale University Press 1970, 2nd edn), also arguing that the social choice aggregated from the voting decisions need not provide the most optimal outcome for all participants.

150 See also William O'Barr and John M Conley, *Fortune and Folly* (NY: McGraw-Hill, 1992).

151 Paul H Edelman, Randall S Thomas and Robert B Thompson, 'Shareholder Voting in an Age of Intermediary Capitalism' (2014), above.

that institutions, who are not motivated to exercise the vote anyway, would not be compelled to play an unwilling role that achieves efficiencies for neither the company nor the shareholders. Presumably other mechanisms in governing directors would also have to be instituted to ensure that their powers are exercised responsibly. The recognition that institutions lack business interests in their corporate governance roles would result in more enlightened policy solutions, and avoid simply forcing institutions to engage in the traditional suite of shareholder powers in the company law framework.

Edelman et al's proposal above is not without traction. In the UK, shareholders' powers and rights have evolved from a partnership framework, and only in the post-war period has the separation of ownership from control taken off.[152] Thus, the presumed level of involvement and interest on the part of shareholders may not hold in a changed landscape of dispersed shareholders who are largely 'financier capitalists' or 'agency' intermediaries. Further, the FCA study into the asset management industry casts doubt on whether institutional shareholder voting really adds much value. This is because much of institutional voting, especially in the US, is motivated by asset managers' relationships with rival asset managers. For example, asset management teams place pressure on their corporate governance colleagues to vote in a certain way so as not to upset other asset managers who are fellow shareholders. Hence, mutual back-scratching may motivate voting behaviour rather than substantive concerns with investee companies.[153] Such motivations for voting are disengaged from the objectives of good corporate equity ownership and it may not be meaningful to keep shareholder voting as a fundamental tenet of company law.

It may be argued that moving away from shareholder rights to vote would cause uproar and negative perceptions in capital markets. However, this should be part of comprehensive rethinking of the optimal level of investor protection in capital markets, such rethinking including perspectives on the importance and rights of non-shareholder stakeholders in view of how they may be affected by and may affect corporate decision-making. The path-dependent inertia that resists changing the institution of shareholder rights (such as in voting) is not necessarily constructive where shareholders are apathetic in their corporate governance rights and non-shareholder stakeholders remain voiceless. For

---

[152] Brian R Cheffins, *Corporate Ownership and Control: British Businesses Transformed* (Oxford: OUP 2010).

[153] 'Fund houses favour rivals at annual general meetings', *Financial Times* (24 April 2016).

example, in the UK, company restructuring and takeovers are exclusively governed by shareholders' votes.[154] It can be questioned whether such a position is still sound when stakeholders such as employees are acutely affected by these events, while shareholders may be transient, or worse, instrumental in using events such as takeovers to extract a premium. Hedge fund activists who bet on or drive disruptive events such as corporate restructurings, mergers and takeovers have been the most successful in extracting enormous premia for their own investment purposes.[155] Neville asks '[can] we get the right shareholders to be more active?',[156] recognising that not all shareholder engagement is beneficial, and that it remains uncertain who the 'right' shareholders are, and whose engagement is desirable from the point of view of the company's good as well as the wider good. There is a case for arguing that what we need are active monitors, shareholders or stakeholders, of corporate decision-making in order to contend for the long-term well-being of the corporation and the corporate economy more widely. This role may not be fulfilled only by shareholders today.

However, the trajectory ahead seems to be adhering to the incumbent legal framework of shareholders' rights to vote. This may be due to path-dependence and inertia to change, as well as fears that the first-mover to overhaul these laws may suffer a backlash in terms of the appeal of its capital markets. The other perspective however, is that the importance of voting rights relates to institutions' duties in investment management.

By engaging in voting in investee companies, institutions show their beneficiaries that they are duly discharging their duties in monitoring investments diligently. Hence, the duty to vote has been adopted as part of the legal duties owed by institutions to their beneficiaries in the US. The Department of Labor in the US issued guidance[157] expressly interpreting the duty to vote on stock owned by employee retirement

---

[154] The aggrandisement of shareholder rights as a mistaken approach is also discussed in Alan Dignam, 'The Future of Shareholder Democracy in the Shadow of the Financial Crisis' (2013), above.

[155] Marco Becht, Julian Franks, Jeremy Grant and Hannes Wagner, 'The Returns to Hedge Fund Activism: An International Study' (2014), above.

[156] Mette Neville, 'The Suspicious Shareholder' in Hanne Birkmose, Mette Neville and Karsten Engsig Sørensen (eds), *The European Financial Market in Transition* (Alpen aan den Rijn: Kluwer Law International, 2011).

[157] See http://www.dol.gov/ebsa/publications/acemer.htm, William L Scogland, 'Fiduciary Duty: What Does it Mean?' (1989) 24 *Tort and Insurance Law Journal* 803.

schemes as a matter of trustees' fiduciary responsibility.[158] This position is however not adopted in the UK with regard to the regulatory rules for pension funds, leaving it open for funds to determine how best to manage plan assets in accordance with general duties of loyalty and care and skill. That said, UK pension funds are nudged in no uncertain terms towards improving their voting levels as low voting levels and the general lack of engagement are decried.[159] From the 1990s, academic commentators have provided empirical evidence on levels of attendance at general meetings[160] and called for voting to be taken on as a form of 'responsibility'.[161] European legislation has now introduced a harmonised provision to compel all retail collective investment schemes (UCITs)[162] to engage in the considered exercise of their voting rights.[163] This has provided another form of impetus to compel those funds whose business models would not have motivated engagement with their corporate governance roles to refrain from neglecting them.

Voting records have, according to the annual surveys by the Investment Management Association, improved significantly over the years. By 2008, over 80 per cent of investment managers managing institutional funds would exercise their votes at general meetings.[164] The IMA[165]

---

[158] Employee Retirement Income Security Act of 1974, 29 US Code Chapter 18, Sections 1101–14.

[159] Paul Myners, *Institutional Investment in the UK: A Review* (2001), above at paras 5.80, 5.85.

[160] Bernard S Black and John C Coffee, 'Institutional Investor Behaviour in the UK' (1993–94) 92 *Michigan Law Rev* 1999; Edward B Rock, 'The Logic and (Uncertain) Significance of Institutional Shareholder Activism' (1990–91) 91 *Georgetown Law Journal* 445; Chris Mallin, 'Institutional Investors and Voting Practices: An International Comparison' (2001) 9 *Corporate Governance* 118.

[161] Chris Mallin, 'Institutional Investors and Voting Practices: An International Comparison' (2001), above.

[162] Discussed in Chapter 5.

[163] Art 21, Commission Directive 2010/43/EU of 1 July 2010 implementing Directive 2009/65/EC of the European Parliament and of the Council as regards organisational requirements, conflicts of interest, conduct of business, risk management and content of the agreement between a depositary and a management company.

[164] Investment Management Association, *Annual Survey of Engagement for Years Ending 2008* (2008).

[165] Investment Management Association, *Adherence to the FRC's Stewardship Code Survey* (as of 31 Dec 2014) at p. 7 records that voting levels are at about 84 per cent, increasing from 78 per cent the year before. According to the IMA, levels of voting have been hovering about the 80 per cent mark for several years.

continues to report a high level of voting by institutions although an OECD report[166] seems to suggest that this figure is rather optimistic.

Although institutions' voting levels have been reported to increase, this could be due to the perception that they would be forced to engage in voting by regulation if no improvement is perceived by policy-makers. The Myners report had mooted a similar approach to the US Department of Labor's approach.[167] The introduction of a duty to consider exercise of voting rights for UCITs also highlights the possibility of more general regulation, which, as will be argued below, is embodied in the proposed EU Shareholders' Rights Directive 2014.[168] The expectation of a compliance basis for voting may have been key to the increased levels of institutional voting that funds would otherwise neglect (largely pension and mutual funds, as discussed in the earlier Section) if left to their own incentives.

There are two possible developments ahead in relation to shareholder voting. One is that shareholder voting may become an explicit and mandatory duty or obligation. The other is that incentives may be introduced by law to encourage voting. We offer some critical views in relation to both.

On the first, it may be argued that UK company law has always maintained the position that shareholders are free to vote as they choose,[169] including voting as bound to certain shareholder agreements (hence fettered discretion)[170] or abstention from voting. Hence it is unlikely that a duty to vote would be introduced as this is contrary to fundamental tenets in company law. However, the UK Corporate Governance and Stewardship Codes encourage institutions to vote as a matter of best practice,[171] and it may be questioned as to whether such best

---

[166] Paul Hewitt, 'The Exercise of Shareholder Rights: Country Comparison of Turnout and Dissent', *OECD Corporate Governance Working Papers*, No. 3, (OECD Publishing 2011) at http://dx.doi.org/10.1787/5kg54d011lvf-en suggests that the average turnout in the UK is just over 65 per cent and levels of dissent or attendance at extraordinary general meetings are low.

[167] Paul Myners, *Institutional Investment in the UK: A Review* (2001), above at para 5.89, p. 92.

[168] Directive (EU) 2017/828 of the European Parliament and of the Council of 17 May 2017 amending Directive 2007/36/EC as regards the encouragement of long-term shareholder engagement.

[169] *Northern Counties Securities Ltd v Jackson & Steeple Ltd* [1974] 1 WLR 1133.

[170] *Halton International v Guernroy* [2005] EWHC 1968.

[171] Section E, UK Corporate Governance Code, Principle 6, UK Stewardship Code.

practice would 'harden' in due course to become a legitimate expectation or norm.[172] However, we sound a couple of reservations with regard to making voting mandatory.

First, we doubt that a compliance basis for voting would promote the objectives underlying the spirit of voting, i.e. the investment culture of diligent monitoring, long-termism and good corporate equity ownership. An empirical study in another area shows that an optimal culture is attained not just by complying with rules and regulations, but by a genuine desire to gain public trust and putting in place institutions that go beyond compliance.[173] Where funds have self-interests and their private objectives, a compliance basis may only exert distorting effects that do not necessarily improve their desire to internalise the ethos of good corporate equity ownership or public interest.

Further, a compliance basis would necessarily boost the increasing importance of the proxy voting industry. The business model of the industry is dedicated to research and making recommendations for voting, and managing funds' exercise of voting rights in myriad companies. The initial growth of the industry was arguably in response to the US Department of Labor's introduction of mandatory voting for retirement scheme trustees. Proxy voting agencies have helped overcome the inertia and high transaction costs of engaging in voting by providing a service that leverages upon economies of scale. However, as will be discussed below, they are in a powerful position to influence funds' voting decisions and can therefore make a significant impact on corporate governance. The power of proxy voting agencies is thus being scrutinised as the industry is also very concentrated. More will follow in our discussion on the European Shareholders' Rights Directive below.

Next, we turn to the development in some jurisdictions that creates incentives for institutions to vote. In a bid to encourage shareholders to be long-termist and constructively engaged, increased voting rights could be seen to be a key incentive.[174] Such a measure would *prima facie*

---

172 G-P Calliess and M Renner, 'From Soft Law to Hard Code: The Juridification of Global Governance' (2007) available at http://ssrn.com/abstract=1030526 and (2009) 22 Ratio Juris 260 generally discusses the conditions for hardening soft law.

173 Mark Yarborough, Kelly Fryer-Edwards, Gail Geller and Richard R Sharp, 'Transforming the Culture of Biomedical Research From Compliance to Trustworthiness: Insights From Nonmedical Sectors' (2009) 84 *Culture of Biomedical Research* 472.

174 John H Matheson and Brent A Olson, 'Corporate Law and the Long Term Shareholder Model of Corporate Governance' (1991–92) 76 *Minnesota Law*

depart from the principle of equality between shareholders, embodied in 'one-share-one-vote', and could be seen as compromising investor protection for minority shareholders.[175]

Some commentators[176] support dual class voting rights, which generally entrench the power of founder or key shareholders in a company. In particular, there is a growing trend for founders of Silicon Valley technology companies to retain control through a dual-class share structure in which voting rights exceed cash flow rights. Founder shareholders may be motivated to insist on such voting structures due to concerns about the potential risk of short-termism in widely-held corporations where hedge funds or other short-term oriented institutions can easily gain influence through the acquisition of equity stakes. For example, Google's founder shareholders Larry Page and Sergey Brin have retained significant control of 55.7 per cent after the initial public offer of shares, despite having only 15 per cent of the cash flow rights.[177] They cite their long-term perspective as rationale for supporting the issue of a class of non-voting shares, which controversially started trading in April 2014.[178] Although dual class voting rights may be viewed with suspicion by some minority shareholders,[179] successful companies such as Berkshire Hathaway, News Corp, Google, Facebook, Amazon and a host of other

Review 1313 argue from empirical research that corporate monitoring is observed where shareholders own at least 25 per cent of the company's equity and are long-termist. A number of commentators call for it, e.g. Hanne Søndergaard Birkmose, 'European Challenges for Institutional Investor Engagement – Is Mandatory Disclosure the Way Forward' (2014) *European Company and Financial Law Review* 214.

[175] Paolo Santella, Enrico Baffi, Carlo Drago and Dino Lattuca, 'A Comparative Analysis of the Legal Obstacles to Institutional Investor Activism in the EU and in the US' (2009), above; Mette Neville, 'Active Ownership and the Competition for International Capital – Recent Trends and Some Implications for Company Law' (2002), above.

[176] Marc T Moore and Edward Walker-Arnott, 'A Fresh Look at Stock Market Short Termism' (2014) 41 *Journal of Law and Society* 416.

[177] John Plender, 'Google takes us back to Old Europe', *Financial Times* (9 May 2004).

[178] 'Google founders look to cement control with novel share split', *Financial Times* (2 April 2014).

[179] See earlier article by Vijay Jog and Allan L Riding, 'Price Effects of Dual-class Shares' (1986) *Financial Analysts Journal* 58. Also see Paul A Gompers, Joy Ishii and Andrew Metrick, 'Extreme Governance: An Analysis of Dual-Class Firms in the United States' (2010) 23 *Review of Financial Studies* 1051; 'The Cost of Control', *The Economist* (21 July 2011) at http://www.economist.com/node/18988938.

internet-based companies such as LinkedIn, Zynga, Groupon and JD.com and Alibaba.com from China continue to attract investors who wish to share in the upside of successful companies led by talented founders.

Increased voting rights for shareholders may also be awarded on the basis of loyalty – i.e. those who remain with a company for more than a certain number of years are regarded as likely to be more 'loyal' and concerned for the long-term well-being of the company. This has been adopted in French reforms that have introduced double voting rights for shareholders who have remained with the company for more than two years.[180] This is not necessarily the most optimal means for identifying genuinely constructive and long-termist shareholders as length of time of shareholding does not necessarily mean more constructive engagement with the company. Further, the 'wrong' sort of shareholders can still be attracted to the company in order to build up key stakes in the company for extraction of private benefits. French companies are characterised by controlling instead of dispersed ownership, the reward for long-termist shareholders, who are likely controlling shareholders, could be seen as a means of merely entrenching their already substantial power over listed companies.

Policy-makers should exercise discretion before embarking on legal reform that tinkers with voting rights as incentives. It is instructive that the European Council and Parliament ultimately decided to remove a proposal inserted in the passage of the EU Shareholders' Rights Directive 2017 that related to encouraging long-term shareholding through enhanced voting powers. As discussed, shareholders have different motivations and reasons for their instrumental assumption of corporate governance roles and policy-makers should examine them more carefully in the wider public interest of securing soundly governed corporations for the future.

Next, we turn to examine the UK's drive towards turning institutions into 'stewards', a role that integrates engaged corporate governance roles into investment management practice in order to meet the twin objectives of delivering long-term returns to savers and supporting a wealth-creating corporate economy over the long term. We critically examine below

---

[180] The Florange Law, discussed in 'Short Term or Short Changed?', *The Economist* (2 May 2015), at http://www.economist.com/news/business/21650149-enhanced-rights-loyal-investors-are-increasingly-touted-way-make-companies-think.

whether the Stewardship Code initiative is likely to transform institutional shareholders into the benevolent corporate equity owners with the characteristics that we have described in Section B.[181]

The UK Stewardship Drive: The Stewardship Code

In the wake of the UK banking crisis 2007–09, the role of institutional shareholders was again brought to the fore, in particular by the Walker Review of 2009.[182] The critique is that institutional shareholders have been uncritical of risky business practices in their investee banks[183] and should have monitored Board risk management. Although institutional shareholder apathy is not regarded as the key cause of the UK banking crisis, the Walker Review on corporate governance in banks and financial institutions is of the view that shortcomings in institutional shareholder oversight provided a tolerant or indeed encouraging context for misjudgments of risk made at the Board level of the failed UK banks. In response, the Institutional Shareholders Committee, the trade association representing institutions, developed a broadly framed Code to encourage institutions to be more active and engaged.[184] Such 'activeness' extends beyond attendance at general meetings and voting, and entails informal dialogue and monitoring, as well as intervention by shareholders where relevant. As this Code has received bottom-up acceptance among institutions, the Financial Reporting Council in the UK adopted this formally as a 'Stewardship Code' in 2010,[185] to reflect the expectations for institutions – that to engage with their investee companies is a matter of 'stewardship'. The Code is subject to a comply-or-explain regime, and only applies to voluntary signatories.[186]

---

[181] Iris H-Y Chiu, 'Turning Institutional Investors into "Stewards" – Exploring the Meaning and Objectives in "Stewardship"' (2013) *Current Legal Problems* 1.

[182] David Walker, *A Review of Corporate Governance in Banks and Financial Institutions* (HM Treasury Nov 2009).

[183] 'FSA Chief Lambasts Uncritical Investors', *Financial Times* (11 March 2009) and 'Myners Lashes out at Landlord Institutional shareholders', *Financial Times* (21 Apr 2009). Also 'Institutional shareholders Admit Oversight Failure on Banks', *The Daily Telegraph* (27 Jan 2009).

[184] Institutional Shareholders' Committee Code 2010.

[185] https://www.frc.org.uk/Our-Work/Codes-Standards/Corporate-governance/UK-Stewardship-Code.aspx, last revision 2014.

[186] J G Parkinson and G Kelly, 'The Combined Code of Corporate Governance' (1999) *The Political Quarterly* 101.

In addition to the definition that we have offered in Section B, investor stewardship can also be defined as '... the process through which institutional shareholders, directors and others seek to influence companies in the direction of long-term, sustainable performance that derives from contributing to human progress and the well-being of the environment and society.'[187] The key notions in 'stewardship' seem to be long termism and taking a more holistic view of the well-being and performance of the company, very much reflecting the type of 'good corporate equity ownership' described in Section B. As one of us has written extensively,[188] it is uncertain what the legal basis for 'stewardship' is – whether it is in the investment management duties owed by institutions or in the corporate governance paradigm with the investee company. If 'stewardship' is intended to articulate the desirability of institutions being engaged with their investee companies as a matter of discharging their duties in investment management, then it is queried why a step further like that taken by the Department of Labor in the US was not taken in this instance. Further, it is uncertain whether the 'stewardship' notion is an entirely 'private' concept which merely repackages best practice in institutions' investment management and corporate governance practices or indeed a concept that responds to wider societal expectations of institutions' roles as key economic actors. If wider societal expectations are at stake, Davies has rightly queried:

> There are two central issues about governments' recent promotion of institutional shareholder activism. The first is whether governments wish the institutions to become more active because they consider that the private goals of the institutions coincide with public policy or because they seek to modify those private goals so as to align them better with government's conception of public policy.[189]

'Traditional' institutions such as pension funds are perceived, rightly or wrongly by policymakers, as the 'right' type of investors who ought to be

---

[187] Arad Reisberg, 'The Notion of Stewardship from a Company Law Perspective: Re-Defined and Re-Assessed in Light of the Recent Financial Crisis?' (2011) *Journal of Financial Crime* 126.

[188] Iris H-Y Chiu, 'Institutional shareholders as Stewards: Towards a New Conception of Corporate Governance?' (2012) 6 *Brooklyn Journal of Financial, Corporate and Commercial Law* 387; 'Turning Institutional Investors into "Stewards" – Exploring the Meaning and Objectives in "Stewardship"' (2013) *Current Legal Problems* 1.

[189] Paul Davies, 'Shareholders in the United Kingdom' (2015) at http://ssrn.com/abstract=2557680.

active. This perception could be due to the long-term horizon of pension funds' liabilities, therefore causing them to be seen as natural champions for the long-term wealth creating role of the corporate sector which is a wider social good. However, Davies suggests that this may be a naïve assumption, and policy-makers may be indeed concerned that 'traditional' institutions do not play a sufficiently salutary role in their investee companies' corporate governance. Hence the Code could indeed be an instrument of soft law to govern institutional behaviour. Such governance is framed in soft law as the UK has always adopted a business-led bottom-up approach to governing business,[190] in order to ensure that efficient and proportionate measures, not top-down and unpopular measures, are adopted. Dignam however criticises such an approach as being in thrall to business interests and dominated by a circle of business and financial elites.[191] The Stewardship Code may suffer from its ambivalent nature because of the unique political context in the UK, in terms of the balance of power between the State and City in governing business. Hence, even if policy-makers wish to champion optimal investment behaviour, it is gently introduced via soft law with bottom-up consensus.

Despite the ambivalent nature of the 'stewardship' notion and the broadly framed nature of the Code, the Code has attracted over 300 signatories in the UK to its comply-or-explain regime. Further, it has attracted international attention. The Code inspired similar international developments in the institution of Stewardship Codes in many other countries, including the Netherlands, Switzerland, Japan, Malaysia and Hong Kong.[192]

---

190 Alan Dignam, 'Exporting Corporate Governance: UK Regulatory Systems in a Global Economy' (2000) *Company Lawyer* 70.

191 Alan Dignam, 'A Principled Approach to Self-Regulation? The Report of the Hampel Committee on Corporate Governance' (1998) 19(5) *Company Lawyer* 140; 'Capturing Corporate Governance: The End of the UK Self-regulating System' (2007) 4 *International Journal of Disclosure and Governance* 24.

192 See the Japanese Code at http://www.fsa.go.jp/en/refer/councils/stewardship/20140407/01.pdf; the Malaysian Code at http://www.sc.com.my/wp-content/uploads/eng/html/consultation/140115_PublicConsultation_1.pdf; the Hong Kong 'Principles of Responsible Ownership' at http://www.sfc.hk/edistributionWeb/gateway/EN/consultation/openFile?refNo=15CP2, see discussion in Iris H-Y Chiu, 'Learning from the UK in the Proposed Shareholders' Rights Directive 2014? European Corporate Governance Regulation from a UK Perspective' (2015) 114 *ZVglRWiss* 1.

The Code's Principles

Under the UK Stewardship Code, institutions are required to establish certain policies to guide their engagement behaviour with investee companies. Principle 1 requires that institutions develop stewardship policies to explain how they intend to integrate stewardship into their investment management and discharge those responsibilities, and publicly disclose the policies. Principle 2 requires institutions to supplement the above-mentioned stewardship policy, which is of an overarching nature, with specific policies that show how institutions manage conflicts of interest that may affect their stewardship. Principle 6 also requires institutions to develop a policy for voting and disclosure of voting behaviour.

Further, the Code provides guidance on best or optimal practices in engagement behaviour. Stewardship involves 'monitoring and engaging with companies on matters such as strategy, performance, risk, capital structure, and corporate governance, including culture and remuneration' through voting and the development of a 'purposeful dialogue' with the investee companies on these matters. Principle 3 requires institutions to 'monitor' their companies. This Principle illustrates examples of monitoring activities, such as keeping abreast of corporate disclosures, considering the quality and implications of corporate disclosure and meeting company representatives, as well as attending general meetings. Such monitoring need not be interactive with the company management as 'monitoring' includes becoming prepared for interaction and it generally refers to being sufficiently informed. Principle 4 then provides for the development of an appropriate escalation and intervention policy. It emphasises that the pursuit of passive investment strategies and/or being underweight in any particular stock should not prevent the undertaking of appropriate escalation and intervention activities. The illustrations of escalation and intervention activities, including meeting company representatives, making public statements, submitting proposals for general meetings and requisitioning general meetings, are of a nature that is more interactive with company management or at least compels company management to respond. Principle 5 then envisages that institutions may step up engagement in collective terms especially 'at times of significant corporate or wider economic stress, or when the risks posed threaten the ability of the company to continue.'[193] Collective engagement, as we will discuss shortly, is likely to become a key means for institutions to

193 Principle 5. Also supported by the Kay Review, see BIS, *The Kay Review of UK Equity Markets and Long-Term Decision Making* (Final Report, 23 July 2012) at paras 7.8ff.

demonstrate engagement in a cost-effective manner. In sum, the Code provides a means of legitimation for the acceptable forms of shareholder engagement which would be treated as stewardship.

The Achievements of the Stewardship Code

The UK's soft law on shareholder engagement introduces standards for what policy-makers would perceive as constructive engagement. In this way, policy-makers have articulated the expectations of 'optimal' institutional shareholder behaviour, as relating both to investment management practice and therefore accountability to beneficiaries, and to institutions' roles in the corporate governance fabric of publicly traded companies. This intervention attempts to 'moderate' institutions' shareholder behaviour so that such is not merely left to institutions' own incentives to determine. By providing Principles in the Code, institutions are given guidance as to how their behaviour ought to be shaped.

Hence, it could be said that barriers to institutional engagement are overcome by the Code, as uncertainties relating to acceptable or expected engagement behaviour are clarified. Further, the Code provides a facilitative framework for engagement so that, for example, institutions facing conflicts of interest could still carry out engagement legitimately as long as they have a policy in place to manage such conflicts. Further, institutions concerned about whether shareholder engagement would be regarded as relevant to investment management could be more assured that the Code supports the link between shareholder engagement and investment management.

For funds that use their corporate governance rights in an instrumentally active manner, the Code provides moderation and guidance on what acceptable behaviour is, besides legitimising the notion of shareholder engagement more broadly beyond voting. Relatively disconcerting forms of hedge fund activism that are rocking the corporate sector in the US may have to be moderated in light of what the Stewardship Code views as legitimate behaviour, therefore protecting companies and markets from potentially disruptive tendencies introduced by such activism. Sergakis is of the view that the Code has achieved much in terms of 'educational' purposes with respect to optimal forms of shareholder engagement.[194]

The Code's openness to collective engagement under Principle 5 may also be regarded as welcome by institutions not otherwise motivated to

---

194 Konstantinos Sergakis, 'The UK Stewardship Code: Bridging the Gap Between Companies and Institutional Investors' (2013) 47 *RJTUM* 109.

incur the cost of shareholder monitoring and engagement. When collective engagement was first endorsed in the Stewardship Code 2010 'at times of significant corporate or wider economic stress, or when the risks posed threaten the ability of the company to continue,'[195] institutions seemed lukewarm to the idea, concerned that collective action would incur further cost of coordination.[196] This is entirely in sync with economists' prediction that coordinated actions among funds are unlikely where dispersal of ownership in stock is high and the landscape comprises many funds to coordinate with. Low levels of holding and high numbers of funds to coordinate with encourage inertia and free-riding behaviour, thus, less likelihood of successful coalitions.[197] Further, there remain concerns about whether collective engagement would trigger the mandatory takeover bid threshold applicable to parties 'acting in concert'.[198] It is to be noted that this principle does not legitimate a phenomenon known as 'wolf packs'. 'Wolf packs' are joint efforts between usually activist hedge funds which use shareholder engagement as a focused strategy to influence management to take certain decisions, usually related to extracting immediate value from the company, such as in the payment of dividends or share buybacks or relating to purported business or governance improvement for the company, such as in the form of demanding the departure of senior executives or Board members to be replaced by the funds' representatives.[199] Principle 5 does not legitimate 'wolf-pack' behaviour as it is qualified by situations of 'significant corporate or wider economic stress', meaning that institutions' collective engagement can only be legitimately supported under the Code if pursuant to the common good of shareholders in general in

---

[195] See n 193 above.

[196] The Financial Reporting Council clarified that it was not sufficient for institutions to demonstrate collective engagement by common membership in a collective body. The FRC has clarified that the Principle actually requires institutions to consider joining forces with other institutions at critical moments and developing policies to show how collective engagement may be achieved. See Financial Reporting Council, *Revisions to the UK Stewardship Code* (Consultation Paper, April 2012) at para 12.

[197] Andreas Schäfer and Urs von Arx, 'The Influence of Pension Funds on Corporate Governance' (2014) 46 *Applied Economics* 2316.

[198] This area is likely to be subject to clearer clarification in the UK, and see clarification in Australia, ASIC, *Regulatory Guide 128: Collective Action by Investors* (June 2015) at http://download.asic.gov.au/media/3273670/rg128-published-23-june-2015.pdf?_ga=1.4889715.1711037398.1455118322.

[199] See Chapter 6.

difficult times. Hence, 'profit-seeking' behaviour on the part of activist hedge funds in wolf packs would not be regarded as in the spirit of the Code.

By the end of 2014, institutions had warmed up to the idea and welcomed collective engagement through a new body initiated by the Association of British Insurers, whose investment affairs division has now merged into the Investment Management Association – the Investor Forum.

The Forum is a body led by asset managers to coordinate instances of collective engagement. The Forum[200] is not only to coordinate voting decisions in the AGM seasons but also facilitate constructive dialogue with investee companies away from the AGM, hence working for asset owners to realise Principle 4 of the Stewardship Code that deals with informal engagement and discussions. The Forum on the face of it dispels any impression of legitimating collective voting behaviour on the back of proxy advisor recommendations, and seems poised to be actively engaged. The Forum will comprise three groups, one to serve advisory purposes for institutional members on a case by case basis under confidentiality, the second to facilitate collective engagement in a pro-active manner where long-term prospects at an investee company may be at risk, and the third to coordinate dialogue and action on shareholder rights under event-driven circumstances such as impending acquisitions. The collective engagement initiative under the Investor Forum is gaining acceptance among the Forum's members, who collectively own about 40 per cent of the UK's listed equity, to the extent that members have agreed to formalise a Forum agreement on their inter-relationships in conducting collective engagement.[201]

Collective engagement is arguably welcome as it is a means to pool information and resources in order to carry out shareholder engagement. The collective wisdom in the consensus among key institutions provides motivation for engagement, and the sharing of resources improves the cost-effectiveness of engagement. Other commentators[202] have also

---

[200] Investor Forum, *Facilitate Dialogue, Create Long-term Solutions and Enhance Value* (Oct 2014).

[201] 'Big Investment Groups Flex Muscles in Boardroom', *Financial Times* (30 August 2016).

[202] Jean-Pascal Gond and Valeria Piani, 'Organizing the Collective Action of Institutional Investors: Three Case Studies from the Principles for Responsible Investment Initiative' in Suzanne Young and Stephen Gates (eds) *Institutional Investors' Power to Change Corporate Behavior: International Perspectives*

affirmed the role of bodies that facilitate that collective pooling of information and resources for shareholder engagement, such as in social responsibility matters. The United Nations Principles for Responsible Investment secretariat and the Investor Climate Change Network[203] are examples of such coordinating and enabling bodies:

> triggering the initiative for collective action; (b) … offering through their networks mobilizing structures that allow potentially interested investors to network and to identify partners in engaging the collective action; (c) … diminishing incentives to free-ride in engaging the reputation of investors as PRI signatories; and (d) … providing a monitoring context and an administrative structure that bear a significant amount of the coordination cost for the collective engagement process.'[204]

It is noted that other commentators have proposed other forms of collective and enabling institutions such as an online company information and ratings system that institutions can use to share information with each other.[205] It is also suggested that institutions can collectively fund delegate agencies to identify potential engagement opportunities and such agencies could be dedicated to coordinating such engagement activities.[206] Hannes[207] also rightly suggests that proxy voting agencies may be in a position to play such a role, and in this light, the proper governance of such agencies may need to be considered, a point taken up in Section D.

Drawbacks of the Stewardship Approach

There are however several reservations that can be articulated in view of the UK's soft law approach to moderating and guiding institutional shareholder behaviour under the Stewardship Code.

First, in championing informal engagement and dialogue between institutions and investee companies, the Code may undermine the collective decision-making of the general meeting, which ensures parity of

---

(Critical Studies on Corporate Responsibility, Governance and Sustainability, Volume 5, Emerald Group Publishing Limited, 2013), pp. 19–59.

203 www.incr.com.

204 See note 202 above.

205 Eva Micheler, 'Facilitating Investor Engagement and Stewardship' (2013) 14 *European Business Organisation Law Review* 29.

206 Sharon Hannes, 'Brave New World: A Proposal for Institutional Investors' (2015) 16 *Theoretical Inquiries in the Law* 245.

207 Above.

treatment of shareholders at a formally organised forum in accordance with company law. The more resourced shareholders or the ones who regard the assumption of corporate governance roles as instrumental to their investment management purposes could assume such 'stewardship' and more effectively influence corporate decision-making through informal engagement episodes, creating an uneven playing field in the market for corporate influence. This has implications for the balance of power in the body of shareholders, a point of warning raised by Anabtawi and Stout[208] who are of the view that more legal governance of such shareholders is needed.

Further, many institutions that do not in reality regard engagement as key to their investment management approach may nonetheless feel pressured to conform and thus sign up to the Code (which may explain the high number of signatories). These institutions may take a minimalist and cosmetic approach to the Code, in order not to incur too much cost. But they use their signatory status to 'brand' themselves to investors.[209] This would be rather pertinent for retail collective investment schemes that are in fierce competition for investment flows. The Financial Reporting Council has identified this as a hazard and has, after several years from the introduction of the Stewardship Code, made its concerns louder with regard to the patchy compliance that funds have demonstrated vis-à-vis the Code.[210] The FRC has decided to introduce a system of classification for institutional signatories so that those that are genuinely active may be distinguished from those that free-ride on the stewardship brand.[211] Classifying institutions into different tiers of commitment to engagement is intended to create a clearer distinction between institutions that walk the talk of stewardship and those that merely free-ride upon the brand. The tiering approach has immediately resulted

---

208 See Chapters 4 and 5, Iris H-Y Chiu, *The Foundations and Anatomy of Shareholder Activism* (2010), above; Iman Anabtawi and Lynn Stout, 'Fiduciary Duties for Activist Shareholders' (2008), as above. See also Matthew R Denes, Jonathan M Karpoff and Victoria B McWilliams, 'Thirty Years of Shareholder Activism: A Survey of Empirical Research' (2015) at http://ssrn.com/abstract=2608085.

209 'Activism has become a marketing strategy', *Financial Times* (10 August 2014).

210 FRC, Developments in Corporate Governance and Stewardship 2015 (Jan 2016) at https://www.frc.org.uk/Our-Work/Publications/Corporate-Governance/Developments-in-Corporate-Governance-and-Stewa-(1).pdf.

211 FRC, Developments in Corporate Governance and Stewardship 2015 (Jan 2016), above.

in the loss of signatories[212] but can also be seen as producing a winnowing effect that helps maintain the integrity of the notion of 'stewardship'.

A more fundamental criticism of the Code is that it deals with the procedural aspects of engagement, such as acceptable modes of 'monitoring' or 'escalation'. But it does not deal with the substance of what institutional investors will raise with companies during the engagement process. As we have observed, funds are likely to view their corporate governance activities as instrumental to their specific business objectives and incentives. Their demands may not therefore be always in the best interests of the company as a whole over the longer term. This conflict of interest between the company's best interests and the immediate commercial interests of institutional investors is observed most acutely in the case of hedge funds' demands to restructure or sell companies, accept or facilitate a takeover bid, cut expenditure on research and development type expenditures or to carry out share buybacks.[213]

Hence we believe that well-meaning attempts to implant a stewardship orientation into institutional shareholders is likely to produce mixed success, with perhaps only a genuine minority that hold to the ethos of 'good corporate equity ownership' described in Section B. In terms of long-termism, Chapter 2 has discussed how persistently short termist most funds are, given their structures and incentives and regulatory compliance requirements. It is uncertain how a call to 'stewardship' in soft law that introduces procedural but not substantive change of their business models would fundamentally change that orientation. Although Denes et al[214] report that greater corporate performance impact is achieved by more powerful shareholder activism, this may be a stock-market rather than an operational phenomenon. Markets may rally when they perceive an engaged shareholder in place, but whether this is likely to be associated with improved operating performance or longer-term corporate success remains questionable. One of us has also argued[215] that

---

212 FRC, 'Tiering of Signatories to the Stewardship Code' (14 Nov 2016) at https://www.frc.org.uk/News-and-Events/FRC-Press/Press/2016/November/Tiering-of-signatories-to-the-Stewardship-Code.aspx.

213 See also John Plender, 'Blowing the whistle on buybacks and value destruction', *Financial Times* (2 March 2016).

214 Matthew R Denes, Jonathan M Karpoff and Victoria B McWilliams, 'Thirty Years of Shareholder Activism: A Survey of Empirical Research' (2015), above.

215 Iris H-Y Chiu, 'Institutional shareholders as Stewards: Towards a New Conception of Corporate Governance?' (2012), above.

shareholder stewardship further embeds the conventional wisdom of shareholder primacy.[216] The championing of shareholder primacy has the potential to marginalise stakeholder and wider concerns and fundamentally constrains efforts to develop a more responsible system of capitalism.[217] We are thus sceptical that shareholder stewardship should be regarded as a panacea for either corporate governance or wider socio-economic concerns.

That said, the European Commission has forged ahead to endorse shareholder engagement as a norm in corporate governance in its proposed Directive of 2014. However, the European provisions have a different tenor, as will be explored, and may pave the way for more balanced regulation of shareholder behaviour. Nevertheless, casting these provisions in the paradigm of the 'Shareholders' Rights Directive', i.e. as a measure in corporate governance, is arguably misplaced.

European Shareholder Rights Directive 2017

The European Commission has, in a recent round of revisions to the Shareholder Rights Directive, introduced further reforms to encourage and realise the exercise of cross-border shareholder rights. One aspect of these reforms is the introduction of a regime that deals with shareholder engagement.[218] These reforms have now been agreed by the key EU institutions. It is noted that the term 'stewardship' is not used in the proposed European legislation but shareholder engagement is actively encouraged along lines similar to those in the UK Stewardship Code.

The final text of the legislation provides that Member States shall require institutional investors and asset managers to develop an engagement policy, which will state, *inter alia*, how institutional investors and asset managers intend to integrate shareholder engagement in their investment strategy, monitor their investee companies' performance, exercise their voting rights, use proxy advisors' services and cooperate

---

216 Maria Goranova and Lori Verstegen Ryan, 'Shareholder Activism: A Multidisciplinary Review' (2014) 40 *Journal of Management* 1230; but see Anastasia O'Rourke, 'A New Politics of Engagement: Shareholder Activism for Corporate Social Responsibility' (2003) 12 *Business Strategy and the Environment* 227.

217 Lynn Stout, *The Shareholder Value Myth: How Putting Shareholders First Harms Investors, Corporations, and the Public* (2012), above.

218 Directive (EU) 2017/828 of the European Parliament and of the Council of 17 May 2017 amending Directive 2007/36/EC as regards the encouragement of long-term shareholder engagement.

with other shareholders. The engagement policy must set out how institutions:

(a) integrate shareholder engagement in their investment strategy;
(b) monitor investee companies in relation to strategy, financial and non-financial performance and risk, capital structure, social and environmental impact and corporate governance;
(c) conduct dialogues with investee companies;
(d) exercise voting rights;
(e) cooperate with other shareholders;
(f) communicate with other stakeholders of the investee companies; and
(g) manage actual and potential conflicts of interest.

Institutions are required to publicly disclose their engagement policy, how it is implemented and the results achieved. If they decide not to institute an engagement policy or to disclose the matters above, they need to provide a clearly reasoned explanation for doing so. Further, institutional investors should annually disclose to the public their investment strategies and explain how such strategies are aligned with the duration of their liabilities and with the medium to long-term performance of their assets.[219]

Additionally, the Directive imposes disclosure obligations on asset managers, who must disclose on a yearly basis to their institutional clients how their investment strategies and policies intend to meet their clients' investment objectives and duration of liabilities.[220] The disclosures are to be made public, with reference to:

(a) key material medium to long-term risks associated with the investments;
(b) portfolio composition, turnover and turnover costs;
(c) the use of proxy advisors for the purpose of engagement activities;

---

[219] In particular, if institutions appoint asset managers, institutions must disclose how such arrangements would meet their objectives, their policies and strategies in evaluating asset managers and portfolio turnover, the duration of the appointment and how the agreed performance yardsticks and asset management charges and fees accord with their objectives. See Art. 3h, Shareholder Rights Directive 2017.

[220] Art. 3i, Shareholder Rights Directive 2017.

(d) policy on securities lending and how it is applied to fulfil its engagement activities if applicable, particularly at the time of the general meeting of the investee companies;
(e) information on whether, and if so how, they make investment decisions based on evaluation of medium to long-term performance of the investee company, including non-financial performance;
(f) whether, and if so which, conflicts of interests have arisen in connection with engagement activities and how the asset managers have dealt with them.

Finally, transparency obligations are also imposed on proxy advisory agencies.[221] They must disclose whether they adhere to a code of conduct issued by an industry body and provide a clear and reasoned explanation for any deviation from the code. Further, they are required to make public disclosure on a yearly basis of the following in order to shed light on their roles in assisting investment funds and asset managers in research and voting:

(a) the essential features of the methodologies and models they apply;
(b) the main information sources they use;
(c) the procedures put in place to ensure quality of the research, advice and voting recommendations and qualifications of the staff involved;
(d) whether and, if so, how they take national market, legal, regulatory and company-specific conditions into account;
(e) the essential features of the voting policies they apply for each market;
(f) whether they have dialogues with the companies which are the object of their research, advice or voting recommendations and with the stakeholders of the company, and if so, the extent and nature thereof.

The new European legislation introduces a soft law approach for governing institutions' engagement as a comply-or-explain approach is adopted, and only a voluntary code of conduct is to be developed for proxy advisory agencies. Such provisions may be seen to be extensions of the UK stewardship approach of 'moderated' norms in corporate governance. However, the Directive's public disclosure requirements imposed on institutions, asset managers and proxy advisers all speak of public

221 Article 3j, Shareholders Rights Directive 2017.

interest and scrutiny, and these sit uneasily with the soft law approach it adopts. This chapter will argue that the Directive has conflated and possibly confused the corporate governance aspects of shareholder engagement (which the UK Code focuses on) and the public interest in subjecting investment management practices to regulatory scrutiny (which the UK has to date avoided). These somewhat conflicting premises have resulted in provisions which are unclear as to accountability and enforcement. We suggest that it is more optimal to set out a clearer and more coherent regulatory regime for investment management practices including corporate governance behaviour. These will be explored below.

The Objectives of the European Shareholder Rights Directive

The Commission explains[222] that improving shareholder engagement is likely to address the issue of excessive short termism on the part of the asset management industry in managing institutional funds. In the Commission's view, short termism is not conducive for meaningful monitoring of corporate behaviour. Shareholders' short-term demand for financial performance puts pressure on companies, compromising their long-term wealth creation potential. Further, short termism on the part of asset managers adversely affects ultimate returns for institutional beneficiaries. The Commission's concerns are rooted in public interest concerns regarding the viability of pension savings through investment. Hence, subjecting institutional investment management to standards and scrutiny is arguably a form of re-regulation, in order to ensure that the privatised and financialised form of social welfare provision may deliver public interest objectives.[223] In this regard, the introduction of shareholder engagement norms in the Directive serves the public interest purpose, and is a form of regulation of investment management practices, although

---

[222] Commission Proposal 2014, at pp. 4, 5, 7 and 8.

[223] John Broadbent, Michael Palumbo and Elizabeth Woodman, 'The Shift from Defined Benefit to Defined Contribution Pension Plans – Implications for Asset Allocation and Risk Management' (*BIS Working Paper* 2006) at http://www.bis.org/publ/wgpapers/cgfs27broadbent3.pdf; Simone Polillo, 'Wildcats in Banking Fields: The Politics of Financial Inclusion' (2011) 40 *Theor Soc* 347; Ismail Erturk, Julie Froud, Sukhdev Johal, Adam Leaver and Karel Williams, 'The Democratization of Finance? Promises, Outcomes and Conditions' (2007) 14 *Review of International Political Economy* 553.

such norms are expressed as corporate governance standards.[224] The main objective of the Directive is clearly to address the public interest concerns surrounding the optimality of investment management practices, the assumption of corporate governance roles being one such aspect. However, the confused premises of the Directive are demonstrated by its comply-or-explain approach, which shows deference to the private paradigm of corporate governance where shareholders should choose how best to engage with their rights and roles. Yet the deference is limited as the Directive clearly wishes to subject investment funds and their asset managers to scrutiny by mandating public disclosure of their policies and activities, and to account for how wider interests such as stakeholders are taken into account. We turn to critically analyse the European legislation's approach and argue that there are inherent contradictions in the concurrent soft law and quasi-regulatory approach. These confused premises result in a regime that lacks clarity and effectiveness.

The Limitations of the European Shareholders' Rights Directive

First, the institution of an engagement policy on the part of institutional investors and asset managers is similar to Principle 1 of the Stewardship Code. It adopts a comply-or-explain approach, i.e. that institutions should comply with the practice of developing an engagement policy as outlined in the Article, but if they choose not to, they should explain how the lack of an engagement policy would still enable them to achieve their objectives. In this way, the Directive adopts the presumption that engaged shareholder behaviour *is equivalent* to optimal investment management practice and the onus is on institutions to show otherwise. As discussed earlier, we do not think this presumption is well-founded, given the different motivations behind and consequences of funds assuming the instrumental use of their corporate governance roles. This policy position puts faith in institutional shareholder behaviour beyond what is expressed by the UK. The UK's Stewardship Code is open to signatories who *voluntarily* regard their corporate governance roles as part of their investment management practice, leaving those who do not take this view with freedom not to sign. The Directive however more strongly presumes in favour of the good of institutional shareholder engagement, which we urge should still be examined with caution.

---

224 Policy underlying the Financial Services Action Plan 1999, Financial Services: Implementing the Framework for Financial Markets – Action Plan (1998) COM (1999)232.

Given the understandable interest in ensuring that modern investment management is not short-termist and can ultimately deliver the social good of long-term savings, we suggest that the right approach should not be to presume the optimality of investment management practice through adopting shareholder engagement, but to bring about more comprehensive regulatory standards for investment management practice to ensure that its perverse incentives are mitigated and that the regulatory objectives for investor protection in the short and long terms are clarified.

The European legislation now clarifies that institutions and their asset managers should disclose how their investment strategies meet medium to long-term investment performance needs, reflecting the public interest concern that investment management has become too short-termist.[225] However, the socially-oriented concerns that Parliament wished to address via shareholder engagement have been dropped in the final legislation, signalling that shareholder engagement is still primarily regarded as a 'private corporate governance' matter although policy-makers are concerned about how it is carried out and its implications for the corporate economy.

It may be argued that institutions' policies and their implementation are subject to public disclosure and hence public and beneficiaries' scrutiny. These may provide bottom-up driving forces to shape institutions' investment management practice. Institutions are obliged to publicly disclose the implementation and achievement of any engagement on their part in relation to their investment strategies, profile and duration of their liabilities and how such contributes to long-term corporate performance. Key elements of institutions' arrangements with their asset managers need to be disclosed. Public disclosure is also required in respect of the exercise of institutions' voting rights. Asset managers also have to account to their institutional clients in terms of how they meet their clients' needs with respect to investment horizon and maturity of liabilities. It is to be noted that part of asset managers' accountability to their institutional clients is now required to be publicly disclosed.

The public interest permeating the above provisions in the Directive underlies the nature of these public disclosure obligations. On the whole, it could be argued that the public disclosure by institutions and their asset managers would reveal the nature of their investment management practice and such can be scrutinised in terms of their effectiveness in

---

[225] Arts 3g, 3h, Directive (EU) 2017/828 of the European Parliament and of the Council of 17 May 2017 amending Directive 2007/36/EC as regards the encouragement of long-term shareholder engagement.

meeting eventual liabilities. The transparency is useful for generating pressures to reduce perverse incentives and agency problems that do not cohere with beneficiaries' long-term interests. However, we are not certain that public disclosure will galvanise such bottom-up governing forces to shape investment management practice. This is because such disclosures do not address the problems in weak beneficiaries' governance – which is a result of the structuration of the investment management chain, the lack of incentives to pursue enforcement (based on regulatory protection for liquidity rights), and the difficulties in making out a case anyway. If such disclosures are meant for regulatory scrutiny, then regulators have no basis for action as the regime in the Directive does not confer powers of regulatory governance upon any public authority.

The Directive as drafted weakly hints at the underlying public interest in the Commission's objectives. Its framing does not advance the form of governance that the Commission purports to be needed over investment management practice that delivers for long-term savers and supports a long-term wealth-creating corporate economy. The 'private' corporate governance paradigms used in the Directive contradict and are unable to accommodate the public interest underlying the Commission's concern for the nature and promises of investment management. The Directive's provisions aim at an optimal type of market behaviour on the part of shareholders but leave it to the private paradigms of 'comply or explain' in corporate governance to bring this about.

Within the essentially private nature of the corporate governance framework, many of these regulative aspects cannot or will not be enforced to achieve the desired governance effects. In this light, we suggest that there is a case to be made for thinking about investment management regulation in a more comprehensive manner. In the next Section, we sketch our thoughts for a regulatory framework.

E. REGULATING INVESTMENT MANAGEMENT PRACTICES AS THE WAY AHEAD?

As the private sector steps into the role of long-term provision for the financial needs of many through intermediating their savings, policy-makers are right to be concerned about the social outcomes of financialisation. Such concerns have only sharpened with passing decades with clearer focus upon the adverse effects of corporate short termism, the self-serving nature of the financial intermediation industry, the limitations of market-based financial capitalism and the inadequacy of investor financial literacy.

It is time to consider if investment management practices ought to be more coherently regulated to meet the objectives of long-term public interest in the intermediation of savings. In this respect, a patchwork of regulatory provisions has been introduced in the UK and EU to address various aspects of investment management. Prudential regulation has been introduced for defined benefit pension schemes for some time now,[226] and although the development of defined contribution schemes removes the financial pressures that apply to defined benefit schemes, regulatory governance has been introduced for defined contribution schemes in terms of scheme governance[227] and oversight, as well as fair management fees.[228] EU legislation has indeed extended prudential regulation to retail investment funds that are open-ended[229] and alternative investment funds.[230] Further, regulation has introduced standardised duties for

---

[226] An annual regulatory obligation is placed on pension funds to carry out actuarial valuations in order to ensure that they meet a 'statutory funding' requirement which assures that they are on track to meet their long-term liabilities, s226 Pensions Act 1995, which evolved from an earlier minimum funding requirement obligation.

[227] DWP, *Better Workplace Pensions: Further Measures for Savers* (March 2014) introduces employee oversight of workplace defined contribution schemes to ensure that the schemes appoint desirable asset managers, are properly managed and overseen and provide value for money. Such oversight is carried out by 'Independence Governance Committees' for the schemes.

[228] See FCA, *Charges in Workplace Personal Pension Schemes: A Consultation Paper* (Oct 2014) and *Final rules for Charges in Workplace Personal Pension Schemes and Feedback on CP14/24* (March 2015) on the charge cap of 0.75 per cent of assets under management, excluding transaction costs.

[229] EU-wide approved mutual funds known as UCITs are to have an initial capital at 125,000 euros and own funds at 0.02 per cent of assets under management, Art 7, Directive 2009/65/EC of the European Parliament and of the Council of 13 July 2009 on the coordination of laws, regulations and administrative provisions relating to undertakings for collective investment in transferable securities (UCITS) (recast) (UCITs Directive 2009).

[230] Hedge and private equity funds that are internally managed must have an initial capital of 300,000 euros, or if externally managed, have an initial capital of 125,000 euros. Funds are to maintain 0.02 per cent of assets under management exceeding 250 million euros as own funds, Art 9, Directive 2011/61/EU of the European Parliament and of the Council of 8 June 2011 on Alternative Investment Fund Managers and amending Directives 2003/41/EC and 2009/65/EC and Regulations (EC) No 1060/2009 and (EU) No 1095/2010 (AIFMD 2011).

investor protection[231] and boosted the rights of investor accountability and enforcement.[232] These are areas that would not have been developed in private law, and indeed would have been increasingly eclipsed by the structure of the investment chain discussed in Chapter 2.[233] The new European Shareholders' Rights Directive 2017 also fits into this mosaic, but more joined-up thinking is required in order to address the range of public interest concerns in investment management.

We support the case for developing a coherent and comprehensive regulatory regime for investment management, clearly debating the dilemmas in regulatory objectives and the tradeoffs. The existing patchwork of regulatory governance currently in force should be part of such a holistic exercise. We also point out that the following aspects remain inadequately dealt with under current regulatory frameworks:

(a) the match between savers' expectations and investment management practices;
(b) identifying aspects of self-serving opportunities in investment management and how to mitigate them;
(c) identifying perverse incentives in investment management that undermine savers' long-term goals; and

---

[231] See Arts 13, 17–18, 20–23 of Commission Directive 2010/43/EU of 1 July 2010 implementing Directive 2009/65/EC of the European Parliament and of the Council as regards organisational requirements, conflicts of interest, conduct of business, risk management and content of the agreement between a depositary and a management company. These relate to management of conflicts of interest, duties of diligence in management, treating investors fairly and acting in their best interests, and considering using the rights to vote in investee companies. The Alternative Investment Fund Managers Directive also provides for investor protection duties, see Art 12, AIFMD 2011 on care, skill and diligence, to employ resources effectively for the performance of due functions, to manage conflicts of interest, to act in the best interests of investors, to comply with all regulatory requirements and to treat investors fairly.

[232] Regular reporting is mandated under the UCITs Directive 2009, e.g. Arts 68, 69, 73 and the AIFMD 2011, Arts 22–23 for investors in terms of annual and periodic reporting, and specific reporting to regulators, see Art 24, and Arts 110–11, Commission Delegated Regulation (EU) No 231/2013 of 19.12.2012 supplementing Directive 2011/61/EU of the European Parliament and of the Council with regard to exemptions, general operating conditions, depositaries, leverage, transparency and supervision (19 Dec 2012).

[233] Discussed in John Morley, 'The Separation of Funds and Managers: A Theory of Investment Fund Structure and Regulation' (2013–14) 123 *Yale Law Journal* 1228.

(d) identifying the scope of entities in the investment chain that should be subject to regulatory governance.

In light of the above themes, we highlight a few key areas that ought to be considered for regulatory governance in respect of funds' assumption of corporate governance roles as part of their investment management.

Regulatory Governance for Entities in the Investment Chain

Many commentators referred to in Chapter 2 voice concerns regarding the length and complexity of the investment chain, and it is arguable that there are market failures and gaps in public interest that are unlikely to be met via the private law relations (in contract, corporate or trust law) that govern the different entities in the chain. Thus, a thorough study is needed to identify the entities in the chain, their functions and purpose and the public interest implications of their roles. The market failures or public interest gaps that surface in relation to each link of the chain should be determined, in order to consider appropriate regulatory governance that may be extended. For example, it may be necessary to consider if investment or pension consultants should be subject to regulatory governance. The Law Commission highlights how much power pension consultants wield over pension funds, and warn of the concentrated nature of the industry.[234] Further, as consultants are increasingly offering fiduciary management services, i.e. a one-stop service from consultancy to asset management, conflicts of interest may abound[235] and it is uncertain if private law such as contract or trust can adequately deal with the perverse incentives and potential compromises in such arrangements. It is timely to consider whether regulatory governance may be able to introduce proscriptive duties to deal with managing or avoiding conflicts

---

[234] The Law Commission, *Fiduciary Duties of Investment Intermediaries* (1 July 2014) at para 11.4 et seq; 'Pension consultants face fresh calls for regulatory oversight', *Financial Times* (19 Oct 2014).

[235] Eric R W Knight and Adam D Dixon, 'The Role of Investment Consultants in Transforming Pension Fund Decision Making: The Integration of Environmental, Social, and Governance Considerations into Corporate Valuation' in James Hawley, Shyam Kamath and Andrew Williams (eds), *Corporate Governance Failures* (University of Pennsylvania Press 2014) at Chapter 10, 217. But see 'Willis Towers Watson reveals fiduciary performance figures', *Financial Times* (31 Jan 2016) that reveals good performance.

of interests and prescriptive duties extended to the interests of ultimate beneficiaries.[236]

Next, there may also be a case for subjecting proxy advisory agencies to regulatory governance. Proxy advisory agencies are in a position to influence one aspect of funds' investment management – i.e. the assumption of their corporate governance roles in respect of exercising voting rights. As many funds are widely diversified, and pension and retail collective investment funds are in particular required by regulation to be so structured, diversification increases the cost and burden of monitoring and exercising voting rights at company general meetings. Proxy advisory agencies provide a useful service of collating research, advising on the exercise of votes and carrying out the execution of voting.

However, these agencies may become too powerful if funds and their asset managers rubberstamp their voting advice. This would mean that such agencies would effectively wield significant power over corporations, depending on their voting advice, without the need to demonstrate much accountability.[237] Empirical research[238] finds that many institutions follow proxy voting advice although funds with larger stakes may carry out independent research and deviate from the advice. Some commentators therefore voice concerns about whether proxy advisers' recommendations are based on sound research, and whether they make standardised assumptions that support one-size-fits-all recommendations.[239] Further, the proxy advisory industry is highly concentrated, dominated by a few large players. They also face conflicts of interest as they provide advisory services to companies too, and it remains uncertain if the management of their conflicts of interest is adequate to ensure that voting advice is impartial and objective.[240] One study finds that conflicts of interest affect

---

[236] 'Asset Managers Turn Against Investment Consultants', *Financial Times* (27 Feb 2017).

[237] David Larcker and Allan McCall, 'The Power of Proxy Advisory Firms', *Harvard Law School Forum* (13 Jan 2014).

[238] Michael C Schouten, 'Do Institutional Investors Follow Proxy Advice Blindly?' (2012) at http://ssrn.com/abstract=1978343; Stephen J Choi, Jill E Fisch and Marcel Kahan, 'The Power of Proxy Advisors: Myth or Reality?' (2010) 59 *Emory Law Journal* 869.

[239] Paul J Rose, 'The Corporate Governance Industry' (2007) 32 *Journal of Corporation Law* 887; David Larcker and Allan McCall, 'The Power of Proxy Advisory Firms' (13 Jan 2014), above.

[240] Daniel M Gallagher, 'Outsized Power & Influence: The Role of Proxy Advisers', *Harvard Law School Forum* (5 Sep 2014); Paul J Rose, 'The Corporate Governance Industry' (2007), above.

the proxy advisers' voting advice, usually in the direction of bias towards management.[241]

In the EU, the European Securities and Markets Authority has already voiced concerns about the proxy advisory industry, its unregulated nature and its accountability deficit compared to its power. Hence, ESMA has called for the industry to demonstrate more robust self-regulation by adopting a code of best practices and to demonstrate adherence to it.[242] The Code was drafted by the 'Best Practices Principles Group' under ESMA's auspices, and contained three broadly framed principles. The Code was to apply on a comply-or-explain basis to voluntary signatories. To date all key proxy advisory agencies are signatories including Glass Lewis, ISS, Manifest and PIRC. Principle One requires signatories to provide services that are delivered in accordance with agreed client specifications. Signatories should have and publicly disclose their research methodology and, if applicable, 'house' voting policies. They should put in place a constructive system of client disclosure and accountability, and management of client relations. Principle Two requires signatories to have and publicly disclose a conflicts-of-interest policy that details their procedures for addressing potential or actual conflicts of interest that may arise in connection with the provision of services. Finally, Principle Three requires signatories to have and publicly disclose their policy (or policies) for communication with issuers, shareholder proponents, other stakeholders, media and the public. ESMA is keenly monitoring agencies' adherence to the Principles and finds that the comply-or-explain landscape is still patchy due to the lack of an ultimate body for accountability. ESMA is in the process of turning the Best Practices Principles Group into such a quasi-governance body.[243]

The eventual hardening of a governance regime for proxy advisory agencies is probably not far off given that the EU Shareholders' Right Directive discussed above has already embarked on identifying areas of concern. We suggest that more exact framing of prescriptive and proscriptive duties for proxy advisory agencies is warranted in due course, such as in relation to avoiding conflicts of interest, just as credit rating

---

[241] Tao Li, 'Outsourcing Corporate Governance: Conflicts of Interest in the Proxy Advisory Industry' (2016) at http://papers.ssrn.com/sol3/papers.cfm?abstract_id=2828690.

[242] ESMA, *Final Report on The Proxy Advisor Industry* (19 Feb 2013).

[243] ESMA, *Report: Follow-up on the Development of the Best Practice Principles for Providers of Shareholder Voting Research and Analysis* (2015).

agencies are now subject.[244] Further prescriptions of duty such as backward validation of key voting recommendations, or due diligence in research, may also be useful.

Some commentators are of the view that instead of strengthening the governance mechanisms over the chain of intermediaries, perhaps the ultimate beneficiaries should be empowered to participate in the corporate governance of their funds' investee companies.[245] This would address the concerns for the disempowered ultimate investor and would introduce new forms of accountability and discipline for corporations. We are sceptical of such suggestions.

We have every sympathy for the apparently disempowered investor whose capital is pooled into a fund and therefore relies on the fund's investment management, including its assumption of corporate governance roles, to realise returns. However, it is contrary to the principle of the pooling mechanism and also counterproductive for its cost-effectiveness to then decentralise one aspect of investment management (i.e. the assumption of corporate governance roles) for direct participation by ultimate beneficiaries. This begs the question of why other aspects of investment management are not decentralised, for example, the portfolio allocation? Such an approach unravels the benefits of the collective investment process and its transaction-cost efficiencies. Further, we are of the view that it is not the *ad hoc* say that ultimate savers can have in the funds' investee companies that would introduce market discipline for their investee companies or investment intermediaries. Individual investors bring with them personal incentives and agendas, and cannot be assumed to be better 'stewards' than funds. Further, they may be apathetic about having such a say if asking them to participate is perceived as a 'hassle'. The cost of having to facilitate their participation, for example at AGMs, would likely be wasteful in light of their likely passivity and apathy. We suspect that it is an arguably hopeless and misplaced cause to look at directly empowering the ultimate beneficiaries to exercise corporate governance rights as a way to provide market discipline for funds and companies.

---

244 Annex 1.B.4, Regulation (EC) No 1060/2009 of the European Parliament and of the Council of 16 September 2009 on credit rating agencies.

245 Ewan McGaughey, 'Participation in Corporate Governance' (2014) at http://ssrn.com/abstract=2593904; Stephen Davis, Jon Lukomnik and David Pitt-Watson, 'Active Shareowner Stewardship: A New Paradigm for Capitalism' (2009) 2 *Rotman International Journal of Pension Management* 10; Anne M Tucker, 'The Outside Investor: Citizen Shareholders and Corporate Alienation' (2013–2014) 11 *U. St. Thomas L.J.* 99.

Instead, a regime to govern practices of investment management could cover all aspects of investment management, and not just their corporate governance roles. That is best designed, supervised and enforced by a regulator. The regulator should clearly articulate the objectives in question and invite debate as to how dilemmas in objectives and interests may be resolved. Such a regulatory regime can overcome the partitioning of legal duties caused by the investment chain structuration and articulate standards that compel chain entities to act in the ultimate long-term interests of savers. The public interest can overtly shape regulatory duties, and can serve as a means of introducing fundamental cultural and behavioural change into investment management. The introduction of a regulatory regime is transaction-cost efficient, providing a centralised system of governance and enforcement against the investment chain entities, and would likely reflect the common interests of many savers. Individual savers are not prevented from taking private enforcement action to address particular interests, whether in private law or in breach of statutory duty.[246] It could even be conceived that the Financial Ombudsman service could extend to dispute resolution between investors and entities in the investment chain on the basis of breaches of investment management duties in regulation. The ultimate investor need not be disempowered in the complex environment of investment management if adequately supported by regulatory duties and avenues to seek redress.

Regulation of Securities Lending?

We are also of the view that the securities lending activities carried out by institutions should be appropriately scrutinised by regulators in order to consider if regulatory governance is needed. This is because securities lending affects the assumption of corporate governance roles by institutions and their borrowers. If institutions' assumption of corporate governance roles should be regarded as a matter of public interest and be increasingly likely to be subject to regulatory governance, then their securities lending activities should accordingly be subject to regulatory scrutiny.

Securities lending by institutions takes place on a massive scale in global markets.[247] This is because securities lending supports short selling activities as well as the need for wholesale market borrowers to pledge collateral in order to obtain short term money market funding.

---

[246] Already existing in s150, UK Financial Services and Markets Act 2000.

[247] Tobias Adrian, Brian Begalle, Adam Copeland and Antoine Martin, 'Repo and Securities Lending' (2011) http://ssrn.com/abstract=1976327.

Early commentators reported how high quality government securities were the mainstay in the market for collateral to access short term wholesale funding.[248] The acceptable range of collateral has expanded over the years and now includes a wide range of corporate securities and structured products.[249]

When institutions engage in securities lending, they earn a fee for the loan of securities while transferring to the borrower the securities and all attendant rights, including corporate governance rights in investee companies. The borrower is obliged to redeliver an equivalent amount of the securities to the lender at an agreed date in the future plus the fee for borrowing. Institutions earn significant amounts of revenue through securities lending.[250]

Thus, when institutions lend their securities, voting rights attached to the securities are transferred to the borrower, and the borrower may be able to exercise those rights even if the underlying economic interest in the securities remains with the lender. This is the situation described by Hu and Black as 'empty voting',[251] and they caution that empty voting can be undertaken with perverse incentives due to the decoupling of economic from corporate governance rights. Empty voting involving perverse incentives, i.e. when the exercise of votes is patently not in the company's interest, has been observed in a few, but not many, cases as Ali et al discuss in relation to the US and Hong Kong.[252] Further, the logic of empty voting extends to what Hu and Black call 'empty vote-buying',[253] which is the deliberate engagement in borrowing securities to vote just before the company's general meeting. Most commentators[254] agree that empty

---

[248] Paul Lipson, Bradley K Sabel and Frank M Keane, 'Securities Lending' (Federal Reserve Bank of NY 1989) at http://ssrn.com/abstract=2030418.

[249] Zoltan Poszar, 'Levered Betas and Wholesale Funding in the Context of Secular Stagnation' (2015) at http://ssrn.com/abstract=2558945.

[250] Geert T M J Raaijmakers, 'Securities Lending and Corporate Governance' (2005) at http://ssrn.com/abstract=928312.

[251] Henry T C Hu and Bernard Black, 'The New Vote Buying: Empty Voting and Hidden (Morphable) Ownership' (2006) 79 *Southern California Law Review* 811

[252] Paul Ali, Ian Ramsay and Benjamin B Saunders, 'Securities Lending, Empty Voting and Corporate Governance' (2014) at http://ssrn.com/abstract=2443217.

[253] Henry T C Hu and Bernard Black, 'Equity and Debt Decoupling and Empty Voting II: Importance and Extensions' (2008) 156 *University of Pennsylvania Law Review* 625.

[254] Carl Clottens, 'Empty Voting: A European Perspective' (2012) 9 *European Company and Financial Law Review* 446; Geert T M J Raaijmakers,

voters or empty vote-buyers are not necessarily always acting to a company's detriment, and both beneficial and adverse outcomes can occur as a result of empty voting or empty vote-buying.

However, when institutions lend their securities, they are unable to assume their corporate governance roles or unable to control how the corporate governance rights attached to their shares would be exercised. If institutional shareholder engagement, and not just any shareholder engagement, matters in the public interest, as is seen in the continued policy exhortation to institutions in the UK and EU, then it is of paramount importance how securities lending affects the exercise of corporate governance roles and rights. Regulators need to consider to what extent securities lending should be curtailed in order to ensure that institutions assume their engagement roles, and to what extent borrowers of securities should or should not be allowed to exercise certain corporate governance rights.

Most commentators agree that banning securities lending is too draconian. Securities lending provides benefits in terms of improving liquidity in the markets, supporting wholesale funding, and allowing funds to generate revenue in order to smooth out the vicissitudes of investment performance.[255] However, imposing some responsibilities on institutions may be appropriate, such as making it mandatory for institutions to make disclosure of securities lending activities. But as some commentators[256] rightly point out, disclosure may not be an effective regulatory tool, as information about securities lending is not necessarily a subject matter for facilitating efficient market discipline. It is uncertain how the market would perceive a notification that the institutional owner

---

'Securities Lending and Corporate Governance' (2005) at http://ssrn.com/abstract=928312; Alon Brav and Richmond D Mathews, 'Empty Voting and the Efficiency of Corporate Governance' (2011) 99 *Journal of Financial Economics* 289.

[255] Jesse Blocher and Robert E Whaley, 'Passive Investing and Securities Lending' (2015) at http://ssrn.com/abstract=2474904; Reena Aggarwal, Jennie Bai and Luc Laeven, 'The Securities Lending Market and the Collateral Channel of Monetary Policy Transmission' (2016) at http://ssrn.com/abstract=2692251; Savina Rizova, 'Securities Lending by Mutual Funds' (2011) at http://ssrn.com/abstract=2056651. Rizova in particular shows how lacklustre past performance in investment drives funds to increase securities lending in order to smooth out returns.

[256] Paul Ali, Ian Ramsay and Benjamin B Saunders, 'Securities Lending, Empty Voting and Corporate Governance' (2014), above; Wolf-Georg Ringe, 'Hedge Funds and Risk-Decoupling – The Empty Voting Problem in the European Union' (2013) 36 *Seattle University Law Review* 1027.

is not exercising its corporate governance rights while the borrower may do so. Would this result in a market price spike or decline in share price? A spike could be likely if a hedge fund borrower is seen as agitating for change that may pay out in short termist gains. But a share price decline could also result if the institutional owner's neglect to assume its corporate governance role is perceived negatively by the market.

Perhaps institutions could be made to recall lent shares around the date of finalisation of membership for voting eligibility at the general meeting. This is however difficult to monitor and enforce, although Christofferson et al[257] report that this is usually done as a matter of best practice anyway. It is also questioned whether such a mandatory requirement would cause adverse knock-on effects for the economic activities supported by securities lending. Many AGMs could converge within a certain period of time and the mandatory requirement to recall would place constraints on the economic activities that securities lending supports, such as the provision of collateral for the smooth functioning of short term money markets that depend on rehypothecation of collateral.

Further, we could consider the possibility of making it mandatory that the borrowers of securities should not borrow them in order to vote on them,[258] or should not vote on them *per se*.[259] This prohibition would not prevent securities lending from being carried out for other economic purposes, and would avoid distorting the investee company's corporate governance fabric. However, commentators also opine that allowing a market for corporate governance rights to arise through securities lending is not a bad thing, as corporate governance rights can then be apportioned by the market to those who are most motivated to use them. Those that do not regard the assumption of corporate governance rights as relevant to their investment management model need not be compelled to do so, and would be able to participate in the market for corporate governance

---

[257] Susan E K Christoffersen, Christopher C Geczy, David K Musto, and Adam V Reed, 'Vote Trading and Information Aggregation' (2007) 62 *Journal of Finance* 2897.

[258] International Securities Lending Association (ISLA), *Voting Issues for Beneficial Owners* (2015) at p. 3, see http://www.isla.co.uk/wp-content/uploads/2015/08/SecuritiesLendingVotingIssuesforBeneficalOwners.pdf, also see Bank of England and ISLA, *Securities Lending and Corporate Governance* (2000) at p. 5, at http://www.bankofengland.co.uk/markets/Documents/gilts/slcgjun05.pdf.

[259] Hedge Fund Working Group, *Hedge Fund Standards: Final Report* (2008).

rights through securities lending. Indeed, Blocher et al[260] and Rizova[261] find that passively managed funds such as indexed or exchange-traded funds are the keenest securities lenders and adopt securities lending as a major part of their business model. However, encouraging a market for corporate governance rights to arise may be argued to be an extreme form of commoditising share ownership. This market provides for a relatively inexpensive way of gaining corporate governance rights, without the full extent of capital commitment required for the purchase of shares. It is susceptible to being used and abused by opportunistic entities who see the assumption of corporate governance rights as serving some instrumental purpose.

Although there is no conclusive evidence that securities lenders are necessarily shirkers in the assumption of their corporate governance rights or that securities borrowers are opportunistic vote buyers that imperil companies at general meetings, the extent to which securities lending *ought* to be part of investment management should be debated upon and determined.[262] At the very least, we should continue to observe how securities lenders and borrowers assume corporate governance roles and the impact of such upon investee companies, in order to determine if they should be subject to regulatory control over their exercise of corporate governance rights.

F. CONCLUSION

This chapter draws together a high level perspective of the instrumental assumption of corporate governance roles by institutions, and shows that both neglect of such roles or the use of them in a self-interested manner by short-term oriented financial actors produces a mixture of beneficial and deleterious effects for investee companies. The desirability of promoting greater shareholder engagement in a world of institutional share ownership is far from obvious, and should not necessarily be seen as the key to an optimal system of corporate governance, as the UK Stewardship Code and the European Shareholder Rights Directive seem to assume.

---

260 Jesse Blocher and Robert E Whaley, 'Passive Investing and Securities Lending' (2015), above.

261 Savina Rizova, 'Securities Lending by Mutual Funds' (2011), above.

262 Simon C Y Wong, 'Is Institutional Investor Stewardship Still Elusive?' (2015) *Butterworths Journal of Banking and Financial Law* 508.

We are of the view that the new European Shareholder Rights Directive has not taken a bold step forward in addressing the public interest aspects of investment management in relation to their corporate governance roles, falling back upon the private paradigm of economically-driven corporate governance to do so. We wonder if the time is near for more comprehensive thinking about the governance and regulation of investment management practices. We would welcome the exploration of such a regulatory approach. Such a framework could build upon the existing patchwork of UK and EU prudential and conduct of business regulation, but also more thoroughly deal with issues hitherto unaddressed, such as the investment chain structuration and the role of the various entities of which it is composed, appropriate conduct in securities lending, and more broadly the mitigation of agency problems and perverse incentives in the investment chain.

Regulation may be the only means, albeit not necessarily perfect, to address the long-term needs of savers reliant on the investment management industry, and its impact on the long-term wealth-creating potential of the corporate economy. We do not believe that a soft law approach of shareholder stewardship which situates the underlying public interest notions in a private 'corporate governance' paradigm is an adequate one. Given commentators' persistent scepticism[263] of the effectiveness of 'shareholder stewardship', we urge UK and EU regulators to look in a different direction.

---

[263] Above, Iris H-Y Chiu, 'Turning Institutional Investors into "Stewards" – Exploring the Meaning and Objectives in "Stewardship"' (2013), above; Arad Reisberg, 'The UK Stewardship Code: On a road to Nowhere' (2015) 15 *The Journal of Corporate Law Studies* 217.

4. Pension funds as corporate governance actors

A. INTRODUCTION

Clark[1] has documented a stellar rise in Anglo-American pension funds as a source of investment capital for corporations since the 1980s. Pension fund capitalism was here to stay, and would be dominated by Anglo-American pension funds and their asset managers, from the US, UK, Canada and Australia.[2] With the notable exception of the Netherlands, occupational pension funds from other jurisdictions and emerging jurisdictions are less significant forces in the global investment market.[3] Commentators suggest that for non-Anglo-American developed jurisdictions, factors such as the state's greater role in social welfare, the dominance of bank-based corporate finance structures and social culture in employment relations have shaped the nature of pension saving; and where emerging jurisdictions are concerned, low levels of income and capital wealth are the main reasons for the relative insignificance of their pension funds on the global stage.[4]

In the UK, occupational pensions are the mainstay of pension provision although personal, group and stakeholder pensions have grown in market share.[5] The key occupational pension funds are the funded public

---

[1] Gordon L Clark, *Pension Fund Capitalism* (Oxford: OUP, 2000), at Chapter 2.

[2] *Ibid.*

[3] Willis Towers Watson. 'Global Pension Assets Study 2016', February 2016. https://www.willistowerswatson.com/en/insights/2016/02/global-pensions-asset-study-2016

It should be noted however that countries such as Japan, South Korea, Norway, China and Singapore operate significant state pension funds. We consider these funds in Chapter 8 in relation to sovereign wealth funds.

[4] Gordon L Clark, *Pension Fund Capitalism* (2000), above at Chapter 3.

[5] The NAPF notes that public and private sector defined benefit pension schemes make up about £1 trillion of assets, and 98 per cent of private sector schemes are occupational schemes. See NAPF, *Trends in Defined Benefit Asset Allocation: The Changing Shape of UK Pension Investment* (July 2013) at p. 5.

sector pension funds which are structured as defined benefit schemes, the private sector defined benefit schemes and the private sector defined contribution schemes.[6] Insurance companies are significant players in the personal and stakeholder pensions market and are annuity writers. These groups have been significant corporate equity owners in the UK but this is a declining trend as will be discussed shortly.

Under defined benefit schemes, employers and employees both contribute to a scheme where employers guarantee fixed pension benefits tied to a proportion of final salary or a career average formula, taking on investment risk and longevity risk in meeting ultimate maturing pension liabilities. Under defined contribution schemes, employers and employees agree to a fixed rate of contribution to an individual pension fund which is then built up to (usually) buy an annuity on retirement.[7] The employee is given an option as to how the individual pension fund may be invested within a range of funds selected by the employer or in self-invested personal pensions appropriate for wealthy and experienced individuals. Employers may also arrange to enrol employees into stakeholder pensions or the National Employment Savings Trust (NEST) accountable to the Department for Work and Pensions and to Parliament.[8] Employees bear the investment risk of the scheme and hence have no guaranteed benefits when liabilities mature in the scheme at retirement. At retirement, retirees use their 'pension pot', valued at that time, to buy an annuity for lifetime payouts, usually underwritten by an insurer. However, the Chancellor introduced a major pension reform in his 2014 budget, permitting pensioners to withdraw 25 per cent of their pension pots tax-free upon retirement and to provide them with freedom of choice as to whether the pension pot should be withdrawn totally or partially (a process known as drawdown) and used for unrestricted investment or to purchase annuities. The FCA's initial market study indicates that pensioners are not making much use of the new choices open to them and tend towards purchasing annuities from the existing provider, hence not

---

[6] There are also defined contribution schemes offered to members in the public sector but these schemes are not significant in size.

[7] The use of the pension pot has been liberated since April 2014 as pensioners can choose to withdraw lump sums instead and avail themselves of investment opportunities other than annuities.

[8] Pensions Act 2008 reforms providing for auto-enrolment and the establishment of an independent NEST accountable to Parliament through the Department of Work and Pensions.

necessarily obtaining value for money.[9] The FCA's persistent competition drive in this area,[10] coupled with increased conduct of business regulation, may in time affect the annuities market.

UK pension institutions invest in corporate equity in the UK, but increasingly, their share of corporate equity in the UK has given way to investment in foreign assets. In turn, foreign institutions are becoming significant owners of UK corporate equity.[11] Despite the diminishing influence of UK pension funds, this chapter discusses UK pension institutions and their corporate governance roles as part of their investment management practice. However, we also take stock of the corporate governance behaviour of pension institutions in relation to UK corporate equity at a more general level in Section C. We are of the view that although the landscape of pension institution investors in UK corporate equity is dominated by foreign Anglo-American institutions, there are many similarities and cross-fertilisations in corporate governance behaviour. This could be due to the fact that a highly international asset management industry is delegated with much of the investment management of pension assets whether those assets are based in the UK or otherwise. Further, a unifying effect in institutional shareholder behaviour may be achieved by significant subscription to the UK Stewardship Code,[12] as well as international shareholder best practices such as the UN Principles of Responsible Investment.[13]

A Survey of UK Pensions Institutions and Trends

A high percentage of public sector pensions in the UK are unfunded defined benefit schemes, such as the centrally administered National Health Service, Teachers and Armed Forces Pension Schemes, and the locally administered police and firefighters' schemes.[14] These represent a contingent liability for the Treasury. The Local Government Pensions

---

[9] FCA, *Retirement Income Market Study: Final Report – Confirmed Findings and Remedies* (March 2015).

[10] FCA, *Retirement Outcomes Review: Terms of Reference* (July 2016).

[11] At 54 per cent, according to the statistics of the 2015 ONS Survey. The share of UK equity held by insurance companies in the UK is at 6 per cent and pension funds at 3 per cent. See http://www.ons.gov.uk/ons/dcp171778_415334.pdf.

[12] Over 300 signatories, both UK based and foreign.

[13] https://www.unpri.org/.

[14] *Independent Public Service Pensions Commission Final Report* (March 2011) (aka Hutton Report), at p. 123. The Hutton Report recognises the hazards of unfunded schemes and the need to take financial stock of the maturing

Scheme (LGPS) is however funded and is an umbrella term that encompasses 89 local government and authority employers including London boroughs.[15] Valued in 2013, the LGPS had assets of about £178 billion[16], representing about 7 per cent[17] of pension assets in the UK, and its largest fund, at about £11 billion, is comparable to the largest private sector defined benefit schemes. Private sector defined benefit pension schemes (DB schemes) represent the majority of pension funds in the UK although the trend is towards closure of defined benefit schemes and the rise of defined contribution schemes (DC schemes).[18] The Pensions Policy Institute reports that large private sector defined benefit schemes with over 10 000 members are few but dominant, with size of assets dwarfing the massive numbers of smaller schemes.[19] As of 2013, total pension assets in the UK exceed £1 trillion,[20] representing about 38 per cent[21] of institutional assets in the UK. Defined benefit pension schemes constitute about 55 per cent of pension assets while defined contribution schemes represent 45 per cent.[22]

This chapter first discusses the broad trends in asset allocation to equities and their ramifications for pension funds as corporate governance actors. It then discusses key issues and factors that shape funds and their asset managers as corporate governance players. A high level of

---

liabilities of the schemes regularly. However, it does not advocate the schemes' movement to a fully-funded basis, see pp. 103, 115.

15 Department for Communities and Local Government, *Local Government Pension Scheme: Opportunities for Collaboration, Cost Savings and Efficiencies* (May 2014) at para 2.4.

16 Above, and NAPF, *Local Government Pension Scheme 2013: Investing in a Changing World* (May 2013) at p. 15.

17 IMA, *Investment Asset Management Survey 2013–14* (2014) at p. 39.

18 PPI, *The Changing Landscape for Private Sector Defined Benefit Pension Schemes* (2007); Gordon L Clark and Ashby HB Monk, 'The "Crisis" in Defined Benefit Corporate Pension Liabilities: Current Solutions and Future Prospects' (2006) at http://ssrn.com/abstract=907291. This trend is also observed in most OECD countries, see Frank Eich, 'The Importance of Defined-Benefit Occupational Pension Schemes in Selected OECD Countries' (2010) at http://ssrn.com/abstract=1660996; Joshua D Rauh and Irina Stefanescu, 'Why Are Firms in the United States Abandoning Defined Benefit Plans?' (2009) 2 *Rotman International Journal of Pension Management* 18.

19 PPI, *The Changing Landscape for Private Sector Defined Benefit Pension Schemes* (2007), above at p. 17.

20 IMA, *Asset Management in the UK 2014–15* (2015) at pp. 2–3.

21 Above.

22 http://www.pensionsworld.co.uk/pw/article/uk-pension-fund-assets-at-%C2%A317-trillion-hit-record-high-12323301.

granularity is not possible as it is intended to provide a broad level of analysis and perspective.

The role of pension institutions in corporate governance is broadly dependent upon their allocations to equity investments. Equity ownership provides the basis for pension institutions as corporate governance actors, and the significance of such ownership would affect pension institutions' perception of the relevance of corporate governance roles to their investment management. We find the following to be the broad trends in pension institutions' asset allocation to equities:

(a) the LGPS has a significant asset allocation in favour of equities,[23] especially domestic equity,[24] although there is a gradual trend of diversification away from equities into alternative asset classes such as infrastructure.[25] The widening deficit in LGPS funds may however result in greater risk-taking behaviour being sought for higher returns,[26] and this could entail greater allocation to equities as is observed in the US. But the pursuit of higher gains could equally mean withdrawal out of equity into alternative asset classes as has been adopted by private sector DB schemes.

(b) The LGPS is undergoing restructuring in terms of the amalgamation of administration of funds in order to take advantage of economies of scale and save on administration, transaction and management costs.[27] The key impetus driving the structural reforms, i.e. cost-savings, is one of the measures to tackle fund

---

[23] NAPF, *Local Government Pension Scheme 2013: Investing in a Changing World* (May 2013) at p. 18 showing that most LG funds allocate more than half of their assets to equities.

[24] Above at p. 19.

[25] Above at p. 21. The NAPF has coordinated the Pensions Infrastructure Platform (PIP) to assist in major pension funds' investment in infrastructure, including a few LGPS members and the BAE, BT and British Airways Pension Schemes. Further, LGPS Regulations have been amended to allow increased asset allocation from 15 to 30 per cent to partnership structures, which are often used by alternative asset classes and infrastructure investments. See DCLG, *Local Government Pension Scheme: Investment in Partnerships* (Consultation Nov 2012) which was implemented in The Local Government Pension Scheme (Management and Investment of Funds) (Amendment) Regulations 2013.

[26] Nancy Mohan and Ting Zhang, 'An Analysis of Risk-Taking Behavior for Public Defined Benefit Pension Plans' (2011) at http://ssrn.com/abstract=1992009.

[27] First referred to in the Hutton Report, Chapter 6; Hymans Robertson, *LGPS Structure Analysis* (Dec 2013); Department for Communities and Local

deficits.[28] At the same time, it indicates an increased preference for passive management for its equities assets, as the investment management fees for passive management are lower than for active management. These trajectories could affect funds' corporate governance roles.

(c) Private sector DB schemes have taken marked steps to move out of UK equities[29] at a notable pace, in response to 'de-risking' and 'liability driven management'[30] for schemes that are increasingly costly and unsustainable due to investment and longevity risks. DB schemes also suffer from high regulatory costs that emanate from accounting rules affecting disclosure, prudential frameworks and

---

Government, *Local Government Pension Scheme: Opportunities for Collaboration, Cost Savings and Efficiencies* (May 2014). See steps taken, e.g. 'London local government pension schemes to pool £25bn', *Financial Times* (22 Nov 2015).

[28] Above.

[29] E.g. Charles Sutcliffe, 'The Cult of the Equity for Pension Funds: Should it Get the Boot?' (2004) at http://ssrn.com/abstract=544862.

[30] Andrew Bridgen, Andrew Clare and Shamik Dhar, 'By How Much Can a Diversified Approach to Investing Improve the Prospects of Reducing a DB Pension Deficit?' (2007) at http://ssrn.com/abstract=1102149. The increased likelihood of unsustainability of private sector defined benefit schemes has prompted closure of many schemes to new entrants, new accruals and even altogether. Thus the closed schemes have adopted liability driven management measures to ensure that liabilities that mature can as far as possible be met. Such measures include allocating away from risky equities into index-linked gilts and corporate bonds, see Zvi Bodie, 'Pension Funds and Financial Innovation' (*NBER Working Paper* 1989) at http://ssrn.com/abstract=256079; Joshua D Rauh, 'Risk Shifting versus Risk Management: Investment Policy in Corporate Pension Plans' (2007) at http://ssrn.com/abstract=931237 (arguing that scheme deterioration forces poorly funded plans to shift to safer assets such as government bonds); while also allocating a small portion of assets to alternatives that may chase higher returns than equities. See NAPF, *Trends in Defined Benefit Asset Allocation: The Changing Shape of UK Pension Investment* (July 2013), pp. 7–13. This is consistent with findings from empirical research suggesting that pension fund allocations change in response to the need to meet deficit pressures, see note below, see Paul Rose and Jason S Seligman, 'Alternative Investments? State & Local Pension Portfolio Use and Performance' (2013) at http://ssrn.com/abstract=2407538; V Bouvatier and S Rigot, 'Pension Funds' Allocations to Hedge Funds: An Empirical Analysis of US and Canadian Defined Benefit Plans' (2013) 45 *Applied Economics* 3701; Aleksandar Andonov, Rob Bauer and Martijn Cremers, 'Pension Fund Asset Allocation and Liability Discount Rates' (2014) at http://ssrn.com/abstract=2070054.

tax treatment.[31] What remains of allocations to equities may be managed in such a way as to chase higher returns.[32] Moreover, DB schemes, besides moving into foreign assets and fixed income securities, are also increasingly invested in alternative asset classes such as hedge funds and private equity. Hence, they may become 'indirect' owners of equity through investments in these funds.

(d) Defined contribution schemes are growing at a phenomenal pace,[33] especially after the introduction of auto-enrolment,[34] and are

---

[31] Commentators have documented that the bearish stock markets in the early 2000s have, together with other factors, caused many defined benefit schemes to fall into deficit. Regulatory controls to govern deficits, together with other tax and accounting rules, as well as longevity risks have forced many employers to consider defined benefit schemes to be no longer financially sustainable. Commentators in Canada even warn of such liabilities adding too much of a burden to firms' balance sheets and threatening the solvency of the corporation, see Stephen Bonnar, 'How Vulnerable are Private Pensions?' (2008) 34 *Canadian Public Policy* 21. For discussion on the UK, see Charles Sutcliffe, 'The Cult of the Equity for Pension Funds: Should it Get the Boot?' (2004), above; Andrew Bridgen, Andrew Clare and Shamik Dhar, 'By How Much Can a Diversified Approach to Investing Improve the Prospects of Reducing a DB Pension Deficit?' (2007), above; Gordon L Clark and Ashby H B Monk, 'The "Crisis" in Defined Benefit Corporate Pension Liabilities: Current Solutions and Future Prospects' (2006), above; Srichander Ramaswamy, 'The Sustainability of Pension Schemes' (BIS Working Paper Jan 2012) at http://ssrn.com/abstract=1980094.

[32] Empirical research suggests that the desire to manage pension deficits should prompt higher risk-taking behaviour in asset allocation to chase higher potential returns and therefore equities should still be favoured, see David McCarthy and David Miles, 'Optimal Portfolio Allocation for Corporate Pension Funds' (2009) at http://ssrn.com/abstract=1440872; Nancy Mohan and Ting Zhang, 'An Analysis of Risk-Taking Behavior for Public Defined Benefit Pension Plans' (2011), above, suggesting that active management of equities may be the preferred approach.

[33] This trend is unlikely to be rolled back even after the global financial crisis, see Edward A Zelinsky, 'The Defined Contribution Paradigm' (2004) 114 *Yale Law Journal* 451; Allianz Global Investors, *Defining the Direction of Defined Contribution in Europe: Results of an Expert Survey* (2009).

[34] Pensions Act 2008, sections 3–8. IMA estimates that defined contributions assets will swell to at least £900 billion by 2050, see PPI, *Retirement Income and Assets: How Can Pensions and Financial Assets Support Retirement?* (Oct 2009), at p. 4.

managed in a variety of mandates[35] in order to cater to individual choice. They seem to continue to be significant investors in UK equities.[36]

(e) Insurance companies have withdrawn from UK equities in significant measure, and this was exacerbated in the global financial crisis 2007–09 as annuity writers took to assets with less perceived volatility such as index-linked gilts.[37] Further, as annuity writers face uncertain futures now that pension withdrawal rules have been relaxed,[38] the significance of their allocation to equities depends on their assets under management and the need to compete with other savings options open to pensioners.

The broad trends above seem to indicate that the LGPS and private sector DC schemes may still remain significant holders of UK corporate equities. However, as private sector DB schemes and insurance companies withdraw from UK listed equity to chase higher returns in foreign equity, the ownership of UK listed equity by UK institutions has fallen to under 20 per cent in 2015.[39] Although DB schemes made up about 72 per cent of pension assets in the UK in 2013,[40] only about 16 per cent of private sector DB schemes remain open; most of them have shut to new

---

[35] IMA, *Investment Asset Management Survey 2013–14* (2014) at pp. 40–41. Such as diversified growth or asset allocation strategies and lifestyle strategies, with the former being the most popular with DC scheme members, see Cerulli Associates, *European Defined Contributions Market* (2013), reported in http://www.wealthandfinance-intl.com/diversified-asset-allocation-strategies-cement-place-as-uk-s-most-popular-dc-pension-default-funds.

[36] Above at p. 45; Towers Watson, *Pension Adequacy: The Challenge for Defined Contribution Pension Plans* (2010); John Broadbent, Michael Palumbo and Elizabeth Woodman, 'The Shift from Defined Benefit to Defined Contribution Pension Plans – Implications for Asset Allocation and Risk Management' (2006) providing aggregate observations on Australia, Canada and the US.

[37] Bank of England and Procyclicality Working Group, *Procyclicality and Structural Trends in Investment Allocation by Insurance Companies and Pension Funds* (July 2014).

[38] '£17m a Day Withdrawn under New Pensions Freedoms', *The Telegraph* (2 Sep 2015).

[39] Office of National Statistics, *Ownership of UK Quoted Shares for UK Domiciled Companies, 2014* (2015) at http://www.ons.gov.uk/ons/dcp171778_415334.pdf.

[40] Towers Watson survey (2014) quoted in Bank of England and Procyclicality Working Group, *Procyclicality and Structural Trends in Investment Allocation by Insurance Companies and Pension Funds* (July 2014) at p. 14.

members or even to new accruals.[41] The number of employees actively contributing to private sector DC schemes is projected to reach over 16 million in 2020 while the number of employees actively contributing to private sector DB schemes is projected to be about 1 million at the same time.[42] Hence, we could even see a reversal of the trend of foreign ownership of UK listed equity as private sector DC schemes become more important as UK equity investors. Indeed, the IMA reports a 'bottoming-out' of UK pension institutions' shift out of UK corporate equities generally.[43]

In the next section, we discuss the key factors affecting pensions institutions in the UK in terms of their investment management trends and practices. These provide a context for us to consider how corporate governance roles in investee companies are likely to be shaped.

B. FUNDED PENSION INSTITUTIONS IN THE UK AND KEY FACTORS AND TRENDS IN THEIR INVESTMENT MANAGEMENT

LGPS

The LGPS is a significant pensions institution and corporate equities owner in the UK, and to a degree emblematic of changes that are occurring elsewhere in the sector. It is currently in the process of embracing change in terms of its scheme provision, structure, internal governance and investment management approach.

First, in order to manage its pension deficits and the investment risks from longevity of its members, the LGPS in 2014 introduced a new scheme of pension provision for members, a career average defined benefit deal instead of a final salary deal as proposed in the Hutton Report.[44] The impetus for cost-cutting also drove structural reform[45] and changes in investment approach following the recommendations of the

---

[41] PPI, *The Changing Landscape of Pension Schemes in the Private Sector in the UK* (2012), above at p. 17.

[42] Above at p. 8.

[43] IMA, *Asset Management in the UK 2014–15* (2015) at p. 5.

[44] Hutton Report, at Chapter 3; and LGPS information at http://www.lgps2014.org/.

[45] Department for Communities and Local Government, *Local Government Pension Scheme: Opportunities for collaboration, cost savings and efficiencies* (May 2014).

Hymans Robertson Report.[46] The LGPS is taking steps to restructure its myriad local pension funds into larger amalgamated funds (in the region of five to ten centrally administered funds) that can be administered with the benefit of economies of scale and cost-savings.[47] Further, as the Hymans Report finds that returns to funds from active management do not outperform passive investing, the LGPS funds should move into predominantly passive investing in order to generate returns at lower cost.

Cost concerns have also driven the centrally administered LGPS funds to carry out its investment management in-house instead of outsourcing. This is reportedly the trajectory with the London Pension Fund Authority which is a significant LGPS fund.[48] However, the balance between in-house management and outsourcing remains an interesting question as the LGPS is influenced by countervailing factors. The increasingly stringent requirements of 'good governance' may induce the LGPS to delegate to professional asset managers, a point we will return to shortly. But the need to keep cost low would support an in-house set-up for investment management. Nevertheless, governance requirements will likely shape the practice of in-house managers.

Performance pressures are profoundly affecting the LGPS' asset allocation decisions and investment management approach.[49] Such pressures influence asset allocation towards riskier/high return assets such as equities (domestic and international) and alternative classes of assets. The Bank of England 2014 survey[50] of asset allocations by pension funds and insurers reports that pension funds demonstrate a variety of behaviour in asset allocations, unlike liability-driven institutions such as insurers. LGPS funds were reported to have behaved counter-cyclically, buying UK listed equity at low prices in the bearish equity markets in the global financial crisis and planning for longer-term holding.[51] The LGPS' continued support for UK corporate equities may hence place it in a position to be a significant corporate governance actor.

---

[46] Hymans Robertson, *LGPS Structure Analysis* (Dec 2013).

[47] See steps taken, e.g. 'London local government pension schemes to pool £25bn', *Financial Times* (22 Nov 2015).

[48] 'London Pensions Fund Authority to take half of assets in-house', *Financial Times* (4 Oct 2015); 'LPFA Plans to Double the Size of its In-house Investment Team', *Financial Times* (14 Dec 2014).

[49] Matt Dubra and Bruce H Lubich, 'Public Pension Governance and Asset Allocation' (2013) 6 *Journal of Centrum Cathedra* 83.

[50] Bank of England and Procyclicality Working Group, *Procyclicality and Structural Trends in Investment Allocation by Insurance Companies and Pension Funds* (July 2014).

[51] Above at p. 33.

However, the LGPS is increasingly shifting towards passive management for its corporate equities holdings. Active management, which used to be the predominant mode of investment management, has come under increasing scepticism as to its value for money. Although active management may generate 'alpha' or excess returns that beat the market,[52] such returns may be insufficient to offset the cost of active management,[53] depending on how economies of scale may reduce the impact of such cost.[54] As studies suggest that passive investing aligned with established stock market benchmarks would produce more long-term returns for pension funds, the higher cost and fees associated with active management are arguably less justifiable.[55] For the LGPS, cost pressures are the foremost factor for the adoption of passive investment management. It remains uncertain whether passive investment management could provide

---

[52] Michel Aglietta, Marie Brière, Sandra Rigotc and Ombretta Signori, 'Rehabilitating the Role of Active Management for Pension Funds' (2012) at http://ssrn.com/abstract=1948726; 'Almost 90% of UK active managers beat the stock market', *Financial Times* (3 August 2014).

[53] Hymans Robertson, *LGPS Structure Analysis* (Dec 2013); Gordon L Clark, *Pension Fund Capitalism* (Oxford: OUP 2000) at Chapter 5; 'EU Asset Managers Offer Bad Value for Money', *Financial Times* (7 Dec 2014) citing Financial Services User Group, *Asset Management and FSUG Position Paper* (Nov 2014) at http://ec.europa.eu/finance/finservices-retail/docs/fsug/papers/1411-asset-management_en.pdf.

[54] Alexander Dyck and Lukasz Pomorski, 'Is Bigger Better? Size and Performance in Pension Plan Management' (2011) at http://ssrn.com/abstract=1690724. Contrary empirical evidence is offered in 'Fund investors find small is beautiful', *Financial Times* (27 Feb 2014); Rob M M J Bauer, K J Martjin Cremers and Rik G P Frehen, 'Pension Fund Performance and Costs: Small is Beautiful' (2010) at http://ssrn.com/abstract=965388.

[55] Ajay Shah and Kshama Fernandes, 'The Relevance of Index Funds for Pension Investment in Equities' (*World Bank Research Paper* 1999); Andrew Clare, Keith Cuthbertson and Dirk Nitzsche, 'An Empirical Investigation into the Performance of UK Pension Fund Managers' (2009) at http://ssrn.com/abstract=1325410; Alexander Dyck, Karl V Lins and Lukasz Pomorski, 'Does Active Management Pay? New International Evidence' (2011) at http://ssrn.com/abstract=1957783; *Better Workplace Pensions: Further Measures for Savers* (2014) Cm 8840 p. 48; John C Bogle, *Common Sense on Mutual Funds* (Chichester: John Wiley & Sons, 2011) arguing that passive and cost-effective investing is the preferred way that delivers reliable long-term returns; Mary Bange, Kenneth Khang and Thomas W Miller Jnr, 'Benchmarking the Performance of Recommended Allocations to Equities, Bonds, and Cash by International Investment Houses' (2008) at https://ideas.repec.org/a/eee/empfin/v15y2008i3p363-386.html, suggesting that benchmarks outperform investment houses' actively managed portfolios.

less or more incentive for funds to assume an engaged corporate governance role. Passive investment management is intended to be cost-effective and undertaking costly corporate governance research and engagement seems contradictory to that approach. However, passive investment places restrictions upon divestment in order to maintain a balance of assets consistent with the chosen established benchmarks. Hence funds could become sticky investors who have no choice but to engage if unhappy with the investee companies. For example, passive asset managers such as Vanguard have put in place shareholder engagement policies that seek to combine corporate governance involvement with low cost, but it remains uncertain if such manoeuvres are merely 'window dressing' in response to demand-side pressures.[56] The LGPS' funds move towards passive investing may also mean that positions would not be taken in smaller cap and less liquid stocks.[57] Such a change in portfolio composition could have an impact upon funds' corporate governance activities as smaller cap stocks may offer more opportunities for engagement in order to generate value and better performance.

Performance pressures have also driven LGPS funds towards alternative asset classes such as infrastructure,[58] but not necessarily in hedge funds, whose high fee structures are a deterrent. For example, CalPERS, the American public pension scheme for public sector employees in the state of California,[59] has publicly withdrawn from hedge funds due to the high fees. The lack of uptake by LGPS funds of alternative investment funds such as hedge and private equity funds could have an impact upon their approach to corporate governance roles more generally. Alternative investment fund managers are more likely to champion shareholder activism as a key investment management modus in the search for higher absolute returns.

Next, the enactment of the Public Service Sector Pensions Act 2013 brings all unfunded public sector funds and the funded LGPS funds under the purview of the Pensions Regulator, and also subjects public

---

[56] Large passive investment managers are frequently in support of the Board and not very critical in their corporate governance roles, see 'Fund Houses Back the Boss too Often', *Financial Times* (17 May 2015).

[57] 'Baillie Gifford: Passive Funds Could Damage the Economy', *Financial Times* (13 Dec 2014).

[58] Department for Communities and Local Government, *Local Government Pension Scheme: Opportunities for Collaboration, Cost Savings and Efficiencies* (May 2014) at para 2.12.

[59] 'Calpers to Exit Hedge Funds, Divest $4 Billion Stake', *Bloomberg* (15 Sep 2014).

service sector funds to certain internal governance frameworks, standards, and reporting and communication requirements. The introduction of more stringent governance requirements would likely put pressure upon how LGPS funds govern themselves, the extent of their delegation to professional asset managers and their embrace of external corporate governance roles, which could push them in the direction favoured by UK policy-makers, as discussed in Chapter 3.

LGPS funds are already generally well-regarded in terms of their internal governance structures. Now, they will be consolidated into larger structures each to be managed by a scheme manager overseen by a Pensions Board for each fund. Scheme managers are full-time appointments looking after the internal control of funds. The pensions boards are responsible for deciding the investment policies and approaches of the funds. The Pensions Regulator's review of the LGPS states that the pensions boards of LGPS funds are adequately represented by competent directors. Board members have generally acquired adequate training and knowledge, and have plans for continuing learning and development; they meet sufficiently regularly in order to discharge their functions (generally quarterly) and use financial sector professionals extensively, such as investment consultants, managers, actuaries, custodians and legal advisers.[60] As LGPS funds become amalgamated into five to ten larger funds, we are of the view that there would be further pressures to enhance the sophistication of internal governance. The need to demonstrate sophisticated internal governance may be a response to the initial discontent resulting from the dismantling of certain local pension boards. Affected local employers and employee beneficiaries may scrutinise the large centrally administered funds in terms of governance and performance with greater interest and hence generate pressures for the governance and administration of the centrally administered funds. Or even if local employers and employee beneficiaries become less interested or motivated to scrutinise the centrally administered funds due to cognitive distance, the Pensions Regulator may carry out more careful scrutiny at least in the early stages post the structural reforms.

There are a few possible ramifications from the new regulatory, governance and accountability pressures on the LGPS. Some commentators suggest that there could be a relationship between enhanced internal

[60] The Pensions Regulator, *Public Service Pension Schemes: A Summary of Governance and Administration* (Sep 2013) at 10.

governance and scrutiny, and risk aversion in investment policies.[61] If so, risk aversion pressures may trigger shifts into safer assets such as fixed income. This would have negative implications for LGPS' interest and motivation in corporate governance roles in their investee companies. Further, as cost concerns have driven scheme and structural changes to the LGPS, its predominantly in-house investment management teams may be unwilling to extend beyond modest recognition of the funds' corporate governance roles, due to the expensive nature of corporate governance research and engagement. However, as fund trustees and managers have become more sophisticated and competent since being placed under the supervisory oversight of the Pensions Regulator,[62] carrying out investment management in-house does not necessarily correspond with less inclination to engage in corporate governance roles.

Further, the soft law requirements with regard to 'stewardship' may motivate such engagement, as many LGPS funds have signed up to the UK Stewardship Code.[63] Adherence to the Code and meaningful engagement with funds' corporate governance roles may be a way to show good internal governance. Funds may feel enhanced pressures to show good internal governance as a result of the confluence of the new regulatory regime and scrutiny into post-restructuring dynamics and performance. These factors would indeed motivate LGPS funds to take a more engaged corporate governance position in their UK investee companies.

Where delegation to professional pension consultants or asset managers is still in place, the LGPS' corporate governance roles would likely be shaped by their influence. Outsourcing to established external professionals is a way of showing good internal governance, as the co-option of appropriate professional help is consistent with the duty of care (which

---

61 Christian E Weller and Jeffrey B Wenger, 'Prudent Investors: The Asset Allocation of Public Pension Plans' (2008) at http://ssrn.com/abstract=1298654.

62 The Pensions Regulator, *Public Service Pension Schemes: A Summary of Governance and Administration* (Sep 2013) at 10.

63 https://www.frc.org.uk/Our-Work/Codes-Standards/Corporate-governance/UK-Stewardship-Code.aspx. On the concept of stewardship see Iris H-Y Chiu, 'Turning Institutional Investors into "Stewards" – Exploring the Meaning and Objectives in "Stewardship' (2013) *Current Legal Problems* 1; Simon C Y Wong, 'Why Stewardship is Proving Elusive for Institutional Investors' [2010] *Butterworths Journal of Banking and Financial Law* 406; Iris H-Y Chiu, 'Institutional Shareholders as Stewards: Toward a New Conception of Corporate Governance' (2012) 6 *Brooklyn Journal of Corporate, Financial and Commercial Law* 387. For a highly critical discussion see Daniëlle Adriana Maria Melis, 'The Institutional Investor Stewardship Myth' (2014) at http://ssrn.com/abstract=2445997.

has in case law been interpreted as a duty to seek professional advice[64]). Where external professionals are used, the impact of such input into fund allocation and management cannot be over-estimated.[65] Pension consultants may play a determinative role on asset allocation policies.[66] A handful of pension consultants in the industry – such as Towers Watson, Mercer and Aon Hewitt – have become dominant market players wielding substantial influence over fund investment allocation decisions.[67] For example, pension consultant input has been crucial[68] to the rapid withdrawal of UK institutional investment from UK listed equity,[69] and it is questioned whether such an approach will similarly be taken in the LGPS' investment approach. Empirical research in the US has also suggested that public sector fund trustees are relatively less sophisticated than their private sector counterparts and hence may be very reliant on professional asset managers'[70] advice on investment management

---

[64] *Martin v City of Edinburgh District Council* [1988] SLT 329.

[65] Clark views this as a challenge as trustees' competence is often not matched with that of their intermediary agents. The reliance of the pension fund industry upon professional financial intermediation is crucial to pension fund governance in both the public and private sectors, see Gordon L Clark, 'Pension Fund Governance: Expertise and Organisational Form' in John Evans, Michael Orszag and John Piggott (eds), *Pension Fund Governance: A Global Perspective on Financial Regulation* (Cheltenham: Edward Elgar, 2008).

[66] A number of empirical studies are of the view that asset allocation is key to investment performance, see Craig W French, 'Another Look at the Determinants of Portfolio Performance: Return Attribution for the Individual Investor' (2003) at https://papers.ssrn.com/sol3/papers.cfm?abstract_id=706603; Gary Brinson et al, 'Determinants of Portfolio Performance' (1986) *Financial Analysts Journal* pp. 39–44; 'Determinants of Portfolio Performance II: An Update' (1991) *Financial Analysts Journal* pp. 40–48.

[67] The Law Commission has flagged up the potential need to subject them to regulation in order to bring any conflicts of interests under a framework of governance. There is also the potential question of whether consultant recommendations may result in homogenous practices that could be systemically damaging. Law Commission, *Fiduciary Duties of Investment Intermediaries* (1 July 2014) at pp. 216–18; 'Investment consultants' stranglehold on pensions questioned', *Financial Times* (6 July 2014); 'Pension consultants face fresh calls for regulatory oversight', *Financial Times* (19 Oct 2014).

[68] NAPF survey, at http://www.napf.co.uk/PressCentre/Press_releases/0389-Schemes-satisfaction-with-investment-consultants-remains-steady.aspx.

[69] Noted in Bank of England and Procyclicality Working Group, *Procyclicality and Structural Trends in Investment Allocation by Insurance Companies and Pension Funds* (July 2014) at p. 36.

[70] Susan Mangiero, 'Pension Risk Management: Derivatives, Fiduciary Duty and Process' (2008) at http://ssrn.com/abstract=128332; Stephen J Choi and Jill

approach. Clark has made a similar comment in the UK context.[71] Hence, the LGPS' approach to its corporate governance roles may be subject to the extensive influence of asset managers where delegation occurs. The nature of asset managers' approach to corporate governance roles has been critically discussed in Chapter 3.

A final question is whether public pension funds such as the LGPS would be more disposed towards corporate governance engagement with investee companies on issues related to public policy, ethics and ESG (environmental, social and governance issues).[72] Commentators in the US have pointed out this tendency on the part of public pension funds.[73] However the appropriateness of public sector pension fund engagement in these issues has been questioned – some commentators regard such engagement as progressive behaviour[74] but contrary opinions have been offered with regard to the dubious[75] motivations for championing these concerns. There is no marked tendency on the part of the LGPS funds to engage with investee companies on ESG issues, but this may be due to

---

E Fisch, 'On Beyond Calpers: Survey Evidence on the Developing Role of Public Pension Funds in Corporate Governance' (2008) 61 *Vanderbilt Law Review* 315.

[71] Gordon L Clark, 'Pension Fund Governance: Expertise and Organizational Form' (2004) 3 *Journal of Pension Economics and Finance* 233.

[72] R Kent Weaver, 'Whose Money Is It Anyhow?: Governance and Social Investment in Collective Investment Funds' (2003) at http://ssrn.com/abstract=1136876.

[73] See for example Rui Albuquerque, Zicheng Lei, Jörg Rocholl and Chendi Zhang, 'Institutional Investors and Corporate Political Activism' (*ECGI Working Paper* 2016) on public pension funds' interest in political activism at http://www.ecgi.org/wp/wp_id.php?id=785&mc_cid=faf516730b&mc_eid=bad7753e00.

[74] Claire Woods and Roger Urwin, 'Putting Sustainable Investing into Practice: A Governance Framework for Pension Funds' (2010) 92 *Journal of Business Ethics* 1; David Hess, 'Public Pensions and the Promise of Shareholder Activism for the Next Frontier of Corporate Governance: Sustainable Economic Development' (2007) 2 *Virginia Law and Business Review* 222; Benjamin Richardson, *Socially Responsible Investment Law* (New York: OUP, 2008). See also David H Webber, 'The Use and Abuse of Labor's Capital' (2015) *NYU Law Review* forthcoming, interpreting the fiduciary duty as permitting additional considerations so long as they are in the best interests of the beneficiaries, such best interests including considerations for current employment security and not just relating to retirement benefits.

[75] Roberta Romano, 'Public Pension Fund Activism in Corporate Governance Reconsidered' (1993) *Columbia Law Review* 795.

trustees' risk aversion in light of case law such as *Cowan v Scargill.*[76] A changed attitude is now encouraged in the Freshfields report[77] which sought to clarify the limited interpretation in *Cowan* and to re-interpret the parameters of trustees' duty of care. Nonetheless, the leadership of the LGPS in the advocacy for such issues within the framework of corporate governance has so far been limited and its future influence remains to be seen.

Private Sector Defined Benefit Schemes

Private sector DB schemes are sponsored by employers and hence, although they are managed for meeting the promises made to employee beneficiaries, the risks of meeting maturing liabilities under the schemes lie with the employer.[78] Private sector DB schemes in most of the developed world are facing challenges in terms of investment risks and longevity risks that may make the schemes unsustainable.[79] Stock market volatility in the last two decades, the global financial crisis 2007–09 and continued geo-political uncertainty in much of the developed world[80] have caused huge losses to private sector DB schemes that have allocated significant assets to equities.[81] Many private sector DB schemes in the

---

76 [1985] 1 Ch 270.

77 Freshfields Bruckhaus Deringer, *A Legal Framework for the Integration of Environmental, Social and Governance Issues into Institutional Investment* (October 2005).

78 Jacob A Bikker, Thijs Knaap and Ward E Romp, 'Measuring and Explaining Implicit Risk Sharing in Defined Benefit Pension Funds' (2014) 46 *Applied Economics* 1996.

79 Srichander Ramaswamy, 'The Sustainability of Pension Schemes' (*BIS Working Paper* Jan 2012) at http://ssrn.com/abstract=1980094.

80 For example, terrorist attacks on Western cities and targets with the rise of Islamic fundamentalism, the exit of the UK from the European Union and the rise of competing emerging markets in the East.

81 The allocation to equities is largely adherent to the 60 per cent equity–40 per cent fixed income formula offered by economists. Discussed in Gordon L Clark, *Pension Fund Capitalism* (2000), above at Chapter 6; Barry Riley, 'Pension Funds and the Capital Markets' in Paul Thornton and Donald Fleming (eds), *Good Governance for Pension Funds* (Cambridge: Cambridge University Press, 2011) at pp. 28, 46; Article 18, Directive 2003/41/EC of the European Parliament and of the Council of 3 June 2003 on the activities and supervision of institutions for occupational retirement provision, *Official Journal* L 235, 23/09/2003 (IORP Directive 2003).

UK are in deficit,[82] this situation having been exacerbated shortly after the EU Referendum vote.[83]

Deficits exert immediate pressures upon company sponsors in terms of balance sheet holes, financial market reporting and share price. Further, longer term threats of insolvency may loom.[84] As a result many private sector DB schemes have closed to new members, or even to new accruals, or have sold out the schemes to insurers who would manage the closed schemes much like maturing annuities.[85] In this landscape, many private sector DB schemes, especially the closed or partially closed ones, are managed towards meeting maturing liabilities. Many of them have adopted liability-driven strategies.[86] This is largely driven by the pressures of regulation and fiduciary law.

Private sector DB schemes are required to adopt mark-to-market accounting in valuing pension fund assets[87] for balance sheet reporting in mandatory financial disclosure and for the purposes of scheme funding requirements introduced in the Pensions Act 2004.[88] However, these regulatory requirements have forced measures to be taken towards deficit reduction in the short term even if liabilities are not maturing until the longer term. Although the duties imposed on pension fund trustees under the Trustees Act 2000 are sufficiently widely-worded to allow trustees to manage according to the long-term investment performance of the funds

---

[82] Pensions Policy Institute, *The Changing Landscape for Private Sector Defined Benefit Pension Schemes* (2007); Gordon L Clark and Ashby H B Monk, 'The "Crisis" in Defined Benefit Corporate Pension Liabilities: Current Solutions and Future Prospects' (2006), above. This trend is also observed in most OECD countries, see Frank Eich, 'The Importance of Defined-Benefit Occupational Pension Schemes in Selected OECD Countries' (2010) at http://ssrn.com/abstract=1660996; Joshua D Rauh and Irina Stefanescu, 'Why Are Firms in the United States Abandoning Defined Benefit Plans?' (2009), above. See 'Pension funds target 'unrealistically' high returns', *Financial Times* (9 Nov 2014).

[83] 'Pensions stretched to breaking point after Brexit vote', *Financial Times* (17 July 2016).

[84] E.g. see Stephen Bonnar, 'How Vulnerable are Private Pensions?' (2008), above.

[85] Pensions Policy Institute, *The Changing Landscape for Private Sector Defined Benefit Pension Schemes* (2007).

[86] IMA for example, report the dominance of liability-driven mandates to asset managers by those schemes, IMA, *Investment Asset Management Survey 2013–14* (2014), at p. 43; Auke Plantinga, 'Performance Measurement for Pension Funds' (2005) at http://papers.ssrn.com/sol3/papers.cfm?abstract_id=900427.

[87] IAS17.

[88] Sections 222–26.

and to take into account all relevant considerations in investment management for meeting the maturing liabilities,[89] the immediate pressures of regulatory compliance often compel pension trustees to adopt short termist investment management approaches. In particular, short termist decisions such as asset allocation changes and asset manager turnover are employed in response to short-term under-performance.[90] In a way, regulatory compliance may overshadow the content of trustees' duty of care to act in an ordinarily prudent way.[91] Further, regulatory compliance may drive plan trustees to risk manage and tailor investment decisions towards shorter time frames.[92]

Although the Kay Review[93] questioned the adequacy of fiduciary law in governing pension fund investment management towards the long-term interests of beneficiaries, we are of the view that the pressures exerted upon pension scheme management from regulation have far outstripped the general law of trustees' duties,[94] as regulation has imposed specific requirements of prudential management and these need to be complied with on a yearly basis regardless of the horizons for maturing liabilities. One may argue that regulation provides precise terms for prescriptive monitoring which general law is unable to develop, such as in prudential regulation, and is thus consistent with the fiduciary spirit of keeping trustees in check. Nevertheless, the minimum funding requirement that

---

89 Law Commission, *Fiduciary Duties of Investment Intermediaries* (2014) at para 6.1. Freshfields Bruckhaus Deringer, *A Legal Framework for the Integration of Environmental, Social and Governance Issues into Institutional Investment* (October 2005).

90 Sharad Asthana and Roland Lipka, 'Management of Defined-Benefit Pension Funds and Shareholder Value' (2003) 41 *Quarterly Journal of Business and Economics* 49; Law Commission, *Fiduciary Duties of Investment Intermediaries* (2014) at para 2.76.

91 Sections 1 and 2, Trustees Act 2000, *Learoyd v Whiteley* (1887) 12 App Cas 727; TPR Code 03, para 94 (2014).

92 See comments in http://www.ipe.com/europes-pension-consultants-playing-the-long-game/44232.fullarticle. Also see Dorothee Franzen, 'Managing Investment Risk in Defined Benefit Pension Funds' (OECD Working Paper, 2010) at http://www.oecd-ilibrary.org/docserver/download/5kmjnr3sr2f3.pdf?expires=1413966718&id=id&accname=guest&checksum=EA1A737DD90414C2DD21383B56ABACF0.

93 Kay Review, see BIS, *The Kay Review of UK Equity Markets and Long-Term Decision Making* (Final Report, 23 July 2012) at p. 69.

94 Such as a duty to consider the suitability of any investment, a duty to review suitability, a duty to ensure diversification of assets consistent with the portfolio management theory and a duty to obtain and consider proper advice, see sections 4 and 5, Trustees Act 2000, s36, Pensions Act 1995.

was imposed on defined benefit plans from 1995 to 2004 imposed short termist pressures on pension funds as a certain level of assets had to be maintained even if long term obligations had not yet matured. Regular runs of prescriptive monitoring induce short termism as compliance is absolute and unforgiving, and lacks the wider breadth and adaptability in general law. Although the minimum funding requirement has been replaced by a statutory funding objective requirement[95] which requires trustees to submit a statement of funding principles, a schedule of contributions consistent with these principles and a recovery plan setting out the steps that will be taken to address the shortfall where the statutory funding objective is not met, trustees are not relieved of short termist pressures as the level of assets still needs to be maintained in accordance with certain technical prescriptions. Moreover, European initiatives such as stress testing pension funds' balance sheets[96] is not regarded as being helpful towards alleviating short termist pressures on funds. In other words, the need for regular monitoring of scheme trustees, in mitigating the 'agency problem', could entail contrary effects for the spirit of managing pensions investments for maturity over the longer term (which should allow for greater tolerance of volatility and funding fluctuations). However, existing fund deficits and hence current 'distrust' of the sustainability of schemes are likely to force more short termist scrutiny into the financial states of funds, inducing more short termist investment behaviour.[97] This is a difficult issue, as the navigation between the Scylla and Charybdis of accountability in the short term and outcomes in the long term inevitably affects investment management and corporate governance practices.

Empirical research suggests that private sector DB scheme trustees are willing to take significant risks in asset allocations and investment management approaches in order to meet short-termist pressures. Hence scheme trustees, their pension consultants and asset managers are largely driven by the need to secure compliance with regulatory requirements such as the statutory funding requirement. One may query whether the longer term nature of general law, which is broadly worded, organic in

[95] Section 222ff, Pensions Act 2004.

[96] 'Stress Tests of European Pensions Hotly Opposed', *Financial Times* (17 May 2015).

[97] See critique in 'Cure for UK Pension Fund Deficits Inflicts More Pain', *Financial Times* (5 Sep 2016).

nature and adaptable to changing times,[98] could provide a countervailing tendency to prevent myopic focus on the short term. However, securing compliance with regulatory requirements arguably constitutes the best interests of beneficiaries *prima facie* and hence general law could be interpreted to support regulatory compliance. This is arguably consistent with the Law Commission's conclusion that the content of fiduciary law could be modified or delineated by explicit regulatory rules that act as specific 'contractual terms' in fiduciary relationships.[99] Further, scheme trustees' appetite for risk-taking may be shaped by their perception that risks are underwritten by the company anyway[100] and risk-taking could be augmented if the company is perceived to be financially robust.[101] Further, where pension fund trustees are company insiders, increased risk-taking in pension schemes could achieve the effect of shareholder wealth maximisation, as risks are shifted onto creditors,[102] and the management of pension assets and liabilities could achieve short term

---

[98] Freshfields Bruckhaus Deringer, *A Legal Framework for the Integration of Environmental, Social and Governance Issues into Institutional Investment* (October 2005).

[99] In 1995, the Law Commission undertook a study of the relationship between the general law of fiduciary duties and its relationship to the regulatory rules that may be imposed on financial intermediaries. In particular, the Law Commission was concerned that fiduciary rules such as that financial intermediaries had to avoid conflicts of interest would logically mean that they could not serve multiple principals who might put them into conflicts of interest. A strict application of fiduciary law would be incongruent with the financial intermediaries' business which is to serve multiple investors and act as the bridge between them and financial markets. The Law Commission's conclusion is that regulatory rules could modify the scope of fiduciary duties that financial intermediaries are subject to, as they are more precise and would be read as contractual usages modifying the nature and scope of the general fiduciary duty. See Law Commission, *Fiduciary Duties and Regulatory Rules* (1995).

[100] David McCarthy and David Miles, 'Optimal Portfolio Allocation for Corporate Pension Funds' (2009), above.

[101] Christina V Atanosova and Evan Gatev, 'Risk-taking of Institutional Investors: Evidence from US Defined Benefit Pension Plans' (2010) at http://ssrn.com/abstract=1570925; Joshua D Rauh, 'Risk Shifting versus Risk Management: Investment Policy in Corporate Pension Plans' (2007), above.

[102] João F Cocco and Paolo F Volpin, 'The Corporate Governance of Defined Benefit Pension Plans: Evidence from the United Kingdom' (*ECGI Working Paper* 2005) at http://ssrn.com/abstract=670685.

payoffs for the company in financial reporting,[103] or in avoiding takeover threats.[104] These driving factors have been found to be important in empirical studies.

In terms of asset allocation to equities, empirical evidence is mixed. Commentators suggest that private sector DB schemes that take on greater risks to generate more returns are equally likely to allocate more assets to equity,[105] or shift from domestic equity into riskier assets such as foreign equity and alternative asset classes.[106] Surveys of the trends in the UK suggest that the latter has been taking place.[107] Even where allocation to equities continues, it is likely that active management of the equities portfolios would be pursued, in order for asset managers to generate short term returns through stock-picking[108] and market movements.[109] The holding out for payoffs over the longer term through shareholder activism may be less appealing.[110] In sum, where private sector DB schemes remain invested in UK corporate equity, it seems that their focus is short-termist performance through active management that focuses on trading. There is generally a lack of incentive on the part of

---

103 Daniel Bergstresser, Mihir Desai, and Joshua Rauh, 'Earnings Manipulation, Pension Assumptions and Managerial Investment Decisions' (2006) 121 *Quarterly Journal of Economics* 157.

104 Jayesh Kumar, 'Impact of Pension Plan Funding Status on M&A Activity' (Watson Wyatt, 2006).

105 Christina V Atanosova and Evan Gatev, 'Risk-taking of Institutional Investors: Evidence from US Defined Benefit Pension Plans' (2010), above; Zvi Bodie, 'Pension Funds and Financial Innovation' (1989), above; Nancy Mohan and Ting Zhang, 'An Analysis of Risk-Taking Behavior for Public Defined Benefit Pension Plans' (2011), above.

106 Andrew Bridgen, Andrew Clare and Shamik Dhar, 'By How Much Can a Diversified Approach to Investing Improve the Prospects of Reducing a DB Pension Deficit?' (2007), above; Aleksandar Andonov, Rob Bauer and Martijn Cremers, 'Pension Fund Asset Allocation and Liability Discount Rates' (2014), above.

107 See point (c) under Section A.

108 Sharad Asthana and Roland Lipka, 'Management of Defined-Benefit Pension Funds and Shareholder Value' (2003), above.

109 Michel Aglietta, Marie Brière, Sandra Rigotc and Ombretta Signori, 'Rehabilitating the Role of Active Management for Pension Funds' (2012), above.

110 Although it may be argued that these funds are well poised to act as key corporate governance actors, especially collectively, see Gordon L Clark and Tessa Hebb, 'Pension Fund Corporate Engagement: The Fifth Stage of Capitalism' (2004) 59 *Industrial Relations* 142.

asset managers to be engaged in their corporate governance roles in investee companies.[111]

We turn however to whether the governance requirements of private sector DB schemes and the pressures of the UK Stewardship Code may change their investment management approaches. Private sector DB schemes are provided by employers who are plan sponsors. The schemes are required[112] to be independent of the company sponsor, but are generally administered by the company plan sponsor's appointees, who could be directors or other managers of the employer.[113] Some private sector schemes are completely outsourced to fiduciary managers – these take on the roles of both investment strategy and management.[114] Private sector DB schemes are structured as trusts, and plan trustees are governed by the duties imposed under the Trustees Act 2000 which provide for fiduciary duties and duties of care and skill. Plan trustees also have to ensure compliance with the Pensions Acts and Regulations, a framework that provides for the prudential management of schemes and accountability to the Pensions Regulator. The investment strategy of private sector DB schemes is generally determined by plan trustees in consultation with pension consultants.[115] These consultants advise on which asset managers to use for the funds' portfolios and hence wield incredible influence in the investment management decisions trustees make.[116] Many private sector DB schemes, upon advice, would appoint asset managers for a range of portfolios. These may be boutique managers such as Woodford Investment, or larger fund houses that manage mandates for a wide variety of funds, such as Legal & General,

[111] Ronald J Gilson and Jeffrey N Gordon, 'Agency Capitalism: Further Implications of Equity Intermediation' (2014) at http://ssrn.com/abstract=2359690; also see Iris H-Y Chiu, 'Turning Institutional Investors into "Stewards" – Exploring the Meaning and Objectives in "Stewardship' (2013), above.

[112] Article 2, 8, IORP Directive 2003 which is transposed in the UK.

[113] Gordon L Clark, *Pension Fund Capitalism* (2000), above at Chapter 6.

[114] For example, see Ernst & Young, *What is Fiduciary Management* (2015) at http://www.ey.com/UK/en/Services/Specialty-Services/Pensions/Fiduciary-Management-1-What-is-Fiduciary-Management.

[115] 'Pension consultants face fresh calls for regulatory oversight', *Financial Times* (19 Oct 2014).

[116] Law Commission, *Fiduciary Duties of Investment Intermediaries* (2014) at paras 11.40ff.

Insight, BlackRock and Pimco.[117] The investment chain on the one hand brings about professionalisation in pensions management but on the other hand generates cost. Trustees' focus on cost is understandable given the regulatory (and short-termist) financial pressures placed on schemes and the general state of pension deficits. Given the general trend of liability-driven management strategies, it seems unlikely the schemes would be prepared to take on costly corporate governance roles in their investee companies. However, this also depends on their asset managers' positions, whose willingness to be engaged may be affected by economies of scale in corporate governance activities,[118] and the pressures generated by the soft law of the Stewardship Code and wider public opinion.[119] However, we are of the view that funds may 'posture' towards making their corporate governance roles visible but seek to do so in as cost-effective a manner as possible.

First, we think that pension funds and the asset management industry would likely tend to support transaction-cost reducing measures through the regulatory standardisation of enhanced minority shareholder protection.[120] There is likely to be significant support for increasing regulatory prescription for minority shareholder protection, as regulation imposed on issuers has the effect of passing the cost of ensuring good governance to the company. Compliance by issuers substitutes[121] for the efforts that shareholders have to make in engagement for good governance. The cost and burden of ensuring good governance would thus shift from funds through engagement and activism, to companies through standardisation of corporate governance standards and minority shareholder protection. The authors have also discussed elsewhere that Anglo-American pension

---

[117] These are the most highly ranked funds by volume of assets under management, see Ftfm's 11th Annual Survey of Asset Managers, 2014, quoted in 'Pensions in flux boost asset managers', *Financial Times* (10 August 2014).

[118] Michael J Rubach and Terrence C Sebora, 'Determinants of Institutional Investor Activism: A Test of the Ryan-Schneider Model (2002)' (2009) 21 *Journal of Managerial Issues* 245.

[119] Iris H-Y Chiu, 'Turning Institutional Investors into "Stewards" – Exploring the Meaning and Objectives in "Stewardship"' (2013), above.

[120] Discussed in Section D, Roger Barker and Iris H-Y Chiu, 'Protecting Minority Shareholders in Blockholder-Controlled Companies – Evaluating the UK's Enhanced Listing Regime in Comparison with Investor Protection Regimes in New York and Hong Kong' (2015) *Capital Markets Law Journal* forthcoming.

[121] Note the box-ticking tendencies that may be generated from compliance with the Corporate Governance Code, and critique in Marc Moore, 'Whispering Sweet Nothings: The Limitations of Informal Conformance in UK Corporate Governance' (2009) 9 *Journal of Corporate Law Studies* 77.

funds' investments in foreign equity are also likely to trigger support for the convergence of international corporate governance standards as transaction-cost reducing measures for achieving a sufficiently high and comforting level of minority investor protection.[122] Such convergence may take place under listing rules and/or securities regulation regimes,[123] as inroads into domestic company law regimes could be trickier.

Moreover, the inertia or reluctance on the part of asset managers to engage in their corporate governance roles may be in part mitigated by adopting proxy advisory agencies' recommendations in voting at annual general meetings and in other forms of less onerous engagement.[124] Proxy advice may also facilitate and reduce the costs of funds' corporate governance roles, and also provides a common platform for collective voting or engagement. Although the roles of proxy advisory agencies may be subject to more regulatory scrutiny in the future, as discussed in Chapter 3, the rise of these services provides a key transaction-cost reducing incentive for funds and their asset managers to become more engaged corporate governance actors.

Further, least-cost engagement with corporate governance roles may be demonstrated via forms of collective engagement at appropriate times. As Principle 5 of the Stewardship Code encourages collective engagement between institutions in times of 'significant corporate or wider economic stress, or when the risks posed threaten to destroy significant value', pension schemes and their asset managers' concerns for cost may be

---

122 Above.

123 See for example Mathias Siems, 'Convergence in Corporate Governance: A Leximetric Approach' (2010) 35 *Journal of Corporation Law* 729; Carsten Gerner-Beuerle, 'Determinants of Corporate Governance Codes' (2014) at http://papers.ssrn.com/sol3/papers.cfm?abstract_id=2346673; Weil Gotshal and Manges, *Comparative Study Of Corporate Governance Codes Relevant to the European Union and Its Member States* (2002) at http://ec.europa.eu/internal_market/company/docs/corpgov/corp-gov-codes-rpt-part1_en.pdf (pointing out significant convergence in Codes although not in company law) and in the EU, Paul Davies and Klaus J Hopt, 'Boards in Europe: Accountability and Convergence' (2013) 61 *American Journal of Comparative Law* 301.

124 The influence of proxy advisers is discussed in Stephen J Choi, Jill E Fisch and Marcel Kahan, 'The Power of Proxy Advisors: Myth or Reality?' (2010) 59 *Emory Law Journal* 869. They argue that the ISS wields significant corporate governance monitoring powers as it is very influential with institutions. In the EU, there also seem to be high levels of consistency between proxy advice and voting outcomes, although larger institutions evaluate the proxy advice with internal resources and may retain more than one advisor, discussed in paras 52, 56, ESMA, *Discussion Paper: An Overview of the Proxy Advisory Industry. Considerations on Possible Policy Options* (Dec 2012).

mitigated by pooling resources and efforts together. This chapter will shortly discuss the likely popularity of this form of engagement as a means to demonstrate schemes' and their asset managers' corporate governance roles. However, it remains to be seen how far such corporate governance roles can be truly engaged and meaningful when they are driven by 'compliance' pressures under the Code and the need to incur minimal expense.

An oft-discussed impediment to pension funds and their asset managers taking more engaged corporate governance roles is that of the conflicts of interest faced by funds. A common situation is where the pension fund invests in the sponsoring company, and although such investment is capped by regulation,[125] pension fund trustees may face conflicts of interest in relation to engagement with the company plan sponsor. Fund trustees may have to strike a balance between protecting members' interests and protecting the financial viability of the plan sponsor, and decisions such as risk-taking and management of the schemes, imposing higher contributions on members or negotiating with the employer plan sponsor may be affected by trustees' conflict of interests.[126] Further, adopting an active corporate governance stance against the sponsoring employer may be unlikely if the trustees are also in senior management positions at the sponsoring employer. The Stewardship Code has called upon pension fund trustees to draw up clear conflicts of interest policies,[127] while the OECD Guidelines[128] and Pension Regulator's Code[129] recommends that trustees take specific measures such as abstention from voting and disclosure in order to manage conflicts of interest impinging on decision-making for the benefit of scheme members. Moreover, conflicts of interest may also arise on the part of asset managers who may wish to refrain from corporate engagement in one particular company for fear of losing management mandates with that company or with others in the same sector.[130]

---

[125] To 5 per cent of the plan sponsor or 10 per cent of the group. Article 18, IORP Directive 2003.

[126] Ian Gault, Samantha Brown and Sam Wilkins, 'Conflicts of Interest' in Paul Thornton and Donald Fleming (eds), *Good Governance for Pension Funds* (Cambridge: Cambridge University Press, 2011) at pp. 85, 93.

[127] Principle 2, UK Stewardship Code 2012.

[128] *OECD Guidelines for Pension Fund Governance* (2009) at para 9, p. 12.

[129] Paras 29–30, TPR Code 03 (2014).

[130] Other conflicts of interest are in relation to asset managers' relationships with each other as fellow shareholders in many companies, see 'Fund houses favour rivals at annual general meetings', *Financial Times* (24 April 2016).

Another way for private sector DB schemes to be involved in corporate governance roles, albeit indirectly, is via allocation to alternative classes such as private equity and hedge funds. In their risk-taking bid to generate more returns consistent with their liability-driven strategies, private sector DB schemes may invest in alternative funds[131] and become indirectly part of these funds' investment management approaches that involve the use of their corporate governance roles and rights, as discussed in Chapter 3. However, 'leveraging' alternative funds' activist corporate governance strategy is not the same as behaving like active investors on the part of pension funds themselves. As Chapter 3 discusses, alternative funds are heavy instrumental users of their corporate governance roles and rights, and their incentives are not always aligned with long-term value creation or the wider public good.

Insurance Companies

Insurance companies are significant players in the pensions market as they are the dominant providers of personal and stakeholder pensions products and annuities in the UK. The relationship between product provider and beneficiary is a contractual one, not governed by the law of trusts. The Kay Review states in strong terms that 'While defined benefits pension schemes normally have trustees, defined contribution schemes are normally governed by contract rather than by a trust deed. We do not believe that the fiduciary character of the management of pensions should be affected by this change.'[132] The sentiment in this statement presumably extends to schemes managed by insurance companies largely structured under contract too. The level of protection for beneficiaries presumably depends on the strength of contractual terms. Moreover, there is extensive regulatory prescription for conduct of business for such schemes, and schemes are also subject to supervision by the Financial Conduct Authority.

---

[131] Paul H Edelman, Randall S Thomas and Robert B Thompson, 'Shareholder Voting in an Age of Intermediary Capitalism' (ECGI Working Paper 2014) at http://ssrn.com/abstract=2401746.

[132] BIS, *The Kay Review of UK Equity Markets and Long-Term Decision Making* (Final Report, 23 July 2012) at para 9.10.

The Equitable Life scandal[133] in the UK demonstrated that contractual provision for high levels of protection could be upheld in courts.[134] Insurance companies in the annuities business thus are compelled to meet their obligations to provide their guaranteed levels of benefits for pensioners who have bought annuities from them. These pressures are much like those applicable to defined benefits schemes discussed above, and thus, similar liability-driven pressures exist for insurance companies in the annuities business. Further, insurance companies in the personal and stakeholder pensions business are in a highly competitive market. An IMA survey documents a declining share of assets flowing into insurance companies as choices for pensions and investment have grown over the last two decades.[135] Hence, there are pressures to outperform as the market is highly competitive.[136] Mandatory disclosure imposed in respect of these funds on an annual and periodic basis entails a form of regular scrutiny that augments competitive pressures.[137]

Insurance companies have, like private sector defined benefit schemes, been in need of chasing higher returns and performance. In particular, they have decamped from UK listed equity into foreign equity and alternative asset classes, in the context of declining returns and losses from UK listed equity discussed above.[138] The Bank of England survey for example finds that international insurance companies have by and large fled from equity, in herd-like behavioural patterns in the wake of

---

[133] See Lord Penrose's report on the failure of Equitable Life, at http://news.bbc.co.uk/1/hi/business/3543549.stm, where the report is available in full.

[134] *Equitable Life Assurance Society v Hyman* [2002] 1 AC 408 (HL). The scandal arose as guaranteed benefits could not be met by Equitable Life which then sought to amend its company constitution and vary the guaranteed benefits promised to policy-holders. Policy-holders challenged these manoeuvres and were successful in court in preventing their guaranteed benefits from being changed.

[135] IMA, Asset Management in the UK Survey 2013–14 (2014) at pp. 31–32.

[136] Bank of England and Procyclicality Working Group, *Procyclicality and Structural Trends in Investment Allocation by Insurance Companies and Pension Funds* (July 2014) at p. 20, para 64.

[137] FCA Handbook, COBS 16 generally, and COBS 20.4.7 for with-profits products.

[138] Gregario Impavido and Ian Tower, 'How the Financial Crisis Affects Pensions and Insurance and Why the Impacts Matter' (IMF Working Paper 2009) at http://ssrn.com/abstract=1442253 report high holdings of marketable securities such as equities in the last two decades, but in declining proportion.

the global financial crisis.[139] This could be due in part to similar investment consultant input into insurers, resulting in herding behaviour. Such herding behaviour has been characterised as pro-cyclical and short-termist.[140] There is also marked behaviour on the part of insurance companies meeting annuities liabilities to rely on index-linked gilts,[141] even if the low interest rate environment is prompting diversification away from fixed income. In the context of these liability-driven pressures and insurance companies' asset allocation, the characterisation of insurance companies' roles in the corporate governance of investee corporations could to a certain extent be similar to that discussed for defined benefit pension schemes and their asset managers – that such a role becomes less relevant to their business model and more costly to assume. We note for example that the insurance company shareholder constituency of AstraZeneca was keener to sell out to Pfizer in its ultimately failed 2014 bid than many other investors who were more committed to the longer term prospects of AstraZeneca as an independent corporate entity.[142]

FCA regulation of insurance companies in relation to personal and stakeholder pensions products is unlikely to affect their corporate governance roles. As most personal and stakeholder pensions are unit-linked, or non-linked or with-profits products, they are essentially similar in nature to defined contribution products where the ultimate investment risk largely lies with investors although insurers may bear some partial risks for life products such as in guarantees, or in goodwill payments to mitigate the shock of investment losses for policy-holders.[143] Regulatory intervention does not protect the level of benefits for investors, but seeks to protect them in terms of conduct of advice and sale, pre and post-sale communications, transparency in fees and charges.[144] The conduct of

---

[139] Bank of England and Procyclicality Working Group, *Procyclicality and Structural Trends in Investment Allocation by Insurance Companies and Pension Funds* (July 2014) at p. 21.

[140] Above at p. 24, para 75.

[141] IMA, Asset Management in the UK Survey 2013–14 (2014) at p. 47. Pimco is of the view that Solvency II Directive will impose prudential requirements that steer the direction of insurers towards fixed income, see http://www.pimco.co.uk/EN/Insights/Pages/The-New-Normal-in-European-Insurance-Asset-Management.aspx.

[142] 'AstraZeneca divides shareholders with rejection of Pfizer's 'final' offer', *The Telegraph* (19 May 2014).

[143] Gregario Impavido and Ian Tower, 'How the Financial Crisis Affects Pensions and Insurance and Why the Impacts Matter' (2009), above.

[144] FCA Handbook, Insurance Conduct of Business, ICOBS.

investment management as such is not regulated. This should be distinguished from the general duty of 'prudence' imposed on pension scheme trustees. However, insurance companies managing personal and stakeholder pensions, and annuities, are subject to regulatory prescriptions as to the institution of adequate internal control and risk management.[145] It can be argued that such forms of regulation[146] make internal decision-making and conduct more robust[147] and hence could improve investor protection.[148] This is especially important after the Penrose report's findings on weak risk management, internal control and corporate governance at Equitable Life. Regulation is indeed silent on governing the nature and character of investment management that should be adopted, such as in schemes' assumption of their corporate governance rights and roles. This may be regarded as slightly backward in view of EU legislation that already articulates some expectations for mutual funds, as will be discussed in Chapter 5.

However, the soft law of the Stewardship Code could provide some influence for equity-investing insurance companies' behaviour. The Association of British Insurers, the ABI, has a track record of showing interest in championing good corporate governance in investee companies in order to reflect the investment performance expectations on the part of members. Insurance companies predominantly adopt in-house management of funds instead of delegation to asset managers,[149] and they can work closely with the ABI in developing their corporate governance positions. The ABI is responding to the needs for demonstration of stewardship by helping their members identify key issues in good

---

145 Article 16(5), MiFID II Directive 2014, as transposed by the FCA Handbook SYSC which imposes these requirements generally on all of its regulated entities.

146 Also internationally recommended in the *OECD Guidelines on Insurer Governance 2012*, pursuant to IAIS and OECD study on internal governance attributes and shortfalls in insurers, see *Issues Paper on Corporate Governance* (July 2009).

147 John Ashcroft, Juan Yermo and Fiona Stewart, 'Regulatory and Supervisory Context for Occupational Pension Provision' in Paul Thornton and Donald Fleming (eds), *Good Governance for Pension Funds* (Cambridge: Cambridge University Press, 2011) at 3, 11.

148 See above and, generally, FCA Handbook PRIN and SYSC, and specific provisions for with-profits policies, which are common in stakeholder and personal pensions, see COBS 20.5 where a policy committee must be appointed as the governing body for each fund, and the arrangement could be similar to a Board of trustees for pension schemes.

149 IMA, Asset Management in the UK Survey 2013–14 (2014) at p. 43.

corporate governance. For example, the ABI's investment affairs division is now merged with the Investment Management Association, and actively promoting one voice in influencing best practices in corporate governance.[150] The ABI has also instituted an Investor Exchange[151] as a platform to facilitate collective engagement. Insurers are likely to move towards collective engagement as a visible and transaction-cost reducing way of engaging in their corporate governance roles, in order to show their adherence to the UK Stewardship Code. However, we expect the nature of their corporate governance interest to be limited and likely to be demonstrated only in a cost-effective and minimalist manner. Further, there is also significant reliance on proxy advisory firms to identify the issues for engagement. For example, the input of proxy advisory firms such as PIRC or ISS is crucial to homogenous voting decisions by insurers against high executive pay.[152]

In response to increased competition, insurance companies have gradually become more open to exploring multiple asset classes, in particular, alternative asset classes such as hedge funds and private equity.[153] As discussed in relation to private sector DB schemes that invest in these funds, insurance companies investing in them could be indirectly involved in the shareholder activism undertaken by hedge funds.[154]

Defined Contribution Schemes

The likely prospect of unsustainable DB schemes has caused many private sector employers to disavow pension risks and to shift to defined contribution schemes completely. Defined contribution schemes have started to become popular in developed countries but the seismic shift in risk-bearing may not be fully comprehended and managed by the

---

150 Above, and see for example Investment Management Association (which merged with ABI Investment Affairs), IMA Principles of Remuneration 2014 at https://www.ivis.co.uk/media/10277/Principles-of-Remuneration-2014.pdf which provides for best practices in controlling executive pay.

151 ABI, *Improving Corporate Governance and Shareholder Engagement* (July 2013) at p. 25.

152 'Shareholder Revolts: Timeline', *The Guardian* (17 July 2014), taking stock of key revolt events in 2014 and their drivers.

153 See interview comments in https://www.clearpathanalysis.com/general/iam-0514-a3/. Pimco's analysis, see http://www.pimco.co.uk/EN/Insights/Pages/The-New-Normal-in-European-Insurance-Asset-Management.aspx.

154 Paul H Edelman, Randall S Thomas and Robert B Thompson, 'Shareholder Voting in an Age of Intermediary Capitalism' (2014), above.

employee sector.[155] This trend, according to Zelinsky,[156] is however likely to be irreversible. In Anglo-American countries where such an extreme shift in risk-bearing has largely taken place, there is only nascent dialogue on whether and how boundaries should be redrawn in risk-shifting.[157] However, in the UK, DC schemes are set to replace DB schemes in pensions savings, and their growth is forecast as likely to be very substantial.[158]

DC schemes are pension plans under which benefits to members are based on the investment returns on the amounts contributed to the plan by the sponsor and member.[159] Employers in the UK may offer DC schemes in the form of individual choices to save into one of several funds that employees could opt into, complemented by an employer's contribution. These funds are likely to be managed professionally by an insurer or asset manager. The employee would have a direct contractual relationship with the fund entity in which her contributions are placed.

---

155 See Evert Carlsson, Karl Erlandzon and Jonas Gustavsson, 'A Tale of Two Systems: Winners and Losers when Moving from Defined Benefit to Defined Contribution Pensions' (2008) at http://ssrn.com/abstract=1088016 for the profiles of likely 'winners' and 'losers' in the shift from DB to DC. On the lack of consumer ability or competence in understanding the nature of risks in DC schemes, see discussion on DC schemes in this section and the citations therein.

156 Edward A Zelinsky, 'The Defined Contribution Paradigm' (2004), above.

157 For example, Policy-makers are also mooting reforms to DC schemes, perhaps moving away from employer-provided schemes to independently managed schemes with no employment nexus. Policy-makers are also considering learning from countries that have embraced more communitarian ideologies in risk-bearing, such as in the Dutch collective pension schemes. The Dutch collective DC scheme has become an object of interest in study. They are dedicated institutions that collectively manage DC assets, and may be better governed and more accountable to member participants. Collective DC institutions are subject to different internal governance frameworks and ethos, and such would shape their roles in corporate governance as equity investors. Hans Blommestein, Pascal Janssen, Niels Kortleve, and Juan Yermo, 'Moving Beyond the 'DB vs. DC' Debate: The Appeal of Hybrid Pension Plans' (2009) 2 *Rotman International Journal of Pension Management* 66; Eduard H M Ponds and Bart van Riel, 'The Recent Evolution of Pension Funds in the Netherlands: The Trend to Hybrid DB-DC Plans and Beyond' (2007) at http://ssrn.com/abstract=964428.

158 Allianz Global Investors, *Defining the Direction of Defined Contribution in Europe: Results of an Expert Survey* (2009).

159 Allianz Global Investors, *Defining the Direction of Defined Contribution in Europe: Results of an Expert Survey* (2009).

Employers are now subject to mandatory legislation[160] to enrol employees into pensions saving schemes, and so employees are likely to be auto-enrolled into a DC scheme by choice or into one chosen by default if no express choice is made. Employees may also be enrolled into NEST, a National Pension Savings DC scheme. NEST is a trust-based occupational pension scheme overseen by a Trustee Corporation (NEST Corporation) which is a not-for-profit entity. It is a non-departmental public body (NDPB) that operates at arm's length from government and is accountable to Parliament through the Department for Work and Pensions.[161]

DC schemes appeal to pension savers in terms of choice. Individuals may choose a fund according to risk appetite, such as 'growth' or 'safety', but empirical research shows that individual savers do not engage in intelligent or informed selection, as studies have shown that individual savers face cognitive challenges choosing a suitable fund.[162] Subsequently, savers are 'stuck' with a fund they have by and large 'selected' or been enrolled into. Such savers rely extensively on investment intermediaries to control and manage their savings for an ultimate pension pot but they often do not monitor investment performance with mandatory reporting and accountability. Hence, although pension accounts for individuals are framed by individual choice,[163] the investment management process generally results in the disengagement and disempowerment of the individual saver.[164] This is particularly disturbing as empirical research does not forecast optimism in DC schemes providing adequately for pensioners. It is speculative but certainly of relevance to consider that much sceptical and pessimistic research on DC scheme is already forecasting the likelihood of a low replacement ratio of

---

[160] Pensions Act 2008.

[161] http://www.nestpensions.org.uk/schemeweb/NestWeb/public/home/contents/homepage.html.

[162] Office of Fair Trading, *Defined Contribution Workplace Pension Market Study* (Sep 2013); Lars Bovenberg, 'Frontiers in Pension Finance and Reform: Institutional Innovation in the Netherlands' (2007) at http://ssrn.com/abstract=13077081; Thomas Post, Helmut Gründl, Joan T Schmit and Anja Zimmer, 'The Impact of Investment Behaviour for Individual Welfare' (2014) 81 *Economica* 15.

[163] Edward A Zelinsky, 'The Defined Contribution Paradigm' (2004), above.

[164] Gordon L Clark and Roger Urwin, 'DC Pension Fund Best-practice Design and Governance' (2010) at http://ssrn.com/abstract=1652680.

income at retirement, as the final values of pension pots are unpredictable.[165] In this context, DC schemes are being subjected to regulatory governance to ensure that investment management is carried out in the best interests of savers. Such regulation of DC schemes also plays a significant role in influencing their corporate governance roles.

DC schemes, usually structured as contractual schemes, are regulated by the Financial Conduct Authority in the UK and are subject to conduct of business rules. General conduct of business rules require that information be communicated in a fair, clear and not misleading manner, investment advice is given that is suitable for the saver, and that customers are treated fairly.[166] Some DC schemes are trust-based, where a master trust is established over a number of schemes and trustees are subject to the regime in the Trustees Act 2000 governing their investment management discretion.[167] In general, scheme participants are passive in nature, and instinctively trust and rely[168] on the employer's role to govern the DC schemes. Hence, the personal investor protections in conduct of business regulation may be somewhat of a white elephant for DC scheme participants.

Until early 2015 employers were not under any formal obligation in the employment relationship to monitor the DC schemes and the employer had no investment relationship with the funds. Commentators[169] have pointed out that many employment DC schemes are administered in companies as part of general human resources. The dedication

---

165 Roger Charlton and Roddy McKinnon, 'Beyond Mandatory Privatization]: Pensions Policy Options for Developing Countries' (2000) 12 *Journal of International Development* 483; Evert Carlsson, Karl Erlandzon and Jonas Gustavsson, 'A Tale of Two Systems: Winners and Losers when Moving from Defined Benefit to Defined Contribution Pensions' (2008), above; Edmund Cannon and Ian Tonks, 'The Value and Risk of Defined Contribution Pension Schemes: International Evidence' (2013) 80 *Journal of Risk and Insurance* 95; Towers Watson, *Pension Adequacy: The Challenge for Defined Contribution Pension Plans* (2010).

166 Generally, FCA Handbook COBS.

167 Trustees' duties are not dissimilar to trustees' duties in general for DB schemes, see for example The Pensions Regulator, *Governance and Administration of Occupational Trust-Based Schemes Providing Money Purchase Benefits* (July 2016) at http://www.thepensionsregulator.gov.uk/docs/code-13.pdf.

168 Evidenced in Alastair Byrne, 'Employee Saving and Investment Decisions in Defined Contribution Pension Plans: Survey Evidence from the UK' (2007) at http://www.actuaries.org.uk/system/files/documents/pdf/byrne_pensions.pdf.

169 Gordon L Clark and Roger Urwin, 'DC Pension Fund Best-practice Design and Governance' (2010), above; Dietrich Hauptmeier and Graham Mannion, 'Effective Investment Governance in Defined Contribution Schemes' in

of resources to help employees choose a suitable fund, or monitor the funds they have participated in, is extremely thin and limited. Where investors are themselves passive and employers do not actively monitor the DC schemes, there is a real governance deficit. In response to this perceived deficit, the Department of Work and Pensions[170] has introduced reforms to mandate the establishment of 'Independent Governance Committees' in employers to oversee the DC schemes and monitor aspects of conduct such as value for money, fees, charges and accountability. For trust-based schemes, a committee of trustees subject to similar responsibilities has to be appointed.[171] A charge cap of 0.75 per cent of funds under management was also imposed from April 2015, excluding transaction costs.[172] Even before the introduction of the charge cap, the ABI's Independent Project Board[173] had also produced a report to identify funds that were at risk of reducing yield for savers over 1 per cent and undertook to contact funds to review their charging structures. The IGC[174] is to be instituted in all firms that operate schemes that are sizeable or complex. Where the nature, size and scale of schemes do not warrant the institution of an IGC, firms could establish a less prescriptive 'governance advisory arrangement'. Whether DC schemes are overseen by an IGC or a committee of trustees, there are similar requirements for governing body appointees to be knowledgeable, adequately resourced and largely independent and to have in place a policy to manage conflicts of interest. These appointees have to oversee investment strategies, act in beneficiaries' best interests and consider ongoing issues such as value for money, and costs and charges borne by schemes. This significant change

---

Paul Thornton and Donald Fleming (eds), *Good Governance for Pension Funds* (Cambridge: Cambridge University Press, 2011) at p. 267.

170 DWP, *Better Workplace Pensions: Further Measures for Savers* (March 2014).

171 The Pensions Regulator, *Governance and Administration of Occupational Trust-Based Schemes Providing Money Purchase Benefits* (July 2016) at http://www.thepensionsregulator.gov.uk/docs/code-13.pdf.

172 See FCA, *Charges in Workplace Personal Pension Schemes: A Consultation Paper* (Oct 2014) and *Final rules for Charges in Workplace Personal Pension Schemes and Feedback on CP14/24* (March 2015) on the charge cap, the exclusion of transaction costs and the prohibition of differential charges or certain inducements.

173 Independent Project Board, ABI, *Defined Contribution Workplace Pensions: The Audit of Charges and Benefits In Legacy Schemes* (Dec 2014).

174 FCA Handbook, COBS 19.5, see also FCA, 'Final Rules for Independent Governance Committees, Including Feedback on CP14/16' (Feb 2015), above.

in the internal governance of DC schemes could affect funds' corporate governance roles in several ways.

First, it remains to be seen how these newly empowered governing bodies may affect asset allocation by schemes. Large DC schemes may also be able to influence how funds are managed to be more tailor-made to their purposes. Commentators[175] report funds' tendency to be heavily equity-based, and invest in conventional asset classes such as bonds and real estate trusts. Allocation decisions have been relatively unimaginative so far and it remains to be seen whether scrutiny by the governing body may change patterns of asset allocation. If the institution of this new level of monitoring and accountability in DC schemes results in anxiety on the part of DC schemes to demonstrate good performance, this could drive schemes to opt for more risky asset allocations or drive short-termism in the investment management process.[176] The framework of regular monitoring and scrutiny is important to alleviate agency problems but, as mentioned in Chapters 2 and 3, very often perpetuates unintended incentives and consequences that distort schemes' long-maturing nature into nevertheless short-termist cycles.[177] Further, given the background of volatile and low returns environments in investment markets in the last decade or so, DC schemes could be incentivised[178] to seek higher returns in the earlier stages of schemes, and hence engage in riskier asset allocations in order to be prepared for maturation of the schemes. This may mean moving into foreign equities and alternative asset classes, thereby marginalising their importance as UK equity owners.

It is queried whether the charge cap for investment management of DC schemes would affect funds' corporate governance roles. We expect funds' corporate governance roles to be very much determined by their own calculus of cost and benefit. Empirical research shows that pension

---

[175] Dietrich Hauptmeier and Graham Mannion, 'Effective Investment Governance in Defined Contribution Schemes' in Paul Thornton and Donald Fleming (eds), *Good Governance for Pension Funds* (Cambridge: Cambridge University Press, 2011) at p. 267.

[176] Short termism is a widespread behaviour in funds managing DC assets, see Fiona Stewart, 'Proving Incentives for Long-Term Investment by Pension Funds: The Use of Outcome-based Benchmarks' (*World Bank Research Paper*, 2014).

[177] Gordon L Clark and Roger Urwin, 'DC Pension Fund Best-practice Design and Governance' (2010), above.

[178] Given that real wage growth in developed countries has stagnated, advocating increased employee contributions for better future pensions is unlikely to be popular.

schemes, conscious of cost, have switched in droves into passive investing.[179] This may also be more comfortable for members of newly formed governing bodies who are yet uncertain of the extent of their obligations. We are sceptical of funds' interest in assuming corporate governance roles as the attendant research and engagement are costly. Nevertheless, even if schemes invest passively, passive asset managers may not shy away from corporate governance roles, especially in voting[180] or where collective engagement brings economies of scale.

Gelter[181] is of the view that the shift from DB to DC would augment the importance of shareholder primacy as employees become more aware of the importance of shareholder wealth for retirement and would therefore support policies that favour shareholder primacy. This could influence law and policy towards providing more scope for shareholder rights and corporate governance engagement. We are of the view that the general ideological context for favouring shareholder primacy would facilitate schemes' corporate governance roles, but whether schemes assume such roles is still dependent on rather practical factors such as cost/benefit, and the pressures perceived from regulatory compliance. As the UK has embraced shareholder stewardship as a best practice, the IGCs may influence scheme management towards that. This could create a driving factor towards taking corporate governance roles seriously within the accountability parameters of the schemes and the charge cap.

However, schemes' corporate governance roles may also be affected by conflicts of interest. Next, DC schemes may invest, subject to the limits in legislation,[182] in the employer's securities. With such conflicts of interest, schemes and their asset managers may be unwilling to engage in corporate governance roles that may be contrary to the employer company's interests. This is a widely observed phenomenon in many developed countries' private sector DC schemes.[183] This is an area which has

---

[179] 'European pension funds to double passive use', *Financial Times* (9 Nov 2014).

[180] Although the charge cap may make voting more challenging if proxy advisors can't be used in a cost-effective manner.

[181] Martin Gelter, 'The Pension System and the Rise of Shareholder Primacy' (2012) at http://ssrn.com/abstract=2079607.

[182] To 5 per cent of the plan sponsor or 10 per cent of the group. Article 18, IORP Directive 2003.

[183] John Broadbent, Michael Palumbo and Elizabeth Woodman, 'The Shift from Defined Benefit to Defined Contribution Pension Plans – Implications for Asset Allocation and Risk Management' (2006) at http://bis.hasbeenforeclosed.com/publ/wgpapers/cgfs27broadbent3.pdf.

however been picked up by the Stewardship Code[184] that requires funds and their managers to develop conflicts of interest policies. Even if funds remain reluctant to be antagonistic to the employer company, they may be compelled to be more transparent and subject their engagement or otherwise to scrutiny. Such may or may not result in changes to behaviour. IGCs may need to be careful on this issue, as antagonistic corporate governance roles may adversely affect their personal interests such as job security. It is to be noted that reforms were introduced in Australia[185] to mitigate conflicts of interest by introducing a more independent composition to the Board of trustees. However, can independent committee members better overcome conflicts of interest? Critique has been levied in such terms: '[Independent trustee-directors] will gravitate towards those with the power of appointment, and be vulnerable to capture by the full-time management of the scheme, because of insufficient resources and lack of information necessary to act as an effective constraint on their actions.'[186]

One particular DC scheme to watch is NEST which is accountable to the government and Parliament. NEST is able to pool together DC assets from enrolled employees and invests assets into life-cycle funds. It is highly likely that NEST outsources to asset managers while monitoring and supervising such delegation. Stewart is of the view that NEST may provide a leading model for investment management of DC assets as NEST has put in good governance frameworks, being accountable to the DWP and to the public, and is likely to be ahead in dealing with financial as well as governance issues.[187] As a matter of best practice, NEST funds and asset managers would likely be encouraged to support the Stewardship Code, and may develop forms of optimal engagement within low cost boundaries. We predict that these would converge around collective engagement and support for transaction-cost reducing regulatory prescriptions in good corporate governance and minority shareholder protection. However, this is not to preclude other practices that may achieve both the aims of stewardship and cost-effectiveness in investment management. It is pertinent going forward to observe any leadership that NEST provides in this area.

---

[184] Principle 2.

[185] Ronald B Davis, 'Reflections on Representation in Australian Superannuation Governance' (2013) 25 *Australian Superannuation Law Bulletin* 51.

[186] Above at p. 53.

[187] Fiona Stewart, 'Proving Incentives for Long-Term Investment by Pension Funds: The Use of Outcome-based Benchmarks' (2014), above.

Now that we have sketched the contours of key factors and trends that will likely shape the governance, investment management and corporate governance roles of the main players in the pensions management industry, Section C discusses the observed corporate governance behaviour of the pensions sector as a whole. This Section draws from empirical, normative and doctrinal legal research to present an aggregate view of pension funds as corporate governance actors in a variety of governance roles. We present a spectrum of typologies of corporate governance roles and discuss observed behaviour in relation to them.

We conclude that on the whole, although pension funds, both global and UK, are significant owners of UK corporate equity, their corporate governance roles have been largely peripheral and have taken a long period of time to be visible. The increased importance of these roles is however being shaped by their asset managers, whose incentives, in the context of contesting forces, shape these roles. Hence these roles are increasingly characterised as instrumental for purposes measured in relation to financial performance and internal business models, and not pursuant to wider social expectations of such roles. We are on the whole sceptical that pension fund capitalism provides leadership in showing how long-term commitment to and engagement with investee companies contributes to the public interest of a well-functioning corporate economy for the long term.

C. THE TYPOLOGIES OF PENSION FUNDS' CORPORATE GOVERNANCE ROLES IN THE UK

We have teased out the key drivers that shape different pension funds in terms of asset allocations and investment practices, and their likely positions on their corporate governance roles. Some common themes affecting funds across the board are cost pressures which have heightened in the low yield environment since the 2000s, and increased regulatory pressures, particularly in ensuring good governance and regular scrutiny. Turning to observed corporate governance behaviour, we suggest that there are ten typologies of investor behaviour among pension fund asset owners and their asset managers. In this Section, we set out the following typologies and explore the factors that drive each type of investor behaviour:

(a) Voting at the annual general meeting, through proxies or otherwise;
(b) Individual informal dialogue and escalation activities;
(c) Collective engagement with other mainstream institutions in voting;

(d) Collective engagement with other mainstream institutions in other events;
(e) Collective engagement with alternative investment funds such as hedge funds;
(f) Investment in hedge or private equity funds as a 'surrogate' means of engaging in corporate governance roles;
(g) Engagement driven by events, mainly mergers and takeovers;
(h) Engagement within the policies of socially responsible investing;
(i) Securities or derivative litigation which may be privately settled; and
(j) Exit over voice.

This Section will examine the nature of investor behaviour in each of the above typologies and seek to offer analytical insights into the factors that shape behaviour. Our analysis is based on desk-based research into existing academic and empirical literature and anecdotal evidence in the financial press.

Voting

Pension funds are likely to be diversified minority shareholders, in companies with a largely dispersed ownership structure where the UK listed market is concerned; but where stakes in foreign companies (as well as foreign equity listed in the UK) are concerned, such a minority stake could be sitting alongside controlling block-holders.

Early empirical literature on pension fund voting shows that funds are disengaged and passive[188] and do not regularly vote at annual general meetings. This is largely due to the high cost of voting at so many investee companies in the diversified portfolios of funds, and the prevalent preference for exit if an investee company underperforms.[189] Voting levels have been improving, and we suggest that the decreased reluctance to vote has been largely brought about by policy pressure since the 1990s. Law and soft law reforms compel and cater for greater shareholder engagement, and transaction-cost reducing institutions such as

---

[188] Andrew M Clearfield, '"With Friends Like These, Who Needs Enemies?" The Structure of the Investment Industry and Its Reluctance to Exercise Governance Oversight' (2005) 13 *Corporate Governance* 114; Paul Myners, *Institutional Investment in the UK: A Review* (2001) at paras 5.77 to 5.94.

[189] See also William O'Barr and John M Conley, *Fortune and Folly* (NY: McGraw-Hill, 1992).

proxy voting have arisen. One of us[190] has argued that there has been relentless policy pressure upon institutional investors to exercise their corporate governance roles[191] in order to monitor their investee companies, so that weaknesses in corporate performance and culture (such as remuneration issues[192]) may be addressed.

In response, pension funds have over the years become more involved in voting at the annual general meetings of their investee companies, as voting is a highly visible form of corporate governance participation.[193] By 2013, the National Pension Funds Association had recorded 96 per cent voting participation among its members, even if corporate governance activities were largely delegated to asset managers.[194] Voting seems to have become what is expected of minimum shareholder behaviour. The trend towards increased voting may be described as a decreased reluctance to vote, although there are signs that pension funds are becoming more pro-actively interested in voting.

First, in order to overcome institutions' reluctance to vote, the soft law of corporate governance has evolved to provide a ready-made template for investors to evaluate their investee companies' corporate governance and its likely associations with other symptoms such as corporate (under-) performance, misbehaviour or scandal. The UK Corporate Governance Code describes best practices in corporate governance – particularly in relation to the structure, composition and functioning of the board of directors and its committees. Adherence to the Code is intended to provide minority investors with an adequate *ex ante* level of protection. The current UK Code has evolved since the first Cadbury Code of Corporate Governance and is often seen as a leading standard[195] in the advancement of the 'soft law' approach to corporate governance. Further, the UK Listing Rules have, since the 1990s, maintained a

---

190 Chapter 2, Iris H-Y Chiu, *The Foundations and Anatomy of Shareholder Activism* (Oxford: Hart 2010).

191 Adrian Cadbury, *The Financial Aspects of Corporate Governance* (1992) at paras 6.10, 6.16 for example.

192 Richard Greenbury, *Report: Directors' Remuneration* (17 Jul 1995) for example.

193 See NAPF and IMA surveys on investor engagement, discussed in Chapter 2, Iris H-Y Chiu, *The Foundations and Anatomy of Shareholder Activism* (2010), above; Paul Hewitt, 'The Exercise of Shareholder Rights' (2011) at http://dx.doi.org/10.1787/5kg54d0l1lvf-en.

194 NAPF, *NAPF Engagement Survey: Pension Funds' Engagement with Investee Companies* (Nov 2013) at p. 28.

195 Financial Reporting Council, *Comply or Explain: 20th Anniversary of the UK Corporate Governance Code* (London, 2012).

requirement that listed companies in the highest listing category (now the Premium listing) of the LSE should comply with the provisions of the prevailing Code of Corporate Governance or else explain any deviations. This establishes the credibility and status of the Code. One of us observes that the corporate governance template has become extensively used as the basis for voting decisions by pension funds and their asset managers, either on a *per se* basis or as a reason for raising discontent regarding corporate under-performance.[196] The Code-driven form of voting behaviour was noted in Moore's critical commentary[197] regarding shareholder revolt in the proposed appointment of Stuart Rose as Executive Chairman of Marks & Spencer in 2008 after having served as its Chief Executive, in violation of several of the best practices in the Code, such as recommending the separation of the Chairman and Chief Executive roles and the need for the Chairman to be independent on appointment. He was of the view that such voting behaviour is driven by a formulaic adherence to the Code which is adverse to flexible application. The intelligent and engaged investor should evaluate the actual corporate governance needs of individual companies. However, the decreased reluctance on the part of institutions to vote can only be achieved by transaction cost-reducing measures. These are the soft law standardisation of corporate governance norms and the growth of the proxy advisory and voting industry which further consolidates the information mediation role necessary for facilitating voting decisions.

Choi et al[198] noted the importance of ISS voting advice for institutions in the US, and in the UK the proxy advisory industry is dominated by a few players such as ISS, Glass Lewis, IVIS (which serves the Association of British Insurers and is not merged into the Investment Management Association), PIRC and Manifest.[199] Although empirical research has not found blind adherence to proxy advisors' voting recommendations, the information mediation role of advisors is highly valued and over half of asset owners and managers would follow the voting advice issued.[200]

---

196 Chapter 2, Iris H-Y Chiu, *The Foundations and Anatomy of Shareholder Activism* (2010), above.

197 Marc T Moore, '"Whispering Sweet Nothings": The Limitations of Informal Conformance in UK Corporate Governance' (2009), above.

198 Stephen J Choi, Jill E Fisch and Marcel Kahan, 'The Power of Proxy Advisors: Myth or Reality?' (2010), above.

199 Marc T Moore, '"Whispering Sweet Nothings": The Limitations of Informal Conformance in UK Corporate Governance' (2009), above.

200 Y Ertimur, F Ferri and D Oesch, 'Shareholder Votes and Proxy Advisors: Evidence from Say on Pay' (2013) 51 *Journal of Accounting Research* 951;

Thomas[201] also argues that proxy advisors perform a specialised service and it would be unfair to criticise pension funds for using them in enhancing the information matrix surrounding their voting decisions.

The decreased reluctance to vote has also paved the way for institutions to become more aware of 'defensive' concerns. These relate to pension funds being more pro-active and vocal where they perceive the need to protect shareholders' interests. For example, in the 2008 capital raising exercise conducted by Barclays Plc, institutional shareholders were roused to protest after Barclays proposed to issue favourably-priced preference shares to Qatari investors, thereby diluting institutions' existing stakes. The institutions managed to negotiate an outcome which allowed them to participate in the capital raising exercise in order to protect their minority rights.[202] Hence, institutions are able to benefit from the legitimation and support for shareholder engagement that underlies the legal and soft law frameworks.

These 'defensive' concerns also became heightened in the wake of the global financial crisis. A major governance issue of concern is executive pay, which seems to have remained immune to falling markets, and has exacerbated the perception of rewards for failure. This negative perception of high levels of executive pay is partly affected by the commentary highlighting the adverse effect of generous bankers' remuneration upon excessive risk-taking at banks,[203] contributing to near failures in many financial institutions during the crisis. Thus, institutions have taken up the battle against high executive remuneration to protect their own investment interests. In the 2012 annual general meeting season, the financial press[204] reported an unprecedented level of adverse institutional shareholder votes in the UK against executive pay packages across

---

ESMA, *Final Report: Feedback Statement on the Consultation Regarding the Role of the Proxy Advisory Industry* (Feb 2013).

[201] Randall S Thomas, 'Public Pension Funds as Shareholder Activists: A Comment on Choi and Fisch' (2008) 61 *Vanderbilt Law Review* 1.

[202] Discussed in detail in Chapter 2, Iris H-Y Chiu, *The Foundations and Anatomy of Shareholder Activism* (2010), above.

[203] Sugato Bhattacharyya and Amiyatosh Purnanandam, 'Risk-Taking By Banks: What Did We Know and When Did We Know It?' (November 2011) http://ssrn.com/abstract=1619472; Francesco Vallascas and Jens Hagendorff, 'CEO Remuneration and Bank Default Risk: Evidence from the US and Europe' (July 2010) at http://papers.ssrn.com/sol3/papers.cfm?abstract_id=1799268, arguing that remuneration linked to stock incentivises CEOs of banks to prefer greater risk-taking.

[204] 'Boards Wake up to a Shareholder Spring', *Financial Times* (4 May 2012).

sectors, triggering a 'Shareholder Spring'. That momentum produced such visible and vibrant shareholder engagement that one of the consequences was that 'more law' was encouraged to be put in place in order to facilitate shareholder engagement in that issue. Legislation[205] introduced a binding shareholder vote for executive remuneration policies, and that required companies to seek approval for proposed remuneration approaches in a three yearly cycle or less. Further, shareholders were given a yearly advisory vote on the company's implementation of the existing pay package. This reform mirrors a similar reform introduced in the US by the Securities Exchange Commission.[206] The impact on pay levels and corporate governance is still being monitored, but so far does not appear to be significant.[207]

Funds' interest in defensive concerns also provides the backdrop for another significant reform in UK company law with regard to corporate reporting. Institutions have generally voiced their concerns that corporate reporting showed no sign of the dangers and risks that were to materialise at many banks in the global financial crisis 2007–09.[208] Hence, funds' interest in more meaningful corporate reporting has sharpened. In response, the UK overhauled the regime for directors' annual reporting. Directors of quoted companies have been subject to a requirement to produce a yearly business review that is a form of narrative reporting of the company's performance as well as of its social and environmental impact.[209] In August 2013, the Companies Act 2006 was amended by the Companies Act 2006 (Strategic Report and Directors' Report) Regulations 2013 to introduce the Strategic Report to replace the directors' business review in the now superseded section 417 of the Companies Act 2006.[210] The Strategic Report incorporates the former requirements of the

---

205 s439A, Companies Act 2006 inserted by the Enterprise and Regulatory Reform Act 2013.

206 Section 951 of the Dodd-Frank Act amending the Securities Exchange Act of 1934 by adding Section 14A.

207 Jie Cai and Ralph A Walkling, 'Shareholders' Say on Pay: Does it Create Value?' (2009) *Journal of Financial and Quantitative Analysis* 299; Fabrizio Ferri and David A Maber, 'Say on Pay Votes and CEO Compensation: Evidence from the UK' (2013) 17 *Review of Finance* 527.

208 Findings in the Sharman Inquiry, see The Sharman Inquiry, *Going Concern and Liquidity Risks: Lessons for Companies and Auditors, Final Report and Recommendations of the Panel of Inquiry* (June 2012), at http://www.frc.org.uk/getattachment/591a5e2a-35d7-4470-a46c-30c0d8ca2a14/Sharman-Inquiry-Final-Report.aspx.

209 Previous s417 Companies Act 2006.

210 Section 414A, 414C, Companies Act 2006.

superseded directors' business review, as well as a description of the company's strategy, business model and gender diversity on the Board, in senior management and in employees. The Strategic Report is a move towards enhanced narrative reporting which sets financial reporting in context so that shareholders can engage with companies bearing in mind their unique strategic and operating contexts. Narrative reporting is seen as a way to encourage intelligent and 'tailor-made' shareholder engagement.[211] Further, the Financial Reporting Council has also issued guidelines on directors' business and financial reporting that directors should include a longer-term viability statement in the Strategic Report in order to advise shareholders of any longer term risks and outlooks that may affect the viability of the company in a period exceeding 12 months.[212] Hence, shareholder voice in voting is flanked by greater and more intelligent forms of transparency to assist shareholder engagement.

Finally, the UK also introduced enhanced protection of minority shareholders in a block-held listed company so that their voice would not be drowned and that their votes would count towards crucial decisions in the issuer. A package of notable reforms in the Listing Rules was introduced to protect the minority shareholder's vote in a block-held listed company.[213] First, such companies' relations with their block-holders must be regulated via a 'Mandatory Agreement' subject to

---

[211] Critically discussed in Iris H-Y Chiu, 'Reviving Shareholder Stewardship: Critically Examining the Impact of Corporate Transparency Reforms in the UK' (2014) 38 *Delaware Journal of Corporate Law* 983.

[212] FRC, *Guidance on Risk Management, Internal Control and Related Financial and Business Reporting* (Sep 2014) at https://www.frc.org.uk/Our-Work/Publications/Corporate-Governance/Guidance-on-Risk-Management,-Internal-Control-and.pdf. This initiative was in response to the critique levied by institutions in the wake of the global financial crisis that going-concern statements of certain banks before the onset of the crisis were not accurate. The state of the going-concern certification was the subject of the Sharman Inquiry which advocated that the concept of 'going concern' did have to be clarified, and that shareholders needed more context-rich information in which to thoroughly assess companies' future prospects. See The Sharman Inquiry, *Going Concern and Liquidity Risks: Lessons for Companies and Auditors, Final Report and Recommendations of the Panel of Inquiry* (June 2012), above; and the FRC's feedback statement, https://www.frc.org.uk/Our-Work/Headline-projects/The-Sharman-Inquiry.aspx.

[213] Financial Services Authority, *Enhancing the Effectiveness of the Listing Regime and Feedback on CP12/2* (Oct 2012); Financial Conduct Authority, *Enhancing the Effectiveness of the Listing Regime and Further Consultation* (November 2013); FCA, 'Response to CP13/15 – Enhancing the Effectiveness of the Listing Regime' (16 May 2014); UK Listing Rules 6.1.4ff.

independent director and shareholder scrutiny; second, minority independent shareholders are to be regarded as a separate class whose approval must be sought where appointing independent directors is concerned or when a cancellation of the Premium listing is proposed.[214]

The legal reforms mentioned above are meant to further facilitate the use of institutions' voting rights, by enriching the information environment for shareholders through more context-rich narrative reporting, and by empowering institutions through making their votes count – in the especially scrutinised area of executive remuneration and where institutions find themselves as minority shareholders in block-held listed companies in the UK equity market.

Institutions have now been nudged and compelled into regular voting behaviour, and one of the signs of pensions' trustees' increased interest in voting is the establishment of the 'Red Lines' initiative by the Association of Member-Nominated Trustees (AMNT).[215] The initiative sets out the preferences of pension trustees in terms of AGM voting. However, we observe that pension institutions are still highly constrained by cost-effective concerns in taking on engaged corporate governance roles.[216]

Even if Codes and law could reduce transaction-costs to a large extent by enriching the information environment and by standardising corporate governance norms, information analysis that translates into decision-making is still a costly job requiring specialised human capital, whether internalised or delegated to proxy advisory agencies. Context-specific narrative reporting may mitigate against investors making superficial and standardised judgments, but they need to be more carefully analysed. Cost pressures remain a challenging factor for funds and their asset managers in engaging with voting. In view of the competing pressures of cost and the need to demonstrate stewardship in voting, it is likely that asset owners will, to a large extent, continue to rely on easy to identify metrics as proxy indicators of governance soundness, and on standardised voting recommendations by proxy advisory agencies when the general meeting seasons kick in. This may explain why institutions in engagement often converge on key issues like executive remuneration. Pension

---

214 See detailed discussion in Roger Barker and Iris H-Y Chiu, 'Protecting Minority Shareholders in Blockholder-Controlled Companies – Evaluating the UK's Enhanced Listing Regime in Comparison with Investor Protection Regimes in New York and Hong Kong' (2015), above.

215 AMNT, *Red Lines Voting* (2016) at http://amnt.org/red-line-voting/.

216 Tessa Hebb, 'The Economic Inefficiency of Secrecy: Pension Fund Investors' Corporate Transparency Concerns' (2006) 63 *Journal of Business Ethics* 385.

asset owners and managers may also look increasingly to collective engagement in order to straddle the competing pressures of cost-effectiveness and need to demonstrate more meaningful stewardship, a point to be taken up shortly.

Further, where external asset managers are used to manage portfolios, cost concerns also constrain pensions institutions' corporate governance roles. This is because asset managers, already constrained by fee pressures, are unlikely to deploy costly resources to engage extensively in corporate governance roles. Further, voting may be affected by conflicts of interest, a point that has been discussed in Chapter 3. Asset managers also pool pension institutions' funds into collective vehicles, so that the right to vote belongs to the collective entity, which cannot represent any particular pensions institutions' corporate governance mandate. This is the case with small pension schemes that cannot afford to instruct dedicated mandates of investment management tailored to meet their needs. In achieving cost-effectiveness and economies of scale in investment management, pensions institutions may be disempowered from exercising any particular corporate governance rights which are no longer attributable to them specifically.[217]

Voting activism is likely to remain rare with pensions institutions. The NAPF survey of 2013[218] commented that pension fund asset owners are not in favour of confrontation with their investee companies and that the unpleasantness of the Shareholder Spring of 2012 was unlikely to be a recurring phenomenon. The exercise of voice through voting is likely to be reactive and for the necessary defensive concerns only, unlikely in most cases to become visibly pro-active and aggressive.

It may be queried whether stock lending, which generates revenue for pension asset owners, could prove to be inhibitory to voting. We note that the Large review in the UK strongly advocated against hedge funds borrowing stock to vote (although voting on borrowed stock is not illegitimate per se)[219] and the NAPF survey highlights a significant number of funds either recalling stock in the voting season or not engaging in lending at all.[220] As discussed in Chapter 3, empty voting

---

[217] 'Asset Managers Push Back against Activist Pension Funds', *Financial Times* (31 July 2016).

[218] NAPF, *NAPF Engagement Survey: Pension Funds' Engagement with Investee Companies* (Nov 2013).

[219] Hedge Funds Standards Board, *Standards* (2012) at para 28.1.

[220] NAPF, *NAPF Engagement Survey: Pension Funds' Engagement with Investee Companies* (Nov 2013).

and securities lending have not caused significant scandals in corporate governance so far, but may need to be revisited in due course.

We turn to consider whether pension funds and their asset managers would utilise other shareholder rights related to the general meeting in order to demonstrate stewardship. Although the company law framework supports shareholder rights in terms of putting items on the agenda for the annual general meeting,[221] circulating statements for support and even calling a general meeting,[222] empirical researchers have found such pro-active behaviour to be relatively rare[223] in the institutional quarter in UK listed equity markets, compared to the more dramatic proxy contests in the US[224] where shareholders' company law rights are ironically more limited.[225] That said, Choi and Fisch document that pension funds in the US often exercise their defensive voting activism by just withholding votes. Truly activist behaviour such as putting on proxy contests is relatively rare, as it is just too difficult for pension funds to find suitable directorial nominees to field.[226] The UK's institutional investor sector remains relatively restrained, albeit enjoying rather powerful company law rights,[227] and this may go to show that the nature of voting by pension fund asset owners is likely to be reactive, responding to issues

---

221 s338, dealing with resolutions and s338A dealing with matters other than resolutions.

222 Where there is a minimum 5 per cent stake in the company, s303, Companies Act 2006.

223 Peter Cziraki, Luc Renneboog and Peter Szilagyi, 'Shareholder Activism through Proxy Proposals: The European Perspective' (*ECGI Finance Working Paper* 2009) at http://papers.ssrn.com/sol3/papers.cfm?abstract_id=1413125.

224 Discussed in Bonnie Buchanan, Jeffry M Netter and Tina Yang, 'Are Shareholder Proposals an Important Corporate Governance Device? Evidence from US and UK Shareholder Proposals' (2010) at http://papers.ssrn.com/sol3/papers.cfm?abstract_id=1572016; Rajeev Kumar, '2014 Corporate Governance Review', reporting on the rise of shareholder proxies in the 2014 AGM season, at http://blogs.law.harvard.edu/corpgov/2014/10/30/2014-corporate-governance-review/.

225 Lucian Ayre Bebchuk, 'The Case for Increasing Shareholder Power' (2005) 118 *Harvard Law Review* 833; Christopher M Bruner, *Corporate Governance in the Common Law World* (Cambridge: Cambridge University Press, 2013).

226 Stephen J Choi and Jill E Fisch, 'On Beyond Calpers: Survey Evidence on the Developing Role of Public Pension Funds in Corporate Governance' (2008), above.

227 Discussed in Iris H-Y Chiu, 'A Confidence Trick: Ex Ante versus Ex Post Frameworks in Minority Investor Protection in the UK' (2014) 11 *European Company Law* 6.

arising from company reporting and perhaps public opinion,[228] taking the path of least-cost and unlikely to be in the vein of taking much leadership and initiative in the interests of long-term value creation.

Collective Engagement as a Way Forward

As mentioned, the competing pressures of cost for shareholder engagement and the need to demonstrate stewardship in the light of policy exhortation have culminated in the 'collectivisation' of 'facilities' for shareholder stewardship. For example, the National Pension Funds' Association established stewardship guidelines[229] in voting and informal engagement to provide a standard template for pension fund owners to determine how stewardship should be carried out. These cost reduction measures help funds to demonstrate compliance with the Stewardship Code. Further, asset managers have also established collective engagement forums in order to enjoy economies of scale and maximise voice at the same time. Chapter 3 has discussed the Investor Forum, an initiative under the auspices of the Investment Management Association, which assists asset managers in meeting their clients' needs for demonstrating stewardship.

As the Investor Forum is an initiative led by asset managers, we predict that asset managers will increasingly dominate the stewardship agenda and processes,[230] and they will manage the balance of cost control in investment management with the needs of their clients in demonstrating effective stewardship. We therefore predict that stewardship will be increasingly delegated to asset managers. Further, reports of pension funds signing up to 'fiduciary management' mandates show that

[228] See Reena Aggarwal, Isli Erel and Laura T Starks, 'Influence of Public Opinion on Investor Voting and Proxy Advisors' (2014) at http://papers.ssrn.com/sol3/papers.cfm?abstract_id=2447012 that finds that proxy advisers are very much influenced by public opinion in making their voting recommendations.

[229] See for example, NAPF, *Corporate Governance Policy and Voting Guidelines* (2014-5) at http://www.napf.co.uk/PolicyandResearch/DocumentLibrary/~/media/Policy/Documents/0418_NAPF_corporate_governance_policy_voting_guidelines_2014_2015_DOCUMENT.pdf.

[230] See Gordon L Clark, 'Pension Fund Governance: Expertise and Organisational Form' in John Evans, Michael Orszag and John Piggott (eds), *Pension Fund Governance: A Global Perspective on Financial Regulation* (Cheltenham: Edward Elgar, 2008).

governing bodies in funds are not really engaged with rigorous monitoring of the investment management process.[231] The lack of strong 'principles' on the part of funds would pave the way for domination over the stewardship processes by asset managers and 'fiduciary managers'. Although we think funds may remain interested in visible engagement activities such as voting, much of the ongoing, behind-the-scenes stewardship would be carried out in informal engagement and collective engagement largely undertaken by asset managers.

We suggest that asset managers' approaches to stewardship are likely to be shaped by the ease of monitoring by their clients.[232] These approaches could be rather measurement-oriented, for example using the numbers of votes cast at company meetings, votes for and against management, votes in adherence to proxy advice etc. These approaches could also be rather standardised, in line with best practices such as adhering to the norms in the Corporate Governance Code, or following other institutional investors. Engagement in collective engagement with other like-minded institutions could have the beneficial effect of reinforcing each other's best practices in stewardship. Collective best practices can be fostered, such as the practice of recalling of lent stock for voting.[233] The converging impact of asset managers' engagement of such character could be beneficial for investee companies' governance, although we caution against a one-size-fits-all approach as discussed earlier. However, what asset managers can do is to a large extent dependent on the contractual terms in their mandates. Further recouping the cost of corporate governance engagement may be less easy now the passing on of cost in relation to corporate access through dealing commissions is prohibited[234] by the Financial Conduct Authority.[235]

---

[231] Note disquiet over the competitiveness of fiduciary management mandates, e.g. see '80% of fiduciary contracts not assigned on competitive basis', *Financial Times* (2 Nov 2014) and 'Willis Towers Watson reveals fiduciary performance figures', *Financial Times* (31 Jan 2016). FCA, *Asset Management Market Study Final Report* (2017) at Chapter 10, at https://www.fca.org.uk/publication/market-studies/ms15-2-3.pdf proposes to bring investment consultants including those acting as fiduciary managers within the regulatory perimeter.

[232] See tendency reported in BIS, *Metrics and Models Used to Assess Company and Investment Performance* (Oct 2014).

[233] Reported to be on the increase in NAPF, *NAPF Engagement Survey: Pension Funds' Engagement with Investee Companies* (Nov 2013).

[234] FCA, *Policy Statement: Changes to the Use of Dealing Commission Rules: Feedback to CP13/17 and Final Rules* (May 2014).

[235] 'Corporate Access Rules still Flouted', *Financial Times* (26 Oct 2014).

However, collective engagement can also facilitate a new type of herding behaviour in stewardship. This may be the case where a hedge fund leads in shareholder activism, galvanising other institutions such as pension funds' asset managers to tag along. Hedge funds often engage in 'wolf packs' with other hedge funds to compel investee companies to cave in to their demands,[236] such as restructuring and share buybacks. If other institutions jump on the bandwagon, this may be more opportunistic behaviour than collective engagement to amplify a beneficial stewardship force. Hence, there is potential, especially where hedge fund activism is involved, for collective engagement to be an amplified instance of instrumental use of corporate governance rights, not necessarily in the long-term best interests of the investee company. That said, many collective episodes in the UK involving institutions and hedge funds have been based on corporate governance issues, and not simply value-extraction behaviour.[237] This may show that institutions are cautious of assuming instrumental corporate governance behaviour in league with hedge funds, and prefer to be associated with them only where the engagement basis is familiar and clear, such as revolving around corporate governance issues. That would ensure that such stewardship adheres to Principle 5 of the Stewardship Code. This tendency may go to show that pension funds and their asset managers place a lot of emphasis on the perceived legitimacy and acceptability of their engagement activities, and may indicate that their stewardship is chiefly for compliance purposes.

Engagement for Environmental, Social and Governance Issues

Many pension fund owners and asset managers sign up to the United Nations Principles of Responsible Investment (UNPRI 2005) and either refer to concerns for 'Environmental, Social and Governance' (ESG) criteria in their investment principles or have dedicated funds towards socially responsible investing (SRI). The interest in ESG matters at investee companies could turn pension funds into a wider force for social

---

236 Discussed in William W Bratton, 'Hedge Funds and Governance Targets' (2007) 95 *Georgetown Law Journal* 1375.

237 For example, pension funds have been cautious of joining hedge fund activism against Alliance Trust Plc led by US hedge fund Elliott Investments, until three proxy advisers advised institutions generally to back Elliott's call for the then CEO, Katherine Garrett-Cox, to go, see 'Elliott Advisers wins shareholder group's backing in Alliance Trust boardroom battle', *The Evening Standard* (16 April 2015).

good, shaping the behaviour at investee companies to be more responsible, culminating in a paradigm of 'fiduciary capitalism'.

In the US, ESG proposals used to be on the backburner but are currently reported to be on the rise on investors' agendas.[238] In the UK, the corporate transparency regime has made ESG transparency important under the directors' business review introduced in 2006 and now reinforced in the Strategic Report required annually of companies.[239] UK pension fund asset owners and managers have been dogged many years by case law such as the decision in *Cowan v Scargill* which could sometimes be interpreted as compelling investment trustees and their delegates only to consider financial rationales for investment in their 'fiduciary duty' and not wider ESG issues. However, with strong support from the Freshfields report[240] and the Law Commission[241] in re-interpreting antecedent case law and providing an organic interpretation of the 'fiduciary duty' that adapts to changing times, the legitimacy of ESG issues is much less in doubt as part of investment management. There are increasing reports of investor scrutiny of Boardroom composition, especially diversity issues, and sustainability issues.[242] However at the moment we do not see a marked difference between engagement behaviour relating to ESG and engagement behaviour in the vein of defensive concerns as discussed earlier, i.e. that shareholder attention to ESG issues would be defensive in nature in relation to breaches of Code or law, or as bearing a relationship to corporate underperformance. It is to be noted that the more politically motivated forms of union-based

[238] Stuart Gillan and Laura T Starks, 'A Survey of Shareholder Activism: Motivation and Empirical Evidence' (1998) at http://papers.ssrn.com/sol3/papers.cfm?abstract_id=663523; KPMG, *Rethinking Shareholder Engagement in the Age of Activism* (2014) at http://www.kpmg-institutes.com/institutes/aci/articles/2014/07/rethinking-shareholder-engagement-in-the-age-of-activism.html.

[239] Discussed earlier.

[240] Freshfields Bruckhaus Deringer, *A Legal Framework for the Integration of Environmental, Social and Governance Issues into Institutional Investment* (October 2005).

[241] Law Commission, *Fiduciary Duties of Investment Intermediaries* (1 July 2014).

[242] For example, a letter was sent by the UK Sustainable Investment and Finance Association to all FTSE350 Chairmen to disclose the proportion of diversity in Board Composition in 2011. See http://www.graftonhaymes.co.uk/2011/09/22/ftse-350-to-lay-open-their-plans-for-female-board-representation/.

activism[243] observed, as led by US public pension funds, are not similarly observed in the institutional quarter in the UK.

Individual Engagement

As discussed earlier, the appeal of collective engagement lies in meeting pension funds' needs to demonstrate stewardship in a cost-effective manner. In this light, we surmise that individual engagement, which would be rather costly, may be very limited. This is in spite of Principles 3 and 4 of the Stewardship Code urging investors to monitor their investee companies and to take escalation action in stewardship if necessary. Although much has been said[244] about the US public pension fund CalPERS' activist approach of drawing up yearly focus lists and targeting companies on the list for engagement, much of which is carried out on an informal and dialogic basis, CalPERS has a significant number of staff dedicated to its corporate governance role and is unique among pension funds. The CalPERS' practices of activism are far from being the standard practice among US pension funds, and do not seem to have been widely exported to pension funds elsewhere.[245] The European Shareholder Rights Directive 2017 may compel institutions in Europe to develop engagement policies but it is likely that funds and asset managers may word their policies broadly and choose to be involved in pragmatic forms of engagement as the occasion arises.

Nevertheless, individual shareholder responses would still be required for certain events, such as takeovers and acquisitions, as each fund owner

---

243 Discussed in Urwana Coiquaud and Lucie Morisette, 'Union Renewal Through Involvement in the Financial Sector' (2010) 65 *Industrial Relations* 2; Ashwini K Agrawal, 'Corporate Governance Objectives of Labor Union Shareholders: Evidence from Proxy Voting' (2011) 25 *Review of Financial Studies* 187.

244 E.g. see Michael P Smith, 'Shareholder Activism by Institutional Investors: Evidence from CalPERS' (1996) 51 *Journal of Finance* 227; Claire E Crutchley, Carl D Hudson and Marlin RH Jensen, 'The Shareholder Wealth Effects of CalPERS' Activism' (1998) 7 *Financial Services Review*, available at http://findarticles.com/p/articles/mi_qa3743/is_/ai_n8786737; S Nesbitt, 'Long-term Rewards from Shareholder Activism: A Study of the CALPERS Effect' (1994) 6 *Journal of Applied Corporate Finance*, pp. 75–80; Philip C English II, Thomas I Smythe and Chris R MacNeil, 'The CalPERS' Effect Revisited' (2004) 10 *Journal of Corporate Finance* 157.

245 Stephen J Choi and Jill E Fisch, 'On Beyond Calpers: Survey Evidence on the Developing Role of Public Pension Funds in Corporate Governance' (2008), above.

needs to contemplate whether selling out for the takeover premium is in the optimal investment interests of beneficiaries, or whether it is better to hold out for the longer term. The aborted takeover of AstraZeneca by Pfizer in 2014 was an episode which saw institutional shareholders having divergent views regarding support of the takeover or otherwise, and at what price. Pfizer, the American drugs giant, approached AstraZeneca for talks of a merger in late 2013, but such talks were purportedly dropped by AstraZeneca which thought the initial offer price of $46 per share too low. In April 2014, Pfizer approached AstraZeneca again with a higher offer but was rebuffed. It nevertheless went public with its intentions to take over AstraZeneca at $50 per share. Although Pfizer pledged to base its European operations in the UK and to have 20 per cent of the merged company's research workforce in Cambridge for at least five years, fears that Pfizer was cutting costs and using the UK as a tax jurisdiction to avoid heftier American taxes were reported in the press. Scepticism surrounded the media and public perception of Pfizer's intentions in the acquisition.[246] Pfizer then adjusted the final offer to $55 per share but shareholders on the whole did not support the bid.[247] The episode however revealed faultlines among institutional shareholders, some of whom would have sold out to Pfizer, and some of whom believed in the potential longer term value of AstraZeneca. For example, asset managers such as Schroders, BlackRock, Jupiter Asset Management and insurers Axa and Legal & General backed the takeover while insurer Fidelity, and asset managers Aberdeen Asset Management, Investor AB, Threadneedle and Neil Woodford, whose stake is controlled by certain funds, backed AstraZeneca.[248]

It remains uncertain to what extent the larger public interest issues such as preserving science and research in the UK and protecting UK jobs affected individual investors' perspectives in this episode. Although Macey[249] is of the view that the market for corporate control presents the best opportunities for investors to exercise corporate governance discipline, this episode seems to indicate that those ready to sell may be

---

246 See for example 'Lord Sainsbury calls for government to stop Pfizer buying AstraZeneca', *The Guardian* (8 May 2014).

247 'AstraZeneca rejects Pfizer's final £69bn takeover bid', *The Guardian* (19 May 2014).

248 'AstraZeneca divides shareholders with rejection of Pfizer's 'final' offer', *The Telegraph* (19 May 2014).

249 Jonathan Macey, 'Institutional Investors and Corporate Monitoring: A Demand-Side Perspective' (1997) 18 *Managerial and Decision Economics* 601.

merely short-termist. It has to be queried whether selling-out behaviour may be regarded as a form of stewardship at all!

In sum, we predict that individual engagement would likely be limited to situations where institutions need to respond individually, such as in a situation of takeovers. Cost pressures would likely deter pension fund owners and their asset managers from individually engaging in particular issues. It remains open as to whether individual engagement would be carried out in response to acute defensive concerns, such as in the Barclays fund-raising episode in 2008 discussed earlier. But where such a situation arises, a number of shareholders may be affected and collective engagement would likely be a more cost-effective way forward.

Litigation

Chapter 3 has earlier discussed the rarity of derivative litigation in the UK, as well as the quiet UK landscape for securities litigation.

That said, it has been pointed out[250] that significant numbers of pension funds do assert their ownership roles via securities litigation. Many such cases are carried out as class litigation, particularly in the US where class securities litigation is much more common and is even regarded as part of the appeal[251] of the securities markets. For example, pension funds in the US and Germany have taken out a class suit against Petrobas for losses caused by the company's misstatements regarding its anti-corruption controls, the suit to be led by the UK pension fund the Universities Superannuation Scheme.[252] Choi and Fisch[253] find that pension funds do play a significant part in the litigation-led activism landscape, as the Private Securities Litigation Reform Act of 1995 favours institutional plaintiffs as leads of class securities litigation against issuers. Both large and small pension funds engage actively in this landscape as they have much to gain financially from damages or settlements.

---

[250] NAPF, *NAPF Engagement Survey: Pension Funds' Engagement with Investee Companies* (Nov 2013) at p. 37, reporting that 71 per cent of members had participated in some form of securities litigation.

[251] R La Porta, F Lopez-De-Silanes and A Shleifer, 'What Works in Securities Laws' (2006) 71 *Journal of Finance* 1.

[252] 'Petrobras scandal prompts wave of investor lawsuits', *Financial Times* (5 April 2015).

[253] Stephen J Choi and Jill E Fisch, 'On Beyond Calpers: Survey Evidence on the Developing Role of Public Pension Funds in Corporate Governance' (2008), above 315.

Many cases are privately settled and hence the settlement has become a major driving factor for investor litigation. Individual investor litigation by funds may also be carried out if the individual fund is of the view that the terms of settling the individual suit may exceed those offered for the class litigants.[254] Although such litigation does discipline issuers in terms of ensuring accurate corporate reporting, investors are possibly acting out of self-interest for the settlement windfalls. One could be sceptical of such a corporate governance role as the settlements paid out by issuers merely represent a transfer of wealth from non-litigating shareholders to litigating ones.

Exit

Chapter 2 has generally discussed the incentives that cause investor myopia on the part of pension funds and their asset managers. As trading is a key investment management practice to generate short-term investment performance, portfolio turnover and hence exit from investee companies is frequently carried out.

The right to exit, to sell one's proprietary holding of securities, is a fundamental proprietary right, and the exercise of such a right to meet specific investment needs should not per se be frowned upon. The concern is with short termist and excessive portfolio churning which generates transaction costs, such activity not actually being related to the long term investment objectives of pension funds.

As long as the prevailing practices of short-termism persist in a landscape of fierce market competition, it is unlikely that asset managers will deviate from this. Policy-makers need to engage in truly heavy lifting in order to change deeply entrenched incentives and the resulting trading culture in investment management practice. The Kay Review suggests that quarterly reporting should be abolished, but we do not think this addresses fundamental issues, as periodic reporting half-yearly and yearly is still regarded as important. Perhaps the premise for reporting should be changed, such as is advocated in the proposed Shareholders' Rights Directive, i.e. on how long-term liabilities are being managed, so that will force a focus on the longer term. Further, tax-based measures could be considered, such as favourable tax policies for dividends. Dividends have become more volatile and less fashionable than share

[254] For example, the Swedish pension fund decided to sue Petrobas in the US on its own, despite a class action against Petrobas led by the UK USS pension fund. See above.

buybacks which achieve various objectives for management and shareholders. The revival of regular dividends may have the potential to encourage holding for the longer term. For reasons explained in Chapter 3, we are however cautious of tinkering with voting rights as an incentive for stimulating long-term holding.

Overall Analysis

Pension schemes, whether in the private or public sector, are under immense pressure to be able to honour their long term obligations. The financialisation of long term savings through investment has largely compromised the long-termism in managing such savings, by succumbing to short termist pressures of performance, exacerbated by regulatory obligations. Defined benefit schemes and annuities are however under considerable pressure as the need to meet maturing liabilities drives the adoption of certain investment management approaches.

The social expectations of pension funds taking on engaged corporate governance roles, and thereby bringing about a fiduciary capitalism which promotes long-term value creation is largely misplaced. In the face of liability-driven and short-termist pressures, it is a struggle for pension funds to internalise an investment management model that treats its corporate governance roles in listed companies as a key part of the business model. This is based on the relatively high cost of such a corporate governance role and the uncertain relationship of such roles to ultimate financial performance. Even if regulatory law, soft law and pressure from public opinion facilitate funds and their asset managers' corporate governance engagement, compulsion may produce a minimalist and compliance-based response, and worse, we could encourage funds and their asset managers to use their corporate governance roles in an instrumental manner for financial gain or to achieve public relations benefits.

It may be argued that by forcing pension funds to think about how corporate governance affects even short termist financial performance concerns, pension funds could provide a driving force for corporate behaviour to fall in line with standardised norms of good corporate governance, thereby mitigating the extreme and perverse perspectives in financialisation that merely assetise corporations for trading and financial engineering. However, one may argue that standardised norms of good corporate governance revolve around shareholder primacy and accountability to shareholders, and asking pension funds to ensure that their interests are met in corporate governance is merely self-referential in nature. Such influence holds limited promise in shaping corporate governance towards ultimately beneficial social ends such as sustainable or responsible corporate behaviour. In other words, financier capitalism is not likely to deliver on the social expectations of fiduciary capitalism.

We do not think that pension funds, under the slew of pragmatic pressures upon them, will embrace an ethos of investment that transcends financial concerns. So we do not think that pension funds as owners of corporate equity will play a major role in leading corporate behaviour towards social responsibility, long-term value creation and stakeholder-oriented concerns, although it remains to be seen how far the development of sustainable finance and investment[255] can change the way business is carried out in mainstream investment management.

D. CONCLUSION

This chapter provides an overview of public and private sector pension schemes, and the key factors that shape their investment management approaches and their corporate governance behaviour. A key aspect is funds' reliance on asset managers to discharge their corporate governance roles. Asset managers are likely to professionalise and standardise notions of 'stewardship' for cost-effective engagement and to achieve at least an appearance of effective engagement with investee companies. We

---

[255] Hung-Gay Fung, Sheryl A Law and Jot Yau, *Socially Responsible Investment in a Global Environment* (Cheltenham: Edward Elgar 2010); Iveta Cherneva, 'The Business Case for Sustainable Finance: Beyond Public Relations, Reputation and Philanthropy' in Iveta Cherneva ed., *The Business Case for Sustainable Finance* (Oxford: Routledge 2012) at p. 1; Rory Sullivan and Craig MacKenzie (eds), *Responsible Investment* (Sheffield: Greenleaf Publishing 2006) showcase how the integration of mainstream financial investment with socially responsible values may be possible under a wider appreciation of the business case. But these are incremental visions of the objectives of investment, and still do not transcend a mainstream paradigm. More radical thinking can be found in Pascal Glémain, 'The Strategy and Fundamentals of Sustainable Finance Serving Sustainable Development' in Special Issue, Finance and Sustainability: Towards a New Paradigm? A Post-Crisis Agenda (2011) 2 *Critical Studies on Corporate Responsibility, Governance and Sustainability* 187; William Sun, Céline Louche and Roland Pérez, 'Finance and Sustainability: Towards a New Paradigm? A Post-Crisis Agenda' (2015) 3 *Finance and Sustainability* 15; Garvin Jabusch, 'Redefining Sustainable Investing: a "Next Economy" Model Approach' (Green Alpha Advisers LLC, 2013); Henry Schäfer, 'Sustainable Finance: A Conceptual Outline' (2012) at http://ssrn.com/abstract=2147590; Roger Urwin, 'Sustainable Investing Practice: Simplified Complexity' (2010) at http://ssrn.com/abstract=1656988.

posit that such corporate governance roles are to be predominantly shaped by the interface between keeping investment management cost low while demonstrating the achievement of shareholder stewardship to wider society, at least superficially. The likely dominant forms of stewardship are likely to revolve around voting subject to proxy advisers' recommendations, collective engagement organised around defensive concerns or norms in corporate governance but not amounting to polarised and confrontational relations with investee companies. However, we are of the view that opportunistic forms of stewardship are also welcomed by pension funds, as observed in their involvement in securities litigation, especially in the US, and some support for hedge fund activism.

We remain sceptical as to whether pension funds and their asset managers can fulfil the aspiration of playing a corporate governance role that is necessary for the long term well-being of the corporate economy.[256] Moreover, we also need to recognise that calling for pension funds and their asset managers to engage in their investee companies' corporate governance need not be an unequivocal good. Instrumental exercises of corporate governance power could cause more harm than good.[257]

---

[256] BIS, *The Kay Review of UK Equity Markets and Long-Term Decision Making* (Final Report, 23 July 2012) at paras 6.27ff. In particular, the Kay Review encourages more concentrated holdings over a longer period of time, favouring voice over exit, and advocates that market and regulatory structures should be reformed to favour liquidity, rapid trading and constant information disclosure.

[257] LSE Roundtable, 'Shareholder Rights and Short Termism', 21 May 2015, examining critically the role of shareholders in transmitting undesirable influences for corporate governance and behaviour.

5. Mutual funds as corporate governance actors

A. INTRODUCTION

Collective retail investing is a growing industry in the UK, as consumer interest in non-bank based saving products is helped by sustained low interest rates and an increasingly pro-consumer regulatory environment in investment regulation. Collective retail investments represent a breakthrough model for many to access financial investment and this model is arguably one of the most important means by which finance can be democratised.[1] An ordinary retail saver is unlikely to be able to access investment management expertise unless via collective investment channels such as mutual funds, as it is too costly to secure a dedicated investment manager unless one has sufficient amounts of private wealth. As bank-based maturity transformation is unlikely to produce the level of long-term returns needed for savings intended for major expenditure such as college tuition fees or a house deposit, saving through retail collective investments such as mutual funds caters for the savings needs of many. As retail collective investing becomes a staple form of saving for many in the developed jurisdictions in the West, and increasingly in emerging economies,[2] global assets under management have swelled. The estimated mutual fund assets under management in the US at end-2013 stands at USD$15 trillion, the largest mutual fund market in the world.[3] In Europe, retail mutual funds known as UCITs (Undertakings in Collective Investments in Transferable Securities) and non-UCITs assets under management stood at 10 trillion euros at the end of 2014.[4] The

---

[1] Robert Pozen and Theresa Hamacher, *The Fund Industry: How Your Money is Managed* (John Wiley & Sons 2011) at Chapter 1.

[2] Price Waterhouse Coopers, *Asset Management 2020: A Brave New World* (2014) at http://www.pwc.com/gx/en/asset-management/publications/asset-management-2020-a-brave-new-world.jhtml.

[3] See http://www.icifactbook.org/fb_ch2.html.

[4] European Fund and Asset Management Association, 'Toral Assets of European Investment Funds Broke through the EUR 10 trillion Mark at end of

sheer quantity of pooled retail savings from all over the world under the management of many global asset managers represents an increasingly important source of finance for capital formation, maturity and liquidity transformations.[5]

In the UK, retail savers have increasingly poured savings into mutual funds.[6] Further, the pension reforms of 2015 that allow pensioners to decide how their pension pots may be used in lieu of buying annuities may also lead to a boost in the retail collective investment fund market. Pensioners now have the choice to put part of their pension pots in such funds.[7]

The operation of collective investment schemes is a regulated activity in the UK,[8] i.e. it is unlawful to operate a collective investment scheme without securing the approval of the Financial Conduct Authority. A collective investment scheme is defined as 'any arrangements with respect to property of any description, including money, the purpose or effect of which is to enable persons taking part in the arrangements (whether by becoming owners of the property or of any part of it or otherwise) to participate in or receive profits or income arising from the acquisition, holding, management or disposal of the property or sums paid out of such profits or income.

The arrangements must be such that the persons who are to participate ('participants') do not have day-to-day control over the management of the property, whether or not they have the right to be consulted or to give directions.

The arrangements must also have either or both of the following characteristics –

(a) the contributions of the participants and the profits or income out of which payments are to be made to them are pooled;

Q1 2014' at http://www.efama.org/Pages/Total-assets-of-European-investment-funds-broke-through-the-EUR-10-trillion-mark-in-Q1-2014.aspx.

[5] See Clara Furse, 'Liquidity Matters', speech at Regional Business Contacts, Birmingham, 11 Feb 2015 in which she mentioned that investment funds have become a key source of liquidity for financial markets, outstripping the role of banks.

[6] 'Sales of retail mutual funds soared to £20.4bn in 2013 and the highest since 2000', at http://www.mindfulmoney.co.uk/investment-insight/investing-strategy/sales-of-retail-mutual-funds-soared-to-20-4bn-in-2013-and-the-highest-since-2000/.

[7] 'Pensions in flux boost asset managers', *Financial Times* (10 August 2014).

[8] S19, Financial Services and Markets Act 2000, read with Schedule 2.

(b) the property is managed as a whole by or on behalf of the operator of the scheme.[9]

A wide interpretation of what may be regarded as 'collective investment schemes' has been adopted by the Financial Conduct Authority as well as courts in order to secure a high level of protection for consumers entering into arrangements of such a nature. Over the years, various arrangements that may be perceived as 'borderline' have been held to fall within the scope of collective investment schemes, thus requiring authorisation and oversight. For example, they have included purchases of real estate interests by individuals under an understanding that there would be a centrally managed process to secure planning and development permission over the plot;[10] purchases of sub-lease interests in foreign real estate for the purposes of securing income generated by the land in terms of agricultural or carbon credit income;[11] services organised to place horse-racing bets on behalf of subscribers;[12] collective financing of a film venture;[13] and collective financing to acquire patent rights.[14] In other words, most forms of collective financing or financing that is to an extent managed centrally would fall within the definition of collective investment scheme. The Financial Conduct Authority's powers to enforce against unauthorised exotic arrangements have inevitably shaped the market for legitimate products.

In the EU, the market for collective retail investment funds is dominated by the UCITs product (Undertakings in Collective Investments in Transferable Securities). The UCITs is a mutual fund vehicle that invests in transferable securities products and money market instruments on a liquid market that is authorised in a Member State. A UCITs fund, underpinned by regulatory compliance with minimum standards in EU legislation, could be marketed to the retail sector in other Member States without further national obstruction from host Member States.[15] Such

[9] S235, Financial Services and Markets Act 2000.

[10] *In re Sky Land Consultants Plc* [2010] EWHC 399 (Ch); *FSA v Asset LI Inc* [2014] EWCA Civ 435, affirmed in the Supreme Court, *Asset Land Investment Plc and another (Appellants) v The Financial Conduct Authority (Respondent)* [2016] UKSC 17.

[11] *FCA v Capital Alternatives Ltd and Ors* [2014] EWHC 144 (Ch); [2015] EWCA Civ 284.

[12] *Financial Services Authority v Fradley* [2005] EWCA Civ 1183 CA.

[13] *Raymond Bieber v Teathers Ltd (in liquidation)* [2012] EWHC 190 (Ch).

[14] *Brown 7 Ors v Innovator One Plc and Ors* [2012] EWHC 1321

[15] In 2001, the Directive was amended to also allow the fund's management company to be passported as the fund may otherwise run into the costly obstacles

cross-border marketing rights are on the basis of compliance with European legislation that allows funds and management companies for funds to be 'passported' across the EU.[16] Since 1985, European legislation for the UCITs has harmonised rules regarding the composition and authorisation of such funds.[17] The UCITs is a perceived 'safe' mutual fund that is open-ended in nature, and has become the most popular and dominant mutual fund product across the European Economic Area. As UCITs invest in largely liquid transferable securities, they are the most common form of equities-owning mutual fund in the EU. The UK market for collective retail investing is, at the time of writing, dominated by the UCITs product, but the UK also allows non-UCITs products to be offered to domestic investors. Following the UK's Referendum vote of 23 June 2016 favouring exit of the UK from the EU, it is uncertain to what extent funds incorporated in the UK will gain recognition and passporting status across the EU in a post-Brexit environment. Much of this will depend on the settlement that the UK manages to achieve in its exit negotiations with the EU following invocation of Article 50 of the Lisbon Treaty. UK fund managers who wish to ensure that their products remain marketable in the EU would likely need to set up subsidiaries in EU jurisdictions such as Ireland, to conduct EU marketing operations. The future prospects for UCITs-based fund management in the UK are hence rather uncertain. We predict that, going forward, a bifurcation may develop between a UK mutual fund industry that serves domestic investors and one that operates more globally. At the time of writing, our discussion of the investment management of the retail collective investment industry in the UK necessarily draws from past rather than future UCITs experience.

In Section B, this chapter will highlight key factors that shape the investment management and governance of retail collective investment

---

of having to appoint national fund managers in host jurisdictions. Directive 2001/107/EC of the European Parliament and of the Council of 21 January 2002 amending Council Directive 85/611/EEC on the coordination of laws, regulations and administrative provisions relating to undertakings for collective investment in transferable securities (UCITS) with a view to regulating management companies and simplified prospectuses.

[16] Directive 2009/65/EC of the European Parliament and of the Council of 13 July 2009 on the coordination of laws, regulations and administrative provisions relating to undertakings for collective investment in transferable securities (UCITS) (recast) (aka UCITS III, superseding the first and second UCITs legislative initiatives in 1985 and 2001).

[17] Council Directive 85/611/EEC of 20 December 1985 on the coordination of laws, regulations and administrative provisions relating to undertakings for collective investment in transferable securities (UCITS).

funds that are owners of corporate equity, in relation to funds' assumption of corporate governance roles in their investee companies. Section C then discusses the typologies of corporate governance behaviour that such funds engage in.

B. KEY FACTORS THAT SHAPE THE CORPORATE GOVERNANCE ACTIVITIES OF COLLECTIVE RETAIL INVESTMENT SCHEMES THAT OWN CORPORATE EQUITY

In this section, we argue that two key factors that shape retail collective investment scheme management are the separation structure and the regulatory regime. Retail collective investment schemes such as the UCITs and other schemes are structured in a way that separates the fund from fund managers, a phenomenon discussed at length in Chapter 2. This gives rise to certain implications for investor protection as well as funds' investment management approaches.

The Structuration of Retail Collective Investment Schemes

In the UK, collective retail investment schemes may be structured as trusts, open-ended companies or closed-ended companies. The fund is the vehicle for pooling together retail savers' capital, and savers thus become shareholders in the corporate vehicle, or beneficiaries in the trust vehicle. The fund does not carry out investment management operations itself, as this is usually outsourced to a fund management company. The fund management company's relationship with the fund is structured under contract. This is typical of the separation structure discussed in Chapter 2.

In terms of constituting the fund, the open-ended company structure[18] has been the most popular with UCITs products as such a structure is more easily exportable for EU-wide marketing than the trust structure, which is not a recognised legal form in a number of continental jurisdictions.[19] The fund is set up as a company and investors subscribe for units in the fund, in the form of shares in the company. The fund appoints a Board of directors

[18] Open-Ended Investment Companies Regulations 2001 (SI 2001/1228)31.

[19] Philip Wood, *Comparative Financial Law* (London: Sweet & Maxwell, 1995), now updated into *Maps of World Financial Law* (London: Sweet & Maxwell 2008).

who oversee the management of the fund, but actual fund management is usually carried out by a fund management company appointed by the Board. Funds could be products designed by management companies which incorporate the fund and appoint management company executives to staff the Board of the fund. In that sense, the fund is branded by and is almost inextricable from the management company. This seems to be the case with fund products offered by banking groups in the EU and UK, and is the case with most mutual funds in the US.[20] However, funds can also be incorporated independently of any particular management company and outsource the investment management to professional asset managers.

The dominant structure for UK non-UCITs schemes is the trust structure whereby a trust is set up to hold the assets of investors, who are the beneficiaries under the trust, and to manage these assets. The assets are managed by trustees according to the terms of the trust, and subject to the Trustees Act 2000. The management of assets can be done in-house or outsourced to professional asset managers.

The Board of directors in the corporate fund structure and the trustees in the trust fund structure both owe fiduciary duties in their management and governance of the fund. The directors of the corporate fund Board owe their fiduciary duties to the fund as a legal person, while the trustees in the trust fund structure owe their fiduciary duties to the beneficiaries of the fund. The corporate fund structure and internal governance is subject to domestic company law and the terms of the company constitution. The UK also provides a specific regulatory framework for funds such as in relation to the objects of the fund in the fund company's constitutional document, the investment powers of the fund, the base currency of the fund, the name of the fund, duration of the fund if applicable, classes of units in the fund, fund managers' charges and expenses, policies relating to issue, cancellation, sale and redemption of units/shares, distribution of income policies, how share/unit-holders' meetings may be organised and held, valuation and pricing policies, and how directors of the fund company may be removed.[21]

Where the UK trust is concerned, trustees are subject to duties in the Trustees Act 2000 and the duties laid down in private law such as fiduciary, tort and contract law. Further, FCA regulation also governs such funds in similar matters as discussed in relation to the corporate

---

[20] Jerry W Markham, 'Mutual Funds Scandals – Comparative Analysis of the Role of Corporate Governance in the Regulation of Collective Investments' (2010) at http://ssrn.com/abstract=1706317.

[21] FCA Handbook COLL 3.

structure above.[22] Specific terms of the trust could be further agreed upon by all parties.

The fund manager is governed by terms of contract with the fund entity. However, FCA regulation has provided for some regulatory prescriptions in view of the governance deficits due to the separation structure, and these are intended chiefly for investor protection. A broad framework of terms between the fund and fund manager is provided in regulation, similar to those for the corporate structure mentioned above. Other regulatory prescriptions for the contractual instrument between funds and fund managers include the contractual scheme of ownership of the assets, policies regarding eligible investors and responsibility of the contractual manager for the register of unit-holders.[23] The FCA[24] is however proposing to strengthen the governance of funds and fund managers by introducing mandatory independence requirements on fund Boards so that a more critical element can be brought in to scrutinise fund managers' performance in the interests of investors.

There is a significant level of regulatory competition among EU Member States in terms of the different business vehicle options open to retail collective investment schemes, and the regulatory and tax costs associated therewith. It is arguable that certain aspects relating to internal governance and structures of funds have become subject to a race to the bottom. This is not wholly inconsistent with the discussion in Chapter 2 about how separation structures and the growth of the investment chain result in governance deficits and agency problems in the fund management enterprise. We survey these in the next Section, and argue that these governance deficits and agency problems reinforce UCITs funds' investment management approach towards trading and short-termist behaviour, and therefore a largely passive and apathetic position in the corporate governance of their investee companies.

Regulatory Competition, Scheme Structure and Implications for Investment Management Practices and Corporate Governance Roles

Dublin and Luxembourg have grown in popularity as the originating jurisdictions for authorised funds which can then be marketed across the

---

[22] As well as unique terms pertaining to the trust e.g. a declaration of trust, trustees' responsibility for the register of unit-holders and trustees' remuneration. Above.

[23] FCA Handbook COLL 3.

[24] FCA, *Asset Management Market Study Final Report* (2017) at Chapter 10 at https://www.fca.org.uk/publication/market-studies/ms15-2-3.pdf.

rest of the European Economic Area. The growth of Dublin and Luxembourg as major UCITs originating jurisdictions is due to smooth and reliable authorisation procedures,[25] favourable tax regimes[26] and specifically tailored corporate governance regimes for the constitution of funds.

Compared to the requirements imposed by the Financial Conduct Authority in the UK, Ireland and Luxembourg offer arguably friendlier internal governance regimes tailored for investment funds. The UK regime requires not only that funds be authorised but also that certain individuals be subject to approval. Senior management and Board members are subject to individual approval,[27] and a rather onerous senior persons responsibility regime.[28] Under this regime, senior persons could incur personal liability[29] for failure of responsibilities or breaches of the Code of Conduct.[30] Besides, the FCA imposes requirements in respect of organisational soundness, risk control and internal governance for fund trustees and fund Boards.[31]

Irish funds are not subject to similar onerous individual approval and liability regimes, and until 2010, the internal governance of funds was largely left to the discretion of the fund and its management company, allowing cost-effective approaches to be adopted. A Code of Corporate Governance tailored for the needs of investment funds has been introduced in 2010 by the relevant trade body, the Irish Funds Industry Association. The Code is soft law, subject to a 'comply or explain' approach. Luxembourg funds are also not subject to mandatory governance requirements, and funds have adopted the cost-effective measure of appointing small Boards staffed largely by employees of the fund

---

[25] Friedrich Heinemann, 'The Benefits of Creating an Integrated EU Market for Investment Funds' (2002) at http://ssrn.com/abstract=309099; Elias Bengtsson and Bernard Delbeque, 'Revisiting the European Asset Management Industry' (2011) *Financial Markets, Institutions and Instruments* 163.

[26] Above.

[27] Section 59, 59ZA of the UK Financial Services and Markets Act 2000 amended as of 2013; FCA Handbook FIT module.

[28] PRA and FCA, *Strengthening Accountability in Banking: A New Regulatory Framework* (July 2014); *Strengthening Accountability in Banking: A New Regulatory Framework for Individuals – Feedback on FCA CP14/13/PRA CP14/14 and consultation on additional guidance* (March 2015). This is now codified in FCA Handbook COCON.

[29] Section 66A and 66B of the UK Financial Services and Markets Act 2000 amended as of 2013, 2015.

[30] FCA Handbook, COCON module sets out the standards for conduct.

[31] Generally, the FCA Handbook, SYSC and PRIN modules.

management company. In 2009 however, a Corporate Governance Code was introduced by the fund industry trade body, the Association of the Luxembourg Fund Industry (ALFI), which is tailor-made to the needs of funds. These initiatives in soft law are intended to boost investor confidence while maintaining the cost-efficiencies that Ireland and Luxembourg have achieved in the UCITs industry.[32]

The cost-efficiency concern has arguably shaped the internal governance structures at Luxembourg and Irish UCITs funds. Left to funds' discretion, the internal governance of funds would be dominated by the fund management company.[33] The fund management company may appoint its directors or employees to sit on the fund's Board, consolidating the power of the fund management company and allowing little independent scrutiny of the fund management company's practices and performance. The domination of the fund management company in the internal governance structures of UCITs funds has resulted in funds largely being passive in their corporate governance positions[34] in relation to investee companies.

In this highly competitive industry, UCITs fund management companies are arguably concerned with short term performance achieved with the lowest possible cost. This is because short term results affect fund inflows, an important concern for management companies.[35] Fund management companies may therefore prefer to trade and engage in portfolio turnover instead of engagement in corporate governance. Fund management company domination on fund Boards also means that fund expense ratios are less scrutinised by fund Boards and hence trading and portfolio turnover behaviour may be less constrained. In this context, funds would not be incentivised to take on engaged corporate governance

---

[32] However, Roiter argues that corporate governance is not that relevant for investor protection as investors are protected by regulatory provisions in disclosure, conduct of business and most importantly liquid exit rights. See Eric D Roiter, 'Disentangling Mutual Fund Governance from Corporate Governance' (2015) 6 *Harvard Business Law Review* 1 at http://www.hblr.org/wp-content/uploads/2016/06/HLB101_crop.pdf.

[33] Jan Jaap Hazenberg, 'Independence and Focus of Luxembourg UCITS Fund Boards' (*LSF Research Working Paper* 2012).

[34] Hanne S Birkmose, 'The Transformation of Passive Institutional Investors to Active Owners – Mission Impossible?' in Hanne Birkmose, Mette Neville and Karsten Engsig Sørensen (eds), *The European Financial Market in Transition* (Alphen aan den Rijn: Kluwer Law International 2011).

[35] John C Bogle, 'The Challenge to Mutual Fund Stewardship' in John D Haslem (ed.), *Mutual Funds: Portfolio Structures, Analysis, Management, and Stewardship* (Chichester: John Wiley & Sons 2010) at Chapter 15, 283ff.

positions in their investee companies as exercising voice may be long drawn-out and costly.[36] It can be argued that such a passive corporate governance position is not unwarranted as investors in UCITs also vote with their feet, redeeming from funds if they are unhappy with short-term performance. Hence, investors may arguably not expect funds to take on long-term oriented and costly shareholder engagement activities in such liquid markets.

As the UK is embarking on a minimum mandatory requirement of two independent directors on fund Boards,[37] it remains to be seen if the introduction of stronger governance requirements will change the corporate governance position of retail funds.

Next, we turn to discuss the fund's relationship with the fund management company, a crucial aspect that determines much of the governance quality of the fund and its corporate governance position vis-à-vis investee companies.

Fund-Fund Management Company Relationship

The UCITs fund and its management company are usually so inextricably related that the 2001 UCITs amendment Directive gave this structural phenomenon recognition by allowing both the UCITs fund to be marketed across the EU and the fund management company to passport its management services to the fund. The dominance of the fund management company over the fund has been earlier discussed in relation to management company executives sitting on the fund's Board. Further, management company dominance may also manifest itself in terms of the Board's possibly subdued role in overseeing the management company. Boards are unlikely to (a) replace management companies even if performance is lacklustre; or (b) monitor and moderate management company's fees and charges. These are two areas that frequently highlight a low level of robustness from the Board in exercising governance oversight over the fund management company.

In the US, it is opined that the replacement of fund management companies for mutual funds is unthinkable as the fund is branded by the management company (aka investment adviser) and therefore completely

[36] Christoph van der Elst and Erik P Vermeulen, 'Europe's Corporate Governance Green Paper: Do Institutional Investors Matter?' in Hanne Birkmose, Mette Neville and Karsten Engsig Sørensen (eds), *The European Financial Market in Transition* (Alphen aan den Riljn: Kluwer Law International 2011).

[37] FCA, *Asset Management Market Study Final Report* (2017), above at Chapter 10.

entwined with the management company.[38] The Board of the fund is therefore unlikely to be able to develop its own objective investment management policies and potentially execute, even in extreme cases, the nuclear option of terminating the mandate of the fund management company. A similar situation exists for the Luxembourg and Irish UCITs discussed above. It therefore follows that the Board's investment objectives would inevitably be developed to dovetail with the fund management company's expertise and preferences, and this would also be the case in terms of the fund's corporate governance activities vis-à-vis its investee companies.

The fund management company's policy in relation to its corporate governance role in investee companies is likely to be influenced by its general corporate governance policy across similar portfolios. For well-diversified portfolios in equity holdings, it may be cost-ineffective to exercise voice in the investee companies due to the relative insignificance of the equity stake and the collective action problems inherent in coordinating other shareholders that can achieve critical mass in terms of voting power. Further, the fund management company's general corporate governance policy can be influenced by the conflicts of interests it faces. For example, if the fund management company is retained by a corporate client to manage its defined contribution pension schemes, and is also an investor in the corporate client through its pension or collective retail investment portfolios, its corporate governance position in relation to such a client/investee company would be shaped by its multifaceted relationships with the company.[39] This usually translates into corporate governance positions biased towards the client/investee company.[40] However, it is not necessarily easy to detect the corporate governance perspectives adopted by any particular fund under the influence of its

---

[38] William Birdthistle, 'Compensating Power: An Analysis of Rents and Rewards in the Mutual Fund Industry' (2006) 80 *Tulane Law Review* 1402.

[39] Jennifer S Taub, 'Able but Not Willing: The Failure of Mutual Fund Advisers to Advocate for Shareholders' Rights' (2009) 34 *Journal of Corporation Law* 101.

[40] Dragana Cvijanovic, Amil Dasgupta and Konstantinos E Zachariadis, 'Ties that Bind: How Business Connections Affect Mutual Fund Activism' (2014) at http://ssrn.com/abstract_id=2317212.

fund management company, as skewed influences are often subtle and may not be immediately apparent to external observers.[41]

Nevertheless, in response to policy-makers' call to funds and their managers to demonstrate stewardship and engagement, the fund management enterprise has to adapt. As the European Shareholder Rights Directive 2017 will apply to UCITs funds and fund managers, there would be a need to incorporate shareholder engagement policies and activities infused with wider ESG and stakeholder concerns, as well as meet public disclosure and scrutiny needs. On balance, we think that UCITs funds and fund managers may undertake the least cost approach to such engagement as the UCITs institution defined by investor protection regulation so far does not cohere with the needs of long-term oriented and publicly accountable shareholder engagement. We predict that funds will adopt a least cost approach in shareholder engagement by (a) using proxy advisers to determine how to vote at general meetings and (b) engaging in collective engagement with other asset managers if the opportunity arises. For example, Cotter et al[42] find in the US that mutual funds rely heavily on proxy advisers such as ISS in order to demonstrate voting but maintain a low level of cost associated with voting. The use of proxy advisers is also on the rise in the EU,[43] although fund management companies do not seem to automatically rely on advice, treating such advice as a form of information enhancement that assists the voting decision.[44] However, the European Shareholder Rights Directive 2017 may result in greater cost in using proxy advisers due to the regulatory obligations of disclosure to be imposed on them. Further, as will be discussed in greater detail in the next section, collective engagement may be a cost-effective way forward for fund management

[41] Marc Kruitof, 'Conflicts of Interest in Institutional Asset Management: Is the EU Regulatory Approach Adequate?' in Luc Thévenoz and Rashid Bahar (eds), *Conflicts of Interest and the Duty of Loyalty* (Zurich: Schultess Verlag 2007).

[42] James Cotter, Alan Palmiter, and Randall Thomas, 'ISS Recommendations and Mutual Fund Voting on Proxy Proposals' (2010) 55 *Villanova Law Review* 56. Also supported in Angela Morgan, Annette Poulsen, Jack Wolf, Tina Yang, 'Mutual Funds as Monitors: Evidence from Mutual Fund Voting' (2009) at http://ssrn.com/abstract=1431072.

[43] ESMA, 'An Overview of the Proxy Advisory Industry. Considerations on Possible Policy Options', ESMA/2012/212, http://www.esma.europa.eu/system/files/2012-212.pdf.

[44] ESMA, *Final Report: Feedback Statement on the Consultation Regarding the Role of the Proxy Advisory Industry* (Feb 2013) reporting high correlations between advice and voting but not in a mindless manner.

companies demonstrating engagement and stewardship, and informal forums are being set up by trade associations for the investment management industry to facilitate such engagement.

Due to the inherent apathy that funds and their managers are likely to have in relation to corporate governance roles in investee companies, compulsion by regulation to engage with these roles may produce perverse incentives to use these roles in an instrumental manner. For example, fund managers may charge funds, and hence investors, for taking on corporate governance roles in relation to funds' investee companies, such as paying for corporate access. Many fund management companies pass these costs on as part of execution charges that funds have to bear.[45] The motivations for and the quality of corporate governance roles taken on by fund management companies are therefore questionable. Fund management companies compelled to demonstrate engagement could even turn these into rent extraction opportunities and make fund management more expensive for the ultimate investors. The fund management company's dominance in funds usually means that fund Boards are relatively weak in moderating or negotiating management company's fees and charges.[46] Although investors can vote with their feet if the charges and fees are too high, such information is not always presented in a manner that is easy to understand. The UK FCA has now intervened to prohibit payments for corporate access out of execution charges,[47] but it remains to be seen if the EU will take a harmonised stance on this.

Although the separation structure has a marked impact on funds' and fund management companies' lack of interest in corporate governance engagement, regulation, underlined by an investor protection focus, has hence played a crucial role in both reinforcing and counteracting the natural tendencies discussed above.

---

45 'Fears rise over cash for access', *Financial Times* (3 March 2013).

46 Gordon Gemmill and Dylan C Thomas, 'The Impact of Corporate Governance on Closed-end Funds' (2006) 12 *European Financial Management* 725 opining that fees and charges manifest rent extraction by the fund management company and are the key principal-agent problem in the fund-fund management company relationship.

47 FCA, *Changes to the Use of Dealing Commission Rules: Feedback to CP13/17 and Final Rules* (May 2014).

The Role of Regulation in Shaping Investment Management at Retail Collective Investment Schemes

We focus on the regulatory regime led by EU legislative harmonisation in the UCITs Directives. This is because the Directives permeate many aspects of governance, structure and investment management of UCITs funds and their management companies. The relatively high level of harmonised regulation for retail collective investment schemes has its roots in the objectives intended to be met by the EU legislation for a harmonised mutual fund product – the UCITs. The regulatory objective in introducing the UCITs in European legislation is to create a pan-European retail fund vehicle that can be attractive to retail savers in Europe. In order to stimulate the growth of a deep European market for retail collective investment products, harmonised legislation for governing UCITs formation and governance, and high standards for investor protection are seen as necessary.

The legislative legacy of the UCITs Directives will remain relevant for the UK, even after Brexit. Depending on trade negotiations, the UK may be able to maintain a UCITs industry. Where this is not viable, we are of the view that the domestic mutual fund industry may also take its cue from much of the UCITs legislation. The UCITs regulatory template has become recognised as the 'gold standard' in retail investor protection, influencing the market for other collective retail investment products.[48] The UCITs model of disclosure regulation that is aimed at producing meaningful and succinct investor information is widely embraced for other forms of 'packaged' retail collective investment products i.e. combining a few financial elements such as insurance and investment.[49]

---

[48] Such as exchange-traded funds. See London Stock Exchange, *Exchange-Traded Funds: Introducing and Operating ETFs in the UK* at http://www.londonstockexchange.com/specialist-issuers/etfs/how-to-issue-etfs/listingandadmissionguide.pdf requires exchange-traded funds listed on the London Stock Exchange to be UCITs-compliant. See also Eddy Wymeersch, 'The Regulatory Regime for Exchange-Traded Funds in the EU' (2011) at http://ssrn.com/abstract=1986852 on the extensive influence of the UCITs regime on the growth of the exchange-traded fund industry in the EU.

[49] See the Regulation (EU) No 1286/2014 of the European Parliament and of the Council of 26 November 2014 on key information documents for packaged retail and insurance-based investment products (PRIIPs).

The UK has also, very early on, adopted into its regulatory framework for non-UCITs funds, such as those investing in assets that are not permitted under UCITs legislation (e.g. in real estate),[50] similar provisions as under the UCITs regulatory template.[51] The UK may maintain a significant convergence of retail collective investment regulation with the EU as this is relevant to its industry needs. In light of this, the UK FCA is keen to continue importing EU legislation on packaged products (PRIIPS) to govern aspects of non-UCITs (or NURS) products offered in the UK.[52]

However, it has to be noted that the UCITs' regime focuses on investor protection, particularly in supplying investors' needs for 'safety' and liquidity, and this would foster a kind of investment management approach that does not tend towards long-term oriented and active shareholder engagement with investee companies. This is beginning to change in the UK and EU with the rise of the stewardship rhetoric and the European Shareholder Rights Directive 2017 discussed in Chapter 3. We, however, still see a dilemma in terms of the regulatory objectives that shape the frameworks for retail collective investment schemes, and posit that these schemes will likely play a minimal role in relation to their corporate governance rights and powers.

We turn first to discuss how the UCITS Directives have established the investor protection tenets for the most popular mutual fund product in the UK and EU, and the implications for investment management practices and corporate governance roles.

---

[50] Simon Clark, Tim Hackemann, Olivier Mesmin, Matthias Roche, and Tom Road, 'Progress on REIT Regimes in Europe' in Graeme Newell and Karen Sieracki (eds), *Global Trends in Real Estate Finance* (Blackwell, 2010) at Chapter 3.

[51] For example, the UK FCA has imposed similar disclosure regulation in the form of the Key Investor Information Document for non-UCITs retail schemes (NURS), see http://www.fca.org.uk/firms/firm-types/fund-authorisation-and-supervision/kiid-nurs-kii-requirements.

[52] FCA, *Changes to Disclosure Rules in the FCA Handbook to Reflect the Direct Application of the PRIIPS Regulation: A Consultation Paper* (18 July 2016) at http://fca.org.uk/news/cp16-18-changes-to-disclosure-rules-for-priips-regulation.

The Impact of UCITs Directives 1985–2009 (recast)

The regulatory framework has achieved much success in branding the UCITs as an investor-friendly product in the EU and beyond.[53] UCITs funds have become popular with retail savers,[54] and the growth in UCITs assets under management reflects the need on the part of retail savers in Europe for yield as well as long-term saving. The growth in the UCITs markets across the EU also addresses the European policy concern[55] for developing the capital markets of Europe, which remain relatively under-developed due to the dominance of bank-based finance.

The 1985 Directive first streamlined certain aspects of internal governance structures of UCITs funds for the purposes of setting minimum standards of investor protection. These relate to: the portfolio limits of funds; accountability of funds to investors; the management mandate of fund managers; and the rights of investors in relation to redemption. This section will argue that the investor-friendly features inevitably shape funds' investment management approach and their corporate governance roles.

Under the 1985 Directive, the composition of UCITs funds has to comply with certain portfolio diversification and prudential risk management requirements. The UCITs fund is not allowed to invest in securities issued by a single issuer beyond 5 per cent of its portfolio; it has to avoid exotic and potentially illiquid assets such as real estate, commodities and precious metals; and it has to comply with prudential risk management in terms of capital adequacy (to have initial capital at 125,000 euros and own funds at 0.02 per cent of assets under management) and avoid leverage. These requirements therefore define the management mandate of UCITs funds to a certain extent, based on low risk and highly liquid marketable securities. Policy-makers then decided to liberalise UCITs funds in 2001, allowing UCITs funds more choice in investment strategies, and investors more choice in the market. Hence in 2001, the UCITs Directive was amended to introduce more classes of financial

---

[53] Douglas Cumming, Gael Imad'Eddine and Armin Schwienbacher, 'Harmonized Regulatory Standards, International Distribution of Investment Funds and the Recent Financial Crisis' (2011) 18 *European Journal of Finance* 261.

[54] Roger Otten and Kilian Thevissen, 'Does Industry Size Matter? Revisiting European Mutual Fund Performance' (2011) at http://ssrn.com/abstract=1741197.

[55] European Commission, 'Financial Services Action Plan: Implementing the Framework for Financial Markets' (Communication) COM (1999) 232.

instruments that UCITs funds could invest in, albeit maintaining the portfolio diversification and prudential management principles in the 1985 Directive. The 2001 Directive[56] permits UCITs funds to invest in bank deposits; a wide range of wholesale money market instruments such as treasury and local authority bills, certificates of deposit, commercial paper, medium-term notes and bankers' acceptances; and other UCITs or non-UCITs collective investment schemes which could invest in a range of exotic assets such as real estate, foreign assets and so on. UCITs funds are also permitted to trade in derivative products including over-the-counter derivatives, envisaged for hedging purposes. They may also be structured as index-based or index-replicating products. The expansion in the eligible assets for UCITs investment would remain consistent with portfolio diversification, but it is important to note that such an expansion also increases the risk profile of UCITs products[57] albeit offering investors more choice. The diversification opportunities for UCITs funds allow funds to shift away from corporate securities into some highly liquid money market instruments and also relatively less liquid and exotic asset classes. Although such reforms are appealing for investor choice, the importance of ownership of corporate equity is de-emphasised and there is certainly no particular focus on corporate equity-related investment management practices such as funds' corporate governance roles.

Funds and their managers are governed and incentivised towards producing periodic investment performance, and the mode of trading-based investment management which could be regarded as short-termist (discussed in Chapter 2) is largely staple practice. This is underpinned by regulatory standards for investor protection such as regular accountability. First, investors in UCITs are entitled to a prospectus of the fund as pre-sale information. Such prospectuses offer comprehensive disclosure based on what a reasonable investor would need to know in terms of: the nature of the investment and the risks, fund rules at incorporation,[58] and

---

[56] Directive 2001/108/EC of the European Parliament and of the Council of 21 January 2002 amending Council Directive 85/611/EEC on the coordination of laws, regulations and administrative provisions relating to undertakings for collective investment in transferable securities (UCITS), with regard to investments of UCITS.

[57] Christian Szylar, 'UCITS TO UCITS III/IV' in Christian Szylar, *Risk Management under UCITs III/IV* (Chichester: John Wiley & Sons 2010).

[58] Art 71, Directive 2009/65/EC of the European Parliament and of the Council of 13 July 2009 on the coordination of laws, regulations and administrative provisions relating to undertakings for collective investment in transferable securities (UCITS) (recast) "recast UCITs Directive 2009".

specifically prescribed items for disclosure.[59] Further, the categories of assets for investment must be disclosed and prominent warnings are to be made where financial derivatives are used; where replication of index strategies is used; where asset categories are comprised of other than transferable securities and money market instruments and where the portfolio composition may be subject to high volatility.[60] However, as prospectuses are often lengthy and technical in terms of the financial information provided and are not readily accessible to many retail investors, the disclosure regime could be comprehensive but on the whole not very effective in terms of achieving investor protection.[61] Thus, in 2001,[62] the European Commission introduced an accompanying 'simplified prospectus' to help retail investors.

The 'simplified prospectus' must contain a summary of the information in the full prospectus in such a way as to be readily comprehensible, and must include information pertaining to the UCITs management company, depositary and auditors, the UCITs' objectives, risk profile, historical information and typical investor profile, as well as information regarding the applicable tax regime, relevant commissions, charges and fees, how to buy units and redemption information, frequency of publication of unit prices and dividend distribution policies. It was envisaged that the 'simplified prospectus' would present the most salient information to investors in a more accessible document. Investors are also entitled to ongoing disclosure documents in the form of an annual long report and

---

[59] Art 69, and Schedule A, recast UCITs Directive 2009.

[60] Art 70, recast UCITs Directive 2009.

[61] Problems regarding information overload and lack of accessibility in investment disclosure have been discussed generally, see for example Troy A Paredes, 'Blinded by the Light: Information Overload and its Consequences for Securities Regulation' (2003) 81 *Washington University Law Quarterly* 417 at pp. 431–62.

[62] Art 27(1), Directive 2001/107/EC of the European Parliament and of the Council of 21 January 2002 amending Council Directive 85/611/EEC on the coordination of laws, regulations and administrative provisions relating to undertakings for collective investment in transferable securities (UCITS) with a view to regulating management companies and simplified prospectuses. See FCA Handbook, COLL 4.6 which has applied this scheme across to many non-UCITs products, such as domestic schemes or overseas 'recognised' schemes. However, as will shortly be discussed, the EU regulatory regime has moved onto a more simplified and prescribed document, known as the KIID – the key investor information document.

half-yearly short report.[63] The annual report must contain audited financial statements[64] while the half-yearly report is also highly prescribed in terms of financial and technical information.[65] The focus on financial categories of information for fund profile and performance reflects the overwhelming emphasis on financial performance in investment management. But this may be reflective of investors' demands.

Investors' needs in liquidity are further protected as a key tenet in investor protection. Liquidity pressures would add to fund management tending towards trading and short-termist horizons, as discussed in Chapter 2. Investors are assured that UCITs funds have to publish their prices whenever there is an issue, sale, repurchase or redemption of shares, or at least twice a month.[66] Investors are also guaranteed the right to redeem at request,[67] upon principles of valuation laid down in national law.[68]

The inaugural tenets of investor protection have achieved a successful branding of the UCITs product, and such features of investor protection have certainly shaped funds' and their managers' investment management preferences. In sum, the portfolio composition constraints imposed by regulation mean that UCITs funds will not hold significant concentrated stakes in any corporation and hence may be disincentivised from taking a long termist and engaged corporate governance position. Further, the guaranteed right of investors to redeem incentivises investors to vote with their feet if unhappy with fund performance. As investors can redeem units in such schemes very easily, the tendency to vote with their feet causes investors to care little beyond the superficial headline performance of a fund, and investors are unlikely to delve too much into fund practices such as funds' corporate governance roles. Further, investors' outlook of short termism reinforces fund short termism[69] in relation to performance and hence there is little interest in being engaged with investee companies over a longer term.

This creates pressure for funds to be managed for short term performance. These attributes entail a trading emphasis on the part of fund

---

[63] Art 68, recast UCITs Directive 2009, see FCA Handbook COLL 4.5.

[64] Art 69, 73, recast UCITs Directive 2009, see FCA Handbook COLL 4.5.

[65] Art 69, recast UCITs Directive 2009, see FCA Handbook COLL 4.5.

[66] Art 76, recast UCITs Directive 2009, see FCA Handbook COLL 6.3.

[67] Art 84, recast UCITs Directive 2009, see FCA Handbook COLL 6.3.

[68] Art 85, recast UCITs Directive 2009, see FCA Handbook COLL 6.3.

[69] Richard B Evans and Rüdiger Fahlenbrach, 'Institutional Investors and Mutual Fund Governance: Evidence from Retail–Institutional Fund Twins' (2012) *Review of Financial Studies* 3530.

management and funds are less likely to favour taking engaged corporate governance roles in investee companies as such engagement may be costly and does not necessarily bring about quick results for investment performance. The IMA Stewardship Survey of 2015 reports that mandates to fund management companies seldom include stewardship issues.[70]

It may be questioned whether these characterising features of UCITs will endure for UK mutual funds as the UK prepares to exit from the European Union. Many of the UK's equity owning funds are structured as UCITs at the moment, and it remains uncertain how many of them will continue to be based in the UK. We envisage that at least a parallel industry of mutual funds will arise to serve the domestic market. We believe that the key investor needs served under the UCITs regime, revolving around mandatory disclosure, periodic accountability, periodic evaluation of financial performance and a generally liquid profile are unlikely to change. This is because these are highly convergent investor preferences and representative of a global mutual fund industry model, such as that in the US. We are of the view that whether or not the UK continues to adopt the UCITs regime for investor protection, very similar features will continue to define regulation of its mutual funds industry.

Post-Crisis Reforms to Retail Collective Investing and How Enhanced Investor Protection Affects Funds' Corporate Governance Roles

Post-crisis, investor protection has risen high on the agenda of EU and UK policy-makers. Commentators regard increased investor protection as being swept up in the general momentum in financial regulation reform, particularly in terms of prudential regulation. Evans[71] argues that regulatory intervention in consumer protection is an attractive option for policymakers who wish to be seen to be doing something important to redress the crisis even if consumer protection may not be directly relevant to the causes of the crisis. Moloney[72] sees consumer protection reforms, that are apparently unrelated to the financial stability-inspired reforms in

---

[70] IMA, *Adherence to the FRC's Stewardship Code* (2015) at http://www.theinvestmentassociation.org//assets/files/surveys/20150526-fullstewardshipcode.pdf.

[71] David S Evans, 'Why Now Is Not the Right Time to Revamp Consumer Financial Protection' (January 2010) http://ssrn.com/abstract=1538005 accessed 6 January 2013.

[72] Niamh Moloney, 'The Legacy Effects of the Financial Crisis upon Regulatory Design in the EU' in Eilis Ferran, Niamh Moloney, Jennifer G Hill

the immediate aftermath of the global financial crisis, as a second wave or as caught up in the 'backwash' of financial stability-inspired reforms. Reforms aimed at consumer and investor protection have thus become more paternalistic[73] in nature, justified by the general tenor relating to more prescriptive prudential regulation.

Further, the wave of conduct scandals in the UK has also created impetus towards enhanced consumer protection in general, and not just in relation to collective investment schemes. Such conduct scandals include the long-running mis-selling of payment protection insurance,[74] credit card identity theft protection,[75] consumer add-ons[76] and derivative products.[77] The heightened social aversion to misdemeanour in the miss-selling of financial products (albeit long-running problems not unique to these times) has given rise to media and academic articulation of public interest narratives underlying consumer protection in financial regulation.[78] As such, the tenor of consumer protection reforms has changed from merely dealing with market access or market failures to a more

---

and John C Coffee Jnr, *The Regulatory Aftermath of the Global Financial Crisis* (Cambridge: Cambridge University Press, 2012), pp. 111, 112.

[73] See Chapter 8, Mads Andenas and Iris H-Y Chiu, *The Foundations and Future of Financial Regulation* (Oxford: Routledge, 2014).

[74] FSA, 'The Assessment and Redress of Payment Protection Insurance Complaints: Feedback on the further consultation in CP10/6 and final Handbook text' (August 2010) PS10/12 http://www.fsa.gov.uk/pubs/policy/ps10_12.pdf. See Eilis Ferran, 'Regulatory Lessons from the Payment Protection Insurance Mis-Selling Scandal in the UK' (2012) *European Business Organisation Law Review* 248.

[75] For example, the FCA set up a Credit Card Protection mis-selling redress scheme involving a large number of banks that had mis-sold card protection insurance to persons who were already protected under legislation for card and identity theft.

[76] 'FCA fines Swinton Group Limited £7.38 million for mis-selling monthly add-on insurance policies' (17 Sep 2013) at https://www.fca.org.uk/news/press-releases/fca-fines-swinton-group-limited-%C2%A3738-million-mis-selling-monthly-add-insurance.

[77] FSA, 'FSA Confirms Full Review of Interest Rate Swap Misselling' (31 January 2013) at http://www.fsa.gov.uk/library/other_publications/interest-rate-swaps; *Bailey v Barclays Bank* [2014] EWHC 2882 (QB).

[78] Eric S Belsky and Susan S Wachter, 'The Public Interest In Consumer and Mortgage Credit Markets' (2010) at http://papers.ssrn.com/sol3/papers.cfm?abstract_id=1582947; Folarin Akinbami, 'Retail Financial Products in the Global Financial Crisis' (2012) at http://papers.ssrn.com/sol3/papers.cfm?abstract_id=2087548.

protective stance. New consumer protection reforms include powers of product intervention[79] and the regulation of investment advice.[80]

European reforms in instituting a new financial regulatory architecture have also put the consumer protection mandate much more prominently on the agenda. In 2009, The de Larosière Report to the European Commission provided a comprehensive analysis of the weaknesses in the financial sector in the EU and recommended stronger regulatory governance in many areas, thus kickstarting much substantive regulatory reform at the EU level. The Report also recommended the institution of a European System of Financial Supervision in order to provide more robust regulation and supervision of the internal market for financial services. The ESFS comprises three pan-European financial regulators (the European Banking Authority (EBA),[81] the European Securities and

---

[79] Product intervention allows regulators to ban products completely or place limits upon distribution or compel re-design where regulators are sceptical of their intended purpose or risks. Financial Services Act 2012, inserting sections 1H and 107 into the Financial Services and Markets Act. See also FSA, 'The FCA's Use of Temporary Product Intervention Rules' (March 2013) at http://www.fsa.gov.uk/static/pubs/policy/ps13-03.pdf; ESMA also has such powers, see European Parliament and Council Regulation (EU) 1095/2010 of 24 November 2010 establishing a European Supervisory Authority (European Securities and Markets Authority), amending Decision No 716/2009/EC and repealing Commission Decision 2009/77/EC [2010] OJ L331/84 (ESMA Regulation 2010), Art 9(3).

[80] This was undertaken first in the UK, in the form of banning product provider commissions for investment advisers. Advisers also have to label themselves as independent or restricted and be remunerated by their clients, thereby removing conflicts of interest and aligning their interests with their clients'. See FSA, 'Distribution of Retail Investments: Delivering the RDR – Feedback to CP09/18 and final rules' (March 2010) PS10/6 http://www.fsa.gov.uk/pubs/policy/ps10_06.pdf; FCA Handbook COBS 6.1A generally; and reviews by the regulator, see FSA, *Assessing the Quality of Investment Advice in the Retail Banking Sector: A Mystery Shopping Review* (February, 2013). European legislation does not go this far but imposes a duty on dependent advisers to survey the whole market before offering advice see Art 24(7) Directive 2014/65/EU of the European Parliament and of the Council of 15 May 2014 on markets in financial instruments and amending Directive 2002/92/EC and Directive 2011/61/EU (recast).

[81] European Parliament and Council Regulation (EU) 1093/2010 of 24 November 2010 establishing a European Supervisory Authority (European Banking Authority), amending Decision No 716/2009/EC and repealing Commission Decision 2009/78/EC [2010] OJ L331/12 (EBA Regulation 2010).

Markets Authority (ESMA)[82] and the European Insurance and Occupational Pensions Authority (EIOPA)[83]), a Joint Committee of the European Supervisory Authorities and national regulators, and a pan-European macro-prudential supervisor (the European Systemic Risk Board (ESRB)[84]) formed under the auspices of the European Central Bank. The EBA, ESMA and EIOPA are tasked with the continuing mandate of market integration and legal convergence but also protective objectives, such as systemic stability and consumer protection. As such, consumer protection regulation has risen on the agenda as the three European sectoral agencies have a specific mandate to provide a single rule-book on this aspect and lead policy-making in this area.

In light of the abovementioned momentum, investor protection has been greatly enhanced for retail collective investing in the UCITs and PRIIPS. Regulatory prescriptions have been enhanced to improve pre-sale investor disclosure. Further, regulatory prescriptions have enhanced UCITs fund management companies' duties to investors directly, mitigating the problems of weak governance of funds under the separation structure. Finally, this section will discuss regulatory reforms designed to improve investor scrutiny and enforcement. These reforms will be examined critically in terms of their impact upon internal governance, structures and investment management at funds and consequently funds' corporate governance roles.

The above regulatory reforms have the potential to bring about radical changes to the way investment management is carried out in UCITs funds. In particular, they will flank the provisions in the European Shareholder Rights Directive 2017. As the UK promotes the Stewardship Code, the same effects may be experienced by UK-based retail collective investment funds that invest in corporate equity.

---

[82] European Parliament and Council Regulation (EU) 1095/2010 of 24 November 2010 establishing a European Supervisory Authority (European Securities and Markets Authority), amending Decision No 716/2009/EC and repealing Commission Decision 2009/77/EC [2010] OJ L331/84 (ESMA Regulation 2010).

[83] European Parliament and Council Regulation (EU) 1094/2010 of 24 November 2010 establishing a European Supervisory Authority (European Insurance and Occupational Pensions Authority), amending Decision No 716/2009/EC and repealing Commission Decision 2009/79/EC [2010] OJ L331/48 (EIOPA Regulation 2010).

[84] European Parliament and Council Regulation (EU) 1092/2010 of 24 November 2010 on European Union macro-prudential oversight of the financial system and establishing a European Systemic Risk Board [2010] OJ L331/1 (ESRB Regulation 2010).

We first discuss a key reform EU regulation has introduced in relation to funds' corporate governance roles. This is in the context of the imposition of direct duties on fund management companies to investors, overcoming the structural barriers of the separation structure. Such regulation[85] now provides that management companies have a duty to exercise their voting rights in a considered manner, as part of the overall fabric of conduct of business to secure investors' best interests. We examine the enhancement of investor protection and the EU's articulation of funds' interest in corporate governance roles as part of that fabric. One may question policy-makers' assumption that investors are interested in funds' corporate governance roles or indeed that funds' engagement with these roles would secure investors' best interests, given that investor protection has been framed in ways that encourage myopic focus on short-termist financial performance and immediate liquidity needs. However, the framing of funds' corporate governance roles in the context of regulatory governance over their investment management for the purposes of investor protection could serve two normative purposes. One is to educate investors and funds towards the wider good of the retail collective investment enterprise, in terms of how the corporate economy is influenced and shaped. Hence, regulation frames what investors *ought* to treat as in their best interests and what funds *ought* to incorporate into their investor protection focus and their compliance obligations. Second, such regulatory framing serves to bring about a cultural shift in the *modus* of modern short-termist and trading-based investment management, reflecting public policy concerns in the well-being of the corporate sector and making funds as investors play a salutary and not damaging part. However, regulators, in trying to achieve the latter, need to reconcile the competing investor protection needs of the near term.

Conduct of Business Regulation and Duty to Vote

Post-crisis regulatory reforms have introduced direct statutory duties that fund management companies owe fund investors. Fund management companies would not otherwise owe duties to fund investors, as the management company is appointed by the fund and therefore owes duties only to the fund as a separate legal person. But as funds are dominated

[85] Commission Directive 2010/43/EU of 1 July 2010 implementing Directive 2009/65/EC of the European Parliament and of the Council as regards organisational requirements, conflicts of interest, conduct of business, risk management and content of the agreement between a depositary and a management company (Commission Directive 2010), Art 21.

by the management company, this channel of accountability is by and large weak.

In 2010, the European Commission introduced an initiative to improve investor protection by imposing conduct of business obligations on management companies of UCITS funds.[86] These regulatory duties in conduct of business seem to be able to give rise to regulatory enforcement if breached, and could form the basis of unit-holder/investor civil actions against the management company for a breach of statutory duties.[87]

The conduct of business regime includes rules on robust and prudent organisation, and the institution of sound internal control mechanisms, including permanent and effective compliance, risk management and internal audit functions.[88] Further, senior management is to be responsible for developing and reviewing investment policies and strategies and for having oversight of all internal control functions.[89] Significant detail is provided on how risk management policies are to be developed and the aspects of risks and exposures that need to be managed.[90] The prudential management of UCITs funds was further flanked by legislative amendments in 2014[91] prescribing that the remuneration policies of management companies should be in line with sound risk management and should not provide incentives for excessive risk-taking.

Next, certain proscriptive duties on the part of management companies are prescribed so that the interests of the investors in the UCITs funds will be secured. Management companies need to effectively prevent personnel from engaging in personal transactions that may compromise funds' interests or make illegitimate use of confidential information.[92] Management companies also need to develop conflicts of interest policies that will help identify areas of conflicts of interest, and specify how those

---

[86] As above. These are implemented in the UK in the FCA Handbook COLL 6.6A.2-7.

[87] S150, UK Financial Services and Markets Act 2000.

[88] Arts 4, 10–12, Commission Directive 2010. See FCA Handbook COLL 6.11, 6.12.

[89] Art 9, Commission Directive 2010. See FCA Handbook, COLL 6.10.

[90] Art 38ff, Commission Directive 2010, FCA Handbook COLL 6.12.

[91] Directive 2014/91/EU of the European Parliament and of the Council of 23 July 2014 amending Directive 2009/65/EC on the coordination of laws, regulations and administrative provisions relating to undertakings for collective investment in transferable securities (UCITS) as regards depositary functions, remuneration policies and sanctions, Arts 14a and 14b (UCITs Directive 2014).

[92] Art 13, Commission Directive 2010, FCA Handbook COLL 6.13.6.

will be effectively managed and disclosed.[93] Conflicts of interest need to be stringently recorded and detrimental impact to unit-holders in funds needs to be avoided.[94] Management companies also need to ensure that any inducements, i.e. payments received by or paid by them from or to third parties do not compromise the best interests of the fund and must be designed to enhance the quality of the service provided to the funds.[95]

Further, certain duties are imposed on management companies to secure the best interests of unit-holders in funds. Management companies are to develop fair and transparent pricing models for asset valuation, and to treat all fund unit-holders fairly and equally.[96] Management companies are subject to extensive information recording duties for subscriptions and redemptions and have to ensure that subscriptions and redemptions are dealt with fairly and in an accountable manner.[97] Management companies are subject to detailed recording duties[98] relating to their portfolios and all portfolio transactions have to be recorded in terms of the prescribed detail. Such information recording is used to underpin the duty imposed on management companies to undertake all due diligence in monitoring their portfolios and to ensure that the portfolios are managed within the investment limits and risk appetite. Management companies should also undertake due diligence in selecting and reviewing investments.[99] Further, management companies are also subject to a duty of best execution when dealing with execution decisions on behalf of funds.[100] The duty requires management companies to consider how the optimal execution for any trade should be carried out in terms of choice of execution venue, nature of counterparty, size of trade, price and costs and any other relevant consideration.

In terms of funds' corporate governance role in relation to their investee companies, management companies are to develop policies on how their voting rights in investee companies should be exercised for the benefit of the funds. Management companies are also to consider how forms of shareholder engagement or activism may be carried out in order

---

[93] Arts 17-18, Commission Directive 2010, FCA Handbook COLL 6.6.17-18.
[94] Art 20, Commission Directive 2010, FCA Handbook COLL 6.6.17-18.
[95] Art 29, Commission Directive 2010.
[96] Art 22, Commission Directive 2010, FCA Handbook COLL 6.6A.2.
[97] Art 15, Commission Directive 2010, FCA Handbook COLL 6.13.
[98] Art 14, 24, Commission Directive 2010, FCA Handbook COLL 6.13.
[99] Art 23, Commission Directive 2010, FCA Handbook COLL 6.6A.4.
[100] Art 25, Commission Directive 2010, FCA Handbook COLL 6.6A.2.

to secure the best interests of the funds.[101] The corporate governance role of funds is now subject to a regulatory duty that regards appropriate shareholder engagement through voting as part of the suite of conduct of business duties owed to investors in the funds. This is complementary to the proposed EU Shareholders' Rights Directive as well as the UK Stewardship Code.

The demands of the regulatory duty for UCITs fund management companies could change their corporate governance roles going forward, as the assumption of corporate governance roles can now be regarded as a matter for compliance. Regulatory enforcement could be a real threat that incentivises funds to engage with their corporate governance roles, although it is questioned as to whether compliance can be demonstrated superficially, and whether regulatory enforcement is indeed a real threat given that there are many more pressing competing demands for regulatory resources in enforcement. However, we think it is unlikely that investors would be able or motivated to sue fund managers in relation to their corporate governance roles, as any causal relationship between those roles and investment losses could be tenuous except in the clearest of cases.

There may concomitantly be increased market demand for shareholder engagement by investors in funds, and this may provide an area of market pressure for fund managers to demonstrate stewardship. In light of sustained low interest rates in the US and EU, and the continuous search for yield by funds with swelling assets under management,[102] investors are paying more attention to what drives performance. Although the link between shareholder activism and better investee company performance is tenuous,[103] investors are paying greater attention to the potential of such activism. Further, there are several convincing studies

---

[101] Art 21, Commission Directive 2010, FCA Handbook, COLL 6.6A.6.

[102] The Price Waterhouse Coopers survey of Asset Management reports that global assets under management stood at about USD$64 trillion at end of 2013. That related to assets managed by professional asset managers and did not include those managed in-house. PwC, *Asset Management 2020: A Brave New World* (2013), above. Haldane estimated in 2014 a figure of total global assets managed by insurance companies, pension funds, mutual funds and others as representing about twice the size of global gross domestic product, estimated to be USD$87 trillion, at http://www.bankofengland.co.uk/publications/Documents/speeches/2014/speech723.pdf.

[103] See Jonathan M J M Karpoff, 'The Impact of Shareholder Activism in Target Companies: A Survey of Empirical Findings' (Sep 2001) at http://ssrn.com/abstract=885365; Stuart Gillan and Laura T Starks, 'The Evolution of Shareholder Activism in the United States' (2007) at http://papers.ssrn.com/sol3/

linking good investee company performance with sound corporate governance in those companies,[104] so funds and asset managers are perceived to have an immediately relevant role to play in championing better corporate governance at investee companies.

However, one should note that the conduct of business duties discussed above apply to UCITs fund management companies only. The FCA has not imported these duties to other collective investment scheme structures under its oversight. It may be argued that other schemes are unlikely to be corporate equity owners and hence the provisions are irrelevant, since most equity-owning schemes are likely structured as UCITs. As the UK begins to negotiate its exit from the European Union, UK-based UCITs fund management companies may only remain viable for the purposes of managing funds marketed throughout the EU, depending on the nature of trade negotiations. If not, we could see the mutual fund industry in the UK shrink by a significant volume. A smaller sector of UK-based only mutual funds may arise. There is nothing preventing such a sector from branding itself differently from the UCITs brand, and also investing in European asset classes. Opportunities arise for the UK mutual funds industry to reposition itself, whether on the basis of highly convergent regulations with the EU, or on the basis of different regulation that provides regulatory competition. A UK mutual funds industry may regard the UCITs provisions as being highly attractive for investors and thus adopt this regime more widely, or may reconsider the cost/benefit aspects of this regime. There is room for the regulation of the UK retail collective investing industry to be repositioned and rebranded, and so these potential moves will inevitably affect funds' investment management approaches and corporate governance roles. Nevertheless, the UK

---

papers.cfm?abstract_id=959670. The results are mixed in Europe too, see Jean-Michel Sahut, Jean-Sebastien Lantz and Sophie Montandrau, 'Activism of Institutional Investors, Corporate Governance Alerts and Financial Performance' (2010) 15 *International Journal of Business* 221 at http://papers.ssrn.com/sol3/papers.cfm?abstract_id=1735797.

[104] There is more support that good corporate governance, such as is measured by Board independence, has a positive relationship with firm performance, see Sanjai Bhagat and Brian Bolton, 'Corporate Governance and Firm Performance: Recent Evidence' (2009) at http://www.econ.upf.edu/docs/seminars/bhagat.pdf although optimal governance structures may differ from jurisdiction to jurisdiction. Optimal governance structures, however, generally have a positive impact on the health of the corporate sector and general economic development, see Maria Maher and Thomas Andersson, 'Corporate Governance: Effects on Firm Performance and Economic Growth' (OECD, 2009) at http://www.ecgi.org/research/accession/cgeu.pdf.

mutual funds industry would continue to grapple with the somewhat conflicting objectives of meeting investor protection needs in the short term, such as reducing cost and improving liquidity and accountability while encouraging funds to take a long-term oriented stewardship stance vis-à-vis their investee companies. As we have relied so far on the soft law of stewardship to nudge institutions into a meaningful corporate governance role, there may not be significant appetite to extend UCITs-based conduct of business rules in a wholesale manner to domestic mutual funds.

Fund Management Charges and Fees

The pressures faced by retail collective investment schemes to keep fees and charges affordable to investors are a significant factor influencing their investment management practices and corporate governance roles.

Mutual fund fees are being scrutinised increasingly by investors in this low-interest rate and low yield environment. In the US, investors have taken class actions against mutual funds for charging excessive fees,[105] although mutual fund fee litigation remains a challenging environment and it is not easy to implicate the fund management company.[106]

Although the EU and UK do not adopt investor litigation as a key governance measure in investor protection against excessive expenses, reforms have been made to make fee charging more transparent, less discretionary and more accountable. In 2010, the European Commission decided to improve the UCITs investor disclosure regime by further simplifying and prescribing the format of the shorter document accompanying the full-length prospectus. The 'Key Investor Information Document' (KIID) is introduced to replace the simplified prospectus.[107] The KIID is a short, two page A4 document that contains five key sections

[105] Quinn Curtis and John Morley, 'An Empirical Study of Mutual Fund Excessive Fee Litigation: Do the Merits Matter?' (2014) at http://papers.ssrn.com/sol3/papers.cfm?abstract_id=1852652.

[106] Quinn Curtis and John Morley, 'The Flawed Mechanics of Mutual Fund Fee Litigation' (2014) at http://papers.ssrn.com/sol3/papers.cfm?abstract_id=2405307; Enzo Incandela, 'Recourse Under § 10(b) on Life Support: The Displacement of Liability and Private Securities Fraud Action after Janus v First Derivative' (2012) 43 *Loyola University Chicago Law Journal* 935.

[107] Commission Regulation (EU) No 583/2010 of 1 July 2010 implementing Directive 2009/65/EC of the European Parliament and of the Council as regards key investor information and conditions to be met when providing key investor information or the prospectus in a durable medium other than paper or by means of a website (Commission Regulation 2010).

whose presentation and format is highly prescribed. The prescribed format has been developed as a result of empirical research with consumers in order to find out the optimal presentation formats for information delivery to consumers.[108] In one of the key sections, funds need to disclose all fees and charges in a tabular format, showing a percentage figure for entry and exit charges and a single total figure for all other charges.[109] This will be accompanied by narrative explanations of the charges and charging structure. The KIID is intended to simplify and de-mystify charging information for investors in order to empower investor scrutiny. The KIID format has proved to be very popular with EU policy-makers who have also adopted it in the PRIIPS regulation.[110]

Further, UK and EU regulation has introduced greater control over what fund managers can pass on to investors as charges and cost. In particular, the regime on third-party inducements has been tightened up. Third-party inducements are payments made to the portfolio manager or from the portfolio manager. Where third party inducements are paid to the portfolio manager, such as kickbacks and commissions, they create conflicts of interest and may result in investment decisions that compromise investor interests. Where third party inducements are paid out to third parties, this could result in the bulging of cost charged to investors and as such affects yield for investors. Regulatory reforms are afoot[111] that demand greater transparency in terms of the break-down of third-party inducements such as brokers' research charges, and rigour in justifying that the inducements enhance services to clients.[112] Clients and regulators are increasingly being provided with the opportunity to scrutinise inducements that affect cost of services and perhaps exert negotiating power to effect desired changes. The FCA is also proposing an all-in fee for asset management based on estimated cost in order to

---

108 IFF Research and YouGov, 'UCITS Disclosure Testing Research Report' (June 2009) at http://ec.europa.eu/internal_market/investment/docs/other_docs/research_report_en.pdf.

109 Arts 10–11, Commission Regulation 2010.

110 Arts 6–8, Regulation (EU) No 1286/2014 of the European Parliament and of the Council of 26 November 2014 on key information documents for packaged retail and insurance-based investment products (PRIIPs).

111 ESMA, *Draft Regulatory Technical Standards for the MiFID II and MiFIR* (Dec 2014) at http://www.esma.europa.eu/system/files/2014-1569_final_report_-_esmas_technical_advice_to_the_commission_on_mifid_ii_and_mifir.pdf.

112 FCA, *Inducements and Conflicts of Interest Thematic Review: Key Findings* (April 2016) at http://www.fca.org.uk/news/inducements-conflicts-interest-thematic-review-key-findings; 'Crackdown on golf alarms fund industry', *Financial Times* (6 May 2016).

motivate better cost control.[113] These new regimes would also mean that the cost for taking on corporate governance roles would have to be more clearly accounted for.

There is an intensifying call from the investor quarter to justify and moderate cost[114] as cost affects yield and investors have been conscious of the difficulty of achieving sustained yield in the current environment. Some of the trends towards cost moderation include investors' increased preference for low cost fund management, such as in passive index tracking funds[115] or exchange traded funds,[116] switching away from active management of funds.[117]

---

113 FCA, *Asset Management Market Study Final Report* (2017), above at Chapter 13.

114 'End 'heads we win, tails you lose' fees', *Financial Times* (16 Nov 2014). See also John Authers, 'Fees matter more than asset allocation', *Financial Times* (6 March 2015) quoting Mebine Faber, *Global Asset Allocation: A Survey of the World's Top Asset Allocation Strategies* (2014) at http://mebfaber.com/2014/12/03/global-asset-allocation-white-paper/.

115 See Kevin R James, 'The Price of Retail Investing in the UK' (FSA Occasional Paper 2000) arguing that passive investing works out better for investors as cost is low and eats less into yield. Also Hymans Robertson, *LGPS Structure Analysis* (Dec 2013); Department for Communities and Local Government, *Local Government Pension Scheme: Opportunities for Collaboration, Cost Savings and Efficiencies* (May 2014) applying to pension funds; 'Vanguard's record inflows prove passive is massive', *Financial Times* (11 Jan 2014).

116 Ilan Guedj and Jennifer Huang, 'Are ETFs Replacing Index Mutual Funds?' (2009) at http://ssrn.com/abstract=1108728.

117 There are inconclusive debates regarding the merits and disadvantages of active and passive investing. Although active management delivers, cost is generally too high and affects yield; Larry E Swedroe, 'Active versus Passive Investing' in John D Haslem (ed.), *Mutual Funds: Portfolio Structures, Analysis, Management, and Stewardship* (Chichester: John Wiley & Sons 2010) at Chapter 6; 'Active share revealed to have feet of clay', *Financial Times* (where Nomura research doubts the benefits of active investing) (25 Jan 2015). But see more nuanced assessment in Edward D Tower, 'Performance of Actively Managed versus Index Funds: The Vanguard Case' in John D Haslem (ed.), *Mutual Funds: Portfolio Structures, Analysis, Management, and Stewardship* (Chichester: John Wiley & Sons 2010) at Chapter 12 and also see generally warnings against making active or passive a binary choice as performance determinations are based on certain assumptions, see Michael W Crook, 'A Stochastic Portfolio Perspective on Utilizing Active and Passive Fund Management' (2012) at http://ssrn.com/abstract=2170776. It is explained that the outperformance of passive funds is largely due to efficient markets in many parts of the world, making it difficult for active managers to beat the market, see Burton G Malkiel, 'Efficient Markets and Mutual Fund Investing: The Advantages of Index Funds'

Market demand may be low for funds and management companies to engage in corporate governance, i.e. apathetic investors may not wish to pay for funds to take on corporate governance roles, and this would be contrary to policy-makers' calls for institutions and asset managers to be engaged with corporate governance. The desire to keep costs low and coalescing around standardised products may mean that there is less appetite for less predictable management techniques involving corporate governance engagement. If so, fund management companies may find it difficult to balance the regulatory expectation of shareholder engagement with the need to convince investors to bear the cost.

On the other hand, we may see something more optimistic i.e. greater clarity in fees and cost structures, and therefore corporate governance engagement is priced more clearly in investment charging, improving funds' commitment to corporate governance roles. Further, the use of investors' money for opportunistic activities would be limited, for example, cash for corporate access is now outlawed by the UK. The UK has identified cash for corporate access as a third party inducement that should not be paid out of client's execution charges.[118] Also, investment management charges may more honestly reflect the efforts in investment management, so that closet index trackers may not be able to charge fees as high as those of actively managed funds.[119]

---

in John D Haslem (ed.), *Mutual Funds: Portfolio Structures, Analysis, Management, and Stewardship* (Chichester: John Wiley & Sons 2010) at Chapter 7. But there is also research affirming the superior performance of real active managers, see 'Almost 90% of UK active managers beat the stock market', *Financial Times* (3 Aug 2014); Robert C Jones, 'Active Management in Mostly Efficient Markets' (2011) 67 *Financial Analysts Journal* 29; Valery Polkovnichenko, Kelsey Wei and Feng Zhao, 'Cautious Risk-Takers: Investor Preferences and Demand for Active Management' (2012) at http://ssrn.com/abstract=2022416; Lubos Pastor, Robert F. Stambaugh and Lucian A. Taylor, 'Scale and Skill in Active Management' (Jan 2014) at http://ssrn.com/abstract=2390285 arguing that small specialist funds can add value although that value may be eroded with fund scale. See also a report that boutique fund managers can add significant value through active investing, 'Fund investors find small is beautiful', *Financial Times* (27 Feb 2014).

[118] FCA, *Changes to the Use of Dealing Commission Rules: Feedback to CP13/17 and Final Rules* (May 2014); 'Six fund groups misused cash for access', *Financial Times* (26 Jan 2014).

[119] John Authers, 'Active fund managers are closet index huggers', *Financial Times* (12 March 2014); 'European markets watchdog examines closet trackers', *Financial Times* (23 Nov 2014); Aron Gottesman and Matthew Morey, 'Getting What You Paid For: Using Mutual Fund Governance to Predict the Activeness of Mutual Funds' (2014) at http://ssrn.com/abstract=2422270.

Passive Investing and Exchange-traded Funds

As investors are increasingly scrutinising cost in order to boost yield, funds have (a) more loudly voiced doubts over the merits of active management and switched into passive investing and (b) called for pseudo-active managers who charge high fees for closet index-hugging to be exposed.

On (a), one would think that there is less scope for passive funds to take on active corporate governance positions in investee companies. This is due to the built-in need for trading in order to follow the index, the relative ease of trading in such a liquid sector and cost constraints.[120] However, stewardship pressures from policy makers and public opinion have been brought to bear on passive funds, and passive fund leaders such as BlackRock and Vanguard have all developed engagement policies in response,[121] although it remains to be seen if such moves are merely window dressing.[122] Nevertheless cost constraints would mean that such funds are likely motivated to find the least costly methods of demonstrating shareholder engagement, and collective forms of engagement therefore look the most promising, as will be shortly discussed.[123]

The growth of the market for exchange-traded funds is another manifestation of how the market caters for investor needs in reducing cost of investment management. As discussed in Chapter 2, investors have become attracted to exchange-traded funds and the market has grown phenomenally in the UK.[124] The fund is listed and benefits from the transparency requirements imposed on listed entities. Further, the fund can be traded at any time during the trading day, and such intra-day liquidity is highly desired by investors, when compared to mutual funds that allow daily redemptions with one published price every day.[125]

---

[120] The IMA Survey seems to prove this point as more stewardship is associated with active management mandates. See IMA, *Adherence to the UK FRC's Stewardship Code* (2015), above.

[121] 'Compulsory stewardship by passive managers moves closer', *Financial Times* (26 April 2015).

[122] 'Fund Houses Back the Boss Too Often', *Financial Times* (17 May 2015).

[123] In the next section, and also see above.

[124] 'Rapid expansion across UK exchange traded funds industry', *Financial Times* (22 Feb 2011); globally see Exchange traded funds make strongest ever start to a year', *Financial Times* (12 April 2015).

[125] Gary L Gastineau, *The Exchange-Traded Funds Manual* (Chichester: John Wiley & Sons 2010) at Chapter 1. But empirical research has also found that exchange-traded funds do not consistently outperform the mutual fund that is passively managed, see Mohamed Sharifzadeh and Simin Hojat, 'An Analytical

Where the exchange-traded fund is based on an index and is passively managed, the liquidity and transparency features seem to be superior to mutual funds that are index-hugging and passively managed too. Exchange-traded funds have also been able to charge lower fees than passively managed mutual funds,[126] thus ensuring that yield is not taken up by fees.

Investors' preferences for low cost and liquidity chime with regulators' investor protection rationales and shape regulatory design. However, these preferences are in our view contrary to the incentives needed for a long-term oriented and engaged corporate governance involvement in investee companies. We suggest that trading in exchange-traded funds allows investors to be yet another step removed from being engaged as equity investors. Investors buy into a fund portfolio and are distanced from each corporate security in the basket. They are thus disengaged from being 'investors' or 'owners' in firms and behave more like traders in whole portfolios. It is arguable that exchange-traded fund investors are largely attracted to the trading freedoms and this reinforces a trading and short-termist culture rather than an investing culture with retail savers. That said, in response to stewardship calls, there is some effort on the part of exchange-traded funds to demonstrate voting, and empirical research[127] shows that most ETF sponsors have written policies in place to exercise voting rights. However, the largest sponsors seem to be pro-management voters, doing very little to 'rock the boat'.[128] Such a position arguably reflects a degree of under-investment in corporate governance research, consistent with funds' and investors' cost concerns, and a willingness to take the path of the least resistance, i.e. voting with management.

However, we also present some factors that may encourage investors, funds and their management companies to take investee companies'

Performance Comparison of Exchange-Traded Funds with Index Funds: 2002–2010' (2012) 13 *Journal of Asset Management* 196–209; Adam Turner, 'Exchange-Traded Funds vs. UK Investment Trusts: A Comparison of Performance' (2010) at http://papers.ssrn.com/sol3/papers.cfm?abstract_id=1689534.

[126] Forbes.com, 'What's the Difference? Mutual Funds and Exchange-traded Funds Explained' (July 2013) at http://www.forbes.com/sites/feeonlyplanner/2013/07/18/whats-the-difference-mutual-funds-and-exchange-traded-funds-explained/.

[127] IRRC Institute, *Proxy Voting by Exchange-Traded Funds: An Analysis of ETF Voting Policies, Practices and Patterns* (2009) at http://www.irrcinstitute.org/pdf/FINAL%20ETF%20Study%20-%20June%2030,%202009.pdf.

[128] That said, a small number of sponsors, such as Rydex, do seem to vote in a considered manner, demonstrating some form of engagement.

corporate governance more seriously. The overall environment of emphasis on good investee company corporate governance in the UK and EU (brought about by the UK Stewardship Code and the proposed EU Shareholders' Rights Directive 2014) may create an overall effect of 'educating' investors concerning the importance of staying engaged, and hence they may put more pressure on funds to do so and scrutinise funds more closely in that regard.

Investors' Appetite for Better Fund Governance

There is increasing investor appetite for funds to be well-governed and for funds to take on appropriate shareholder engagement positions. It could be said that investors' appetite for funds to be better governed itself creates a spillover effect to an enhanced interest in funds' assumption of corporate governance roles in their investee companies. There is empirical research to suggest that better governed funds tend to have and impose higher governance expectations upon investee companies, resulting in a benign monitoring effect.[129] For example, Luxembourg and Irish trade bodies have introduced soft law on corporate governance in funds in 2009 and 2010 respectively. Such corporate governance reforms are likely to have an impact upon the funds' internal governance and could affect their roles as corporate governance actors in their investee companies.

The Luxembourg AIFI Corporate Governance Code now imposes high level duties and responsibilities on fund Boards to act with due diligence, to act fairly and independently for the interests of investors irrespective of the directors' affiliations, to ensure fair and equal treatment of investors such as in the conveyance of information, to ensure that shareholder rights can be exercised in a considered way, to ensure effective management of conflicts of interest, to ensure compliance with laws and that effective risk management is in place, and that the Board is remunerated fairly and proportionately.[130] It is noted that there is no explicit recommendation to institute independent or non-executive directors, and no explicit discussion of oversight of the fund management company. Hazenberg's survey[131] shows that in Luxembourg, fund Board

[129] Wen-Hsiu Chou, Lilian Ng, and Qinghai Wang, 'Are Better Governed Funds Better Monitors?' (2011) at http://ssrn.com/abstract=1913430.

[130] See the 10 principles in http://www.alfi.lu//sites/alfi.lu/files/files/Alfi%20guidelines%20and%20recommendations/Code-of-Conduct-2013-3-final.pdf.

[131] Jan Jaap Hazenberg, 'Independence and Focus of Luxembourg UCITS Fund Boards' (LSF Research Working Paper 2012).

directors still see themselves mainly as taking on a role that complies with the needs of the corporate structure, and are involved in general risk management. They do not see themselves as investors' watchdogs. The issue of independence may even be regarded as irrelevant in Luxembourg funds as fund performance is not affected by it.[132] That is not to say that fund performance is necessarily unaffected by fund governance in general, quite the contrary according to empirical research.[133] Nevertheless, the PriceWaterhouseCoopers survey[134] shows that some funds have become responsive to investor pressures and have started to introduce one independent director onto each fund Board. The survey also finds that directors are adequately trained, meet on average six to seven times a year, and that Board meetings are generally well-attended. Boards are focused mainly on risk management and internal control but oversight of fund management companies remains an area in need of improvement. The internal governance of Luxembourg-domiciled funds is slowing changing.

The IFIA Corporate Governance Code[135] introduced by the Irish trade body is on a comply-or-explain basis and requires fund Boards to be structured and run according to certain standards. Fund Boards need to have a minimum of three directors, of whom at least a majority are to be non-executive and one is to be independent. The non-executive directors may be appointed from the fund management company but the Board is required to act in the overriding interests of investors in the fund. Board directors are also to undergo adequate training and ensure adequate time commitment to the fund they are appointed to. Board directors are not ordinarily able to take on more than eight fund directorships, and this prevents jumbo directors whose appointments are mere formalities from being a prevalent phenomenon.

---

[132] Jan Jaap Hazenberg, 'Effectiveness of Independent Boards of Luxembourg Funds' (2013) at http://ssrn.com/abstract=2276849.

[133] Jay Wellman and Jian Zhou, 'Corporate Governance and Mutual Fund Performance: A First Look at the Morningstar Stewardship Grades' (2007) at http://ssrn.com/abstract=714303. Also see how structure affects charges and governance, See A Joseph Warburton, 'Should Mutual Funds Be Corporations? A Legal & Econometric Analysis' (2008) 33 *Journal of Corporation Law* 745; Lawrence He, Martin Kusy, Deepak Singh and Samir Trabelsi, 'Mutual Fund Fees, Performance, and Governance Structure in Canada' (2013) at http://ssrn.com/abstract=2201213.

[134] PwC, *Luxembourg Fund Governance Survey 2014* (2015).

[135] See Corporate Governance Code for Collective Investment Schemes and Management Companies, http://www.ecgi.org/codes/documents/code_cg_ifia_14dec2011_en.pdf.

The FCA has also embarked on governance reforms and in 2017 proposes a minimum of two independent directors on fund Boards in order to improve governance of funds generally and oversight of fund managers.[136]

Market demand for better governed funds may in time shape the symbiotic relationship between fund governance and funds' corporate governance positions. Funds could become more sensitive to investee companies' corporate governance as reflecting investors' preferences, and become more engaged. In a competitive fund market, if investors' appetite for better fund governance becomes more pronounced, funds may distinguish themselves by more pronounced engagement with investee companies' corporate governance, as such corporate governance engagement could reinforce the impression that fund governance is also being taken seriously. As funds' internal governance becomes part of the matrix of attributes for investor appeal, bottom-up pressures from investors may go some way towards supporting the regulatory duty to exercise voting rights and the obligations imposed under the European Shareholder Rights Directive 2017.

Improving Investors' Rights of Recourse

Finally, this section argues that the reforms that improve investors' ease of enforcement in civil litigation against fund management companies and depositaries could play a part in causing an impact on fund corporate governance roles.

First, the duty to exercise voting rights in investee companies (as discussed above) by UCITs funds is a statutory duty, and so it is conceivable that courts will allow investors to sue fund management companies for a breach of such statutory duty, under the tortious action of breach of statutory duties in section 150 of the UK Financial Services and Markets Act. Although there is no action recorded to date, the passivity of investors in bringing such actions may change. This is because the regime for investor litigation has been greatly expanded under the post-crisis reforms. The new context could incentivise more investor civil litigation in light of policy-makers' call to make market discipline a pressing reality.

Investor litigation is a form of market discipline cautiously encouraged by European policy-makers at the moment. We observe that new avenues

[136] FCA, *Asset Management Market Study Final Report* (2017), above at Chapter 10.

of investor litigation have been created, such as against credit rating agencies,[137] and against depositaries of UCITs[138] and alternative investment funds.[139] For example, in the area of depositaries, UCITs fund Boards have been likely to appoint the group's depositary institution as the fund's depositary. Such arrangements would ensure that the fund management company has the ease of dealing with another member in the fund management enterprise group. The relative insulation of the fund management company from scrutiny has been subject to reform pressures since the Madoff scandal,[140] and the EU has thus introduced legislation to compel funds to appoint independent third-party depositaries to safeguard fund assets.[141] Regulators now require that the UCITs fund management company appoints a single depositary for each UCITs fund it manages, and such appointments are on prescribed terms in regulation. The depositary will focus on custodial functions and effective reconciliation of accounts and registers.[142] The extent of oversight duties may elevate depositaries' functions to the status of an independent

---

[137] Regulation (EU) No 462/2013 of the European Parliament and of the Council of 21 May 2013 amending Regulation (EC) No 1060/2009 on credit rating agencies Text with EEA relevance, Art 35a. See commentary in Brigitte Haar, 'Civil Liability of Credit Rating Agencies – Regulatory All-or-Nothing Approaches between Immunity and Over-Deterrence' (2012) at http://ssrn.com/abstract=2198293.

[138] Discussed shortly.

[139] European Parliament and Council Directive 2011/61/EU of 8 June 2011 on Alternative Investment Fund Managers and amending Directives 2003/41/EC and 2009/65/EC and Regulations (EC) No 1060/2009 and (EU) No 1095/2010 [2011] OJ L174/1, Art 21.

[140] 'Bernard Madoff: How the scandal worked', *The Telegraph* (19 Jan 2009).

[141] Art 22, Directive 2014/91/EU of the European Parliament and of the Council of 23 July 2014 amending Directive 2009/65/EC on the coordination of laws, regulations and administrative provisions relating to undertakings for collective investment in transferable securities (UCITS) as regards depositary functions, remuneration policies and sanctions (UCITs Directive 2014), FCA Handbook, COLL 6.6.4, 6.6.12, 6.6.13.

[142] Under Article 22, the depositary has a cash flow monitoring function, a custodial function over financial instruments, a function to verify ownership of assets by the UCITs fund, a function to ensure that subscription and redemption orders are duly reconciled, a function to oversee valuation procedures are implemented by the management company in compliance with laws and regulations, a function to ensure that any re-use of the assets of the UCITs fund is carried out is in the interest of unit-holders and covered by high quality and liquid collateral and a duty of diligence to oversee any third parties to whom the depositary delegates any functions. Art 22a, UCITs Directive 2014, FCA Handbook COLL 6.6.4.

gatekeeper that secures the protection of unit-holders' interests in the key areas of valuation, subscription and redemption, generation of income through securities lending and safe custody of money and assets.

Regulators require that the separate depositary should 'act honestly, fairly, professionally, independently and solely in the interest of the UCITS and the investors of the UCITS.'[143] Hence, the contractual limitations that would have prevented unit-holders from holding depositaries to account are overcome by regulation. Regulatory duties are now imposed directly on depositaries to take care of UCITs fund investors' interests and, arguably, this changes the relational construct between depositaries and UCITs management companies from one of contract to one of gate-keeping or oversight. Where depositaries previously owed contractual duties only to the management company by virtue of the terms of appointment, the private relational construct between depositaries and management companies is now changed such that the contractual duties are over-written by regulatory prescription, and depositaries owe regulatory duties to UCITs fund investors directly. This incentivises depositaries to monitor and oversee aspects of management company practices that are within the scope of their responsibilities for the benefit of investors.

The depositary is incentivised to perform its functions in a diligent[144] and uncompromising manner as civil liability may be incurred for loss of financial instruments in the custody of the depositary or its delegate. Depositary duties are by nature statutory duties, they are *prima facie* enforceable by the regulator. In terms of enforcement in private litigation, the management company would have a right of enforcement as the appointing party under contract, but we think there is a case for saying that investors who are owed these duties could have a cause for action too. Previously the UCITs recast Directive of 2009 did state clearly that the depositary could be liable to the management company and investors in the UCITs fund. Case law in Luxembourg[145] has however interpreted this to mean that the depositary is liable to investors generally and such liability should be enforced via the management company's action. A direct right of action is not available to investors unless the jurisdiction's

[143] Art 25, UCITs Directive 2014.

[144] Art 24, UCITs Directive 2014, FCA Handbook COLL 6.6.4.

[145] Vincent Naveaux and Renaud Graas, 'Direct Action by Investors against a UCITS Depositary–A Short-Lived Landmark Ruling?' (2012) 7 *Capital Markets Law Journal* 455.

national law permits it.[146] It is now arguable that the position has changed as Article 24 now allows investors to invoke the liability of the depositary directly as long as the depositary is not subject to double jeopardy.

We are of the view that civil liability seems to be a form of strict liability, subject to the defence of proving that 'the loss has arisen as a result of an external event beyond [the depositary's] reasonable control, the consequences of which would have been unavoidable despite all reasonable efforts to the contrary.' Depositaries could also be civilly liable where investor losses are caused by any negligent or intentional failure in complying with regulatory duties.

Direct duties owed to investors which attract strict liability could create incentives for investors to sue as the mechanism of strict liability helps to overcome the need to prove *mens rea* or negligence, in effect shifting the burden onto the fund management company to adduce the appropriate defence. It can be argued that the duties in conduct of business are susceptible to strict liability. The duty to exercise voting rights does not seem to be only actionable upon proof of negligence, and unless a fund management company demonstrates records of deliberation, the failure to exercise voting rights could be strictly actionable.[147] It remains to be seen if the prospect of easier investor enforcement may galvanise a culture of greater investor discipline of their investment funds.

Some commentators are however of the view that market discipline is unlikely to play a key role in enforcing funds' corporate governance positions, due to the apathy of retail investors and collective action failures. A number of commentators are sceptical that investors would be motivated to take collective litigation to enforce fund and management company duties.[148] Langevoort also argues that collective litigation is not the point as investors are unlikely and unable to successfully sue where fund performance is fine, and so civil litigation is only likely in the

---

[146] Or unless there is a direct action in tort due to the individual harm done to the specific investor in question.

[147] Art 24, UCITs Directive 2014.

[148] Michael C Schouten, 'Why Governance Might Work in Mutual Funds' (2011) 109 *Michigan Law Review* 89; John Morley and Quinn Curtis, 'Taking Exit Rights Seriously: Why Governance and Fee Litigation Don't Work in Mutual Funds' (2010) 120 *Yale L.J.* 84.

clearest cases of egregious behaviour. It is unlikely to act as a credible enforcement mechanism for specific duties such as the duty to vote.[149]

Other commentators are of the view that investor pressure for changes in fund management practice could come from the threat of litigation, whether or not mounted successfully. Litigation provides a context for voice to be exercised and heard, and existence of the regulatory framework, or the making of a threat to litigate could be sufficient to bring investors' demands to bear.[150]

We have outlined the competing forces that shape mutual fund investment management practice in the UK, and argue that cost concerns and investors' overwhelming interest in liquidity reinforce a trading culture that is apathetic towards funds' corporate governance roles. However, the regulatory duty to consider exercise of voting rights by UCITs funds could have a strong compelling effect to demonstrate shareholder engagement. Market demand for funds to demonstrate shareholder engagement may also increase in the overall environment of increased interest in good governance at funds and the corporate sector and empowerment for investor discipline in law and regulation. The next section discusses the typologies of corporate governance engagement by retail collective investment funds, mainly UCITs funds, in the UK corporate sector. This discussion seeks to take stock of the engagement landscape and is drawn from a literature review of empirical findings.

C. THE TYPOLOGIES OF RETAIL COLLECTIVE INVESTMENT FUNDS' ASSUMPTION OF CORPORATE GOVERNANCE ROLES IN THE UK

We suggest that there are eight typologies of shareholder engagement that retail collective investment funds carry out in relation to the UK corporate sector. These are observed in relation largely to UCITs funds.

---

149 Donald Langevoort, 'Private Litigation to Enforce Fiduciary Duties in Mutual Funds: Derivative Suits, Disinterested Directors and the Ideology of Investor Sovereignty' (*ECGI Working Paper* 2006) at http://ssrn.com/abstract=885970.

150 Joseph A McCahery, Laura T Starks and Zacharias Sautner, 'Behind the Scenes: The Corporate Governance Preferences of Institutional Investors', AFA 2011 *Denver Meetings Paper* at 13 (2010), available at http://ssrn.com/abstract=1571046.

The eight typologies are:

(a) Voting at the annual general meeting, through proxies or otherwise;
(b) Individual informal dialogue and escalation activities;
(c) Collective engagement with other mainstream institutions in voting;
(d) Collective engagement with other mainstream institutions in other events;
(e) Collective engagement with alternative investment funds such as hedge funds;
(f) Socially responsible Retail Collective Investment Schemes;
(g) Securities or derivative litigation (which may be privately settled); and
(h) Exit.

Voting at General Meetings

Retail collective investment schemes' (or in the US, mutual funds') general lack of interest in investee company corporate governance has been lamented in the US,[151] UK and EU.[152]

As UCITs fund management companies are now subject to a statutory duty to exercise fund voting rights in a considered manner, UCITs fund management companies have drawn up codes of best practice that relate to development of engagement policies, demonstration of engagement behaviour and exercising voting rights in a considered manner.[153] The UK Investment Management Association, the trade body for most asset managers, also reports increased resources being dedicated to shareholder engagement and an increase in the exercise of voting rights, whether that is in voting for or against management proposals or in abstaining from

[151] John C Bogle, 'The Challenge to Mutual Fund Stewardship' in John D Haslem (ed.), *Mutual Funds: Portfolio Structures, Analysis, Management, and Stewardship* (Chichester: John Wiley & Sons 2010) at Chapter 15, 283ff; John D Haslem, 'Identifying Mutual Fund Stewardship' in John D Haslem (ed.), *Mutual Funds: Portfolio Structures, Analysis, Management, and Stewardship* (Chichester: John Wiley & Sons 2010) at Chapter 16, 305ff.

[152] CEPS-ECMI, 'Rethinking Asset Management from Financial Stability to Investor Protection and Economic Growth' (2012) at http://ssrn.com/abstract=2060134.

[153] *EFAMA Code for External Governance* (2011) at http://www.efama.org/Publications/Public/Corporate_Governance/11-4035%20EFAMA%20ECG_final_6%20April%202011%20v2.pdf.

voting.[154] The 2013 IMA survey reports that, for the last 2 years, voting levels have hovered between 70–90 per cent for asset managers in relation to all stocks held.[155]

We doubt that stewardship would become a mainstay in investment management and think it would be unlikely to change fund managers' preference for trading and portfolio turnover where such would result in quicker impact upon performance.[156] In this light, 'stewardship' activities may be added to the mix of investment management only, and are likely to be carried out within an instrumental framework towards achieving fund performance, since empirical research (as mentioned earlier) still produces mixed findings as to the financial potential of bringing about good governance at investee companies.

Although voting levels are on the rise, the quality of such engagement through voting may be tenuous. The chapter suggests that this is because of cost concerns on the part of fund managers and the uncertain relationship between stewardship and investment performance. Thus, it is surmised that fund managers are likely to adopt a least cost method in demonstrating stewardship.

Some of the cost-effective measures undertaken by fund managers include reliance on proxy advisers' recommendations. The US and EU report high levels of such reliance,[157] although in the EU, mindless reliance is not observed. Next, fund managers are likely to champion regulatory and listing rules reforms[158] to compel companies to institute

---

154 IMA, *Adherence to the FRC's Stewardship Code 2013* (2014) at pp. 6ff, http://www.theinvestmentassociation.org/assets/files/surveys/20140501-01_stewardshipcode.pdf, and *Adherence to the FRC's Stewardship Code* (2015) at http://www.theinvestmentassociation.org//assets/files/surveys/20150526-fullstewardshipcode.pdf too.

155 Above.

156 Michael C Schouten, 'Why Governance Might Work in Mutual Funds' (2011), above; John Morley and Quinn Curtis, 'Taking Exit Rights Seriously: Why Governance and Fee Litigation Don't Work in Mutual Funds' (2010), above.

157 James Cotter, Alan Palmiter, and Randall Thomas, 'ISS Recommendations and Mutual Fund Voting on Proxy Proposals' (2010) 55 *Villanova Law Review* 56; IRRC Institute, 'Proxy Voting by Exchange-Traded Funds: An Analysis of ETF Voting Policies, Practices and Patterns' (2009), above; ESMA, *Final Report: Feedback Statement on the Consultation Regarding the Role of the Proxy Advisory Industry* (Feb 2013).

158 Empirical research has found that mutual funds have grown in countries with sound corporate governance regimes for shareholder protection and securities regulation that favours shareholder protection and accountability, see Ajay

good governance. Such reforms achieve a 'transaction-cost' reduction effect for fund managers as a ready template is provided for fund managers to engage with their investee companies. The cost of private bargains between funds and companies in achieving governance standards unique to each company would likely be too high. As discussed in Chapter 4, policy-makers have introduced such transaction-cost reduction measures in the form of more prescriptive corporate governance requirements in Listing Rules[159] and heightened mandatory transparency in corporate reporting in the UK.[160]

Empirical research finds that voting by retail collective investment schemes is affected by conflicts of interest in relation to the investee company.[161] Investigations have been carried out in the US to determine mutual fund responses to individual shareholder proposals and the findings show a lack of support for individual shareholder proposals resulting either from a lack of interest or due to pro-management behaviour. Hence, it is unlikely that, through voting behaviour, retail collective investment schemes, sticking largely to well-trodden governance issues, will perform significant roles in galvanising change in investee companies. That said, in areas where public opinion has become loud and pervasive, retail collective investment schemes may respond to such pressures in order to demonstrate considered voting behaviour.[162]

Khorana, Henri Servaes, Peter Tufano, 'Explaining the Size of the Mutual Fund Industry Around the World' (2005) 78 *Journal of Financial Economics* 145.

[159] Such as the mandatory relationship agreement between majority shareholders and their Premium-listed companies, FCA Handbook Listing Rules 6.1.4ff.

[160] See Iris H-Y Chiu, 'Reviving Shareholder Stewardship: Critically Examining the Impact of Corporate Transparency Reforms in the UK' (2014) 38 *Delaware Journal of Corporate Law* 983.

[161] Jennifer S Taub, 'Able but Not Willing: The Failure of Mutual Fund Advisers to Advocate for Shareholders' Rights' (2009), above; Dragana Cvijanovic, Amil Dasgupta and Konstantinos E Zachariadis, 'Ties that Bind: How Business Connections Affect Mutual Fund Activism' (2014), above; Angela Morgan , Annette Poulsen, Jack Wolf, Tina Yang, 'Mutual Funds as Monitors: Evidence from Mutual Fund Voting' (2009) at http://ssrn.com/abstract=1431072.

[162] Reena Aggarwal, Isil Erel and Laura Starks, 'Influence of Public Opinion on Investor Voting and Proxy Advisors' (2014) at http://ssrn.com/abstract=2476517.

Individual Informal Dialogue and/or Escalation

Empirical research on individual informal dialogue and engagement is hard to come by as such activities are behind the scenes and not reported. However, the Investment Management Association Survey shows that asset managers are increasingly engaged in company-specific research and using informal channels to provide their views to management through meetings with company representatives, such as with the Senior Independent Directors.[163] Such engagement does depend on the size of holdings, and empirical research seems to confirm that funds with greater stakes would be more involved in behind-the-scenes dialogue, affecting change at informal levels so that such influence is not overt or exercised in an adversarial manner.[164] The common matters for engagement are company performance and corporate governance issues such as executive remuneration.[165]

However, it is to be noted that there is an increasing trend towards collective engagement, whether in voting or informal engagement behaviour, possibly due to the economies of scale of such collective engagement. The next section discusses.

Collective Engagement in Voting at Other Events and with Hedge Funds

As discussed in Chapter 3, collective engagement among fund managers has become an increasingly popular method of shareholder engagement and of demonstrating such engagement. This is due to the economies of scale and transaction-cost efficiencies that such collective engagement achieves. The Investment Management Association's initiative, the Investor Forum, will likely play a key part in bringing together dialogue among fund managers for collective engagement and collective voting to different extents.

Anecdotal evidence from the Investment Management Association's survey of fund manager members' practices shows that a majority of

---

163 IMA, *Adherence to the FRC's Stewardship Code 2013* (2014), above at pp. 3–5 15; *Adherence to the FRC's Stewardship Code* (2015), above continues to affirm that fund managers find informal engagement very useful.

164 Pengfei Ye, 'On Investors' Ownership and Voting Decisions: Evidence from Mutual Funds' (2008) at http://ssrn.com/abstract=1100362.

165 IMA, *Adherence to the FRC's Stewardship Code 2013* (2014), above at pp. 4–5; *Adherence to the FRC's Stewardship Code* (2015), above.

surveyed respondents act collectively in most engagement episodes.[166] Where a common governance issue arises, such as excessive executive pay or discontent with management leadership, collective engagement among other asset managers could be carried out. Collective engagement could take the form of informal initial dialogue. Proxy advisers' recommendations on such issues could also form a key point for the coalescing of such collective engagement[167] in voting or in pre-voting voices.

However, in terms of collective engagement with other types of investors such as hedge funds, whose activism is usually more pro-active and driven by an agenda of value extraction,[168] there seems to be less of such collective engagement observed in the UK and EU. This may be partly because fund management practices differ and UK European hedge funds work rather autonomously. For example, European hedge fund Cevian[169] was crucial to Old Mutual's takeover of Skandia of Sweden in 2005 after having targeted its activism at Skandia. Well-known UK based hedge funds such as Knight Vinke and The Children's Investment Fund have also carried out their activism episodes alone.[170] It is also reported that although US hedge funds are increasingly looking at value extraction through activism activities in UK and European companies, such activism is frequently successfully fended off by company boards and regarded sceptically by other institutional investors in the UK and European corporate sector.[171] For example, New York hedge fund Elliott Management's episode of activism against Alliance Trust in early

---

[166] Above.

[167] For example, the proxy advisory agency Manifest sees its role as part of networks that could help facilitate the collective engagement of their asset manager and institutional clients. See http://www.manifest.co.uk/who-we-are/stewardship-code/.

[168] Chapter 3, Iris H-Y Chiu, *The Foundations and Anatomy of Shareholder Activism* (Oxford: Hart, 2010).

[169] 'Who is Cevian?' (5 Apr 2012) at http://www.investorschronicle.co.uk/2012/04/05/comment/no-free-lunch/who-is-cevian-4LA77D7zEtfA6ypcc1gy9L/article.html; Markus Kallifatides, Sophie Nachemson-Ekwall, Sven-Erik Sjöstrand, *Corporate Governance In Modern Financial Capitalism: Old Mutual's Hostile Takeover of Skandia* (Cheltenham: Edward Elgar 2014). In sum, Cevian agitated for Old Mutual's takeover of Skandia, delivering a healthy return for Cevian upon its divestment of Skandia shares in 2005. However Old Mutual disposed of Skandia eventually in 2011.

[170] E.g. Knight Vinke's engagement with HSBC from 2007–09. See 'TCI goes where other funds fear to tread', *Financial Times* (8 Feb 2012).

[171] 'Hedge fund activism hits a brick wall in Europe', *Financial Times* (10 Nov 2013).

2015,[172] which sought to achieve the appointment of Elliott's directors onto the Alliance Board, was regarded initially with scepticism by other institutional investors in spite of Alliance's lukewarm performance. Elliott however succeeded in its activism as it fielded two directorial candidates who are acceptable to institutional investors.[173] This episode seems to indicate that there is substantial caution in the institutional funds sector in joining up with hedge funds in activism episodes.

In the US however, institutions and mutual funds are warming up to hedge funds' activism and are increasingly joining in to put pressure on companies for change. This is largely due to empirical research showing the correlation between activist successes and enhanced share price performance.[174] It is thus observed that there is increasing dialogue between these different types of investors in the US.[175] It remains to be seen whether the model of collective engagement which is increasingly becoming popular in the UK and EU will feature coalitions only among similar types of investors or will become more inclusive of American style hedge funds. The collective engagement forums, such as the Investor Forum which brings together institutional investors, are likely to foster a 'club' around like-minded institutions and reinforce collective thinking and behaviour among similar types of investors.

Securities or Derivative Litigation

Chapter 3 has earlier discussed the rarity of derivative litigation in the UK, as well as the quiet landscape for securities litigation. There seems to be little involvement of retail collective investment schemes in securities or derivative litigation against investee companies in the EU and UK.

Even in the US, where class securities or derivative litigation against investee companies is much more common, mutual funds may not be incentivised to participate in such litigation as a means of engagement. This may be explained by mutual funds' highly diversified positions and relative disinterest in leading securities litigation. Further, mutual fund investors are also not incentivised to support securities litigation as the potential returns from compensation may not outweigh the negative

[172] 'Alliance Trust investors at heart of hedge fund battle', *Financial Times* (20 March 2015).

[173] 'Alliance Trust agrees truce with Elliott', *Financial Times* (28 Apr 2015).

[174] Many of which are cited in Chapter 6, and in Chapter 3.

[175] 'Activist investors find allies in mutual, pension funds', *Reuters* (9 Apr 2013).

effect on share price and the cost of litigation.[176] Hence mutual funds are unlikely to adopt investor litigation as a key corporate governance mechanism.

Socially Responsible Retail Collective Investment Schemes

Socially responsible retail collective investment schemes could be rather attractive for investors seeking priorities beyond financial performance. However, they could also appeal to investors who believe that 'doing well' can be achieved by 'doing good'. Does the 'social responsibility' focus of the fund affect the fund's corporate governance role in investee companies?

Where socially responsible funds are focused on financial performance and adopt social responsibility branding to either appeal to investors or enhance returns, they are more or less mainstream in character, and we observe the same indifference to funds' corporate governance roles. Empirical research has produced mixed findings[177] as to whether socially responsible mutual funds perform better than conventional mutual funds. Studies have found outperformance,[178] no difference[179] and sub-par performance.[180] Sub-par performance is usually attributed to the high fees in management that wipe out minimal yield.[181] Hence, socially

---

[176] Richard A Booth, 'Class Conflict in Securities Fraud Litigation' (2011) at http://papers.ssrn.com/sol3/papers.cfm?abstract_id=1811768.

[177] Luc Renneboog, Jenke ter Horst and Chendi Zhang, 'The Price of Ethics: Evidence from Socially Responsible Mutual Funds' (*ECGI Working Paper* 2007).

[178] Auke Plantinga and Bert Scholtens, 'Socially Responsible Investing and Management Style of Mutual Funds in the Euronext Stock Markets' (2001) at http://papers.ssrn.com/sol3/papers.cfm?abstract_id=2599238; Luc Renneboog, Jenke ter Horst and Chendi Zhang, 'The Price of Ethics: Evidence from Socially Responsible Mutual Funds' (*ECGI Working Paper* 2007) for certain techniques in socially responsible investing such as activism and index following.

[179] Maria Ceu Cortez, Florinda Silva and Nelson Areal, 'Socially Responsible Investing in the Global Market: The Performance of US and European Funds' (2009) at http://ssrn.com/abstract=1342469; Luc Renneboog, Jenke ter Horst and Chendi Zhang, 'Socially Responsible Investments: Methodology, Risk Exposure and Performance' (2007) at http://ssrn.com/abstract=985267.

[180] Christopher C Geczy, Robert F Stambaugh and David Levin, 'Investing in Socially Responsible Mutual Funds' (2005) at http://ssrn.com/abstract=416380; Luc Renneboog, Jenke ter Horst and Chendi Zhang, 'The Price of Ethics: Evidence from Socially Responsible Mutual Funds' (2007), above for certain techniques such as screening.

[181] Christopher C Geczy, Robert F Stambaugh and David Levin, 'Investing in Socially Responsible Mutual Funds' (2005), above.

responsible investors and funds that are generally focused on mainstream investment performance metrics are unlikely to adopt very different investment management practices. Indeed, a piece of empirical research[182] has found that in the US, socially responsible mutual funds may start with a portfolio packed with investee companies that have demonstrated good environmental social and governance (ESG) behaviour or scored highly on ESG ratings, but this portfolio composition does not endure beyond three years. The portfolio changes are attributed to the value-driven preferences of investors, whose appetite for financial performance may demand portfolio rebalancing in order for the fund to be managed to sustain performance expectations. This may indicate that the demand for socially responsible mutual funds is still highly value-driven and the investment management practice adheres to mainstream approaches based on trading and short-termism. Hence, the 'socially responsible' mutual fund may not regard shareholder engagement as pertinent to its investment management practice.

Empirical research to date shows that 'socially responsible' funds follow rather than lead investee companies in the area of social responsibility. Socially responsible funds generally employ a screening technique for investment or follow major socially responsible indexes such as the FTSE4Good.[183] It is rare for funds to invest in socially underperforming companies to agitate for change or engage in social activism generally.[184] In the UK and EU, socially responsible shareholder activism is relatively rare, and this could be due to the potentially high cost of such activism which may then make the funds unattractive to investors. Further, the general landscape of apathy for socially responsible activism, manifested in the lack of popularity of socially responsible proxy proposals at general meetings,[185] may discourage such activism.

---

[182] Maximilian Wimmer, 'ESG-Persistence in Socially Responsible Mutual Funds' (2012) at http://ssrn.com/abstract=2138882.

[183] Luc Renneboog, Jenke ter Horst and Chendi Zhang, 'Is Ethical Money Financially Smart?' (*ECGI Working Paper* 2006).

[184] Although shareholder advocacy is discussed in the more radical funds in sustainable finance and investing, see Mark L Trevitt, 'Jupiter Ecology' in Cary Kronsinsky, Nick Robins and Steven Veiderman, *Evolutions in Sustainable Investing* (Chichester: John Wiley & Sons 2012) at pp. 11, 20; Julie Fox Gorte, 'Investors a Force for Sustainability' in Cary Kronsinsky and Nick Robins (eds), *Sustainable Investing* (Earthscan 2008) at p. 31.

[185] Peter Cziraki, Luc Renneboog and Peter Szylaygi, 'Shareholder Activism through Proxy Proposals: The European Perspective' (2009) at http://www.ccfr.org.cn/cicf2010/papers/20091216064910.pdf.

However, where socially responsible funds clearly embrace alternative values, it is observed in the US that social responsibility activism is on the rise.[186] The investor base cares about the ethos of holistic investing and investors are willing to support shareholder activism in investee companies although such activism is rather costly and could affect yield.

It is however unlikely that we will see increased social activism supported by conventional investors in view of the mixed evidence for better return and the high cost of such activism. Investors dedicated to supporting shareholder activism and investing accordingly would likely remain a minority.

Exit

Frequent portfolio turnover in retail collective investment management is commonplace, as the pressures of short-termist performance often compel fund managers to trade[187] instead of holding and engaging over a longer term. Short termist pressures are inevitable given the competition amongst myriad funds for inflows and the right of investors to redeem fairly quickly and easily.[188] Empirical research into US mutual funds has found a general propensity to exit rather than engage where investee companies may have underperformed.[189] A piece of research[190] produced in the UK in 2014 that comprehensively surveyed investment practices on the part of fund managers also reported various incentives that encourage frequent portfolio turnover.

With the duty to exercise voting rights for UCITs fund management companies and greater compulsion for institutions to show shareholder

---

[186] Especially in the US where social responsibility activism is on the rise, see Mary Hunter-McDonnell, Braydon King and Sarah Soule, 'A Dynamic Process Model of Private Politics: Activist Targeting and Corporate Receptivity to Social Challenges' (2014) at http://papers.ssrn.com/sol3/papers.cfm?abstract_id=2432208; Diane Del Guercio and Hai Tran, 'Institutional Investor Activism' in H Kent Baker, John R Nofsinger (eds), *Socially Responsible Finance and Investing* (Chichester: John Wiley & Sons 2010) at Chapter 19.

[187] Vikas Agarwal, Gerald D Gay and Leng Ling, 'Window Dressing in Mutual Funds' (2014) at http://ssrn.com/abstract=1804939.

[188] John C Bogle, 'The Challenge to Mutual Fund Stewardship' in John D Haslem (ed.), *Mutual Funds: Portfolio Structures, Analysis, Management, and Stewardship* (Chichester: John Wiley & Sons 2010) at Chapter 15.

[189] Michael C Schouten, 'Why Governance Might Work in Mutual Funds' (2011), above.

[190] BIS, *Metrics And Models Used To Assess Company And Investment Performance* (Oct 2014).

engagement under the European Shareholder Rights Directive 2017, would investment management behaviour move away from frequent portfolio turnover? Frequent portfolio turnover is not *per se* contrary to investor protection objectives and so it cannot be regarded as a clear antithesis to shareholder engagement. Demonstrating engagement does not mean that a fund cannot sell out of the investee company. Funds could determine that exit is best after attempting engagement or determine that engagement would not be efficacious or cost effective. We are of the view that no easy conclusions can be drawn from exit behaviour and exit should not *per se* be regarded as a potential breach of the duty to vote.

D. CONCLUSION

Retail collective investment schemes that own corporate equities tend to be structured as UCITs and we have discussed how their corporate governance roles may be shaped by their structuration and by regulation.

We are of the view that the investor protection objectives underlying regulation have inevitably shaped funds' short-termist priorities. Such investor protection measures include redemption rights for investors, regular reporting and transparency, and governance in relation to cost and fees. But these measures have not made the corporate governance role of funds relevant to their business model of investment management. Funds face contrary driving forces in terms of shaping their corporate governance roles. The current concern with transparency and moderation in cost and fees could make shareholder engagement relatively expensive and even more unattractive. However, compulsion by regulation and market pressures makes it difficult not to demonstrate some degree of engagement. Although the IMA is of the view that more asset managers show an integrated approach in investment management incorporating stewardship, our view is that regulatory compulsion to engage in such roles would go little further in encouraging funds to internalise such roles as an essential part of their business model. Funds are likely to regard such regulatory compulsion as part of compliance obligations, and this may produce minimalist but compliant engagement, consistent with cost pressures such as using proxy advisory agencies for voting decisions and engaging in collective engagement. Hence, such corporate governance roles are likely to be reactive and not pro-actively instigating change in investee companies. Regulatory imposition that forces funds to reckon with their corporate governance roles is unlikely to be the optimal way of encouraging the development of deep and committed corporate governance roles in a socially beneficial way, as discussed in Chapter 3. Further, we also do not think that shareholder stewardship would exert a mitigating force upon agency-type issues in the fund management enterprise such as portfolio churning and transaction costs.

Ultimately, retail investors are themselves risk averse and relatively fickle. They generally support the investor protection regimes that have been instituted for their protection even if these may put short termist pressures on funds and entail short termist investment management behaviour. Investor clamour for exchange-traded funds is a testament to an ultimately deep disconnect between the beneficiary community and the investee corporations at the other end of the investment chain.

6. Hedge funds as corporate governance actors

A. INTRODUCTION

Hedge funds have been in existence since the 1940s,[1] although their assets under management took off meteorically during the 1990s.[2] Hedge funds operate on an agenda of absolute returns, seeking to generate gains on investment whatever the conditions of the market. They maximise upsides and minimise downsides using a variety of financial strategies, including hedging, leveraging and short selling, and are not necessarily benchmarked to an index (in contrast to orthodox long-only funds).[3] One specific hedge fund strategy is the focus of this book – the carrying out of shareholder activism to stimulate absolute gains on public equity holdings. This chapter focuses on this kind of hedge fund activism as the most significant expression of hedge funds' shareholder rights and corporate governance roles. Hedge fund activism is a form of targeted engagement, usually over certain specific demands relating to corporate structure, capital management and corporate strategy. Hedge fund activism has been lauded by some as performing a much-needed role in 'governance entrepreneurship,'[4] providing leadership in an otherwise moribund landscape of passive institutional ownership of public equity. It also represents a challenge to the traditional model of US corporate

---

[1] Started in the US by Alfred Winslow Jones, see Hedge Funds Standards Board, *What is a Hedge Fund?* at www.hfsb.org.

[2] The amount of investment managed by hedge funds jumped 100 per cent from over US$100bn to over US$200bn, see The Conference Board, *Hedge Fund Activism: Findings and Recommendations for Corporations and Investors* (2008), at p. 12.

[3] Alternative Investment Market Association (AIMA), *Roadmap to Hedge Funds* (2008) at p. 101, Francois S L'Habitant, *Handbook on Hedge Funds* (Chichester: John Wiley & Sons 2006) generally.

[4] Paul Rose and Bernard Sharfman, 'Shareholder Activism as a Corrective Mechanism in Corporate Governance' (2014) *Brigham Young University Law Review* 1015.

governance, which has traditionally seen shareholders defer to the wishes of executive management except in the most egregious cases of misconduct. As a result, the methods of activist hedge funds have in recent years come to be more widely accepted as a justifiable part of the corporate landscape, at least in the US and UK. For example, in December 2013 the Chair of the SEC, Mary Jo White, opined that 'there is widespread acceptance of many of the policy changes that so-called activists seek'.[5]

This chapter reviews a selection of the empirical research relating to the legacy of hedge fund activism, and acknowledges that immediate benefits in share price performance, operating performance and corporate governance can occur in some cases. However, the business motivations for hedge fund activism are hard to reconcile with the ethos underlying the model of good equity ownership discussed in Chapter 3. We thus approach hedge fund activism with some scepticism in terms of its alignment with the 'stewardship' ethos that is likely to underpin a well-functioning and sustainably performing corporate sector for the long term.

What is Hedge Fund Activism?

In 2007, it was estimated that only about 5 per cent of hedge funds' resources, at about US$50bn, were available for shareholder activism;[6] this figure has now risen to over $112bn out of which at least 10 well-established activist hedge funds are managing over $10bn each.[7] Shareholder activism is still a minority strategy[8] for hedge funds, but hedge fund activism has in a number of ways become a unique species of shareholder engagement in investee companies due to their ownership methodologies as well as their underlying motivations.

---

[5] Mary Jo White. 'Remarks at the 10th Annual Transatlantic Corporate Governance Dialogue', Washington, D.C. 3 December 2013.

[6] According to research by JP Morgan, as reported in the OECD Steering Group, *The Implications of Alternative Investment Vehicles for Corporate Governance: A Synthesis of Research about Private Equity Firms and Activist Hedge Funds* (2007) at para 3.1, p. 22.

[7] JP Morgan, *The Activist Revolution* (2015) at https://www.jpmorgan.com/jpmpdf/1320693986586.pdf.

[8] FCA, *Hedge Fund Survey* (June 2015) finds that 40 per cent of hedge funds active in the UK are equity-owning, but only about 17 per cent are 'multi-strategy', including shareholder activism.

Cheffins and Armour argue that much of hedge fund activism is a form of 'offensive shareholder activism'.[9] Offensive shareholder activism is characterised by deliberately taking an equity stake in a publicly-traded company to carry out activism, motivated by the investment returns that may be generated by such activist campaigns in the stock market. Such activist episodes are often followed by prompt exit from the company when the targeted returns have been generated, or if the campaign has not resulted in the expected outcome.

Typically, the aim of activists is to force companies into taking corporate decisions, such as a deal or share buyback, which will impact on the share price. The hedge fund business model is much less oriented to the nurturing of longer-term improvements in the underlying business, although activist managers may often seek to claim that they are motivated by long-term considerations. As we shall see, this is a claim that should be treated with a healthy scepticism in many instances.

It may be argued that hedge fund activism targeted at US companies has developed differently from hedge fund activism observed in the UK and many European countries. In the US, there is a significant amount of activism focused on releasing 'value' from the targeted company, as well as engaging in merger-arbitrage. The former relates to hedge funds seeking to gain one-off windfalls from the company due to a favourable market response to share repurchases or higher dividend payouts, while the latter relates to opportunistically taking a stake at a point when a target company may sell part or all its business, or the fund may agitate for such a transaction to be carried out. In 2008, The Conference Board[10] reported that typical targets for hedge funds would be companies –

a) with excess cash capacity and no compelling investment or innovation plans; such companies are hence vulnerable to demands for the return of capital to shareholders through higher dividends or share buybacks (such as J-Power which was targeted by the UK Children's Investment Fund in 2008);
b) with high levels of expenditure in R&D or capital expenditure that can be significantly reduced, with short-term cash-flow benefits for shareholders;

---

[9] Brian Cheffins and John Armour, 'The Past, Present and Future of Shareholder Activism by Hedge Funds' (2012) *Journal of Corporation Law* also at http://papers.ssrn.com/sol3/papers.cfm?abstract_id=1932805.

[10] The Conference Board, *Hedge Fund Activism: Findings and Recommendations for Corporations and Investors* (2008).

c) with significant asset diversification, hence giving activists the opportunity to call for sales of non-core assets that may result in a generation of cash for shareholders in terms of redistribution; and
d) with high institutional ownership, and takeover defences or corporate governance practices that are sub-optimal and not yet challenged, allowing hedge funds to bundle up a few issues appealing to institutional investors, to garner support for its activism package (such as in the case of Knight Vinke and HSBC).

A more recent study by Activist Insight found that four major factors made a company vulnerable to the attention of activists. These included total shareholder return over a 12-month period that was much weaker than most of its peers, and return on equity that was below average for its sector. Other factors included a high level of institutional ownership and the existence on the shareholder register of hedge funds that have previously run activist campaigns.[11]

Merger arbitrage was very much favoured in the early 2000s; for example, the 2007 campaign led by Trian Fund against Cadbury Schweppes in the UK saw the spinoff of its beverage business. In March 2007, Trian amassed a close to 3 per cent stake in Cadbury Schweppes and vocally called for the split of the beverage business to take place as soon as possible to boost investment value. Two days after the announcement of Trian's close to 3 per cent stake, Cadbury Schweppes announced the decision to split its beverage business, apparently accelerating its decision due to Trian's exertion of pressure.[12] This decision resulted in investors owning two shares for one, and increased Cadbury's cash by a massive amount. However, in the aftermath of the global financial crisis 2007–09, the landscape for mergers and acquisitions became quiet and hedge fund activism in this area also slowed.[13] However, with economic recovery in the US, activist hedge funds are once again engaged in this strategy.[14]

Merger arbitrage also involves taking a stake in a company in the hope of imminent restructuring such as being merged or acquired. Dan Loeb's

---

[11] 'The challenge of predicting where activist investors will pounce', Financial Times (23 January 2017).

[12] 'Cadbury Confirms Plans to Split' *BBCNews* (15 March 2007).

[13] John Armour and Brian Cheffins, 'The Rise and Fall (?) of Shareholder Activism by Hedge Funds' (2009) at http://papers.ssrn.com/sol3/papers.cfm?abstract_id=1489336.

[14] 'Hedge Fund Investors Fall in Love with Merger Arbitrage (Again)', *Bloomberg* (27 April 2016).

Third Point, a well-established activist hedge fund, is involved in many episodes of merger arbitrage, such as forcing pharma companies Amgen and Allergan to merge. The hedge fund could also have profited immensely from Pfizer's purported takeover of Allergan which was ultimately aborted due to the intervention of the Obama administration in relation to 'tax inversion' mergers, which are driven by a desire to shift the tax domicile of the merged entity from the United States to a lower-tax jurisdiction (in this case Ireland).

In terms of 'value' release from the target company in the form of share repurchases or dividends, there are countless examples from the US. Large companies like General Motors,[15] Apple,[16] and Yahoo[17] have all been targeted by activist investors for share buybacks or dividends, and even FANUC, the Japanese robot-maker, has been targeted by Third Point to distribute a sizeable dividend.[18] These returns of capital to shareholders are not necessarily carried out due to efficiency considerations in the company's use of resources. Empirical research has cast doubt on the economic wisdom of activist-fuelled share repurchase programmes in terms of both the wisdom of the repurchase itself and the longer-term financial implications for the company.[19] Indeed, share-buybacks can also be viewed as a sign that a company has run out of ideas for the profitable deployment of capital. In some sectors – such as technology or life sciences – this would reflect negatively on management and innovation capabilities at the company.

Between 2012 and 2014, ADT, the US alarms business, bought back more than $2bn of its shares following demands from the activist fund Corvex. However, the buybacks were then followed by a profit warning that ADT blamed on its failure to match the marketing investments of its competitors. Corvex could sell back the bulk of its stake to the company before the profit warning took place, but the share price subsequently fell to a level far below that prevailing at the time of the buy-back (from

---

15 'General Motors Plans $5bn Stock Buyback, Avoids Showdown with Hedge Funds', *Reuters* (9 March 2015).

16 See 'Apple, Cisco and IBM Prove Stock Buybacks are a Sham', *MarketWatch* (1 Feb 2016); 'Apple Raises $7 Billion in Bond Market to Finance Share Buybacks', *Bloomberg* (28 Jul 2016).

17 'Yahoo to Buy Back 40 Million Shares from Third Point', *CNBC.com* (23 July 2013).

18 'Japanese Robot Maker Fanuc to Double Dividend', *Wall Street Journal* (27 April 2015).

19 Jon Handy, 'Hedge Fund Activists and Share Repurchases' (2015) 7 *Banking and Finance Review* 113.

which it has yet to recover). Overall, the episode was highly profitable for the hedge fund activist but disastrous for its corporate target and its longer-term shareholders.[20]

To achieve value extraction, hedge fund activists often concurrently ask for governance changes or involvement in management such as obtaining a Board seat. A classic case of this kind of hedge fund intervention occurred in 2013 at Sotheby's, the venerable US auction house. Two hedge funds – Third Point and Marcato – each took a 9 per cent stake in the company, and began agitating for management and strategic changes, and a return of cash to shareholders. Dan Loeb of Third Point justified his campaign as follows: 'Sotheby's is like an old master painting in desperate need of restoration.' In May 2014, Loeb and two of his associates joined the board and subsequently forced the ejection of the long-standing Chairman and CEO, William Ruprecht. A new CEO, Tad Smith, was brought into the company with a strategic mandate to increase the focus on the Asian and contemporary art markets. The roles of Chairman and CEO were also split between two individuals. The changes have not yet generated significantly improved results at the operational level, although it is still too soon to assess their longer-term impact.[21]

We will shortly appraise the contribution made by hedge fund activists' involvement in corporate governance in this manner, but we suggest that activist hedge funds' corporate governance roles are pursuant to their returns objectives in relation to the target company, and hence these roles are assumed in an 'instrumental' manner as motivated by their profit objectives.

In the UK and Europe, aggressive hedge fund activism has not been as successful. For example, Knight Vinke's activism against HSBC has simply not yielded any results. Knight Vinke Asset Management is a Monaco-based hedge fund that specialises in shareholder activism. In September 2007, Knight Vinke acquired a close to 1 per cent stake in HSBC and, supported by CalPERS, it started a campaign against HSBC urging HSBC to review –

(a) Its highly diversified business consisting of many non-majority stakes in institutions worldwide; and

[20] 'Activist hedge funds found wanting in essential tasks', *Financial Times* (29 March 2016).

[21] 'Sotheby's taps Tad Smith to be chief executive', *Financial Times* (16 March 2015).

(b) Its insufficient focus on emerging markets where it has comparative advantages.[22]

Knight Vinke took the view that the above failures in strategy had caused the group to underperform over the previous years.[23] HSBC responded by arranging a meeting between senior independent director Simon Robertson and Knight Vinke, but Knight Vinke's request for an independent review of the group's strategy was turned down.[24] On 16 October 2007, Knight Vinke wrote an open letter to all shareholders explaining its perception of HSBC's deficiencies and underperformance, and took out large advertisements in leading newspapers to draw shareholders' attention to the matter.[25] Several institutional investors did voice support for Knight Vinke's recommendations for HSBC which included the disposal of non-core minority stakes in companies around the world and a greater focus on emerging markets where HSBC's revenue growth had been the highest. Although HSBC did not concede to Knight Vinke, the activist stepped up its campaign by highlighting further corporate governance issues such as generous share plans to be awarded to executives in November 2007.[26] Furthermore, from March 2008 to May 2008, Knight Vinke called specifically for HSBC to sell its consumer credit subsidiary in the US which specialised in sub-prime lending, in order to minimise losses for the group.[27] HSBC had not met any of Knight Vinke's demands after 14 months of activism and in light of the extraordinary financial and banking crisis that started in late 2008, institutional support also waned. However, by mid 2009, HSBC has sold its US sub-prime business, and then relocated its Group Chief Executive to Hong Kong.[28] Knight Vinke did not manage to gain HSBC's acquiescence in any of its

---

22 Knight Vinke's letter to Stephen Green, 30 Nov 2007, at http://www.knightvinke.com/includes/documents/2009/2/20071130_letter.html. Other letters are available to see at http://www.knightvinke.com/media_centre/hsbc/.

23 'Knight Vinke Goes for Jugular in New HSBC Attack', *The Observer* (11 Sep 2007).

24 'HSBC Rebuffs Attempt by Activist Knight Vinke to Force Shake-Up', *The Independent* (20 Sep 2007).

25 Eric Knight, at the *Shareholder Activism in the UK Conference* (2008), however explains this as a way to evade insider dealing prohibitions.

26 'Knight Vinke Attacks HSBC over Bonuses', *The Financial Times* (23 Nov 2007).

27 'Knight Vinke Tells HSBC to Shed US Loan Arm', *The Telegraph* (13 May 2008).

28 25 September 2009, see http://www.knightvinke.com/includes/documents/2009/k/kv_web_hsbc_250909.pdf.

demands but some of HSBC's strategic changes may have been kick-started by this episode.

In fact, Katelouzou's survey of the non-US hedge fund activism landscape[29] seems to show that many activist hedge funds are only likely to achieve success with their target companies if they significantly adapt their behavioural profile to the local business environment. For example, Alliance Trust, a 120-year-old investment trust company based in the UK, had been targeted by activist hedge fund Laxey Partners in 2011 in a campaign that called for a change in business model and the departure of its Chief Executive Katherine Garrett-Cox. Garrett-Cox won the support of institutional investors and defended Alliance Trust against Laxey which exited its stake. However, continued lacklustre performance at Alliance Trust then made it vulnerable to Elliott Management, another hedge fund that approached its activism in a gentler but more persistent manner, persuading Alliance to accept its Board nomination and convincing other shareholders of the need to change. Elliott's 'soft' and more co-operative approach won accession to its requests and saw the departure of Garrett-Cox in 2015.[30] One of Europe's most celebrated activist hedge funds, Cevian Capital, is known for taking less confrontational and dialogue-based approaches to target companies, and avoids the more antagonistic approaches prevalent in US hedge fund activism.[31]

Further, hedge fund activism in the UK and Europe, although featuring interest in 'value' extraction such as through business restructuring or distributions,[32] is arguably less singularly focused on those ends. Such activism is generally framed around activist concerns for corporate governance and performance, and activists often ask to become involved in management via Board appointments. These activist investors may thus attempt to be seen to be more constructive and less instrumental which is important if they are to build a coalition of support and legitimacy amongst other investors and the wider business community.[33]

---

[29] Dionysia Katelouzou, 'Myths and Realities of Hedge Fund Activism: Some Empirical Evidence' (2013) 7 *Virginia Law and Business Review* 459.

[30] 'How Alliance Trust's long battle with activists has unfolded', *The Telegraph* (1 Oct 2015), 'Activist hedge fund Elliott scores successes in UK', *Financial Times* (19 August 2016).

[31] 'Meet Europe's best activist investor', *Fortune* (27 August 2015).

[32] Véronique Bessière, Michael Kaestner and Anne-Laurence Lafont, 'Hedge Fund Activism: Insights from a French Clinical Study' (2011) 21 *Applied Financial Economics* 1225.

[33] Dionysia Katelouzou, 'Myths and Realities of Hedge Fund Activism: Some Empirical Evidence' (2013), above.

Although hedge fund activism in the US and UK may be 'styled' differently, shareholder activism is essentially an investment strategy used by these hedge funds, and is a quintessential representation of the 'instrumental' form of shareholder engagement we discussed in Chapter 3. Partnoy and Thomas point out that hedge fund activism coupled with the use of innovative financial strategies is a form of 'financial innovation'[34] that raises challenges for corporate governance policy. We will discuss empirical researchers' appraisal of the effects and outcomes of hedge fund activism, but caution at this stage that short-term beneficial financial performance effects do not provide a complete legitimating basis for such activism. Furthermore, activist investment strategies give rise to questions of principle in relation to whether corporate governance rights should be so exploited for the purposes of short-term value extraction.

B. CRITICALLY ANALYSING THE DRIVERS OF HEDGE FUND ACTIVISM AND FACTORS THAT SHAPE SUCH ACTIVISM

Hedge fund activism is driven by its perceived potential profitability. Such strategies may be driven by a combination of factors; the firm-specific potential for 'value' increase or extraction at target companies, as well as hedge funds' own internal governance structures and incentives, and the legal and regulatory contexts that are benign to funds' strategies and do not create impeding cost to funds.

Firm Characteristics

Commentators have found that hedge fund activists target companies with 'spare capacity', either in the sense of under-performance in stock market value[35] or in operational efficiency.[36] In doing so, one could argue that hedge funds perform the collective good of improving firm value for all investors by their activist efforts, and so, even if hedge funds are

---

[34] Frank Partnoy and Randall S Thomas, 'Gap Filling, Hedge Funds, and Financial Innovation' (2006) at http://papers.ssrn.com/sol3/Papers.cfm?abstract_id=931254.

[35] John C Coffee and Darius Palia, 'The Impact of Hedge Fund Activism: Evidence and Implications' (2014) at http://ssrn.com/abstract=2496518.

[36] Zhongzhi He, Jiaping Qiu and Tingfeng Tang, 'Hedge Fund Activism and Corporate Innovation' (2014) at http://ssrn.com/abstract=2411739.

focused on their returns, the alignment of their interests with other investors results in the provision of a collective good. Further, firms with such spare capacity may also be under the leadership of a less than effective Board and management, so hedge fund intervention in the governance of the company can be regarded as a form of useful monitoring, overcoming agency problems, and delivering improved firm value at the same time. In such hedge fund activism, the likely alignment of the activist's interests with other investors is likely to produce an overall beneficial effect which is often observed in empirical research on hedge fund activism, which we discuss below in Section C.

Hedge fund activists also typically target companies with a dispersed institutional investor base, as such an investor base is less likely to oppose hedge fund activism effectively or may indeed support such activism.[37] Further, pursuant to hedge funds' interest in returns gained from corporate share repurchases, distributions or merger arbitrage, they target companies with substantial cash holdings and where opportunities loom for merger arbitrage.[38] In these situations it is less clear that corporate share repurchases or distributions, or indeed business restructuring, are unequivocally good for the business of the corporation in the longer term, but they are frequently supported by other investors as immediate returns on investment are very attractive and appeal to the short-termist pressures faced by many institutions.

Although there is support[39] for corporate share repurchases and distributions to control the agency problem, viz reducing spare cash in a corporation helps to mitigate managerial slack with respect to the spare cash and prevents managers from deploying such spare cash in a value-destroying manner, yet there are also many discussions supporting the holding of cash within a company. Cash holding could be deployed for longer-term purposes such as research and investment opportunities that arise,[40] as well as for the purposes of creating buffers for the

---

[37] John C Coffee and Darius Palia, 'The Impact of Hedge Fund Activism: Evidence and Implications' (2014), above.

[38] The Conference Board, *Hedge Fund Activism: Findings and Recommendations for Corporations and Investors* (2008).

[39] Chuan-San Wang, Norman Strong, Samuel Tung and Steve Lin, 'Share Repurchases, the Clustering Problem, and the Free Cash Flow Hypothesis' (2009) 38 *Financial Management* 487.

[40] Lee Pinkowitz, Rene M Stultz and Rohan Williamson, 'Is There a U.S. High Cash Holdings Puzzle after the Financial Crisis?' (2012) at http://papers.ssrn.com/sol3/papers.cfm?abstract_id=2064046; Nicoletta Batini and Joshua Felman, 'Why are US Firms Hoarding Money?' IMF, *Country Report* 11/202 (2011).

company to overcome future unforeseen stresses and fluctuations.[41] Blair[42] also argues that the purpose of incorporation is to be able to hold capital over the long term without being subject to return demands and expropriation from short-termist and transient shareholders. Hence, the necessary wisdom of activist demands towards capital repurchases and distributions cannot always be assumed. Moreover, there is a behavioural aspect to activist demands for capital repurchases and distributions – managers often engage in these tactics in order to signal (or indeed 'pump up') a company's strength,[43] and to improve earnings per share which can then improve managers' compensation performance metrics.[44] Hence, such activist demands merely align with short-termist institutions'[45] and managers' preferences, and can be fundamentally decoupled from the business success of the company in the long term.

Merger arbitrage is very much affected by market sentiment, and hedge fund activism in this area rises in a landscape of active deals. Stout doubts that activist hedge funds' interest in merger arbitrage necessarily

---

[41] Andrés Ramirez, 'Risk and the Multinational Corporation Revisited: The Case of Natural Disasters and Corporate Cash Holdings' (2011) at http://ssrn.com/abstract=1772969; Tom W Bates, Kathryn M Kahle and Rene M Stultz, 'Why Do U.S. Firms Hold So Much More Cash than They Used To?' (2009) 64 *Journal of Finance* 1985 on precautionary planning by managers.

[42] Margaret Blair, 'The Neglected Benefits of the Corporate Form: Entity Status and the Separation of Asset Ownership From Control' (2014) at http://ssrn.com/abstract=563307.

[43] Elisabeth Dedman, Thanamas Kungwal and Andrew W Stark, 'The Information Content of Regular Dividends and Share Buybacks for Market Value and Future Earnings in the UK' (2012) at http://ssrn.com/abstract=2188291; Leah Kaniampuram, 'Beneficiaries of Stock Buybacks: Tendering Shareholders or Non-Tendering Shareholders' (2008) at http://papers.ssrn.com/sol3/papers.cfm?abstract_id=1287123; Alice A Bonaimé and Michael A Ryngaert, 'Insider Trading and Share Repurchases: Do Insiders and Firms Trade in the Same Direction?' (2013) at http://ssrn.com/abstract=1361738; Harrison Liu and Edward P Swanson, 'Are Corporate Share Repurchases Used to Support Overvalued Equity?' (2013) at http://papers.ssrn.com/sol3/papers.cfm?abstract_id=2283764.

[44] Sheng-Syan Chen, Yanzhi Wang, 'Financial Constraints and Share Repurchases' (2012) 105 *Journal of Financial Economics* 311; Jesse M Fried, 'Share Repurchases, Equity Issuances, and the Optimal Design of Executive Pay' (2011) 89 *Texas Law Review* 1113.

[45] José-Miguel Gaspar, Massimo Massa, Pedro Matos, Rajdeep Patgiri and Zahid Rehman, 'Can Buybacks be a Product of Shorter Shareholder Horizons?' (2005) at http://papers.ssrn.com/sol3/papers.cfm?abstract_id=649482.

improves a company's future business success.[46] Business restructuring such as mergers, acquisitions or spin-offs often create huge adjustment and transaction costs after the deal is done, and shareholders have left with their premia in their pockets.[47] Further, activists agitating for mergers and acquisitions often perpetuate share price inflation in the markets due to speculation and expectations, without regard for anti-trust implications which may crystallise to block the merger at a late stage (for example, the proposed Dow Chemicals and Du Pont merger in 2014, the Halliburton acquisition of Baker Hughes in 2014 and the Office Depot and Staples proposed merger in 2015). Merger arbitrage activists would have left with their stock price returns but other investors caught holding the stock for too long suffered the consequences.[48]

Hedge fund activism has come to exert a significant impact on short-term market sentiment. Partly because of early successes in the 2000s,[49] empirical researchers have found increasingly that an announcement of a hedge fund stake *as such* causes stock price to rise in anticipation of hedge fund activism.[50] Hence, regardless of the substance of activist efforts and intended outcomes, stake acquisition alone, for activist hedge funds with a track record, already performs a self-fulfilling function to generate early returns in the stock market. However, the popularity of hedge fund activism may also cause it to decline beyond a

---

[46] Lynn Stout, 'Shareholders Unplugged' (2006) *Legal Affairs* 21.

[47] John C Coffee and Darius Palia, 'The Impact of Hedge Fund Activism: Evidence and Implications' (2014), above.

[48] Ronald Orol, 'Activists Also to Blame for Mega-Deal Failures', *Realmoney.com* (14 May 2016).

[49] Nicole M Boyson and Robert M Mooradian, 'Hedge Funds as Shareholder Activists from 1994-2005' (2007) at http://ssrn.com/abstract=948907; Alon Brav, Wei Jiang, Randall S Thomas and Frank Partnoy, 'Hedge Fund Activism, Corporate Governance and Firm Performance' (2007) at http://ssrn.com/abstract=948907.

[50] Marco Becht, Julian Franks, Jeremy Grant and Hannes Wagner, 'The Returns to Hedge Fund Activism: An International Study' (2014) at http://ssrn.com/abstract=2376271; John C Coffee and Darius Palia, 'The Impact of Hedge Fund Activism: Evidence and Implications' (2014), above; Dionysia Katelouzou, 'Myths and Realities of Hedge Fund Activism: Some Empirical Evidence' (2013), above; April Klein and Emanuel Zur, 'Entrepreneurial Shareholder Activism: Hedge Funds and Other Private Investors' (2006) at *ECGI Finance Working Paper* No. 140/2006.

certain point as the level of returns generated declines.[51] During the last few years, the performance of the hedge fund sector has deteriorated, and it has generally underperformed the overall stock market. Activist funds generated a return of just 2.8 per cent per annum over the three years to 2016, a period when the broader US stock market returned 10.8 per cent per annum. The industry's most high-profile managers also experienced difficulties. Daniel Loeb's activist portfolio lost 3 per cent in 2015; Carl Icahn lost 18 per cent; and Bill Ackman suffered a 20 per cent meltdown.[52] This highly dynamic landscape is being watched closely by investors. The largest US public pension fund, CalPERS, announced in 2014 that it was withdrawing entirely from hedge funds due to concerns about performance and fees, and this change gathered pace among other investors in 2015 and 2016.[53]

Internal Governance Factors

Hedge funds are not highly regulated in terms of their internal governance structures, as their client base, professional and sophisticated investors, are seen to be able to design optimal bargains with hedge funds.[54] The freedoms associated with their internal governance may be an important factor for hedge funds' adoption of various unconventional return strategies, including shareholder activism.

Many hedge funds are structured in such a way as to reflect the separation of funds from managers as described in Chapter 2. Hedge funds may be incorporated or formed as limited partnerships in offshore jurisdictions or jurisdictions that have tax friendly regimes for investors'

---

[51] For example, activist funds were overall down 7.7 per cent in 2015, reported in McKinsey, *Activist Investing Annual Review* (2016); Dan Bernhardt and Ed Nosal, 'Gambling for Dollars: Strategic Hedge Fund Manager Investment' (2013) at http://ssrn.com/abstract=2367475.

[52] 'Activist hedge funds found wanting in essential tasks', *Financial Times* (29 March 2016).

[53] 'Majority of big investors disappointed by hedge fund returns', *Financial Times* (15 February 2017).

[54] This has been the prevailing view in the UK, until the global financial crisis prompted major regulatory reform in the EU bringing about an extent of hedge fund regulation in the form of the Alternative Investment Managers Directive 2011. Eilis Ferran, 'The Regulation of Hedge Funds and Private Equity: A Case Study in the Development of the EU's Regulatory Response to the Financial Crisis' (February 2011) *ECGI Law Working Paper* No 176/2011 <http://ssrn.com/abstract=1762119. We will discuss further if the Directive introduces significant impact into investment regulation for funds.

income. Investors have direct relationships with the funds themselves, which offer investor protection based on contractual terms, partnership agreements or the corporate constitution where the fund is incorporated. The funds delegate investment management to fund management companies. Investors do not have a direct relationship with the hedge fund managers. The difficulties for investors in calling the fund managers to account have been highlighted in a key case in the UK.[55] In that case, the fund is a limited partnership with some of the fund managers as general partners and investors as limited partners. The general partners delegate fund management to the company they have incorporated, but fund performance was lacklustre. Investors were of the view that fund management was negligent but the general partners were unlikely to take any enforcement action against the fund management company of which they were part. Hence the investors sought judicial clarification as to their rights. The court concluded that the investors could sue the fund management company, but in so doing they would forgo their 'limited liability' privilege as limited partners and be regarded as general partners in the fund, assuming the obligations and liabilities of the fund itself. This put the investors in a rather unfavourable position and they have subsequently lobbied the UK government for changes to the law.[56] A special private fund limited partnership[57] vehicle is now created under law, to be distinguished from general limited partnerships for treatment of limited partners' legal rights. Limited partners in a private fund can now take certain actions such as making changes to the general partner composition, enforcing the partnership's entitlements and investor rights, advising on the prospects of the partnership including disposals and winding up and acting as surety for the partnership. These rights boost investor protection as they allow for monitoring of general partners' investment management, participating in decision-making such as by appointing a representative to a committee for decision-making purposes

---

[55] *Certain Limited Partners In Henderson PFI Secondary Fund II LLP (A Firm) Claimant v Henderson PFI Secondary Fund II LP (A Firm), Henderson Equity Partners Limited (sued on its own behalf and on behalf of all creditors of Henderson PFI Secondary Fund II LP from time to time) Henderson Equity Partners (GP) Limited (sued on its own behalf and on behalf of all creditors of Henderson PFI Secondary Fund II LP from time to time)* [2012] EWHC 3259.

[56] HM Treasury, Proposal on Using Legislative Reform Order to Change Partnership Legislation for Private Equity Investments (March 2016) at https://www.gov.uk/government/uploads/system/uploads/attachment_data/file/509841/PU 1924_Final.pdf. Law reform was enacted in the Legislative Reform (Private Fund Limited Partnership) Order 1907.

[57] The Legislative Reform (Private Fund Limited Partnerships) Order 2017.

and in relation to exercise of the partnership's investor rights, and acting on behalf of the limited partnership in perhaps suing the negligent asset manager. These inroads into the opacity and exclusivity of general partners' management will boost investor protection significantly.

If the hedge fund is incorporated as a company, the position of investors may be worse and less flexible than under the limited partnership discussed above. This is because the company is a separate legal entity and would only take enforcement action in its own name against a negligent fund manager. Such actions are to be decided by the Board,[58] and empirical research shows that hedge fund directors are not generally effective as monitors as they have been nominated and placed by the fund manager,[59] and many of them act as 'jumbo' directors[60] for hundreds of funds, unable to pay dedicated attention to monitoring the fund manager's activities and performance in any one fund.[61] Investors are structured as shareholders and would not have the power to sue in the company's name.[62] The governance deficits in hedge funds have been well-canvassed but these give rise to a great breadth of freedom for fund managers to pursue many strategies to achieve absolute returns, something investors may be willing to trade off for. Besides, it may be argued that other structures protect investors, such as remuneration incentives for fund managers, discussed below.

Hedge funds have been able to design bargains with investors in such a way as to facilitate their activism activities. The key structures that

---

[58] *Quinn & Axtens v Salmon* [1909] 1 Ch 311 (CA) (aff. [1909] AC 442); *Breckland Group Holdings Ltd v London & Suffolk Properties Ltd* [1989] BCLC 100, (1988).

[59] Peter Szilagyi and Chong Wei Chong, 'The Board of Directors in Hedge Fund Governance' (2012) at https://www.aeaweb.org/conference/2013/retrieve.php?pdfid=412 argue that Board governance can improve much more to secure a greater level of fund monitoring and performance for protecting investors' interests.

[60] See 'Fund 'jumbo' directors and their many seats', *Financial Times* (20 Nov 2011); 'Cayman directors sit on hundreds of boards', *Financial Times* (2 Oct 2016).

[61] This was the point of contention in litigation in the Cayman Islands over the failure of Weavering Fixed Income Macro Fund which had jumbo directors on Board, who investors alleged were not able to scrutinise fraudulent activity carried out by the fund manager. Investors won the case at first instance successfully alleging wilful neglect on the part of directors, but the Court of Appeal reversed the finding. See *Weavering Macro Fixed Income Fund Limited (In liquidation) (the "Fund") vs Stefan Peterson and Hans Ekstrom* (CA, 2015).

[62] *Shaw v Shaw* (1935) 2 KB 113.

support hedge fund activism are (a) the ability to take concentration risks, i.e. devote fund resources to only a few target companies, taking not insignificant albeit minority stakes in the target company; (b) the ability to prevent redemptions for perhaps at least a year or so, the locking up of such capital allowing activists to dedicate themselves to an activism agenda over a pronounced period of time in order to produce success;[63] and (c) the structure of remuneration that entitles fund managers to a significant percentage of performance gains. The hedge fund remuneration structure is usually based on a 2 and 20 per cent basis, which means that a fixed management charge of 2 per cent of assets under management is levied, plus a performance element of 20 per cent of gross profits earned. The performance element motivates hedge fund managers to achieve absolute returns to the funds[64] and drives hedge fund activists towards focused behaviour in achieving positive results from their activist efforts. It has also proved to be highly lucrative to the hedge fund managers themselves; for example, the 25 highest paid hedge fund managers shared around $21.5 bn in personal remuneration in 2013, although this declined to $11.6 bn in 2014 and $12.9 bn in 2015.[65] This remuneration basis underlies the 'governance entrepreneurship' of hedge fund activists.[66] The changes to limited partnership law mentioned above could have an impact on fund strategy as investors have greater monitoring and, to an extent, participation powers. However, we think that investors are unlikely to interfere until necessary and likely in an *ex post* manner. We will also shortly return to examine whether increasing levels of securities and investment fund regulation have significantly affected these internal structures that support hedge fund activism. The key

---

[63] Houman B Shadab, 'Hedge Fund Governance' (2013) 19 *Stanford Journal of Law, Business & Finance* 141; Nicole M Boyson and Robert M Mooradian, 'Corporate Governance and Hedge Fund Activism' (2011) 14 *Rev Deriv Res* 169; Douglas Cumming and Na Dai, 'A Law and Finance Analysis of Hedge Funds' (2010) 39 *Financial Management* 997; Chris Clifford, 'Value Creation or Destruction? Hedge Funds as Shareholder Activists' (2007) at http://ssrn.com/abstract=971018.

[64] Robert C Illig, 'The Promise of Hedge Fund Governance: How Incentive Compensation Can Enhance Institutional Investor Monitoring' (2008) 60 *Alabama Law Review* 41.

[65] 'Hedge fund geeks outshine activists in earnings bonanza', *Financial Times* (10 May 2016).

[66] Paul Rose and Bernard Sharfman, 'Shareholder Activism as a Corrective Mechanism in Corporate Governance' (2014), above; Bernard Sharfman, 'Activist Hedge Funds in a World of Board Independence: Creators or Destroyers of Long-Term Value?' (2015) *Columbia Business Law Review* 813.

dilemma is that regulatory interventions that address imbalances in investor protection could create cost and disincentives for hedge funds to adopt flexible strategies such as shareholder activism.

Corporate Law and Shareholder-Friendly Frameworks

A key determinant of hedge fund activism is the framework for corporate law as well as securities and investment regulation. These are to a large part affected by prevailing ideologies, policies and socio-political factors that shape the corporate sector and its relationship with society,[67] as well as regulatory interventions that could be affected by topical demands,[68] international standards[69] and competitive needs. Where law and regulatory regimes provide facilitative frameworks, these greatly reduce the cost of activists' activities and may indeed provide legitimacy for such activities. These frameworks are based on the social and policy acceptance for shareholder-primacy led ideologies in the framing of the company as an essentially private and efficient economic organisation.[70] However we will assess the impact of regulation in securities and investment regulation which address countervailing notions of public interest and frame the corporation's role and responsibilities in a different manner.

---

[67] Such as the shareholder-focused or stakeholder-focused corporate governance systems explained under the varieties of capitalism thesis, see David Solskice and Peter A Hall, *Varieties of Capitalism* (Oxford: OUP 2001); Lucian A Bebchuk and Mark J Roe, 'A Theory of Path Dependence in Corporate Ownership and Governance' in Jeffrey Gordon and Mark J Roe (eds), *Convergence and Persistence in Corporate Governance* (Cambridge: CUP 2004).

[68] See discussion of the evolution of corporate governance standards being a relatively 'local' issue to the UK in Iris H-Y Chiu, 'Learning from the UK in the Proposed Shareholders' Rights Directive 2014? European Corporate Governance Regulation from a UK Perspective' (2015) 114 *ZVglRWiss* 1.

[69] Such as the OECD Corporate Governance Standards (2015).

[70] Ronald H Coase, 'The Nature of the Firm' (1937) 4 *Economica* 386 is the foundational work for regarding the firm as a nexus of contracts to reduce transaction costs in the market; M Jensen and W Meckling, 'Theory of the Firm: Managerial Behavior, Agency Costs and Ownership Structure' (1976) 3 *Journal of Financial Economics* 305 further develops an agency-based model of the relationships subsumed under the firm which has become the foundation for shareholder primacy.

Katelouzou[71] finds that corporate law that provides greater shareholder rights and protection is perceived to be friendly for hedge fund activism. Jurisdictions that facilitate shareholder participation at general meetings, the exercise of shareholder rights such as tabling resolutions at general meetings, or access to derivative litigation find more instances of hedge fund activism in their corporate sector. There is arguably a connection between these corporate law regimes and an ideological embrace of 'shareholder primacy', where it is generally accepted that the company is an efficient organisation that produces wealth on the back of locked-up capital provided by shareholders, and therefore should be managed to maximise shareholder value.[72] Both the UK and US have corporate law regimes characterised by shareholder primacy, although the UK provides a greater extent of shareholder rights than the US, for example in relation to director removal rights, ratification rights etc.[73] However, there is a very vibrant landscape for hedge fund activism in the US despite less extensive shareholder protection rights (in Delaware and under federal securities law),[74] perhaps because derivative and securities litigation are more accessible in the US, and so form the basis for activists' more credible threats of litigation against the Board.[75] Corporate governance rules that are favourable for shareholder protection as part of securities regulation (such as the UK Corporate Governance Code for premium-listed companies) are also attractive to hedge fund activists, as these rules indicate the manoeuvrable space for hedge funds to make demands of the Board and assess the likelihood of support from other investors and the company.[76] In the UK, the impracticality and rarity of accessing derivative or securities litigation[77] as a way to exert pressure on target boards means that other avenues of shareholder protections and frameworks become more important in a hedge fund activist's consideration of the

---

[71] Dionysia Katelouzou, 'Worldwide Hedge Fund Activism: Dimensions and Legal Determinants' (2015) 17 *University of Pennsylvania Journal of Business Law* 789.

[72] Andrew Keay, 'Shareholder Primacy in Corporate Law: Can it Survive? Should it Survive?' (2009) at http://ssrn.com/abstract=1498065.

[73] See Chapter 3.

[74] Christopher Bruner, *Corporate Governance in the Common Law World* (Cambridge: CUP 2015).

[75] Above.

[76] Iris H-Y Chiu, 'A Confidence Trick: Ex Ante versus Ex Post Frameworks in Minority Investor Protection in the UK' (2014) 11 *European Company Law* 6.

[77] John Armour, Bernard Black, Brian Cheffins and Richard Nolan, 'Private Enforcement of Corporate Law: An Empirical Comparison of the UK and US' (2009) 6 *Journal of Empirical Legal Studies* 687.

total matrix of shareholder-friendliness in a jurisdiction. The UK and US systems, representatives of a strong shareholder primacy tradition, have developed in a manner which suggests that the market discipline provided by hedge fund activists is desirable, and regard this movement as a 'market for corporate influence'.[78] The general ideological and policy support for shareholder activism is relatively high in the US and UK compared to jurisdictions that do not embrace shareholder primacy to the same extent.[79]

Pro-shareholder ideology can be utilised by hedge funds as they use and manipulate ownership rights in stock to their logical extreme. We may say that activist hedge funds merely act within the boundaries of their ownership and shareholder rights and so hedge fund activism is *prima facie* legitimate. However, as Bratton[80] points out, activist hedge funds do exert real pressure and create impact upon the company, shareholders and other stakeholders, and their legal and social legitimacy should not necessarily be taken for granted. We observe gradual shifts in the development of policy and ideology regarding the legitimacy of shareholder activism and the underlying support of the shareholder primacy ideology. In the US, Bratton comments that the Delaware court's support for managerial use of defensive arsenal derived from takeover law against activist hedge funds signals development in corporate law doctrine,[81] as well as underlying policy against the self-interested and

---

[78] Brian R Cheffins and John Armour, 'The Past, The Present and Future of Shareholder Activism by Hedge Funds' (2011), above; Paul Rose, 'Shareholder Proposals in the Market for Corporate Influence' (2014) 66 *Florida Law Review* 2179; and see Chapters 5 and 8, Maria Goranova and Lori Vestegen Ryan (eds), *Shareholder Empowerment: A New Era in Corporate Governance* (Palgrave Macmillan 2015).

[79] John Buchanan et al (eds), *Hedge Fund Activism in Japan: The Limits of Shareholder Primacy* (Oxford: OUP 2012).

[80] See William W Bratton, 'Hedge Fund Activism, Poison Pills, and the Jurisprudence of Threat' (2016) at http://ssrn.com/abstract=2835610.

[81] Bratton argues that the *Third Point LLC v Ruprecht* case 2014 WL 1922029, at 9 (Del. Ch.) could be interpreted as developing a mechanism to compel hedge funds to make a case for justifying their activism, instead of riding on the presumed legitimacy of shareholder rights to make demands, see above. Corporate law ought to respond doctrinally although activist hedge funds do not seek control and merely 'play' the rules on shareholder rights. Their taking of shareholder rights to new levels of expression and the exertion of actual influence upon the company should be considered as important aspects that company law ought to respond to.

relatively short-termist objectives that activists bring to disrupt companies. The Chief Justice in Delaware, Leo Strine, has called for a rollback of shareholder powers as boards have become increasingly deluged by activist demands. In Strine's view, investors 'turn the corporate governance process into a constant "Model United Nations" where managers are repeatedly distracted by referenda on a variety of topics proposed by investors with trifling stakes'.[82] Further, questions loom in the UK over the future of shareholder primacy,[83] and whether such a basis for corporate governance and company law is sustainable and acceptable.

Hedge funds often purchase shares or use their shareholder rights in ways that are cost-effective to them, but which generate concerns for the market. They may for example purchase instruments such as contracts for differences rather than long equity positions outright as the former are less costly and could potentially obscure fund ownership information until the fund needs to make its stake public to the regulators and markets (a point we return to below).[84] They may also contemplate hedging away their economic exposure to the target company so that their economic interest is decoupled from their ownership position; this may be a matter of risk management for funds, but could nevertheless call into question their incentives as shareholders. These manipulations of share ownership rights exploit gaps in corporate law, which has not caught up with the permutations of financial instruments in commoditising shareholder rights.

One phenomenon, known as 'empty voting',[85] has played out before and has raised some concerns. In 2004, Perry Corp, an activist hedge fund in the US, bought a 10 per cent stake in King Pharmaceuticals on its anticipated merger with Mylan Laboratories. The fund hedged its stake

---

[82] 'Delaware judge calls for end to 'deluge' of activist votes'. *Financial Times* (24 March 2014).

[83] For example, the UK Parliament Committee on Business Skills and Innovation launched a public inquiry into corporate governance reforms in September 2016, see Terms of reference at http://www.parliament.uk/business/committees/committees-a-z/commons-select/business-innovation-and-skills/news-parliament-2015/corporate-governance-inquiry-launch-16-17/.

[84] Dionysia Katelouzou, 'Worldwide Hedge Fund Activism: Dimensions and Legal Determinants' (2015), above.

[85] Henry T C Hu and Bernard B S Black, 'The New Vote Buying: Empty Voting and Hidden (Morphable) Ownership' (2006) 76 *Southern California Law Review* 811; Henry T C Hu and Bernard B S Black, 'Equity and Debt Decoupling and Empty Voting II: Importance and Extensions' (2008) 156 *University of Pennsylvania Law Review* 625.

using swaps, and bought Mylan shares which were similarly hedged using swaps. Hence the fund could vote in any manner in the proposed merger as the economic interest in Mylan shares was hedged. Perry supported the merger although it ultimately fell through. Although Perry was taken to task for disclosure failures by the Securities and Exchange Commission, the issue of concern that arose in this episode was the disconcerting nature of an activist hedge fund's stake in a company and the perverse and misaligned incentives in exercising any corporate governance influence or power. Ringe highlights that such decoupling of economic from ownership interest can also be achieved by borrowing securities to vote, a practice that has been observed in Europe,[86] although voting on borrowed securities is not regarded as good practice.[87] Empty voting has not presented itself as a prevalent problem in hedge fund activism so far,[88] but the sophistication of hedge funds in using financial instruments to skirt the boundaries of corporate law raises the question of whether facilitative corporate law is indeed useful for such 'corporate governance' monitoring, or is merely an arena for opportunists to manipulate or indeed abuse shareholder rights in the corporate sector.

Securities Regulation

Securities regulation plays a highly important role in driving hedge fund activism. Jurisdictions that have strong securities markets supported by high levels of mandatory corporate transparency are attractive to hedge fund activists as access to research for opportunities is made easier.[89] Such jurisdictions are also more likely to have dispersed ownership structures that make activism more likely to be unimpeded or supported.

Securities regulation traditionally demands that companies make mandatory disclosures to the market to overcome information asymmetry

---

[86] Wolf-Georg Ringe, 'Hedge Funds and Risk Decoupling: The Empty Voting Problem in the European Union' (2013) 36 *Seattle University Law Review* 1027.

[87] International Securities Lending Association (ISLA), Voting Issues for Beneficial Owners (2015) at p. 3, see http://www.isla.co.uk/wp-content/uploads/2015/08/SecuritiesLendingVotingIssuesforBeneficalOwners.pdf, Bank of England and ISLA, Securities Lending and Corporate Governance (2000) at http://www.bankofengland.co.uk/markets/Documents/gilts/slcgjun05.pdf.

[88] Dionysia Katelouzou, 'Myths and Realities of Hedge Fund Activism: Some Empirical Evidence' (2013), above.

[89] Dionysia Katelouzou, 'Worldwide Hedge Fund Activism: Dimensions and Legal Determinants' (2015), above.

with investors,[90] but does not require so much of investors. Such disclosures are a necessary inconvenience for hedge fund activists but are complementary to the favoured regime of general corporate and market transparency. Activist hedge funds thus seek to maximise their returns within the constraints of disclosure regimes for stake acquisition. The fundamental question for policy-makers in designing stake acquisition disclosures is the balance that needs to be struck in terms of mandating high levels of market transparency and confidence, and supporting what may be perceived as beneficial hedge fund activism. Comparing the US and UK, investors are required to disclose a significant stake in a company, which is defined as 3 per cent and above of voting rights in the UK, but 5 per cent and above of a beneficial interest in shares in the US.[91] The US allows investors a 10 day period to make the disclosure upon acquisition of the threshold stake, but is proposing to reduce this to one business day.[92] The UK requires such disclosure within two trading days or four trading days for a non-European issuer.[93] The US applies mandatory disclosure to beneficial interests, while the UK extends disclosure to arrangements that could give rise to ownership interests, including using contracts for differences.[94] This distinction has proved important to some hedge fund campaigns. For example, Bill Ackman's Pershing Square hedge fund, together with Vornado Realty Trust, could acquire 27 per cent of the US retailer JC Penney in 2010 before having to disclose its stake, which drew criticism from various commentators.[95] Finally, the US requires a form of intentions-based disclosure where the acquirer informs the market of intentions towards the company, while the UK does not require such disclosure.[96]

---

[90] John C Coffee, 'Market Failure and the Economic Case for a Mandatory Disclosure System' (1984) 70 *Virginia Law Rev* 717; Merritt B Fox, 'Rethinking Disclosure Liability in the Modern Era' (1997) *Washington U Law Quarterly* 903.

[91] FCA Handbook DTR 5.1.2; section 12 of the US Securities Exchange Act 1934.

[92] 17 CFR 240.13d-1 on the timeframe for a Schedule 13D filing; see Ronald J Gilson and Jeffrey N Gordon, 'The Agency Costs of Agency Capitalism: Activist Investors and the Revaluation of Governance Rights' (2013) 113 *Columbia Law Review* 863.

[93] FCA Handbook DTR 5.8.3.

[94] From 5 per cent onwards, see http://www.fsa.gov.uk/pubs/cp/cp07_20_update.pdf, and FCA Handbook, DTR 5.3ff.

[95] 'Pershing and Vornado reveal JC Penney stake', *Financial Times* (8 October 2010).

[96] Schedule 13D, Securities Exchange Act 1934.

The different calibrations of disclosure rules for activist hedge funds may affect their incentives as the timeframe, scope and mode of disclosure all affect the potential level of profits hedge fund activists can make. As will be discussed shortly, a substantial amount of activist hedge fund returns is made upon disclosure of the fund's stake (and/or intentions) as the market adjusts its expectations towards what activists can achieve in a company. The stock price increase following announcement of a hedge fund stake is usually significant,[97] even before the market assesses the achievements and outcomes. Hence, hedge funds need to reap their market rewards in good time before public disclosure erodes their gains. Some commentators argue that preservation of hedge funds' advantage before disclosure is essential to incentivise their useful corporate governance roles,[98] but it should be recognised that their gains must be made at the expense of others in the market.

The Impact of Investment Fund Regulation

Finally, investment fund regulation may affect hedge fund activism as such regulation may facilitate, or impose barriers or cost on the undertaking of such activities.

Prior to the introduction of the European Alternative Investment Fund Managers Directive 2011 (AIFMD),[99] hedge funds were not regulated in terms of their investment management practices and their arrangements with their investors. However, that is not to say that their practices did not raise concerns. These concerns relate to two areas: one, the conduct of funds vis-à-vis their investors, and two, the corporate governance roles

---

[97] Marco Becht, Julian Franks, Jeremy Grant and Hannes Wagner, 'The Returns to Hedge Fund Activism: An International Study' (2014), above; John C Coffee and Darius Palia, 'The Impact of Hedge Fund Activism: Evidence and Implications' (2014), above; Dionysia Katelouzou, 'Myths and Realities of Hedge Fund Activism: Some Empirical Evidence' (2013), above; April Klein and Emanuel Zur, 'Entrepreneurial Shareholder Activism: Hedge Funds and Other Private Investors' (2006), above.

[98] Christian Alexander Mecklenburg-Guzmán, 'The Reason for the Regulation of Contracts for Difference and Its Impact on Hedge Fund Activism' (2013) 14 *Journal of Banking Regulation* 61; Alexandros Seretakis, 'Hedge Fund Activism Coming to Europe: Lessons from the American Experience' (2014) 8 *Brooklyn Journal of Corporate, Financial & Commercial Law* 438.

[99] European Parliament and Council Directive 2011/61/EU of 8 June 2011 on Alternative Investment Fund Managers and amending Directives 2003/41/EC and 2009/65/EC and Regulations (EC) No 1060/2009 and (EU) No 1095/2010 [2011] OJ L174/1 (AIFMD).

of activist hedge funds. In terms of policy design, regulatory intervention in these areas may create impediments and cost concerns for hedge funds, and policy-makers must consider the balance between the public interest in these areas of concern, vis-à-vis preserving the incentives of hedge funds to engage in activism where such may be regarded as economically beneficial.[100]

The UK instituted a working group led by Sir Andrew Large to flesh out best practices for hedge funds regarding their relations with investors and some aspects of their investment management practices.[101] One of the best practices identified by the Large Report was that hedge funds should not borrow securities from institutional investors to vote on company proposals and exercise shareholder rights in an opportunistic manner. This was later enshrined in the Hedge Fund Standards Board set of best practices.[102] The Hedge Fund Standards also recommend that hedge funds should make their proxy voting policies and engagement practices transparent to their investors, and should not abuse their shareholder positions in companies for the purposes of benefiting from insider dealing.[103] It has therefore been recognised early on that hedge funds' corporate governance roles can be pursuant to opportunism, but it may be seen to be too prescriptive to govern their corporate governance roles except where specific concerns such as insider dealing and voting on borrowed securities arise.

The introduction of the AIFMD has not put the best practice of 'not borrowing securities to vote' on a legislative footing. In fact, there is very little in the AIFMD that directly addresses shareholder activism as a hedge fund strategy and how it should be conducted. It may nevertheless be argued that certain provisions in the AIFMD on investor protection may affect hedge funds' incentives to engage in shareholder activism.

First, the AIFMD only affects hedge fund managers who wish to market funds in the EU. As the UK has transposed the Directive,[104] fund managers who wish to market funds in the UK, regardless of the UK's exit from the EU, would be subject to this regulatory regime as it applies

---

100 See discussion below.

101 Hedge Fund Working Group (led by Sir Andrew Large), 'Hedge Fund Standards: Final Report' (January 2008) http://www.hfsb.org/sites/10188/files/final_report.pdf.

102 Standard 28, Hedge Fund Standards at http://www.hfsb.org/wp-content/uploads/2016/04/Hedge-Fund-Standards-as-at-November-2015.pdf.

103 Standards 23–26, Hedge Fund Standards at http://www.hfsb.org/wp-content/uploads/2016/04/Hedge-Fund-Standards-as-at-November-2015.pdf.

104 FCA Handbook, FUND module.

here. However, this regulatory regime does not affect a foreign hedge fund which has not been marketed in the EU/UK, but has taken stakes in EU/UK companies.

The AIFMD introduces prudential regulation for hedge fund managers, who need to ensure that each fund meets the requisite capital adequacy requirements.[105] There is however no limit placed on concentration risk, and so activist hedge funds can carry on their practice of purchasing a minority but significant stake in a target company to commence activism. However, the AIFMD requires fund managers to establish a maximum amount of leverage[106] to be employed for each fund they manage, and such leverage levels must be disclosed.[107] Activist hedge funds could employ leverage to finance their stake to maximise returns, and so setting up maximum leverage levels up front could impede the flexibility activist hedge funds enjoy. Further, short selling restrictions may be imposed from time to time by regulators,[108] as may restrictions upon leverage,[109] as these are often seen to be connected to systemic risk. These potential interventions could limit activist hedge funds' flexibility in conducting their strategies.

Next, Article 16 of the AIFM Directive provides that AIFMs must have liquidity management systems and procedures and must regularly stress test their systems and procedures. The European Securities and Markets Authority (ESMA) specifies that AIFMs should establish a liquidity policy to manage the liquidity risks arising from different profiles of assets and to monitor the liquidity risks of each AIF under management.[110] This is for the purpose of being aligned with redemption policies so that the fund's liquidity profile and redemptions may be managed in order to prevent fund stresses and to secure a certain extent of investor protection in terms of their freedom to exit. It is queried whether these provisions interfere with activist hedge funds' freedom to arrange for lock-ups with their investors. Empirical research suggests that if investors are prevented from withdrawing their capital in, perhaps, a year, the commitment of funds to hedge fund activism will make activism more effective and likely profitable.[111] Hence the regulatory pressures for

---

[105] Art 9, AIFMD, FCA Handbook, IFPRU module.
[106] Art 15(4), AIFMD, FCA Handbook FUND 3.2.6, 3.7.7.
[107] Art 24(4), AIFMD, FCA Handbook, FUND 3.4.5.
[108] Art 25(3), AIFMD, FCA Handbook FUND 3.4.6a, 3.4.7.
[109] Art 25(3), AIFMD, FCA Handbook FUND 3.7.10.
[110] Art 16, AIFMD, FCA Handbook FUND 3.6.2, 3.6.3.
[111] Zhongzhi He, Jiaping Qiu and Tingfeng Tang, 'Hedge Fund Activism and Corporate Innovation' (2014) at http://ssrn.com/abstract=2411739.

liquidity certainty as a form of investor protection may interfere with hedge funds' strategies in designing a period of shareholder activism to coincide with capital lock-up.

Further, the remuneration policies of hedge funds, which generally follow the 2 and 20 model discussed earlier, although not subject to precise regulatory interference, are now mandated to be 'consistent with and promote sound and effective risk management'.[112] The scope of application of Article 13 extends to 'senior management, risk takers, control functions and any employee receiving total remuneration that takes them into the same remuneration bracket as senior management and risk takers, whose professional activities have a material impact on the risk profiles of [any alternative investment fund] they manage.' There are specific prescribed best practices[113] of awarding at least 50 per cent of variable remuneration in the form of securities instruments linked to the fund, with at least 40 per cent of such being deferred. The non-deferred instruments must also be subject to at least 6 months' retention. These prescriptive best practices are harmonised across the EU for banks, investment firms and mutual funds.

These remuneration principles could affect the freedom of hedge funds' business models, and in January 2014, the FCA issued a guidance[114] to allow certain funds to disapply the prescriptive rules on remuneration. Hedge funds managing less than £1bn in total assets may have the discretion to disapply the remuneration rules in whole or in part. However significant hedge funds in terms of size, employment, scope of activities and levels of risk should institute a remuneration committee to give considered justification for any disapplication of the remuneration rules above. Hedge funds have, reportedly, started to moderate their remuneration arrangements in a highly competitive market,[115] but this may not necessarily be in response to regulatory provisions.

We do not see the AIFMD and its UK transposition as significantly affecting the key incentives and freedoms that hedge funds enjoy in

---

[112] Art 13, AIFMD, FCA Handbook FUND 3.3.5A and 3.7.4. Also see AIFM Remuneration Code in SYSC 19B, FCA Handbook which set out the principles for remuneration to be consistent with risk management, appropriate control and holistic assessment of performance.

[113] Principles 5(e) and (f), AIFM Remuneration Code, SYSC 19B, FCA Handbook.

[114] FCA, *General Guidance on the AIFM Remuneration Code (SYSC 19B)* (January 2014) at https://www.fca.org.uk/publication/finalised-guidance/fg14-02.pdf.

[115] 'The 2 and 20 Hedge Fund Model is Dead', *CNBC news* (2 May 2016).

conducting shareholder activism. Nevertheless, general increase in cost of compliance, due to regulatory requirements in relation to capital adequacy, organisational soundness such as instituting an independent compliance function, the need to appoint independent valuers and depositaries and to maintain robust oversight of outsourcees[116] could all add cost to the hedge fund investment management outfit, and thus affect their strategies, including shareholder activism.

For activist hedge funds not affected by the AIFMD but who have taken stakes in target companies in the UK, there is arguably another soft law regime that may moderate their behaviour, and that is the Stewardship Code instituted by the Financial Reporting Council.[117] The Code only compels voluntary signatories to comply or explain and if the hedge fund activist concerned is not a signatory, it is technically able to ignore the Code. However, the Code may have rather persuasive 'moral' force in articulating what acceptable shareholder engagement conduct should look like, therefore exerting mitigating influence upon the relatively 'brasher' forms of American-style hedge fund activism which could escalate to visible and antagonistic levels.

Chapter 3 has discussed the Code in relative detail, and so we will only highlight the Code provisions most relevant to hedge fund activism. The Code provides a legitimating basis for shareholder engagement, making both formal (i.e. attendance at general meetings and voting) and informal engagement with the investee company (through dialogue with Board members, meetings etc) acceptable forms of shareholder engagement. However, it requires that shareholder engagement be carried out based on 'monitoring' (Principle 3 of the Code) which means at least being adequately informed. Hence, diligence and research must form the basis of meaningful and constructive engagement, implying perhaps that opportunistic forms of engagement are not encouraged. Although Principle 4 of the Code legitimates forms of escalation such as open letters or tabling of resolutions at the general meeting, such should be preceded by more collaborative forms of engagement and dialogue. Principle 5 permits collective engagement by shareholders, but envisages that such should be in response to wider corporate and economic stresses faced by the investee company. The limitation to 'defensive forms' of activism[118]

---

[116] Articles 12–21, AIFMD, FCA Handbook FUND 3 has transposed these.

[117] As of 2012, see https://www.frc.org.uk/Our-Work/Codes-Standards/Corporate-governance/UK-Stewardship-Code.aspx.

[118] E.g. see Andreas Jansson, 'No Exit!: The Logic of Defensive Shareholder Activism' (2014) 10 *Corporate Board: Roles, Duties and Composition* 16 and discussion in Chapter 3.

in Principle 5 shows that the Code does not endorse hedge funds' 'wolf-pack' behaviour,[119] where funds join forces in initiating changes at a company as a form of 'offensive activism'. Finally, Principles 6 and 7 of the Code on appropriate disclosures of voting and accountability to beneficiaries are consistent with the transparency best practices in the Hedge Funds Standards[120] that envisage hedge fund investors, being of a certain level of sophistication, monitoring and exerting governing influence upon funds' practices, including their shareholder activism behaviour. The moderating influence of the Code upon signatories' behaviour, and its role as a broader benchmark for what is 'legitimate' or 'acceptable' shareholder engagement behaviour, could go some way towards conditioning the type of shareholder activism in the UK. The international emulation[121] of the Stewardship Code may also reflect the kind of balance that other jurisdictions wish to achieve – in terms of encouraging shareholder engagement, but in a constructive manner.

The changing landscape of regulation, particularly securities and investment fund regulation, would have a significant influence upon funds' incentives to engage in activist strategies. Anabtawi and Stout[122] are already calling for such players in the 'market for corporate influence' to be subject to fiduciary duties, as such engagement behaviour is driven by commercial motivations and commoditises shareholder rights. Chiu and Katelouzou[123] argue that shareholder activists should be regulated as part of overall accountability for their investment management

[119] Discussed in David J Berger and Kenneth M Murray, 'As the Market Turns: Corporate Governance Litigation in an Age of Stockholder Activism' (2009) 5 *NYU Journal of Law & Business* 207; William W Bratton, 'Hedge Funds and Governance Targets' (2007) 95 *Georgetown Law Journal* 1375; Thomas W Briggs, 'Corporate Governance and the New Hedge Fund Activism: An Empirical Analysis' (2007) 32 *Journal of Corporation Law* 681; John C Coffee and Darius Palia, 'The Wolf at the Door: The Impact of Hedge Fund Activism on Corporate Governance' (2015) at http://ssrn.com/abstract=2656325.

[120] Standard 1, 25, 26, Hedge Funds Standards at http://www.hfsb.org/wp-content/uploads/2016/04/Hedge-Fund-Standards-as-at-November-2015.pdf.

[121] Such as adapted by the Japanese public pension fund, the Italian and Malaysian stock exchanges, the Swiss investors' association, see Iris H-Y Chiu, 'Learning from the UK in the Proposed Shareholders' Rights Directive 2014? European Corporate Governance Regulation from a UK Perspective' (2015), above.

[122] Iman Anabtawi and Lynn Stout, 'Fiduciary Duties for Activist Shareholders' (2008) 60 *Stanford Law Rev* 1255.

[123] Iris H-Y Chiu and Dionysia Katelouzou, 'Making a Case for Regulating Institutional Shareholders' Corporate Governance Roles' (2017) *Journal of Business Law*, forthcoming.

practices. It is even arguable that the European Shareholder Rights Directive 2014 is edging towards that direction.[124] Further, the Financial Stability Board's focus on asset managers and their impact on systemic risk, chiefly in terms of redemption and liquidity mismatches,[125] could affect activist strategies that work best with limited redemption rights and capital lock-ups. On a countervailing note, policy-makers may be unwilling to exert downward pressure on shareholder activism as it is a much-needed form of market discipline in the corporate sector[126] which has been replete with different types of scandals since the 1990s in the US and UK. Nevertheless, as Chapter 3 points out, there is less unequivocal praise for the desirability of institutions' shareholder roles now with empirical research showing the negative impact of their short-termist influences upon corporations. In the UK, the Financial Reporting Council has embarked on a more holistic 'business and society' rhetoric, encouraging companies to engage with stakeholder concerns, seeming to move away from an exclusive endorsement of the shareholder primacy ideology that so fundamentally supports shareholder activism.[127]

C. EVALUATING THE ACHIEVEMENTS OF HEDGE FUND ACTIVISM

One of the strongest arguments that support the legitimacy of hedge fund activism (and possibly less regulatory intervention to disincentivise it) is the beneficial impact upon corporate performance. Much of the empirical research agrees that the initiation and outcome of many hedge fund activist episodes produce significant stock price increases and, therefore, market returns.[128] Hence, there is an overall beneficial effect for *all*

---

[124] Iris H-Y Chiu, 'European Shareholder Rights Directive Proposals: A Critical Analysis in Mapping with the UK Stewardship Code?' (2016) 17 *ERA Forum* 31, DOI: 10.1007/s12027-016-0415-6.

[125] FSB, *Proposed Policy Recommendations to Address Structural Vulnerabilities from Asset Management Activities* (22 June 2016).

[126] Discussed in Chapter 3 in relation to UK policy makers' perspectives since the Cadbury Committee was instituted in 1991 to look into corporate scandals.

[127] FRC, 'Aligning the Interests of Business and Society' (5 Oct 2016) at https://www.frc.org.uk/News-and-Events/FRC-Press/Press/2016/October/Aligning-the-interests-of-business-and-society.aspx.

[128] Marco Becht, Julian Franks, Jeremy Grant and Hannes Wagner, 'The Returns to Hedge Fund Activism: An International Study' (2014), above; Nicole

shareholders due to the improved market valuation of the target company. However, what may be more important is longer-term corporate performance in terms of stock market valuation as well as operational efficiency. We are keen to know if the improved stock market valuation is sustainable or whether it is merely a bubble responding to anticipated hedge fund activism. More importantly, has the company's productivity, competitiveness and wealth creating capacity improved in terms of its operational efficiency? Many empirical studies show that longer term enhanced stock market valuation holds,[129] and indeed that operational efficiency has improved.[130] Such results may benefit not only shareholders but stakeholders as the company may benefit from improved efficiencies, productivity and prospects over the longer term. Some empirical research indicates that hedge fund activism reduces the agency problem, for example excessive managerial slack[131] and opaque financial reporting,[132] and these positive governance effects could have fed into better management and improved operational efficiency. However, it may be argued that many of the empirical studies on long-term performance of the company after hedge fund activism do not extend beyond five years,[133] and there is thus insufficient conclusive evidence to support the

M. Boyson and Robert M. Mooradian, 'Corporate Governance and Hedge Fund Activism' (2011) 14 *Rev Deriv Res* 169.

[129] Lucian Bebchuk, Alon Brav and Wei Jiang, 'The Long-Term Effects of Hedge Fund Activism' (2015) 115 *Columbia Law Review* 2085.

[130] Above and Alon Brav, Wei Jiang and Hyunseob Kim, 'The Real Effects of Hedge Fund Activism: Productivity, Asset Allocation, and Labor Outcomes' (2015) at http://ssrn.com/abstract=1551953; Zhongzhi He, Jiaping Qiu and Tingfeng Tang, 'Hedge Fund Activism and Corporate Innovation' (2014), above.

[131] Shane Goodwin, 'Corporate Governance and Hedge Fund Activism' (Aug 2015) at http://ssrn.com/abstract=2646293; Laura Kabler, 'Money in the Game: Executing a Governance-Based Hedge Fund Strategy' (2006) 12 *Stanford Journal of Law, Business & Finance* 121; Heqing Zhu, 'The Preventive Effect of Hedge Fund Activism' (2013) at http://ssrn.com/abstract=2369533.

[132] C S Agnes Cheng, Henry He Huang and Yinghua Li, 'Hedge Fund Intervention and Accounting Conservatism' (2013) at http://ssrn.com/abstract=2519286; Jing Chen and Michael J Jung, 'Activist Hedge Funds and Firm Disclosure' (2015) Review of Financial Economics 52 at http://ssrn.com/abstract=2666783.

[133] Marco Becht, Julian Franks, Jeremy Grant and Hannes Wagner, 'The Returns to Hedge Fund Activism: An International Study' (2014), above; Nicole M. Boyson and Robert M. Mooradian, 'Corporate Governance and Hedge Fund Activism' (2011), above; Lucian Bebchuk, Alon Brav and Wei Jiang, 'The Long-Term Effects of Hedge Fund Activism' (2015), above.

thesis that beneficial effects of hedge fund activism are contributing to long-term value creation.

It may also be questioned whether hedge fund activism comes at a price, such as cost-cutting, reduction of employment and research and development, and the taking of undue risks such as leverage by the target company. In this area, there are mixed findings[134] as commentators warn that improved market valuations are often superficially justified and do not reflect some of the externalities that follow from hedge fund activism, such as the erosion of long-term potential that affects stakeholders.

Four other concerns from the perspective of principle should be raised against over-emphasising the outcome-legitimacy of hedge fund activism.

One, even if hedge fund activism creates abnormal returns for all shareholders, the distribution of wealth is skewed in favour of the activist funds. Where that skewed distribution does not feature, it is unlikely that there will be sufficient incentive to motivate hedge fund activism.[135] Should such a distributive outcome be accepted on the basis that major returns go to the most entrepreneurial 'governance' actors, and that the 'trickle-down' effects to other shareholders who free-ride on those efforts is justifiably less? This is related also to the second question of whether hedge fund activism undermines shareholder democracy which is provided in the general meeting framework in company law. Company law provides a forum for shareholders to make decisions collectively, i.e. in the general meeting.[136] If certain shareholders could gain disproportionate influence over the Board by informal engagement and persistent focused activism, would this not contradict the general meeting framework and unfairly undermine other shareholders' voices in their corporate governance roles?[137] Indeed this concern was addressed by Pacces[138]

---

[134] John C Coffee and Darius Palia, 'The Impact of Hedge Fund Activism: Evidence and Implications' (2014), above; Marcel Kahan and Edward B Rock, 'Hedge Funds in Corporate Governance and Corporate Control' (2007) 155 *University of Pennsylvania Law Review* 1021; Frank Partnoy, 'U.S. Hedge Fund Activism' (2015) at http://ssrn.com/abstract=2585290; Nick W A Stokman, 'Influences of Hedge Fund Activism on the Medium Term Target Value' (2007) at http://ssrn.com/abstract=1019968 on the short-lived 'pop' in share price.

[135] April Klein and Emanuel Zur, 'Entrepreneurial Shareholder Activism: Hedge Funds and Other Private Investors' (2006), above.

[136] Part 13, Chapter 3 of the Companies Act 2006.

[137] Chapter 4, Iris H-Y Chiu, *The Foundations and Anatomy of Shareholder Activism* (Oxford: Hart 2010).

[138] Alessio M Pacces, 'Exit, Voice and Loyalty from the Perspective of Hedge Funds Activism in Corporate Governance' (2016) 9 *Erasmus Law Review* 199.

who argues that different governance preferences may indeed lead to conflict between shareholders as activism heightens and sharpens such conflict, and proposes that companies should be able to issue different classes of voting rights so that only those 'loyal' to the company will prevail in terms of voice. Undesirable activism that is not preferred by other shareholders may thus be kept under control in this model, but equally constructive activism could be rewarded. This is an interesting proposal but the departure from the one-share-one-vote principle cherished by minority shareholders may be resisted by policy-makers and the investment industry. Nevertheless, what is highlighted is that the informal influence exerted in hedge fund activism lies in a grey area between shareholder rights *in the books of the law* and the implementation of those rights, i.e. *law in action.* Depending on the dynamics of the general meeting body, the persistence of a hedge fund activist's voice could become disproportionately distorting in terms of the general meeting – management dialogue. It is clear from the experience of many activist campaigns that, in situations of contested corporate governance, activists tend to speak with the loudest voice and are skilled in dominating the public narrative.[139] The legal framework which is focused upon ensuring shareholders' fair and informed participation in the general meeting[140] does not go further in controlling for exuberant or overbearing behaviour.

Next, it is queried whether hedge fund activists should be treated like other shareholders as their business models dictate that there is certainty of their exit, in the short or medium term. Hedge fund activists are certain to exit upon the successful conclusion or otherwise of the activism episode. This is because the negotiated capital lock-up with investors usually comes to an end in a year or two, coinciding with the end of a successful activism episode where hedge funds could cash out their gains. Alternatively, hedge fund activists exit very quickly if the activism is unlikely to yield results to move on to another target, so that it can take full advantage of the capital lock-up period for activism to yield results. One of us has earlier argued[141] that as hedge fund activists are certain to exit, their position as shareholders is rather different from other shareholders or institutions whose long holdings are generally open-ended whether they choose to sell out. Hence, there may be a case for curtailing such necessarily transient activists' shareholder powers in

[139] 'Hedge funds should not be the only activist investors', John Gapper, *Financial Times* (26 February 2014).

[140] See discussion in Chapter 3.

[141] Chapter 4, Iris H-Y Chiu, *Foundations and Anatomy of Shareholder Activism* (2010), above.

the interests of the company overall. Blair[142] argues that the corporate form is designed to preserve capital for long term use so the ownership of corporate equity should be framed in the ethos of long-termism in spirit even if a liquid secondary market allows a shareholder to transfer shares. The hedge fund activist is arguably only buying into a company based on an ultimate transfer, at a premium. It is queried if such transient involvement which nevertheless maximises the use of shareholder rights, should be regarded as supportable and legitimate within the principles of company law.[143] Bratton[144] has rightly pointed out that activists have been minority shareholders playing within the rules but pushing the rules to their extreme. Perhaps it is time for corporate law doctrines to respond robustly with reform to such changes equity ownership. Hedge fund activism, as dictated by their business model and needs, also seems not to be imminently reflected in the stewardship ethos of good corporate equity ownership, as such activists are *prima facie* not incentivised to take a long-term view of either the company's well-being or their investment holdings.

Finally, Stout is of the view that support for shareholder activism ultimately reflects shareholder primacy ideologies and would inevitably marginalise stakeholder concerns.[145] There are mixed findings on whether hedge fund activism has caused companies to improve shareholder value at the expense of stakeholders' interests,[146] where the interests are not so aligned, stakeholder interests are bound to be sacrificed.[147]

We are of the view that hedge fund activism is a relatively extreme form of instrumental assumption of corporate governance rights and roles. Its self-interested pursuit of short-term shareholder value maximisation cannot be readily assumed to align with social good, and its

---

142 Margaret Blair, 'The Neglected Benefits of the Corporate Form: Entity Status and the Separation of Asset Ownership From Control' (2014), above.

143 Ronald J Gilson and Jeffrey N Gordon, 'Agency Capitalism: Further Implications of Equity Intermediation' (2014) at http://ssrn.com/abstract=2359690.

144 William W Bratton, 'Hedge Fund Activism, Poison Pills, and the Jurisprudence of Threat' (2016), above.

145 Lynn A Stout, 'The Toxic Side Effects of Shareholder Primacy' (2013) 16 *University of Pennsylvania Law Review* 2003.

146 Iris H-Y Chiu, 'European Shareholder Rights Directive Proposals: A Critical Analysis in Mapping with the UK Stewardship Code?' (2016) 17 *ERA Forum* 31, DOI: 10.1007/s12027-016-0415-6.

147 Lynn A Stout, 'The Toxic Side Effects of Shareholder Primacy' (2013), above.

outcome legitimacy ought to be subject to much longer periods of testing in terms of impact on corporate viability and stakeholder interests. Further, it is doubtful that supporting such forms of unabashed shareholder primacy is welfare-enhancing or desirable in the principles of corporate law and the wider context of corporations, economy and society. It also remains to be seen how hedge fund activists are going to develop and mature as an industry.

Next, we turn to a survey of the typologies of corporate governance behaviour that hedge fund activists have engaged in.

D. TYPOLOGIES OF HEDGE FUND ACTIVISTS' ASSUMPTION OF CORPORATE GOVERNANCE ROLES IN THE UK

This section discusses hedge fund activists' corporate governance behaviour. Hedge fund activists perceive corporate governance as an instrument to be wielded for investment returns; hence their corporate governance activities are markedly different from other institutions. These roles are intended to be intensive and focused towards the funds' objectives, although many commentators are prepared to regard their actions as legitimate if performance and governance benefits are concurrently gained by the target company. We however advocate caution in terms of the long-term sustainability of any perceived beneficial effects and urge that holistic consideration be given to the company's position vis-à-vis their stakeholders.

General Meetings

Hedge fund activists are highly visible at the general meeting level of their target companies. Instead of assuming 'defensive' stances like other institutions in voting, and relying on proxy advisers' voting advice, hedge fund activists have, based on their research, already formed an agenda of what they are seeking to achieve in the target company. Hence, they frequently utilise in full their shareholder rights pursuant to the general meeting to make their demands known. These rights include the right to ask questions,[148] the right to table resolutions,[149] including in the UK to make nominations for directorial positions, and even the right to call a

[148] Section 319A, Companies Act 2006.

[149] Sections 338-340B, Companies Act 2006.

general meeting if they own a stake exceeding 5 per cent of voting interests in the target company.[150]

Activist hedge funds formulate precise objectives for the company, and seek to make the target company acquiesce to their demands. In the UK, home-grown, European and US hedge funds all operate in the publicly listed market, issuing similar demands in terms of business restructuring, governance changes and return of capital. Whether they succeed is often dependent on support from other shareholders, chiefly other institutions. Other institutions may not always be eager to jump on the bandwagon, unless a clear case has been made, such as the underperformance of the target company (e.g. at Rolls Royce Plc or Alliance Trust Plc) and governance issues (such as at Alliance Trust Plc).

In the case of Rolls Royce Plc,[151] the company had been under-performing for several years, and in 2015, US hedge fund ValueAct took a 10.8 per cent stake in the company, agitating for changes such as business restructuring and disposals, and operational efficiency reviews for cost savings. In 2016 when the company announced a further dividend cut, institutions were prepared to support ValueAct's proposal to put one of its nominee directors on the Rolls Royce Board. The chief operating officer of ValueAct was appointed as a Rolls Royce director. However, this was only a partial victory as Rolls Royce agreed to the appointment subject to a formal arrangement with ValueAct that prevented ValueAct from unduly disrupting its business. ValueAct agreed to a two-year standstill in its activist demands and would refrain from demanding business restructuring at Rolls Royce or tabling any proposals to that effect or openly criticising the company. ValueAct's nominee would not be regarded as independent and cannot sit on the nomination, audit or remuneration committees. It would also vote in favour of management during that time. This settlement has secured crucial time for Rolls Royce executives to execute their business strategy plans to convince other shareholders of their continued viability. This episode goes to show that there is still a degree of scepticism in the UK as to hedge fund activists' motivation and the impact upon other shareholders.[152] The case also highlighted that it could not be taken for granted that institutional investors would automatically support hedge

---

[150] Section 303, Companies Act 2006.

[151] For example, see 'Rolls-Royce Names Activist Shareholder ValueAct to Board, Vows No Change to Strategy', *Wall Street Journal* (2 March 2016).

[152] Failed episodes of activism include Sandell Asset Management's failure to get FirstGroup Plc to spin off its US business in 2014 for example.

funds whenever change is agitated even if the breadth of company law rights for shareholders in the UK is very wide.

Elliott Management's activism against Alliance Trust Plc also took a significant amount of time to achieve results. Alliance Trust Plc had been an underperforming investment trust company for some time and by April 2015, Elliott had taken a 12.25 per cent stake and started to agitate for change. Elliott demanded that Alliance Trust's business model had to be restructured and that governance changes be introduced, such as the reduction of executive director pay and the outsourcing of fund management activities. The Board of Alliance Trust undertook extensive dialogue with institutions and finally agreed a truce with Elliott such that two of their nominee directors would be appointed to the Board but Katherine Garrett-Cox was to stay on as Chief Executive.[153] Elliott also agreed to a year long standstill in terms of exerting further pressure on Alliance Trust and Garrett-Cox. In fact, share buybacks took place to boost shareholder returns. However, by February 2016, Alliance Trust's results were still disappointing, and it finally agreed to implement the business restructuring plans proposed earlier, cutting costs and relinquishing Garrett-Cox as Chief Executive.[154]

Although hedge fund activism gains most visibility at the general meeting, achieving success at the general meeting is often an expensive process in terms of time and effort. Despite the extensive range of shareholder rights in UK company law, the scepticism of the wider business community remains a valuable check upon hedge fund activism, forcing such activists to demonstrate a clear case before support is gained. Further, even if hedge fund activists 'succeed', the consequence is often a costly dedication of further engagement time and effort in terms of appointment of a fund manager or two to a Board. This provides an opportunity for both the Board and other shareholders to determine if hedge fund nominated appointees could make a real difference. On balance, despite the potential of significant value gains if markets reward hedge fund activists' engagement efforts to improve an investee company's performance, the cost for hedge fund activists may be substantial. This cost-benefit matrix may provide the necessary filtering mechanism for all but the strongest cases of hedge fund activism to be initiated in the UK.

---

[153] 'Alliance Trust Strikes Deal with Elliott Advisers', *The Guardian* (28 Apr 2015).

[154] 'Alliance Trust's Garrett-Cox to leave in March' *The Telegraph* (15 Feb 2016).

Individual Informal Dialogue and Escalation Activities

The Stewardship Code's recommended best practice of monitoring, dialogue and escalation by engaged shareholders is often exemplified by hedge fund activists, although their persistence and insistence is not always well-regarded.

Activist hedge funds generally target their communications and escalation ahead of general meetings as they push for changes to be implemented at the meetings. An example of this point is the case of Sandell Asset Management's activism against FirstGroup Plc in late 2013.[155] Sandell, a US hedge fund, took a 3 per cent stake in Firstgroup, asking for its US business to be spun off to improve corporate performance, and for governance changes such as the reduction of excessively high executive pay. Sandell sent open letters to the company ahead of the general meeting and galvanised other investors in its cause. However, only 25 per cent of other shareholders supported Sandell's proposal to vote down the remuneration report at the general meeting. The FirstGroup Chairman insisted on not breaking up the business and did not see any value in adopting the strategy change demanded by the hedge fund. Ultimately institutions supported the Board's strategy and by November 2014, Sandell started to reduce its stake in FirstGroup to below 3 per cent.

Unlike the Code's vision of monitoring, dialogue and escalation, which is a continuous and open-ended form of engagement between an investor and a company over the long term, hedge fund activists' performance of those activities is generally targeted, intensive and likely to terminate rapidly if there is no sign of success. It has been reported that hedge fund activist The Children's Investment Fund took a stake of over 5 per cent at Royal Mail after its partial privatisation in October 2013, but after a series of reported informal dialogues, the Fund cut its stake by January 2014, with no apparent changes in Royal Mail's strategy.[156] The retreat episodes involving hedge fund activists raise queries as to whether the activists were acting for the long-term good of the company. It is observed that these retreats are usually quick, and take place within a year.

---

155 'FirstGroup Investor Sandell Pushes for Business Split', *The Telegraph* (10 Dec 2013).

156 'Hedge Fund TCI is Royal Mail's Biggest Shareholder', *The Telegraph* (22 Oct 2013); 'Hedge Fund TCI Cuts Stake in Royal Mail', *The Telegraph* (20 Jan 2014).

Collective Engagement

Hedge funds tactically engage in collective activism, or what is called 'wolf-pack' behaviour. An empirical study found that over 20 per cent of activism instances over a 10-year period involved 'wolf packs',[157] with hedge funds coordinating with similarly-minded players to boost the collective voice represented by their total voting rights. This is important in the US for proxy solicitation to put forward Board nominees and in the UK for exercising shareholder rights that require a minimum threshold, such as calling a general meeting. Wolf packs have been associated with higher initial stock market returns and with greater success in compelling the target company to acquiesce to the activist hedge funds' demands.[158]

The collective activism by Atticus Capital and the Children's Investment Fund against Deutsche Börse is an example of wolf pack behaviour that has been maintained over several years against the German stock exchange, with mixed results. In late 2004, The Children's Investment Fund took a 5 per cent stake at Deutsche Börse and openly made known its objection to a proposed acquisition of the London Stock Exchange, claiming that the price offered was too high. Deutsche Börse purported to ignore the fund's demands. However, Atticus Capital then threw its support behind blocking the bid, and so did institutions Fidelity and Merrill Lynch. The bid was ultimately aborted and both the Chairman and Chief Executive left the company.[159] In 2008, Atticus and the Children's Investment Fund again pressured Deutsche Börse to make business restructuring changes by selling off Clearstream and to improve governance by replacing directors on the supervisory board.[160] The funds amassed a 19 per cent stake at the height of their combined efforts, but Deutsche Börse refused to accede to the demands and the Board appealed to investors to trust in their strategy. The funds' struggle with Deutsche Börse took almost a year but institutional investors were sceptical and did not step up support. Ultimately both funds sold off their stakes in Deutsche Börse[161] and in fact, Atticus shut down its flagship US fund in

---

157 Marco Becht, Julian Franks, Jeremy Grant and Hannes Wagner, 'The Returns to Hedge Fund Activism: An International Study' (2014), above.

158 Above.

159 'Seifert falls on sword after failed bid for LSE', *The Telegraph* (10 May 2005).

160 'Hedge funds team up to pressure Deutsche Börse', www.marketwatch.com (2 Sep 2008).

161 'Atticus Ends Battle with Deutsche Börse', *New York Times* (1 Apr 2009); 'D Börse Struggle Ends as TCI Bows Out', *Financial Times* (2 Apr 2009).

2009 after suffering massive losses from concentrated positions in the market downturn during the global financial crisis.

It may be argued that in the UK and Europe, collective activism by hedge fund activists may not go very far unless there is significant institutional support too. Institutional investors, though reactive in nature, need to be convinced of the business case of such activism for their interests. Further the long-termism ethos in the Stewardship Code provides a benchmark with which to assess institutional shareholder behaviour and they may be cautious as to joining with hedge fund activists in case they appear to be supporting short-termist measures or measures that may adversely affect stakeholders. In a way, institutions in the UK and Europe, perhaps than in the US, act as quasi-gatekeepers for the legitimacy of hedge fund activism. Thus, 'wolf-pack' hedge fund activism is less reported in the UK and EU, and as the episode surrounding Deutsche Börse had shown, less easily susceptible to success.

Securities or Derivative Litigation

The use of derivative litigation in the UK is exceedingly rare as procedural barriers are rather high, requiring minority shareholders to prove a *prima facie* case for directors' breach of duties in preliminary proceedings.[162] Armour et al have found in an empirical study that derivative litigation against large public companies is not a realistic prospect for shareholder redress.[163] Further, the prospect of securities litigation is also remote due to the need to prove relatively difficult elements in allegations of breaches of continuing disclosure to the securities markets.[164]

There is an example of an activist hedge fund using the threat of litigation to exert pressure on a UK Plc that ended in the fund's spectacular failure in the activism episode. British Energy was an electricity provider in the UK, privatised in 1996. From 2002, its share

---

[162] Section 263, UK Companies Act 2006. See *Prudential Assurance Co Ltd v Newman Industries Ltd* (No 2) [1982] Ch 204; critical reflections by Arad Reisberg, 'Derivative Claims under the Companies Act 2006: Much Ado About Nothing?' in J Armour and J Payne (eds), *Rationality in Company Law: Essays in Honour of DD Prentice* (Oxford: Hart Publishing, 2009) at p. 17.

[163] John Armour, Bernard Black, Brian Cheffins and Richard Nolan, 'Private Enforcement of Corporate Law: An Empirical Comparison of the UK and US' (2009), above.

[164] Schedule 10A, Financial Services and Markets Act 2000, which requires a mis-disclosure or omission to be dishonest, see discussion in Chapter 3.

price had been performing weakly due to falling electricity prices. In mid 2004, British Energy had to propose a restructuring of the company's capital to stave off administration. It proposed accepting a government bailout which would allow the government to take a majority stake in the company, and to convert bondholders' rights into equity. This would result in existing shareholders being diluted to about 2.5 per cent of the equity holding in the company.[165] One of its then shareholders was activist hedge fund Polygon Master Global Opportunities Fund. Polygon, which held 5.6 per cent of British Energy, opposed the restructuring as it was a raw deal for shareholders. It threatened to take a derivative action against the management of British Energy claiming breaches of fiduciary duties, and requisitioned an extraordinary general meeting in order to obtain a resolution opposing the restructuring.[166] In retaliation, British Energy decided to delist from the London Stock Exchange a day before the extraordinary general meeting and such delisting was permitted to be carried out without the need for shareholder approval.[167] British Energy and its creditors also launched a series of legal actions against Polygon. Hence, three months after the activist campaign started, Polygon backed down and agreed to vote against its own proposals at the extraordinary general meeting. British Energy and its creditors then withdrew the legal action against Polygon. Polygon subsequently unwound its position in British Energy and exited the company.[168] Shortly after the approval of the restructuring, British Energy relisted its shares on the London Stock Exchange in January 2005.

The Polygon episode not only demonstrates that litigation is an ineffective tool in engaging target companies in the UK but also that it is widely seen as *unwelcome* and *unconstructive*, and likely to backfire upon the activist campaign. The wide breadth of shareholder rights and the UK's generally friendly attitude towards shareholder engagement tolerates constructive engagement and long-termism; but it is not generally supportive of blatantly self-interested exercises of legalistic shareholder rights or disruptive or wealth transferring actions such as individualistic litigation. Thus, unlike in the US, hedge fund activism in

---

[165] 'Rebel Investors Attack British Energy Rescue', *The Independent* (26 July 2004).

[166] 'Polygon Calls in Lawyers to Halt British Energy Restructuring', *The Independent* (1 Aug 2004).

[167] 'British Energy Pre-empts Polygon by Delisting Shares', *The Independent* (24 Sep 2004).

[168] Polygon Backs Down over British Energy', *The Independent* (1 Oct 2004).

the UK needs to be anchored within the fabric of the body of the general meeting and other institutions' support to gain traction.

Exit

Hedge fund activists typically exit the target company whether their campaign has been successful or not. If the campaign appears unlikely to be successful and further resources dedicated to this effort may be futile or costly, hedge funds exit quickly, such as the sale of Sandell's stake in FirstGroup or The Children's Investment Fund's stake in Deutsche Börse as discussed above. Such sales may not always be in hedge funds' advantage as large stakes are not easy to unwind; where a campaign has not been progressing well, losses may be incurred upon sale. However, the hedge fund activist would have to weigh up the cost/benefit of continuing to keep such a stake in view of likely poor reports of its performance to investors and investors' desire to redeem capital. As discussed above, some activist hedge funds may impose capital lock-ups for a year or so, so hedge funds are under some pressure to generate success within a relatively short period of time in their activism. They would not be able to hold shares for too long as investor redemption rights and indeed redemptions could materialise following the lack of activism success.

Even if a campaign has been successful or partially so, hedge funds typically exit a target company within five years. A successful campaign may have improved market valuation for the investee company, but such improved valuation could easily taper off after the episode of activism 'to unlock value' has passed. Activist hedge funds would need to seek out new targets to generate their desired high levels of absolute returns. This is because they face competitive pressures to retain the confidence of investors and to maintain a low level of investor redemptions, as well as liquidity pressures associated with redemptions; as a result, they need to be unwinding concentrated stakes at regular intervals. Some commentators regard hedge fund activists' involvement in a company over a couple or few years as sufficiently 'long-termist'[169] but it should be queried whether that perspective is sound.

---

[169] Such as Lucian Bebchuk, Alon Brav and Wei Jiang, 'The Long-Term Effects of Hedge Fund Activism' (2015), above 115 *Columbia Law Review* 2085. For sceptics see John C Coffee and Darius Palia, 'The Wolf at the Door: The Impact of Hedge Fund Activism on Corporate Governance' (2015) at http://ssrn.com/abstract=2656325.

E. CONCLUSION

Hedge fund activism is fundamentally instrumental towards the funds' performance needs, and its strategies as well as duration of activism are shaped in the light of these needs. Performance and governance benefits have sometimes ensued for certain investee companies that have succumbed to activist pressure, thus eliciting praise from some quarters for the effective market discipline that hedge funds have introduced to the sleepy landscape of corporate governance. The positive externalities generated by hedge funds are not universally accepted as other research has shown, and we remain sceptical about viewing such activism as a manifestation of 'stewardship' in the context of good corporate equity ownership we discussed in Chapter 3. The Stewardship Code's endorsement of engagement escalation under Principle 4, where the investee company has not responded to informal engagement, seems approving of strategies that hedge fund activists use, such as demanding to meet members of the Board or even going public with grievances. However, the 'wolf pack' type of collective activism by hedge funds seen largely in the US would not likely align with the sort of collective engagement envisaged in the Stewardship Code.[170] We acknowledge that hedge fund activism has provided in some cases the catalyst for change. However, as a model of corporate governance 'entrepreneurship' we think the beneficial tenets of stewardship upheld in the UK and Europe have provided checks upon the more instrumental aspects of their behaviour, and hedge fund activism has necessarily become more nuanced to respect the engagement norms that prevail in local markets. This could be crucial to the avoidance of externalities to stakeholders and undesirable disruption for companies. However, there should be no easy assumption of the public good consequences of such instrumental activity that is geared towards private profit-making in the short term. In this respect, the importance of the Stewardship Code in normalising what is acceptable behaviour or otherwise cannot be overstated.

[170] Principle 5.

7. Private equity funds and their corporate governance actors

A. INTRODUCTION

A private equity fund invests in equity securities which are not traded on public equity markets. The idea is to buy equity stakes in private businesses, actively managing those businesses, and then realise the value created by selling or floating the business on the stockmarket. The 2015 Preqin Global Private Equity and Venture Capital Report estimates total assets under management in global private equity funds to be around USD$3.8 trillion.[1] Assets under private equity continue to swell for the best performing funds as institutional and wealthy investors are pressured to seek return opportunities in the low-growth, low interest rate environment of recent years.

Private equity funds operate in two key business models. One is venture capital, where private equity funds provide capital to start-up and scale-up companies in order to allow them to grow and become profitable and mature;[2] the other is buy-out where private equity funds buy out a mature company, sometimes a listed company which they take private, in order to resolve some of its operational problems, and turn it around as a healthy and profitable company, to be resold or listed in due course.[3] The Preqin survey estimates that about USD$300–400 billion are invested in buyout on a yearly basis, while the venture capital market attracts on

[1] Preqin, *2015 Preqin Global Private Equity & Venture Capital Report* (2015) at https://www.preqin.com/docs/reports/2015-Preqin-Global-Private-Equity-&-Venture-Capital-Report-Sample-Pages.pdf.

[2] For example, see T Bradford and R Smith, 'Private Equity: Uses and Sources' (1997) 10 *Journal of Applied Corporate Finance* 89; M Wright and K Robbie, *Management Buy-Outs and Venture Capital: Into the Next Millennium* (Cheltenham: Edward Elgar 1999).

[3] M Wright, L Renneboog et al, 'Leveraged Buy-outs in the UK and Continental Europe: Retrospect and Prospect' (2006) 18 *Journal of Applied Corporate Finance* 38; M Wright and K Robbie, *Management Buy-Outs and Venture Capital: Into the Next Millennium* (1999), above.

average about USD$100 billion of inflows yearly.[4] Where the UK is concerned, a 2013 survey estimates the private equity sector to be managing about £190 billion worth of assets.[5]

Private equity funds take a different ownership approach to many of the institutions discussed in this book. After raising funds from investors and investing in private companies, PE fund managers become hands-on managers of their investments. While they do not generally exercise day-to-day control, fund managers are actively involved in setting and monitoring the implementation of company strategy. They also play a key role in appointing and incentivising senior management and the board of directors. As well as chasing improved operational efficiencies, higher debt levels at investee companies are also employed as a means of amplifying investment returns. The PE fund's returns are mainly realised by selling or floating the company at a profit. The industry generally works on the basis of a four to six year exit horizon, meaning that the investment will be made with the explicit assumption that it will be sold to a trade buyer or taken through an IPO process within that timeframe.

Hence, although they are only temporary owners, PE fund managers are closely involved in portfolio companies' corporate governance over the medium term, where they typically enjoy management responsibilities and in many cases controlling shareholder rights. This contrasts with the governance role played by many institutions in public equity, which is normally short-term oriented, arm's-length or passive.

Private equity emerged as both an asset class and a terminology in the lexicon of finance in the 1980s. During the 1970s, it had become illegal in many countries to use the assets of a target company to give security to a bidder for that company. This was designed to stop asset stripping. However, an unintended consequence of this change was to prevent the rescue of viable companies, many of which were subsidiaries of larger failing businesses. In the UK, the Companies Act 1981 attempted to alleviate this situation by allowing companies to support other struggling companies under certain defined circumstances. In the US, a market for subprime 'junk' bonds was created which enabled investors to issue high yield debt to fund acquisitions. The peak of this initial growth in private equity activity was the well-documented buy-out of RJR Nabisco in 1988 for approximately $23bn. However, following the impact of the recession

---

[4] Preqin, *2015 Preqin Global Private Equity & Venture Capital Report* (2015), above.

[5] Department of Trade and Investment, *Fund Management in the UK* (2013) at https://www.gov.uk/government/uploads/system/uploads/attachment_data/file/478378/UKTI_Asset_mgmt_broch_B5_RC_AW_DIGIAL.pdf.

of the early 1990s, many leveraged private equity investments struggled or collapsed. Appetite to support in-house private equity declined, and virtually all in-house private equity departments rebranded themselves as separate private equity or buy-out firms which raised designated PE funds from institutional and high net worth investors.[6]

By the late 1990s, the market had split into two segments: the largest private equity funds were increasingly international in their outlook, while the mid-market PE funds focused on specific sectors or types of business. A prolonged period of economic growth from the mid-1990s to the financial crisis of 2007–09 was characterised by ever larger funds, larger deals, greater complexity in deal structures, and greater use of leverage to amplify returns. Much of this expansion was driven by the growth of global debt markets. Banks that had previously held loans on their own balance sheets now sold them into the wholesale market. Such an accelerating process of financial disintermediation increased the funds that were available to private equity players. But when this market dried up during the global financial crisis, the negative impact on the private equity market – which had grown dependent on ever larger infusions of leverage – was substantial.

However, this proved to only be a temporary setback. Since the crisis, institutional investors have turned to private equity in search of returns. Record numbers of buyout deals were achieved in 2014 and 2015, and by 2016 levels of cash available for investment by PE funds (so-called 'dry powder') reached record levels ($754 bn),[7] based on investor hopes that private equity as an asset class will continue to outperform public equity as it appears to have done in the 1980s, 1990s and 2000s.[8]

Venture Capital Funds

Private equity venture capital funds specialise in investing in start-up companies in their early stages. These companies may be founded by

---

[6] John Gilligan and Mike Wright. 'Private Equity Demystified – An Explanatory Guide' (3rd edn, ICAEW, 2014).

[7] Cat Rutter Pooley and Attracta Mooney, 'US pension funds halve private equity allocations', *Financial Times*, 5 March 2017.

[8] Robert S Harris, Tim Jenkinson, and Steven N Kaplan. 'Private equity performance: What do we know?' *The Journal of Finance* 69.5 (2014), 1851–82. According to this study, buyout funds have outperformed the S&P 500 by at least 3 per cent per year, net of fees, over the period. Venture capital funds have performed less impressively: they outperformed public markets substantially in the 1990s, but have underperformed in the 2000s.

entrepreneurs with certain ideas or inventions but who lack experience in developing their ideas or innovations for commercialisation and success. Private equity venture capital funds invest with the intention of taking on a hands-on role in working with the less experienced entrepreneurs in development, commercialisation and management in order to grow the business from a bottom-up level. Private equity venture capital funds structure their arrangements (and fee levels) with their portfolio companies in order to reflect their intense involvement and to protect their own interests.[9] Such arrangements are first protected by confidentiality and exclusivity obligations during negotiations, and even when an investment arrangement is agreed upon, the fund is usually only liable to provide financing in stages, in order to ensure that key target milestones are defined and achieved before further investment is committed.

Private equity venture capital funds often structure their investment in the form of a mixture of different types of securities issued by the target company in order to maximise their protection, rights and returns,[10] in view of agency costs. They usually take a significant but minority stake in a company, and such a stake may be structured as a mixture of ordinary, preference and convertible stock, with convertible preferred stock being the most commonly adopted.[11] The preferred component in stock carries fixed and higher dividend entitlements even if they are non-voting or have less weighting in voting rights. Such preferred stock maximises the fund's return objectives especially if the company achieves good performance. The convertible instrument may be in the form of convertible stock or debt, usually the former.[12] The equity component maximises cash flow rights, but funds rely on debt-based instruments to achieve a predictable stream of income from regular repayments and to protect their interests in an environment of asymmetry with the entrepreneur. Further, debt-based instruments offer the fund protection in case the company fails to fare well. In that case, part of the fund's interest may be converted into debt, allowing the fund to step into the shoes of a creditor, having higher priority for distribution rights over shareholders in

[9] T Bradford and R Smith, 'Private Equity: Uses and Sources' (1997), above.

[10] Thomas J Chemmanur and Zhaohui Chen, 'Venture Capitalists versus Angels: The Dynamics of Private Firm Financing Contracts' (2006) at https://papers.ssrn.com/sol3/papers.cfm?abstract_id=342721.

[11] Andrew Metrick and Ayako Yasuda, 'Venture Capital and Other Private Equity: A Survey' (2010) at https://papers.ssrn.com/sol3/papers.cfm?abstract_id=1723882.

[12] Above.

case of insolvency of the company. Convertible instruments thus allow adaptation by funds throughout the process of investment to maximise funds' cash flow rights and protection, and to exert the requisite discipline upon the entrepreneurs. Further, funds may bargain for early redemption rights in case of certain triggers such as the performance of the project, failure of certain representations or warranties, or failure of the personalities in the funds and company to work together.

Private equity venture capital funds bargain for intensive monitoring rights over the entrepreneurs and strong corporate governance rights to protect their interests. Board appointments for fund representatives are the norm in order to facilitate monitoring at the level of key decision-making. Funds and entrepreneurs may agree to a fund-approved Chief Executive, and to putting in place systems, policies and controls such as hiring, marketing, information reporting and internal control in order to ensure that the governance of the company is transparent, led by competent personnel and focused on key strategic areas. On corporate governance rights, funds may insist on veto rights over certain decisions, and anti-dilution and pre-emption rights so that their shareholding interests are adequately protected.[13]

Buy-out Funds

Private equity buy-out funds generally target a mature business which is unlikely to be insolvent (low Tobin qs), with high cash flows that may give the impression of not being used efficiently, and enjoying less analyst coverage. The last factor incentivises such firms to go private as they have not been attracting sufficient investor attention on the public securities markets anyway.[14] Buy-out funds may operate singly or in 'clubs', and although much public attention has been paid to their 'public-to-private' activities i.e. the buyout of a public, usually listed company, to take it private, Metrick et al report that such deals only represent fewer than 10 per cent of buy-out deals.[15]

Buy-out funds may, unlike in venture capital funds, take controlling stakes in the portfolio company, usually in a mixture of ordinary, preferred and convertible stock like that discussed above. They also engage in staged financing, defining key performance targets for the

---

[13] Above and T Bradford and R Smith, 'Private Equity: Uses and Sources' (1997), above.

[14] Andrew Metrick and Ayako Yasuda, 'Venture Capital and Other Private Equity: A Survey' (2010), above.

[15] Above.

portfolio company before committing further finance. As managerial slack is one of the main perceived problems in a buy-out fund's portfolio target, the corporate governance structures designed by buy-out funds are key to the investment in order to impose high levels of discipline while maximising the fund's potential returns.

Buy-out funds normally put fund representatives on the portfolio companies' Board while at the same time reducing Board size and independent representation in order to keep the Board small, insider-based and focused on generation of value and performance.[16] However, unlike in venture capital funds' relationships with entrepreneurs, buy-out funds are reportedly less hands-on and personally involved in the business. One of the key tactics employed by buy-out funds is a form of substitute discipline for managers, achieved through financial engineering – i.e. significant levels of leverage are taken on by the portfolio company, at least partly to fund the buy-out fund's acquisition of the company in the first place. Leverage is seen as a useful and stringent discipline on cash flows and, therefore, managerial slack,[17] a point that we will return to in assessing the corporate governance roles of buy-out funds and their implications. Further, buy-out funds bargain for certain veto rights in key decision-making at the portfolio company and have key say in exit options such as in flotation, re-selling of the company or debt conversion.

In order to protect their returns objectives, funds usually charge to the portfolio companies a range of management and monitoring fees, something which is not observed in the arrangements between venture capital funds and their portfolio companies. Metrick et al report[18] that such fixed income flows protect funds' return objectives but frequently represent the bulk of returns on their investment, raising the query as to whether buy-out funds systemically expropriate from their controlling stakes (an issue that we will explore further below).

Before we move on to evaluate venture capital and buy-out funds' corporate governance roles and their implications, we discuss the structures of governance between funds and their investors as a key factor that

---

[16] Francesca Cornelli and Oĝuzhan Karakas, 'Corporate Governance of LBOs: The Role of Boards' (2012) at http://ssrn.com/abstract=1875649. Michael Jensen, 'The Economic Case For Private Equity' (2007) at http://ssrn.com/abstract=963530.

[17] Ronald W Masulis and Randall S Thomas, 'Does Private Equity Create Wealth?' (2009) *University of Chicago Law Review* 1; Michael Jensen, 'The Economic Case For Private Equity' (2007), above.

[18] Andrew Metrick and Ayako Yasuda, 'Venture Capital and Other Private Equity: A Survey' (2010), above.

shapes funds' corporate governance roles as part of their investment strategies. Further, we also discuss how increased regulatory intervention in the fund-investor relationship may affect their external corporate governance roles.

B. PRIVATE EQUITY FUNDS AND THEIR RELATIONSHIPS WITH INVESTORS

The ability of private equity funds to engage in tailor-made corporate governance arrangements with their portfolio companies is in part derived from the freedoms they enjoy under the investment arrangements between funds and their investors.

Limited Partnership Structure

Private equity funds, whether venture or buy-out funds, are frequently structured[19] as 'limited partnerships', oftentimes in an offshore jurisdiction with favourable tax regimes. In these arrangements, investors are limited partners who supply investment capital, while taking no powers of management at all. The private equity fund managers are the general partners in the limited partnership, having all powers of management and also liability arising out of their management roles. Many legal regimes that offer the limited partnership as a business vehicle do not stipulate at length[20] how the general and limited partners' relationships should be conducted; this is frequently left to the investment agreements made by each investor with the fund. The relatively light governance of the limited partnership business vehicle allows funds a significant amount of freedom to structure their relationships with investors in such a way as to facilitate their investment strategies as described briefly above. The general partners typically have the discretion to appoint the fund management company which would make the relevant investment decisions. This structure is again in the vein of the 'separation of fund manager from funds' structure we discussed in Chapter 2. The UK has reformed its limited partnership regime in favour of allowing private fund limited partnerships to be recognised as a separate category of limited partnerships.[21] The reform also allows a 'white list' of limited partner rights that

---

[19] See generally, Guy Fraser-Sampson, *Private Equity as an Asset Class* (Wiley Finance 2007).

[20] For example, the UK Limited Partnerships Act 1907.

[21] The Legislative Reform (Private Fund Limited Partnerships) Order 2017.

can be exercised without running the risk that limited partners would lose their limited liability status. This measure improves investor protection in such funds but if the funds are established outside of the UK under other limited partnership laws, the extent of investor protection may be different from under the UK's model.

Impact of Regulation in the Alternative Investment Fund Managers' Directive

Where investors in the funds are not a monitoring force for the conduct of investment management and the fund's corporate governance role in their portfolio companies, it may nevertheless be queried whether the European Alternative Investment Fund Managers' Directive (AIFM Directive), largely transposed in the UK,[22] may offer certain mandatory levels of investor protection that affect private equity funds' freedoms.

Private equity funds enjoy a key freedom of being typically close-ended with a finite life span of ten years or less. Investors usually do not enjoy redemption rights until at least the medium term, such as five years, as funds do not have ready access to the liquidity of a secondary market for private company shares. The mechanism of locking up investors' capital ensures that the funds can carry out their strategies without undue pressure from investor redemptions.[23] The AIFM Directive does not make prescriptive recommendations about funds' redemption policies, leaving it to funds to determine what is appropriate as long as disclosure is made to investors.[24]

Although the AIFM Directive fills in perceived gaps in this highly unregulated area of fund-investor relationships, seeking to redress imbalances and to ensure that funds conduct themselves properly and safely, there are two caveats. One is that these protections do not apply to a small fund, which will be explained shortly. Another is that many of the investor protection duties are owed to the regulator and not to the investor directly, and investors may face a tortuous path if they decide to embark on civil enforcement against the fund manager directly.

First, the AIFM Directive regards funds whose investors do not have redemption rights of at least five years and which are unleveraged to be

---

22 Financial Services (Alternative Investment Fund Managers) Regulations 2013.

23 Ulf Axelson, Per Strömberg and Michael S. Weisbach, 'Why Are Buyouts Levered? The Financial Structure of Private Equity Funds' (2009) 64 *Journal of Finance* 1549.

24 Art 23, AIFMD.

generally of less concern in respect of issues of systemic risk. As long as these funds manage less than 500 million euros in total assets, they can be exempt from the AIFM Directive. The UK applies these thresholds to 'small AIFMs'[25] and exempts them from the AIFM Directive and the obligations transposed in the UK. Small 'AIFMs' are required to be registered in the UK and have to make periodic reports to the FCA in terms of their main trading strategies and principal exposures, but there are very few mandatory provisions in relation to such fund managers' conduct. This means that investors are largely left to their own devices in terms of protecting themselves when they invest in small private equity funds. It may be argued that small funds may be in a less powerful position vis-à-vis potential clients, and have fewer investors, so investors have greater room to bargain for the appropriate monitoring and accountability mechanisms. However, investors may not do so, or do so adequately, as highly rational and optimal contracting behaviour is but an ideal; it is typical for medium to long-term contracts to leave gaps due to information asymmetry and uncertainties at the point of contract. Further, small funds, being systemically less important, are more likely to be allowed to fail if they run into difficulties. Thus, although it may seem – on the face of it – that exempting small funds is a more proportionate approach to the AIFM Directive, regulation seems to necessitate an all-or-nothing approach in this context; the current carve-out does not address investor protection needs, which can indeed be heightened in a small fund context. Nevertheless, in the UK, there are only about 100 small funds on the FCA's register,[26] and there is no further breakdown information on assets under management for each fund; indeed, it is uncertain which funds are private equity as opposed to other kinds of fund. It is surmised that the scope of small funds is therefore relatively minimal, and so most private equity funds are within the scope of the AIFM Directive.

Conduct of Business Duties

In addition to regulation, soft law standards in the UK have been developed by the British Venture Capital Association in the form of the Walker Guidelines on Disclosure and Transparency in Private Equity

---

[25] Section 9, Financial Services (Alternative Investment Fund Managers) Regulations 2013.

[26] https://www.fca.org.uk/publication/systems-information/aifmd-small-register.pdf.

2007.[27] These guidelines promote best practices in terms of structuring private equity arrangements with investors and their portfolio companies, and apply to all private equity funds. They require yearly reporting by funds to investors on issues such as leverage levels, buyout activity, performance measures, fee payments and the receipt of legal, audit and other advice and valuation methodologies. These Guidelines and industry practices are monitored by the BVCA which promises to be a custodian for best practices. The Guidelines also deal with buy-out funds' conduct in their portfolio companies, a point we will return to shortly.

Where the AIFM Directive applies, Article 12 provides that fund managers owe conduct of business duties such as: duties in care, skill and diligence, duty to employ resources effectively for the performance of due functions, duty to manage conflicts of interest, duty to act in the best interests of investors, duty to comply with all regulatory requirements and duty to treat investors fairly. These are further fleshed out in Commission Delegated Regulation 2013,[28] which has been directly applicable to the UK. The Commission Regulation explains that fund managers are expected to be duly diligent in terms of their investment plans and transactions, and in selecting relevant counterparties such as prime brokers.[29] They have to act honestly and fairly in terms of adequate competence, time commitment, integrity and use of resources.[30] They are to treat investors fairly so that no one group of investors suffers from a material disadvantage.[31] They are to manage conflicts of interests appropriately with an upfront policy and disclosure, and to ensure that any inducements do not affect their service to their clients.[32] They should ensure best execution is achieved in the transactions made for their clients.[33]

It is pertinent to note that such duties are not owed directly to investors by the relevant fund manager, except perhaps the duty to treat investors fairly. This is because the separation structure insulates the fund manager

---

[27] http://www.bvca.co.uk/ResearchPublications/Publications/WalkerGuidelines.aspx.

[28] Articles 17–37, Commission Delegated Regulation (EU) No 231/2013 of 19 December 2012 supplementing Directive 2011/61/EU of the European Parliament and of the Council with regard to exemptions, general operating conditions, depositaries, leverage, transparency and supervision.

[29] Articles 18–20, above.

[30] Articles 21–22, above.

[31] Article 23, above.

[32] Articles 24, 30–36, above.

[33] Article 27, above.

from such responsibilities to investors directly unless legislation imposes a direct obligation, which is arguably in the duty to treat investors fairly. These are largely regulatory duties owed to the relevant regulator, to be enforced by regulatory actions such as fines and censure. In the UK, investors may only have benefit of the protection of these duties if they sue on the basis of breach of statutory duty,[34] riding upon a regulatory enforcement action. One of the issues arising in practice is that private equity funds that have not committed all of their capital may, towards the end of the lock-up period, quickly find opportunities for investment in order to deploy such capital,[35] and investment decisions made this way may not be in investors' best interests. It is uncertain as to whether the AIFM Directive's duties would address this issue – perhaps where there is a failure of due diligence or if the investment made is arguably not considered as achieving best execution.

Investors may be protected by mandatory annual reporting that is imposed on fund managers, which is subject to some prescription in order to ensure that the information is salient and comparable.[36] Further, investors are protected by a mandatory obligation on the part of fund managers to maintain a separate depositary for each alternative investment fund under management, with extensive obligations imposed on the depositary to gatekeep against potential wrong-doing vis-à-vis assets or money to be protected for the benefit of investors.[37] In the UK, the depositaries' liability is clarified as to be actionable between depositaries, fund managers and investors, thus seemingly giving investors a right of action.[38]

Conduct of business duties, increased compliance, record-keeping for purposes of diligence and reporting requirements add cost to private equity fund management, not to mention the imposition of prudential requirements for initial capital and the need to maintain a form of insurance to meet prudential requirements.[39] These are likely to have a

---

[34] S150, Financial Services and Markets Act 2000.

[35] Sridhar Arcot, Zsuzsanna Fluck and José-Miguel Gaspar and Ulrich Hege, 'Fund Managers under Pressure: Rationale and Determinants of Secondary Buyouts' (2014) at http://ssrn.com/abstract_id= 2332801.

[36] Article 23, AIFMD; Article 109 of the Commission Delegated Regulation 2013; FCA Handbook FUND 3.3.2ff.

[37] Article 21, AIFMD; Articles 83-102, Commission Delegated Regulation 2013; and FCA Handbook FUND 3.11.1ff.

[38] Section 29, Financial Services (Alternative Investment Fund Managers) Regulations 2013.

[39] Article 9, AIFMD.

knock-on effect upon the cost charged to investors whether or not the benefits of investor protection conferred exceed the cost to funds and fund managers. Private equity funds continue to enjoy great freedoms in bargaining for favourable financial terms with their investors, and as they can generate rather high returns in this low-growth environment,[40] these terms have remained firmly in favour of funds.[41]

Fees and Remuneration for Private Equity Funds

One of the incentives[42] for private equity funds' business model is their '2-and-20' fee model which allows them to charge a 2 per cent fixed fee over the total assets under management, plus a 20 per cent carried interest upon profits generated by the fund on a yearly basis (which in many jurisdictions is subject to favourable tax treatment – treated as capital gains rather than income for the PE manager). Further, as mentioned above, other fund management costs could be charged to investors, such as the maintenance of a separate depositary. Buy-out funds also charge their portfolio companies management charges and fees. However, the AIFM Directive potentially interferes with fund managers' remuneration models as the Directive requires remuneration policies to be consistent with sound risk management,[43] and prescribes mandatory aspects of remuneration structures between fixed and variable remuneration and deferral of remuneration, in the same vein as discussed in Chapter 6.[44] These are further to be disclosed in prescribed detail to investors.[45] The Ernst & Young Survey in 2012 reported significant disincentivising effects generated by the AIFM Directive's remuneration regime, which is harmonised from banking and investment firm regulation.[46] Hence, in the UK, the FCA has relaxed the remuneration rules for certain funds: i.e. unleveraged funds with no redemption rights for

---

[40] To be discussed in the next Section.

[41] 'Private equity clings to '2 and 20' fee model', *Financial Times* (12 Aug 2016).

[42] Robert C Illig, 'What Hedge Funds Can Teach Corporate America: A Roadmap for Achieving Institutional Investor Oversight' (2007) 57 *American University Law Review* 225 in discussing the similar model used by private equity funds.

[43] Article 16, AIFMD.

[44] Annex II, AIFMD, transposed in FCA Handbook, SYSC 19B.

[45] Articles 107–8, Commission Delegated Regulation 2013.

[46] EY Survey on AIFMD: Ernst and Young, 'Game-changing Regulation? The Perceived Impact of the AIFM Directive on Private Equity in Europe' (2012).

investors of at least five years, and funds that are not small but manage less than £5billion in total assets. These funds would be given the discretion to determine whether to apply the prescriptive remuneration regime at all or in part.[47]

Nonetheless, regulators have expressed significant concerns about the fees being charged by PE funds, often without the knowledge of their investors. In 2014, the SEC issued a warning to the industry after finding numerous examples of fees and expenses being charged inappropriately to investors. Since then, Blackstone, KKR, Fenway Partners, Clean Energy Capital and Lincolnshire Management have all been issued with fines and penalties by the US regulator.[48] Ludovic Phalippou and colleagues researched the accounts of 592 US companies that were bought by private equity managers between 1981 and 2013. They found that $20bn in hidden fees (for costs described as financing costs, underwriting services, monitoring and transaction fees, and consulting fees) were paid to private equity managers by investee companies due to clauses in the master services agreements which govern the relationship between the company and the PE manager. As a result, the official expense ratio reported by PE managers was significantly understated. The study found, for example, that US fund manager CalPERS paid around $2.6bn in hidden fees on private equity investments made between 1991 and 2014 on top of its $3.4bn bill for carried interest (although $1.3bn was subsequently repaid to CalPERS as a rebate against its annual management fees).[49]

In sum, although law and regulation have to an extent intervened in the internal governance of funds' relationships with their investors, such intervention has not brought about major changes in their business model and investment management strategies. Payne[50] argues that the AIFM Directive, in its attempt to apply equally to hedge and private equity fund managers, has created an over-inclusive regime where private equity fund managers are subject to the same obligations as hedge fund managers,

---

[47] FCA, *General guidance on the AIFM Remuneration Code (SYSC 19B)* (January 2014). For leveraged funds, the threshold for discretionary disapplication of the Remuneration Code is £1 billion of total assets under management.

[48] Chris Flood, '$20bn cost of hidden private equity fees', *Financial Times*, 13 December 2015.

[49] Ludovic Phalippou, Christian Rauch, and Marc P. Umber. 'Private Equity Portfolio Company Fees' (2016). https://papers.ssrn.com/sol3/papers.cfm?abstract_id=2703354

[50] Jennifer Payne, 'Private Equity and its Regulation in Europe' (2011) at http://ssrn.com/abstract=1886186.

even if the contexts they are operating in do not warrant such treatment. However, although the Directive makes no specific distinction in most of its provisions, one could treat irrelevant provisions as being inapplicable, thus not affecting the private equity fund manager. Further, the regulatory measure of potentially greatest impact, remuneration regulation, is likely disapplied to most funds unless they have in excess of £1bn in total assets under management (and leveraged) or £5bn in total assets management (unleveraged with investors having no redemption rights for at least five years). These high thresholds require only the largest funds to be subject to remuneration regulation in proportion to their risk profiles, therefore indicating regulators' willingness to leave funds the freedom to bargain with their investors as long as they are not significant enough to entail systemic stability implications.

C. PRIVATE EQUITY FUNDS' CORPORATE GOVERNANCE ROLES

Private equity funds' corporate governance roles, whether in venture capital or buyout funds, are exercised for the purpose of generating value from the portfolio company in order to deliver investment returns. In the context of venture capital funds, such involvement amounts to a form of entrepreneurial or business management, while in the context of buy-out funds, such involvement is 'instrumental' in nature, as discussed in Chapter 3.

Venture Capital and Fund Managers' Corporate Governance Roles

Commentators have generally regarded private equity fund managers involvement in the corporate governance of portfolio companies as a constructive and value-adding phenomenon. Private equity fund managers are actively involved in restructuring board composition,[51] bringing in suitable executives and independent directors with requisite industry

[51] Natee Amornsiripanitch, Paul A Gompers and Yuhai Xuan, 'More than Money: Venture Capitalists on Boards' (2015) at http://ssrn.com/abstract=2586592; Viral V Acharya, Moritz Hahn and Conor Kehoe, 'Corporate Governance and Value Creation: Evidence from Private Equity' (2009) at http://ssrn.com/abstract=1324016.

skills and competence.[52] They are also usually in favour of hiring an external Chief Executive (who is granted a significant equity stake in the company) so that the founder entrepreneur may be supported in terms of building a professional management structure or checked in terms of unrealistic ideas or empire building.[53] The efficiencies achieved in decision-making at Board level are often cascaded down into operational efficiencies, as private equity fund managers reportedly affect hiring, retention and remuneration policies for employees and not just executives, seeking to maximise the performance of the firm.[54] Various studies suggest that the effectiveness of firms' systems, policies and controls are generally enhanced under private equity fund managers' influence. In sum, the governance and operational restructuring carried out reflects a form of mentoring offered by the private equity fund managers to their portfolio companies. Further, fund managers are generally crucial in bringing in networks of contacts for the portfolio company and in expanding their business opportunities.[55] These valuable and hands-on approaches are reflective of a type of corporate governance role that takes meaningful ownership of the business, fusing the fund's monitoring role with entrepreneurship and management.

Of course many portfolio companies fail, or the relationship between the private equity fund manager and the founder entrepreneur may disintegrate under the weight of the fund manager's intrusive agenda.[56] However, where such intensive involvement succeeds in creating a healthy partnership between the private equity fund manager and the founder entrepreneur/s of the portfolio company, such companies have benefited greatly in terms of performance and growth.[57] Nevertheless the model of venture capital is singularly focused on returns to equity capital over a relatively short period of time, and unabashedly works to favour shareholders over all other stakeholders. Such a corporate governance

---

[52] Stefano Casselli and Stefano Gatti, 'Corporate Governance and Independent Directors: Much Ado About Nothing? The Evidence behind Private Equity Investment Performance' (2007) at http://ssrn.com/abstract=968465.

[53] Natee Amornsiripanitch, Paul A Gompers and Yuhai Xuan, 'More than Money: Venture Capitalists on Boards' (2015), above.

[54] Above, and Stefano Bonini, 'The Effects of Private Equity Investors on the Governance of Companies' (2015) at http://ssrn.com/abstract=2647219.

[55] Viral V Acharya, Moritz Hahn and Conor Kehoe, 'Corporate Governance and Value Creation: Evidence from Private Equity' (2009), above.

[56] *Boughtwood v Oak Investment Partners XII Ltd Partnership.* [2010] EWCA Civ 23.

[57] Viral V Acharya, Moritz Hahn and Conor Kehoe, 'Corporate Governance and Value Creation: Evidence from Private Equity' (2009), above.

ethos may work while the company is small and has few stakeholders, but the impact on stakeholder welfare (particularly that of employees) in the context of venture capital invested companies remains unclear. One report suggests that the operational efficiencies and increased wealth creation by portfolio companies are partly achieved by cutting cost, such as labour cost, and thus negatively impacts on stakeholders.[58] Further, venture capital funds are likely only to be able to remain invested for a finite period, in tandem with their contractually-defined investor redemption rights, so the portfolio company is pressured to be in a position for sale or flotation within a ten year period, a rather demanding timeline for a start-up. Oxera's report in 2006[59] indicated that many venture capital fund-backed companies in the UK do float successfully, generating consistent returns even after the exit of the fund, indicating the sustainability of the funds' contributions to the company's governance and operational efficiencies and wealth-creation productivity. However, after the global financial crisis, funds have found it more difficult to float their portfolio companies and more trade sales have been conducted.[60]

As stated above, a ten year time horizon – from entry to exit – for venture capital funds can create an impetus for the generation of short-term performance. In some industries – particularly those focused on innovation, technology and the exploitation of intellectual property – such a time horizon may be inimical to ultimate business success in the investee company. In the UK, this has led to the launch of so-called patient capital funds which seek to fund similar ventures to those traditionally served by venture capital funds, but without the constraints of a ten year partnership structure. Industry data suggest that, by 2016, venture capital funds had been overtaken by these investors as a source of funding for start-ups and early stage ventures in the UK technology sector. Such investors include Woodford Patient Capital, an £880m investment trust launched in April 2015, which has been active in the biotech sector, and several investment companies spun out of UK

---

[58] Timothy Dore, 'Venture Capital and the Performance of Incumbents' (2015) at https://papers.ssrn.com/sol3/papers.cfm?abstract_id=2666529.

[59] Oxera, *The London Markets and Private Equity Backed IPOs* (March 2006) at http://www.oxera.com/Oxera/media/Oxera/The-London-markets-and-private-equity-backed-IPOs.pdf?ext=.pdf.

[60] Preqin Special Report, *Exits in Private Equity* (2011) at https://www.preqin.com/docs/reports/Preqin_Special_Report_Exits_in_Private_Equity.pdf.

universities, such as Imperial Innovations and Oxford Sciences Innovation. All of these sources of patient capital emphasise their more stable ownership approach compared to a typical venture capital fund.[61]

In the United States, venture capital funds have played an important role in the recent growth of the technology sector. Various rounds of funding have underpinned the emergence of the highly valued 'Unicorn' companies – like Uber and Airbnb – which remain in private hands despite achieving estimated valuations in excess of $1 bn. However, the structuring of these equity financing deals has created difficult corporate governance issues. Many of the investments in more mature start-ups have been legally structured to give investors guaranteed returns and protection against losses. This has given rise to a variety of share classes with differing ownership rights, which makes such companies extremely complex and difficult to value. Such a structure may also serve to dilute early employees and founders, and may ultimately push Silicon Valley companies towards an IPO purely to 'clear the decks' from such convoluted ownership rights. These issues partly reflect the success of the venture-funding industry in the US – technology companies have preferred to stay in private hands rather than go public due to the abundant availability of venture and private equity funding (which is often much less available in other countries). But it may also reflect the reduced risk appetite of the venture capital industry and the increased role of non-traditional venture capital investors (such as mutual funds and hedge funds) in directly financing early-stage transactions.[62]

Buy-out Funds and Fund Managers' Corporate Governance Roles

Buy-out funds often take controlling stakes in their portfolio companies, and are in a position to nominate directors to the Board of the portfolio company. However, as buy-out funds deal with mature businesses, whether to assist a management buy-out, or to take a publicly listed company private, the extent of governance rights is a matter for delicate bargaining. The intimate involvement of fund managers cannot be assumed, as is often the case with venture capital funds where founder-entrepreneurs of portfolio companies rely to a greater extent on their investors' expertise.

---

[61] Murad Ahmed, 'Patient capital overtakes VC for UK tech groups', *Financial Times* 1 November 2015.

[62] Leslie Hook, 'Technology: Unicorns face end of the 'steroid era', *Financial Times*, 10 November 2015.

Buy-out funds rely significantly upon the governance/discipline effects of debt upon the portfolio company, in order to keep management under check. Buy-out funds often fund their purchase of the company by the company's own borrowing, sometimes up to 70 per cent of the purchase price.[63] The high level of leverage is a form of financial engineering that allows buy-out funds to maximise their returns on their investment by committing as little of their capital as possible.[64] A number of commentators have also opined that the high level of leverage acts as a form of 'management check', in order to mitigate agency problems.[65] High levels of leverage force companies into a debt servicing burden, which creates incentives for companies to manage their cash flow carefully in order not to default. The fund manager hopes that this will result in operational efficiencies, as well as the reduction of idle cash overall in the company that could be misused by corporate management.[66] Further, Fontenay opines that buy-out funds act as a reputational 'gatekeeper' for portfolio company debt, and may attract more favourable terms for such debt than would otherwise be available.[67]

The corporate governance 'discipline' effect of high levels of leverage in the portfolio company has also been empirically tested in a number of studies suggesting that improved governance can be observed. Masulis and Thomas discuss how high levels of portfolio company leverage cause managers' incentives to be aligned with the funds, in terms of improving

---

[63] Jules Domenichini, 'Public to Private Transactions, Private Equity Ownership and IPOs: A Case Study of Debenhams' (2012) at http://ssrn.com/abstract=1516293.

[64] Ulf Axelson, Per Strömberg and Michael S. Weisbach, 'Why Are Buyouts Levered? The Financial Structure of Private Equity Funds' (2009), above; Stephen F Diamond, 'Beyond the Berle and Means Paradigm: Private Equity and the New Capitalist Order' in Cynthia Williams and Peer Zumbansen (eds), *The Embedded Firm: Corporate Governance, Labour and Finance Capitalism* (Cambridge: Cambridge University Press 2012) at p. 151.

[65] Ronald W Masulis and Randall S Thomas, 'Does Private Equity Create Wealth?' (2009), above; Michael Jensen, 'The Economic Case For Private Equity' (2007), above.

[66] Ann-Kristin Achleitner, André Betzer and Jasmin Gider, 'Do Corporate Governance Motives Drive Hedge Funds and Private Equity Activities?' (2009) at http://ssrn.com/abstract=1292896.

[67] Elizabeth Fontenay, 'Private Equity as Gatekeepers' (2013-14) 33 *Review of Banking and Financial Law* 115.

performance and shareholder value.[68] There is also some discussion[69] on a wider improvement to portfolio companies' corporate governance in the sense that monitoring and scrutiny of the Board is generally improved. It has been found that buy-out funds target companies with weaker governance, such as entrenched CEOs and insider-filled Boards. These companies would then be revamped in terms of their Board size and composition upon buy-out.[70] Gong et al found that, of their sample study of 126 buy-out portfolio companies, at least 51 per cent experienced a CEO turnover attributable to the need to reduce agency cost, showing that buy-out funds exercise a form of scrutiny and discipline over the Board.[71] Even where buy-out funds have retained previous management, Achleitner et al[72] report that corporate governance can be improved to benefit operational efficiency, as leadership is taken robustly over strategic matters for value creation. In their case study on New Look, governance improvements post buy-out allowed the retailer to carry out strategic expansion and growth without the burdens of regulatory compliance and reporting, greatly improving operational efficiency and performance.

However, there is also a significant amount of scepticism with respect to buy-out funds' roles in enhancing the corporate governance of portfolio companies. First, Anabtawi found that management buy-outs assisted by buy-out funds tend to depress the purchase price of the company in order to reduce the premia to be paid to existing shareholders. There may be a case for saying that buy-out funds encourage the

---

[68] Ronald W Masulis and Randall S Thomas, 'Does Private Equity Create Wealth?' (2009), above.

[69] Guy Schofield, 'Private Equity: Governance Arbitrage and Lessons for Public Corporate Governance' (2014) at http://ssrn.com/abstract=2441166; Steven Toms, Nick Wilson and Mike Wright, 'The Evolution of Private Equity: Corporate Restructuring in the UK, c.1945-2010' (2012) at http://ssrn.com/abstract=2145445.

[70] Andrew Tellam, Peter Clarkson and Shams Pathan, 'Do Private Equity Target Firms Exhibit Less Effectual Governance Structures?' (2013) at http://ssrn.com/abstract=2339482.

[71] James Jianxin Gong and Steve Yuching Wu, 'CEO Turnover in Private Equity Sponsored Leveraged Buyouts' (2011) 19 *Corporate Governance: An International Review* 195.

[72] Ann-Kristin Achleitner, Eva Lutz, Kerry Herman and Josh Lerner, 'New Look: Going Private with Private Equity Support' (2009) at http://ssrn.com/abstract=1120230.

buy-out managers to behave opportunistically.[73] Next, a number of studies have also found that buy-out funds nominate their representatives on Boards and tend to influence Board composition in such a way that Boards are predominantly composed of insiders.[74] The independent directorial representations on portfolio company Boards falls significantly. It may be argued that the monitoring role is supplied by the funds' representatives and so there is no need for independent representation on the Board. However, such insider CEOs and Board directors increasingly become less sensitive to performance as there is hardly any threat to tenure or remuneration.[75] Of course, the private status of the portfolio company means that its governance structure can be more flexible and would not have to be in compliance with the Corporate Governance Code[76] which applies to all UK premium-listed companies. Commentators have however argued that buy-out funds benefit from the lack of market and regulatory scrutiny of the governance structures of portfolio companies largely in order to benefit themselves.[77]

For example, the high levels of leverage that portfolio companies take on have been observed in some cases to be used to pay out dividends to the buy-out funds, therefore allowing buy-out funds to extract value from portfolio companies in the near-term, which could be at the expense of

---

[73] Iman Anabtawi, 'Predatory Management Buy-outs' (2015) 49 UC *Davis Law Review* 1287 at http://ssrn.com/abstract=2649192.

[74] Francesca Cornelli and Oĝuzhan Karakas, 'Corporate Governance of LBOs: The Role of Boards' (2012), above; Viral V Acharya, Moritz Hahn and Conor Kehoe, 'Corporate Governance and Value Creation: Evidence from Private Equity' (2009) at http://ssrn.com/abstract=1324016.

[75] Although Cornelli and Karakas argue that operating performance is improved which may be a justifiable trade-off with inside entrenchment, Francesca Cornelli and Oĝuzhan Karakas, 'Corporate Governance of LBOs: The Role of Boards' (2012), above.

[76] The Code mandates at least 50 per cent non-executive representation on Boards and independent directors are often responsible for key committees of the Board.

[77] In this respect, the Financial Reporting Council has called for law reform to subject significant large private companies to the corporate governance code so that Board composition will not be dominated by insiders and will work in the stakeholders' and the company's overall interests. See 'FRC responds to Green Paper on Corporate Governance Reforms' (21 Feb 2017) at https://www.frc.org.uk/News-and-Events/FRC-Press/Press/2017/February/FRC-responds-to-Green-Paper-on-Corporate-Governmen.aspx.

the company's long-term performance.[78] It has been commented that Phones4U, the failed UK mobile phone company, paid large dividends to their buy-out fund owners despite bleak business prospects and reduced market share.[79] The opportunistic behaviour of buy-out funds in favouring their own interests while assuming a position of power and discipline in portfolio companies has also been observed in Denmark where extraordinarily high levels of dividends have been paid out by portfolio companies in the early years of buy-out fund ownership.[80] Lemstra,[81] in his case study of the buy-out of Eircom of Ireland, also documents that buy-out investors have loaded Eircom with high levels of debt without any intention of repayment, tying Eircom's cash flow to debt repayment and making it impossible for Eircom to invest in product and market development. Eircom neared bankruptcy in 2012, and Lemstra's analysis attributed much of that to buy-out fund investors' predatory behaviour in prioritising return of capital to themselves.

It could be argued that buy-out funds' 'creaming' off of value creation by the portfolio company is justified in view of the usually extraordinary performance gains made by the company. Before carried interest can be earned, funds typically need to achieve a hurdle rate of return of 8 per cent (although this has been declining in recent years as investor money has flooded into the asset class).[82] Acharya et al found that buy-out funds consistently outperform the stock market indices by up to 80 per cent.[83] Cumming et al found that returns to fund investors are generally at levels of 30 per cent or more.[84] One can view buy-out funds' extraction of value

---

78 Richard P Nielsen, 'The Private Equity-Leveraged Buyout Form of Finance Capitalism: Ethical and Social Issues, and Potential Reforms' (2008) 18 *Business Ethics Quarterly* 379.

79 Jonathan Ford, 'Private equity, not the mobile, killed Phones 4U', *Financial Times* (21 Sep 2014).

80 Frederik Vinten, 'The Performance of Private Equity Buyout Fund Owned Firms' (2007) at http://ssrn.com/abstract=1114603.

81 Wolter Lemstra and John P M Groenewegen, 'Private Equity Leveraged Buyout and Public Values: The bankruptcy of Eircom, Ireland' (2012) at http://ssrn.com/abstract=2032222.

82 John Gapper. 'The private equity party is overcrowded', *Financial Times*. 1 March 2017.

83 Viral V Acharya, Conor Kehoe and Michael Reyner, 'Private Equity vs PLC Boards in the U.K.: A Comparison of Practices and Effectiveness' (*ECGI Working Paper*, 2008).

84 Douglas Cumming, Donald Siegel and Mike Wright, 'Private Equity, Leveraged Buyouts and Governance' (2007) at http://papers.ssrn.com/sol3/papers.cfm?abstract_id==983802.

as akin to those that controlling shareholders engage in, as a form of incentive for them to take on the risk of holding a relatively illiquid and concentrated stake.[85] However, buy-out funds' portfolio companies have not always performed well. Bratton studied 321 buy-out exits between 1995–2004 in the UK and found that almost 40 per cent of buy-out portfolio companies became distressed or bankrupt. In such cases, if the fund has not performed poorly, it is only because they have extracted sufficiently, and passed the burden of the company on to long-term creditors of the company. Further, it can also be argued that the elevated performance sustained under buy-out fund ownership is not exactly a lasting phenomenon. This is because much of it can come about by short-term structuring such as selling off freeholds,[86] selling off ancillary (though viable) businesses for a short-term gain[87] or cutting cost, such as reduction of workforce and investment. Cohn et al[88] are highly sceptical of improved operational efficiencies under buy-out fund ownership, after carrying out empirical research for US portfolio companies over ten years between 1990–2000. Over the longer term, short-term restructuring such as selling off freeholds would only generate rent expenses which could become expensive for the company.[89] Further, the overhang effects of high levels of leverage can be very damaging as the cash flow discipline reduces managers' discretion to spend on investment, and research and development, therefore dampening the company's long-term prospects. High levels of leverage also render the company much more vulnerable to distress should circumstances change.[90]

In view of the amount of portfolio company leverage that is taken on, one can argue that buy-out funds have minimised the assumption of their risk, transferring such risks to the portfolio company and its creditors. The extraction behaviour carried out by buy-out funds is thus a transfer of wealth from creditors to shareholders, even if the buy-out fund

---

[85] Ronald J Gilson, 'Controlling Shareholders and Corporate Governance: Complicating the Comparative Taxonomy' (2006) 119 *Harvard Law Review* 1641.

[86] Jules Domenichini, 'Public to Private Transactions, Private Equity Ownership and IPOs: A Case Study of Debenhams' (2012), above.

[87] Jonathan Ford, 'Private equity, not the mobile, killed Phones 4U', *Financial Times* (21 Sep 2014).

[88] Jonathan B Cohn, Lillian F Mills, Erin M Towery, 'The Evolution of Capital Structure and Operating Performance After Leveraged Buyouts: Evidence from U.S. Corporate Tax Returns' (2013) at http://ssrn.com/abstract=1764406.

[89] Jules Domenichini, 'Public to Private Transactions, Private Equity Ownership and IPOs: A Case Study of Debenhams' (2012), above.

[90] Above.

remains invested for five to ten years.[91] Indeed, it could be argued that such transfer of wealth to shareholders may be at the expense of stakeholders such as suppliers, employees and customers too.[92] For example, Goergen et al's study[93] in the UK found that job losses and wage reductions were more pronounced in portfolio companies in the year immediately after being subject to buy-out investment compared to control groups of companies, suggesting that improved near-term performance is usually at the expense of stakeholder welfare. Masulis and Thomas also find that portfolio companies may trim their pension surpluses and a certain extent of wealth transfer is observed on the part of US companies following buy-out investment.[94] Ultimately, if portfolio companies are left weaker after buy-out funds have achieved their extraction objectives, the bankruptcy of the company would leave many stakeholders adversely affected, such as suppliers, unsecured creditors etc.[95]

A particular concern from investors in PE funds arises through the use of so-called 'secondaries', i.e. sale of an investee company to another PE manager to realise the value from the investment. This has occurred to a significant extent since the financial crisis, as PE funds have sought to offload their pre-crisis investments and crystallise a return for their investors. However, the ultimate investors may find themselves on both sides of this deal but minus a significant 20 per cent cut in carried interest for the selling PE fund manager. Furthermore, such a scenario offers much reduced opportunities for operational improvement compared to an initial buy-out. Between 2004 and 2014, for example, UK

---

[91] Richard P Nielsen, 'The Private Equity-Leveraged Buyout Form of Finance Capitalism: Ethical and Social Issues, and Potential Reforms' (2008), above.

[92] Above and William W Bratton, 'Private Equity's Three Lessons for Agency Theory' (2008) 3 *Brooklyn Journal of Corporate, Financial & Commercial Law* 1.

[93] Marc Goergen, Noel O'Sullivan and Geoffrey Wood, 'The Employment Consequences of Private Equity Acquisitions: The Case of Institutional Buy Outs' (2014) at http://ssrn.com/abstract=2459890.

[94] Ronald W Masulis and Randall S Thomas, 'Does Private Equity Create Wealth?' (2009), above.

[95] Sudi Sudarsanam, Mike Wright and Jian Huang, 'Going Private Buyouts and Shareholder Wealth Gains: Impact of Bankruptcy Risk' (2007) at http://ssrn.com/abstract=967731.

company Pets at Home was passed through the hands of three PE owners before eventually achieving an IPO.[96]

Buy-out funds' corporate governance behaviour is based unabashedly on the shareholder primacy that is supported by the company law framework. As long as company law entrusts key decision-making to a Board accountable to shareholders and frames shareholders as the only entity to make certain key decisions – in relation to issues like Board appointment and removal,[97] substantial and related-party transactions,[98] capital restructuring[99] and general ratification of directors' conduct[100] – shareholders need not account further for the exercise of their powers. In a private company context with controlling shareholders, shareholder power is magnified to an extreme, away from any scrutiny of markets or regulators. Perhaps some portfolio companies are not insignificant in size or stakeholder footprint, such as in public-to-private deals, but the pursuit of extreme forms of shareholder primacy exposes the overall marginalisation of stakeholders and brings to question whether such imbalances in power and wealth distribution are socially acceptable.[101] Indeed researchers have found that buy-out funds thrive in jurisdictions which provide strong protections in contract and property rights and relatively weak labour rights. Legal frameworks that protect strong private law rights such as contracts and property allow buy-out funds relative freedom to structure their relationships with investors and portfolio companies, and are favourable to high levels of corporate leverage.[102]

The relative opacity and unaccountability of buy-out funds' roles in their portfolio companies, as well as allegations of wealth transfer, have caused concern. In 2007, Sir David Walker recommended that buy-out owned portfolio companies with a market capitalisation exceeding £300 million, with over 1000 full-time equivalent UK employees and generating at least 50 per cent of revenues in the UK should make yearly

---

[96] The Economist. 'Buy in Barons'. 18 January 2014. http://www.economist.com/news/finance-and-economics/21594331-buy-out-firms-selling-each-other-much-their-investors-annoyance-buy

[97] S168, Companies Act 2006.

[98] S190ff, Companies Act 2006.

[99] S641ff, 690ff, 709ff, Companies Act 2006.

[100] S239, Companies Act 2006.

[101] Kevin Morrell and Ian Clark, 'Private Equity and the Public Good' (2010) 96 *Journal of Business Ethics* 249.

[102] Nicholas Bedu and Matthieu Montalban, 'Analysing the Uneven Development of Private Equity in Europe: Legal Origins and Diversity Of Capitalism' (2014) 12 *Socio-Economic Review* 33.

enhanced disclosures to the public in addition to yearly financial information filing. Such disclosures include a business review, such as in section 414A of the Companies Act, which discusses non-financial performance and the company's engagement with and impact upon a range of stakeholders.[103] These are to apply on a comply-or-explain basis and capture portfolio companies managed by fund managers who fall outside of the scope of the AIFM Directive, which to an extent also addresses the above concerns.

The AIFM Directive, transposed into Regulations in the UK,[104] provides for regulatory scrutiny by compelling disclosure by fund managers leading up to the buy-out, as well as post buy-out. Leading up to the buy-out, fund managers have to make disclosure of acquisition thresholds from 10 per cent of voting rights, and at every additional 10 per cent thereafter.[105] Where a buy-out fund has obtained control of the non-listed portfolio company, disclosures have to be made to the company (in particular its employees), shareholders and the Financial Conduct Authority in relation to: the identity of the fund managers and funds that have acquired control, their policies in managing conflicts of interest between the funds, managers and portfolio company, and their policies relating to employees and employment in the portfolio company.[106] Further, the fund managers have to disclose their business intentions in the portfolio company, including whether there are any repercussions on employment and changes in employment policy.[107] However, the UK regulator allows exemption from disclosure of any of the above information if serious prejudice would be occasioned to the company.[108] These ex ante forms of disclosure may on the one hand be argued to be minimalist as they do not necessarily change buy-out funds' agenda or behaviour and could provide the opportunity for funds to frame them in acceptable and self-justifying

---

[103] Walker Working Group, Disclosure and Transparency in Private Equity-Final Report (Dec 2007) at www.walkerworkinggroup.com, adopted as the Walker Guidelines by the BVCA, at http://www.bvca.co.uk/Research Publications/Publications/WalkerGuidelines.aspx.

[104] Financial Services and Markets (The Alternative Fund Managers) Regulations 2013, Part 5, s34ff.

[105] Article 27, AIFMD; sections 36, 38, Financial Services and Markets (The Alternative Fund Managers) Regulations 2013.

[106] Art 28, AIFMD; section 39, Financial Services and Markets (The Alternative Fund Managers) Regulations 2013.

[107] Art 28(4), AIFMD; s40, Financial Services and Markets (The Alternative Fund Managers) Regulations 2013.

[108] Section 41, Financial Services and Markets (The Alternative Fund Managers) Regulations 2013.

ways. However, it is also possible that such disclosures invite public and regulatory scrutiny, and may exert a form of moral suasion against blatantly extractive behaviour.

The AIFM Directive also requires yearly annual reporting that the portfolio company makes to shareholders to be made available to employees.[109] In fact, the AIFM Directive's provision is arguably weak as shareholder-focused disclosures would not necessarily be useful to stakeholders such as employees. The UK has strengthened such disclosure requirements to include a business review, such as suggested under the Walker Guidelines, and narrative reporting highlighting key events in the company in the past year, the company's likely future development and the extent and reasons for any acquisition or disposal of the company's capital.[110] Again, yearly transparency subjects buy-out funds' roles in portfolio companies to wider scrutiny, and may highlight the chasms of wealth distribution in the company. However, transparency does not necessarily translate into policies or actions against the ownership impact of PE funds on their investee companies. In the overall context of shareholder primacy in company law and capital markets, it remains questionable what transparency can achieve.

The AIFM Directive's most robust and direct attack upon buy-out funds' extractive behaviour is found in Article 30 which prohibits fund managers in a period of 24 months after the buy-out, from supporting in any way asset stripping of the portfolio company by way of capital reductions, distributions, redemption of shares or acquisition of own shares. Fund managers are prevented from voting in favour of such resolutions and are held to a duty to use best efforts to prevent asset stripping from taking place.[111] This provision protects portfolio companies from asset stripping and excessive extraction by buy-out funds in the first two years after acquisition, but the scope of asset stripping extends only to distributions that exceed the company's profits that year or which would cause net assets to fall below the amount of subscribed capital and reserves. Hence, asset stripping damaging to the company's financial strength is prevented, but buy-out funds could still prioritise wealth transfers towards themselves. Moreover, the prohibition lasts only 24 months after which the buy-out fund is free to determine capital and

---

[109] Art 29, AIFMD; section 42, Financial Services and Markets (The Alternative Fund Managers) Regulations 2013.

[110] Section 42, Financial Services and Markets (The Alternative Fund Managers) Regulations 2013.

[111] Art 30, AIFMD; section 43, Financial Services and Markets (The Alternative Fund Managers) Regulations 2013.

distribution decisions in favour of itself. This provision does not arguably go far enough to protect stakeholders from being expropriated or marginalised, and does not sufficiently instil long-termism in buy-out funds' corporate governance roles.

It may be argued that it is in buy-out funds' interests to make the portfolio company successful and profitable in order that the fund may exit in due course. If the company were to be floated on the stock exchange,[112] its profitability, prospects and governance need to be healthy in order to do so, and mandatory disclosure required under securities regulation extends to at least three years of company information prior to flotation. The need for such disclosure would ensure that the company is maintained in a state fit for flotation.[113] However, Harbula's empirical research points out that many buy-out funds do not achieve greatly increased disposal value as many portfolio companies with struggling debt burdens are not that attractive.[114] Further, not all buy-out funds manage their portfolio companies well or with dedication, and Bratton[115] reports that private equity funds pass their 'junk targets' to one another when exit is required, and trade-sales, a very common private equity exit route, can obscure the lacklustre performance or indeed failures of the selling fund in relation to the portfolio company. Such a market failure is sustained largely because funds are not sufficiently monitored or controlled by their locked-in investors even if the law and regulation for limited partnerships and under the AIFM Directive have improved investor scrutiny and expressions of rights. Indeed, a number of commentators report that large numbers of buy-out portfolio companies become bankrupt in buy-out fund management or soon after exit.[116]

In sum, private equity funds' immensely powerful and significantly involved corporate governance roles in portfolio companies, whether in

---

112 Viral V Acharya, Conor Kehoe and Michael Reyner, 'Private Equity vs PLC Boards in the U.K.: A Comparison of Practices and Effectiveness' (2008), above.

113 Götz Müller, Manuel Vasconcelos, 'Listed Private Equity and the Case of Exits' (2010) at http://ssrn.com/abstract=1557007.

114 Peter Harbula, 'Operating Performance, Valuation, Leverage and Corporate Governance of Leveraged Buy-Out Transactions: A Continental European Perspective' (2011) at http://ssrn.com/abstract=1876454.

115 William W Bratton, 'Private Equity's Three Lessons for Agency Theory' (2008), above.

116 Above and Sudi Sudarsanam, Mike Wright and Jian Huang, 'Going Private Buyouts and Shareholder Wealth Gains: Impact of Bankruptcy Risk' (2007), above.

the venture capital or buy-out context, are instrumental towards their investment objectives – the need to deliver high returns within a fixed time-frame. Such an instrumental corporate governance approaches raises questions regarding the sidelining of stakeholders' interests and highly skewed wealth distributions towards the funds and their managers. Such an instrumental approach is also reliant upon a context of law and ideology that is pro-shareholder primacy, a precept that is not beyond question.

D. CONCLUSION

In his 2014 letter to investors, legendary US investor Warren Buffet described private equity as a misnomer. In his view, the industry brands itself 'private equity' to divert attention from its primary focus on debt – the 1980s terminology 'leveraged buyout firm' remains a more accurate description of such funds. In Buffet's words: 'In truth, "equity" is a dirty word for many private-equity buyers; what they love is debt. And, because debt is currently so inexpensive, these buyers can frequently pay top dollar. Later, the business will be resold, often to another leveraged buyer. In effect, the business becomes a piece of merchandise.'[117]

For the critics, PE funds make money in an entirely instrumental manner – by cutting jobs, taking on excessive debt, and passing on a fatally weakened enterprise after a few years following the extraction of massive fees. The role of PE funds in their investee companies' corporate governance is not inconsistent with the above business model. Nonetheless, PE funds offer investee companies a far more engaged approach to ownership than their peers in public equity markets. Arguably, private equity is responding to the short-term pressures that afflict listed companies; it provides a safe haven which – for a while at least – can be used to implement operational improvements that would not be tolerated if the shares were still exposed to the fluctuating sentiments or regulatory demands of capital markets. Although the approach taken by private equity fund managers is hardly akin to the stewardship philosophy described in the early chapters of this book, it nonetheless introduces a measure of 'voice' into equity ownership. Nevertheless, due to a lack of liquidity, PE funds seek to exploit to the maximum possible extent the

---

[117] Berkshire Hathaway, '50th Annual Letter to Shareholders', February 2015.

ownership and governance privileges that come with equity ownership, and are therefore a logical consequence of a governance system centred on the primacy of the shareholder constituency.

8. Sovereign wealth funds and their corporate governance roles

A. INTRODUCTION

Sovereign wealth funds (SWFs) are a small but not insignificant segment of the international investment community. Compared to global pension and mutual fund assets standing at about USD$212 trillion as of 2014, SWF assets are only a fraction at USD$4.5 trillion in total.[1] Although SWF assets are expected to continue to grow,[2] they are unlikely to become the dominant global investors in the immediate future. However, they attracted much attention through episodes of significant investment in a number of international banking groups during the global financial crisis, notwithstanding the fact that they have only taken minority stakes.[3] They have also drawn attention to themselves in relation to certain foreign acquisitions that were regarded by national governments as being in sensitive or strategic industries.[4] This chapter is dedicated to examining a particular aspect of SWF influence, in the corporate governance of investee companies and the implications of such influence.

[1] William L Megginson and Veljko Fotak, 'Rise of the Fiduciary State: A Survey of Sovereign Wealth Fund Research' (2014) at http://ssrn.com/abstract=2432623.

[2] Filipa Sá and Francesca Viani, 'Shifts in Portfolio Preferences of International Investors: An Application to Sovereign Wealth Funds' (*Bank of England Working Paper* 2011), commenting that the commodities boom, balance of payments imbalance and increase in foreign exchange reserves for some emerging economies continue to create surpluses that can be funnelled into SWFs.

[3] Benjamin J Cohen, 'Sovereign Wealth Funds and National Security: The Great Tradeoff' (2009) 85 *International Affairs* 713 documenting the total amount of SWF investment in global banks in the global financial crisis at USD$60 bn in total.

[4] Bruce Winfield Bean, 'Attack of the Sovereign Wealth Funds: Defending the Republic from the Threat of Sovereign Wealth Funds?' (2009) 18 *Michigan State Journal of International Law* 65 discussing the objections to Dubai Ports World having the rights to manage six US ports after acquisition, in 2006, of P&O, a UK company that managed those ports. Dubai Ports World's American

SWFs are defined as

> special purpose investment funds or arrangements, owned by the general government. Created by the general government for macroeconomic purposes, SWFs hold, manage, or administer assets to achieve financial objectives, and employ a set of investment strategies which include investing in foreign financial assets. … SWFs are commonly established out of balance of payments surpluses, official foreign currency operations, the proceeds of privatizations, fiscal surpluses, and/or receipts resulting from commodity exports.'[5]

They are however distinguished from central banks or state-owned enterprises. SWFs are created by governments to participate in domestic and global investment opportunities, albeit as part of their long-term fiscal management, thereby connecting public financial objectives with private financial methodologies, conflating state-market or public-private distinctions.[6] It may of course be argued that such distinctions are artificial and meaningless as states are intertwined with their economies and markets are shaped by socio-political forces.[7] That said, SWFs represent a paradigmatic creature in this interface, and take on both statecraft-like[8] as well as market-based behaviour,[9] as this chapter will explore. Such behaviour is driven by a number of factors discussed in

---

operations were wholly hived off and then divested eventually. Also discussed is CNOOC's failed bid for UNOCAL due to political pressure in the US.

[5] International Working Group of Sovereign Wealth Funds, IMF, *Generally Accepted Principles and Practices: Santiago Principles* (October 2008) at http://www.iwg-swf.org/pubs/eng/santiagoprinciples.pdf.

[6] Fabio Bassan, *The Law of Sovereign Wealth Funds* (Cheltenham: Edward Elgar, 2011) at Chapter 1.

[7] Above, and see Michel Aglietta, 'Sovereign Wealth Funds and the Mutation of Global Finance' (2014) 8 *Law and Financial Markets Review* 282.

[8] See notion of 'economic diplomacy' discussed in Henry Wai-Chung Yeung, 'From National Development to Economic Diplomacy? Governing Singapore's Sovereign Wealth Funds' (2011) 24 *The Pacific Review* 625; Friedrich Wu and Koh De Wei, 'From Financial Assets to Financial Statecraft: The Case of China and Emerging Economies of Africa and Latin America' (2014) 23 *Journal of Contemporary China* 781.

[9] Discussed in Rolando Avendaño, Javier Santiso. 'Are Sovereign Wealth Funds Politically Biased? A Comparison with other Institutional Investors' in Narjess Boubakri, Jean-Claude Cosset (eds), Institutional Investors in Global Capital Markets (Emerald Group, 2011); Christopher Balding, 'A Portfolio Analysis of Sovereign Wealth Funds' (2008) at http://ssrn.com/abstract=1141531 discusses this as investment behaviour focused on financial returns, and therefore not dissimilar from other institutions in the capital markets.

Section B, which shape SWFs' corporate governance roles where they invest in corporate equity.

Table 8.1[10] below maps the current count of SWFs in the world, and although many SWFs come from emerging economies, developed economies such as Norway and the US also have significant SWFs.

Table 8.1 Current count of SWFs in the world

Asia Pacific
Australian Future Fund
Brunei Investment Agency
China – Africa Development Fund
China Investment Corporation
China – National Social Security Fund
China – SAFE Investment Company
Hong Kong – Monetary Authority IP
Indonesia – Government Investment Unit
Kiribati – Revenue Equalization Reserve Fund
Korea Investment Corporation
Malaysia – Khazanah Nasional
Mongolia – FSF
New Zealand Superannuation Fund
Papua New Guinea – SWF
Singapore – GIC Private Limited
Singapore – Temasek Holdings
Timor-Leste Petroleum Fund
Vietnam – State Capital Investment Corporation
Middle East and North Africa
Bahrain – Mumtalakat Holding Company
Algeria – Revenue Regulation Fund
National Development Fund of Iran
Iraq DFI
Kuwait Investment Authority
Libyan Investment Authority
Oman Investment Fund
Oman – State General Reserve Fund

[10] Taken from the Sovereign Wealth Fund Institute website at http://www.swfinstitute.org/sovereign-wealth-fund-profiles/.

Palestine Investment Fund	
Qatar Investment Authority	
Saudi Arabia – Public Investment Fund	
Saudi Arabia – SAMA Foreign Holdings	
UAE – Abu Dhabi Investment Authority	
UAE – Abu Dhabi Investment Council	
UAE – Emirates Investment Authority	
UAE – IPIC	
UAE – Investment Corporation of Dubai	
UAE – Mubadala Development Company	
UAE – RAK Investment Authority	
Europe	
France – Strategic Investment Fund	
Ireland Strategic Investment Fund	
Italian Strategic Fund	
Norway – Government Pension Fund – Global	
Russian Direct Investment Fund	
Russia – National Welfare Fund	
Russia – Reserve Fund	
Central Asia	
Azerbaijan – State Oil Fund	
Kazakhstan – Samruk-Kazyna	
Kazakhstan National Fund	
Kazakhstan NIC	
Turkmenistan Stabilization Fund	
Sub-Saharan Africa	
Angola – Fundo Soberano de Angola	
Botswana – Pula Fund	
Equatorial Guinea – FFG	
Gabon – Sovereign Wealth Fund	
Ghana – Petroleum Funds	
Mauritania – NFHR	
Mauritius – SWF	
Nigerian Sovereign Investment Authority	
Nigeria – Bayelsa Development and Investment Corporation	
Senegal FONSIS	

Table 8.1 (continued)

Latin America and the Caribbean
Bolivia – FINPRO
Brazil – Sovereign Fund of Brazil
Chile – ES Fund
Chile – Pension Reserve Fund
Fondo Mexicano del Petroleo
Mexico – Stabilization Fund
Panama Sovereign Wealth Fund
Peru – FEF
Trinidad and Tobago – HSF
UK – ODF – Falkland Islands
Venezuela – FIEM
North America
Canada – Alberta's Heritage Fund
USA – Alabama Trust Fund
USA – Alaska Permanent Fund
USA – LEQTF
USA – New Mexico State IC
USA – North Dakota Legacy Fund
USA – Texas Permanent School Fund
USA – Texas Permanent University Fund
USA – Permanent Wyoming Mineral Trust Fund
USA – West Virginia Future Fund

Source: Adapted from SWF Institute at http://www.swfinstitute.org/sovereign-wealth-fund-profiles/ (accessed 6 Oct 2015).

Of the numerous SWFs in the world, this chapter is specifically concerned with corporate equity-owning SWFs that have the opportunity to take on corporate governance roles. Such roles are placed directly at the public-private interface we mentioned above, as SWFs take on a private sector and market-facing position as shareholders, while bound to pursue their state-based objectives too.

Corporate equity-owning SWFs tend to be the larger and most internationally significant ones. SWFs with greater volumes of assets are likelier to diversify in their investments, taking on higher risk assets such as corporate equity. They are also likelier to invest beyond domestic corporate equity, in foreign capital markets. The largest SWFs as at end

2015 are the Norway Global Pension Fund (USD$873 bn), the Abu Dhabi Investment Authority (USD$773 bn), the China Investment Corporation (USD$746.70 bn), Saudi Arabia's SAMA Holdings (USD$671 bn) and the Kuwait Investment Authority (USD$592 bn).[11]

In determining the asset allocation of SWFs, and in particular, whether they hold corporate equity in domestic and/or foreign markets, the raison d'être of the fund is important. The objective of the fund's creation, rooted in certain fiscal policies, plays a key role in determining asset allocation and investment strategy. One commentator also found that SWF creation can be a result of peer emulation between states, and hence the objectives of such SWFs and their investment strategies may also be influenced by such emulation and trend-following.[12]

Objectives of SWFs

The IMF has typologised five types of SWFs, namely, the stabilisation fund, savings fund, reserve investment corporation, development fund and pension reserve fund.[13] These types are not fixed and mutually exclusive categories; rather, they represent a continuum of objectives that SWFs can grow and mature into.[14] The stabilisation fund may be regarded as a basic 'starter' vehicle. Stabilisation funds are instituted to insulate the economy against commodity or oil price swings, so that government revenues can be smoothed out even in volatile markets. Stabilisation funds can be used for fiscal purposes during recessions,[15] and for the management of domestic economic phenomena.[16] As stabilisation funds are a fiscal instrument, conservative investment and the

---

[11] The rankings can be found on the Sovereign Wealth Funds Institute website at http://www.swfinstitute.org/fund-rankings/.

[12] Jeffrey Chwieroth, 'Fashions and Fads in Finance: Contingent Emulation and the Political Economy of Sovereign Wealth Fund Creation' (2010) at http://ssrn.com/abstract=1643861.

[13] IMF, 'Sovereign Wealth Funds – A Work Agenda' (2008), available at http://www.imf.org/external/np/pp/eng/2008/022908.pdf.

[14] Edwin M Truman, 'Sovereign Wealth Funds: The Need For Greater Transparency And Accountability' (*Peterson Inst. For Int'l Econ, Policy Brief* No. Pb07-6) 4 (2007) available at http://www.iie.com/publications/pb/pb07-6.pdf.

[15] For example, see Aniaka Oluchi, 'Infrastructural Development: The Vision of Nigerian Sovereign Wealth Fund' (2013) at http://ssrn.com/abstract=2232974.

[16] For example, discussion on the role of the Kuwait Investment Authority during economic recessions and more particularly in economic rebuilding after the expulsion of Iraq in the invasion episode of 1991. Kyle Hatton and Katharina

maintenance of high liquidity are of fundamental importance for the fund to respond quickly to fiscal needs.[17] Smaller stabilisation funds are generally invested in conservative asset classes such as high grade short-term debt securities, money market instruments[18] and foreign currency.[19] SWFs that are principally characterised as having stabilisation purposes are unlikely to be major investors in corporate equity.

Along the continuum, stabilisation funds may grow into larger multi-purpose funds, or into distinct new funds with other objectives.[20] For example, stabilisation funds can take on savings and other objectives. Savings funds are purposed towards converting non-renewable assets, such as extractible commodities and oil, into a more diversified portfolio of assets generating income for future generations, thus serving the purposes of inter-generational equity and avoiding 'Dutch disease'.[21] Such funds, in pursuit of diversification, tend to favour investment in foreign corporate equity in developed economies, as these are regarded as

Pistor, 'Maximizing Autonomy in the Shadow of Great Powers: The Political Economy of Sovereign Wealth Funds' (2011) *Columbia Journal of Transnational Law* 2. Further, major oil price declines in early 2016 have also caused a few governments to decide to use their SWF reserves to smooth out economic cycles, see reports on Qatar and Kuwait having to cut back on SWF investments, or liquidate holdings in order to use reserves, 'Lower Oil Tests Sovereign Wealth Funds', *Financial Times* (22 March 2016).

[17] IMF, 'Sovereign Wealth Funds – A Work Agenda' (2008), above at p. 6.

[18] Ingilab Ahmadov and Kenan Asnali, 'State Oil Fund of Azerbaijan Republic: Past, Present and Future' in Ingilab Ahmadov et al, Sovereign Wealth Funds: New Challenges for Caspian Countries (Baku 2011) at http://www.resourcegovernance.org/sites/default/files/SWFs-Caspian-Countries.pdf.

[19] Sergey Drobeyshevsky, 'Russian Sovereign Wealth Funds' in Ingilab Ahmadov et al, Sovereign Wealth Funds: New Challenges for Caspian Countries (2011), above.

[20] E.g. David Kemme, 'Sovereign Wealth Fund Issues and The National Fund(s) of Kazakhstan' (2012) at http://ssrn.com/abstract=2188391; Yelena Kalyuzhnova, 'The National Fund of the Republic of Kazakhstan(NFRK): From Stress-test to Global Future' in Ingilab Ahmadov et al, *Sovereign Wealth Funds: New Challenges for Caspian Countries* (2011), above.

[21] E.g. The Australian Reserve Fund, see Gordon Clark, 'Temptation and the Virtues of Long-Term Commitment: The Governance of Sovereign Wealth Fund Investment' (2009) at http://ssrn.com/abstract=1349123; Gordon Clark, Adam Dixon and Ashby H B Monk, *Sovereign Wealth Funds: Legitimacy, Governance and Global Power* (Princeton: Princeton University Press 2013) at Chapter 4; the Gulf Funds and the Norway Fund too, see Rawi Abdelal, 'Sovereign Wealth in Abu Dhabi' (2009) 14 *Geopolitics* 317; Gordon Clark, Adam Dixon and Ashby H B Monk, *Sovereign Wealth Funds: Legitimacy, Governance and Global Power* (2013), above at Chapter 5.

safer long-term assets that represent clear diversification from the economic model of resource extraction and export. Investing abroad also avoids the problem of domestic investment causing asset price inflation in the domestic economy.[22]

As SWFs grow and mature, the savings objective may be adopted in addition to the stabilisation objective, thus changing the investment strategy and asset allocation of the fund, such as in Kazakhstan[23] and Russia,[24] and SWFs can further develop absolute returns objectives (reserve investment corporations) to increase the reserve level of funds, such as practised by Australia[25] and China.[26] SWFs that adopt savings and reserve investment objectives generally diversify their asset allocation and invest more significantly in corporate equities. Norway in particular sees investing in foreign corporate equity as an essential part of such diversification.[27] This asset allocation policy is also adopted by the Government Investment Corporation of Singapore and the China Investment Corporation.[28] Commentators find that many SWFs report an asset

---

[22] William L Megginson and Veljko Fotak, 'Rise of the Fiduciary State: A Survey of Sovereign Wealth Fund Research' (2014), above.

[23] Yelena Kalyuzhnova, 'The National Fund of the Republic of Kazakhstan-(NFRK): From Stress-test to Global Future' in Ingilab Ahmadov et al, *Sovereign Wealth Funds: New Challenges for Caspian Countries* (2011), above.

[24] Sergey Drobeyshevsky, 'Russian Sovereign Wealth Funds' in Ingilab Ahmadov et al, *Sovereign Wealth Funds: New Challenges for Caspian Countries* (2011), above.

[25] Gordon Clark, 'Temptation and the Virtues of Long-Term Commitment: The Governance of Sovereign Wealth Fund Investment' (2009), above.

[26] For example, the Chinese SWFs are described by Dixon and Monk as rentier and productivity funds, aimed at capturing value in an entrepreneurial way in order to boost returns to reserves. See Adam D Dixon and Ashby H B Monk, 'Rethinking the Sovereign in Sovereign Wealth Funds' (2011) 37 *Transactions of the Institute of British Geographers* 104.

[27] The Fund allocates over half of its assets to foreign corporate equity, over 30 per cent to the US and 12 per cent to the UK, see Mehmet Caner, Turanay Caner and Thomas Grennes, 'Determinants of Investment by the Norwegian Sovereign Wealth Fund: GDP versus Institutions' (2009) at http://ssrn.com/abstract=1534697.

[28] Henry Wai-Chung Yeung, 'From National Development to Economic Diplomacy? Governing Singapore's Sovereign Wealth Funds' (2011), above; Charlie Cai and Iain Clatcher, 'Chinese Investment Goes Global: The China Investment Corporation' (2009) 17 *Journal of Financial Regulation and Compliance* 9.

allocation of as much corporate equity as debt,[29] moving towards an increasing allocation to equity and higher risk classes of assets.[30] In particular, the Norwegian Fund is reported to own at least 1 per cent of global stock across all equity markets, although its internal governance rules prohibit it from holding more than 10 per cent of any individual company.[31]

As part of the extension of fiscal policy management, SWFs can also play a part in developmental objectives and in the promotion of national champions. In this regard, SWFs may be significant investors in domestic corporate equity, such as the ABU Dhabi Mubadala Corporation,[32] Temasek Holdings of Singapore,[33] the Korea Investment Authority[34] and the French Strategic Fund.[35] The US funds also play a large part in funding school education in states.[36] Finally, SWFs can also fund contingent public liabilities such as pension fund liabilities, as in the case of Norway, and may adopt asset allocation and investment strategies that

---

[29] D G Fernandez and B Eschweiler, 'Sovereign Wealth Funds: A Bottom Up Primer', JP Morgan Research 2008, quoted in Christopher Balding, 'Framing Sovereign Wealth Funds: What We Know and Need to Know' (2009) at http://ssrn.com/abstract=1335556; Dyck and Morse also report similar findings, see Alexander Dyck and Adair Morse, 'Sovereign Wealth Fund Portfolios' (2011) at http://ssrn.com/abstract=1792850.

[30] William L Megginson and Veljko Fotak, 'Rise of the Fiduciary State: A Survey of Sovereign Wealth Fund Research' (2014), above report a typical portfolio profile of 60–65 per cent equities with increased holdings in alternative asset classes such as real estate and infrastructure.

[31] Larry Cata Backer, 'Sovereign Investing and Markets-Based Transnational Rule of Law Building: The Norwegian Sovereign Wealth Fund in Global Markets' (2013) 29 *American University International Law Review* 1.

[32] Rawi Abdelal, 'Sovereign Wealth in Abu Dhabi' (2009), above.

[33] Wilson Ng, 'The Evolution of Sovereign Wealth Funds: Singapore's Temasek Holdings' (2010) 18 *Journal of Financial Regulation and Compliance* 6.

[34] Woochan Kim, 'Korea Investment Corporation: Its Origin and Evolution' (2012) 17 *Journal of the Asia Pacific Economy* 208.

[35] Described by Dixon and Monk as 'territorial SWFs' that are aimed at boosting national strategic industries, see Adam D Dixon and Ashby H B Monk, 'Rethinking the Sovereign in Sovereign Wealth Funds' (2011), above.

[36] Paul Rose, 'North American Dream: The Rise of U.S. and Canadian Sovereign Wealth' (2014) at http://ssrn.com/abstract=2423113.

are similar to institutions managing for long term maturation of liabilities,[37] which includes a significant allocation to corporate equities. Looking forward, some commentators see SWFs as being capable of expanding into more significant roles as lenders or supporters of the last resort for not only domestic but also international markets, in order to protect global financial stability. Such a role would have far-reaching implications in terms of their investment in global corporate equities.[38]

This chapter now focuses on equity-owning SWFs in both the domestic and international spheres. Our literature survey shows that SWFs' investment management policies are shaped by their internal structures and governance which reflect the political and constitutional contexts of various states, in order to effect investment management policies that meet political, social and constitutional objectives. However, the soft law embodied in the Santiago Principles,[39] which provide best practices in the internal governance and structures for SWFs, also have some impact upon SWF investment management practices such as their corporate governance roles. One may query whether SWFs' investment management practices and hence their corporate governance activities, are therefore inextricably politicised. The creation of SWFs is a means of extending fiscal management into the sphere of globalised financial markets, engaging with the benefits that financialisation can offer. As SWFs operate within the context of their domestic political and economic purposes, their engagement with global financial markets is unlikely to be on completely the same footing as market-based actors.

SWFs are rooted in multiple and more complex objectives than those governing market-based funds. At a descriptive level, we observe that SWFs conform to a certain extent to the expectations of market behaviour in terms of investment allocation and conduct, and this may be

---

[37] For example see Rolando Avendaño, Javier Santiso, 'Are Sovereign Wealth Funds Politically Biased? A Comparison with other Institutional Investors' in Narjess Boubakri, Jean-Claude Cosset (eds), *Institutional Investors in Global Capital Markets* (2011), above; Christopher Balding, 'A Portfolio Analysis of Sovereign Wealth Funds' (2008), above.

[38] Katharina Pistor, 'Sovereign Wealth Funds, Banks and Governments in the Global Crisis: Towards a New Governance of Global Finance?' (2009) *European Business Organisation Law Review* 333; Massimilliano Castelli and Fabio Scacciavillani, 'SWFs and State Investments: A Preliminary General Overview' in Fabio Bassan (ed.), *Research Handbook in Sovereign Wealth Funds and International Investment Law* (Cheltenham: Edward Elgar 2015) at p. 9, Chapter 1; Tao Sun and Heiko Hesse, 'Sovereign Wealth Funds and Financial Stability – An Event Study Analysis' (*IMF Working Paper* 2009).

[39] To be discussed later in this Chapter.

important as SWFs may not be able to engage with markets successfully unless they behave in a manner acceptable to markets. However, their investment allocation and corporate governance conduct cannot be explained by market-based paradigms exclusively, as this chapter will explore. We observe that the market's inability to fully grasp the more complex contextual fabric for SWFs results in suspicions against SWFs and has culminated in calls to make SWFs more clearly market-based.[40] However, if SWFs behave in a clearly market-based manner, such as in some of the investment decisions and corporate governance activities pursued, for example, by the Qatar Investment Authority and its subsidiaries, such market-based behaviour can also raise suspicions as to what other motives SWFs are entertaining.[41]

As investors that operate within a more complex context than market-based actors, SWFs open up the thinking space for investment management and conduct in that they are not constrained by, nor do they herd towards, market-cherished concepts such as liquidity and short termism. Perhaps these differences in the SWF approach alienate them from other market players which have been forced to embrace such tenets – due to their own business imperatives and the constraints of their regulatory environment – even if such behaviours are ultimately sub-optimal for long-term value creation. Hence, the differences that certain SWF approaches bring in terms of long term orientation or sustainability become cast in an unnecessarily negative light by envious competitors that cannot afford the luxury of such 'uncommercial' investment parameters. The differences SWFs bring could hence countervail to some degree the insular and sub-optimal effects of financialised markets and therefore we argue that narrow-minded and insular economic constructions for SWFs 'as investors' should not be unconditionally supported at the normative level. We take the view that although we do not necessarily regard SWFs as model investors, there is much to learn from SWFs in not being so rigidly held hostage to insular and financialised market incentives and behaviours.

We turn next to survey how SWFs are constituted, structured and governed to provide the background context for understanding SWFs' investment management approaches.

[40] One of the tenets of the Santiago Principles, to be discussed shortly.
[41] As will be discussed later in this Chapter.

The Structures and Governance of SWFs

The structures and governance of SWFs crucially affect the asset allocation and investment strategies of funds. In particular, we observe from our literature review that the accountability structures and professionalism in funds are important factors that shape asset allocation and investment strategies.

SWFs are created by national governments, but they may be structured differently in order to entail different extents of formal and/or substantive independence from their political masters. The legal basis of SWFs may be found in constitutive law or company law. For example, SWFs could be a statutory body independent of government and have their own legal personalities. SWFs could also be set up as private companies with their own separate legal personalities. In both cases some form of accountability structure would lead back to the government. Alternatively, SWFs may be pools of assets owned by the central bank or ministry of finance, without a separate legal personality.[42] One may be inclined to think that funds with separate legal personalities may be more independent and hence their governance subject to less opaque and political interference. However, the form of separate legal personality does not necessarily correlate with funds' substantive independence, i.e. formal independence through the creation of a separate legal personality does not guarantee substantive independence. This is due to the structures of governance and accountability adopted for the funds and the practical implementation of these structures.

Referring to Bassan's typology of SWFs[43] in respect of their governance structures, SWFs may (a) have a separate legal personality or otherwise and (b) have clearly defined governance structures or otherwise. The four typologies representing different combinations of the above attributes are shown in the diagram below. Utilising Bassan's framework in surveying the relationship between legal basis and substantive independence in funds, we observe that separate legal personalities may not always coincide with substantive independence.

The Australian Future Fund is an example of separate legal personality used to protect the Fund's substantive independence. The Fund is set up to avoid political interference and represents cross-party consensus. Hence its separate legal personality and its clearly defined and high

---

42 IWG Secretariat, 'Sovereign Wealth Funds: Current Institutional and Operational Practices' (2008) at http://www.iwg-swf.org/pubs/eng/swfsurvey.pdf.

43 Fabio Bassan, *The Law of Sovereign Wealth Funds* (2011), above at Chapter 2.

Figure 8.1 Typologies of SWF governance structures

standards of corporate governance allow the Fund to achieve a high level of substantive independence, such as in the appointment of six independent members of the Board, including an independent Chairman. Such independence is likely to prevent the Fund from being made to succumb to political interference with its investment strategy,[44] which is important, as short-lived parliaments in democracies may interfere with SWFs to meet near-term fiscal needs. This also means that the investment behaviour of the Fund is likely to be less politically motivated. Grounded within its constitutional context, the Fund may exhibit more predictable characteristics that are consistent with market-based behaviour.

Where Norway is concerned, the Global Pension Fund is not a separate legal personality. It is a government account opened by the Ministry of Finance at the central bank which is managed by its in-house Fund manager, the NBIM. However, high standards of governance and accountability can be achieved in this case as the Ministry of Finance owes direct accountability to the Norwegian Parliament which approves the Fund's investment strategy. Hence, although the Fund is not a separate legal personality, its substantive independence seems to be high

---

[44] Gordon Clark, 'Temptation and the Virtues of Long-Term Commitment: The Governance of Sovereign Wealth Fund Investment' (2009), above; Gordon Clark, Adam Dixon and Ashby H B Monk, *Sovereign Wealth Funds: Legitimacy, Governance and Global Power* (2013) at Chapter 4.

as a result of accountability mechanisms owed by the Ministry to Parliament, ensuring democratic scrutiny of the Fund's investment objectives and strategies. The Fund's focus on ethical investments and divestments are very much a reflection of its social legitimacy and parliamentary accountability.[45]

Next, the Government of Singapore Corporation is a separate legal personality that is tasked as fund manager to the government.[46] However, the formal independence of the Corporation as a separate legal personality does not always give rise to substantive independence. A number of commentators[47] have discussed how GIC may have been used in forms of economic diplomacy, international statecraft and the furtherance of domestic political objectives. Further, another example, the Chinese Investment Corporation, is also a separately incorporated entity. It is however headed by persons intricately connected with the Chinese Communist Party and their political interests.[48] Such leadership has influenced the CIC's investments domestically as well as abroad. Formal independence is therefore overshadowed by the lack of substantive independence. The Korea Investment Corporation is also a separate legal personality but controlled by government elites and political interests, manifesting in its largely political domestic investments.[49]

The lack of high levels of substantive independence for SWFs in spite of independent constitutive structures may be attributed to the political

---

[45] Gordon L Clark and Ashby H B Monk, 'The Legitimacy and Governance of Norway's Sovereign Wealth Fund: The Ethics of Global Investment' (2009) at http://ssrn.com/abstract=1473973; Øyvind Ytrestøyl Foldal, 'Mitigating Tensions between Domestic Politics and Global Finance – A Study of the Decision Making Process of Norway's Sovereign Wealth Fund' (2010) at http://ssrn.com/abstract=1664344. More will be discussed in Section B.

[46] Yvonne C L Lee, 'The Governance of Contemporary Sovereign Wealth Funds' (2010) 6 *Hastings Business Law Journal* 197.

[47] Victor Shih, 'Tools of Survival: Sovereign Wealth Funds in Singapore and China' (2009) 14 *Geopolitics* 328; Kyle Hatton and Katharina Pistor, 'Maximizing Autonomy in the Shadow of Great Powers: The Political Economy of Sovereign Wealth Funds' (2011), above and Gordon Clark, Adam Dixon and Ashby H B Monk, *Sovereign Wealth Funds: Legitimacy, Governance and Global Power* (2013), above.

[48] Victor Shih, 'Tools of Survival: Sovereign Wealth Funds in Singapore and China' (2009), above; Gordon Clark, Adam Dixon and Ashby H B Monk, *Sovereign Wealth Funds: Legitimacy, Governance and Global Power* (2013), above at Chapter 7.

[49] Woochan Kim, 'Korea Investment Corporation: Its Origin and Evolution' (2012), above.

context of these SWFs. Some of these SWFs are formed by authoritarian states. Further, the structures for some SWFs may reflect complex political relations and bargaining. For example, the Chinese Investment Corporation is an independent entity that is responsible for paying the People's Bank of China (the central bank) for the debt issued by the Ministry of Finance in acquiring its foreign currency reserve assets.[50] Its accountability to the Ministry and underlying obligations to the central bank are complex structures that meet complex political bargains in political turf wars in Chinese bureaucracy.[51] Some commentators argue that political factionalisation underlies the structures and accountability of Chinese SWFs. The number of Chinese SWFs reflects the different factions of bureaucratic power in China that seek to exercise control over China's vast sovereign wealth. These SWFs have exhibited unpredictable investment behaviour[52] due to the changes in political tide and perceived manoeuvres by bureaucrats in their power dynamics.

The structures of certain SWFs may also be used to mask the political nature of certain investment activities. For example, SWFs constituted with independent status could be used to serve as devices to insulate political leaders from their states' wealth, but in reality actually strengthen and legitimate these leaders' control over state wealth. Hatton and Pistor[53] argue that the Kuwait and Abu Dhabi funds have been instituted so as to create perceptions of the separation of state wealth from the ruling families of these states, but are in fact cleverly used to consolidate ruling families' and individuals' power and to placate domestic constituencies.[54] They argue that the Singapore SWFs perform a

---

[50] Leong H Liew and Liping He, 'Operating in an Inharmonious World: China Investment Corporation' (2012) 17 *Journal of the Asia Pacific Economy* 253; Ming Zhang and Fan He, 'China's Sovereign Wealth Fund: Weakness and Challenges' (2009) 17 *China and the World Economy* 101.

[51] Leong H Liew and Liping He, 'Operating in an Inharmonious World: China Investment Corporation' (2012), above.

[52] Victor Shih, 'Tools of Survival: Sovereign Wealth Funds in Singapore and China' (2009), above; Ming Zhang and Fan He, 'China's Sovereign Wealth Fund: Weakness and Challenges' (2009), above.

[53] Kyle Hatton and Katharina Pistor, 'Maximizing Autonomy in the Shadow of Great Powers: The Political Economy of Sovereign Wealth Funds' (2011), above.

[54] See also Gordon Clark, Adam Dixon and Ashby H B Monk, *Sovereign Wealth Funds: Legitimacy, Governance and Global Power* (2013), Chapter 3 on the Kuwait Investment Authority and the Brunei SWF.

similar function in consolidating the power of the ruling party, the People's Action Party. The investment strategy of these SWFs therefore could potentially reflect the interests of domestic power consolidation, cronyism, and also international relations and diplomacy.[55]

In more egregious cases, commentators have found that despite formal structures that seem to bestow certain extents of independence on SWFs, real political interference often manifests itself in the funds' investment allocations.[56] For example fund allocations to certain corporations may be a smokescreen for a form of domestic corruption.[57] It is also observed that many smaller and emerging African funds are both poorly governed and enjoy a low level of substantive independence, being more susceptible to manipulation by powerful ruling entities.[58] Where funds are more susceptible to domestic political interference and/or are used as instruments in international statecraft, investment strategy and asset allocation may be less susceptible to commercially objective explanations. We will explore this in greater detail in Section B.

Professionalism in Fund Management

The level of professionalism in investment management adopted by the SWF also affect its asset allocation and investment strategy. There is no necessary relationship between legal personality, governance structures and the level of professionalism in SWF fund management. Funds that

---

[55] E.g. see Sofia A Johan, April Knill and Nathan Mauck, 'Determinants of Sovereign Wealth Fund Investment in Private Equity vs Public Equity' (2013) 44 *Journal of International Business Studies* 155 find that SWFs invest in companies of high risk where political relations may be weak, and such investment behaviour cannot be explained on objective commercial criteria. See also April Knill, Bong Soo Lee and Nathan Mauck, 'Bilateral Political Relations and Sovereign Wealth Fund Investment' (2011) at http://ssrn.com/abstract=1498518.

[56] Shai Bernstein, Josh Lerner and Antoinette Schoar, 'The Investment Strategies of Sovereign Wealth Funds' (2013) 27 *The Journal of Economic Perspectives* 219.

[57] David Kemme, 'Sovereign Wealth Fund Issues and The National Fund(s) of Kazakhstan' (2012), above.

[58] Thouraya Triki and Issa Faye, 'Africa's Quest for Development: Can Sovereign Wealth Funds Help?' in Narjess Boubakri and Jean Claude Cosset (eds), *Institutional Investors in Global Capital Markets* (2011), above.

are not separate legal personalities may employ professional fund managers (Norway[59]) or otherwise (Timor-Leste[60]). Funds with high levels of substantive independence (e.g. Australia[61]) and funds that enjoy lower levels of substantive independence seem equally to employ professional fund managers, for example, the Singapore[62] and Gulf Funds.[63] There may be funds that enjoy a high substantive level of independence that do not employ professional fund managers, such as Chile,[64] and funds that have a low level of substantive independence that do the same, such as Russia,[65] Kazakhstan,[66] China[67] and Korea.[68]

Professional management in SWFs may be in-house or outsourced. Some SWFs, such as GIC of Singapore, employ a mixture of in-house investment teams and outsourcing of some portfolios to external asset

---

[59] Trude Myklebust, 'The Norwegian Government Pension Fund: Moving Forward on Responsible Investing and Governance' (2010) 3 *Rotman International Journal of Pension Management* 20, but see Gordon L Clark and Ashby H B Monk, 'The Norwegian Government Pension Fund: Ethics over Efficiency' (2010) 3 *Rotman Journal of International Pension Management* 14.

[60] Andrew Ang, 'The Four Benchmarks of Sovereign Wealth Funds' (2010) at http://ssrn.com/abstract=1680485, also see introduction to the Petroleum Fund of Timor Leste which is managed exclusively by its central bank, at https://www.mof.gov.tl/budget-spending/petroleum-fund/.

[61] Above at Chapter 4.

[62] Gordon Clark, Adam Dixon and Ashby H B Monk, *Sovereign Wealth Funds: Legitimacy, Governance and Global Power* (2013), above Chapter 6.

[63] Rawi Abdelal, 'Sovereign Wealth in Abu Dhabi' (2009), above; Bader Alhashel, 'Sovereign Wealth Funds: A Literature Review' (2015) 78 *Journal of Economics and Business* 1; Alexander Dyck and Adair Morse, 'Sovereign Wealth Fund Portfolios' (2011), above.

[64] http://www.hacienda.cl/english/sovereign-wealth-funds/about-the-funds.html.

[65] Sergey Drobeyshevsky, 'Russian Sovereign Wealth Funds' in Ingilab Ahmadov et al, *Sovereign Wealth Funds: New Challenges for Caspian Countries* (2011), above.

[66] David Kemme, 'Sovereign Wealth Fund Issues and The National Fund(s) of Kazakhstan' (2012), above.

[67] Jing Li, 'State As An Entrepreneur: A Study of the Investment Contractual Terms and Level of Control of China's Sovereign Wealth Fund in its Portfolio Firms' (2014) at http://ssrn.com/abstract=2617150; Ming Zhang and Fan He, 'China's Sovereign Wealth Fund: Weakness and Challenges' (2009), above.

[68] Woochan Kim, 'Korea Investment Corporation: Its Origin and Evolution' (2012), above.

managers.[69] Some SWFs outsource asset management completely to a variety of asset managers, such as the Australia Future Fund[70] and Alaska Permanent Fund.[71] Some SWFs are managed exclusively in-house, such as the Abu Dhabi funds which employ highly qualified and well-educated local elites to manage the funds in-house.[72] The outsourcing to professional asset managers may also wax and wane depending on states' economic needs. In late 2015, a number of Gulf funds withdrew from asset managers so that states could have more flexibility in drawing upon wealth funds to meet domestic economic needs after a sustained period of low oil prices.[73]

Professional management has a direct impact on asset allocation and investment management practice, and tends to introduce market-focused behaviour to SWFs. Nevertheless, the use of in-house investment management teams, albeit professionally qualified, is often associated with relatively greater fund opacity, and the market may remain sceptical as to what extent the use of professional in-house fund management demonstrates market-based behaviour on the part of these SWFs.[74] On the whole, professionally managed portfolios of SWFs behave in greater alignment with other institutional investors than politically motivated investors do.

SWFs that employ professional management, whether outsourced or in-house, diversify from conservative fixed income and money market instruments into corporate equity, especially those offered in developed markets.[75] The favourite sectors of corporate equity in developed markets often relate to key industries such as finance, energy, transportation and

---

[69] See GIC Investment Report 2014–15, at http://www.gic.com.sg/report/report-2014-2015/managing_portfolio.html.

[70] http://www.futurefund.gov.au/investment/investment_managers.

[71] http://www.apfc.org/home/Content/investments/managers2009.cfm.

[72] Rawi Abdelal, 'Sovereign Wealth in Abu Dhabi' (2009), above.

[73] 'Sovereign Wealth Funds Withdraw £19bn from Asset Managers', *Financial Times* (6 Dec 2015).

[74] Anthony Wong, 'Sovereign Wealth Funds and the Problem of Asymmetric Information: The Santiago Principles and International Regulations' (2009) 34 *Brooklyn Journal of International Law* 1081.

[75] Above, Mehmet Caner, Turanay Caner and Thomas Grennes, 'Determinants of Investment by the Norwegian Sovereign Wealth Fund: GDP versus Institutions' (2009), above; William L Megginson and Veljko Fotak, 'Rise of the Fiduciary State: A Survey of Sovereign Wealth Fund Research' (2014), above.

telecommunications.[76] As these are also strategic industries, it may be queried whether political interests underlie these investments, a point that will be discussed in greater detail in Section B. Empirical research has also found that levels of foreign corporate equity ownership are higher where external managers are used, and more risky asset classes are also engaged with.[77] For example, distressed firms that seem undervalued are targeted for investment, and such behaviour is consistent with market-based investment behaviour.[78] Commentators opine that the use of external asset managers shapes SWF investment tendencies into more commercially-oriented and hence recognisable market-based investment behaviour.[79]

Where in-house professional management dominates or is exclusively used, corporate equity investments show a regional bias[80] or orientation towards countries that are culturally similar, for example in having a similar dominant religious belief.[81] This may be due to more limited knowledge and exposure on the part of in-house investment teams, who are more comfortable with what is familiar. Professional investment teams also invest in corporate equity in highly developed markets, where higher levels of transparency provide comfort for SWF managers. However, with the growth of emerging economies, more SWFs are investing in these economies in general.[82]

---

[76] Alexander Dyck and Adair Morse, 'Sovereign Wealth Fund Portfolios' (2011), above; William L Megginson and Veljko Fotak, 'Rise of the Fiduciary State: A Survey of Sovereign Wealth Fund Research' (2014), above.

[77] Shai Bernstein, Josh Lerner and Antoinette Schoar, 'The Investment Strategies of Sovereign Wealth Funds' (2013), above.

[78] Jason Kotter and Ugur Lel, 'Friends or Foes? Target Selection Decisions of Sovereign Wealth Funds and Their Consequences' (2010) at http://ssrn.com/abstract=1292407.

[79] James Faulconbridge, 'Rebalancing the Geographies of Financial Services Power: The Role of Sovereign Wealth Funds' (2010) 42 *Environment and Planning* 2271.

[80] Alexander Dyck and Adair Morse, 'Sovereign Wealth Fund Portfolios' (2011), above.

[81] Vidhi Chhaochharia and Luc Laeven, 'The Investment Allocation of Sovereign Wealth Funds' (2009) at http://ssrn.com/abstract=1262383.

[82] Javier Santiso, 'Sovereign Development Funds: Key Financial Actors of the Shifting Wealth of Nations' (OECD *Emerging Markets Network Working Paper* 2008) at http://ssrn.com/abstract=1300288; Javier Santiso, 'Sovereign Funds Are Helping Strike A New World Economic Balance' (2011) at http://ssrn.com/abstract=1877224.

Where SWFs are less professionally managed, largely dominated by bureaucrats[83] who may be appointed to safeguard governments' interests, the investment behaviour of SWFs may be more erratic and less commercially justifiable. This may be the case especially in relation to domestic corporate equity investments where SWFs may be used to further cronyism, prop up ailing companies that are important to state industries, support local monopolies[84] or engage in financial decisions that do not seem commercially supported.[85] In sum, the extent of professional management employed by funds affects their inclination to own corporate equity, domestic and foreign, as well as funds' investment strategies and level of market-based behaviour, as illustrated in Figure 8.2.

In sum, we do not observe predictable or easily typologised patterns of structures and governance of SWFs that relate to certain types of investment strategies and corporate governance behaviour. SWFs seem to adopt structures to implement as well as to obfuscate objectives. In the next section, we turn to the factors in different observed profiles of corporate governance behaviour on the part of SWFs that reflect both strategic and commercially explicable agendas.

---

[83] E.g. the CIC and Korean Investment Corporation, see Woochan Kim, 'Korea Investment Corporation: Its Origin and Evolution' (2012), above; Ming Zhang and Fan He, 'China's Sovereign Wealth Fund: Weakness and Challenges' (2009), above; Jing Li, 'State As An Entrepreneur: A Study of the Investment Contractual Terms and Level of Control of China's Sovereignwealth Fund in its Portfolio Firms' (2014), above; but see Guo Li, 'Demystifying the Chinese Sovereign Wealth Fund – A Perspective of the U.S. Financial Regulation' (2010) at http://ssrn.com/abstract=1641628; Friedrich Wu and Arifin Seah, 'Would China's Sovereign Wealth Fund Be a Menace to the USA?' (2008) 16 *China and the World Economy* 33.

[84] David Kemme, 'Sovereign Wealth Fund Issues and The National Fund(s) of Kazakhstan' (2012), above.

[85] Larry Cata Backer, 'Sovereign Investing in Times of Crisis: Global Regulation of Sovereign Wealth Funds, State Owned Enterprises and the Chinese Experience' (2009) *Transnational Law and Contemporary Problems* 101; Shai Bernstein, Josh Lerner and Antoinette Schoar, 'The Investment Strategies of Sovereign Wealth Funds' (2013), above; Joshua Aizenmann and Reuven Glick, 'Sovereign Wealth Funds: Stylized Facts About Their Determinants and Governance' (*NBER Working Paper* 2008) at http://www.nber.org/papers/w14562.

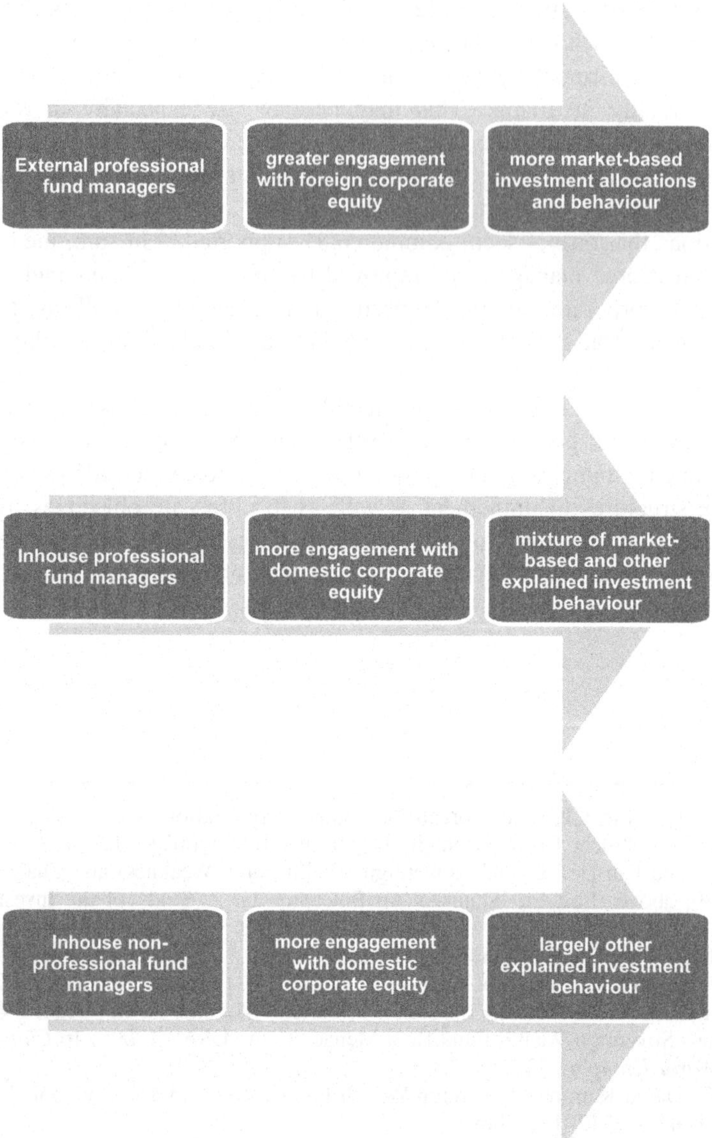

Figure 8.2 Professionalisation of SWF and market behaviour

B. DRIVERS AND FACTORS SHAPING THE CORPORATE GOVERNANCE ROLES OF SWFS

The corporate governance roles of SWFs are part of their investment strategies. First, we suggest that SWFs' corporate governance roles in their domestic investments differ somewhat from their foreign investments. SWFs' domestic corporate equity investments are often influenced by factors other than market-based commercially explicable behaviour. Their corporate governance activities in relation to domestic corporate equity investments manifest those mixed objectives.

We suggest that SWFs' corporate governance roles as foreign corporate investors are shaped by both their strategic interests and commercially objective market-based assessments. We also suggest that SWFs' corporate governance roles are affected by host country responses and developments at the international level in the political-legal sphere. Taken together, SWFs' corporate governance roles are a manifestation of the navigation of their political interests in the transnational paradigm of the global economy, finance and law.

This book is written from an unavoidably UK perspective and therefore concerned with the corporate governance role of foreign SWFs in UK publicly traded companies. However, in order to provide a more compelling understanding of foreign SWFs' corporate governance roles, it is instructive to compare with their corporate governance roles in domestic corporate investments.

SWF Investments in Their Domestic Corporate Equity

SWFs may invest in domestic corporate equity for a number of reasons, for example to support national fiscal and industrial policy.[86] Commentators have observed that such investments are strategically targeted at grooming national champions into globally competitive companies.[87] The French Strategic Fund is patently for the purposes of investing in significant French companies, such as Aéroports Paris, Alcatel-Lucent,

---

[86] Alan Gelb, Silvano Tordo, Havard Halland, Noora Arfaa and Gregory Smith, 'Sovereign Wealth Funds and Long-Term Development Finance' (*World Bank Policy Research Working Paper* 2014).

[87] E.g. in China and Russia, see Justin O'Brien, 'Barriers to Entry: Foreign Direct Investment and the Regulation of Sovereign Wealth Funds' (2008) 42 *International Lawyer* 1231.

Danone, Nexans etc.[88] These stakes are long-term oriented but minority stakes. There is little evidence of the Fund's corporate governance role in these companies and it can be surmised that the passive corporate governance role is itself strategic in order to provide a form of stable equity support for French companies that are otherwise expected to operate along largely commercial lines.

Singapore's Temasek Holdings is also a domestic strategic investor,[89] but it takes significant or majority shareholdings in Singapore's key industrial companies and national champions, some of which are local monopolies, such as the Singapore Mass Rapid Transit Corporation (the subway system), PSA International (port management), Singapore Airlines, Singapore Technologies and a number of subsidiaries, Singapore Telecommunications, Mediacorp (major television services provider) and the Development Bank of Singapore.[90] Such strategic investments often entail engaged corporate governance roles. Where Temasek is a majority shareholder in the national champion concerned, its corporate governance role could extend into decision-making as it holds the rights of directorial appointment and removal. However, Gourevitch and Shinn have observed that although in possession of strong corporate governance control in its investee companies, Temasek's profile is one of restraint and exemplary conduct for sustaining a good reputation.[91] Nevertheless, practical evidence of Temasek's corporate governance role in its investee companies is difficult to obtain as disclosure is scarce in that context.

SWFs' domestic investments can also be pursuant to politically motivated reasons such as cronyism or for the purposes of consolidating domestic ruling power. One commentator claims that the domestic investments made by Chinese sovereign wealth funds could be politically motivated as enterprise leaders and political leaders are closely linked by

---

88 http://www.nexans.com/eservice/Corporate-en/navigatepub_205133_-21794/The_Fonds_Strategique_d_Investissement_French_Sove.html for example; also see Adam D Dixon and Ashby H B Monk, 'Rethinking the Sovereign in Sovereign Wealth Funds' (2011), above.

89 Henry Wai-Chung Yeung, 'From National Development to Economic Diplomacy? Governing Singapore's Sovereign Wealth Funds' (2011), above; Larry Catá Backer, 'SWFs in Five Continents and Three Narratives: Similarities and Differences' in Fabio Bassan (ed.), *Research Handbook in Sovereign Wealth Funds and International Investment Law* (2015), above at p. 57, Chapter 3.

90 See Temasek Review 2015 at http://www.temasekreview.com.sg/index.html.

91 Peter A Gourevitch and James Shinn, *Political Power and Corporate Control* (Princeton University Press 2005) at pp. 201–206.

party membership and by being part of the same elite cohort.[92] Further, such investments could also entail indirect extraction of benefit and exercise of influence.[93] However, the perception of Chinese SWFs may be negatively affected by those of Chinese State-owned Enterprises which are subject to well-documented political interference resulting in tunnelling, expropriation of minority shareholders and generally poor standards of corporate governance.[94]

Empirical research seems to suggest that on average, even if SWFs invest significantly in domestic enterprises, or act as capital injectors of the last resort,[95] they do not assume glaring corporate governance powers and roles. However, this conclusion is tentative at best as little information transparency is offered regarding SWF relations with their domestic investee companies. Much exercise of influence could well be behind the scenes, but it may be argued that this opacity regarding the exercise of their power is not a matter for concern as long as the companies benefit from such influence. However, at a wider level, it is uncertain if SWF influences ultimately provide an unfair advantage for SWF-invested companies and are therefore prejudicial to other enterprises. SWF investment and influence may also help maintain certain monopolies.

Dyck and Morse[96] are of the view that SWFs are active investors, but in a more defensive manner, focused upon the protection of investment value. However, there are also reports of SWFs' investments being used to bail out domestic companies, and indeed the lack of assumption of corporate governance monitoring in those cases may create moral hazard for the companies, such as in the episode of the Korean Investment Corporation's issuance of foreign currency swaps with Korean banks in

---

[92] Larry Cata Backer, 'Sovereign Investing in Times of Crisis: Global Regulation of Sovereign Wealth Funds, State Owned Enterprises and the Chinese Experience' (2009), above.

[93] Jing Li, 'State As An Entrepreneur: A Study of the Investment Contractual Terms and Level of Control of China's Sovereign Wealth Fund in its Portfolio Firms' (2014), above.

[94] Jonathan G S Koppell, 'Political Control for China's State-Owned Enterprises: Lessons from America's Experience with Hybrid Organizations' (2007) 20 *Governance* 255–78; Peter A Gourevitch and James Shinn, *Political Power and Corporate Control* (2005), above at pp. 192–200.

[95] Bader Alhashel, 'Sovereign Wealth Funds: A Literature Review' (2015), above.

[96] Alexander Dyck and Adair Morse, 'Sovereign Wealth Fund Portfolios' (2011), above.

order to finance their borrowings.[97] There are anecdotal stories of SWFs' subtle but powerful influences behind the scenes of investee companies. We are also aware of reports of modest and ineffective engagement of SWFs with their corporate governance roles, in spite of friendlier conditions for the assumption of such roles at home. This mixture of ambivalent but unconfirmed observations of SWF behaviour as governance actors perhaps goes towards showing that SWF investments in domestic corporate equity are based on a complex fabric of rationale and motivations and are less discernible in terms of their investment management conduct and behaviour.

SWF Investments in Foreign Corporate Equity

SWF investments in foreign corporate equity are often viewed with unease by domestic governments and media, as questions often loom as to whether such investments are strategic in nature. The negative connotations associated with strategic foreign investments revolve around industrial, commercial and military espionage, potential threat to the economic stability or 'way of life' in the host country, fears of asset or job stripping from investee companies, or relocation of operations or technical know-how to the country of the investor.[98] There may also be concerns that SWFs may cause financial instability if they sell their large stakes, and their strategic interests could be in conflict with the national security interests of their host countries.[99] However, as a number of commentators acknowledge,[100] the negative connotations are more imagined than real at the moment. SWF foreign investments are often

---

[97] Woochan Kim, 'Korea Investment Corporation: Its Origin and Evolution' (2012), above.

[98] Bruce Winfield Bean, 'Attack of the Sovereign Wealth Funds: Defending the Republic from the Threat of Sovereign Wealth Funds?' (2009), above.

[99] Justin O'Brien, 'Barriers to Entry: Foreign Direct Investment and the Regulation of Sovereign Wealth Funds' (2008), above. But see A Blundell-Wignall, Y Hu and J Yermo, 'Sovereign Wealth and Pension Fund Issues', *OECD Working Papers on Insurance and Private Pensions* 2008; Tao Sun and Heiko Hesse, 'Sovereign Wealth Funds and Financial Stability – An Event Study Analysis' (2009), above.

[100] Ronald J Gilson and Curtis J Milhaupt, 'Sovereign Wealth Funds and Corporate Governance: A Minimalist Response to the New Mercantilism' (2008) 60 *Stanford Law Review* 1345; Harry McVea, 'Corrupting Capitalism? Sovereign Wealth Funds and the United Kingdom's Regulatory Framework' (2013) *Journal of Business Law* 434.

commercially explicable even if they may be made with strategic purposes in mind.

Commercially Explicable and Market-Based Investment Behaviour

Investment in foreign corporate equity is often seen as an ideal means of diversifying from state reliance on certain sources of wealth creation, such as in commodities or oil. SWF investments in foreign corporate equity in mature capital markets such as the US and UK are commercially explicable and rational.[101] As we have already observed, the Norwegian Fund is reported to own at least 1 per cent of global stock, much of which is concentrated in the US and Europe.

Hence, many commentators[102] report that SWFs behave like institutional investors in their commercially explicable allocations to corporate equity, and also in their passive corporate governance capacities. They generally take diversified and minority stakes, and lack incentives to be activist investors. Further, even when SWFs demonstrate shareholder engagement behaviour, this is usually defensive in character,[103] i.e. reacting to performance or governance problems in an investee company in order to safeguard investment value. Further SWFs may even be highly cautious in such defensive stances as market perceptions surrounding SWFs are often uneasy and may discourage SWFs from assuming any engaged position. In practice, SWFs do exit from their investments, but there have been no reports of such exits triggering massive price declines or instability for investee companies concerned, for example, the exit of the Abu Dhabi Fund investment in Barclays[104] made at the height of the global financial crisis, and the exit of Temasek Holdings from Bank of America after suffering severe losses in its Merrill Lynch stake.[105]

---

101 Bader Alhashel, 'Sovereign Wealth Funds: A Literature Review' (2015), above.

102 Rolando Avendaño and Javier Santiso, 'Are Sovereign Wealth Funds Politically Biased? A Comparison with other Institutional Investors' in Narjess Boubakri, Jean-Claude Cosset (eds), *Institutional Investors in Global Capital Markets* (2011), above; Jason Kotter and Ugur Lel, 'Friends or Foes? Target Selection Decisions of Sovereign Wealth Funds and Their Consequences' (2010), above.

103 Alexander Dyck and Adair Morse, 'Sovereign Wealth Fund Portfolios' (2011), above.

104 See 'Abu Dhabi quietly cashes out of Barclays', *Financial Times* (18 July 2013).

105 'Temasek Counts the Cost of Merrill Stake', *The Wall Street Journal* (18 May 2009).

The following will discuss where we observe strategic forms of investment behaviour in SWFs' foreign corporate equity investments. Such strategic forms of behaviour may sometimes be very subtle. However, ethical investing led by the Norwegian Global Pension Fund is an example of overt and unabashed strategy, and purports to lead the market in investment management behaviour.

Strategic Investing in Foreign Corporate Equity

Strategic investing can be carried out in foreign corporate equity as an extension of domestic industrial policy. For example, investing in regional corporations may strengthen the competitive position of national champions in the region. Temasek Holdings of Singapore for example has a regional focus and invests 40 per cent of its assets in key industries in the Asia-Pacific region. It has minority stakes in three major Chinese banks, a major retailer in Hong Kong (AG Watsons), a property developer in Indonesia (Pulau Indah Ventures Sdn Bhd) and Korean health sciences company Celltrion.[106] Notable episodes of its regional acquisitions include a majority stake in Thai telecommunications company Shincorp that was beneficially owned by former prime minister Thaksin Shiniwatra, which resulted in public revolt against the prime minister, his ousting and the eventual divestment of the Temasek stake at a loss.[107] Temasek also acquired a majority stake in Indonesian bank PT Danamon, which it purported to sell to its national champion DBS Bank in 2013. It may be surmised that the stake acquired by Temasek could be for the purposes of furthering DBS Bank's regional growth and dominance. The Indonesian bank regulators however were sceptical of the deal and DBS Bank's regional ambitions in dominating the financial market. The deal ultimately collapsed although Temasek has maintained its majority stake of 67 per cent to date.[108] The above episodes may be adduced to show that strategic investing by SWFs can be a delicate affair and may easily attract a national backlash.

Another reason for strategic investing may be to ensure supply security for industries that are nationally important. The CIC makes strategic

---

[106] http://www.temasekreview.com.sg/index.html.

[107] Wilson Ng, 'The Evolution of Sovereign Wealth Funds: Singapore's Temasek Holdings' (2010), above; Suntharee, Lhaopadchan, 'The Politics of Sovereign Wealth Fund Investment: The Case of Temasek and Shin Corp.' (2010) 18 *Journal of Financial Regulation and Compliance* 15.

[108] 'DBS Bid for Indonesia's Danamon Collapses', *Financial Times* (31 July 2013).

investments in enterprises in countries that China depends on for energy, commodities and food security. Although not a major part of the CIC's portfolio, CIC investments in Latin America and Africa are largely in agriculture, oil and minerals.[109] However, the CIC's investments are modest compared to government procurement and foreign direct investment schemes that the Chinese government, banks and state-owned enterprises have engaged in with Latin American and African companies.[110] In contrast, the CIC is not a vehicle used for patently strategic purposes although China as a whole has engaged in strategic investment in many emerging economies overseas.

The experiences of Temasek and CIC show that even in forms of strategic investing, SWFs do not assume overt stances of commercial colonisation as some fear. They do seek synergies with domestic industrial policy and it would be naïve to suggest that the strategic aspects of their investments are merely coincidental to market-based commercial objectives. However, they do not often take majority stakes, they seem to work for the success of the investee company as a means of benefiting their industrial policy, and certainly have not produced alarming effects such as the destruction of long-term value or major disturbance to the host country's industrial and economic landscape.[111] For example, the CIC's investment in a non-voting stake in US private equity firm Blackstone demonstrates the Chinese strategic interest in the financial services industry without indications of malevolent influence. The synergies between CIC and Blackstone ultimately culminated in Blackstone being appointed to manage some CIC portfolios[112] as well as Blackstone's significant investments in a few Chinese companies including

---

[109] Gungwu Wang and Yongnian Zhang, 'An Update on Sovereign Wealth Funds' in *China: Development and Governance* (Singapore: World Scientific Publishing 2013) at p. 201. 'China's sovereign wealth fund shifts focus to agriculture', *Financial Times* (17 June 2014).

[110] Barbara Kotschwar, Theodore H Moran, and Julia Muir, 'Chinese Investment in Latin American Resources: The Good, the Bad, and the Ugly' (*Peter Institute for International Economics Working Paper* 2012) at http://www.iie.com/publications/wp/wp12-3.pdf.

[111] Jennifer Cooke, 'Finding the Right Balance for Sovereign Wealth Fund Regulation: Open Investment vs. National Security' (2009) *Columbia Business Law Review* 728; Richard Epstein and Amanda Rose, 'The Regulation of Sovereign Wealth Funds: The Virtues of Going Slow' (2009) 76 *University of Chicago Law Review* 111.

[112] Kyle Hatton and Katharina Pistor, 'Maximizing Autonomy in the Shadow of Great Powers: The Political Economy of Sovereign Wealth Funds' (2011), above.

Blue Star in the chemicals sector.[113] The synergies produced in such strategic investing often show how complex the SWFs' corporate governance role is in achieving win-win results for both parties, and simplistic notions of destructive or opportunistic behaviour on the part of SWFs are often too biased.

SWFs that show a mixture of strategic and commercially explicable objectives in their foreign investments are often structured in a way that projects a market-based, commercially oriented investing image. For example, Singapore's Temasek and China's CIC are incorporated as separate legal entities in order to strengthen their appearance of independence, but they are led and managed by highly qualified individuals who are also politically connected with ruling politicians.[114] Temasek is further subject to an accountability regime which is headed by the elected President of Singapore.[115] Temasek, to a greater extent than CIC, also engages in extensive outsourcing to reputable asset managers, besides managing portfolios in-house by highly qualified teams. The mixture of merit-based and politically connected recruitment, and the hybrid approach of in-house and external fund management[116] translate into investment behaviour that is commercially justifiable and yet also serves politically strategic interests.

In terms of such SWFs' corporate governance behaviour, we observe that funds adopt a generally benign and constructive stance in corporate governance. First, such funds project a supportive stance towards the long-term viability of the company. The long-term viability of the investee company is not only in the commercial interests of the fund, but also in its strategic interests, as the strategic interests lie in combining synergies between foreign investments and the domestic interests of the fund. Hence, Bertoni and Lugo find in their empirical research that

---

[113] Leong H Liew and Liping He, 'Operating in an Inharmonious World: China Investment Corporation' (2012), above.

[114] Kyle Hatton and Katharina Pistor, 'Maximizing Autonomy in the Shadow of Great Powers: The Political Economy of Sovereign Wealth Funds' (2011), above.

[115] Yvonne C L Lee, 'The Governance of Contemporary Sovereign Wealth Funds' (2010), above, but all elected Presidents of Singapore to date have been connected to the ruling party to some extent – two out of the three elected Presidents in Singapore have been former members of the ruling party and ministers of significant position, the remaining one was a senior bureaucrat and former ambassador.

[116] Critically discussed in Alan Gelb, Silvano Tordo, Havard Halland, Noora Arfaa and Gregory Smith, 'Sovereign Wealth Funds and Long-Term Development Finance' (2014), above.

the market welcomes an SWF stake, as it sees the mixture of commercial and strategic interests on the part of the SWF as offering protective goodwill for the investee company concerned.[117] A couple of commentators argue that the positive market reaction to an SWF stake is due to confidence that the SWF will positively contribute to the business prospects of the investee company by providing for it domestic market access and government contract opportunities. Contrary to paranoid commentators who fear that SWFs invest in strategic industries in host states in order to destroy value or threaten social stability, the subtle advantages of SWFs' strategic corporate governance persona seem more evident in many cases.[118] Dewenter et al argue that as part of their strategic interests, SWFs contribute a valuable monitoring role in their corporate governance capacity towards investee companies' long-term success.[119] As SWFs do not have liabilities to meet and are usually only accountable to a single entity, the government, they are not affected by short termist pressures and are able to provide long-termist, stable forms of investment that contribute to the long-term viability of their investee companies.[120] Such a stabilising effect is found in a number of empirical surveys on the impact of SWF investment.[121] However, SWFs' corporate

---

[117] Fabio Bertoni and Stefano Lugo, 'The Effect of Sovereign Wealth Funds on the Credit Risk of their Portfolio Companies' (2014) *Journal of Corporate Finance* forthcoming at http://ssrn.com/abstract=1763173.

[118] Elvira Sojli and Wing Wah Tham, 'The Impact of Foreign Government Investments: Sovereign Wealth Fund Investments in the United States' in Narjess Boubakri and Jean Claude Cosset (eds), *Institutional Investors in Global Capital Markets* (2011), above at p. 207.

[119] Kathryn L Dewenter, Xi Han and Paul H Malatesta, 'Firm Values and Sovereign Wealth Fund Investments' (2009) at http://ssrn.com/abstract=1354252, (2010) 98 *Journal of Financial Economics* 256.

[120] The fear-mongering regarding arbitrary and destabilising capital withdrawal by SWFs is arguably unfounded, see Amy Keller, 'Sovereign Wealth Funds: Trustworthy Investors or Vehicles of Strategic Ambition? An Assessment of the Benefits, Risks and Possible Regulation of Sovereign Wealth Funds' (2009) 7 *Georgetown Journal of Law and Public Policy* 333; Tao Sun and Heiko Hesse, 'Sovereign Wealth Funds and Financial Stability – An Event Study Analysis' (2009), above; Roland Beck and Michael Fidora, 'Sovereign Wealth Funds – Before and Since the Crisis' (2009) *European Business Organisation Law Review* 353; George Kratsas and Jon Truby, 'Regulating Sovereign Wealth Funds to Avoid Investment Protectionism' (2015) I *Journal of Financial Regulation* 95; Michel Aglietta, 'Sovereign Wealth Funds and the Mutation of Global Finance' (2014), above.

[121] Vincent Gasparro and Michael S Pagano, 'Sovereign Wealth Funds' Impact on Debt and Equity Markets during the 2007–09 Financial Crisis' (2010)

governance roles in foreign investee companies may nevertheless be conditioned by perceptions in the host country, a point that will be taken up shortly.

We turn next to discuss the Norwegian Global Pension Fund which has pursued a relentlessly strategic agenda[122] and at times aggressive corporate governance role, an investing style that is markedly different from the strategic investors discussed above. We argue that this is due to the increasing market acceptance of the Fund's strategic interest in ethical investing, which has become a globally aspirational investment standard.[123]

Strategic Investing by the Norway Global Pension Fund

The Norwegian Fund invests principally in developed capital markets such as the US and UK and it has taken on very active corporate governance roles. We argue that the unique characteristics of the Norwegian Fund's governance and accountability are critical for its investment strategy and behaviour. As the Fund is accountable to the Ministry of Finance and its objectives determined by Parliament, the Fund's corporate governance role needs to appeal to the electorate in order to provide legitimacy for its investment management. Hence it has adopted a strategic role of championing ethics and social responsibility in its investee companies.

The Norwegian Fund's strategic agenda is based on a broad notion of 'Ethics'. Unlike the funds discussed above, the strategic agenda is not an extension of domestic industrial policy or economic interests; it is a product of the needs of domestic social legitimacy and political accountability. As already discussed above, the Norwegian Fund is owned by the Ministry of Finance whose accountability for the Fund is to Parliament. As Parliament has the power to approve of the investment strategy of the Fund, the Ministry has instituted mechanisms to ensure that their oversight of fund management meets the needs of parliamentary and

---

66 *Financial Analysts Journal* 92; Roland Beck and Michael Fidora, 'Sovereign Wealth Funds – Before and Since the Crisis' (2009), above.

[122] Larry Cata Backer, 'Sovereign Wealth Funds as Regulatory Chameleons: The Norwegian Sovereign Wealth Funds and Public Global Governance Through Private Global Investment' (2010) 41 *Georgetown Journal of International Law* 425.

[123] Gordon Clark, Adam Dixon and Ashby H B Monk, *Sovereign Wealth Funds: Legitimacy, Governance and Global Power* (2013), above at Chapter 5.

wider social accountability.[124] One such mechanism is the independent Council of Ethics which provides advice to the Ministry on the ethical guidelines for investment, and the ethical evaluation of investee companies. On the basis of such advice, the Ministry may direct the central bank (which delegates fund management to NBIM) to formulate its investment strategy including its corporate governance position vis-à-vis investee companies. The actions that the NBIM can be directed to take include divestment from existing investee companies, placing an investee company under observation, which is then publicly announced, or engagement in other forms of shareholder activism. At a broader level, the independent Council of Ethics is a form of 'procedural legitimacy'[125] adopted by the Ministry to facilitate a form of participative democracy[126] in its decision-making, so that it may achieve a high standard of accountability to Parliament and foster a perception of social legitimacy in its role.

The rhetoric of ethics chimes with wider social acceptance and legitimacy and is also seen to be consistent with commercial objectives, as investing in companies with poor environmental, social and governance track records could result in long-term losses.[127] Six areas of priorities have been identified in the Fund's ethical investment agenda: equal treatment of shareholders, shareholder influence and Board accountability, well-functioning, legitimate and efficient markets, children's rights, climate change,[128] and water management.[129] The ethical strategy is reflected in the Fund's corporate governance roles.

---

[124] Øyvind Ytrestøyl Foldal, 'Mitigating Tensions between Domestic Politics and Global Finance – A Study of the Decision Making Process of Norway's Sovereign Wealth Fund' (2010), above.

[125] Gordon L Clark and Ashby H B Monk, 'The Legitimacy and Governance of Norway's Sovereign Wealth Fund: The Ethics of Global Investment' (2009), above; Gordon L Clark and Ashby H B Monk, 'The Norwegian Government Pension Fund: Ethics over Efficiency' (2010), above.

[126] Gordon Clark, Adam Dixon and Ashby H B Monk, *Sovereign Wealth Funds: Legitimacy, Governance and Global Power* (2013), above at Chapter 5.

[127] Trude Myklebust, 'The Norwegian Government Pension Fund: Moving Forward on Responsible Investing and Governance' (2010), above.

[128] See also Anita M Halvorssen, 'Addressing Climate Change Through the Norwegian Sovereign Wealth Fund (SWF) – Using Responsible Investments to Encourage Corporations to take ESG Issues into Account in their Decision-making' (2010) at http://ssrn.com/abstract=1712799.

[129] Gordon L Clark and Ashby H B Monk, 'The Legitimacy and Governance of Norway's Sovereign Wealth Fund: The Ethics of Global Investment' (2009), above.

The Norwegian Fund's corporate governance role has been admired by many commentators and we argue that this is because (a) the Fund is clearly a minority investor, (b) it connects its strategic agenda with universally acceptable rhetoric in ethics and (c) its strategy is carried out in highly acceptable expressions of shareholder engagement endorsed by western institutional investors.

The Fund employs a range of corporate governance strategies pursuant to its ethical focus. One strategy is the public announcement of divestment and blacklisting of companies that the Fund considers to be contrary to its ethical focus. The Fund does explain in what respects the companies are not compatible with its ethical focus. Companies that the Fund has divested from include Walmart for alleged human rights violations in its supply chain and Rio Tinto for its allegedly environmentally unsustainable practices. The Fund is also able to publicly announce that it is placing certain investee companies under observation for incompatibility with its ethical principles.[130] To date the Fund has placed only Alstom under observation for corruption allegations made against it.

At one level, divestment, blacklisting and placing under observation are the Fund's unique investment decisions, but on the other hand, such blacklists do create a benchmark for ethical investments, and negatively impact upon the investibility of the firms on the list. Backer[131] and Chesterman[132] argue that the Fund's ethical investment decisions, such as divestment, are a projection of strategic state capitalism upon the private corporate sector and seek to influence the formation of transnational investment norms. They query if such a form of strategic exercise of transnational power is legitimate. Moreover, the Council of Ethics' deliberations on these companies are not made public and the application of their ethical criteria is somewhat opaque.[133] Chesterman criticises the ethical evaluation undertaken by the Council of Ethics as a form of

---

[130] To date, only Alstom has been placed under observation for corruption allegations.

[131] Larry Cata Backer, 'Sovereign Investing and Markets-Based Transnational Rule of Law Building: The Norwegian Sovereign Wealth Fund in Global Markets' (2013), above.

[132] Simon Chesterman, 'The Turn to Ethics: Disinvestment from Multinational Corporations for Human Rights Violations – The Case of Norway's Sovereign Wealth Fund' (2008) 23 *American University International Law Review* 577.

[133] Jenni Maria Nossum, 'Corporate Governance in Oil-lubricated Norway: Regulation, Practice, Ethics and Incoherence' (2015) at http://ssrn.com/abstract=2622072; Anita M Halvorssen, 'Investing in Sustainability: Reform Proposals for

juridification of ethical investment norms without being subject to the legal processes of judicial review.[134] However, it may also be argued that the leadership taken by the Fund in setting transnational investment norms promotes best practices in long term investing and will bring about both better corporate practice and investment performance in the long run.[135] In this respect, the Fund is only behaving like a commercially sensible long-term investor and is arguably providing a free collective good for all other institutional investors.

The Fund is not shy of vocal shareholder activism that is consistent with its ethical strategy. But as it only takes minority stakes (limited to 10 per cent as mandated by the Ministry) across an immense range of global companies, involved engagement in shareholder activism would be very demanding in terms of resources. It is reported[136] that the Fund is increasingly voting on proposals of its investee companies and engaging in dialogue where relevant, but it remains to be seen if any significant episodes of intensive engagement will occur in the future.

We suggest that due to the Fund's wide range of investments and the high cost of dedicated monitoring, the Fund is unlikely to be able to undertake intense and tailor-made shareholder activism to change corporate behaviour. The Fund therefore engages in broad level strategies such as discussed above, or reacts to bad news, such as the placing of Alstom on observation after corruption allegations emerged. The Fund also uses ISS as its proxy voting advisor. Although the Fund claims that ISS advises the Fund based on a unique set of policy parameters defined by NBIM,[137] we are sceptical about NBIM's undertaking much pre-emptive monitoring and shareholder engagement, as these require dedicated resources and are costly. However, its selective activism and highly

---

the Ethics Guidelines of the Norwegian Sovereign Wealth Fund' (2014) 11 *European Company Law* 107.

[134] Simon Chesterman, 'The Turn to Ethics: Disinvestment from Multinational Corporations for Human Rights Violations – The Case of Norway's Sovereign Wealth Fund' (2008), above.

[135] Gurneeta Vasudeva, 'Weaving Together the Normative and Regulative Role of Government: How the Norwegian Sovereign Wealth Fund's "Responsible" Conduct is Shaping Firms' Cross-Border Investments' (2013) *Organisation Science* 1662 at http://www.hbs.edu/faculty/conferences/2013-paulrlawrence/Documents/OS_Gurneeta_%20SWF_Final_Jan2_2013.pdf.

[136] Anita M Halvorssen, 'Using the Norwegian Sovereign Wealth Fund's Ethical Guidelines as a Model for Investors, be They Private or Government-Owned' (2011) at http://ssrn.com/abstract=1774748.

[137] See http://www.nbim.no/en/transparency/external-service-providers-/ as of 30 June 2015.

visible episodes are effective in creating an overall impression of responsible and active ownership.

Next, we argue that although SWFs' strategic agendas drive much of their investment strategies and corporate governance behaviour in investee companies, certain other factors are playing a critical role in shaping funds' investment management approaches and corporate governance roles. One, the reception of host countries could be important in influencing funds' corporate governance roles, as funds may deliberately restrain their corporate governance roles and visibility in the face of potentially suspicious or hostile reception. Second, the development of international standards of governance and transparency for SWFs, due to scepticism regarding SWFs' investment motives, can play a part in shaping SWFs' relations with the world through modifications to its investment management approaches. Such changes would affect SWFs' corporate governance roles.

The Impact of Host Country Reception on SWFs' Corporate Governance Roles

Although many host countries see the economic benefits of foreign investment,[138] protectionist instincts can arise against SWF investment. This is largely due to fear of the unknown,[139] where host countries are not certain what interests, strategic and/or commercial, are at play in motivating the investment, and how such interests will impact the host country's corporate sector and wider economy more broadly.[140] Such suspicions and fear are not helped if there is lack of transparency on the part of the investing SWF.[141]

---

[138] Robert Kimmitt, 'Public Footprints in Private Markets: Sovereign Wealth Funds and the World Economy' (2008) 87 *Foreign Affairs* 119.

[139] Jennifer Cooke, 'Finding the Right Balance for Sovereign Wealth Fund Regulation: Open Investment Vs. National Security' (2009), above.

[140] The suspicions regarding the interests of SWFs have to do with the opacity of their internal governance structures and their different and unfamiliar national governance cultures. See Joshua Aizenmann and Reuven Glick, 'Sovereign Wealth Funds: Stylized Facts About Their Determinants and Governance' (2008), above at http://www.nber.org/papers/w14562.

[141] Although some SWFs publish information voluntarily, such as the Temasek yearly review that provides an overview of its portfolio and performance, many SWFs, such as the Abu Dhabi, Kuwaiti Funds and the CIC, do not provide adequate disclosures of who they are, or their investment objectives and strategies.

Empirical research has found that where an SWF takes a stake in a foreign company, the market reacts positively, but the positive market reaction is often discounted, i.e. less than the positive market reaction to a stake acquired by a private sector institutional investor.[142] This is due to markets being unsure as to what the SWF's investment objectives may be and thus the long-term performance of the investee company is viewed with ambivalence. A number of researchers have also found that SWF investments are correlated with no impact[143] or weaker long-term returns,[144] and this is because the markets may look upon SWF-invested companies with overall disfavour. On the one hand, the long-termist nature of SWFs may indicate a stable source of capital, and even long-term monitoring in their corporate governance roles. Indeed, as pointed out earlier, empirical research seems to indicate an overall positive impact that SWFs have on the long-term performance of investee companies. However, in the near term, markets are unsure how the strategic objectives of the SWF may affect a company's motivation to pursue short-term profitability and hence value the company with some reservations.

In light of markets' ambivalent reactions to SWF investments, it could be argued that SWFs may find it at least commercially sensible to act as restrained investors, adopting a low profile in corporate governance roles, in order not to jeopardise the long-term value of their investments. Li finds that the CIC for example, acts mostly as a passive investor in its foreign investments.[145] The general passivity of SWFs as shareholders is noted in the US,[146] and more generally.[147] Hatton and

---

[142] Bernardo Bertolotti, Veljko Fotak and William L Megginson, 'The Sovereign Wealth Fund Discount: Evidence from Public Equity Investments' (2015) at http://ssrn.com/abstract=2322745.

[143] See Jason Kotter and Ugur Lel, 'Friends or Foes? Target Selection Decisions of Sovereign Wealth Funds and Their Consequences' (2010), above.

[144] April Knill, Bong Soo Lee and Nathan Mauck, 'Is Sovereign Wealth Fund Investment Destabilizing?' (2010) at http://ssrn.com/abstract=1328045; Jennifer Kim Chau Hua, Francis In, Viet Do and Xibin Zhang, 'Stock Liquidity, Intractable Information and Sovereign Wealth Fund Investment' (2015) at http://ssrn.com/abstract=2625902.

[145] Jing Li, 'State As An Entrepreneur: A Study of the Investment Contractual Terms and Level of Control of China's Sovereign Wealth Fund in its Portfolio Firms' (2014), above.

[146] Paul Rose, 'Sovereigns as Shareholders' (2008) *North Carolina Law Review* 84.

[147] Andrew Ang, 'The Four Benchmarks of Sovereign Wealth Funds' (2010), above; Jason Kotter and Ugur Lel, 'Friends or Foes? Target Selection Decisions

Pistor[148] argue that adopting passivity is the optimal position as SWFs do not wish to incur the ire of host countries and attract protectionist responses, which would be counter-productive to both their strategic and commercial objectives. Further, passivity is indeed consistent with the needs of the domestic political economy and foreign relations. Where the domestic political economy is concerned, the projection of the SWF as a commercially-focused and sensible investor that is passive for long-term returns helps to consolidate domestic legitimacy and support for the SWF. Where foreign relations are concerned, passivity is consistent with the unspoken understanding with developed but indebted economies that countries benefiting from trade or balance of payments imbalances will do their part in recycling dollars and maintaining a stable global economic order.[149] Further, SWF investments may also be a form of reciprocity for American protection, whether military or economic (such as applicable to the Gulf States and Singapore for example). In light of such sensitivities, a passive corporate governance role would be most appropriate for SWF investments.[150]

In the US, many commentators treat SWFs as powerful investors whose behaviour is not trusted by markets,[151] and suggestions have been

---

of Sovereign Wealth Funds and Their Consequences' (2010), above; William L Megginson and Veljko Fotak, 'Rise of the Fiduciary State: A Survey of Sovereign Wealth Fund Research' (2014), above; Mark Mietzner, Dirk Schiereck and Denis Schweizer, 'The Role of Sovereign Wealth Funds as Activist or Passive Fund Managers' (2015) 16 *Journal of Asset Management* 303.

148 Kyle Hatton and Katharina Pistor, 'Maximizing Autonomy in the Shadow of Great Powers: The Political Economy of Sovereign Wealth Funds' (2011), above.

149 Eric Langland, 'Misplaced Fears Put to Rest: Financial Crisis Reveals the True Motives of Sovereign Wealth Funds' (2009) 18 *Tulane Journal of International and Comparative Law* 263; Kyle Hatton and Katharina Pistor, 'Maximizing Autonomy in the Shadow of Great Powers: The Political Economy of Sovereign Wealth Funds' (2011), above. But see Aaditya Mattoo and Arvind Subramanian, 'Currency Undervaluation and Sovereign Wealth Funds: A New Role for the World Trade Organization' (*Peterson Institute Working Paper Series* 2008) who argue that it is in the self-interest of SWF countries to recycle dollars.

150 Kyle Hatton and Katharina Pistor, 'Maximizing Autonomy in the Shadow of Great Powers: The Political Economy of Sovereign Wealth Funds' (2011), above.

151 Bruce Winfield Bean, 'Attack of the Sovereign Wealth Funds: Defending the Republic from the Threat of Sovereign Wealth Funds?' (2009), above; Joel Slawotsky, 'Sovereign Wealth Funds as Emerging Financial Superpowers: How U.S. Regulators Should Respond' (2009) 40 *Georgetown Journal of International Law* 1239.

made about curtailing SWFs' corporate governance powers, such as the suspension of voting rights advocated by Gilson and Milhaupt,[152] the mandatory channelling of investment through third party intermediaries suggested by Keller,[153] the use of securities regulation to force intentions-based disclosure at lower thresholds of stake acquisition suggested by Rose[154] and more draconian measures such as investment restrictions.[155] The US and Canada also have rather comprehensive regimes of investment vetting where national security issues may arise,[156] and such measures form an arsenal to deal with less welcome forms of foreign, including SWF, investment.[157] Even where US banks needed the stabilising quality of SWF investment in the global financial crisis, many rescuing SWFs took non-voting or passive stakes in order to show support without incurring possible backlashes.[158] Against this background, it is observed that SWFs are already non-voting investors in

---

152 Ronald J Gilson and Curtis J Milhaupt, 'Sovereign Wealth Funds and Corporate Governance: A Minimalist Response to the New Mercantilism' (2008), above.

153 Amy Keller, 'Sovereign Wealth Funds: Trustworthy Investors or Vehicles of Strategic Ambition? An Assessment of the Benefits, Risks and Possible Regulation of Sovereign Wealth Funds' (2009), above.

154 Paul Rose, 'Sovereigns as Shareholders' (2008), above.

155 Mooted but not supported by George Kratsas and Jon Truby, 'Regulating Sovereign Wealth Funds to Avoid Investment Protectionism' (2015), above.

156 Discussed in Benjamin J Cohen, 'Sovereign Wealth Funds and National Security: The Great Tradeoff' (2009), above; Jennifer Cooke, 'Finding the Right Balance for Sovereign Wealth Fund Regulation: Open Investment Vs. National Security' (2009), above; Paul Rose, 'Sovereigns as Shareholders' (2008), above; Gil Lan, 'Foreign Direct Investment in the United States and Canada: Fractured Neoliberalism and the Regulatory Imperative' (2014) *Vanderbilt University Law Review* 1262.

157 On whether the legal framework in the US deals proportionately with unwelcome investments, see Edward F Greene and Brian A Yeager, 'Sovereign Wealth Funds – A Measured Assessment' (2008) 3 *Capital Markets Law Journal* 247.

158 Cohen documents a total of USD$60 bn in SWF injection in crisis-stricken banks during the global financial crisis, see Benjamin J Cohen, 'Sovereign Wealth Funds and National Security: The Great Tradeoff' (2009), above. The stabilising effect of such injections is discussed in Vincent Gasparro and Michael S Pagano, 'Sovereign Wealth Funds' Impact on Debt and Equity Markets during the 2007–09 Financial Crisis' (2010) 66 *Financial Analysts Journal* 92; Massimilliano Castelli and Fabio Scacciavillani, 'SWFs and State Investments: A Preliminary General Overview' in Fabio Bassan (ed.), *Research Handbook in Sovereign Wealth Funds and International Investment Law* (2015), above at p. 9, Chapter 1. The low corporate governance profile of such

some US companies,[159] or passive investors in many others. In this way, SWFs are hampered from assuming 'stewardship' profiles[160] even though they are less subject to short-termist pressures like those apparent at other more commercially-driven institutions.

Where the EU is concerned,[161] there is no EU-wide legal framework for vetting SWF investments except in the case of competition scrutiny. The EU has articulated a skeletal communication[162] on SWF investments that very much supports international developments discussed below, but in practice, it is very much up to Member States how they relate to SWF investment, and levels of protectionism are, for example, much higher in France than in Germany.[163]

Where the UK is concerned, the official stance is arguably too open and liberal, although there are in place mechanisms for investment vetting based on national security or competition grounds.[164] As the UK actively encourages institutional investors to engage with their investee

---

investments was discussed in Kyle Hatton and Katharina Pistor, 'Maximizing Autonomy in the Shadow of Great Powers: The Political Economy of Sovereign Wealth Funds' (2011), above; Friedrich Wu and Arifin Seah, 'Would China's Sovereign Wealth Fund Be a Menace to the USA?' (2008), above.

159 For example, CIC's non-voting stake in its first tranche of investment in Blackstone, Qatar Holdings' preference stakes in Volkswagen, Songbird Plc, as examples of stakes that are redeemable after a fixed period, in 2009 and 2012 respectively; and Abu Dhabi Fund's stake in Barclays which was also a redeemable preference stake, see 'Abu Dhabi quietly cashes out of Barclays', *Financial Times* (18 July 2013).

160 Paul Rose, 'Sovereign Shareholder Activism: How SWFs Can Engage in Corporate Governance' (2014) at http://ssrn.com/abstract=2461227.

161 Anna de Luca, 'The EU and Member States: FDI, Portfolio Investments, Golden Powers and SWFs' in Fabio Bassan (ed.), *Research Handbook in Sovereign Wealth Funds and International Investment Law* (2015), above at p. 178, Chapter 7.

162 Communication from the Commission to the European Parliament, the Council, the European Economic and Social Committee and the Committee of the Regions – A common European approach to Sovereign Wealth Funds (2008) at http://eur-lex.europa.eu/legal-content/EN/ALL/?uri=CELEX:52008DC0115. See also Seth Robert Lindberg, 'Sovereign Wealth Fund Regulation in the E.U. and U.S.: A Call for Workable and Uniform Sovereign Wealth Fund Review within the E.U.' (2009) 37 *Syracuse Journal of International Law and Commerce* 95.

163 Daniel Haberly, 'White Knights from the Gulf: Sovereign Wealth Fund Investment and the Evolution of German Industrial Finance' (2014) 90 *Economic Geography* 293.

164 Harry McVea, 'Corrupting Capitalism? Sovereign Wealth Funds and the United Kingdom's Regulatory Framework' (2013), above.

companies, as part of good corporate governance,[165] SWFs have responded to this welcoming environment by engaging in episodes of more visible shareholder engagement. They have followed the cue of institutional investors, and demonstrated the same concerns for minority shareholder protection and good corporate governance standards, and have avoided being overly aggressive or confrontational. The Qatar Investment Authority's subsidiary fund, Qatar Holding, an investor in London Stock Exchange listed company Xstrata, engaged in an episode of shareholder activism when the merger deal between Glencore and Xstrata was being discussed in 2012.[166] The Qatari Fund was of the view that Xstrata had been offered a poorer deal than it deserved and was vocal with this opinion at its 3 per cent stake, leading other sovereign wealth funds such as the Norwegian Fund and GIC of Singapore to oppose the deal. The Qatari Fund then proceeded to build up its Xstrata stake to almost 11 per cent before Glencore offered a better deal for Xstrata shareholders.[167] Another example is that of Temasek, the Singapore SWF that owns 18 per cent of London listed Standard Chartered, which has openly opposed the re-election of four executive directors of the bank in light of inadequate non-executive representation on the Board, consistent with the UK Corporate Governance Code.[168] This episode of shareholder activism, consistent with good standards of corporate governance and acceptable to other institutional shareholders, has been supported. These episodes show that SWFs' corporate governance roles have the potential to be active and monitoring in nature, but the extent of assumption of such roles is highly sensitive to the host country's environment of receptiveness.

Next, we turn to international developments on standard-setting for SWFs, and discuss how these may affect SWFs' investment management and corporate governance positions in the future. At the international level, host countries have been calling for SWFs to be more transparent, as the transparency of their objectives and internal governance could to

---

[165] UK Stewardship Code, Chapter 3, and background and context therein discussed.

[166] 'Qatar to oppose Glencore-Xstrata merger', *Financial Times* (30 Aug 2012).

[167] Discussed in Anna Sandor, 'Leveraging International Law to Incentivize Value-Added Shareholding: Why Foreign Sovereign Wealth Funds Still Matter and How They Can Improve Shareholder Governance' (2015) 46 *Georgetown Journal of International Law* 947.

[168] 'Temasek fails to back Standard Chartered executive directors', *The Telegraph* (8 May 2013).

an extent assuage suspicions surrounding the nature of SWF investments. This has culminated in the development of an international set of best practices for SWFs, commonly called the Santiago Principles.

The Impact of the Santiago Principles

The Santiago Principles are a set of 24 broadly framed Generally Accepted Principles and Practices for SWFs developed by a working group of 26 SWFs under the sponsorship of the International Monetary Fund.[169] These Principles reflect the best practices that the 26 SWFs already practise or aspire to practise, and set a benchmark for the rest of the SWFs in the world. The Santiago Principles are further supported by the ongoing commitment of the International Forum of Sovereign Wealth Funds formed by the 26 SWFs behind the Principles, by virtue of the Kuwait Declaration.[170]

The Principles deal with the internal governance and accountability of the SWF. The Principles recommend that SWFs be constituted upon a certain legal basis, be operationally independent from the government, have a clear delineation of responsibilities, coordinate in a predictable manner with fiscal and monetary authorities, have clear appointment procedures for the management of the SWF, have clear accountability channels and a clear framework[171] for risk management and investment performance measurement, engage in yearly professional audit and reporting to the fund owner, and uphold professional and ethical standards within the SWF.[172] The Principles also provide that the SWF's investment policies should be clear and consistent with defined objectives, risk tolerance and investment strategy; their investment decisions should be for the purposes of maximising risk-adjusted returns on economic and financial grounds; they should not take advantage of privileged information or their privileged positions and should behave as shareholders in a manner consistent with their investment interests. They should deal with third parties in accordance with clear rules and on the basis of commercial interests, and this may apply to service providers

---

[169] International Working Group on Sovereign Wealth Funds, *Generally Accepted Principles and Practices: Santiago Principles* (2008) at http://www.iwg-swf.org/pubs/eng/santiagoprinciples.pdf.

[170] 'Kuwait Declaration': Establishment of the International Forum of Sovereign Wealth Funds, http://www.iwg-swf.org/mis/kuwaitdec.htm.

[171] Principles 18–23.

[172] Principles 1, 3, 5–13.

such as proxy voting agencies.[173] In order to signal clear intentions to third parties, host countries and investee companies, SWFs are also required to make public disclosures of various aspects, such as the purpose of the SWF,[174] policies and rules with regard to its funding, withdrawal or spending operations of the SWF,[175] the governance framework and operational independence of the SWF,[176] relevant financial information with regard to its economic and financial orientation and its role in international financial stability,[177] and the exercise of its voting rights.[178] SWFs must ensure that their operations comply with host state laws and regulations,[179] and be subject to regular review as regards their adherence to the Santiago Principles.[180]

The Principles would in essence require SWFs to focus on commercially explicable interests only and to make disclosures so that any strategic objectives may be apparent to all. The governance structures and the disclosure obligations imposed under the Principles would also compel SWFs to edge towards internationally accepted standards of good corporate governance which require independent representation and scrutiny at Board level and the entry of external auditors to provide financial assurance. The public disclosures required of SWFs are aimed not only to ensure that they are accountable to their domestic polities but also to signal non-threatening intentions to host countries.

Norton forcefully points out that the Santiago Principles can give rise to an effective form of international economic governance for SWFs,[181]

---

173 Principle 14.
174 Principle 2.
175 Principle 4.
176 Principle 16.
177 Principle 17.
178 Principle 21.
179 Principle 15.
180 Principle 24.
181 Joseph J Norton, 'The "Santiago Principles" and the International Forum of Sovereign Wealth Funds: Evolving Components of the New Bretton Woods II Post-Global Financial Crisis Architecture and Another Example of Ad Hoc Global Administrative Networking and Related "Soft" Rulemaking?' (2010) 29 *Review of Banking and Financial Law* 465; Joseph J Norton, 'The 'Santiago Principles' for Sovereign Wealth Funds: A Case Study on International Financial Standard Setting Processes' (2010) 13 *Journal of International Economic Law* 645. We do not agree that the Principles are a thin rule of financial law as suggested in Yvonne C L Lee, 'A Reversal of Neo-Colonialism: The Pitfalls and Prospects of Sovereign Wealth Funds' (2009) 40 *Georgetown Journal of International Law* 1103. They are demanding and constitute powerful constraints

but remain a body of soft law that is insufficiently plugged into the international networked governance of various bodies and institutions such as the OECD, IOSCO and FSB. The elevation of the Santiago Principles into a fundamental plank of international networked economic governance, perhaps by instituting forms of international enforcement[182] or dispute resolution,[183] could greatly enhance the implementation and effectiveness of these Principles. It is however observed[184] that the implementation of the Principles has been uneven among SWFs, even including the 26 founding SWFs behind the Principles. Full implementation of the Principles would force SWFs to disclose their strategic intentions, which may have national interest implications. SWFs may also perceive it to be unfair that they are subject to intentions-based disclosure for an equity stake of any measure when similar disclosures are seldom asked of other shareholders in most jurisdictions.[185] Jimenez et al[186] have critically argued that the extent of disclosure expected of SWFs under the Santiago Principles exceeds those expected of private sector institutions, even to their beneficiaries. SWFs may perceive the full implementation of the Principles as having the effect of forcible 'neutering' of SWFs' strategic aspects in their foreign investments, which would be inconsistent with the hybrid motivations that are the very basis for SWFs' existence. The imposition of double standards on SWFs could be a disincentive for the assumption of their corporate governance roles.

---

upon SWFs if fully implemented and this explains why the Principles are unevenly implemented in practice, even by the 26 founding SWFs.

[182] Benjamin J Cohen, 'Sovereign Wealth Funds and National Security: The Great Tradeoff' (2009) 85 *International Affairs* 713; Locknie Hsu, 'Santiago GAPPs and Codes of Conduct: Limits and Chances of Negotiated Rules' in Fabio Bassan (ed.), *Research Handbook in Sovereign Wealth Funds and International Investment Law* (2015), above at p. 99 Chapter 4.

[183] George Kratsas and Jon Truby, 'Regulating Sovereign Wealth Funds to Avoid Investment Protectionism' (2015), above; Aaditya Mattoo and Arvind Subramanian, 'Currency Undervaluation and Sovereign Wealth Funds: A New Role for the World Trade Organization' (2008), above.

[184] Adam D Dixon, 'Enhancing the Transparency Dialogue in the "Santiago Principles" for Sovereign Wealth Funds' (2014) 37 *University of Seattle Law Review* 581.

[185] Unless an acquisition of 5 per cent or more is made of a listed issuer, which triggers intentions-based disclosure under the Securities Exchange Act 1934 in the US, or in relation to takeover legislation, such as in the UK.

[186] Javier W Ibanez Jimenez and Antonio Partal Urena, 'Sovereign Wealth Fund (SWF) Global Regulation and Transparency: A Preliminary Private-Investment Law Approach' (2010) *Journal of International Banking Law and Regulation* 441.

On the other hand, SWFs could, on the basis of compliance with the Santiago Principles, become less inhibited from being active shareholders consistent with market-based interests as adherence to the Principles could give them an aura of legitimacy.[187] Moreover, as doubts are expressed as to the effectiveness of the Santiago Principles as a body of soft law,[188] the legitimacy quotient added by adhering to the Principles may be overstated.

We predict that there may be no significant impact on SWFs' corporate governance positions or that SWFs may indeed become more inhibited in their corporate governance positions. Signing up to the Principles may force SWFs to be even more opaque about their strategic objectives, and they may seek a balance of thin adherence so as to maintain strategic privacy while still appearing as viable investors for opportunities in foreign markets. In maintaining such a delicate balance of interests, it is likely that SWFs would continue to opt for passive corporate governance roles and a low profile in order not to attract attention to themselves. Further, it is queried if the Santiago Principles have set higher and more forbidding thresholds for SWFs to engage in corporate governance roles. It may be argued that in order for SWFs to engage in more visible corporate governance roles, much more[189] is now required on SWFs' part in demonstration of adherence to the Principles. SWFs could be even less engaged in corporate governance as a result of trying to avoid having to adhere fully to the Principles.

This section has discussed the key drivers that shape SWFs' corporate governance positions, and we posit that such roles, as part of SWFs' investment strategy, are a manifestation of SWFs' mixture of strategic and commercial interests in their investments. Even their appearance of being commercially-focused may itself be strategic in nature. However, our findings from literature review suggest that SWFs' strategic interests are not of the destructive and destabilising type. They generally seek synergies and win-win solutions that attain both their strategic interests as well as the long-term success of their investee companies. With their long-term orientation and usually benign interests, one would have

[187] Above; Ashby H B Monk, 'Sovereignty in the Era of Global Capitalism: The Rise of Sovereign Wealth Funds and the Power of Finance' (2011) 43 *Environment and Planning* 1813.

[188] Anthony Wong, 'Sovereign Wealth Funds and the Problem of Asymmetric Information: The Santiago Principles and International Regulations' (2009), above.

[189] Paul Rose, 'Sovereign Wealth Fund Investment in the Shadow of Regulation and Politics' (2009) 40 *Georgetown Journal of International Law* 6.

supposed that SWFs are ideal for assuming the monitoring role in corporate governance.[190] However, such roles are downplayed more than is necessary in order to assuage fears and suspicions surrounding SWFs. We predict that SWFs remain unlikely to assume activist positions unless markets or host countries are receptive to such behaviour, such as in relation to the ethical investing leadership assumed by the Norwegian Fund or in markets such as the UK where constructive shareholder engagement is welcomed. As such, any beneficial effects of monitoring by SWFs as long-term patient owners in the agency paradigm may be curtailed.[191]

C. TYPOLOGIES OF SWF ENGAGEMENT WITH THEIR CORPORATE GOVERNANCE ROLES

We suggest that there are six typologies of shareholder behaviour observed on the part of SWFs invested corporate equity. Our discussion spans SWFs' domestic and international investments, but the UK context will also be specifically discussed, especially in relation to the Qatari SWF which has made many investments in the UK.

The six typologies are:

(a) Voting at the annual general meeting, through proxies or otherwise;
(b) Collective engagement with other mainstream institutions in voting;
(c) Collective engagement with other mainstream institutions in other events;
(d) Indirect engagement through activist hedge funds;
(e) Informal influence; and
(f) Exit over voice.

---

[190] Maria Ungureanu, 'The Corporate Governance of Sovereign Wealth Funds', *Harvard Law School Forum on Corporate Governance* (7 August 2014).

[191] Jennifer Kim Chau Hua, Francis In, Viet Do and Xibin Zhang, 'Stock Liquidity, Intractable Information and Sovereign Wealth Fund Investment' (2015), above. Although it is doubted that those SWFs that manage mostly in-house would have the capacity and resources to be effective monitors, see William L Megginson and Veljko Fotak, 'Rise of the Fiduciary State: A Survey of Sovereign Wealth Fund Research' (2014), above; Paul Rose, 'Sovereign Shareholder Activism: How SWFs Can Engage in Corporate Governance' (2014), above.

Voting at General Meetings

Other than disclosures made by the Norwegian Fund, there are relatively scarce disclosures by SWFs on their voting records. That said, Gong[192] and Li[193] document that many SWF stakes are non-voting or come with restraints on the exercise of shareholder power, such as in relation to directorial appointments or removals. As the exercise of voting rights may be perceived as a signal for furthering strategic interests, SWFs that can exercise such rights may be more restrained than is necessary. The relative lack of disclosure may mean scarce exercise of such rights (which does not mean that the SWF does not exercise other soft forms of corporate governance influence), or the opacity can be perceived to be necessary in order not to highlight any strategic interests (even if they may create benign outcomes for the company).

However, greater visibility is available where an SWF perceives that its voting decisions are likely to be treated as convergent with accepted best practices in minority shareholder protection or corporate governance. Ghahramani[194] argues that SWF activism is likelier where their portfolios emulate institutional investors' portfolios or are indexed. Such SWFs project a high level of consonance with commercial objectives, and hence their investment behaviour is more likely to be perceived as a natural outworking of those commercial objectives. The other example is Temasek's refusal to re-elect four executive directors of Standard Chartered as it considered this did not conform to best corporate governance practices, an episode discussed earlier. We also think that where a portfolio is externally managed, the assumption of corporate governance positions consistent with the asset manager's recommendations is also likely to be regarded without negativity. However, such shareholder engagement would likely revolve around the commercially explicable issues of minority shareholder rights and corporate governance, which are consonant with other institutional shareholders' concerns.

---

[192] Bo Gong, 'Institutional Investment in the UK and China' in *Understanding Institutional Shareholder Activism: A Comparative Study of the UK and China* (Oxford: Routledge 2014) at p. 88.

[193] Jing Li, 'State As An Entrepreneur: A Study of the Investment Contractual Terms and Level of Control of China's Sovereignwealth Fund in its Portfolio Firms' (2014), above.

[194] Salar Ghahramani, 'Sovereign Wealth Funds and Shareholder Activism: Applying the Ryan-Schneider Antecedents to Determine Policy Implications' (2013) 13 *Corporate Governance: The International Journal of Business in Society*, pp. 58–69.

That said, the Norwegian Fund adopts a completely different approach altogether. It seeks to justify its ethics-led shareholder activism by being transparent with its ethical strategies and its voting records.[195] Such a high level of transparency may condition us into accepting the legitimacy of its corporate governance role, even if we know that it is strategic in character. Nevertheless, the Norwegian Fund reports that the Institutional Shareholders Services (ISS), a proxy advisory agency, is retained to assist in voting decisions.[196] Seeking advice from the ISS may be necessary given the Norwegian Fund's wide-ranging holdings in global equity and the demands placed on it at voting season. Although the ISS is placed under a tailor-made mandate to meet the NBIM's needs, the retention of the ISS may also give rise to the perception that the Fund's voting decisions are in accordance with the best practices in corporate governance which most proxy advisory agencies uphold.

As the exercise of shareholder rights in voting would be scrutinised in relation to SWFs' investment motives, funds are likely to be cautious about any exercise of such rights unless they, like the Norwegian Fund, are prepared to anchor their corporate governance roles in high levels of transparency. In general, we predict that SWFs may be willing to make their corporate governance positions visible only within the 'safe' boundaries of convergent behaviour with other institutions. Hence, they may more likely assume visible corporate governance positions in episodes of collective engagement or through increased investment in activist hedge funds in order to benefit indirectly from their engagement activities.

Collective Engagement with Other Institutions in Voting or Other Activities

SWFs are not natural partners for collective engagement. Mainstream institutions do not treat SWFs as being part of the institutional investor cohort they can work together with, and SWFs may not wish to send any signals about themselves by working with private sector institutions. In terms of collaboration between SWFs and other institutions, this is an emerging development only, under the umbrella of the Co-investment Roundtable of Sovereign and Pension Funds.[197] The Roundtable features many of the world's largest SWFs, seeking opportunities to co-invest

---

[195] http://www.nbim.no/en/responsibility/voting-records/.

[196] See http://www.nbim.no/en/transparency/external-service-providers-/ as of 30 June 2015.

[197] As of 2014, http://www.ifswf.org/pst/6thamiwswf/crosapf.pdf.

together with pension funds in long-term projects, and so these are not confined to corporate equity investments.

We have witnessed only a rare episode of collective activism in the UK, between Qatar Holdings, a subsidiary fund of the Qatar Investment Authority and several institutions including Fidelity, Schroders and Standard Life, in relation to improving the takeover premium offered by Glencore International.[198] This rare episode is often described as not characteristic of the passive nature of Gulf SWFs. This may be unique to the Qatar Investment Holdings approach, as they have been taking highly visible approaches to acquiring assets. Some of their high profile acquisitions include three Mayfair Hotels[199] previously subject to a tussle between the Barclay brothers and Paddy McKillen, and London's Canary Wharf,[200] which belonged to London-listed Songbird in which Qatar Holdings held a previous minority stake. This section will shortly discuss Qatar Holdings' corporate governance position in many UK investments, which look relatively more active than other SWFs.

Indirect Activism through Hedge Fund Investments

Ghahramani argues that SWFs have a natural propensity to be activist shareholders,[201] and it is conceivable that SWFs may see investment in activist hedge funds as a way to indirectly carry out their shareholder engagement intentions.

SWFs have been increasing allocations to hedge funds, largely to benefit from diversification of investments.[202] Event-driven hedge funds are a popular destination for SWF investment, and SWFs could be leveraging upon activist funds to achieve shareholder engagement with companies. We think this is largely commercially motivated, as it would be unwarranted to presume that any SWF that invests in an activist hedge

---

[198] Earlier discussed, also see 'Qatar in spotlight over merger activism', *Financial Times* (1 July 2012).

[199] 'Barclay brothers sell stake in three luxury London hotels', *The Guardian* (23 April 2015).

[200] 'Canary Wharf to be bought by Qatar Investment Authority', *The Guardian* (28 January 2015).

[201] Salar Ghahramani, 'Sovereign Wealth Funds and Shareholder Activism: Applying the Ryan-Schneider Antecedents to Determine Policy Implications' (2013), above pp. 58–69.

[202] Preqin, 'Sovereign Wealth Fund Investors in Hedge Funds', in *Hedge Fund Spotlight* (June 2015) at https://www.preqin.com/docs/newsletters/hf/Preqin-HFSL-June-15-Sovereign-Wealth-Fund-Investors-in-Hedge.pdf.

fund is able to influence its activist strategy.[203] As hedge funds act as intermediaries for SWFs, their independence and own agendas dominate and it is unlikely that SWFs would use hedge fund activism as a cover for their own strategic activism.

However, as the Korean Investment Corporation episode[204] with Elliott Management Corp, the US hedge fund, has shown, strategic interests can overwhelm SWF investment behaviour. The KIC has invested in activist hedge fund Elliott Management Corp, but has openly called upon Elliott not to intervene in Korean national champion Samsung. The KIC seems to be caught between its strategic and commercial objectives in that episode, but this did not stop Elliott from mounting an episode against Samsung, which was subsequently defeated.

Informal Influence

The main channel of influence exerted by SWFs in their investee companies is likely to be informal and relatively opaque. As discussed in Section B, SWF investments in their domestic economies, largely driven by strategic motivations such as to support national champions or as part of cronyism, may bring about benefits to the investee company in terms of access to markets, government procurement and other support. Even SWF investments in foreign companies can bring about these informal advantages, whether the investment is punctuated by strategic or commercial purposes or a mix of these.[205] The subtlety of informal influence may be the reason why empirical researchers have found mixed evidence[206] on the impact of SWF investments on the long term operating performance of their investee companies – positive aspects such as monitoring and constructive input are acknowledged, but negative aspects

---

[203] For example, an interview with NBIM shows that they are not necessarily in dialogue with hedge funds and regard themselves as having different activist strategies and purposes. See Patrick Bolton, Joseph Samama and Joseph E Stiglitz, *Sovereign Wealth Funds and Long Term Investing* (New York: Columbia University Press 2012) at p. 118.

[204] 'Korean Sovereign Fund Asks Elliott to Stop Investing in Korea', *The Wall Street Journal* (18 Aug 2015). But see 'Complicated: KIC Invested in Hedge Fund which is against Samsung Merger', SWF Institute, 8 July 2015.

[205] Elvira Sojli and Wing Wah Tham, 'The Impact of Foreign Government Investments: Sovereign Wealth Fund Investments in the United States' in Narjess Boubakri and Jean Claude Cosset (eds), *Institutional Investors in Global Capital Markets* (2011), above at p. 207.

[206] Discussed earlier in n109–112, 135–136.

such as the opacity of SWF influence and the unspoken nature of their strategic interests dampen the positive perceptions.

SWFs are unlikely to become more substantively transparent with their strategic interests,[207] unlike in the case of the Norwegian Fund whose strategy is very much fashioned by social and parliamentary accountability. In the post-Santiago Principles era, we continue to expect SWFs to comply moderately with the Principles in terms of transparency regarding their motivations, internal governance and voting behaviour. SWFs desire to continue to access highly developed capital markets, and given this context, we expect their investment behaviour to be guided by their strategic interests, while being commercially justifiable. They are likely to continue being sensitive to the needs of their host environment while appearing to be convergent with international standards.[208] Such a balance is not always easy to achieve.

Exit

SWFs are long-term patient investors with no explicit liabilities and hence there is no need for them to exit investments due to short termist pressures. Many commentators are of the view that they are unlikely to exhibit short termist herding behaviour and can hold out in an investment even in trough periods.[209] That said, oil price declines have put pressure on many governments and it is reported that such governments have raided their SWFs and have been engaged in selling activity in order to liquidate SWF holdings.[210] Hence, SWF exits are generally normally connected to their strategic interests and not intended to be a form of corporate governance 'discipline'.

For example, Singapore's Temasek Holdings bought a 3.8 per cent stake in Merrill Lynch which merged with Bank of America at the height

---

[207] Post-Santiago surveys show a low uptake of the Principles among existing and new SWFs, see 'Time for SWFs to show greater transparency', *Financial Times* (2 Sep 2012).

[208] Such as the Abu Dhabi Fund's adoption of annual reporting since 2010, but such reporting can be regarded as rather superficial. Gulf funds continue to be scored rather modestly on the Truman Transparency scoreboard, see Edwin M Truman et al, 'Accountability and Transparency: The Sovereign Wealth Fund Scoreboard' (*Peterson Institute for International Economics* 2010) at pp. 72–73.

[209] Michel Aglietta, 'Sovereign Wealth Funds and the Mutation of Global Finance' (2014), above; Roland Beck and Michael Fidora, 'Sovereign Wealth Funds – Before and Since the Crisis' (2009), above.

[210] See 'Sovereign wealth funds drive turbulent trading', *Financial Times* (1 Feb 2016).

of the global financial crisis in 2007.[211] Hatton and Pistor[212] argued that this was politically motivated, likely at the request of the US. Temasek's swift divestment of the large stake at a loss two years later was explained as being in line with their portfolio focus on the Asia-Pacific. The stake was possibly never aligned with Temasek's strategic objectives, and divestment should not be interpreted as a form of corporate governance discipline. Further, the Abu Dhabi funds' and Sheikh Mansour's stakes in Barclays, acquired in 2008 during the global financial crisis, have also been quietly sold in 2013,[213] indicating perhaps that the stake was purchased as a form of stabilising support for Barclays. As Barclays returned to profitability, the stake was sold as there may no longer be any strategic reason to maintain it.

Divestment is however treated as a form of corporate governance discipline by the Norwegian Fund. Divestment by the Norwegian Fund signals to the market the Fund's opinion that the investee company falls short on ethical or sustainable behaviour. As discussed in Section B, the Norwegian Fund's divestments are usually made based on one of their ethical criteria, which includes environmental sustainability. The Fund's divestment from coal, from companies that have been embroiled in alleged human rights violations (such as Singapore Technologies, Walmart etc) are statements made by the Fund in disapproval of certain corporate behaviour and activities. The slightly less draconian measure of placing companies under observation also intends to achieve a similar effect of bringing the Fund's influence to bear upon corporate behaviour. It may be argued that divestment does not achieve anything pursuant to the Fund's corporate governance role as no constructive activism is brought to bear. However, if divestment affects share price or corporate profitability, market discipline may to a certain extent be achieved.[214]

---

211 'Temasek defends BofA stake sale', *Financial Times* (22 May 2009).

212 Kyle Hatton and Katharina Pistor, 'Maximizing Autonomy in the Shadow of Great Powers: The Political Economy of Sovereign Wealth Funds' (2011), above.

213 'Abu Dhabi quietly cashes out of Barclays', *Financial Times* (18 July 2013).

214 There is some empirical evidence that negative ESG disclosures affect sales and therefore corporate profitability, see Les Coleman, 'Losses from Failure of Stakeholder Sensitive Processes: Financial Consequences for Large US Companies from Breakdowns in Product, Environmental, and Accounting Standards' (2011) 98 *Journal of Business Ethics* 247.

In other cases, commentators[215] argue that the Norwegian Fund behaves as an engaged investor that conducts informal dialogue and exchange with its investee companies. Its threat of divestment or placing under observation could indeed be a means to pave the way for informal shareholder engagement.[216]

Unique to Norway and contrary to the usual perception of exit as disengagement, divestment, the role of the Norwegian Fund may be seen as providing a collective, almost public, good in shareholder engagement for common causes in ethics and social responsibility at international companies.

SWFs in the UK – Spotlight on Qatari SWFs

Qatar's sovereign wealth funds have extensive investments in the UK, including in real estate (Canary Wharf, the Shard, the Olympic Village, luxury hotels such as the Connaught, Berkeley and Claridges in London and other prime real estate in Central London), significant private companies such as Harrods Ltd and significant investments in publicly listed companies on the London Stock Exchange. These include a 26 per cent holding in Sainsbury's, a 20 per cent stake in the London Stock Exchange itself, a 10 per cent stake in British Airways, a 12.7 per cent stake in Barclays Plc, and a 20 per cent stake in BAA holdings, the major operator of the UK's airports. It is also to be noted that the Qatari funds do not only invest in the UK's national champions. They also invest extensively in French national champions such as Lagardère (12 per cent), Total (4 per cent), EADS (6 per cent), Technip, Air Liquide, Vinci SA (5 per cent), GDF Suez, Veolia (5 per cent), Vivendi, Royal Monceau, France Telecom and Areva. They also hold stakes in Credit Suisse (6 per cent) and Royal Dutch Shell (3 per cent).

---

[215] Maria Ungureanu, 'The Corporate Governance of Sovereign Wealth Funds', Harvard Law School Forum on Corporate Governance (7 August 2014); Anita M Halvorssen, 'Using the Norwegian Sovereign Wealth Fund's Ethical Guidelines as a Model for Investors, be They Private or Government-Owned' (2011), above.

[216] Although the impact of socially responsible investors on corporate behaviour is arguably negligible, see Matthew Haigh and James Hazelton, 'Financial Markets: A Tool for Social Responsibility?' (2004) 52 *Journal of Business Ethics* 59.

The nature of the funds' holdings provides diversification from their oil-based economy by investing in developed capital markets,[217] boosting the potential for reserve investment growth. The funds' significant holdings in several publicly listed companies also put the funds in a position to exercise their corporate governance roles.

Qatar Holdings, the subsidiary of the Qatar Investment Authority, is the main SWF investor in the UK companies mentioned above. Its corporate governance footprint has been more pronounced than many SWFs. This may be attributed to the 'aggressive' corporate and deal-making culture in the QIA.[218] For example, the episode involving Qatar Holdings' role in leading Xstrata minority shareholders to demand a higher takeover premium from Glencore showed the fund's willingness to take vocal leadership for the protection of minority shareholders. Further, the activism carried out by Qatar Holdings has extended to management rights, such as securing Board appointment rights via its 20 per cent BAA stake.[219] Qatar Holdings has also made bold corporate governance moves such as demanding to nominate a Board member to Songbird Estates, a listed UK real estate company,[220] where the Holdings owned a 24 per cent stake in the free float of ordinary shares. However, the motivations for the appointment were less clear, as the Fund was also wrestling for control of the ownership of Canary Wharf, of which Songbird Estates owned 70 per cent.[221] Such a move was not pursuant to the upholding or enhancement of corporate governance standards, but could be motivated by their commercial interest in Canary Wharf. As disclosure and transparency on the part of the Qatar Investment Authority is relatively scarce,[222] it is uncertain how many other investments have translated into Board seats.

---

217 'Qatar: what's next for the world's most aggressive deal hunter?', *Financial Times* (4 July 2013).

218 Above.

219 Source: 'Time for SWFs to show greater transparency', *Financial Times* (2 Sep 2012).

220 Qataris appoint Ken Costa to Songbird Estates board', *Financial Times* (11 Dec 2014).

221 Canary Wharf was ultimately jointly bought by Qatar Holdings and a Canadian entity from Songbird Estates.

222 QIA has a low score of 17 on Truman's scoreboard, see Allie E Bagnall and Edwin M Truman, 'Progress on Sovereign Wealth Fund Transparency and Accountability: An Updated SWF Scoreboard' (*Peterson Institute for International Economics*, August 2013) at https://piie.com/publications/pb/pb13-19.pdf.

The Qatar funds have so far taken stakes and corporate governance positions in important and profitable UK companies. Their corporate governance roles seem aligned with commercial motivations, which explain the 'defensive' behaviour in the Glencore-Xstrata episode. Nevertheless, securing Board seats and being able to exert influence from the driving seat could give rise to opportunities to inject strategic interests in their investments. Would Qatar Holdings behave like the shareholder activists who carry out 'offensive' activism discussed in Chapters 3 and 6? We do not see similar behaviour on the part of the Qatari SWFs as the attainment of Board seats is not related to driving specific demands and changes, as carried out by activist hedge funds. Further, we also do not see ultimate exit after agitating for change, which is often the trajectory of hedge fund activism. As such, the Qatar funds' corporate governance roles would bear greater resemblance to private sector institutional investor activism, although they behave in a more active manner than institutions.

D. CONCLUSION

SWFs, with swelling assets under management, are growing to become significant investors in developed capital markets. Although some fear that such investments are politically or strategically motivated and may bring negative consequences to the investee companies and host country markets, SWFs' investments in foreign corporate equity, especially corporate equity in developed capital markets, can be attributed to the needs of diversification from their economic models. Further, as SWFs seek to attain objectives that are beneficial to their own economies such as stabilisation, savings and inter-generational equity, their investments in foreign corporate equity tend to be constructive, long-term oriented and stabilising in nature.

The qualities of long-termism and constructive monitoring could almost place SWFs in the position of being an optimal corporate governance actor in their investee companies. In this light, the Norwegian Global Pension Fund, the world's largest SWF, uses its investment strategy to pursue its wider mission of enhancing ethical and sustainable practices in the global corporate sector. Although some may see such a corporate governance role as supplying a useful collective good on behalf of most institutions, it can nevertheless be criticised as a projection of strategic state priorities onto global capitalism.[223] Most SWFs therefore steer clear of assuming visible corporate governance roles, although the extent of informal influence that can be exercised remains opaque. Such informal influence has been documented by some empirical researchers[224] as being constructive and beneficial, although we suggest that a mixture of strategic motivations may be at play too. We argue that SWFs have actually been behaving with great restraint in their corporate governance roles, perhaps more restrained than necessary, as it is impossible for them to shed suspicions of association with strategic or politically-driven behaviour, and their activist gestures if any, could easily be magnified in more negative light than warranted. Hence, we do not think that many SWFs will become leading examples of engaged shareholders in the coming years, and the Norwegian model is not necessarily regarded as the template to follow by many others.

The perhaps unnecessarily risk averse and suspicious attitude of the markets vis-à-vis SWFs' foreign investments is likely to curtail the benefits of SWFs' corporate governance roles in long-termist monitoring. We do not think that adhering to the Santiago Principles would bolster SWFs in their corporate governance roles, as SWFs are likely to continue strategically complying with certain aspects of the Principles as far as such align with their interests. SWFs are unlikely to be able to become as objectively commercially-motivated as is demanded under the Principles, and perhaps they do not believe that thick compliance with the Santiago Principles will gain them much more favour in the markets anyway, as public perception is not a matter of rational judgment. Further, the Santiago Principles are unlikely to be hardened further in international legal order. In sum, we see most SWFs as carrying out a balancing act between investing effectively in foreign markets and quietly achieving their strategic interests.

It may be argued that the Qatar Investment Authority and its subsidiary funds provide an example of how SWFs can project themselves as acting commercially, and exhibiting behaviour similar to activist institutional

[223] Larry Cata Backer, 'Sovereign Investing and Markets-Based Transnational Rule of Law Building: The Norwegian Sovereign Wealth Fund in Global Markets' (2013), above.

[224] For example, Elvira Sojli and Wing Wah Tham, 'The Impact of Foreign Government Investments: Sovereign Wealth Fund Investments in the United States' in Narjess Boubakri and Jean Claude Cosset (eds), *Institutional Investors in Global Capital Markets* (Emerald Group 2011) at p. 207.

shareholders. Although they have not completely won over public perception,[225] and it remains uncertain what strategic motivations they have, they seem to have persistently engaged at a corporate governance level in a way that is not dissimilar from what can legitimately be done by private sector institutions. The QIA's active ownership behaviour challenges the Western markets' imposition of double standards – that exhort SWFs to behave only in a commercial capacity and yet be regulated like state-owned strategic entities.

---

[225] For example, 'How much of London is owned by Qatar's royal family?', *The Guardian* (9 Dec 2014); 'How London is being Sold off to Qatar', *The Daily Mail Online* (25 April 2015).

9. Conclusion: Beyond shareholder stewardship – visions for responsible investment management and a new corporate governance

The UK[1] and EU[2] have expressed faith in the capacity of institutional shareholders to act as 'stewards' of listed and, to a lesser extent, private companies, and have over the last few years adopted policies aimed at encouraging them to become more engaged in their corporate governance roles. Policy makers are convinced that if institutions can be persuaded to adopt a meaningful corporate governance role, the resulting impact on corporate performance, behaviour and accountability will be beneficial for the companies themselves and the economy as a whole.

In this book, we have examined the major institutional shareholders in UK corporate equity, including pension funds (of which we have focused on UK-based pension schemes), retail collective investment funds, alternative investment funds and sovereign wealth funds. The rise of institutions as owners of corporate equity is in no small part due to the general trend of financialisation in developed economies, a trend that compels individuals, households, corporations and public bodies to increasingly undertake their financial activities via the private financial intermediation sector. Collective investment has grown to become a main *modus* for saving, and institutions which manage funds as pools of capital have arisen to become significant allocators of investment capital. Corporate equities in both the developed and emerging economies are an

---

[1] The UK Stewardship Code 2012; the exploration by the Department of Business, Energy and Industrial Strategy, *Green Paper: Corporate Governance Reforms* (Nov 2016) at https://www.gov.uk/government/uploads/system/uploads/attachment_data/file/584013/corporate-governance-reform-green-paper.pdf to further involve shareholders in the control of executive pay which is still excessive, particularly from a social distribution perspective.

[2] Directive (EU) 2017/828 of the European Parliament and of the Council of 17 May 2017 amending Directive 2007/36/EC as regards the encouragement of long-term shareholder engagement.

important destination for such investment, and hence, institutions have, due to their investment management activities, also become dominant owners of corporate equity. The ownership of such corporate equity brings with it historically-defined legal and economic rights to participate in corporate decision-making in the general meeting, the exercise of voice in corporate governance, and certain rights in litigation as well as the right to sell out and exit the investment in the company concerned.

Corporate equity ownership also arguably brings with it moral rights and obligations relating to the practice of good corporate ownership which policy-makers call 'stewardship'. Such a vision of 'good ownership' includes engaging in corporate governance roles meaningfully for the well-being of the investee company over the long term, which in theory is an objective aligned with the investment performance objective of many institutions. The ownership of corporate equity cannot (and should not) be viewed as merely a private proprietary right that can be exercised in any way the shareholder sees fit. Although there is case law endorsement for the freedom to vote,[3] courts have also introduced doctrines that exert a degree of control over such freedom, being mindful that the company is a collective body and the overall well-being of the company is important.[4] Mandatory company law has also, over the years, been introduced to curtail what may be regarded to be objectionable exercises of otherwise legal power by majority shareholders.[5] Increasingly, ownership of corporate equity by institutions is regarded as a 'representative' economic right on behalf of myriad savers.[6] A public interest dimension has become more pronounced in both public and academic discourse in relation to the ownership of corporate equity and the corporate governance roles this entails. This was articulated as early as in the 1990s, in Useem's 'investor capitalism' model[7] and in Hawley and Williams' 'fiduciary capitalism' model introduced in 2000.[8] As

---

[3] *Northern Counties Securities Ltd. v Jackson & Steeple. Ltd.* [1974] 1 WLR 1133.

[4] *Allen v Gold Reefs of West Africa Ltd* [1900] 1 Ch 656; *Brown v British Abrasive Wheel Co* [1919] 1 Ch 290 and modern interpretation in *Arbuthnott v Bonnyman & Ors* [2015] EWCA Civ 536.

[5] E.g. the exception to *Foss v Harbottle* (1843) 67 ER 189, now the derivative action s260–263, Companies Act 2006; s994, Companies Act 2006.

[6] Ewan McGaughey, 'Participation in Corporate Governance' (2014) at http://ssrn.com/abstract=2593904.

[7] Michael Useem, *Investor Capitalism: How Money Managers are Rewriting the Rules of Corporate America* (Basic Books, 1999).

[8] J P Hawley and A T Williams, 'Shifting Ground: Emerging Global Corporate-Governance Standards and the Rise of Fiduciary Capitalism' (2005)

owners of corporate equity, institutions *should*, in their corporate governance roles, reflect the social interest in the long-term performance, well-being and perhaps even sustainability of their investee companies, contributing their influence to shaping a healthy and sound corporate sector to deliver long-term savers' needs through long-term value creation.

However, for a variety of reasons (described in this book), the optimal corporate governance role envisaged above is often not realised in modern investment management. We are of the view that most pension schemes, whether defined benefit or defined contribution schemes, are subject to short-termist pressures that may make the expenditure of significant time or resources on the corporate governance of any particular investee company incompatible with their commercial imperatives and regulatory obligations. Indeed, regulatory obligations are often a key source of the short termist pressures that pension schemes face even though these obligations are well-intentioned for beneficiary protection and prudential objectives. Retail collective investment schemes are also tightly regulated, and increasingly converge on low-cost, passive models or exchange-traded funds where adherence to an Index is the key investment management strategy. These are the funds, which along with their asset managers, can be seen – due to their ubiquity as private savings vehicles – as 'representing' the economic and social interests of retail savers. Yet they are often found to be subject to short-termist pressures or are unwilling or unable to expend significant time and resources on a long-term 'stewardship' role. Their attitudes derive both from the commercial imperatives of their business models and the ways in which regulation has shaped the industry (which are often based on well-meaning attempts to promote investor protection). Hence, policy-makers' reliance on institutions to play their part in corporate governance in order to bring about the optimal social effects of well-functioning, well-governed and performing corporations blithely ignores the dilemmas faced in the investment management sector and fail to fully appreciate the implications of these limitations.

As for alternative investment funds, it may be observed that private equity funds that play an engaged corporate governance role in unlisted companies have achieved significant economic and governance impact on their investee companies, and activist hedge funds can also exert a

---

37 *Environment and Planning* 1995–2013, *The Rise of Fiduciary Capitalism: How Institutional Investors Can Make Corporate America More Democratic* (University of Pennsylvania Press, 2000).

positive effect upon corporate performance by using their corporate governance powers and rights to make certain specific demands of boards and management. However, we are sceptical that these models can be used to promote a long-term ownership approach based on stewardship and long-term value creation across the corporate sector as a whole (although there may be individual cases of beneficial impact). This is because most alternative investment funds are single-mindedly geared towards realisation of short-term (or at best medium term) profits, and their assumption of corporate governance roles has to be understood in the context of the instrumental pursuit of their business models. As the business models of alternative fund managers are relatively less regulated than pension and retail schemes, they are at liberty to engage in more exotic investment management strategies. In the case of activist hedge funds, it has been opined that they create a market for corporate influence in order to extract value from investee corporations.[9] Empirical evidence is mixed as to the long-term well-being of companies that have been targeted by activist hedge funds,[10] or owned by private equity buy-out funds.[11] The corporate governance roles incorporated into these funds' investment strategies could be described as 'instrumental' to their business needs, and hence not necessarily aligned with the socially optimal model of 'stewardship' envisaged in our ideal model of corporate equity ownership based on long-term value creation.

Moving away from private investment funds, sovereign wealth funds examined in Chapter 8 indulge in mixed tendencies – some of their investments are long-termist, reflecting industrial strategy in the interests of usually domestic public policy, while others may be commercially motivated (especially foreign corporate equity investments). However, being free of short-termist pressures, sovereign wealth funds could potentially play the part of long-termist, engaged corporate governance actors that advance the sustainable well-being of their investee companies. We highlighted the Norwegian public pension fund which adopts an overt policy of supporting greater social responsibility in corporations worldwide and uses its ownership rights in corporate equity to exert such influence, although its role is not necessarily beyond critique.[12]

---

[9] John Armour and Brian Cheffins, 'The Rise and Fall (?) of Shareholder Activism by Hedge Funds' (2012) 14 *Journal of Alternative Investments* 17.

[10] Discussed in Chapter 6.

[11] Discussed in Chapter 7.

[12] For example, see Simon Chesterman, 'The Turn to Ethics: Disinvestment from Multinational Corporations for Human Rights Violations–The Case of

In sum, we are sceptical of claims that institutions possess in aggregate the capacity and the willingness to genuinely embrace a 'stewardship' role – based on principles of good company ownership – in their investee companies (notwithstanding the contrary claims of their marketing and corporate governance teams), and hence do not see the modern investment management industry as offering a viable mechanism for delivering a well-functioning, well-governed and performing corporate economy for the long term. Indeed, we are of the view that certain aspects of investment management, including institutions' corporate governance roles, may need to be better governed by standards which should be developed in regulation. These would seek to address areas where the power of investment management service providers is not adequately checked, so that greater transparency and accountability can be achieved. Indeed, the European Shareholders' Rights Directive 2017 has gone some way towards making asset managers and proxy advisers more publicly accountable although not regulated as such.

Despite these reservations about its wider governance role, we nonetheless recognise that the investment management sector performs an increasingly important function of intermediating myriad and voluminous savings needs and should be adequately enabled and governed.[13] Investment management has become and will remain an extremely important business sector – in the United Kingdom, the United States and increasingly elsewhere – and this contribution should be encouraged and nurtured. However, we should be less ready than many current policy makers to expect that the investment management sector as a whole can play a major part in assuming a quasi-governmental business oversight function which is relied upon to bring about a socially optimal corporate sector. Investment management is just one economic sector amongst many, with its own commercial and regulatory concerns. If we could come to view investment management as just a business like any other, rather than as a monitoring and resource allocation mechanism for the entire economy, we might be closer to defining the future path of corporate governance policy.

The question arises as to what measures are needed then to support a socially optimal corporate sector that is well-functioning, well-governed and performing for the long-term? This book does not accept that such an

---

Norway's Sovereign Wealth Fund' (2008) 23 *American University International Law Review* 577.

[13] Iris H-Y Chiu and Dionysia Katelouzou, 'Making a Case for Regulating Institutional Shareholders' Corporate Governance Roles' (2017) *Journal of Business Law*, forthcoming.

important public policy question should rest upon the shoulders of private actors alone, such as institutional shareholders, their asset managers and other financial intermediaries. Indeed, we suggest that this is an issue that requires public policy choices and decisions to be made.

THE FAILURES OF SHAREHOLDER PRIMACY

The question as to whether corporate governance in the UK remains fit for purpose or should be reformed was most recently re-examined by a Parliamentary committee on corporate governance in 2016.[14] This reflects the continuing social appetite for achieving a long-termist and socially optimally corporate sector, an aspiration that is persistently being thwarted by the prevalence of corporate short-termism and corporate scandals.

The legitimacy of the traditional corporate governance ethos in the UK, based on shareholder primacy, is increasingly being questioned. The policy expectation that institutions will embrace 'stewardship' is itself a facet of shareholder primacy, as shareholders, the constituents regarded as most important to the corporate objective, have both the *right* as well as the 'social mandate' to influence corporate decision-making and behaviour. However, shareholder primacy has only furthered shareholders' insular interests in pursuit of short-termist share price performance, regular dividends and financial performance that may be achieved at the expense of wider stakeholder interests and needs. Shareholder primacy is a narrow and limited premise for company law, as it does not take into account the reality that (a) the economic organisation of the company is made up of many more parts than its 'Board', top management and shareholders[15] and (b) the societal institution that is the

---

[14] http://www.parliament.uk/business/committees/committees-a-z/commons-select/business-innovation-and-skills/news-parliament-2015/corporate-governance-inquiry-launch-16-17/.

[15] Many commentators have pointed out that even taking the nexus of contracts view of the company, there are many suppliers of productive capital into the organisational framework and undue focus on shareholders obscures the firm-specific commitment of capital made by other stakeholders whose interests are not as protected. For example, see Margaret Blair, *Ownership and Control: Rethinking Corporate Governance for the Twenty-First Century* (Brookings Institute 1994); Arturo Capasso, 'Stakeholder Theory and Corporate Governance: The Role of Intangible Assets' at http://papers.ssrn.com/sol3/papers.cfm?abstract_id=610661 arguing that a resource-based view allows us to more clearly

corporation serves multifaceted purposes and carries out activities that have impact beyond creating shareholder returns.[16]

We are highly sceptical of the idea that further advancement of shareholder primacy and shareholders' rights and roles in the company is the optimal way to secure a long-termist corporate sector that meets social expectations. The embrace of shareholder primacy in company law has become systemically disempowering and marginalising for other stakeholders in the company.[17] The entrenched imbalance in company law in favour of shareholders has been exploited by various actors – including various types of investment manager discussed in this book – and business and corporate practices have been developed in a manner that does little to ameliorate such an imbalance.

---

see the extent of committed productive capital other stakeholders offer the company.

[16] The sum of the corporation is often greater than its parts, and to an extent the collective entity of the company, or 'the real entity' interfaces with society (in the form of interdependencies, positive and negative externalities and philanthropy), and politics (e.g. in the form of political donations) in such a way that the corporation should not merely be treated as an internalised private bargaining phenomenon. See for example, Carl Kaysen, 'The Corporation: How Much Power? What Scope?' in Edward S Mason (ed.), *The Corporation in Modern Society* (Mass: Harvard University Press 1970) at p. 85; John E Parkinson, *Corporate Power and Responsibility: Issues in the Theory of Company Law* (Oxford: Clarendon Press 1995); Philip Blumberg, 'The Politicization of the Corporation' (1971) 26 *Business Lawyer* 1551; Susanna Kim Ripken, 'Corporations Are People Too: A Multi-Dimensional Approach To The Corporate Personhood Puzzle' (2009) 15 *Fordham Journal of Corporate and Financial Law* 97; Lawrence E Mitchell, 'Groundwork Of The Metaphysics Of Corporate Law' (1993) 50 *Washington and Lee Law Rev* 1477. Also see writings aimed at encouraging the corporation to take up responsible citizenship; Lawrence E Mitchell (ed.), *Progressive Corporate Law* (Boulder: Westview Press 1995); Sally Wheeler, *Corporations and the Third Way* (Oxford: Hart 2002); Kent Greenfield, 'New Principles For Corporate Law' (2005) 1 *Hastings Business Law Journal* 89; *The Failure of Corporate Law* (London: The University of Chicago Press 2006). For globally active multinational corporations, some commentators have referred to their footprint as a form of global citizenship, see for example, Andrew Crane and Dirk Matten, *Business Ethics: Managing Corporate Citizenship and Sustainability in the Age of Globalization* (Oxford: OUP 2015); Judith Richter and John Borton, *Holding Corporations Accountable: Corporate Conduct, International Codes, and Citizen Action* (Zed Books 2001).

[17] Arturo Capasso, 'Stakeholder Theory and Corporate Governance: The Role of Intangible Assets', above; Robert Phillips, 'Stakeholder Legitimacy' (2003) 13 *Business Ethics Quarterly* 25 on the stakeholders who remain unrecognised in company law.

The embrace of shareholder primacy has also raised questions about the raison d'être of incorporation, which is to provide a long-termist framework for the protection of productive activities sustained by investment capital,[18] as discussed in Stout's vision of the corporation as a 'time machine'.[19] Rather, the corporation has become increasingly exploited as a place for extraction of short-term value by those legitimately in power within the corporate structure, i.e. executives in the form of excessive levels of pay[20] and shareholders in the form of dividends or capital return or redemption, even if such wealth transfers exceed the company's profits,[21] or deplete the company's long-term investment potential[22] or remove a cash buffer that can be useful for the company in withstanding stress and volatility in the business environment.[23]

---

[18] Margaret Blair, 'The Neglected Benefits of the Corporate Form: Entity Status and the Separation of Asset Ownership From Control' (2014) at http://ssrn.com/abstract=563307.

[19] Lynn Stout, 'The Corporation as Time Machine: Intergenerational Equity, Intergenerational Efficiency, and the Corporate Form' (2015) at http://papers.ssrn.com/sol3/papers.cfm?abstract_id=2556883.

[20] E.g. William Forbes, 'CEO Pay in FTSE 100: Pay Inequality, Board Size and Performance' (2012) at https://papers.ssrn.com/sol3/papers.cfm?abstract_id=2140204; Lisa Goh and Aditi Gupta, 'Executive Compensation, Compensation Consultants, and Shopping for Opinion: Evidence from the UK' (2010) at https://papers.ssrn.com/sol3/papers.cfm?abstract_id=1577925. Also see High Pay Centre, *Thinking High and Low: Exploring pay disparities in society* at http://highpaycentre.org/pubs/thinking-high-and-low-exploring-pay-disparities-in-society; 'New High Pay Centre report: Executive pay continues to climb at expense of ordinary workers' (2014) at http://highpaycentre.org/pubs/new-high-pay-centre-report-executive-pay-continues-to-climb-at-expense-of-o.

[21] As in the case of BHS, see House of Commons Work and Pensions and Business, Innovation and Skills Committees, *BHS* (2016) at http://www.publications.parliament.uk/pa/cm201617/cmselect/cmworpen/54/54.pdf.

[22] José-Miguel Gaspar, Massimo Massa, Pedro Matos, Rajdeep Patgiri and Zahid Rehman, 'Can Buybacks be a Product of Shorter Shareholder Horizons?' (2005) at http://papers.ssrn.com/sol3/papers.cfm?abstract_id=649482; Lee Pinkowitz, Rene M Stultz and Rohan Williamson, 'Is There a U.S. High Cash Holdings Puzzle after the Financial Crisis?' (2012) at http://papers.ssrn.com/sol3/papers.cfm?abstract_id=2064046; Nicoletta Batini and Joshua Felman, 'Why are US Firms Hoarding Money?' *IMF, Country Report* 11/202 (2011).

[23] Andrés Ramirez, 'Risk and the Multinational Corporation Revisited: The Case of Natural Disasters and Corporate Cash Holdings' (2011) at http://ssrn.com/abstract=1772969; Tom W Bates, Kathryn M Kahle and Rene M Stultz, 'Why Do U.S. Firms Hold So Much More Cash than They Used To?' (2009) 64 *Journal of Finance* 1985 on precautionary planning by managers.

It is time to recognise the negative distortions in company law that arise from shareholder primacy and embrace a case for reform. These imbalances are unlikely to be corrected unless company law intervenes to redress them, thereby ideologically reforming itself. In short, we believe that it is timely to consider introducing a more stakeholder-oriented model in company law and corporate governance.

It may be argued that enrolling stakeholders in company law would necessarily be disruptive for existing legal structures, creating confusion for directors' duties and the corporate objective.[24] Legal reform necessitates adaptation to change and we argue that workable reform is possible. We also do not believe that relying on companies to adopt stakeholder consciousness as a soft form of business or management ethics[25] would be sufficient,[26] as there are no consistent or fundamental motivations for companies to do so, and whether stakeholders can bring their pressure to bear will depend largely on the political economy context relating to particular industry sectors.[27]

---

[24] John Argenti, 'Stakeholders: The Case Against' (1997) 30(3) *Long Range Planning* 442; Elaine Sternberg, *Stakeholding: Betraying the Corporation's Objectives* (*London Social Affairs Unit Research Paper* No 27).

[25] Timothy L Fort, 'Goldilocks And Business Ethics: A Paradigm That Fits "Just Right"' (1998) 23 *Journal of Corporation Law* 245; Michael C Jensen, 'Non-Rational Behavior, Value Conflicts, Stakeholder Theory, and Firm Behavior' in Bradley R Agle, Thomas Donaldson, R Edward Freeman, Michael C Jensen, Ronald K Mitchell and Donna J Wood, *Towards Superior Stakeholder Theory* (2008) 18 *Business Ethics Quarterly* 159; R Edward Freeman, 'Ending the So-Called "Friedman-Freeman" Debate' in Bradley R Agle, Thomas Donaldson, R Edward Freeman, Michael C Jensen, Ronald K Mitchell and Donna J Wood, *Towards Superior Stakeholder Theory* (2008), above.

[26] Donna Wood, 'Corporate Responsibility and Stakeholder Theory: Challenging the Neoclassical Paradigm' in Bradley R Agle, Thomas Donaldson, R Edward Freeman, Michael C Jensen, Ronald K Mitchell and Donna J Wood, *Towards Superior Stakeholder Theory* (2008), above; Tom Donaldson, 'Two Stories' in Bradley R Agle, Thomas Donaldson, R Edward Freeman, Michael C Jensen, Ronald K Mitchell and Donna J Wood, *Towards Superior Stakeholder Theory* (2008), above; Andrew Crane and Trish Ruebottom, 'Stakeholder Theory and Social Identity: Rethinking Stakeholder Identification' (2011) 102 *Journal of Business Ethics* 77; James A Steib, 'Assessing Freeman's Stakeholder Theory' (2009) 87 *Journal of Business Ethics* 401.

[27] Some refer this issue to different varieties of capitalism calibrating different relational paradigms between the company and stakeholders based on political context, economic structures and social culture. See generally Peter A Hall and David Soskice, 'An Introduction to the Varieties of Capitalism' in Peter A Hall and David Soskice, *Varieties of Capitalism* (Oxford: Oxford University

LOOKING FORWARD AT LAW AND POLICY TO SECURE A LONG-TERMIST AND SOCIALLY OPTIMAL CORPORATE SECTOR

In our submission to the Parliamentary Committee Inquiry, we advocated a stakeholder-theory infused blueprint for company law whereby stakeholders may be given more scope for participating in relevant company decision-making. Many stakeholders make firm-specific commitments that are long-termist and ongoing,[28] and would benefit from the establishment of principles for a relational framework *within* and not just *with* the company. We argue in support of such reforms to enhance stakeholders' positions and power in a company, as we believe these will relate ultimately to the substantive outcomes of fairer distribution of responsibility and wealth, mitigation of externalities and improved corporate practices and ethics.

This change of focus towards a more pluralistic corporate governance approach will have implications across multiple dimensions. We do not explore them in detail in this book as they are explored elsewhere,[29] but we envisage changes to company law and legal redress. Stakeholder participation could be structured in many ways, including Board or Board committee representation, and redefinition of the meaning of director independence, as well as dedicated processes for engaging stakeholder voice in the company.[30] Legal reform will be necessary to bring about a pluralistic approach to corporate governance by conceiving of Board responsibilities, duties and powers in different ways, recalibrating exclusive shareholder powers so that corporate decision-making is reformed in favour of wider distribution. For example, the exclusive powers for shareholders to approve of certain transactions or to remove directors would need to be rethought. Specific areas of power distribution, such as

Press 2001); and see critique in Dorothee Bohle and Béla Greskovits, 'Varieties of Capitalism and Capitalism «tout court»' (2009) 50 *European Journal of Sociology* 355.

[28] Margaret Blair, *Ownership and Control: Rethinking Corporate Governance for the Twenty-First Century* (1994), above; Arturo Capasso, 'Stakeholder Theory and Corporate Governance: The Role of Intangible Assets', above.

[29] Iris H-Y Chiu, 'Operationalising A Stakeholder Conception in Company Law', (2017) 10 *Law and Financial Markets Review* at http://dx.doi.org/10.1080/17521440.2017.1309161.

[30] Iris H-Y Chiu and Roger M Barker, 'Submission to The Business Skills and Innovation Commons Select Committee: Corporate Governance Inquiry' (2016) at https://papers.ssrn.com/sol3/papers.cfm?abstract_id=2858903.

in governance, takeovers, capital decisions, board appointments and executive pay, may need to be changed so that stakeholders have a meaningful voice in them – or at the very least, key decisions are no longer taken by directors who are entirely beholden to the shareholder constituency, but by directors who are instead required to adopt a broader vision of the best interests of the company. These may require heavy lifting in reform, but we believe little can be advanced by continuing to rely on a shareholder primacy-based model of shareholder 'stewardship' and the further expansion of shareholder powers. The current policy direction emphasizing the 'empowerment' and stewardship orientation of institutional shareholders will need to be reconceptualised.

We believe that treating corporate governance and company law reforms as public policy choices that need to be made in order to advance a more legitimate corporate economy based on long-term value creation is the correct approach. The investment management industry should not be overly laden with a 'hidden' public policy agenda that it is unlikely to achieve given its nature as a private sector business activity and the regulatory pressures that determine its priorities and objectives. We believe that the investment management industry will continue to flourish as a major industry in many economies – helping savers, providing employment and generating tax revenues – but no longer distorting the wider corporate system in a way that is inconsistent with the social and economic requirement for long-term value creation. At the end of this process, the investment management industry itself may well breathe a sigh of relief that the expectations of society for the sector are now better aligned to its own mission and objectives.

Bibliography

Abdelal, Rawi, 'Sovereign Wealth in Abu Dhabi' (2009) 14 *Geopolitics* 317.

Abner, David J, *The ETF Handbook: How to Value and Trade Exchange-Traded Funds* (Chichester: John Wiley & Sons, 2010).

Acharya, Viral V, Hahn, Moritz and Kehoe, Conor, 'Corporate Governance and Value Creation: Evidence from Private Equity' (2009) at http://ssrn.com/abstract=1324016.

Acharya, Viral V, Kehoe, Conor and Reyner, Michael, 'Private Equity vs PLC Boards in the U.K.: A Comparison of Practices and Effectiveness' (*ECGI Working Paper*, 2008).

Achleitner, Ann-Kristin, Betzer, André and Gider, Jasmin, 'Do Corporate Governance Motives Drive Hedge Funds and Private Equity Activities?' (2009) at http://ssrn.com/abstract=1292896.

Achleitner, Ann-Kristin, Lutz, Eva, Herman, Kerry and Lerner, Josh, 'New Look: Going Private with Private Equity Support' (2009) at http://ssrn.com/abstract=1120230.

Admati, Anat R and Pfleiderer, Paul, 'The "Wall Street Walk" and Shareholder Activism: Exit as a Form of Voice' (2009) 22 *Review of Financial Studies* 2645.

Adrian, Tobias, Begalle, Brian, Copeland, Adam and Martin, Antoine, 'Repo and Securities Lending' (2011) http://ssrn.com/abstract=1976327.

Aggarwal, Reena, Bai, Jennie and Laeven, Luc, 'The Securities Lending Market and the Collateral Channel of Monetary Policy Transmission' (2016) at http://ssrn.com/abstract=2692251.

Agarwal, Vikas, Gay, Gerald D and Ling, Leng, 'Window Dressing in Mutual Funds' (2014) at http://ssrn.com/abstract=1804939.

Aggarwal, Reena, Erel, Isli and Starks, Laura T, 'Influence of Public Opinion on Investor Voting and Proxy Advisors' (2014) at http://papers.ssrn.com/sol3/papers.cfm?abstract_id=2447012.

Agle, Bradley R, Donaldson, Thomas, Freeman, R Edward, Jensen, Michael C, Mitchell, Ronald K and Wood, Donna J, *Towards Superior Stakeholder Theory* (2008) 18 *Business Ethics Quarterly* 159.

Aglietta, Michel, 'Sovereign Wealth Funds and the Mutation of Global Finance' (2014) 8 *Law and Financial Markets Review* 282.

Aglietta, Michel, Brière, Marie, Rigotc, Sandra, Signori, Ombretta 'Rehabilitating the Role of Active Management for Pension Funds' (2012) at http://ssrn.com/abstract=1948726.

Agrawal, Ashwini K, 'Corporate Governance Objectives of Labor Union Shareholders: Evidence from Proxy Voting' (2011) 25 *Review of Financial Studies* 187.

Ahmadov, Ingilab, Tsani, Stela and Aslanli, Kenan, *Sovereign Wealth Funds: New Challenges for Caspian Countries* (Baku 2011) at http://www.resourcegovernance.org/sites/default/files/SWFs-Caspian-Countries.pdf.

Ahmandov, Ingilab and Asnali, Kenan, 'State Oil Fund of Azerbaijan Republic: Past, Present and Future' in Ingilab Ahmadov et al, *Sovereign Wealth Funds: New Challenges for Caspian Countries* (Baku 2011) at http://www.resourcegovernance.org/sites/default/files/SWFs-Caspian-Countries.pdf.

Aizenmann, Joshua and Glick, Reuven, 'Sovereign Wealth Funds: Stylized Facts About Their Determinants and Governance' (*NBER Working Paper* 2008) at http://www.nber.org/papers/w14562.

Akinbami, Folarin, 'Retail Financial Products in the Global Financial Crisis' (2012) at http://papers.ssrn.com/sol3/papers.cfm?abstract_id=2087548.

Albuquerque, Rui, Lei, Zicheng, Rocholl, Jörg and Zhang, Chendi, 'Institutional Investors and Corporate Political Activism' (*ECGI Working Paper* 2016) at http://www.ecgi.org/wp/wp_id.php?id=785&mc_cid=faf516730b&mc_eid=bad7753e00.

Alhashel, Bader, 'Sovereign Wealth Funds: A Literature Review' (2015) 78 *Journal of Economics and Business* 1.

Ali, Paul, Ramsay, Ian and Saunders, Benjamin B, 'Securities Lending, Empty Voting and Corporate Governance' (2014) at http://ssrn.com/abstract=2443217.

Allen, Franklin and Gale, Douglas, 'Asset Price Bubbles and Monetary Policy' (2000) at http://finance.wharton.upenn.edu/~allenf/download/Vita/apbm.pdf.

Allen, Franklin, Qian, Jun Q J, Shan, Susan Chenyu and Zhao, Mengxin, 'The IPO of Industrial and Commercial Bank of China and the 'Chinese Model' of Privatizing Large Financial Institutions' (2012) 20 *European Journal of Finance* 599.

Allianz Global Investors, *Defining the Direction of Defined Contribution in Europe: Results of an Expert Survey* (2009).

Alternative Investment Market Association (AIMA), *Roadmap to Hedge Funds* (2008).

Amadi, Amir A, 'Equity Home Bias: A Disappearing Phenomenon?' (2004) at http://papers.ssrn.com/sol3/papers.cfm?abstract_id=540662.

Amornsiripanitch, Natee, Gompers, Paul A and Xuan, Yuhai, 'More than Money: Venture Capitalists on Boards' (2015) at http://ssrn.com/abstract=2586592.

Anabtawi, Iman, 'Some Skepticism about Increasing Shareholder Power' (2006) 53 UCLA Law Review 561.

Anabtawi, Iman, 'Predatory Management Buy-outs' (2015) 49 *UC Davis Law Review 1287* at http://ssrn.com/abstract=2649192.

Anabtawi, Iman and Stout, Lynn, 'Fiduciary Duties for Activist Shareholders' (2008) 60 *Stanford Law Rev* 1255.

Andenas, Mads and Chiu, Iris H-Y, *The Foundations and Future of Financial Regulation: Governance for Responsibility* (Oxford: Routledge, 2014).

Anderson, Anne-Marie and Myers, David H, 'The Cost of Being Good' (2007) 28 *Review of Business* 5.

Ando, Albert and Modigliani, Franco, 'The "Life Cycle" Hypothesis of Saving: Aggregate Implications and Tests' (1963) 53 *The American Economic Review* 55.

Andonov, Aleksandar, Bauer, Rob and Cremers, Martijn, 'Pension Fund Asset Allocation and Liability Discount Rates' (2014) at http://ssrn.com/abstract=2070054.

Ang, Andrew, 'The Four Benchmarks of Sovereign Wealth Funds' (2010) at http://ssrn.com/abstract=1680485.

Appel, Ian R, Gormley, Todd R and Keim, Donald B, 'Passive Investors not Passive Owners' (2014) at http://www.stern.nyu.edu/sites/default/files/assets/documents/1%20Gormley%20Passive%20Investors%20Not%20Passive%20Owners.pdf.

Arcot, Sridhar, Fluck Zsuzsanna, Gaspar, José-Miguel and Hege, Ulrich, 'Fund Managers under Pressure: Rationale and Determinants of Secondary Buyouts' (2014) at http://ssrn.com/abstract_id= 2332801.

Argenti, John, 'Stakeholders: The Case Against' (1997) 30 (3) *Long Range Planning* 442.

Armour, John and Cheffins, Brian, 'The Rise and Fall (?) of Shareholder Activism by Hedge Funds' (2012) 14 *Journal of Alternative Investments* 17.

Armour, John and Cheffins, Brian, 'The Rise and Fall (?) of Shareholder Activism by Hedge Funds' (2009) at http://papers.ssrn.com/sol3/papers.cfm?abstract_id=1489336.

Armour, John and Payne, Jennifer (eds), *Rationality in Company Law: Essays in Honour of DD Prentice* (Oxford: Hart Publishing, 2009).

Armour, John and Skeel, David Jnr, 'Who Writes the Rules for Hostile Takeovers, and Why-The Peculiar Divergence of US and UK Takeover Regulation' (2006) 95 *Georgetown Law Journal* 1727.

Armour, John and Whincop, Michael, 'The Proprietary Foundations of Corporate Law' (2007) *Oxford Journal of Legal Studies* 429.

Armour, John, Black, Bernard, Cheffins, Brian and Nolan, Richard, 'Private Enforcement of Corporate Law: An Empirical Comparison of the UK and US' (2009) 6 *Journal of Empirical Legal Studies* 687.

Arrow, Kenneth J, *Social Choice and Individual Values* (Conn: Yale University Press 1970, 2nd edn).

Arup, Christopher, 'The Global Financial Crisis: Learning from Regulatory and Governance Studies' (2010) 32 *Law and Policy* 363.

Aspen Institute, *Overcoming Short-termism: A Call for a More Responsible Approach to Investment and Business Management* (2009) at http://www.aspeninstitute.org/publications/overcoming-short-termism-call-more-responsible-approach-investment-business-management.

Assa, Jacob, 'Financialization and its Consequences: The OECD Experience' (2012) 1 *Finance Research* 35.

Association of British Insurers, *Improving Corporate Governance and Shareholder Engagement* (July 2013).

Association of Member Nominated Trustees (AMNT), *Red Lines Voting* (2016) at http://amnt.org/red-line-voting/.

Asthana, Sharad and Lipka, Roland, 'Management of Defined-Benefit Pension Funds and Shareholder Value' (2003) 41 *Quarterly Journal of Business and Economics* 49.

Atanosova, Christina V and Gatev, Evan, 'Risk-taking of Institutional Investors: Evidence from US Defined Benefit Pension Plans' (2010) at http://ssrn.com/abstract=1570925.

Australian Securities and Investments Commission, *Regulatory Guide 128: Collective Action by Investors* (June 2015) at http://download.asic.gov.au/media/3273670/rg128-published-23-june-2015.pdf?_ga=1.4889715.1711037398.1455118322.

Avgouleas, Emilios, 'The Global Financial Crisis, Behavioural Finance and Financial Regulation: In Search of a New Orthodoxy' (2009) 9 *Journal of Corporate Law Studies* 23.

Avgouleas, Emilios, 'Regulating Financial Innovation: A Multifaceted Challenge to Financial Stability, Consumer Protection, and Growth' in *The Oxford Handbook of Financial Regulation* (forthcoming 2015).

Axelson, Ulf, Strömberg, Per and Weisbach, Michael S, 'Why Are Buyouts Levered? The Financial Structure of Private Equity Funds' (2009) 64 *Journal of Finance* 1549.

Back, Kerry, Li, Tao and Ljungqvist, Alexander, 'Liquidity and Governance' (2013) at http://ssrn.com/abstract=2350362.

Backer, Larry Cata, 'Sovereign Investing in Times of Crisis: Global Regulation of Sovereign Wealth Funds, State Owned Enterprises and the Chinese Experience' (2009) *Transnational Law and Contemporary Problems* 101.

Backer, Larry Cata, 'Sovereign Wealth Funds as Regulatory Chameleons: The Norwegian Sovereign Wealth Funds and Public Global Governance Through Private Global Investment' (2010) 41 *Georgetown Journal of International Law* 425.

Baird, Philip L., Geylani, Pinar Celikkol and Roberts, Jeffrey A, 'Corporate Social and Financial Performance Re-Examined: Industry Effects in a Linear Mixed Model Analysis' (2012) 109 *Journal of Business Ethics* 367.

Baker, H Kent, Nofsinger, John R (eds), *Socially Responsible Finance and Investing* (Chichester: John Wiley & Sons 2010).

Balachandran, Balasingham, Chalmers, Keryn, Haman, Janto, 'On-Market Share Buybacks, Exercisable Share Options and Earnings Management' (2008) 48 *Accounting and Finance* 25.

Balding, Christopher, 'A Portfolio Analysis of Sovereign Wealth Funds' (2008) at http://ssrn.com/abstract=1141531.

Bange, Mary, Khang, Kenneth and Miller, Thomas W Jnr, 'Benchmarking the Performance of Recommended Allocations to Equities, Bonds, and Cash by International Investment Houses' (2008) at https://ideas.repec.org/a/eee/empfin/v15y2008i3p363-386.html.

Bank of England, *Securities Lending: An Introductory Guide* at http://www.bankofengland.co.uk/markets/Documents/gilts/sl_intro_green_9_10.pdf.

Bank of England and ISLA, *Securities Lending and Corporate Governance* (2000) at http://www.bankofengland.co.uk/markets/Documents/gilts/slcgjun05.pdf.

Bank of England and Procyclicality Working Group, *Procyclicality and Structural Trends in Investment Allocation by Insurance Companies and Pension Funds* (July 2014).

Barker, Roger and Chiu, Iris H-Y, 'Protecting Minority Shareholders in Blockholder-Controlled Companies – Evaluating the UK's Enhanced Listing Regime in Comparison with Investor Protection Regimes in New York and Hong Kong' (2015) 10 *Capital Markets Law Journal* 98.

Barnett, Michael and Duvall, Raymond (eds), *Power in Global Governance* (Oxford: OUP, 2005).

Barnett, Michael L and Salomon, Robert M, 'Beyond Dichotomy: The Curvilinear Relationship between Social Responsibility and Financial Performance' (2006) 27 *Strategic Management Journal* 1101.

Bassan, Fabio (ed.), *Research Handbook in Sovereign Wealth Funds and International Investment Law* (Cheltenham: Edward Elgar 2015).

Bassan, Fabio, *The Law of Sovereign Wealth Funds* (Cheltenham: Edward Elgar, 2011).

Bates, Tom W, Kahle, Kathryn M and Stultz, Rene M, 'Why Do U.S. Firms Hold So Much More Cash than They Used To?' (2009) 64 *Journal of Finance* 1985.

Batini, Nicoletta and Felman, Joshua, 'Why are US Firms Hoarding Money?' *IMF, Country Report* 11/202 (2011).

Bauer, Rob M M J, Cremers, K J Martjin and Frehen, Rik G P, 'Pension Fund Performance and Costs: Small is Beautiful' (2010) at http://ssrn.com/abstract=965388.

Bauer, Rob, Derwall, Jeroen and Otten, Rogér, 'The Ethical Mutual Fund Performance Debate: New Evidence from Canada' (2007) 70 *Journal of Business Ethics* 111.

Bazot, Guillaume, 'Financial Consumption and the Cost of Finance: Measuring Financial Efficiency in Europe (1950–2007)' (2014) at http://www.ipp.eu/wp-content/uploads/2014/06/working-paper-2014-17-pse-gbazot.pdf.

Bean, Bruce Winfield, 'Attack of the Sovereign Wealth Funds: Defending the Republic from the Threat of Sovereign Wealth Funds?' (2009) 18 *Michigan State Journal of International Law* 65.

Bebchuk, Lucian Ayre, 'The Case for Increasing Shareholder Power' (2005) 118 *Harvard Law Review* 833.

Bebchuk, Lucian A, Brav, Alon A and Jiang, Wei, 'The Long Term Effects of Hedge Fund Activism' (2013) at http://papers.ssrn.com/sol3/papers.cfm?abstract_id=2291577.

Bebchuk, Lucian, Brav, Alon and Jiang, Wei, 'The Long-Term Effects of Hedge Fund Activism' (2015) 115 *Columbia Law Review* 2085.

Bebchuk, Lucian and Spamann, Holger, 'Regulating Bankers' Pay' (2010) 98 *Georgetown Law Journal* 247.

Becht, Marco, Franks, Julian, Grant, Jeremy and Wagner, Hannes, F, 'The Returns to Hedge Fund Activism: An International Study' (2014) at http://ssrn.com/abstract=2376271.

Beck, Roland and Fidora, Michael, 'Sovereign Wealth Funds – Before and Since the Crisis' (2009) *European Business Organisation Law Review* 353.

Bedu, Nicholas and Montalban, Matthieu, 'Analysing the Uneven Development of Private Equity in Europe: Legal Origins and Diversity Of Capitalism' (2014) 12 *Socio-Economic Review* 33.

Bellofiore, Riccardo, 'The Ascent and Crisis of Money-Manager Capitalism' (2011) 40 *International Journal of Political Economy* 5.

Belsky, Eric S and Wachter, Susan S, 'The Public Interest In Consumer and Mortgage Credit Markets' (2010) at http://papers.ssrn.com/sol3/papers.cfm?abstract_id=1582947.

Bengtsson, Elias, 'A History of Scandinavian Socially Responsible Investing' (2008) 82 *Journal of Business Ethics* 969.

Bengtsson, Elias and Delbeque, Bernard, 'Revisiting the European Asset Management Industry' (2011) *Financial Markets, Institutions and Instruments* 163.

Bengtsson, E. 'Fund Management and Systemic Risk – Lessons from the Global Financial Crisis' (*Cityperc Working Paper* 2013).

Benson, Karen L, Brailsford, Timothy J and Humphrey, Jacquelyn E, 'Do Socially Responsible Fund Managers Really Invest Differently?' (2006) 65 *Journal of Business Ethics* 337.

Berger, David J and Murray, Kenneth M, 'As the Market Turns: Corporate Governance Litigation in an Age of Stockholder Activism' (2009) 5 NYU *Journal of Law & Business* 207.

Bergstresser, Daniel, Desai, Mihir, and Rauh, Joshua, 'Earnings Manipulation, Pension Assumptions and Managerial Investment Decisions' (2006) 121 *Quarterly Journal of Economics* 157.

Berle, Adolf A and Means, Gardiner, *The Modern Corporation and Private Property* (NY: Macmillan, 1932).

Bernhardt, Dan and Nosal, Ed, 'Gambling for Dollars: Strategic Hedge Fund Manager Investment' (2013) at http://ssrn.com/abstract=2367475.

Bernstein, Shai, Lerner, Josh and Schoar, Antoinette, 'The Investment Strategies of Sovereign Wealth Funds' (2013) 27 *The Journal of Economic Perspectives* 219.

Bertoni, Fabio and Lugo, Stefano, 'The Effect of Sovereign Wealth Funds on the Credit Risk of their Portfolio Companies' (2014) *Journal of Corporate Finance* forthcoming at http://ssrn.com/abstract=1763173.

Bessière, Véronique, Kaestner, Michael and Lafont, Anne-Laurence, 'Hedge Fund Activism: Insights from a French Clinical Study' (2011) 21 *Applied Financial Economics* 1225.

Bhagat, Sanjai and Bolton, Brian, 'Corporate Governance and Firm Performance: Recent Evidence' (2009) at http://www.econ.upf.edu/docs/seminars/bhagat.pdf.

Bhattacharyya, Sugato and Purnanandam, Amiyatosh, 'Risk-Taking By Banks: What Did We Know and When Did We Know It?' (November 2011) http://ssrn.com/abstract=1619472.

Bikker, Jacob A, Knaap, Thijs and Romp, Ward E, 'Measuring and Explaining Implicit Risk Sharing in Defined Benefit Pension Funds' (2014) 46 *Applied Economics* 1996.

Birdthistle, William, 'Compensating Power: An Analysis of Rents and Rewards in the Mutual Fund Industry' (2006) 80 *Tulane Law Review* 1402.

Birkmose, Hanne Søndergaard, 'European Challenges for Institutional Investor Engagement – Is Mandatory Disclosure the Way Forward' (2014) *European Company and Financial Law Review* 214.

Birkmose, Hanne, Neville, Mette and Sørensen, Karsten Engsig (eds), *The European Financial Market in Transition* (Alphen aan den Riljn: Kluwer Law International 2011).

BIS, *The Kay Review of UK Equity Markets and Long-Term Decision Making* (Final Report, 23 July 2012).

BIS, *Exploring the Intermediated Shareholding Model* (January 2016) at https://www.gov.uk/government/uploads/system/uploads/attachment_data/file/489357/bis-16-20-intermediated-shareholding-model.pdf.

Black, Bernard S, 'Shareholder Passivity Re-examined' (1990) 89 *Michigan Law Review* 520.

Black, Bernard S, 'The Legal and Industrial Preconditions for Strong Stock Markets' (*Stanford Law School Working Paper* No. 179, 2001).

Black, Bernard S and Coffee, John C, 'Institutional Investor Behaviour in the UK' (1993-4) 92 *Michigan Law Rev* 1999.

Black, Julia, 'Critical Reflections on Regulation' (2002) 27 *Australian J of Legal Philosophy* 1.

Black, Julia, 'Mapping the Contours of Contemporary Financial Services Regulation' (2002) 2 *Journal of Corporate Law Studies* 253–87.

Black, Julia, 'Enrolling Actors in Regulatory Systems: Examples from UK Financial Services Regulation' (2003) *Public Law* 2003 63–91.

Blair, Margaret, *Ownership and Control: Rethinking Corporate Governance for the Twenty-First Century* (Brookings Institute 1994).

Blair, Margaret M, 'Making Money: Leverage and Private Sector Money Creation' (2012) 36 *Seattle University Law Review* 417.

Blair, Margaret, 'The Neglected Benefits of the Corporate Form: Entity Status and the Separation of Asset Ownership From Control' (2014) at http://ssrn.com/abstract=563307.

Blake, Christopher R and Morey, Matthew R, 'Morningstar Ratings and Mutual Fund Performance' (1999) at http://papers.ssrn.com/sol3/papers.cfm?abstract_id=168668.

Blocher, Jesse and Whaley, Robert E, 'Passive Investing and Securities Lending' (2015) at http://ssrn.com/abstract=2474904.

Blommestein, Hans, Janssen, Pascal, Kortleve, Niels, and Yermo, Juan, 'Moving Beyond the 'DB vs. DC' Debate: The Appeal of Hybrid Pension Plans' (2009) 2 *Rotman International Journal of Pension Management* 66.

Blumberg, Philip, 'The Politicization of the Corporation' (1971) 26 *Business Lawyer* 1551.

Blundell-Wignall, A, Hu, Y and Yermo, J, 'Sovereign Wealth and Pension Fund Issues', *OECD Working Papers on Insurance and Private Pensions* 2008.

BNY Mellon, *Risk Roadmap: Hedge Funds and Investors' Evolving Approach to Risk* (August 2012), at http://www.thehedgefundjournal.com/sites/default/files/riskroadmap.pdf.

Bodie, Zvi, 'Pension Funds and Financial Innovation' (*NBER Working Paper* 1989) at http://ssrn.com/abstract=256079.

Boersch, Alexander, 'Doing Good by Investing Well? Pension Funds and Socially Responsible Investment: Results of an Expert Survey' (January 2010) *Allianz Global Investors International Pension Paper* No 1/2010 http://papers.ssrn.com/sol3/papers.cfm?abstract_id=1607730.

Boettke, Peter J, 'Teaching Economics, Appreciating Spontaneous Order, and Economics as a Public Science' (2010) at http://papers.ssrn.com/sol3/papers.cfm?abstract_id=1661513.

Bogle, John C, *Common Sense on Mutual Funds* (Chichester: John Wiley & Sons, 2011).

Bohle, Dorothee and Greskovits, Béla, 'Varieties of Capitalism and Capitalism «tout court»' (2009) 50 *European Journal of Sociology* 355.

Bonaimé, Alice A and Ryngaert, Michael A, 'Insider Trading and Share Repurchases: Do Insiders and Firms Trade in the Same Direction?' (2013) at http://ssrn.com/abstract=1361738.

Bonini, Stefano, 'The Effects of Private Equity Investors on the Governance of Companies' (2015) at http://ssrn.com/abstract=2647219.

Bonnar, Stephen, 'How Vulnerable are Private Pensions?' (2008) 34 *Canadian Public Policy* 21.

Booth, Richard A, 'Class Conflict in Securities Fraud Litigation' (2011) at http://papers.ssrn.com/sol3/papers.cfm?abstract_id=1811768.

Bootle, Roger, *The Trouble with Markets: Saving Capitalism from Itself* (London: Nicholas Brealey Publishing, 2012).

Boubakri, Narjess, Cosset, Jean-Claude (eds), *Institutional Investors in Global Capital Markets* (Emerald Group, 2011).

Bouvatier, V and Rigot, S, 'Pension Funds' Allocations to Hedge Funds: An Empirical Analysis of US and Canadian Defined Benefit Plans' (2013) 45 *Applied Economics* 3701.

Bovenberg, Lars, 'Frontiers in Pension Finance and Reform: Institutional Innovation in the Netherlands' (2007) at http://ssrn.com/abstract=13077081.

Boyer, Robert, 'Is a Finance-led Growth Regime a Viable Alternative to Fordism?' (2000) 29 *Economy and Society* 111.

Boyson Nicole M and Mooradian, Robert M, 'Hedge Funds as Shareholder Activists from 1994–2005' (2007) at http://ssrn.com/abstract=948907.

Boyson, Nicole M and Mooradian, Robert M, 'Corporate Governance and Hedge Fund Activism' (2011) 14 *Rev Deriv Res* 169.

Bracking, Sarah, 'How do Investors Value Environmental Harm/Care? Private Equity Funds, Development Finance Institutions and the Partial Financialization of Nature-based Industries' (2012) 43 *Development and Change* 271.

Bradford, T and Smith, R, 'Private Equity: Uses and Sources' (1997) 10 *Journal of Applied Corporate Finance* 89.

Braithwaite, John, *Regulatory Capitalism* (Cheltenham: Edward Elgar, 2008).

Bratton, William W, 'Hedge Funds and Governance Targets' (2007) 95 *Georgetown Law Journal* 1375.

Bratton, William W, 'Private Equity's Three Lessons for Agency Theory' (2008) 3 *Brooklyn Journal of Corporate, Financial & Commercial* Law 1.

Bratton, William W, 'Hedge Fund Activism, Poison Pills, and the Jurisprudence of Threat' (2016) at http://ssrn.com/abstract=2835610.

Bratton, William W and Wachter, Michael L, 'Shareholders and Social Welfare' (2013) 36 *University of Seattle Law Review* 489.

Brav, Alon, Jiang, Wei and Kim, Hyunseob, 'The Real Effects of Hedge Fund Activism: Productivity, Asset Allocation, and Labor Outcomes' (2015) at http://ssrn.com/abstract=1551953.

Brav, Alon A, Jiang, Wei W, Thomas, Randall S R S and Partnoy, Frank F, 'Hedge Fund Activism, Corporate Governance and Firm Performance' (2007) at http://ssrn.com/abstract=948907.

Brav, Alon and Mathews, Richmond D, 'Empty Voting and the Efficiency of Corporate Governance' (2011) 99 *Journal of Financial Economics* 289.

Bridgen, Andrew, Clare, Andrew and Dhar, Shamik, 'By How Much Can a Diversified Approach to Investing Improve the Prospects of Reducing a DB Pension Deficit?' (2007) at http://ssrn.com/abstract=1102149.

Briggs, Thomas W, 'Corporate Governance and the New Hedge Fund Activism: An Empirical Analysis' (2007) 32 *Journal of Corporation Law* 681.

Brinson, Gary, Hood, L Randolph and Beebower, Gary L, 'Determinants of Portfolio Performance' (1986) *Financial Analysts Journal* pp. 39–44.

Brinson, Gary, Hood, L Randolph and Beebower, Gary L 'Determinants of Portfolio Performance II: An Update' (1991) *Financial Analysts Journal* pp. 40–48.

Broadbent, John, Palumbo, Michael and Woodman, Elizabeth, 'The Shift from Defined Benefit to Defined Contribution Pension Plans – Implications for Asset Allocation and Risk Management' (*BIS Working Paper* 2006) at http://www.bis.org/publ/wgpapers/cgfs27broadbent3.pdf.

Bruner, Christopher M, *Corporate Governance in the Common Law World* (Cambridge: Cambridge University Press, 2013).

Bruner, Christopher, *Corporate Governance in the Common Law World* (Cambridge: CUP 2015).

Buchanan, Bonnie G, Netter, Jeffrey M, Poulsen, Annette B and Yang, Tina, 'Shareholder Proposal Rules and Practice: Evidence from a Comparison of the United States and United Kingdom' (2012) 49 *American Business Law Journal* 739.

Buchanan, Bonnie, Netter, Jeffry M and Yang, Tina, 'Are Shareholder Proposals an Important Corporate Governance Device? Evidence from US and UK Shareholder Proposals' (2010) at http://papers.ssrn.com/sol3/papers.cfm?abstract_id=1572016.

Buchanan, John, Chai, Dominic Heesang and Deakin, Simon (eds), *Hedge Fund Activism in Japan: The Limits of Shareholder Primacy* (Oxford: OUP 2012).

Burgess, Stephen, 'Measuring Financial Sector Output and Its Contribution to UK GDP', *Quarterly Bulletin Q3* (2011) at http://www.bankofengland.co.uk/publications/Documents/quarterlybulletin/qb110304.pdf.

Burkhart, Mike and Dasgupta, Amil, 'Activist Funds, Leverage and Procyclicality' (2014) at http://ssrn.com/abstract=2169880.

Burris, Scott, Kempa, Michael and Shearing, Clifford, 'Changes In Governance – A Cross-disciplinary Review of Current Scholarship' (2008) 41 *Akron Law Review* 1.

Busby, Graham, 'Conflicts of Interest and Inducements under MiFID' (2008) *Journal of International Banking Law and Regulation* 1.

Bushee, Brian J, 'Do Institutional Investors Prefer Near-Term Earnings Over Long-Run Value?' (2001) 18 *Contemporary Accounting Research* 207–46.

Business Innovation and Skills, *Metrics and Models Used to Assess Company and Investment Performance* (Oct 2014).

Business Innovation and Skills, *Exploring the Intermediated Shareholding Model* (January 2016) at https://www.gov.uk/government/uploads/system/uploads/attachment_data/file/489357/bis-16-20-intermediated-shareholding-model.pdf.

Business Innovation and Skills, *Proposal on using Legislative Reform Order to Change Partnership Legislation for Private Equity Investments* (March 2016) at https://www.gov.uk/government/uploads/system/uploads/attachment_data/file/509841/PU1924_Final.pdf.

Byrne, Alastair, 'Employee Saving and Investment Decisions in Defined Contribution Pension Plans: Survey Evidence from the UK' (2007) at http://www.actuaries.org.uk/system/files/documents/pdf/byrne_pensions.pdf.

Cadbury Committee, *Financial Aspects of Corporate Governance* (1992).
Cai, Charlie and Clatcher, Iain, 'Chinese Investment Goes Global: The China Investment Corporation' (2009) 17 *Journal of Financial Regulation and Compliance* 9.
Cai, Jie and Walkling, Ralph A, 'Shareholders' Say on Pay: Does it Create Value?' (2009) *Journal of Financial and Quantitative Analysis* 299.
Callen, Jeffrey L and Fang, Xiaohua, 'Institutional Investor Stability and Crash Risk: Monitoring Versus Short-Termism?' (2013) 37 *Journal of Banking and Finance* 3047.
Calliess, G-P and Renner, M, 'From Soft Law to Hard Code: The Juridification of Global Governance' (2007) available at http://ssrn.com/abstract=1030526 and (2009) 22 *Ratio Juris* 260.
Caner, Mehmet, Caner, Turanay and Grennes, Thomas, 'Determinants of Investment by the Norwegian Sovereign Wealth Fund: GDP versus Institutions' (2009) at http://ssrn.com/abstract=1534697.
Cannon, Edmund and Tonks, Ian, 'The Value and Risk of Defined Contribution Pension Schemes: International Evidence' (2013) 80 *Journal of Risk and Insurance* 95.
Capasso, Arturo, 'Stakeholder Theory and Corporate Governance: The Role of Intangible Assets' (2004) at http://papers.ssrn.com/sol3/papers.cfm?abstract_id=610661.
Caporin, Massimiliano and McAleer, Michael, 'The Ten Commandments for Managing Investments' (2009) at http://ssrn.com/abstract=1342265.
Carlsson, Evert, Erlandzon, Karl and Gustavsson, Jonas, 'A Tale of Two Systems: Winners and Losers when Moving from Defined Benefit to Defined Contribution Pensions' (2008) at http://ssrn.com/abstract=1088016
Casselli, Stefano and Gatti, Stefano, 'Corporate Governance and Independent Directors: Much Ado About Nothing? The Evidence behind Private Equity Investment Performance' (2007) at http://ssrn.com/abstract=968465.
Cata Backer, Larry, 'Sovereign Investing and Markets-Based Transnational Rule of Law Building: The Norwegian Sovereign Wealth Fund in Global Markets' (2013) 29 *American University International Law Review* 1.
Çelik, Serdar, Isaksson, Mats, 'Institutional Investors as Owners' (*OECD Corporate Governance Working Paper* 2013).
CEPS-ECMI, 'Rethinking Asset Management from Financial Stability to Investor Protection and Economic Growth' (2012) at http://ssrn.com/abstract=2060134.

Charlton, Roger and McKinnon, Roddy, 'Beyond Mandatory Privatization: Pensions Policy Options for Developing Countries' (2000) 12 *Journal of International Development* 483.

Cheffins, Brian R, *Company Law: Theory, Structure and Operation* (Oxford: OUP 1997).

Cheffins, Brian R, *Corporate Ownership and Control: British Businesses Transformed* (Oxford: OUP 2010).

Cheffins, Brian and Armour, John, 'The Past, Present and Future of Shareholder Activism by Hedge Funds' (2012) *Journal of Corporation Law*, also at http://papers.ssrn.com/sol3/papers.cfm?abstract_id=1932805.

Chemmanur, Thomas J and Chen, Zhaohui, 'Venture Capitalists versus Angels: The Dynamics of Private Firm Financing Contracts' (2006) at https://papers.ssrn.com/sol3/papers.cfm?abstract_id=342721.

Chen, Jing and Jung, Michael J, 'Activist Hedge Funds and Firm Disclosure' (2015) *Review of Financial Economics 52* at http://ssrn.com/abstract=2666783.

Chen, Sheng-Syan, Wang, Yanzhi, 'Financial Constraints and Share Repurchases' (2012) 105 *Journal of Financial Economics* 311.

Cheng, C S Agnes, Huang, Henry He and Li, Yinghua, 'Hedge Fund Intervention and Accounting Conservatism' (2013) at http://ssrn.com/abstract=2519286.

Cherneva, Iveta, 'The Business Case for Sustainable Finance: Beyond Public Relations, Reputation and Philanthropy' in Iveta Cherneva (ed.), *The Business Case for Sustainable Finance* (Oxford: Routledge 2012).

Chesterman, Simon, 'The Turn to Ethics: Disinvestment from Multinational Corporations for Human Rights Violations–The Case of Norway's Sovereign Wealth Fund' (2008) 23 *American University International Law Review* 577.

Chew, Donald S and Gillan, Stuart (eds), *Corporate Governance at the Crossroads: A Book of Readings* (NY: McGraw-Hill Irwin 2005).

Chhaochharia, Vidhi and Laeven, Luc, 'The Investment Allocation of Sovereign Wealth Funds' (2009) at http://ssrn.com/abstract=1262383.

Chiu, Iris H-Y, *The Foundations and Anatomy of Shareholder Activism* (Oxford: Hart, 2010).

Chiu, Iris H-Y, 'Institutional shareholders as Stewards: Towards a New Conception of Corporate Governance?' (2012) 6 *Brooklyn Journal of Financial, Corporate and Commercial Law* 387.

Chiu, Iris H-Y, 'Turning Institutional Investors into "Stewards" – Exploring the Meaning and Objectives of "Stewardship"' (2013) *Current Legal Problems* 1.

Chiu, Iris H-Y, 'A Confidence Trick: Ex Ante versus Ex Post Frameworks in Minority Investor Protection in the UK' (2014) 11 *European Company Law* 6.

Chiu, Iris H-Y, 'Reviving Shareholder Stewardship: Critically Examining the Impact of Corporate Transparency Reforms in the UK' (2014) 38 *Delaware Journal of Corporate Law* 983.

Chiu, Iris H-Y, 'Learning from the UK in the Proposed Shareholders' Rights Directive 2014? European Corporate Governance Regulation from a UK Perspective' (2015) 114 *ZVglRWiss* 1.

Chiu, Iris H-Y, 'The Disruptive Implications of Fintech- Policy Themes for Financial Regulators' (*UCL Centre of Ethics and Law Working Paper* 2016).

Chiu, Iris H-Y, 'European Shareholder Rights Directive Proposals: A Critical Analysis in Mapping with the UK Stewardship Code?' (2016) *ERA Forum* 1, DOI: 10.1007/s12027-016-0415-6.

Chiu, Iris H-Y, 'Operationalising A Stakeholder Conception in Company Law', (2017) 10 *Law and Financial Markets Review* at http://dx.doi.org/10.1080/17521440.2017.1309161.

Chiu, Iris H-Y and Barker, Roger M, 'Submission to The Business Skills and Innovation Commons Select Committee: Corporate Governance Inquiry' (2016) at https://papers.ssrn.com/sol3/papers.cfm?abstract_id=2858903.

Chiu, Iris H-Y and Katelouzou, Dionysia, 'Making a Case for Regulating Institutional Shareholders' Corporate Governance Roles' (2017) *Journal of Business Law*, forthcoming.

Choi, Seung-Doo, Lee, Inmoo and Megginson, William, 'Do Privatization IPO Firms Outperform in the Long Run?' (2006) at http://ssrn.com/abstract=676181.

Choi, Stephen J and Fisch, Jill E, 'On Beyond Calpers: Survey Evidence on the Developing Role of Public Pension Funds in Corporate Governance' (2008) 61 *Vanderbilt Law Review* 315.

Choi, Stephen J, Fisch, Jill E and Kahan, Marcel, 'The Power of Proxy Advisors: Myth or Reality?' (2010) 59 *Emory Law Journal* 869.

Choi, Stephen J, Fisch, Jill E and Pritchard, A C, 'Do Institutions Matter? The Impact of the Lead Plaintiff Provision of the Private Securities Litigation Reform Act' (2005) 83 *Washington University Law Quarterly* 869.

Chou, Wen-Hsiu, Ng, Lilian, and Wang, Qinghai, 'Are Better Governed Funds Better Monitors?' (2011) at http://ssrn.com/abstract=1913430.

Christoffersen, Susan E K, Geczy, Christopher C, Musto, David K and Reed, Adam V, 'Vote Trading and Information Aggregation' (2007) 62 *Journal of Finance* 2897.

Chwieroth, Jeffrey, 'Fashions and Fads in Finance: Contingent Emulation and the Political Economy of Sovereign Wealth Fund Creation' (2010) at http://ssrn.com/abstract=1643861.

Claessens, Stijn, Djankov, Simeon, Fan, Joseph P H, and Lang, Larry H P, 'Expropriation of Minority Shareholders: Evidence from East Asia' (2004) at http://elibrary.worldbank.org/doi/book/10.1596/1813-9450-2088.

Clare, Andrew, Cuthbertson, Keith and Nitzsche, Dirk, 'An Empirical Investigation into the Performance of UK Pension Fund Managers' (2009) at http://ssrn.com/abstract=1325410.

Clark, Gordon L, *Pension Fund Capitalism* (Oxford: Oxford University Press, 2000).

Clark, Gordon L, 'Pension Fund Governance: Expertise and Organizational Form' (2004) 3 *Journal of Pension Economics and Finance* 233.

Clark, Gordon, 'Temptation and the Virtues of Long-Term Commitment: The Governance of Sovereign Wealth Fund Investment' (2009) at http://ssrn.com/abstract=1349123.

Clark, Gordon L, Dixon, Adam D and Monk, Ashby H B (eds), *Managing Financial Risks: From Global to Local* (Oxford: OUP 2012).

Clark, Gordon, Dixon, Adam and Monk, Ashby H B, *Sovereign Wealth Funds: Legitimacy, Governance and Global Power* (Princeton: Princeton University Press 2013).

Clark, Gordon L, Feiner, Andreas and Viehs, Michael, 'From Stockholder to Stakeholder: How Sustainability Can Drive Financial Outperformance' (March 2015) at http://www.arabesque.com/index.php?tt_down=51e2de00a30f88872897824d3e211b11.

Clark, Gordon L and Hebb, Tessa, 'Pension Fund Corporate Engagement: The Fifth Stage of Capitalism' (2004) 59 *Industrial Relations* 142.

Clark, Gordon L and Hebb, Tessa, 'Why Should They Care? The Role of Institutional Investors in the Market for Corporate Global Responsibility' (2005) 37 *Environment and Planning* 2015.

Clark, Gordon L and Monk, Ashby H B, 'The "Crisis" in Defined Benefit Corporate Pension Liabilities: Current Solutions and Future Prospects' (2006) at http://ssrn.com/abstract=907291.

Clark, Gordon L and Monk, Ashby H B, 'The Legitimacy and Governance of Norway's Sovereign Wealth Fund: The Ethics of Global Investment' (2009) at http://ssrn.com/abstract=1473973.

Clark, Gordon L and Monk, Ashby H B, 'The Norwegian Government Pension Fund: Ethics over Efficiency' (2010) 3 *Rotman Journal of International Pension Management* 14.

Clark, Gordon L, Thrift, Nigel and Tickell, Adam, 'Performing Finance: The Industry, the Media and Its Image' (2004) 11 *Review of International Political Economy* 289.

Clark, Gordon L and Urwin, Roger, 'DC Pension Fund Best-practice Design and Governance' (2010) at http://ssrn.com/abstract=1652680.

Clark, Gordon L and Wójcik, Darius, *The Geography of Finance* (Oxford: OUP, 2007).

Clark, Robert C, 'The Four Stages of Capitalism: Reflections on Investment Management Treatises' (1981) 94 *Harvard Law Review* 561.

Clearfield, Andrew M, '"With Friends Like These, Who Needs Enemies?" The Structure of the Investment Industry and Its Reluctance to Exercise Governance Oversight' (2005) 13 *Corporate Governance* 114.

Clifford, Chris C, 'Value Creation or Destruction? Hedge Funds as Shareholder Activists' (2007) at http://ssrn.com/abstract=971018.

Clottens, Carl, 'Empty Voting: A European Perspective' (2012) 9 *European Company and Financial Law Review* 446.

Coase, Ronald H, 'The Nature of the Firm' (1937) 4 *Economica* 386.

Cocco, João F and Volpin, Paolo F, 'The Corporate Governance of Defined Benefit Pension Plans: Evidence from the United Kingdom' (*ECGI Working Paper* 2005) at http://ssrn.com/abstract=670685.

Coffee, John C, 'The Folklore of Investor Capitalism' (1997) 95 *Michigan Law Review* 1970.

Coffee, John C, Jnr, 'The Future as History: The Prospects for Global Convergence in Corporate Governance and Its Implications' (1999) 93 *Northwestern University Law Review* 641.

Coffee, John C and Palia, Darius, 'The Impact of Hedge Fund Activism: Evidence and Implications' (2014) at http://ssrn.com/abstract=2496518.

Coffee, John C and Palia, Darius, 'The Wolf at the Door: The Impact of Hedge Fund Activism on Corporate Governance' (2015) at http://ssrn.com/abstract=2656325.

Cohen, Benjamin J, 'Sovereign Wealth Funds and National Security: The Great Tradeoff' (2009) 85 *International Affairs* 713

Cohn, Jonathan B, Mills, Lillian F, Towery, Erin M, 'The Evolution of Capital Structure and Operating Performance After Leveraged Buyouts: Evidence from U.S. Corporate Tax Returns' (2013) at http://ssrn.com/abstract=1764406.

Coiquaud, Urwana and Morisette, Lucie, 'Union Renewal Through Involvement in the Financial Sector' (2010) 65 *Industrial Relations* 2.

Conaglen, Matthew, 'The Nature and Function of Fiduciary Loyalty' (2005) 121 *L.Q.R.* 453.

Conard, Alfred F, 'Beyond Managerialism: Investor Capitalism?' (1988-1989) 22 *U. Mich. J.L.* Reform 117.

Conference Board, *Hedge Fund Activism: Findings and Recommendations for Corporations and Investors* (2008).

Congdon, Tim, *Money and Asset Prices in Boom and Bust* (London: Institute of Economic Affairs, 2005).

Conyon, Martin and Sadler, Graham 'Shareholder Voting and Directors' Remuneration Report Legislation: Say on Pay in the UK' (2010) 18 *Corporate Governance* 296.

Cooke, Jennifer, 'Finding the Right Balance for Sovereign Wealth Fund Regulation: Open Investment Vs. National Security' (2009) *Columbia Business Law Review* 728.

Cornelli, Francesca and Karakas, Oĝuzhan, 'Corporate Governance of LBOs: The Role of Boards' (2012) at http://ssrn.com/abstract=1875649.

Corporate Values Strategy Group, *Overcoming Short-termism: A Call for a More Responsible Approach to Investment and Business Management* (New York: Aspen Institute Business and Society Programs, 2009), http://www.aspeninstitute.org/publications/overcoming-short-termism-call-more-responsible-approach-investment-business-management.

Cortez, Maria Ceu, Silva, Florinda and Areal, Nelson, 'The Performance of European Socially Responsible Funds' (2009) 87 *Journal of Business Ethics* 573.

Cortez, Maria Ceu, Silva, Florinda and Areal, Nelson, 'Socially Responsible Investing in the Global Market: The Performance of US and European Funds' (2009) at http://ssrn.com/abstract=1342469.

Cotter, James, Palmiter, Alan and Thomas, Randall, 'ISS Recommendations and Mutual Fund Voting on Proxy Proposals' (2010) 55 *Villanova Law Review* 56.

Cox, Paul, Brammer, Stephen and Millington, Andrew, 'An Empirical Examination of Institutional Investor Preferences for Corporate Social Performance' (2004) 52 *Journal of Business Ethics* 27.

Crane, Andrew and Matten, Dirk, *Business Ethics: Managing Corporate Citizenship and Sustainability in the Age of Globalization* (Oxford: OUP 2015).

Crane, Andrew and Ruebottom, Trish, 'Stakeholder Theory and Social Identity: Rethinking Stakeholder Identification' (2011) 102 *Journal of Business Ethics* 77.

Crook, Michael W, 'A Stochastic Portfolio Perspective on Utilizing Active and Passive Fund Management' (2012) at http://ssrn.com/abstract=2170776.

Crook, Michael W and Nick, Brian, 'Equities (still) for the Long Run: A New Look at the Future Equity Premium' (2012) at http://ssrn.com/abstract=2172796.

Crutchley, Claire E, Hudson, Carl D and Jensen, Marlin RH, 'The Shareholder Wealth Effects of CalPERS' Activism' (1998) 7 *Financial Services Review*, at http://findarticles.com/p/articles/mi_qa3743/is_/ai_n8786737.

Cuervo, A, 'Corporate Governance Mechanisms: A Plea for Less Code and More Market Control' (2002) 10 *Corporate Governance; An International Review* 84.

Cumming, Douglas and Dai, Na, 'A Law and Finance Analysis of Hedge Funds' (2010) 39 *Financial Management* 997.

Cumming, Douglas, Imad'Eddine, Gael and Schwienbacher, Armin, 'Harmonized Regulatory Standards, International Distribution of Investment Funds and the Recent Financial Crisis' (2011) 18 *European Journal of Finance* 261.

Cumming, Douglas, Siegel, Donald and Wright, Mike, 'Private Equity, Leveraged Buyouts and Governance' (2007) at http://papers.ssrn.com/sol3/papers.cfm?abstract_id==983802.

Curtis, Quinn and Morley, John, 'An Empirical Study of Mutual Fund Excessive Fee Litigation: Do the Merits Matter?' (2014) at http://papers.ssrn.com/sol3/papers.cfm?abstract_id=1852652.

Curtis, Quinn and Morley, John, 'The Flawed Mechanics of Mutual Fund Fee Litigation' (2014) at http://papers.ssrn.com/sol3/papers.cfm?abstract_id=2405307.

Cvijanovic, Dragana, Dasgupta, Amil and Zachariadis, Konstantinos E, 'Ties that Bind: How Business Connections Affect Mutual Fund Activism' (2014) at http://ssrn.com/abstract_id=2317212.

Cziraki, Peter, Renneboog, Luc and Szilagyi, Peter, 'Shareholder Activism through Proxy Proposals: The European Perspective' (2009) at http://ssrn.com/abstract=1413125.

Dalhuisen, Jan J, *Transnational and Comparative Commercial, Financial and Trade Law*, vol III (5th edn, Oxford: Hart Publishing 2012).

Dallas, Lynne, 'Short-Termism, the Financial Crisis, and Corporate Governance' (2012) 37 *Journal of Corporation Law* 265.

Das, Satyajit, *Extreme Money: Masters of the Universe and the Cult of Risk* (London: Financial Times, 2011).

Dasgupta, Amil and Piacentino, Giorgia, 'The Wall Street Walk when Blockholders Compete for Flows' (2014) at http://ssrn.com/abstract=1848001.

Davies, Paul, 'Shareholders in the United Kingdom' (2015) at http://ssrn.com/abstract=2557680.

Davies, Paul and Hopt, Klaus J, 'Boards in Europe: Accountability and Convergence' (2013) 61 *American Journal of Comparative Law* 301.

Davis, Gerald F, *Managed by the Markets: How Finance Re-shaped America* (New York: OUP, 2009).

Davis, Ronald B, 'Reflections on Representation in Australian Superannuation Governance' (2013) 25 *Australian Superannuation Law Bulletin* 51.

Davis, Stephen, Lukomnik, Jon, Pitt-Watson, David, 'Active Shareowner Stewardship: A New Paradigm for Capitalism' (2009) 2 *Rotman International Journal of Pension Management* 10.

Dedman, Elisabeth, Kungwal, Thanamas and Stark, Andrew W, 'The Information Content of Regular Dividends and Share Buybacks for Market Value and Future Earnings in the UK' (2012) at http://ssrn.com/abstract=2188291.

Del Guercio, Diane and Tkac, Paula A, 'Star Power: The Effect of Morningstar Ratings on Mutual Fund Flow' (2007) at http://papers.ssrn.com/sol3/papers.cfm?abstract_id=286157.

Dembinski, Paul H, *Finance: Servant or Deceiver* (transl. by Kevin Cook, Basingstoke: Palgrave Macmillan 2009).

Denes, Matthew R, Karpoff, Jonathan M and McWilliams, Victoria B, 'Thirty Years of Shareholder Activism: A Survey of Empirical Research' (2015) at http://ssrn.com/abstract=2608085.

Dent, George W Jnr, 'The Essential Unity of Shareholders and the Myth of Investor Short-Termism' (2010) 35 *Delaware Journal of Corporate Law* 97.

Department for Communities and Local Government, *Local Government Pension Scheme: Opportunities for Collaboration, Cost Savings and Efficiencies* (May 2014).

Department for Communities and Local Government, *Local Government Pension Scheme: Investment in Partnerships* (Consultation Nov 2012).

Department of Business, Energy and Industrial Strategy, *Green Paper: Corporate Governance Reforms* (Nov 2016) at https://www.gov.uk/government/uploads/system/uploads/attachment_data/file/584013/corporate-governance-reform-green-paper.pdf.

Department of Trade and Investment, *Fund Management in the UK* (2013) at https://www.gov.uk/government/uploads/system/uploads/attachment_data/file/478378/UKTI_Asset_mgmt_broch_B5_RC_AW_DIGIAL.pdf.

Department of Work and Pensions, *Landscape and Charges Survey 2013: Charges and Quality in Defined Contribution Pension Schemes* (Feb 2014).

Department of Work and Pensions, *Better Workplace Pensions: Further Measures for Savers* (March 2014).

Derwall, Jeroen and others, 'The Eco-Efficiency Premium Puzzle' (2005) 61 *Financial Analysts Journal* 51.

Derwall, Jeroen, Koedijk, Kees and Horst, Jenke ter, 'A Tale of Values-Driven and Profit-Seeking Social Investors' (2011) 35 *Journal of Banking and Finance* 2137.

Deutsche Bank Advisors, Sustainable Investing: Establishing Long Term Value and Performance (2012) at http://www.dbcca.com/research.

Dewenter, Kathryn L, Han, Xi and Malatesta, Paul H, 'Firm Values and Sovereign Wealth Fund Investments' (2009) at http://ssrn.com/abstract=1354252, (2010) 98 *Journal of Financial Economics* 256.

Dhir, Aaron A, 'Shareholder Engagement in the Embedded Business Corporation: Investment Activism, Human Rights and TWAIL Discourse' (2012) 22 *Business Ethics Quarterly* 99.

Diebold, F X, Doherty, N, and Herring, R J (eds), *The Known, The Unknown and The Unknowable in Financial Risk Management* (Princeton University Press, 2010).

Dignam, Alan, 'A Principled Approach to Self-Regulation? The Report of the Hampel Committee on Corporate Governance' (1998) 19(5) *Company Lawyer* 140.

Dignam, Alan, 'Exporting Corporate Governance: UK Regulatory Systems in a Global Economy' (2000) *Company Lawyer* 70.

Dignam, Alan, 'Capturing Corporate Governance: The End of the UK Self-regulating System' (2007) 4 *International Journal of Disclosure and Governance* 24.

Dignam, Alan, 'The Future of Shareholder Democracy in the Shadow of the Financial Crisis' (2013) 36 *University of Seattle Law Review* 639.

Dixon, Adam D, 'Enhancing the Transparency Dialogue in the "Santiago Principles" for Sovereign Wealth Funds' (2014) 37 *University of Seattle Law Review* 581.

Dixon, Adam D and Monk, Ashby H B, 'Rethinking the Sovereign in Sovereign Wealth Funds' (2011) 37 *Transactions of the Institute of British Geographers* 104.

Domenichini, Jules, 'Public to Private Transactions, Private Equity Ownership and IPOs: A Case Study of Debenhams' (2012) at http://ssrn.com/abstract=1516293.

Dore, Timothy, 'Venture Capital and the Performance of Incumbents' (2015) at https://papers.ssrn.com/sol3/papers.cfm?abstract_id=2666529.

Dubra, Matt and Lubich, Bruce H, 'Public Pension Governance and Asset Allocation' (2013) 6 *Journal of Centrum Cathedra* 83.

Duruigbo, Emeka, 'Stimulating Long-term Shareholding' (2011–12) 33 *Cardozo Law Review* 1734.

Duruigbo, Emeka, 'Tackling Shareholder Short-Termism and Managerial Myopia' (2011–12) 100 *Kentucky Law Journal* 531.

Dyck, Alexander, Lins, Karl V and Pomorski, Lukasz, 'Does Active Management Pay? New International Evidence' (2011) at https://papers.ssrn.com/sol3/papers.cfm?abstract_id=1957783.

Dyck, Alexander and Morse, Adair, 'Sovereign Wealth Fund Portfolios' (2011) at http://ssrn.com/abstract=1792850.

Dyck, Alexander and Pomorski, Lukasz, 'Is Bigger Better? Size and Performance in Pension Plan Management' (2011) at http://ssrn.com/abstract=1690724.

Easterbrook, Frank H and Fischel, Daniel R, *The Economic Structure of Corporate Law* (Mass: Harvard University Press, 1991).

Easterbrook, Frank H and Fischel, Daniel, *The Economic Structure of Corporate Law* (Mass: Harvard University Press 1996).

Edelman, Paul H, Thomas, Randall S and Thompson, Robert B, 'Shareholder Voting in an Age of Intermediary Capitalism' (2014) at http://ssrn.com/abstract=2401746.

EFAMA Code for External Governance (2011) at http://www.efama.org/Publications/Public/Corporate_Governance/11-4035%20EFAMA%20ECG_final_6%20April%202011%20v2.pdf.

EFAMA, *Asset Management in Europe: 6th Annual Review* (2013) at http://www.efama.org/Publications/Statistics/Asset%20Management%20Report/Asset_Management_Report_2013.pdf.

Eich, Frank, 'The Importance of Defined-Benefit Occupational Pension Schemes in Selected OECD Countries' (2010) at http://ssrn.com/abstract=1660996.

English, Philip C II, Smythe, Thomas I and MacNeil, Chris R, 'The CalPERS' Effect Revisited' (2004) 10 *Journal of Corporate Finance* 157

Epstein, Gerald A (ed.), *Financialization and the World Economy* (Cheltenham: Edward Elgar, 2005).

Epstein, Richard and Rose, Amanda, 'The Regulation of Sovereign Wealth Funds: The Virtues of Going Slow' (2009) 76 *University of Chicago Law Review* 111.

Ernst & Young, *What is Fiduciary Management* (2015) at http://www.ey.com/UK/en/Services/Specialty-Services/Pensions/Fiduciary-Management-1-What-is-Fiduciary-Management.

Ertimur, Y, Ferri, F and Oesch, D, 'Shareholder Votes and Proxy Advisors: Evidence from Say on Pay' (2013) 51 *Journal of Accounting Research* 951.

Erturk, Ismail, Froud, Julie, Johal, Sukhdev, Leaver, Adam and Williams, Karel, 'The Democratization of Finance? Promises, Outcomes and Conditions' (2007) 14 *Review of International Political Economy* 553.

Erturk, Ismail, Froud, Julie, Johal, Sukhdev, Leaver, Adam and Williams, Karel (eds), *Financialization At Work: Key Tests and Commentary* (Oxford: Routledge, 2008).

European Commission, 'Financial Services Action Plan: Implementing the Framework for Financial Markets' *(Communication) COM* (1999) 232.

European Securities and Markets Authority, 'An Overview of the Proxy Advisory Industry. Considerations on Possible Policy Options', ref. ESMA/2012/212, http://www.esma.europa.eu/system/files/2012-212.pdf.

European Securities and Markets Authority, *Discussion Paper: An Overview of the Proxy Advisory Industry. Considerations on Possible Policy Options* (Dec 2012).

European Securities and Markets Authority, *Final Report: Feedback Statement on the Consultation Regarding the Role of the Proxy Advisory Industry* (Feb 2013).

European Securities and Markets Authority, *Final Report on The Proxy Advisor Industry* (19 Feb 2013).

European Securities and Markets Authority, *Draft Regulatory Technical Standards for the MiFID II and MiFIR* (Dec 2014) at http://www.esma.europa.eu/system/files/2014-1569_final_report_-_esmas_technical_advice_to_the_commission_on_mifid_ii_and_mifir.pdf.

European Securities and Markets Authority, *Final Report: ESMA's Technical Advice to the Commission on MiFID II and MiFIR* (Dec 2014).

European Securities and Markets Authority, *Report: Follow-up on the Development of the Best Practice Principles for Providers of Shareholder Voting Research and Analysis* (2015).

Evans, David S, 'Why Now Is Not the Right Time to Revamp Consumer Financial Protection' (January 2010) at http://ssrn.com/abstract=1538005.

Evans, John, Orszag, Michael and Piggott, John (eds), *Pension Fund Governance: A Global Perspective on Financial Regulation* (Cheltenham: Edward Elgar, 2008).

Evans, Richard B and Fahlenbrach, Rüdiger, 'Institutional Investors and Mutual Fund Governance: Evidence from Retail–Institutional Fund Twins' (2012) *Review of Financial Studies* 3530.

Fama, Eugene F and French, Kenneth R, 'Luck Versus Skill in the Cross Section of Mutual Fund Returns' (2009) at http://papers.ssrn.com/sol3/papers.cfm?abstract_id=1356021.

Fama, Eugene, 'Efficient Capital Markets: A Review of Theory and Empirical Work'(1970) 25 *Journal of Finance* 383.

Faulconbridge, James, 'Rebalancing the Geographies of Financial Services Power: The Role of Sovereign Wealth Funds' (2010) 42 *Environment and Planning* 2271.

FCA, *General Guidance on the AIFM Remuneration Code* (SYSC 19B) (January 2014) at https://www.fca.org.uk/publication/finalised-guidance/fg14-02.pdf.

FCA, *Final rules for Charges in Workplace Personal Pension Schemes and Feedback on CP14/24* (March 2015).

FCA, *Hedge Fund Survey* (June 2015).

Fender, Ingo, 'Institutional Asset Managers: Industry Trends, Incentives and Implications For Market Efficiency' (2003) *BIS Quarterly Review* 75.

Ferguson, Niall, *The Ascent of Money* (London: Penguin, 2008).

Fernandez, D G and Eschweiler, B, 'Sovereign Wealth Funds: A Bottom Up Primer', JP Morgan Research 2008, quoted in Christopher Balding, 'Framing Sovereign Wealth Funds: What We Know and Need to Know' (2009) at http://ssrn.com/abstract=1335556.

Fernandez, Pablo, 'The Equity Premium in 150 Textbooks' (2013) at http://papers.ssrn.com/sol3/papers.cfm?abstract_id=1473225.

Ferran, Eilis, 'The Regulation of Hedge Funds and Private Equity: A Case Study in the Development of the EU's Regulatory Response to the Financial Crisis' (February 2011) *ECGI Law Working Paper* No 176/2011 http://ssrn.com/abstract=1762119.

Ferran, Eilis, 'Regulatory Lessons from the Payment Protection Insurance Mis-Selling Scandal in the UK' (2012) *European Business Organisation Law Review* 248.

Ferran, Eilis, Moloney, Niamh, Hill, Jennifer G and Coffee, John C Jnr, *The Regulatory Aftermath of the Global Financial Crisis* (Cambridge: Cambridge University Press, 2012).

Ferranini, Guido and Ungureanu, Maria Cristina, 'Economics, Politics, and the International Principles for Sound Compensation Practices: An Analysis of Executive Pay at European Banks' (2011) 64 *Vanderbilt Law Review* 432.

Ferri, Fabrizio and Maber, David A, 'Say on Pay Votes and CEO Compensation: Evidence from the UK' (2013) 17 *Review of Finance* 527.

Financial Conduct Authority, *General Guidance on the AIFM Remuneration Code (SYSC 19B)* (January 2014) at https://www.fca.org.uk/publication/finalised-guidance/fg14-02.pdf.

Financial Conduct Authority, *Enhancing the Effectiveness of the Listing Regime and Further Consultation* (November 2013); *Response to CP13/15 – Enhancing the Effectiveness of the Listing Regime* (May 2014).

Financial Conduct Authority, *Changes to the Use of Dealing Commission Rules: Feedback to CP13/17 and Final Rules* (May 2014).

Financial Conduct Authority, *Policy Statement: Changes to the Use of Dealing Commission Rules: Feedback to CP13/17 and Final Rules* (May 2014).

Financial Conduct Authority, *Response to CP13/15 – Enhancing the Effectiveness of the Listing Regime* (16 May 2014).

Financial Conduct Authority, *Strengthening Accountability in Banking: A New Regulatory Framework* (July 2014).

Financial Conduct Authority, *Charges in Workplace Personal Pension Schemes: A Consultation Paper* (Oct 2014).

Financial Conduct Authority, *Final rules for Charges in Workplace Personal Pension Schemes and Feedback on CP14/24* (March 2015).

Financial Conduct Authority, *Retirement Income Market Study: Final Report – Confirmed Findings and Remedies* (March 2015).

Financial Conduct Authority, *Strengthening Accountability in Banking: A New Regulatory Framework for Individuals – Feedback on FCA CP14/13/PRA CP14/14 and consultation on additional guidance* (March 2015).

Financial Conduct Authority, *Inducements and Conflicts of Interest Thematic Review: Key Findings* (April 2016) at http://www.fca.org.uk/news/inducements-conflicts-interest-thematic-review-key-findings.

Financial Conduct Authority, *Guidance on Fund Suspensions* (8 July 2016) at http://www.fca.org.uk/news/guidance-fund-suspensions.

Financial Conduct Authority, *Changes to Disclosure Rules in the FCA Handbook to Reflect the Direct Application of the PRIIPS Regulation: A Consultation Paper* (18 July 2016) at http://fca.org.uk/news/cp16-18-changes-to-disclosure-rules-for-priips-regulation.

Financial Conduct Authority, *Retirement Outcomes Review: Terms of Reference* (July 2016).

Financial Conduct Authority, 'Asset Management Market Study'. *Interim Report*, November 2016.

Financial Conduct Authority, *Asset Management Market Study Final Report* (2017) at https://www.fca.org.uk/publication/market-studies/ms15-2-3.pdf.

Financial Reporting Council, *Comply or Explain: 20th Anniversary of the UK Corporate Governance Code* (London, 2012).

Financial Reporting Council, *Guidance on Risk Management, Internal Control and Related Financial and Business Reporting* (Sep 2014) at https://www.frc.org.uk/Our-Work/Publications/Corporate-Governance/Guidance-on-Risk-Management,-Internal-Control-and.pdf.

Financial Reporting Council, *Developments in Corporate Governance and Stewardship 2015* (Jan 2016) at https://www.frc.org.uk/Our-Work/Publications/Corporate-Governance/Developments-in-Corporate-Governance-and-Stewa-(1).pdf.

Financial Reporting Council, *Tiering of Signatories to the Stewardship Code* (14 Nov 2016) at https://www.frc.org.uk/News-and-Events/FRC-Press/Press/2016/November/Tiering-of-signatories-to-the-Stewardship-Code.aspx.

Financial Services, Building a Framework for Action, *COM* (1998) 625 1.

Financial Services, Communication on Implementing the Framework For Financial Markets: Action Plan, *COM* (1999) (232).

Financial Services, *Final Report of the Committee of Wise Men on the Regulation of European Securities Markets* (15 Feb 2001).

Financial Services Authority, 'Distribution of Retail Investments: Delivering the RDR – feedback to CP09/18 and final rules' (March 2010) PS10/6 http://www.fsa.gov.uk/pubs/policy/ps10_06.pdf

Financial Services Authority, 'Distribution of Retail Investments: Delivering the RDR – Professionalism' (January 2011) PS11/01 http://www.fsa.gov.uk/pubs/policy/ps11_01.pdf

Financial Services Authority, *Enhancing the Effectiveness of the Listing Regime and Feedback on CP12/2* (Oct 2012).

Financial Services Authority, *Assessing the Quality of Investment Advice in the Retail Banking Sector: A Mystery Shopping Review* (February 2013).

Financial Services Authority, 'The FCA's Use of Temporary Product Intervention Rules' (March 2013) at http://www.fsa.gov.uk/static/pubs/policy/ps13-03.pdf.

Financial Stability Board, *Global Shadow Banking Monitoring Report 2013* and *2012*.

Financial Stability Board, *Proposed Policy Recommendations to Address Structural Vulnerabilities from Asset Management Activities: A Consultation Paper* (22 June 2016) at http://www.fsb.org/wp-content/uploads/FSB-Asset-Management-Consultative-Document.pdf.

Financial Stability Board and the International Organisation of Securities Commissioners, *Assessment Methodologies for Identifying Non-Bank Non-Insurer Global Systemically Important Financial Institutions* (March 2015).

Fisch, Jill E, 'The Mess at Morgan: Risk, Incentives and Shareholder Empowerment' (2015) 83 *University of Cincinnati Law Review* 651.

Flannigan, Robert, 'Shareholder Fiduciary Accountability' (2014) *Journal of Business Law* 1.

Flannigan, Robert, 'The Core Nature of Fiduciary Accountability' (2009) *New Zealand Law Review* 375.

Foldal, Øyvind Ytrestøyl, 'Mitigating Tensions between Domestic Politics and Global Finance – A Study of the Decision Making Process of Norway's Sovereign Wealth Fund' (2010) at http://ssrn.com/abstract=1664344.

Foley, C Fritz and Greenwood, Robin, 'The Evolution of Corporate Ownership after IPO: The Impact of Investor Protection' (2010) 23 *Review of Financial Studies* 1231.

Folkman, Peter, Froud, Julie, Johal, Sukhdev and Williams, Karel, 'Working for Themselves: Financial Intermediaries and Present Day Capitalism' (2007) 49 *Business History* 552.

Fontenay, Elizabeth, 'Private Equity as Gatekeepers' (2013-14) 33 *Review of Banking and Financial Law* 115.

Fort, Timothy L, '"Goldilocks And Business Ethics: A Paradigm That Fits "Just Right"' (1998) 23 *Journal of Corporation Law* 245.

Fox, Merritt B, 'Rethinking Disclosure Liability in the Modern Era' (1997) *Washington U Law Quarterly* 903.

Franks, Julian, Mayer, Colin, Volpin, Paolo and Wagner, Hannes F, 'The Life Cycle of Family Ownership: A Comparative Study of France, Germany, Italy and the U.K' (2012) 25 *Review of Financial Studies* 1675.

Franzen, Dorothee, 'Managing Investment Risk in Defined Benefit Pension Funds' (*OECD Working Paper*, 2010) at http://www.oecd-ilibrary.org/docserver/download/5kmjnr3sr2f3.pdf?expires=1413966718&id=id&accname=guest&checksum=EA1A737DD90414C2DD21383B56ABACF0.

Fraser-Sampson, Guy, *Private Equity as an Asset Class* (Wiley Finance 2007).

French, Craig W, 'Another Look at the Determinants of Portfolio Performance: Return Attribution for the Individual Investor' (2003) at https://papers.ssrn.com/sol3/papers.cfm?abstract_id=706603.

Freshfields Bruckhaus Deringer, *A Legal Framework for the Integration of Environmental, Social and Governance Issues into Institutional Investment* (October 2005).

Fried, Jesse M, 'Open Market Repurchases: Signaling or Managerial Opportunism?' (2001) 2 *Theoretical Inquiries in the Law* 865.

Fried, Jesse M, 'Share Repurchases, Equity Issuances, and the Optimal Design of Executive Pay' (2011) 89 *Texas Law Review* 1113.

Fried, Jesse M, 'The Uneasy Case for Favoring Long-Term Shareholders' (2015) 124 *Yale Law Journal* 1554.

Froud, Julie, Johal, Sukhdev, Leaver, Adam and Williams, Karel *Financialization and Strategy: Narrative and Numbers* (Oxford: Routledge 2006).

FSB, *Policy Recommendations to Address Structural Vulnerabilities of from Asset Management Activities* (12 Jan 2017) at http://www.fsb.org/2017/01/fsb-publishes-policy-recommendations-to-address-structural-vulnerabilities-from-asset-management-activities/.

Fung, Hung-Gay, Law, Sheryl A and Yau, Jot, *Socially Responsible Investment in a Global Environment* (Cheltenham: Edward Elgar 2010).

Gallagher, Daniel M, 'Outsized Power & Influence: The Role of Proxy Advisers', Harvard Law School Forum (5 Sep 2014).

Gaspar, José-Miguel, Massa, Massimo, Matos, Pedro, Patgiri, Rajdeep and Rehman, Zahid, 'Can Buybacks be a Product of Shorter Shareholder Horizons?' (2005) at http://papers.ssrn.com/sol3/papers.cfm?abstract_id=649482.

Gasparro, Vincent and Pagano, Michael S, 'Sovereign Wealth Funds' Impact on Debt and Equity Markets during the 2007–09 Financial Crisis' (2010) 66 *Financial Analysts Journal* 92.

Gastineau, Gary L, *The Exchange-Traded Funds Manual* (Chichester: John Wiley & Sons 2010).

Geczy, Christopher C, Stambaugh, Robert F and Levin, David, 'Investing in Socially Responsible Mutual Funds' (2005) at http://ssrn.com/abstract=416380.

Geiger, Uri, 'The Case for the Harmonisation of Securities Disclosure Rules in the Global Market' (1997) 1997 *Columbia Business Law Review* 241.

Gelb, Alan, Tordo, Silvano, Halland, Havard, Arfaa, Noora and Smith, Gregory, 'Sovereign Wealth Funds and Long-Term Development Finance' (*World Bank Policy Research Working Paper* 2014).

Gelter, Martin, 'The Pension System and the Rise of Shareholder Primacy' (2012) at http://ssrn.com/abstract=2079607.

Gelter, Martin, 'The Pension System and the Rise of Shareholder Primacy' (2013) 43 *Seton Hall Law Review* 909.

Gemmill, Gordon and Thomas, Dylan C, 'The Impact of Corporate Governance on Closed-end Funds' (2006) 12 *European Financial Management* 725.

Generation Foundation, UNEP and UNPRI, *Fiduciary Duty for the 21st Century: Statement on Investor Obligations and Duties* (June 2016) at https://www.unpri.org/download_report/19422.

Gerner-Beuerle, Carsten, 'Determinants of Corporate Governance Codes' (2014) at http://papers.ssrn.com/sol3/papers.cfm?abstract_id=2346673.

Gerner-Buerle, Carsten and Kirschmaier, Tom, 'Say on Pay: Do Shareholders Care?' (2016) at http://papers.ssrn.com/sol3/papers.cfm?abstract_id=2720481.

Ghahramani, Salar, 'Sovereign Wealth Funds and Shareholder Activism: Applying the Ryan-Schneider Antecedents to Determine Policy Implications' (2013) 13 *Corporate Governance: The International Journal of Business in Society* 58–69.

Gianetti, Mariassunta and Yu, Xiaoyun, 'The Corporate Finance Benefits of Short Horizon Investors' (*ECGI Working Paper* 2016).

Gillan, Stuart L and Starks, Laura T, 'Corporate Governance, Corporate Ownership, and the Role of Institutional Investors: A Global Perspective' (2003) 13 *Journal of Applied Finance*.

Gillan, Stuart and Starks, Laura T, 'The Evolution of Shareholder Activism in the United States' (2007) at http://papers.ssrn.com/sol3/papers.cfm?abstract_id=959670.

Gilligan, John and Wright, Mike, *Private Equity Demystified – An Explanatory Guide* (3rd edn, ICAEW, 2014).

Gilovich, Thomas, Griffin, Dale and Kahneman, Daniel (eds), *Heuristics and Biases: The Psychology of Intuitive Judgment* (Cambridge: Cambridge University Press 2002).

Gilson, Ronald J, 'Controlling Shareholders and Corporate Governance: Complicating the Comparative Taxonomy' (2006) 119 *Harvard Law Review* 1641.

Gilson, Ronald J and Gordon, Jeffrey N, 'The Agency Costs of Agency Capitalism: Activist Investors and the Revaluation of Governance Rights' (2013) 113 *Columbia Law Review* 863.

Gilson, Ronald J and Gordon, Jeffrey N, 'Agency Capitalism: Further Implications of Equity Intermediation' (2014) at http://ssrn.com/abstract=2359690.

Gilson, Ronald J and Milhaupt, Curtis J, 'Sovereign Wealth Funds and Corporate Governance: A Minimalist Response to the New Mercantilism' (2008) 60 *Stanford Law Review* 1345.

Gilson, Ronald J and Whitehead, Charles K, 'Deconstructing Equity: Public Ownership, Agency Costs, and Complete Capital Markets' (2008) 108 *Columbia Law Review* 231.

Glémain, Pascal, 'The Strategy and Fundamentals of Sustainable Finance Serving Sustainable Development' in *Special Issue, Finance and Sustainability: Towards a New Paradigm? A Post-Crisis Agenda* (2011) 2 Critical Studies on Corporate Responsibility, Governance and Sustainability 187.

Goergen, Marc and Renneboog, Luc, 'Strong Managers and Passive Institutional Investors in the UK' (1998) at http://ssrn.com/abstract=137068.

Goergen, Marc, O'Sullivan, Noel and Wood, Geoffrey, 'The Employment Consequences of Private Equity Acquisitions: The Case of Institutional Buy Outs' (2014) at http://ssrn.com/abstract=2459890.

Goergen, M, Renneboog, Luc and Zhang, Chendi, 'Do UK Institutional Shareholders Monitor Their Investee Firms?' (2007) at http://ssrn.com/abstract_id=1124406.

Gompers, Paul A, Ishii, Joy and Metrick, Andrew, 'Extreme Governance: An Analysis of Dual-Class Firms in the United States' (2010) 23 *Review of Financial Studies* 1051.

Gong, Bo, 'Institutional Investment in the UK and China' in *Understanding Institutional Shareholder Activism: A Comparative Study of the UK and China* (Oxford: Routledge 2014).

Gong, James Jianxin and Wu, Steve Yuching, 'CEO Turnover in Private Equity Sponsored Leveraged Buyouts' (2011) 19 *Corporate Governance: An International Review* 195.

Goodwin, Shane, 'Corporate Governance and Hedge Fund Activism' (Aug 2015) at http://ssrn.com/abstract=2646293.

Goodwin, Shane, Singh, Akshay, Slipetz, Walter and Rao, Ramesh, 'Myopic Investor Myth Debunked: The Long-term Efficacy of Shareholder Advocacy in the Boardroom' (2014) at http://ssrn.com/abstract=2555701.

Goranova, Maria and Ryan, Lori Verstegen, 'Shareholder Activism: A Multidisciplinary Review' (2014) 40 *Journal of Management* 1230.

Goranova, Maria and Ryan, Lori Vestegen (eds), *Shareholder Empowerment: A New Era in Corporate Governance* (Palgrave Macmillan 2015).

Gordon, Jeffrey and Roe, Mark J (eds), *Convergence and Persistence in Corporate Governance* (Cambridge: CUP 2004).

Gospel, Howard, Pendleton, Andrew and Vitols, Sigurt, *Financialization, New Investment Funds and Labour* (Oxford: OUP 2014).

Gottesman, Aron and Morey, Matthew, 'Getting What You Paid For: Using Mutual Fund Governance to Predict the Activeness of Mutual Funds' (2014) at http://ssrn.com/abstract=2422270.

Gourevitch, Peter A and Shinn, James, *Political Power and Corporate Control* (Princeton University Press 2005).

Graves, S and Waddock, S, 'Institutional Ownership and Control: Implications for Long-Term Corporate Strategy' (1990) 4 *Academy of Management Perspectives* 75–83.

Graves, Samuel B and Waddock, Sandra A, 'Institutional Owners and Corporate Social Performance' (1994) 37 *Academy of Management Journal* 1034.

Greenbury, Richard, *Report: Directors' Remuneration* (17 Jul 1995).

Greene, Edward F and Yeager, Brian A, 'Sovereign Wealth Funds – A Measured Assessment' (2008) 3 *Capital Markets Law Journal* 247.

Greenfield, Kent, 'New Principles For Corporate Law' (2005) 1 *Hastings Business Law Journal* 89.

Greenfield, Kent, *The Failure of Corporate Law* (London: The University of Chicago Press 2006).

Grossman, Sanford J and Hart, Oliver D, 'The Costs and Benefits of Ownership: A Theory of Vertical and Lateral Integration' (1986) 94 *Journal of Political Economy* 691.

Guedj, Ilan and Huang, Jennifer, 'Are ETFs Replacing Index Mutual Funds?' (2009) at http://ssrn.com/abstract=1108728.

Guyatt, Danyelle, 'Meeting Objectives and Resisting Conventions: A Focus on Institutional Investors and Long-Term Responsible Investing' (2005) 5 *Corporate Governance: The International Journal of Business in Society* 139.

Haar, Brigitte, 'Civil Liability of Credit Rating Agencies – Regulatory All-or-Nothing Approaches between Immunity and Over-Deterrence' (2012) at http://ssrn.com/abstract=2198293.

Haberly, Daniel, 'White Knights from the Gulf: Sovereign Wealth Fund Investment and the Evolution of German Industrial Finance' (2014) 90 *Economic Geography* 293.

Hall, Peter A and Soskice, David, *Varieties of Capitalism* (Oxford: Oxford University Press 2001).

Halvorssen, Anita M, 'Addressing Climate Change Through the Norwegian Sovereign Wealth Fund (SWF) – Using Responsible Investments to Encourage Corporations to take ESG Issues into Account in their Decision-making' (2010) at http://ssrn.com/abstract=1712799.

Handy, Jon, 'Hedge Fund Activists and Share Repurchases' (2015) 7 *Banking and Finance Review* 113.

Hannes, Sharon, 'Brave New World: A Proposal for Institutional Investors' (2015) 16 *Theoretical Inquiries in the Law* 245.

Hanrahan, Pamela F, 'Fiduciary Duty and the Market: Private Law and the Public Good' (2008) *University of Melbourne Legal Studies Research Paper* No 347 http://ssrn.com/abstract=1184443

Hansmann, Henry and Kraakman, Reinier, 'The End of History for Corporate Law' (2000) 89 *Georgetown Law Journal* 439.

Hansmann, Henry, 'How Close is the End of History' (2005) at http://lesliecaton.com/wordpress/wp-content/uploads/2012/01/7-Hansmann-FINAL.pdf.

Hansmann, Henry and Kraakman, Reinier, 'Reflections on the End of History for Corporate Law' (2011) at http://papers.ssrn.com/sol3/papers.cfm?abstract_id=2095419.

Harbula, Peter, 'Operating Performance, Valuation, Leverage and Corporate Governance Of Leveraged Buy- Out Transactions: A Continental European Perspective' (2011) at http://ssrn.com/abstract=1876454.

Hart, Oliver, 'An Economist's Perspective on the Theory of the Firm' 89 *Columbia Law Review* 1757–1774 (1989).

Haslem, John A, 'Morningstar Mutual Fund Measures and Selection Model' (2014) *Journal of Wealth Management* 19.

Haslem, John D (ed.), *Mutual Funds: Portfolio Structures, Analysis, Management, and Stewardship* (Chichester: John Wiley & Sons 2010).

Hatton, Kyle and Pistor, Katharina, 'Maximizing Autonomy in the Shadow of Great Powers: The Political Economy of Sovereign Wealth Funds' (2011) *Columbia Journal of Transnational Law* 2.

Haugaard, Mark, *The Constitution of Power: A Theoretical Analysis of Power, Knowledge and Structure* (Manchester: Manchester University Press 1997).

Haugaard, Mark (ed.), *Power: A Reader* (Manchester: Manchester University Press 2002).

Hawley, J P and Williams, A T, *The Rise of Fiduciary Capitalism: How Institutional Investors Can Make Corporate America More Democratic* (University of Pennsylvania Press, 2000).

Hawley, J P and Williams, A T, 'Shifting Ground: Emerging Global Corporate-Governance Standards and the Rise of Fiduciary Capitalism' (2005) 37 *Environment and Planning* 1995.

Hawley, James, Kamath, Shyam, Williams, Andrew (eds), *Corporate Governance Failures* (University of Pennsylvania Press 2014).

Hayek, F A, *Individualism and Economic Order* (University of Chicago Press, 1944).

Hayek, F A, *The Constitution of Liberty* (University of Chicago Press, 1960).

Hazenberg, Jan Jaap, 'Independence and Focus of Luxembourg UCITS Fund Boards' (*LSF Research Working Paper* 2012).

Hazenberg, Jan Jaap, 'Effectiveness of Independent Boards of Luxembourg Funds' (2013) at http://ssrn.com/abstract=2276849.

He, Lawrence, Kusy, Martin, Singh, Deepak and Trabelsi, Samir, 'Mutual Fund Fees, Performance, and Governance Structure in Canada' (2013) at http://ssrn.com/abstract=2201213.

He, Zhongzhi, Qiu, Jiaping and Tang, Tingfeng, 'Hedge Fund Activism and Corporate Innovation' (2014) at http://ssrn.com/abstract=2411739.

Hebb, Tessa, 'The Economic Inefficiency of Secrecy: Pension Fund Investors' Corporate Transparency Concerns' (2006) 63 *Journal of Business Ethics* 385.

Hebb, Tessa, *No Small Change: Pension Funds and Corporate Engagement* (Ithaca NY: Cornell University Press, 2008).

Hedge Funds Standards Board, *What is a Hedge Fund?* at www.hfsb.org.

Hedge Fund Working Group (led by Sir Andrew Large), 'Hedge Fund Standards: Final Report' (January 2008) http://www.hfsb.org/sites/10188/files/final_report.pdf.

Hedge Fund Working Group, *Hedge Fund Standards: Final Report* (2008).

Hein, Eckhard, *The Macro-economics of Finance Dominated Capitalism and its Crisis* (Cheltenham: Edward Elgar 2012).

Hein, Eckhard, 'Finance-dominated Capitalism and Redistribution of Income: A Kaleckian Perspective' (2013) at http://ssrn.com/abstract=2198919.

Hein, Eckhard, Niechoj, Torsten, Spahn, Peter and Truger Achim (eds), *Finance-led Capitalism: Macro-economic Effects of Changes in the Financial Sector* (Marburg: Metropolis Verlag 2009).

Heinemann, Friedrich, 'The Benefits of Creating an Integrated EU Market for Investment Funds' (2002) at http://ssrn.com/abstract=309099.

Hellsten, Sirkku and Mallin, Chris, 'Are "Ethical" or "Socially Responsible" Investments Socially Responsible?' (2006) 66 *Journal of Business Ethics* 393.

Helms, Caitlin, Fox, Mark and Kenagy, Robert, 'Corporate Short-Termism: Causes and Remedies' (2012) 23 *International and Comparative Company Law Review* 45.

Hendry, John, Sanderson, Paul, Barker, Richard and Roberts, John D, 'Owners or Traders? Conceptualizations of Institutional Investors and Their Relationship with Corporate Managers' (2006) 59 *Human Relations* 1101.

Hess, David, 'Public Pensions and the Promise of Shareholder Activism for the Next Frontier of Corporate Governance: Sustainable Economic Development' (2007) 2 *Virginia Law and Business Review* 222.

Hetherington, J A C, 'Defining the Scope of Controlling Shareholders' Fiduciary Responsibilities' (1987) 22 *Wake Forest Law Review* 9.

Heuben, Robby and Straetmans, Gert, 'Shareholder Rights and Responsibilities in the Context of Corporate Social Responsibility' (2016) 27 *European Business Law Review* 615.

Hewitt, Paul, 'The Exercise of Shareholder Rights' (2011) at http://dx.doi.org/10.1787/5kg54d0l1lvf-en.

Hewitt, Paul, 'The Exercise of Shareholder Rights: Country Comparison of Turnout and Dissent', *OECD Corporate Governance Working Papers*, No. 3 (OECD Publishing 2011) at http://dx.doi.org/10.1787/5kg54d0l1lvf-en.

High Pay Centre, 'New High Pay Centre report: Executive pay continues to climb at expense of ordinary workers' (2014) at http://highpaycentre.org/pubs/new-high-pay-centre-report-executive-pay-continues-to-climb-at-expense-of-o.

High Pay Centre, *Thinking High and Low: Exploring Pay Disparities in Society* (2015) at http://highpaycentre.org/pubs/thinking-high-and-low-exploring-pay-disparities-in-society.

High Pay Centre, 'Submission to the BIS select committee corporate governance enquiry', October 2016. http://highpaycentre.org/pubs/hpc-submission-to-the-bis-select-committee-corporate-governance-enquiry-oct.

Hill, Jennifer G, 'Images of the Shareholder – Shareholder Power and Shareholder Powerlessness' (2015) at http://ssrn.com/abstract=2664430.

Hirschmann, Albert O, *Exit, Voice and Loyalty: Responses to Decline in Firms, Organizations, and States.* (Cambridge, MA: Harvard University Press 1970).

HM Treasury, *Proposal on Using Legislative Reform Order to Change Partnership Legislation for Private Equity Investments* (March 2016) at https://www.gov.uk/government/uploads/system/uploads/attachment_data/file/509841/PU1924_Final.pdf.

Ho, Karen, 'Situating Global Capitalisms: A View from Wall Street Investment Banks' (2005) 20 *Cultural Anthropology* 68.

Hoepnerab, Andreas G F, Rezec, Michael and Siegl, Sebastian, 'Does Pension Funds' Fiduciary Duty Prohibit the Integration of Environmental Responsibility Criteria in Investment Processes?' (2011) at http://ssrn.com/abstract=1930189.

Hong, Harrison and Kacperczyk, Marcin, 'The Price of Sin: The Effects of Social Norms on Markets' (2009) 93 *Journal of Financial Economics* 15.

Hooghe, Liesbet and Marks, Gary, 'Unraveling the Central State, but How? Types of Multi-level Governance' (2003) 97 *American Political Science Review* 233.

House of Commons Work and Pensions and Business, Innovation and Skills Committees, *BHS* (2016) at http://www.publications.parliament.uk/pa/cm201617/cmselect/cmworpen/54/54.pdf.

Howells, Geraint, 'The Potential and Limits of Consumer Empowerment by Information' (2005) 32 *Journal of Law and Society* 349.

Hu, Henry T C and Black, Bernard B S, 'The New Vote Buying: Empty Voting and Hidden (Morphable) Ownership' (2006) 76 *Southern California Law Review* 811.

Hu, Henry T C and Black, Bernard B S, 'Equity and Debt Decoupling and Empty Voting II: Importance and Extensions' (2008) 156 *University of Pennsylvania Law Review* 625.

Hua, Jennifer Kim Chau, In, Francis, Do, Viet and Zhang, Xibin, 'Stock Liquidity, Intractable Information and Sovereign Wealth Fund Investment' (2015) at http://ssrn.com/abstract=2625902.

Hubbard, Douglas, *The Failure of Risk Management: Why It's Broken and How Do we Fix it?* (Chichester: John Wiley & Sons 2009).

Hudson, Michael, 'From Marx to Goldman Sachs: The Fictions of Fictitious Capital, and the Financialization of Industry' (2010) 38 *Journal of Socialist Theory* 419.

Hudson, Michael, *Finance Capitalism and its Discontents* (Dresden: Islet Verlag, 2012).

Hunter-McDonnell, Mary, King, Braydon and Soule, Sarah, 'A Dynamic Process Model of Private Politics: Activist Targeting and Corporate Receptivity to Social Challenges' (2014) at http://papers.ssrn.com/sol3/papers.cfm?abstract_id=2432208.

Hymans Robertson, *LGPS Structure Analysis* (Dec 2013).

Ibbotson, Roger G, Carr, Richard C and Robinson, Anthony W, 'International Equity and Bond Returns' (1982) 38 *Financial Analysts Journal* 61.

Illiev, Peter, Lins, Karl V, Miller, Darius P and Roth, Lukas, 'Shareholder Voting and Corporate Governance Around the World' (2015) 28 *Review of Financial Studies* 2167.

Illig, Robert C, 'What Hedge Funds Can Teach Corporate America: A Roadmap for Achieving Institutional Investor Oversight' (2007) 57 *American University Law Review* 225.

Illig, Robert C, 'The Promise of Hedge Fund Governance: How Incentive Compensation Can Enhance Institutional Investor Monitoring' (2008) 60 *Alabama Law Review* 41.

Impavido, Gregario and Tower, Ian, 'How the Financial Crisis Affects Pensions and Insurance and Why the Impacts Matter' (*IMF Working Paper* 2009) at http://ssrn.com/abstract=1442253.

Incandela, Enzo, 'Recourse Under § 10(b) on Life Support: The Displacement of Liability and Private Securities Fraud Action after Janus v. First Derivative' (2012) 43 *Loyola University Chicago Law Journal* 935.

Independent Project Board, ABI, *Defined Contribution Workplace Pensions: The Audit of Charges and Benefits In Legacy Schemes* (Dec 2014).

Independent Public Service Pensions Commission Final Report (March 2011) (aka Hutton Report).

Ingley, C B and van der Walt, N T, 'Corporate Governance, Institutional Investors and Conflicts of Interest' (2004) 12 *Corporate Governance* 534.

International Monetary Fund, 'Sovereign Wealth Funds—A Work Agenda' (2008), at http://www.imf.org/external/np/pp/eng/2008/022908.pdf.

International Organisation of Securities Commissioners (IOSCO), *Next Steps on the NBNI G-SIFI Assessment Methodologies* (4 July 2015).

International Securities Lending Association (ISLA), *Voting Issues for Beneficial Owners* (2015) at http://www.isla.co.uk/wp-content/uploads/2015/08/SecuritiesLendingVotingIssuesforBeneficalOwners.pdf.

International Working Group of Sovereign Wealth Funds, IMF, *Generally Accepted Principles and Practices: Santiago Principles* (October 2008) at http://www.iwg-swf.org/pubs/eng/santiagoprinciples.pdf.

Investment Management Association, *Annual Survey of Engagement for Years Ending 2008* (2008).

Investment Management Association, *Adherence to the FRC's Stewardship Code Survey* (as of 31 Dec 2014).

Investment Management Association, *Adherence to the FRC's Stewardship Code 2013* (2014) at http://www.theinvestmentassociation.org/assets/files/surveys/20140501-01_stewardshipcode.pdf.

Investment Management Association, *Investment Asset Management Survey 2013–14* (2014).

Investment Management Association, *Adherence to the UK FRC's Stewardship Code* (2015) at http://www.theinvestmentassociation.org//assets/files/surveys/20150526-fullstewardshipcode.pdf.

Investment Management Association, *Asset Management in the UK 2014–15* (2015).

Investor Forum, *Facilitate Dialogue, Create Long-term Solutions and Enhance Value* (Oct 2014).

Ireland, Paddy, 'The Financialization of Corporate Governance' (2009) at http://ssrn.com/abstract=2068478.

IRRC Institute, *Proxy Voting by Exchange-Traded Funds: An Analysis of ETF Voting Policies, Practices and Patterns* (2009) at http://www.irrcinstitute.org/pdf/FINAL%20ETF%20Study%20-%20June%2030,%202009.pdf.

IWG Secretariat, 'Sovereign Wealth Funds: Current Institutional and Operational Practices' (2008) at http://www.iwg-swf.org/pubs/eng/swfsurvey.pdf.

Jabusch, Garvin, *Redefining Sustainable Investing: A "Next Economy" Model Approach* (Green Alpha Advisers LLC, 2013).

James, Kevin R, 'The Price of Retail Investing in the UK' (*FSA Occasional Paper* 2000).

Jansson, Andreas, 'No Exit!: The Logic of Defensive Shareholder Activism' (2014) 10 *Corporate Board: Roles, Duties and Composition* 16.

Jensen, Michael, 'The Economic Case For Private Equity' (2007) at http://ssrn.com/abstract=963530.

Jensen, M and Meckling, W, 'Theory of the Firm: Managerial Behavior, Agency Costs and Ownership Structure' (1976) 3 *Journal of Financial Economics* 305.

Jimenez, Javier W Ibanez and Urena, Antonio Partal, 'Sovereign Wealth Fund (SWF) Global Regulation and Transparency: A Preliminary Private-Investment Law Approach' (2010) *Journal of International Banking Law and Regulation* 441.

Jog, Vijay and Riding, Allan L, 'Price Effects of Dual-class Shares' (1986) *Financial Analysts Journal* 58.

Johan, Sofia A, Knill, April and Mauck, Nathan, 'Determinants of Sovereign Wealth Fund Investment in Private Equity vs Public Equity' (2013) 44 *Journal of International Business Studies* 155.

Joly, Carlos, 'Why Responsible Investment Falls Short of Its Purpose and What to Do About It' (2010) 10 *Corporate Governance* 18.

Jones, Robert C, 'Active Management in Mostly Efficient Markets' (2011) 67 *Financial Analysts Journal* 29.

Jones, Stewart, van der Laan, Sandra, Frost, Geoff and Loftus, Janice, 'The Investment Performance of Socially Responsible Investment Funds in Australia' (2008) 80 *Journal of Business Ethics* 181.

JP Morgan, *The Activist Revolution* (2015) at https://www.jpmorgan.com/jpmpdf/1320693986586.pdf.

Judge, Kathryn, 'Intermediary Influence' (2015) 82 *University of Chicago Law Review* 573.

Juniper, James, 'A Genealogy of Short-Termism in Capital Markets' (1998) at http://papers.ssrn.com/sol3/papers.cfm?abstract_id=219990.

Kabler, Laura, 'Money in the Game: Executing a Governance-Based Hedge Fund Strategy' (2006) 12 *Stanford Journal of Law, Business & Finance* 121.

Kahan, Marcel and Rock, Edward B, 'Hedge Funds in Corporate Governance and Corporate Control' (2007) 155 *University of Pennsylvania Law Review* 1021.

Kahneman, Daniel and Tversky, Amos (eds), *Choices, Values and Frames* (Cambridge: Cambridge University Press 2003).

Kallifatides, Markus, Nachemson-Ekwall, Sophie, Sjöstrand, Sven-Erik, *Corporate Governance In Modern Financial Capitalism: Old Mutual's Hostile Takeover of Skandia* (Cheltenham: Edward Elgar 2014).

Kamiyama, Tetsuya, 'ASEAN's Investment Trusts Market: Current Conditions and Challenges' (2013) 5 *Nomura Journal of Capital Markets* 1.

Kaniampuram, Leah, 'Beneficiaries of Stock Buybacks: Tendering Shareholders or Non-Tendering Shareholders' (2008) at http://papers.ssrn.com/sol3/papers.cfm?abstract_id=1287123.

Karmel, Roberta, 'Should A Duty To The Corporation Be Imposed On Institutional Shareholders?' (2004) 60 *Business Lawyer* 1.

Karpoff, Jonathan M J M, 'The Impact of Shareholder Activism in Target Companies: A Survey of Empirical Findings' (Sep 2001) at http://ssrn.com/abstract=885365.

Katelouzou, Dionysia, 'Myths and Realities of Hedge Fund Activism: Some Empirical Evidence' (2013) 7 *Virginia Law and Business Review* 459.

Katelouzou, Dionysia, 'Worldwide Hedge Fund Activism: Dimensions and Legal Determinants' (2015) 17 *University of Pennsylvania Journal of Business Law* 789.

Kay, John, *Other People's Money* (London: Profile Books 2015).

Kaysen, Carl, 'The Corporation: How Much Power? What Scope?' in Edward S Mason (ed.), *The Corporation in Modern Society* (Mass: Harvard University Press 1970).

Keay, Andrew, 'Shareholder Primacy in Corporate Law: Can it Survive? Should it Survive?' (2009) at http://ssrn.com/abstract=1498065.

Keller, Amy, 'Sovereign Wealth Funds: Trustworthy Investors or Vehicles of Strategic Ambition? An Assessment of the Benefits, Risks and Possible Regulation of Sovereign Wealth Funds' (2009) 7 *Georgetown Journal of Law and Public Policy* 333.

Kemme, David, 'Sovereign Wealth Fund Issues and The National Fund(s) of Kazakhstan' (2012) at http://ssrn.com/abstract=2188391.

Khorana, Ajay, Servaes, Henri and Tufano, Peter, 'Explaining the Size of the Mutual Fund Industry Around the World' (2005) 78 *Journal of Financial Economics* 145.

Kim, Woochan, 'Korea Investment Corporation: Its Origin and Evolution' (2012) 17 *Journal of the Asia Pacific Economy* 208.

Kimmitt, Robert, 'Public Footprints in Private Markets: Sovereign Wealth Funds and the World Economy' (2008) 87 *Foreign Affairs* 119.

Klein, April and Zur, Emanuel, 'Entrepreneurial Shareholder Activism: Hedge Funds and Other Private Investors' (2006) at *ECGI Finance Working Paper* No. 140/2006.

Knight, Frank H, *Risk, Uncertainty and Profit* (1921, Rep FL: Signalman Publishing, 2009).

Knill, April, Lee, Bong Soo and Mauck, Nathan, 'Bilateral Political Relations and Sovereign Wealth Fund Investment' (2011) at http://ssrn.com/abstract=1498518.

Koppell, Jonathan G S, 'Political Control for China's State-Owned Enterprises: Lessons from America's Experience with Hybrid Organizations' (2007) 20 *Governance* 255–78.

Kotschwar, Barbara, Moran, Theodore H and Muir, Julia, 'Chinese Investment in Latin American Resources: The Good, the Bad, and the

Ugly' (*Peter Institute for International Economics Working Paper* 2012) at http://www.iie.com/publications/wp/wp12-3.pdf.

Kotter, Jason and Lel, Ugur, 'Friends or Foes? Target Selection Decisions of Sovereign Wealth Funds and Their Consequences' (2010) at http://ssrn.com/abstract=1292407.

KPMG, *Rethinking Shareholder Engagement in the Age of Activism* (2014) at http://www.kpmg-institutes.com/institutes/aci/articles/2014/07/rethinking-shareholder-engagement-in-the-age-of-activism.html.

Kratsas, George and Truby, Jon, 'Regulating Sovereign Wealth Funds to Avoid Investment Protectionism' (2015) I *Journal of Financial Regulation* 95.

Kronsinsky, Cary and Robins, Nick (eds), *Sustainable Investing* (Earthscan 2008).

Kronsinsky, Cary, Robins, Nick and Veiderman, Steven, *Evolutions in Sustainable Investing* (Chichester: John Wiley & Sons 2012).

Kumar, Rajeev, '2014 Corporate Governance Review', reporting on the rise of shareholder proxies in the 2014 AGM season, at http://blogs.law.harvard.edu/corpgov/2014/10/30/2014-corporate-governance-review/.

Kumar, Jayesh, 'Impact of Pension Plan Funding Status on M&A Activity' (Watson Wyatt, 2006).

Kumpan, Christoph and Leyens, Patrick C, 'Conflicts of Interest of Financial Intermediaries' (2008) 5 *European Company and Financial Law Review* 72.

Kus, Basak, 'Financialisation and Income Inequality in OECD Nations: 1995-2007' (2012) 43 *The Economic and Social Review* 477.

L'Habitant, Francois S, *Hedge Funds: Myths and Limits* (Chichester: Wiley Finance 2002).

L'Habitant, Francois S, *Handbook on Hedge Funds* (Chichester: John Wiley & Sons 2006).

La Porta, R, Lopez-de-Silanes, F and Shleifer, A, 'What Works in Securities Laws' (2006) 71 *Journal of Finance* 1.

La Porta, R, Lopez-de-Silanes, F, Shleifer, A and Vishny, R, 'Law and Finance' (1998) 106 *Journal of Political Economy* 1113.

Lan, Gil, 'Foreign Direct Investment in the United States and Canada: Fractured Neoliberalism and the Regulatory Imperative' (2014) *Vanderbilt University Law Review* 1262.

Langevoort, Donald C, 'Taming the Animal Spirits of the Stock Markets: A Behavioral Approach to Securities Regulation' (2002) 97 *Northwestern University Law Rev* 135.

Langevoort, Donald, 'Private Litigation to Enforce Fiduciary Duties in Mutual Funds: Derivative Suits, Disinterested Directors and the Ideology of Investor Sovereignty' (*ECGI Working Paper* 2006) at http://ssrn.com/abstract=885970.

Langland, Eric, 'Misplaced Fears Put to Rest: Financial Crisis Reveals the True Motives of Sovereign Wealth Funds' (2009) 18 *Tulane Journal of International and Comparative Law* 263.

Langley, Paul, 'Uncertain Subjects of Anglo-American Financialization' (2007) 65 *Cultural Critique* 67.

Lannoo, K and Levin, M, 'Securities Market Regulation in the EU' (2003) (Research Study Carried out for the Wise Persons' Committee, Centre for European Policy Studies 2003), at http://216.239.51.104/search?q=cache:MDFLRqTml-QJ:www.wise-averties.ca/reports/WPC_4.pdf+gros+lannoo+euro+capital&hl=en&ct=clnk&cd=15&client=opera.

Lapavitsas, Costas (ed), *Financialization in Crisis* (Leiden: Brill Publishers, 2012).

Larcker, David and McCall, Allan, 'The Power of Proxy Advisory Firms', Harvard Law School Forum (13 Jan 2014).

Law Commission, *Fiduciary Duties and Regulatory Rules* (Law Com CP No 124, 1995).

Law Commission, *Fiduciary Duties of Investment Intermediaries* (June 2014) at http://lawcommission.justice.gov.uk/areas/fiduciary_duties.htm.

Lee, Yvonne C L, 'A Reversal of Neo-Colonialism: The Pitfalls and Prospects of Sovereign Wealth Funds' (2009) 40 *Georgetown Journal of International Law* 1103.

Lee, Yvonne C L, 'The Governance of Contemporary Sovereign Wealth Funds' (2010) 6 *Hastings Business Law Journal* 197.

Leibowitz, Martin L, 'The Dedicated Bond Portfolio in Pension Funds Parts 1 and 2' (1986) 42 *Financial Analysts Journal* 68–75 and 47–57 respectively.

Lemstra, Wolter and Groenewegen, John P M, 'Private Equity Leveraged Buyout and Public Values: The Bankruptcy of Eircom, Ireland' (2012) at http://ssrn.com/abstract=2032222.

Levi-Faur, David, 'The Global Diffusion of Regulatory Capitalism' (2005) 598 *ANNALS of the Academy of Political Science* 12.

Lewis, Alan and Juravle, Carmen, 'Morals, Markets and Sustainable Investments: A Qualitative Study of 'Champions'' (2010) 93 *Journal of Business Ethics* 483.

Li, Guo, 'Demystifying the Chinese Sovereign Wealth Fund – A Perspective of the U.S. Financial Regulation' (2010) at http://ssrn.com/abstract=1641628.

Li, Jing, 'State As An Entrepreneur: A Study of the Investment Contractual Terms and Level of Control of China's Sovereign Wealth Fund in its Portfolio Firms' (2014) at http://ssrn.com/abstract=2617150.

Li, Suxiao, de Haan, Jakob, Scholtens, Bert and Yang, Haizhen, 'Are International Fund Flows Pro- or Counter-Cyclical?' (2015) 22 *Applied Economics Letters* 378.

Li, Tao, 'Outsourcing Corporate Governance: Conflicts of Interest in the Proxy Advisory Industry' (2016) at http://papers.ssrn.com/sol3/papers.cfm?abstract_id=2828690.

Liew, Leong H and He, Liping, 'Operating in an Inharmonious World: China Investment Corporation' (2012) 17 *Journal of the Asia Pacific Economy* 253.

Lin, Ken-Hou and Tomaskovic-Devey, Donald, 'Financialization and U.S. Income Inequality, 1970–2008' (2013) 118 *American Journal of Sociology* 1284.

Lindberg, Seth Robert, 'Sovereign Wealth Fund Regulation in the E.U. and U.S.: A Call for Workable and Uniform Sovereign Wealth Fund Review within the E.U.' (2009) 37 *Syracuse Journal of International Law and Commerce* 95.

Lipson, Paul, Sabel, Bradley K and Keane, Frank M, 'Securities Lending' (Federal Reserve Bank of NY 1989) at http://ssrn.com/abstract=2030418.

Liu, Harrison and Swanson, Edward P, 'Are Corporate Share Repurchases Used to Support Overvalued Equity?' (2013) at http://papers.ssrn.com/sol3/papers.cfm?abstract_id=2283764.

Lobe, Sebastian and Walkshäusl, Christian, 'Vice vs. Virtue Investing Around the World' (May 2011) http://ssrn.com/abstract=1089827.

Lobel, Orly, 'The Renew Deal: The Fall of Regulation and the Rise of Governance in Contemporary Legal Thought' (2004-5) 89 *Minnesota Law Rev* 342.

London Stock Exchange, *Exchange-Traded Funds: Introducing and Operating ETFs in the UK* at http://www.londonstockexchange.com/specialist-issuers/etfs/how-to-issue-etfs/listingandadmissionguide.pdf.

Long, Susan and Sievers, Burkard (eds), *Towards a Socioanalysis of Money, Finance and Capitalism* (Oxford: Routledge, 2013).

Macey, Jonathan, 'Institutional Investors and Corporate Monitoring: A Demand-Side Perspective' (1997) 18 *Managerial and Decision Economics* 601.

Maher, Maria and Andersson, Thomas, 'Corporate Governance: Effects on Firm Performance and Economic Growth' (*OECD Working Paper* 1999).

Maher, Maria and Andersson, Thomas, 'Corporate Governance: Effects on Firm Performance and Economic Growth' (OECD, 2009) at http://www.ecgi.org/research/accession/cgeu.pdf.

Malagoli, Andrea and Young, Chris, 'Stocks for the Long Run: Historical Facts and Statistical Fallacies' (2010) at http://ssrn.com/abstract=1904992.

Mallin, Chris, 'Institutional Investors and Voting Practices: An International Comparison' (2001) 9 *Corporate Governance* 118.

Manconi, A, Massa, M and Yasuda, A, 'The Role of Institutional Investors in Propagating The Crisis of 2007–2008' (2012) 104 *Journal of Financial Economics* 491–518.

Mangiero, Susan, 'Pension Risk Management: Derivatives, Fiduciary Duty and Process' (2008) at http://ssrn.com/abstract=128332.

Marchisio, Gaia and Ravasi, Davide, 'Family Firms and the Decision to Go Public: A Study of Italian IPOs' (2001) at http://ssrn.com/abstract=278237.

Marginson, David and McAulay, Laurie, 'Exploring the Debate on Short-Termism: A Theoretical and Empirical Analysis' (2008) 29 *Strategic Management* 273.

Markham, Jerry W, 'Mutual Funds Scandals – Comparative Analysis of the Role of Corporate Governance in the Regulation of Collective Investments' (2010) at http://ssrn.com/abstract=1706317.

Martí-Ballester, Carmen-Pilar, 'A Comparative Analysis of the Performance of Collective Investment Institutions' (2012) *Review of Economics and Finance* 43.

Martin, Randy, 'The Twin Towers of Financialization: Entanglements of Political and Cultural Economies' (2009) 3 *The Global South* 108.

Masulis, Ronald W and Thomas, Randall S, 'Does Private Equity Create Wealth?' (2009) *University of Chicago Law Review* 1.

Matheson, John H and Olson, Brent A, 'Corporate Law and the Long Term Shareholder Model of Corporate Governance' (1991-2) 76 *Minnesota Law Review* 1313.

Mattoo, Aaditya and Subramanian, Arvind, 'Currency Undervaluation and Sovereign Wealth Funds: A New Role for the World Trade Organization' (*Peterson Institute Working Paper Series* 2008).

Mayer, Colin, *Firm Commitment* (Oxford: OUP 2013).

McCahery, Joseph (ed.), *Corporate Governance Regimes: Convergence and Diversity* (Oxford: OUP 2002).

McCahery, Joseph A, Starks, Laura T and Sautner, Zacharias, 'Behind the Scenes: The Corporate Governance Preferences of Institutional Investors', AFA 2011 Denver Meetings Paper at 13 (2010), available at http://ssrn.com/abstract=1571046.

McCarthy, David and Miles, David, 'Optimal Portfolio Allocation for Corporate Pension Funds' (2009) at http://ssrn.com/abstract=1440872.
McCormack, Gerard, 'Conflicts of Interest and the Investment Management Function' (1999) 2 *Company Lawyer* 2.
McGaughey, Ewan, 'Participation in Corporate Governance' (2014) at http://papers.ssrn.com/sol3/papers.cfm?abstract_id=2593904.
McGaughey, Ewan, 'Does Corporate Governance Exclude the Ultimate Investor?' (2016) 16 *Journal of Corporate law Studies* 221.
McVea, Harry, 'Corrupting Capitalism? Sovereign Wealth Funds and the United Kingdom's Regulatory Framework' (2013) *Journal of Business Law* 434.
Mecklenburg-Guzman, Christian Alexander, 'The Reason for the Regulation of Contracts for Difference and Its Impact on Hedge Fund Activism' (2013) 14 *Journal of Banking Regulation* 61.
Megginson, William L and Fotak, Veljko, 'Rise of the Fiduciary State: A Survey of Sovereign Wealth Fund Research' (2014) at http://ssrn.com/abstract=2432623.
Mehra, Rajnish and Prescott, Edward C, 'The Equity Premium: a Puzzle' (1985) 15 *Journal of Monetary Economics* 145.
Melis, Daniëlle Adriana Maria, 'The Institutional Investor Stewardship Myth' (2014) at http://ssrn.com/abstract=2445997.
Mellor, Mary, *The Future of Money: From Financial Crisis to Public Resource* (New York: Pluto Press 2010).
Mendales, Richard E, 'Collateralized Explosive Devices: Why Securities Regulation Failed to Prevent the CDO Meltdown, and How to Fix it' [2009] *University of Illinois Law Review* 1359.
Metrick, Andrew and Yasuda, Ayako, 'Venture Capital and Other Private Equity: A Survey' (2010) at https://papers.ssrn.com/sol3/papers.cfm?abstract_id=1723882.
Micheler, Eva, 'Facilitating Investor Engagement and Stewardship' (2013) 14 *European Business Organisation Law Review* 29.
Mietzner, Mark, Schiereck, Dirk and Schweizer, Denis, 'The Role of Sovereign Wealth Funds as Activist or Passive Fund Managers' (2015) 16 *Journal of Asset Management* 303.
Millon, David, 'Shareholder Social Responsibility' (2012–13) 36 *Seattle University Law Review* 911.
Mitchell, Dalia Tsuk, 'Institutional shareholders as Proxies: The Contours of Shareholder Democracy' (2006) 65 *Washington and Lee Law Rev* 4.
Mitchell, Dalia Tsuk, 'Shareholders As Proxies: The Contours of Shareholder Democracy' (2006) 63 *Washington and Lee Law Review* 1503.
Mitchell, Lawrence E, 'Groundwork Of The Metaphysics Of Corporate Law' (1993) 50 *Washington and Lee Law Rev* 1477.

Mitchell, Lawrence E (ed.), *Progressive Corporate Law* (Boulder: Westview Press 1995).

Mitchell, Lawrence E, 'The Legitimate Rights of Public Shareholders' (2009) 66 *Washington and Lee Law Review* 1635.

Modigliani, Franco, 'Life Cycle, Individual Thrift, and the Wealth of Nations' (1986) 76 *The American Economic Review* 297.

Mohan, Nancy and Zhang, Ting, 'An Analysis of Risk-Taking Behavior for Public Defined Benefit Pension Plans' (2011) at http://ssrn.com/abstract=1992009.

Moloney, Niamh, *How to Protect Investors: Lessons from the EC and the UK* (Cambridge: Cambridge University Press 2012).

Monks, Robert A G, *The New Global Investors* (Capstone, 2001).

Monks, Robert, Miller, Anthony and Cook, Jacqueline, 'Shareholder Activism on Environmental Issues: A Study of Proposals at Large US Corporations (2000–2003)' (2004) 28 *Natural Resources Forum* 317.

Moore, Marc, 'Whispering Sweet Nothings: The Limitations of Informal Conformance in UK Corporate Governance' (2009) 9 *Journal of Corporate Law Studies* 77.

Moore, Marc T and Walker-Arnott, Edward, 'A Fresh Look at Stock Market Short-termism' (2014) 41 *Journal of Law and Society* 416.

Mooschlechner, Peter, Schuberth, Helene and Weber, Beat (eds), *The Political Economy of Financial Market Regulation* (Cheltenham: Edward Elgar 2006).

Morck, Randall (ed.), *A History of Corporate Governance around the World* (NBER Books, 2005).

Moreno, Ramón and Santos, Marjorie, 'Pension Systems in EMEs: Implications for Capital Flows and Financial Markets' (2009) at http://ssrn.com/abstract=1992376.

Morgan, Angela, Poulsen, Annette, Wolf, Jack Yang, Tina, 'Mutual Funds as Monitors: Evidence from Mutual Fund Voting' (2009) at http://ssrn.com/abstract=1431072.

Morley, John, 'The Separation of Funds and Managers: A Theory of Investment Fund Structure and Regulation' (2013–14) 123 *Yale Law Journal* 1228.

Morley, John and Curtis, Quinn, 'Taking Exit Rights Seriously: Why Governance and Fee Litigation Don't Work in Mutual Funds' (2010) 120 *Yale L.J.* 84.

Morrell, Kevin and Clark, Ian, 'Private Equity and the Public Good' (2010) 96 *Journal of Business Ethics* 249.

Mosley, Layna and Singer, David Andrew, 'Taking Stock Seriously: Equity-Market Performance, Government Policy, and Financial Globalization' (2008) 52 *International Studies Quarterly* 405.

Mraović, Branka, 'A Free Market Capitalism or a Speculative Market Capitalism?' (2011) 7 *Social Responsibility Journal* 578.

Mukunda, Gautam, 'The Price of Wall Street's Power' (2014) *Harvard Business Review* 70.

Mülbert, Peter O, 'Corporate Governance of Banks after the Financial Crisis: Theory, Evidence, Reforms' (*ECGI Working Paper* 2010).

Müller, Götz and Vasconcelos, Manuel, 'Listed Private Equity and the Case of Exits' (2010) at http://ssrn.com/abstract=1557007.

Myklebust, Trude, 'The Norwegian Government Pension Fund: Moving Forward on Responsible Investing and Governance' (2010) 3 *Rotman International Journal of Pension Management* 20.

Myners, Paul, *Institutional Investment in the UK: A Review* (2001).

National Association of Pension Funds, *Local Government Pension Scheme 2013: Investing in a Changing World* (May 2013).

National Association of Pension Funds, *Trends in Defined Benefit Asset Allocation: The Changing Shape of UK Pension Investment* (July 2013).

National Association of Pension Funds, *NAPF Engagement Survey: Pension Funds' Engagement with Investee Companies* (Nov 2013).

National Association of Pension Funds, *Corporate Governance Policy and Voting Guidelines* (2014-5) at http://www.napf.co.uk/PolicyandResearch/DocumentLibrary/~/media/Policy/Documents/0418_NAPF_corporate_governance_policy_voting_guidelines_2014_2015_DOCUMENT.pdf.

Naveaux, Vincent and Graas, Renaud, 'Direct Action by Investors against a UCITS Depositary—A Short-Lived Landmark Ruling?' (2012) 7 *Capital Markets Law Journal* 455.

Nesbitt, S, 'Long-term Rewards from Shareholder Activism: A Study of the CALPERS Effect' (1994) 6 *Journal of Applied Corporate Finance* 75.

Neville, Mette, 'Active Ownership and the Competition for International Capital – Recent Trends and Some Implications for Company Law' (2002) *European Business Organisation and Law Review* 440.

Newell, Graeme and Sieracki, Karen (eds), *Global Trends in Real Estate Finance* (Blackwell, 2010).

Ng, Wilson, 'The Evolution of Sovereign Wealth Funds: Singapore's Temasek Holdings' (2010) 18 *Journal of Financial Regulation and Compliance* 6.

Nielsen, Richard P, 'The Private Equity-Leveraged Buyout Form of Finance Capitalism: Ethical and Social Issues, and Potential Reforms' (2008) 18 *Business Ethics Quarterly* 379.

Nitzan, Jonathan and Bichler, Shimshon, *Capital as Power: A Study of Order and Creorder* (Oxford: Routledge, 2009).

Nobles, Richard L, 'The Exercise of Trustees' Discretion under a Pension Scheme' (1992) *Journal of Business Law* 261.

Norton, Joseph J, 'The "Santiago Principles" and the International Forum of Sovereign Wealth Funds: Evolving Components of the New Bretton Woods II Post-Global Financial Crisis Architecture and Another Example of Ad Hoc Global Administrative Networking and Related "Soft" Rulemaking?' (2010) 29 *Review of Banking and Financial Law* 465.

Norton, Joseph J, 'The 'Santiago Principles' for Sovereign Wealth Funds: A Case Study on International Financial Standard Setting Processes' (2010) 13 *Journal of International Economic Law* 645.

Nossum, Jenni Maria, 'Corporate Governance in Oil-lubricated Norway: Regulation, Practice, Ethics and Incoherence' (2015) at http://ssrn.com/abstract=2622072.

O'Barr, William and Conley, John M, *Fortune and Folly* (NY: McGraw-Hill, 1992).

O'Brien, Justin, 'Barriers to Entry: Foreign Direct Investment and the Regulation of Sovereign Wealth Funds' (2008) 42 *International Lawyer* 1231.

O'Horrigan, James, 'The Ethics of the New Finance' (1987) 6 *Journal of Business Ethics* 97.

O'Rourke, Anastasia, 'A New Politics of Engagement: Shareholder Activism for Corporate Social Responsibility' (2003) 12 *Business Strategy and the Environment* 227.

OECD Steering Group, *The Implications of Alternative Investment Vehicles for Corporate Governance: A Synthesis of Research about Private Equity Firms and Activist Hedge Funds* (2007).

Office of Fair Trading, *Defined Contribution Workplace Pension Market Study* (Sep 2013).

Office of National Statistics, *Ownership of UK Quoted Shares for UK Domiciled Companies, 2014* (2015) at http://www.ons.gov.uk/ons/dcp171778_415334.pdf.

Oluchi, Aniaka, 'Infrastructural Development: The Vision of Nigerian Sovereign Wealth Fund' (2013) at http://ssrn.com/abstract=2232974.

Osthoff, Peer C and Kempf, Alexander, 'The Effect of Socially Responsible Investing on Portfolio Performance' (2005) 13 *European Financial Management* 908.

Otten, Roger and Thevissen, Kilian, 'Does Industry Size Matter? Revisiting European Mutual Fund Performance' (2011) at http://ssrn.com/abstract=1741197.

Ownership Commission *Report* (March 2012).

Oxera, *The London Markets and Private Equity Backed IPOs* (March 2006) at http://www.oxera.com/Oxera/media/Oxera/The-London-markets-and-private-equity-backed-IPOs.pdf?ext=.pdf.

Pacces, Alessio M, 'Exit, Voice and Loyalty from the Perspective of Hedge Funds Activism in Corporate Governance' (*ECGI Working Paper*, 2 August 2016) at http://papers.ssrn.com/sol3/papers.cfm?abstract_id=2805982.

Pacces, Alessio M, 'Exit, Voice and Loyalty from the Perspective of Hedge Funds Activism in Corporate Governance' (2016) 9 *Erasmus Law Review* 199.

Pack, Spencer J, *Capitalism as a Moral System* (Cheltenham: Edward Elgar 1991, 2010).

Pagliari, Stefano, 'Who Governs Finance? The Shifting Public-Private Divide in the Regulation of Derivatives, Rating Agencies and Hedge Funds' (2012) 18 *European Law Journal* 44.

Palazzo, Guido and Rethel, Lena, 'Conflicts of Interest in Financial Intermediation' (2008) 81 *Journal of Business Ethics* 193.

Palley, Thomas I, *Financialisation: The Economics of Finance Capital Domination* (Basingstoke: Palgrave Macmillan 2013).

Paredes, Troy A, 'Blinded by the Light: Information Overload and its Consequences for Securities Regulation' (2003) 81 *Washington University Law Quarterly* 417.

Parkinson, John E, *Corporate Power and Responsibility: Issues in the Theory of Company Law* (Oxford: Clarendon Press 1995).

Parkinson, John G and Kelly, G, 'The Combined Code of Corporate Governance' (1999) *The Political Quarterly* 101.

Partnoy, Frank, *Infectious Greed: How Deceit and Risk Corrupted the Financial Markets* (London: Profile Books 2003).

Partnoy, Frank, 'U.S. Hedge Fund Activism' (2015) at http://ssrn.com/abstract= 2585290.

Partnoy, Frank and Thomas, Randall S, 'Gap Filling, Hedge Funds, and Financial Innovation' (2006) at http://papers.ssrn.com/sol3/Papers.cfm?abstract_id=931254.

Pastor, Lubos and Stambaugh, Robert F, 'On the Size of the Active Management Industry' (2012) at http://papers.ssrn.com/sol3/papers.cfm?abstract_id=1532268.

Pastor, Lubos, Stambaugh, Robert F and Taylor, Lucian A, 'Scale and Skill in Active Management' (Jan 2014) at http://ssrn.com/abstract=2390285.

Payne, Jennifer, 'Private Equity and its Regulation in Europe' (2011) at http://ssrn.com/abstract=1886186.

Pensions Policy Institute, *The Changing Landscape for Private Sector Defined Benefit Pension Schemes* (2007).

Pensions Policy Institute, *Retirement Income and Assets: How Can Pensions and Financial Assets Support Retirement?* (Oct 2009).

Pensions Policy Institute, *The Changing Landscape of Pension Schemes in the Private Sector in the UK* (2012).

Petersen, Henry L and Vredenburg, Harrie, 'Morals or Economics? Institutional Investor Preferences for Corporate Social Responsibility' (2009) 90 *Journal of Business Ethics* 1.

Philippon, Thomas, 'Has the U.S. Finance Industry Become Less Efficient? On the Theory and Measurement of Financial Intermediation' (2012) at http://pages.stern.nyu.edu/~tphilipp/papers/Finance_Efficiency.pdf.

Phillips, Robert, 'Stakeholder Legitimacy' (2003) 13 *Business Ethics Quarterly* 25.

Pike, Andy and Pollard, Jane, 'Economic Geographies of Financialization' (2010) 86 *Economic Geography* 29.

Pinkowitz, Lee, Stultz Rene M, and Williamson, Rohan, 'Is There a U.S High Cash Holdings Puzzle after the Financial Crisis?' (2012) at http://papers.ssrn.com/sol3/papers.cfm?abstract_id=2064046.

PIRC, *Survey of Voting Trends* (1998) at http://www.cix.co.uk/~pirc/pubs/pr98.htm.

Pistor, Katharina, 'Sovereign Wealth Funds, Banks and Governments in the Global Crisis: Towards a New Governance of Global Finance?' (2009) *European Business Organisation Law Review* 333.

Plantinga, Auke, 'Performance Measurement for Pension Funds' (2005) at http://papers.ssrn.com/sol3/papers.cfm?abstract_id=900427.

Plantinga, Auke and Scholtens, Bert, 'Socially Responsible Investing and Management Style of Mutual Funds in the Euronext Stock Markets' (2001) at http://papers.ssrn.com/sol3/papers.cfm?abstract_id=2599238.

Polillo, Simone, 'Wildcats in Banking Fields: The Politics of Financial Inclusion' (2011) 40 *Theoretical Society* 347.

Polkovnichenko, Valery, Wei, Kelsey and Zhao, Feng, 'Cautious Risk-Takers: Investor Preferences and Demand for Active Management' (2012) at http://ssrn.com/abstract=2022416.

Ponds, Eduard H M and van Riel, Bart, 'The Recent Evolution of Pension Funds in the Netherlands: The Trend to Hybrid DB-DC Plans and Beyond' (2007) at http://ssrn.com/abstract=964428.

Porter, Michael, *Capital Choices: Changing the way America Invests in Industry* (Mass: Harvard Business School 1994).

Post, Thomas, Gründl, Helmut, Schmit, Joan T and Zimmer, Anja, 'The Impact of Investment Behaviour for Individual Welfare' (2014) 81 *Economica* 15.

Poszar, Zoltan, 'Levered Betas and Wholesale Funding in the Context of Secular Stagnation' (2015) at http://ssrn.com/abstract=2558945.

Poszar, Zoltan and Singh, Manmohan, 'The Non-Bank-Bank Nexus and the Shadow Banking System' (2011) at http://ssrn.com/abstract=1971440.

Powell, Andrew and Rankin, Georgina, 'Investment Management and Occupational Pension Schemes' in Dick Frase (ed.), *Law and Regulation of Investment Management* (2nd edn, London: Sweet & Maxwell, 2011).

Pozen, Robert and Hamacher, Theresa, *The Fund Industry: How Your Money is Managed* (John Wiley & Sons 2011).

Preqin, 2015 Preqin Global Private Equity & Venture Capital Report (2015) at https://www.preqin.com/docs/reports/2015-Preqin-Global-Private-Equity-&-Venture-Capital-Report-Sample-Pages.pdf.

Price Waterhouse Coopers, *US Global Equity Watch 2012.*

Price Waterhouse Coopers, *Asset Management 2020: A Brave New World* (2014) at http://www.pwc.com/gx/en/asset-management/publications/asset-management-2020-a-brave-new-world.jhtml.

Price Waterhouse Coopers, *Luxembourg Fund Governance Survey 2014* (2015).

Price Waterhouse Coopers and Baker & McKenzie, *Cross-border IPOs: Choice in an Uncertain World* (Nov 2012) at http://www.pwc.com/en_GX/gx/audit-services/ipo-centre/assets/pwc-cross-border-ipo-trends.pdf.

Qian, Meijun, Pan, Hongbo and Yeung, Bernard Yin, 'Expropriation of Minority Shareholders in Politically Connected Firms' (2010) at http://papers.ssrn.com/sol3/papers.cfm?abstract_id=1719335.

Raaijmakers, Geert T M J, 'Securities Lending and Corporate Governance' (2005) at http://ssrn.com/abstract=928312.

Ramaswamy, Srichander, 'The Sustainability of Pension Schemes' (*BIS Working Paper* Jan 2012) at http://ssrn.com/abstract=1980094.

Ramirez, Andrés, 'Risk and the Multinational Corporation Revisited: The Case of Natural Disasters and Corporate Cash Holdings' (2011) at http://ssrn.com/abstract=1772969.

Ramirez, Steven A, 'The Virtues of Private Securities Litigation: An Historic and Macroeconomic Perspective' (2014) 5 *Loyola University of Chicago Law Journal* 669.

Rauh, Joshua D, 'Risk Shifting versus Risk Management: Investment Policy in Corporate Pension Plans' (*NBER Working Paper* 2007) at http://www.nber.org/papers/w13240.

Rauh, Joshua D and Stefanescu, Irina, 'Why Are Firms in the United States Abandoning Defined Benefit Plans?' (2009) 2 *Rotman International Journal of Pension Management* 18.

Rebonato, Riccardo, *Plight of the Fortune Tellers: Why we Need to Manage Financial Risk Differently* (NJ: Princeton University Press, 2007).

Reisberg, Arad, 'The Notion of Stewardship from a Company Law Perspective: Re-Defined and Re-Assessed in Light of the Recent Financial Crisis?' (2011) *Journal of Financial Crime* 126.

Reisberg, Arad, 'The UK Stewardship Code: On a road to Nowhere' (2015) 15 *The Journal of Corporate Law Studies* 217.

Renneboog, Luc, Horst, Jenke ter and Zhang, Chendi, 'Is Ethical Money Financially Smart?' (February 2006) *ECGI Finance Working Paper* No 117/2006 http://papers.ssrn.com/sol3/papers.cfm?abstract_id=887162.

Renneboog, Luc, Horst, Jenke ter, and Zhang, Chendi, 'Socially Responsible Investments: Methodology, Risk Exposure and Performance' (June 2007) *ECGI Finance Working Paper* No 175/2007 http://papers.ssrn.com/sol3/papers.cfm?abstract_id=985267.

Renneboog, Luc, Horst, Jenke ter and Zhang, Chendi, 'The Price of Ethics: Evidence from Socially Responsible Mutual Funds' (*ECGI Working Paper* 2007).

Richardson, Benjamin J, 'Do the Fiduciary Duties of Pension Funds Hinder Socially Responsible Investment?' (2007) 22 *Review of Banking and Financial Law* 145.

Richardson, Benjamin J, *Socially Responsible Investment Law* (New York: Oxford University Press 2008).

Richter, Judith and Borton, John, *Holding Corporations Accountable: Corporate Conduct, International Codes, and Citizen Action* (Zed Books 2001).

Ringe, Wolf-Georg, 'Hedge Funds and Risk-Decoupling – The Empty Voting Problem in the European Union' (2013) 36 *Seattle University Law Review* 1027.

Ripken, Susanna Kim, 'Corporations Are People Too: A Multi-Dimensional Approach To The Corporate Personhood Puzzle' (2009) 15 *Fordham Journal of Corporate and Financial Law* 97.

Rizova, Savina, 'Securities Lending by Mutual Funds' (2011) at http://ssrn.com/abstract=2056651.

Roach, Lee, 'The Directors' Remuneration Report Regulations 2002 and the Disclosure of Executive Remuneration' (2005) 25 *Company Lawyer* 141.

Roche, David and McKee, Bob, *New Monetarism* (Independent Strategy, 2007).

Rock, Edward B, 'The Logic and (Uncertain) Significance of Institutional Shareholder Activism' (1990–91) 91 *Georgetown Law Journal* 445.

Roe, Mark J, 'Corporate Short-Termism—In the Boardroom and in the Courtroom' (2013) 68 *Business Lawyer* 977.

Roiter, Eric D, 'Disentangling Mutual Fund Governance from Corporate Governance' (2015) 6 *Harvard Business Law Review* 1 at http://www.hblr.org/wp-content/uploads/2016/06/HLB101_crop.pdf.

Romano, Roberta, 'Public Pension Fund Activism in Corporate Governance Reconsidered' (1993) *Columbia Law Review* 795.

Rose, Paul J, 'The Corporate Governance Industry' (2007) 32 *Journal of Corporation Law* 887.

Rose, Paul, 'Sovereigns as Shareholders' (2008) *North Carolina Law Review* 84.

Rose, Paul, 'Common Agency and the Public Corporation' (2010) 63 *Vanderbilt Law Review* 1355.

Rose, Paul, 'North American Dream: The Rise of U.S. and Canadian Sovereign Wealth' (2014) at http://ssrn.com/abstract=2423113.

Rose, Paul, 'Shareholder Proposals in the Market for Corporate Influence' (2014) 66 *Florida Law Review* 2179.

Rose, Paul and Seligman, Jason S, 'Alternative Investments? State & Local Pension Portfolio Use and Performance' (2013) at http://ssrn.com/abstract=2407538.

Rose, Paul and Sharfman, Bernard, 'Shareholder Activism as a Corrective Mechanism in Corporate Governance' (2014) *Brigham Young University Law Review* 1015.

Rosella, Michael R and Pugliese, Domenick, 'The Evolution of the Exchange-Traded Fund: Is Active Management on the Horizon?' (2006) 7 *Journal of Investment Compliance* 44.

Rosenau, J (ed.), *Governance Without Government* (Cambridge: Cambridge University Press 1992, rep 2000).

Rubach, Michael J and Sebora, Terrence C, 'Determinants of Institutional Investor Activism: A Test of the Ryan-Schneider Model (2002)' (2009) 21 *Journal of Managerial Issues* 245.

Sá, Filipa and Viani, Francesca, 'Shifts in Portfolio Preferences of International Investors: An Application to Sovereign Wealth Funds' (*Bank of England Working Paper* 2011).

Sahut, Jean-Michel, Lantz, Jean-Sebastien and Montandrau, Sophie, 'Activism of Institutional Investors, Corporate Governance Alerts and Financial Performance' (2010) 15 *International Journal of Business* 221 at http://papers.ssrn.com/sol3/papers.cfm?abstract_id=1735797.

Sandberg, Joakim, 'Socially Responsible Investment and Fiduciary Duty: Putting the Freshfields Report into Perspective' (2011) 101 *Journal of Business Ethics* 143.

Sandor, Anna, 'Leveraging International Law to Incentivize Value-Added Shareholding: Why Foreign Sovereign Wealth Funds Still Matter and How They Can Improve Shareholder Governance' (2015) 46 *Georgetown Journal of International Law* 947.

Santella, Paolo, Baffi, Enrico, Drago, Carlo and Lattuca, Dino, 'A Comparative Analysis of the Legal Obstacles to Institutional Investor Activism in the EU and in the US' (2009) 23 *European Business Law Review* 2, at http://ssrn.com/abstract=1137491.

Santiso, Javier, 'Sovereign Development Funds: Key Financial Actors of the Shifting Wealth of Nations' (*OECD Emerging Markets Network Working Paper* 2008) at http://ssrn.com/abstract=1300288.

Santiso, Javier, 'Sovereign Funds Are Helping Strike A New World Economic Balance' (2011) at http://ssrn.com/abstract=1877224.

Santoro, Michael A and Strauss, Ronald J, *Wall Street Values: Business Ethics and the Global Financial Crisis* (Cambridge: Cambridge University Press, 2012).

Schäfer, Andreas and von Arx, Urs, 'The Influence of Pension Funds on Corporate Governance' (2014) 46 *Applied Economics* 2316.

Schäfer, Henry, 'Sustainable Finance: A Conceptual Outline' (2012) at http://ssrn.com/abstract=2147590.

Schofield, Guy, 'Private Equity: Governance Arbitrage and Lessons for Public Corporate Governance' (2014) at http://ssrn.com/abstract=2441166.

Schouten, Michael C, 'Why Governance Might Work in Mutual Funds' (2011) 109 *Michigan Law Review* 89.

Schouten, Michael C, 'Do Institutional Investors Follow Proxy Advice Blindly?' (2012) at http://ssrn.com/abstract=1978343.

Scogland, William L, 'Fiduciary Duty: What Does it Mean?' (1989) 24 *Tort and Insurance Law Journal* 803.

Scott, Colin, 'Analysing Regulatory Space: Fragmented Resources and Institutional Design' (2001) *Public Law* 329.

Scott, John, *Power: Key Concepts* (Cambridge: Citizenry Press, 2001).

Seretakis, Alexandros, 'Hedge Fund Activism Coming to Europe: Lessons from the American Experience' (2014) 8 *Brooklyn Journal of Corporate, Financial & Commercial Law* 438.

Sergakis, Konstantinos, 'The UK Stewardship Code: Bridging the Gap Between Companies and Institutional Investors' (2013) 47 *RJTUM* 109.

Shadab, Houman B, 'Hedge Fund Governance' (2013) 19 *Stanford Journal of Law, Business & Finance* 141.

Shah, Ajay and Fernandes, Kshama, 'The Relevance of Index Funds for Pension Investment in Equities' (*World Bank Research Paper* 1999).

Shamir, Ronen, 'The Age of Responsibilization: On Market-Embedded Morality' (2008) 37 *Economy and Society* 1.

Sharfman, Bernard, 'Activist Hedge Funds in a World of Board Independence: Creators or Destroyers of Long-Term Value?' (2015) *Columbia Business Law Review* 813.

Sharfman, Bernard, 'A Theory of Shareholder Activism and its Place in Corporate Law' (2015) 82 *Tennessee Law Review* 101.
Sharifzadeh, Mohamed and Hojat, Simin, 'An Analytical Performance Comparison of Exchange-Traded Funds with Index Funds: 2002–2010' (2012) 13 *Journal of Asset Management* 196–209.
Shih, Victor, 'Tools of Survival: Sovereign Wealth Funds in Singapore and China' (2009) 14 *Geopolitics* 328.
Shiller, Robert H, 'Bubbles, Human Judgment, and Expert Opinion' (2002) 58 *Financial Analysts Journal* 18.
Shiller, Robert H, *Irrational Exuberance* (Crown Business, 2006).
Siems, Mathias, 'Convergence in Corporate Governance: A Leximetric Approach' (2010) *35 Journal of Corporation Law* 729.
Sievanen, Riikka, Rita, Hannu and Scholtens, Bert, 'The Drivers of Responsible Investment: The Case of European Pension Funds' (2013) 117 *Journal of Business Ethics* 137.
Slawotsky, Joel, 'Sovereign Wealth Funds as Emerging Financial Superpowers: How U.S. Regulators Should Respond' (2009) 40 *Georgetown Journal of International Law* 1239.
Smith, Anne Marie and Nash, Kate (eds), *Globalisation and Contemporary Studies on the Nation State* (Pluto Press 2006).
Smith, Michael P, 'Shareholder Activism by Institutional Investors: Evidence from CalPERS' (1996) 51 *Journal of Finance* 227.
Smithers, Andrew, *The Road to Recovery: How and Why Economic Policy must Change* (Chichester: John Wiley & Sons, 2013).
Solskice, David and Hall, Peter A, *Varieties of Capitalism* (Oxford: OUP 2001).
Spangler, Timothy, *The Law of Private Investment Funds* (Oxford: OUP 2010).
Statman, Meir, 'Socially Responsible Investments' (2007) 17 *Journal of Investment Consulting* 37.
Statman, Meir, 'Quiet Conversations: The Expressive Nature of Socially Responsible Investors' [2008] *Journal of Financial Planning* 40.
Steib, James A, 'Assessing Freeman's Stakeholder Theory' (2009) 87 *Journal of Business Ethics* 401.
Sternberg, E, *Stakeholding: Betraying the Corporation's Objectives* (London Social Affairs Unit Research Paper No 27, 1998).
Stewart, Fiona, 'Proving Incentives for Long-Term Investment by Pension Funds The Use of Outcome-based Benchmarks' (*Word Bank Research Paper*, 2014).
Stokman, Nick W A, 'Influences of Hedge Fund Activism on the Medium Term Target Value' (2007) at http://ssrn.com/abstract=1019968.

Stout, Lynn A, 'The Toxic Side Effects of Shareholder Primacy' (2013) 16 *University of Pennsylvania Law Review* 2003.

Stout, Lynn, *The Shareholder Value Myth: How Putting Shareholders First Harms Investors, Corporations, and the Public* (Berrett-Koehler, 2012).

Stout, Lynn, 'The Corporation as Time Machine: Intergenerational Equity, Intergenerational Efficiency, and the Corporate Form' (2015) at http://papers.ssrn.com/sol3/papers.cfm?abstract_id=2556883.

Stratling, Rebecca, 'General Meetings: A Dispensable Tool for Corporate Governance of Listed Companies?' (2003) 11 *Corporate Governance* 74.

Strivens, M, Espenlaub, S and Walker, M, 'The Influence of Institutional Investors over CEO Turnover in the UK' (2008) at http://ssrn.com/abstract=991595.

Sudarsanam, Sudi, Wright, Mike and Huang, Jian, 'Going Private Buyouts and Shareholder Wealth Gains: Impact of Bankruptcy Risk' (2007) at http://ssrn.com/abstract=967731.

Sullivan, Rory and MacKenzie, Craig (eds), *Responsible Investment* (Sheffield: Greenleaf Publishing 2006).

Sun, Tao and Hesse, Heiko, 'Sovereign Wealth Funds and Financial Stability—An Event Study Analysis' (*IMF Working Paper* 2009).

Sun, William, Louche, Céline, Pérez, Roland, 'Finance and Sustainability: Towards a New Paradigm? A Post-Crisis Agenda' (2015) 3 *Finance and Sustainability* 15.

Suntharee, Lhaopadchan, 'The Politics of Sovereign Wealth Fund Investment: The Case of Temasek and Shin Corp.' (2010) 18 *Journal of Financial Regulation and Compliance* 15.

Sutcliffe, Charles, 'The Cult of the Equity for Pension Funds: Should it Get the Boot?' (2004) at http://ssrn.com/abstract=544862.

Szilagyi, Peter and Chong, Chong Wei, 'The Board of Directors in Hedge Fund Governance' (2012) at https://www.aeaweb.org/conference/2013/retrieve.php?pdfid=412.

Szylar, Christian, *Risk Management under UCITs III/IV* (Chichester: John Wiley & Sons 2010).

Talbot, Lorraine E, 'Why Shareholders Shouldn't Vote: A Marxist-progressive Critique of Shareholder Empowerment' (2013) 76(5) *MLR* 791.

Taub, Jennifer S, 'Able but Not Willing: The Failure of Mutual Fund Advisers to Advocate for Shareholders' Rights' (2009) 34 *Journal of Corporation Law* 102.

Tellam, Andrew, Clarkson, Peter and Pathan, Shams, 'Do Private Equity Target Firms Exhibit Less Effectual Governance Structures?' (2013) at http://ssrn.com/abstract=2339482.

Tett, Gillian, *Fool's Gold: How Unrestrained Greed Corrupted a Dream, Shattered Global Markets and Unleashed a Catastrophe* (London: Abacus Books, 2010).

Thannasoulis, John, 'The Case for Intervening in Bankers' Pay' (2012) 67 *The Journal of Finance* 849.

The Pensions Regulator, *Public Service Pension Schemes: A Summary of Governance and Administration* (Sep 2013).

The Pensions Regulator, *Governance and Administration of Occupational Trust-Based Schemes Providing Money Purchase Benefits* (July 2016) at http://www.thepensionsregulator.gov.uk/docs/code-13.pdf.

The Sharman Inquiry, *Going Concern and Liquidity Risks: Lessons for Companies and Auditors, Final Report and Recommendations of the Panel of Inquiry* (June 2012), at http://www.frc.org.uk/getattachment/591a5e2a-35d7-4470-a46c-30c0d8ca2a14/Sharman-Inquiry-Final-Report.aspx.

Thévenoz, Luc and Bahar, Rashid (eds), *Conflicts of Interest and the Duty of Loyalty* (Zurich: Schultess Verlag 2007).

Thomas, Randall S, 'Public Pension Funds as Shareholder Activists: A Comment on Choi and Fisch' (2008) 61 *Vanderbilt Law Review* 1.

Thompson, John K and Choi, Sang-Mok, 'Governance Systems for Collective Investment Schemes in OECD Countries' *OECD Occasional Paper* (April 2001).

Thornton, Paul and Fleming, Donald (eds), *Good Governance for Pension Funds* (Cambridge: Cambridge University Press, 2011).

Thornton, Rosy, "Ethical Investments: A Case of Disjointed Thinking" (2008) 67 *Cambridge Law Journal* 396.

Tomorrow's Company, *Tomorrow's Stewardship: Why Stewardship Matters* (June 2011).

Toms, Steven, Wilson, Nick and Wright, Mike, 'The Evolution of Private Equity: Corporate Restructuring in the UK, c.1945-2010' (2012) at http://ssrn.com/abstract=2145445.

Towers Watson, *Pension Adequacy: The Challenge for Defined Contribution Pension Plans* (2010).

Trevitt, Mark L, 'Jupiter Ecology' in Cary Kronsinsky, Nick Robins and Steven Veiderman, *Evolutions in Sustainable Investing* (Chichester: John Wiley & Sons 2012).

Truman, Edwin M 'Sovereign Wealth Funds: The Need For Greater Transparency And Accountability' (*Peterson Inst. For Int'l Econ, Policy Brief* No. Pb07-6) 4 (2007) available at http://www.iie.com/publications/pb/pb07-6.pdf.

Tsuk, Dalia, 'From Pluralism to Individualism: Berle and Means and 20th-Century American Legal Thought: The Modern Corporation and

Private Property by Adolf A. Berle; Gardiner C. Means Review' (2005) 30 *Law and Social Inquiry* 179.

Tucker, Anne M, 'The Outside Investor: Citizen Shareholders and Corporate Alienation' (2013–2014) 11 *U. St. Thomas L.J.* 99.

Turner, Adam, 'Exchange-Traded Funds vs. UK Investment Trusts: A Comparison of Performance' (2010) at http://papers.ssrn.com/sol3/papers.cfm?abstract_id=1689534.

Underhill, Geoffrey R D, 'Markets beyond Politics? The State and the Internationalisation of Financial Markets' (1991) 19 *European Journal of Political Research* 197.

Underhill, Geoffrey and Zhang, Xiaoke, 'Norms, Legitimacy, and Global Financial Governance' (2006) *WEF Working Paper* No 13 http://papers.ssrn.com/sol3/papers.cfm?abstract_id=941389.

UNEP Finance Initiative, *A Legal Framework for Integrating Environmental, Social and Governance Issues into Institutional Investment* (2005).

UNEPFI, *Fiduciary Responsibility: Legal and Practical Aspects of Integrating Environmental, Social And Governance Issues Into Institutional Investment* (Geneva: UNEPFI, 2009).

Ungureanu, Maria, 'The Corporate Governance of Sovereign Wealth Funds', Harvard Law School Forum on Corporate Governance (7 August 2014).

Urwin, Roger, 'Sustainable Investing Practice: Simplified Complexity' (2010) at http://ssrn.com/abstract=1656988.

Useem, Michael, *Investor Capitalism: How Money Managers are Rewriting the Rules of Corporate America* (Basic Books, 1999).

Vallascas, Francesco and Hagendorff, Jens, 'CEO Remuneration and Bank Default Risk: Evidence from the US and Europe' (July 2010) at http://papers.ssrn.com/sol3/papers.cfm?abstract_id=1799268.

van der Zwan, Natascha, 'Making Sense of Financialisation' (2014) 12 *Socio-economic Review* 99.

van Setten, Lodewjik, *The Law of Institutional Investment Management* (Oxford: Oxford University Press 2009).

Vanderkerckhove, Wim and others (eds), *Responsible Investment in Times of Turmoil* (Dordrecht: Springer 2011).

Vinten, Frederik, 'The Performance of Private Equity Buyout Fund Owned Firms' (2007) at http://ssrn.com/abstract=1114603.

Wahal, Sunil, 'Pension Fund Activism and Firm Performance' (1996) 31 *Journal of Financial and Quantitative Analysis* 1.

Walker, David, *A Review of Corporate Governance in Banks and Financial Institutions* (Nov 2009).

Walker Working Group, Disclosure and Transparency in Private Equity-Final Report (Dec 2007) at www.walkerworkinggroup.com, adopted as the Walker Guidelines by the BVCA, at http://www.bvca.co.uk/ResearchPublications/Publications/WalkerGuidelines.aspx.

Walter, Ingo and Sisli, Elif, 'The Asset Management Industry in Asia: Dynamics of Growth, Structure, and Performance' (2007) 16 *Financial Markets, Institutions and Instruments* 1.

Wang, Chuan-San, Strong, Norman, Tung Samuel and Lin, Steve, 'Share Repurchases, the Clustering Problem, and the Free Cash Flow Hypothesis' (2009) 38 *Financial Management* 487.

Wang, Gungwu and Zhang, Yongnian, 'An Update on Sovereign Wealth Funds' in *China: Development and Governance* (Singapore: World Scientific Publishing 2013).

Warburton, A Joseph, 'Should Mutual Funds Be Corporations? A Legal & Econometric Analysis' (2008) 33 *Journal of Corporation Law* 745.

Watson, Matthew, *The Political Economy of International Capital Mobility* (Basingstoke: Palgrave Macmillan 2007).

Weaver, R Kent, 'Whose Money Is It Anyhow?: Governance and Social Investment in Collective Investment Funds' (2003) at http://ssrn.com/abstract=1136876.

Webber, David H, 'The Use and Abuse of Labor's Capital' (2015) 89 *NYU Law Review* 2108.

Weil Gotshal and Manges, *Comparative Study Of Corporate Governance Codes Relevant to the European Union and Its Member States* (2002) at http://ec.europa.eu/internal_market/company/docs/corpgov/corp-gov-codes-rpt-part1_en.pdf.

Weller, Christian E and Wenger, Jeffrey B, 'Prudent Investors: The Asset Allocation of Public Pension Plans' (2008) at http://ssrn.com/abstract=1298654.

Wellman, Jay and Zhou, Jian, 'Corporate Governance and Mutual Fund Performance: A First Look at the Morningstar Stewardship Grades' (2007) at http://ssrn.com/abstract=714303.

West, Richard R, 'Conflicts of Interest: Substance or Subterfuge?' (1971) 27 *Financial Analysts Journal* 31.

Wheatley, M, *The Wheatley Review of LIBOR* (Sep 2012).

Wheeler, Sally, *Corporations and the Third Way* (Oxford: Hart 2002).

Wheeler, Sally, 'From Responsible Saver to Stewarded Investor? (2013-4) at http://ssrn.com/abstract=2238612.

Whelan, Charles J, 'Money Manager Capitalism: Still Here but Not Quite as Expected' (2002) 36 *Journal of Economic Issues* 401.

Williams, Colin C, 'A Borderless World Of Hypermobile and Homeless Money?' (2004) 2 *Industrial Geographer* 144.

Williams, Cynthia and Zumbansen, Peer (eds), *The Embedded Firm: Corporate Governance, Labour and Finance Capitalism* (Cambridge: Cambridge University Press 2012).

Williams, Toni, 'Empowerment of Whom and for What? Financial Literacy Education and the New Regulation of Consumer Financial Services' (2009) 29 *Law and Policy* 226.

Willis, Lauren E, 'Against Financial Literacy Education' (2008–9) 94 *Iowa Law Review* 197.

Wilmarth, Arthur E Jnr, 'The Transformation of the Financial Services Industry: 1975–2000, Competition, Consolidation and Increased Risks' (2002) *University of Illinois Law Rev* 215.

Wimmer, Maximilian, 'ESG-Persistence in Socially Responsible Mutual Funds' (2012) at http://ssrn.com/abstract=2138882.

Winter, Jaap, 'Shareholder Engagement and Stewardship: The Realities and Illusions of Institutional Share Ownership' (2011) at http://ssrn.com/abstract=1867564.

Wolf, Martin, *Fixing Global Finance* (Conn: Yale University Press, 2008).

Wong, Anthony, 'Sovereign Wealth Funds and the Problem of Asymmetric Information: The Santiago Principles and International Regulations' (2009) 34 *Brooklyn Journal of International Law* 1081.

Wong, Simon C Y, 'Why Stewardship Is Proving Elusive for Institutional Investors' (2010) 7 *JIBFL* 406.

Wong, Simon C Y, 'Is Institutional Investor Stewardship Still Elusive?' (2015) *Butterworths Journal of Banking and Financial Law* 508.

Wood, Geoffrey and Wright, Mike, 'Wayward Agents, Dominant Elite, or Reflection of Internal Diversity? A Critique of Folkman, Froud, Johal and Williams on Financialisation and Financial Intermediaries' (2010) 52 *Business History* 1048.

Wood, Philip, *Comparative Financial Law* (London: Sweet & Maxwell, 1995), now updated into *Maps of World Financial Law* (London: Sweet & Maxwell 2008).

Woods, Claire and Urwin, Roger, 'Putting Sustainable Investing into Practice: A Governance Framework for Pension Funds' (2010) 92 *Journal of Business Ethics* 1.

Wray, L Randall, 'Money Manager Capitalism and the Global Financial Crisis' (2009) at http://ssrn.com/abstract=1478508.

Wright, John S F and Head, Brian, 'Reconsidering Regulation and Governance Theory: A Learning Approach' (2009) 31 *Law and Policy* 192.

Wright, M and Robbie, K, *Management Buy-Outs and Venture Capital: Into the Next Millennium* (Cheltenham: Edward Elgar 1999).

Wright, M, Renneboog, L et al, 'Leveraged Buy-outs in the UK and Continental Europe: Retrospect and Prospect' (2006) 18 *Journal of Applied Corporate Finance* 38.

Wu, Friedrich and Seah, Arifin, 'Would China's Sovereign Wealth Fund Be a Menace to the USA?' (2008) 16 *China and the World Economy* 33.

Wu, Friedrich and Wei, Koh De, 'From Financial Assets to Financial Statecraft: The Case of China and Emerging Economies of Africa and Latin America' (2014) 23 *Journal of Contemporary China* 781.

Wymeersch, Eddy, 'The Regulatory Regime for Exchange-Traded Funds in the EU' (2011) at http://ssrn.com/abstract=1986852.

Yan, X and Zhang, Z, 'Institutional Investors and Equity Returns: Are Short-Term Institutions Better Informed?' (2009) 22 *Review of Financial Studies* 893.

Yang, Tina, 'Mutual Funds as Monitors: Evidence from Mutual Fund Voting' (2009) at http://ssrn.com/abstract=1431072.

Yarborough, Mark, Fryer-Edwards, Kelly, Geller, Gail, and Sharp, Richard R, 'Transforming the Culture of Biomedical Research From Compliance to Trustworthiness: Insights From Nonmedical Sectors' (2009) 84 *Culture of Biomedical Research* 472.

Ye, Pengfei, 'On Investors' Ownership and Voting Decisions: Evidence from Mutual Funds' (2008) at http://ssrn.com/abstract=1100362.

Yeoh, Peter, 'Socially Responsible Investing: Legal and Related Challenges' (2014) 35 *Company Lawyer* 35.

Yeung, Henry Wai-Chung, 'From National Development to Economic Diplomacy? Governing Singapore's Sovereign Wealth Funds' (2011) 24 *The Pacific Review* 625.

Young, Suzanne and Gates, Stephen (eds), Institutional Investors' Power to Change Corporate Behavior: International Perspectives (*Critical Studies on Corporate Responsibility, Governance and Sustainability*, Volume 5, Emerald Group Publishing Limited, 2013).

Zagzebski, Linda Trinkaus, *Epistemic Authority* (Oxford: OUP 2012).

Zelinsky, Edward A, 'The Defined Contribution Paradigm' (2004) 114 *Yale Law Journal* 451.

Zhang, Ming and He, Fan, 'China's Sovereign Wealth Fund: Weakness and Challenges' (2009) 17 *China and the World Economy* 101.

Zhu, Heqing, 'The Preventive Effect of Hedge Fund Activism' (2013) at http://ssrn.com/abstract=2369533.

Zingales, Luigi, *Capitalism for the People: Recapturing the Lost Genius of American Capitalism* (New York: Basic Books 2012).

Index

2-and-20 fee model 334, 362

accountability 7, 33, 74, 95–9
  consequences of 97–8
accumulation of capital 26
activism 6, 7, 58, 60, 85–6, 132, 156–7
  see also hedge fund activism; shareholder behaviour
  defensive 133–5, 138, 139–40
  hedge fund 59, 84, 86, 143, 147–8, 302–3, 309–10
  indirect 427–8
  investor capitalism, as 13
  offensive 143–51, 311
  retreats 345
  socially responsible investing 118
  voting 224
  vulnerability to 312
agency capitalism 15, 72
  see also intermediary capitalism; money manager capitalism
  fiduciary capitalism as 14
agency problem 7, 15, 85–7, 217
  active management 85–6
  addressing 28
  churning 85
  passive management 88–90
  rent-seeking 85
AIF *see* alternative investment funds
Alternative Investment Fund Managers (AIFM) Directive (2011/61/EU) 72–3, 101, 106–7, 332–3
  Article 12 360
  Article 16 333–4
  Commission Delegated Regulation (2013) 360
  Remuneration Code 334
alternative investment funds 8, 10, 19, 86
  global assets 17–18
  hedge *see* hedge funds
  not regulated under Directive 2011/61/EU 73
  private equity *see* private equity funds
annuities 199–200, 224, 225
  see also insurance companies; pension funds
  regulation 227
arbitrage 32, 69
  merger 148, 312–13, 318, 319–20
  regulatory 62
  value 6, 37, 43
asset classes 37–8, 55
  alternative 202, 204, 209, 219, 225, 233
  corporate bonds 55
  equity *see* equity
  exotic 39, 55, 91, 272, 273
  illiquid 91, 92, 272
  infrastructure 38, 55, 119, 202, 209
  publicly traded corporate equity *see* equity
  securitised 55
asset management 78–9, 93
  agency problem *see* agency problem
  asset managers 78, 85
    expertise 29
    professional 17, 18, 120, 397
    reluctance to engage in corporate governance 222
    short-termism 79–80, 97–8
  constraints on 244, 252
  collective engagement forums 246, 302

disclosure obligations 180–81, 184
exchange-traded funds *see* exchange-traded funds
fees/charges 86–7, 104–5
dealing commissions 103–4
soft dollars 103
investment engineering 83–4
securities lending 84–5
Investor Forum 175, 246
passive 88–90, 209, 222, 234
short-termism 79–83, 219
Association of British Insurers 175, 227
Independent Project Board 232
Investment Management Association merger 228
Investor Exchange 228
atomisation 42
processes 21

beneficial ownership 15
block holdings 54, 57, 237, 242
buy-out funds 351, 355–7
corporate governance behaviour 374–5
leverage levels 368–9, 370–71
management buy-outs, and 369–70
minimising risk 372–3
opportunistic behaviour 371
regulation 375–7
secondaries 373–4
value extraction 371–2
venture capital and 367
buybacks 178, 253–4
hedge fund 313–14, 248
rights 148–9

cheap money 19, 28, 38
Coasean organisation 76
collective investment management 19, 23, 261
see also savings, collective pooling
business models 8, 16, 42–3
adapting for compliance 62
affecting shareholder behaviour 61
coupon pool capitalism, as 25
decentralisation of power 191
discretionary power of 71–2, 130
financialisation *see* financialisation
global phenomenon 11, 18
growth of 17–20
legal basis for 63–7
high net worth individuals, for 19
marketised model of 101
partial intermediation, as 18, 20
professionalised 28–32, 61, 70
regulation *see* regulation
short-termism in 50–51, 79–83
strategies 10–11
structures 16
collective investment schemes
see also mutual funds; UCITs
borderline 259
broad definition of 259
characteristics 258–9
Ireland, in 264
management *see* collective investment management
regulation 258, 259, 270–71
regulatory competition 263–6
retail *see* collective retail investment funds
trusts 262–3
UCITs funds 259–60, 266
fund/management company relationship 266–9
non-UCITs 262
regulation 270–71
collective retail investment funds 70–71, 257, 307–8
corporate governance roles 297–8
collective engagement 301–3
exit 306–7
individual informal dialogue 301
voting at general meetings 298–300
securities/derivative litigation 303–4
socially responsible 304–6
enhanced investor protection, and 276, 279
fund/manager separation 261, 269
investors 291–3
prudent person rule, and 98–9

regulatory reforms 276–80
charges and fees 285–8
conduct of business obligations and duties 280–82, 283–5
corporate governance roles 280, 282–3
exchange-traded funds 289–91
passive investing 289
structures 261–3
competition 26–7, 200, 225
global 56, 60
impact of 34, 61, 86
increasing 228
price 104
regulatory 263–6
conflicts of interest 47, 62, 63, 178, 281–2
see also fiduciary law; regulation
fiduciary law and 64–5
management of 65–6, 107, 172, 232, 291
pension funds, in 223, 234–5
proxy advisors, of 189–90
consumer protection *see* investor protection
corporate equity
fiduciary capitalism, as 14, 122–3
ownership 2, 122–6
good 3, 129, 137–8, 178
regulation 130–31
significance of 126–31
structures 129–30
corporate governance
see also regulation; shareholders
conduct of business 280–85
convergence of standards 222
democratising 14
disempowerment of investors 74
governance entrepreneurs 146
institutional 123
instrumental approach to 58–9, 60
internal 6, 12, 16
investment funds
capacities 3–4
roles 10–12, 13, 16
investment management, and 4, 8
investor protection *see* investor protection
pension funds *see* pension fund corporate governance
regulatory 4, 31–2, 188
accountability 33, 49–50, 74, 95–9
financial consultants, for 188
investment chains, for 188–9
proscriptive duties 188–9
proxy advisory agencies, for 189–91, 222
public-interest oriented 6, 186
reporting 241–2, 243
rights
private litigation, and 151–7
shareholders, of 12
corporate ownership *see* ownership
corporate social responsibility 110
ESG factors 110–11, 248–50
integration 112–13
legitimacy of 113
socially responsible investing *see* socially responsible investing
UN Principles of Responsible Investment 113
Cowan v Scargill 214, 249

defined benefit pension schemes 199
defined contribution shift 43–4
de-risking 203
liability driven management 203–4
private sector schemes *see* private sector defined benefit schemes
unfunded 200, 201
defined contribution pension schemes 199, 228, 229–30
asset allocation 233
auto-enrolment 204, 230
cap on management charges 232, 233
corporate governance 233–5
governance deficit 231–2
growth of 204–5
Independent Governance Committees 232
NEST 199, 235
enrolment in 230
regulation 231–3

retirement income 230–31
savers
appeal to 230
disempowerment of 230
shift toward 43–4, 228–9, 234
trust-based 231
democratic capitalism 14
depositaries 76, 293
independent 335, 361
third party 294–6
derivative litigation 151
costs 154–5
continuing disclosure breach 155–6
good faith in 153
minority investors and 152–3
negligent misstatements 154
representative actions (UK) 155
derivatives 274
innovation in 38
over-the-counter 273
rise of 33–4
Deutsche Bank Advisers report (2012) 119
disclosure
see also transparency
-based regulation 45
continuing disclosure breach 155–6
obligations in EU law 180–81, 184
voting rights and 184

Efficient Capital Markets Hypothesis 39
engagement 7, 59, 138–9
asset manager 222
collective 175–6, 301–3, 346–7, 426–7
environmental, social and governance issues, over 248–50
EU 158–9
least-cost 222, 246
not unequivocal good 142, 157
private corporate governance, as 184
UK
stewardship standards 157–8
US comparison 142
voting *see* voting
epistemic authority 28–30
equity 53–60
corporate ownership *see* ownership
cross-border raising 56
dispersal of 58
finance 54
ownership *see* ownership
premium 53
favoured asset class, as 53
increasing supply 54
ownership 58–9
private 10, 54
publicly traded corporate 37, 39–40, 54, 55–6
assets as investments 58
short-term holdings 53
European Securities and Markets Authority 103–4, 190, 278–9
exchange-traded funds 86, 90–93
growth of 92
UK Listing Rules, and 90–91
executive remuneration 240
corporate governance issue, as 135, 136, 301
shareholder say on pay 135–40, 241
EU regulation
see also corporate governance; regulation
Alternative Investment Fund Managers (AIFM) Directive (2011/61/EU) 72–3, 331, 332–3
Article 12 360
Article 16 333–4
Commission Delegated Regulation (2013) 360
Remuneration Code 334
corporate governance of collective retail investment funds 280
European Securities and Markets Authority 103–4, 278–9
code of best practices 190
harmonisation 50, 52, 55–6, 164
Key Investor Information Document (KIID) 285–6
Lisbon Treaty, Article 50 260
prudential 186

Shareholder Rights Directive (2007) 139, 158, 160
Shareholder Rights Directive (2014) 165, 179, 291, 337
Shareholder Rights Directive (2017) 179–82, 187, 250
disclosure obligations 180–81
engagement policy 180
limitations 183–5
objectives 182–3
reforms 179–80
soft law approach 181–2
transparency obligations 181
soft law approach 181–2, 197
standardised duties 186–7
Undertakings in Collective Interests in Transferable Securities Directive (2009/65/EC) (UCITS) 72–3, 100– 101, 259–60
European System of Financial Supervision
European Banking Authority 278
European Insurance and Occupational Pensions Authority 279
European Securities and Markets Authority 103–4, 190, 278–9
European Systemic Risk Board 279
Joint Committee of the European Supervisory Authorities 279

fiduciary capitalism 5, 14–15, 122, 254, 437
see also investor capitalism
agency capitalism, as 14
corporate equity ownership as 14
intermediary capitalism, as 14
money manager capitalism, as 14–15
fiduciary law 63
see also regulation
conflicts of interest, and 64
liability 64–5
limitation of application 64, 66
proscriptive duty, as 63–4
finance, increasing importance of 22
Financial Conduct Authority 83, 87, 103
audits 107–8
powers 224, 259, 231, 247, 258, 259, 375
financial elite 31
financialisation 2, 5, 8, 15–16, 22
see also financier capitalism
affecting strategic behaviour 41
concerns over 185–6
defining 21–2
financier capitalism as manifestation of 21
legitimation of 46
norms 22–3
acceptance of risk-bearing by individuals 43–6
commoditisation 37–42
detachment of investment returns from real activity 37–42
efficiency through collective pooled investment 25–8
making investment intermediation a business 32–6
professionalisation of collective management 28–32
social importance of investment by private individuals 23–5
private savings, of 66
transactionalisation of relationships 25
financial sector
activity/corporate real productivity balance 25
exclusive jurisdiction 64
output 22
financial stability 19, 102, 389
Financial Stability Board 101–2, 109, 337
financier capitalism 2, 7, 16, 20–23
see also financialisation; shareholder
global phenomenon, as 20
increasing social importance of 25
influence of 22

manifestation of financialisation, as 21
rise of 22
social trust in 24–5, 29
flotation 54–5, 56, 356, 366, 377
foreign exchange market, alleged manipulation in 1
France 130
policy-making 101, 168
protectionism in 418
Strategic Fund 388, 401–2
free market 24
wisdom 130
Freshfields Report 112, 113, 214, 249
fund management sector
see also corporate governance, internal; investment funds
agent of capitalist transformation, as 5
corporate governance role of *see* corporate governance
epistemic authority of 29
global growth 1, 5
incentives 62
internal governance 6
influences on 16
investment intermediary, as 1–2, 5, 8
key source of systemic risk, as 1
managers *see* fund managers
oversight position of 2
structures 62
intermediary chains *see* investment intermediaries
transactionalisation 6, 74
fund managers 14
discretionary powers of 71–2, 130
duties 296
separation from funds 66, 67–72, 73
asset managers *see* asset management
efficiency justifications 69–70
governance deficits of 71
intermediary chains and 69, 75–7
investor exit rights and 73
regulatory support for 72–5
funds *see* investment funds

GDP increases 22
Germany
class actions in 252
policy-making 101
protectionism in 418
wolf pack behaviour against stock exchange 346
global financial crisis (2007–09) 1, 22, 34, 39, 67
conduct of business reforms, post- 102–3
good corporate owner 3, 129, 137–8
golden share 129–30
governance entrepreneurs 146
governance nexus 4–5, 7–8, 9, 61, 62
definition 11
Great Depression 48

hedge fund activism 59, 84, 86, 143, 147–8, 302–3, 309–10, 314–16, 350
buybacks 313–14
corporate governance, and 145–7, 342
collective engagement 346–7
derivative litigation 347–9
exit 349
general meetings 342–4
individual informal dialogue 345
securities litigation 347–9
defining 310–17
dividends 313, 314
drivers of 317
corporate law framework 325, 326–7
firm characteristics 317–21
internal governance 321–5
investment fund regulation 331–7
securities regulation 329–31
shareholder friendliness 325, 327–9

evaluating 337
distribution of wealth 339
exit 340–41
improved market valuation 337–8
long-term performance 338–9
price of 339
shareholder democracy 339–40
shareholder interests 341–2
financial innovation, as 148
merger arbitrage 312–13
minority strategy 310
offensive shareholder activism, as 311
performance 316
retreats 345
short-termist, as 149
UK/US differentiation 311–12, 317
vulnerability to 312
hedge funds 70–71
2-and-20 fee model 334, 362
activism *see* hedge fund activism
corporate governance actors, as 309, 314
publicisation of 59
regulation 150
Hutton Report 206
Hymans Robertson Report 207

incentives 7, 60, 62, 72, 87, 140
see also voting
adverse 105
AIFMD, in 73, 334–5
direct duties 296
dis- 156, 275, 362, 422
misaligned 75, 329
perverse 75–6, 78, 83, 107, 110, 149, 269
reducing 184–8
regulatory enforcement 283, 336
rent-seeking 104
short-termist 99
voting rights 166–8
income
finance-generated/non-finance generated differentiation 24
wealth disparity 25
Independent Governance Committees (IGC) 232, 234, 235
institutionalisation of savings 18
insurance companies
annuities, and 199–200, 224, 225, 227
Association of British Insurers *see* Association of British Insurers
asset management 225–6
in-house 227
Equitable Life scandal 225
investor protection 226
regulation 224–5, 226–7
interbank market
alleged manipulation in 1
intermediary capitalism 15, 20–21
see also agency capitalism; money manager capitalism
fiduciary capitalism as 14
investment
enterprise nature of 33, 36
ramifications 34–5
socially responsible investing *see* socially responsible investing
investment capitalism 123
investment funds
see also fund management sector; fund managers
alternative *see* alternative
close-ended 96, 101
collective retail *see* collective retail investment funds
corporate governance capacities *see* corporate governance
factors shaping 7
hedge *see* hedge funds
intermediary owners, as 13
management *see* collective investment management
mutual *see* mutual funds
open-ended 96, 97, 186, 260, 261
pension *see* pension funds
private equity *see* private equity funds
separation from managers 67–72, 73

intermediary chains *see* investment intermediaries
efficiency justifications 69–70
investor exit rights and 73
governance deficits of 71
regulatory support for 72–5
sovereign wealth *see* sovereign wealth funds
investment intermediaries 25–6
intermediary chains 27, 69, 221
adverse incentives in 105
growth of 74, 75–7
regulatory governance 188–92
savers disparity of power 26, 28–9, 30–31
investment intermediation
business, not service 32–6
dominant structure of 25
expansion of 66
investment management *see* collective investment management
Investment Management Association
Association of British Insurers merger 228
Investor Forum 175, 246
survey 301–2
investor capitalism 5
see also fiduciary capitalism
agency capitalism, as 14
democratic capitalism, as 14
institutional 59–60
intermediary capitalism, as 14
money manager capitalism, as 14–15
shareholder activism as 13
investor protection 11, 12, 50, 57, 226
see also fiduciary law; regulation
against exploitation 103–5
dilemma of 67
enhanced 276, 279
third party depositaries 294–6
voting rights as 159–60
investors
see also shareholders
disempowerment of 74
exit rights 73, 101
institutional 123–5
corporate governance role 125–6
myopia 82–3, 141
prudent 98–9, 111
rights *see* rights
varying perception of 124, 125
Ireland 263, 291
Corporate Governance Code 264, 292
Irish Funds Industry Association 264

Kay Review 5, 76, 93, 216

de Larosière Report 287
law and finance thesis 12
Law Commission 105
Report CP124 (1995) 64–5
LGPS *see* Local Government Pensions Scheme
limited partnerships
light governance of 357
white list 357–8
liquidity 7, 51–2
ill- 91, 92, 272
investor 51–2, 100–102
markets, in 40, 55, 90, 92, 101, 266
litigation 252–3
derivative *see* derivative litigation
private 151–7
rights 293–4
securities/derivative 303–4
Local Government Pensions Scheme 200–201, 206
amalgamation of funds 210
asset allocation 202
corporate governance, and 211–14
cost concerns 206, 207, 211
in-house investment management 207
London Pension Fund Authority 207
Pensions Regulator, and 209–10
performance pressures 207, 209
regulatory governance, and 209, 210–11

restructuring 202–3, 206–7
shift towards passive investing 208–9
Stewardship Code signatories 211
long-term
corporate wealth creation 8, 11, 36, 50, 60, 72
passive investing and 90
hedge fund performance 338–9
investment discretion 95
objectives 7, 63, 120–21, 129, 168
short-termism obscuring 140–41
public interest 107, 123, 186–7
savings 2, 82, 99, 125, 184, 197
stewardship *see* stewardship
value creation 5, 6, 110, 119, 128, 129, 246, 254, 390
long-termism 52, 82, 93, 119, 409, 415, 433, 445
compromised 254
stewardship ethos 341, 347
looking forward 445–6
Luxembourg 264, 265,
Corporate Governance Code 291–2

modern portfolio management theory 6
portfolio diversification 94
money manager capitalism 15
see also agency capitalism; intermediary capitalism
fiduciary capitalism as 14
Morningstar ratings 80
mutual funds 8
see also collective investment schemes; UCITs
charges and fees regulatory reforms 285–8
corporate governance actors, as 257–61
global assets 257–8
non-UCIT 257, 260
UCIT 257, 259–60
UK growth in 258
Myners Report 165

New Finance 44–5
nexus of contracts 127

objectives
business 35, 36, 178
collective investment management, of 32, 47
European Shareholder Rights Directive 182–3
funding 96, 217
investor protection 48, 74, 110, 184, 307
long-term 7, 63, 120–21, 129, 168
short-termism obscuring 140–41
prudential regulatory 94
public interest 102, 157, 182, 185
short-termist 7, 140
social 126
sovereign wealth funds 385–90
OECD 17, 44, 61, 131, 422
Guidelines for Pension Fund Governance (2009) 223
Pension Regulator's Code 223
ownership
beneficial 15
concentrated 143–4
corporate equity 122–6
fiduciary capitalism, as 14
revolution in 2
equity 58–9
shareholder 127–8
universal 10, 14

packaged retail and insurance-based products 271, 279
regulation 286
passivity
fund management 88–90, 209, 222, 234
investment 86, 88–90, 208–9
shareholder 10, 88–90, 132–3, 415–16
Pensions Act (1995)
Statement of Principles 70
pension fund capitalism 198
pension fund corporate governance actors 198–200

collective engagement 246–8
engagement for environmental, social and governance issues 248–50
exit 253–4
individual engagement 250–52
litigation 252–3
roles 202, 236–7
voting 237, 241, 243
activism 244
conflicts of interest, and 244
code-driven 238–9
levels 237–8
proxy advisors' recommendations 239–40
Red Lines initiative 243
pension funds 2, 8, 99, 254–5
annuities, and 199–200, 224, 225
asset management 246–7
stewardship, and 247
CalPERS 59, 250
Co-investment Roundtable of Sovereign and Pension Funds 426
conflicts of interest 223
corporate governance *see* pension fund corporate governance
cost concerns 206, 207, 211, 243, 244
defined benefit *see* defined benefit pension schemes
defined contribution *see* defined contribution pension schemes
diminishing influence of 200, 205
ESG factors, and 110, 111
funded public sector 199
LGPS *see* Local Government Pensions Scheme
global investment 17, 18
insurance companies *see* insurance companies
management as partial intermediation 18
National Employment Savings Trust (NEST) 199, 235
National Pension Funds' Association 246
occupational 198–9
outsourcing investment management 68, 70
Pensions Policy Institute 201
personal 226
prudent person rule, and 98–9
public sector 59
reform 199–200
source of investment capital, as 198
stakeholder 199, 226
stress testing balance sheets 217
trends in 202–6
trustees
Association of Member-Nominated Trustees 243
duty of care 70
unfunded defined benefit 200, 201
policy 16
changes 19
EU 158–9
fixation 11
initiatives 3
UK 157–8
Polygon Master Global Opportunities Fund 348
Prequin Global Private Equity and Venture Capital Report (2015) 351
PricewaterhouseCoopers 19
Asset Management survey 17–18, 20
PRIIPS *see* packaged retail and insurance-based products
private equity funds 70–71, 86, 351, 378–9
AIFM Directive regulatory impact 358–9
business models 351–2
buy-out funds *see* buy-out funds
conduct of business duties 359–62
corporate governance roles 143–5, 364, 377–8
buy-out funds *see* buy-out funds
concentrated ownership 143–4
fund managers 364–6
offensive activism 143
venture capital funds 366–7
emergence of 352–3

expansion of 353
fees and remuneration 362–4
2-and-20 fee model 334, 362
investor relationships 357–62
limited partnerships 357–8
ownership approach 352
venture capital funds 353–5
private sector defined benefit schemes 201, 203–4, 214
asset allocation to equity 219–20
asset allocation to alternative classes 224
asset managers 220–21
conflicts of interest 223
deficits 214–15, 217
liability-driven strategies 215
regulation 215–17
compliance 218, 221
mark-to-market accounting 215
short-termist approaches of 216
trustee risk-taking 217, 218–19
trusts, as 220
privatisation 56, 345
profit disjunction 42
profit-seeking 33
ramifications of 34–5
proxy advisory agencies 180
concerns over 190
International Shareholders Services 426
regulatory corporate governance 189–91, 222
regulatory governance, and 189–90
transparency obligation 181
voluntary code of conduct 181, 190
voting recommendations 222, 239–40, 243, 256
reliance on 228, 268, 299
prudent person rule 98–9
public interest 2, 6, 143, 168, 194, 251
concerns 182–3, 184
corporate equity, and 437–8
corporate governance 123, 125
hedge funds, and 332
investment chains, and 188, 197
long-term 107, 123, 186–7
objectives 102, 157, 182, 185
shaping regulatory duties 192

regulation 8, 11, 31–2, 93–4
see also corporate governance
affecting shareholder behaviour 61–2
conduct of business 62
reforms 102–3
conflicts of interest *see* conflicts of interest
developments 108–10, 185–8
disclosure-based 45
entrenching financialisation 46–7
EU *see* EU regulation
fiduciary law *see* fiduciary law
impact of fund manager duties 106–8
importance of 62
increase in 47–8
intermediary chains, and 75–7, 188–92
investor liquidity *see* liquidity
investor protection *see* investor protection
Irish *see* Ireland
limitation of remedies 64, 68
long-term public interest, and 186–7
Luxembourg *see* Luxembourg
periodic accountability 95–9
portfolio diversification 94–5
prudential 186
reform 105
securities lending *see* securities lending
separation structure, and 72–5
single regulator 192
shortcomings in 187–8
standardisation effects 48–9, 50, 62
UK *see* UK regulation
US *see* US regulation
regulation theory 123–4
regulatory competition 263–6
rent-seeking 75, 85
incentives 104

retail collective investment funds *see* collective retail investment funds
returns
  absolute 32, 209, 309, 323, 324, 349, 387
  generation through trading 32
rights
  exit 306–7
  governance 57, 59
    private litigation and 151–7
    sidelining of 58
  litigation 293–4
  of recourse 293–7
  proprietary 57, 58
  shareholder 162
    quasi-proprietary nature of 13, 127
    reserve power, as 57
    buybacks 148–9
  stakeholder 57–8
  voting *see* voting
rising asset prices 19
risk
  -bearing by individuals 43–6
  legal 64
  management 33–4
  systemic 1, 26–7, 28
  -taking, excessive 141

Santiago Principles 420–24
  soft law in 389, 421–2, 423
saving 23–5
  see also collective investment management
  collective pooling 23, 25–8
  social nature of 33
  through investment 24
savings
  institutionalisation of 18
securities lending 84–5
  regulation of 192–6
self-interest 129, 130, 156, 166, 253, 341
  commercial 143
shadow banking 36
shareholder
  see also financier capitalism; investors capitalism
  activism *see* activism
  behaviour *see* shareholder behaviour
  empowerment 4
  engagement *see* engagement
  institutional 123
  passivity *see* passivity
  power 162
  primacy 140–42, 178–9
    failures of 441–4
  protection 12
  rights *see* rights
  stewardship *see* stewardship
  value ideology 35–6, 40–41
shareholder behaviour 131
  see also engagement
  activism *see* activism
  engagement 7, 59, 138–9
    not unequivocal good 142
    US/UK comparison 142
  individual 250–52
  passivity *see* passivity
  shareholder spring 138, 240–41
shareholders 3–4
  see also investors
  company owners, as 127–8
  corporate governance role of 12
  minority protection 12
  rights *see* rights
  say on pay 135–40
short termism 7, 34, 140–41
  asset management, in 79–83
  collective investment management, in 50–51
  equity holdings, in 53
  hedge fund 149
  private sector DB schemes, of 216
  sovereign wealth funds, of 99
sin stocks 117
smart beta investment 86
socially responsible investing 114, 248
  activism 118
  Deutsche Bank Advisers report (2012) 119–20
  negative screening 115

performance 116, 117–18
positive screening 116
second-generation 116
third-generation 116–17
fourth-generation 118–19
social trust 24–5, 29
sovereign wealth funds 8, 19, 433–5
Australian Future Fund 391–2
behaviour 381–2
central bank distinction 381
Chinese Investment Corporation 393, 394
Co-investment Roundtable of Sovereign and Pension Funds 426
concerns over 416–17
corporate governance roles 150–51, 380, 424
collective engagement 426–7
drivers 401
exit 429–31
host countries, and 414–20
indirect activism 427–8
informal influence 428–9
voting 425–6
corporate equity-owning 384–5
definition 381
French Strategic Fund 401–2
global presence 382–4
governance 391–5
substantive independence 393–4
Government of Singapore Corporation 393
investment
behaviour 405–6
foreign corporate equity, in 404–5
strategic 401–4, 406–10
vetting 417
Korean Investment Corporation 393, 428
Norwegian Global Pension Fund 392–3, 430–31
strategic investing by 410–14
objectives 385–90
passive shareholders, as 415–16
professional management 395–9
professionalisation 400
prudent person rule, and 98–9
Qatar Holding 419
Santiago Principles 420–24
short-termism, and 99
state-owned enterprises distinction 381
structures 391–5
masking nature of investments 394–5
typologies of 391, 392
UK, in 431–3
stakeholders rights *see* rights
stewardship 7, 10, 16, 128–9, 436–41
see also UK regulation
ambivalent nature of 171
Code *see* Stewardship Code
drawbacks of 176–9
shareholder primacy, and 178–9
Stewardship Code (2010) 3, 7, 139, 165–6, 169–71
achievements of 173–6
classification of institutional signatories 177–8
comply-or-explain 169, 171
defining 170
key notions of 170
Principles 172–3
Principle 3 250, 355
Principle 4 250, 255, 350
Principle 5 173, 174–5, 222–3, 355–6
Principle 6 336
Principle 7 336
Shareholders' Rights Directive (2017), and 179–82
standards 3, 7, 139, 157
stock exchanges
cross-listing 55–6
foreign listing 55, 56
second tier markets 55
structures 62
collective investment management 16
collective retail investment funds 261–3
corporate equity 129–30
investment intermediation 25
separation 72–5

sovereign wealth funds 391–5
sub-optimal decisions 34–5, 38–9
systemic risk 26–7, 28
see also risk

third stage of capitalism 21
time horizons 10
transactionalisation of relationships 25
transparency 185, 235, 307, 376
see also disclosure
hedge fund 332, 336
mandatory corporate 249, 300
obligations in EU law 181
pricing, in 282, 285
Walker Guidelines 359–60
trusts 262–3
collective retail investment schemes as 261
private sector defined benefit schemes 220
trust-based DC pension schemes 231
trustees
Association of Member-Nominated Trustees 243
duty of care 70

UCITs 259–60, 266, 268
Directives 72–3, 100–101, 272–6
1985 272
2001 266, 272–4
2009 100
exit rights 73
legislative legacy of 270
exchange-traded funds and 97
fund/management company relationship 261, 266–9
funds in Europe 257–8
non- 260, 262
trusts *see* trusts
regulation 87, 96, 270–71
short-termism of 265
simplified prospectus 274
voting duties 298, 306
UK banking crisis (2007–9) 169
UK regulation 46–7, 48, 57–8, 168–9
see also corporate governance; regulation; stewardship; Stewardship Code
Cadbury Code 238
Companies Act (1981) 352
Companies Act (2006) 96, 151
Section 414A 375
(Strategic Report and Directors' Report) Regulations (2013) 241
Corporate Governance Code 165–6
soft law, as 264, 335
Directors' Remuneration Report Regulations (2002) 136
enhanced protection of minority shareholders 242
Enterprise and Regulatory Reform Act (2013) 137
Financial Conduct Authority 83, 87, 103
audits 107–8
powers 224, 259, 231, 247, 258, 259, 375
Financial Reporting Council 337
Financial Services Action Plan (1999) 55
Financial Services and Markets Act 293
governance reforms 293
Greenbury Committee 136
Hedge Fund Standards Board 332
Listing Rules 90–91, 130, 156, 238–9
reforms 242–3, 299–300
Ownership Commission 125, 128
Pensions Act (1995) 70
Pensions Act (2004) 215
Public Service Sector Pensions Act (2013) 209–10
soft law approach 171, 173, 176, 211, 221, 227, 238, 359–60
Stewardship Code (2010) 3, 7, 139, 165–6, 169–71
Strategic Report 241–2
Trustees Act (2000) 215, 262
Walker Guidelines on Disclosure and Transparency in Private Equity (2007) 359–60

unicorn companies 367
universal ownership 10, 14
UN Principles of Responsible Investment (UNPRI 2005) 113, 248
US regulation 47, 48
see also corporate governane; regulation
Dodd-Franck Act (2010) 137
Private Securities Litigation Reform Act (1995) 252
Securities Exchange Commission 137, 241

Valeant Pharmaceuticals 149–50
value arbitrage 6, 37
value creation, long-term 6
vote buying 194
voting
see also pension fund corporate governance
compliance based 166
defensive concerns, and 240–41
developments 165–6
EU harmonisation 164
Her Majesty's Commissioners of Inland Revenue v Laird Group Plc 159
incentivising 166–7
institutional rights 159–60
reviewing 161–3
levels 160–61, 164–5
pension fund *see* pension fund corporate governance
proxy 160
rights
dual class 167–8
duty to exercise 293
investor protection, as 159–60
legal duty, as 163–4
Shareholder Rights Directive (2007) 160
sovereign wealth funds 425–6

Walker Guidelines on Disclosure and Transparency in Private Equity (2007) 359–60
see also private equity funds
Walker Review (2009) 169
wealth disparities, increasing 25
wealth generation
rentier income, as 38
wolf packs 174, 346

zero sum games 32–3, 34